SELECTED LETTERS OF WILLIAM STYRON

SELECTED LETTERS OF
WILLIAM STYRON

EDITED BY
ROSE STYRON
WITH
R. BLAKESLEE GILPIN

RANDOM HOUSE · NEW YORK

Published in the United States by Random House, an imprint of The Random House Publishing Group, a division of Random House, Inc., New York.

Random House and colophon are registered trademarks of Random House, Inc.

LIBRARY OF CONGRESS CATALOGING-IN-PUBLICATION DATA
Styron, William, 1925–2006.
Selected letters of William Styron / edited by Rose Styron, with R. Blakeslee Gilpin.
p. cm.
Includes index.
ISBN 978-1-4000-6806-7
eBook ISBN 978-0-679-64533-7
1. Styron, William, 1925–2006—Correspondence. 2. Novelists, American—20th century—Correspondence. I. Title.
PS3569.T9Z48 2012 813'.54—dc23
[B] 2012013783

Printed in the United States of America on acid-free paper

www.atrandom.com

246897531

FIRST EDITION

Book design by Simon M. Sullivan

Frontispiece photograph: William Styron working on *Lie Down in Darkness* at Valley Cottage, on a tilt-top desk that had belonged to the radical journalist Randolph Bourne. (Photograph by Sigrid de Lima)

All letters, old and new, are the still-existing parts of a life. To read them now is to be open when some discovery of truth—or perhaps untruth, some flash of light—is just occurring. It is clamorous with the moment's happiness or pain.

—Eudora Welty

INTRODUCTION

Reading Bill's letters has been a journey of surprise for me. As the originals and copies of the thousand-plus handwritten missives began to arrive from friends, colleagues, librarians, and others to whom I had sent hopeful queries about the letters' existence, I opened them with excitement—but then, for a moment, might hesitate, feeling almost as if I were prying into a secret life, the life of a man I'd lived with and loved for fifty-four not uncomplicated years. The "secret life" wasn't a different or parallel life—it was *our* life, one committed to paper, privately, enhanced for me now by a brilliant wordsmith with original thoughts and insights, with generous impulses and particular humor to particular persons he valued: family, close friends from childhood through middle age, writers contemporary and aspiring, mentors, Marine buddies, and neighbors and editors with whom he had deep connections over the years. What a gift! Suddenly, belatedly, I realized that half the endless hours I thought he was working on novels alone at one desk or another he was actually writing letters.

Bill wrote everywhere, it seems. When we met in Italy (a night in a bar with Truman Capote that burgeoned into a crazy romance), he was working in a small high room at the back of the palatial American Academy in Rome, the first fiction writer to be awarded its Prix de Rome. He was surrounded by painters, sculptors, architects, and musicians. Each morning, he said, he was roused by sounds from the Ping-Pong table on the terrace his window overlooked (Lukas and Cornelia Foss doing earliest battle). How different from the couple of years he struggled—even for food—in cheap, New York City rooms before *Lie Down in Darkness* became a bestseller.

Soon we moved in together: a dark basement flat next door to the Academy, where Giuseppe, its big uniformed doorman, would descend the steps to deliver Bill's cherished mail. Bill piled books and yellow legal stretching bar the place where Bill would stand, most often alone, quiet, and spread out the day's pages to contemplate. Rarely in later years did he read aloud the afternoon yellow-page compositions in his beautiful script as he had each evening of our first decades together, often by a fire he built. He'd stay up very late, revising. I would type (two fingers) the next morning as he slept. For years he'd want to discuss at least part of a chapter with me, and then with his treasured editor, Bob Loomis.

An inveterate note-taker but a poor correspondent myself, I was delighted to see Bill's postcards and letters from 1967 to 2002 that detailed our leaving Connecticut quite regularly (*en famille* on school breaks), most often in winter, but often *à deux*. Bill hated cold weather. We might join the Robert Penn Warrens in Egypt, the James Joneses in France, the Sadri Khans in Kenya, the Carlos Fuenteses in Mexico, the John Marquands on Salt Cay, the Mike Nicholses or the Robert Brusteins sailing the Caribbean, or the Gabriel García Márquezes in Colombia, then Cuba. More serious missions—Poland with Kurt Vonnegut, Chile with Arthur Miller—were chronicled, too. Every summer we moved to Martha's Vineyard, where Bill barricaded himself in a little prefab behind the house to write, posting an intimidating VERBOTEN sign on the door. Surely he was creating more than fiction.

Post office visits remained a fact of daily life. Walks to the main post office in Vineyard Haven before lunch and to the little auxiliary one in West Chop with a series of dogs in the afternoons supplanted his Connecticut drives to the small clapboard structure in the center of Roxbury.

Reading these letters, I was moved again and again by the love he expressed for me, for his children, for his friends. He was a kind, physically gentle man who flew into legendary short-lived rages at all of us; hung up the phone on his family's callers, old and young, if they didn't dare to schmooze with him first; invented mesmerizing horror stories to terrify and amuse his children at bedtime; got jealous of the considerable attention I paid to each child—especially, I guess, son Tommy—and would shout unpleasantries from his workrooms at their high-spirited noisiness or perceived misbehavior. By the time Alexandra, much younger, was growing up, his outbursts were becoming more intense. I did not see the handwriting on the wall: incipient depression. Only after he gave up alcohol at fifty-eight—a decision he stuck to as firmly as he had cigarettes at thirty-eight—did I realize disaster lurked.

An extraordinary thinker and artist, Bill put much on paper that he would never say aloud. Though immersing myself in his letters made me miss him more, respect and admire him more, as might be anticipated, it also sparked old doubts, and certain resentments, and regrets about my own responses in later years. Much of his youthful correspondence—which we had to eliminate because of space—made me wish I had known him as a boy—his language crafted so often with funny details of "fooling around." A fourteen-year-old's diary entry: "After supper wrote letters. Went to bed." Discursive teenage missives sent from home and prep school implored recipients for a reply. One quoted an Eaton stationery ad: "To get a letter, send a letter." Often he'd ask a relative to send him special stamps, and he wrote away for rare and exotic stamps himself.

YOU WILL SEE as you read these letters that his chief correspondents, those to whom he opened his mind and heart, were, first, his father, William Styron, Sr., then his Duke mentor, Professor William Blackburn, and his novelist friends such as James Jones, Norman Mailer, and Willie Morris. Others he was very close to, like Peter Matthiessen and Carlos Fuentes, rated only a few because he saw them or phoned them so frequently. Neighbors like Mia Farrow and Philip Roth, with whom we shared so many evenings, did find several: witty litanies about home life, or reassurances about books and performances. His thoughts on his own creative process and those of his fellow writers are profound, discursive, rich. Our eldest daughter unearthed one of the best batches. From age sixteen she frequently lived abroad. To Susanna the letters are humorous and compassionate, full of advice and comments, on family life at home, on news, world politics, and literature, and endless warnings to drive carefully. He shared much of his deeper self with her, as he did with his great friends whom he encouraged with fair and insightful criticism of their works-in-progress, or with readers requesting advice on mental health issues (many wrote back that his personal replies had helped save their sanity). Indeed, it's stunning how often he wrote back to fans—how he loved his fans! It has been difficult to select. Thank heavens for Bob Loomis and Blake Gilpin and their judicious cutting.

So we begin with a series of letters to Pop, who supported him in every way after the death of his mother, from his early teen years through the advent of marriage. Unfortunately, we could not locate letters to James Baldwin, Bill's close friend, who spent most of a year at our home in Connecticut in the sixties. Racial violence and the civil rights movement dominated the news. Bill and Jimmy would sit in the back room each evening discussing the books they were working on that year. Jimmy encouraged Bill to write *Nat Turner* in the first person. A number of black writers published objections to Bill's inhabiting their hero. Though he won a Pulitzer and was supported by Jimmy and John Hope Franklin, Bill, a man who championed civil and human rights as well as fictional license, was hurt. And sad that the film, already in process and starring James Earl Jones, was canceled. It took more than a dozen years before the success of *Sophie's Choice,* novel and film and opera, restored his sense of public appreciation.

Many stories are told in these pages, but inevitably some of the pieces are missing. As this goes to print, I suspect postcards and letters may still be on their way. In an electronic age of immediate communication, does anyone still correspond at such length? Alas.

ROSE STYRON
February 2012

POSTMARK

My personal interactions with William Styron were glancing, but they revolved entirely around his correspondence. For two summers, between the ages of nineteen and twenty-one, I served as the postmaster of a seasonal post office on Martha's Vineyard. My one-room shop intersected one of Bill's walking routes and throughout those summers, I could count on the occasional and nearly wordless encounter as he bought stamps for a postcard to Philip Roth or a package to Carlos Fuentes.

I imagined myself a budding writer and I anticipated our postal exchanges with great interest. I secretly hoped Bill would recognize me as a kindred spirit, but alas, we never muttered more than a few words to each other. I was left to thumb the addresses of his outgoing mail, daydreaming about the exciting literary world he inhabited.

Midway through my doctorate, I discovered Styron's letters to one of my dissertation subjects, Robert Penn Warren. Styron wrote Warren in December of 1946, hoping to study "writing under [him]." This was the beginning of a long friendship, which grew especially close when the two became neighbors in the Connecticut countryside. After stumbling upon Bill's letters to Warren, I began to investigate Styron's friendships with Southern expatriates like C. Vann Woodward and Willie Morris. Chance had met opportunity and I was soon off to Durham, North Carolina, to explore Bill's papers.

At Duke, in a beautifully organized archive, I found the story of a man, a writer, and an American century. Styron's letters intimately document sixty years of his hopes and fears, narrating history that he not only witnessed but touched and changed. Like most writers, Styron explored the challenges of the act of creation in his letters. However, very few writers so powerfully probe the meaning of writing, the constant tug-of-war between a writer and the critical establishment, and the pains and joys of life itself. In other words, in these pages, you will find so much more than reportage about the events of daily life; these letters show the same attention to the human condition that allowed Styron's writing to touch so many lives.

On the individual level, Bill repeatedly reached out to help aspiring writers, took the time to respond to fans who had been touched by his work, and wrote to nearly everyone in the same spirit as his epistles to close friends like James Jones and John Marquand. Particularly noteworthy in this regard are Bill's letters to his eldest child, Susanna. One letter of note, from May 15, 1972, shows the affectionate thoughtfulness that characterizes his correspondence.

> As for your existential "wrassling," I'm sure that I don't have to tell you that your pondering and wondering and troubling are only extensions of what people have been doing ever since they had the capability of thought, which is to say hundreds of thousands of years. Gods and the idea of a God were of course born out of just this troubled pondering, so it may or may not be a consolation to you that your intense wonder and turmoil about the meaning of the human condition is, in fact, a <u>part</u> of the human condition—or at least as it is experienced by sensitive and questing souls like yourself (no joke). It may just be that there is no reason or purpose to existence. Many great men—thinkers and artists—have thought this to be true, yet have not despaired over this assumption but have created great work through their very vision of mankind enduring triumphant over the sheer purposelessness of the universe, and in spite of the bleak and soulless aspect it so often presents. The whole concept of tragedy is of course embodied in this notion.

I am not aware of many parents who would take the time to write to their children with such care and profundity, much less treat the subject and the child with such humor, compassion, and respect. The historian in me revels in other examples. Writing to James Jones on August 12, 1965, Bill recalled writing Lyndon Johnson's Voting Rights Act speech with Vineyard neighbor Richard Goodwin. That letter screams its importance, with juxtapositions of Jackie Onassis water-skiing, Frank Sinatra as a lifeguard, and Bill self-consciously announcing the letter as "Notes of a Waif Astray in the 20th Century."

There is rollicking humor and deep sadness in these letters; signs of towering ego and profound insecurity; sweet affection and stinging bitterness. You will find elements of all in Bill's letter to Philip Roth on January 29, 1973. Ostensibly, Bill wrote to comfort Roth after Norman Podhoretz and Irving Howe viciously attacked Roth's character in an article in *Commentary*. But before Styron addressed the *Commentary* piece, he offered a lengthy excursus about his experiences during the *Nat Turner* controversy and the sheer absurdity of the critical establishment. The nearly 2,000-word letter is a testament to both the isolation and the camaraderie of the modern American novelist. Expressed in classic Styronese, Bill signed off with "Yours in the slime we sometimes find ourselves up to our asses in."

As one follows the vicissitudes of the writerly existence in these pages, it is hard not to develop a deep attraction to Styron's mind and pen. My own passion for this correspondence led to a meeting with Bill's widow, Rose, in the fall of 2007. When Rose asked if I would like to edit Bill's letters, I naively leapt at the chance. Little did I know that the process of gathering, transcribing, and notating those letters would take the better part of five years, but what an incredible journey it has been. Benefiting from serendipitous circumstances and generous support from various institutions, I was able to meet with Rose daily for almost an entire year. Each morning, we would sit together in the Styron home in Vineyard Haven, Massachusetts, and work through my previous day's transcriptions and notations. Rose would retrieve names, books, and obscure events at a constant clip. Working intimately with this sparkling soul, the matriarch who knew about or experienced most of what transpires in these pages, has been a distinct privilege.

As this collection grew in size, scope, and quality, Rose and I shared the joy of uncovering a new narrative about William Styron. Quite distinct from a biography or a memoir, these selected letters narrate one writer's lifelong struggles and joys—captured in private dispatches about professional life, friendship, and family. Indeed, in many ways, the stories in these pages were known only in part to Bill's individual correspondents, and the extent of this writing has surprised even his closest friends.

Of course, across these pages, certain themes emerge. All the ambitious young littérateurs will be touched by Bill's self-conscious journey from the Duke classroom to the *New York Times* bestseller list. Styron's ambitions are captured in a letter to his mentor William Blackburn in February 1950 as he was finishing his first novel, *Lie Down in Darkness*. Acknowledging his conscious restraint in the book, Styron expressed his lifelong distaste for "the Hemingway tight-lipped mumble school." "I believe that a writer should accommodate language to his own peculiar personality," he continued, "and mine wants to use great words, evocative words, when the situation demands them."

Styron would spend the next six decades negotiating the tension between the "orotund" and the "spare." In these intimate snapshots of his interior life, readers will follow the unique circumstances that helped Styron establish himself at the forefront of American letters. These letters are intimate, funny, and profound all at once. One sees his foibles laid bare, his friendships given color and life, and his accomplishments put into sharpest relief. Tracing the deep cultural impact of *The Confessions of Nat Turner* to the harrowingly personal *Darkness Visible,* Styron's letters help us appreciate the swirl of events that contributed to his creative work, and the struggle that took each project from the germ of an idea to a finished product.

Unlike some of his contemporaries, Styron approached letter writing rather haphazardly; he seemed to write only when the epistolary muse struck him. A grudging typist, Styron's handwritten letters are all unique—that is to say, without carbons. With no eye toward posterity, Styron's extensive archive at Duke consists almost entirely of letters written *to,* not *by* him. As such, the process of assembling this collection has been an ongoing and worldwide search for the scattered but precious words he sent to friends and fans alike. We have been unable, despite Herculean efforts, to track down letters Bill wrote to James Baldwin, for instance, though we know such letters exist. There are surely other gaps and omissions, and so these are William Styron's *Selected Letters,* for we fear they could never be made truly complete.

Styron himself spoke to some of these difficulties even in the 1960s. Writing to Blackburn, who was editing the letters of Bill's Duke classmate, the writer Mac Hyman, Bill mentioned his "surprise" at finding some of their letters in his papers. "During these last years we always spoke to each other by telephone," Styron explained on March 30, 1965, "the invention which is in the process of killing off all literary correspondence."

Fortunately, Styron did not cease writing letters altogether, even when the telephone took over more and more of his friendly and professional communication. The hours he would spend on a given day (letters are often clustered in this manner) speak to the psychological space the activity helped create for him in the midst of struggling with a novel. Again and again in these pages, Styron expressed his belief that writing was "a tedious and agonizing process and I loathe [it] with almost a panic hatred."

But in a letter to Hyman in May of 1953, Styron showed his typical ironic self-awareness as he revealed the importance of writing letters to help navigate that tedium and panic.

> All this probably doesn't interest you in the least, but what it narrows down to is this, if it'll give you any comfort—that is, if you need any comfort. What I mean is that I think that any writer who ever lived, who was any good at all, has had long long periods of precisely the same sort of strain and struggle that both you and I are going through; I only comfort myself (and God knows it seems like forlorn comfort at times) that it seems to be true that often such periods of doubt and thrashing around eventually produce the best work. They often eventually produce the best work because it is during such periods of struggle (when one is long unpublished or goes through long periods of tortured sterility) that a writer really suffers. A lot of crap has been written about suffering, and the value of it, and in about two seconds I'll shut up, but every now and then, even in the midst of my most dried-up, sterile depressions, I have a crazy confused moment of joy in the knowledge that anything good I ever did seemed at one time or another impossible of attaining, that it was a hard struggle in getting it out, that it seemed at times to be crushed under the weight of my doubts about it, but if it happened to be good at all it was because of the doubts, and perhaps a little suffering. End of quotation.

It was in his correspondence where Styron not only sounded out his frequent bouts with "melancholy" and "writer's block" but helped ease himself out of both predicaments. Indeed, Bill's self-awareness certainly extended to his letters; he wanted them to be more than scrawled grocery lists. He understood them as part of his oeuvre and expressed definite feelings about the publication of writers' letters. When Blackburn proposed doing a collection of Styron's letters in 1966, Bill wrote that "the publication of personal letters . . . has somewhat the quality of gratuitous exposure." Indeed, responding to a letter he had written to Mac in May of 1957, Styron told Blackburn, "when I read that letter of mine which you sent and thought of it appearing in print, I felt terribly naked all of a sudden."

Fortunately for those reading this volume, Styron added that "when a writer is dead, certainly that becomes a different matter. Presumably then there evolves enough interest in the writer's private self that the very publication of his correspondence wipes out the element of gratuitousness . . . when I myself am dead and someone wants to put my letters together, I couldn't care less one way or another."

Although we have taken Styron at his stated indifference, the hallmark of this volume reveals the very opposite guiding emotion. Styron's care and concern pulse in each word collected here. My hope is that this invitation to see his "private self" will reveal his concern not just for showing love and friendship to those he corresponded with but for making lasting and worthy art for the readers he cared so much about.

R. BLAKESLEE GILPIN
February 2012

EDITORIAL NOTES

After transcribing and annotating more than one thousand letters, it has been necessary to make certain cuts and edits. Ellipses mark infrequent deletions from the text. We have occasionally included incomplete letters, sometimes missing as much as a page, if the extant contents justified inclusion. Errors in punctuation and spelling have been silently corrected, with the exception of intentionally (often humorously) misspelled words. We have tried to keep explanatory notes to a minimum, identifying the people and books that we have deemed worthy of explanation.

A small number of these letters have appeared in print prior to being collected in this volume. Fourteen of Bill's letters to the writer Donald Harington appeared in a special issue of *The Southern Quarterly* in 2002. We have also chosen to reprint several letters that first appeared in Styron's *Letters to My Father*, ed. James L. W. West III (Baton Rouge: Louisiana State University Press, 2009). West's wonderful collection included all of Bill's letters to William C. Styron, Sr., from January 1943 to October 1953.

All the letters follow a basic format:

Recipient　　　　Date Written from

William Styron dated virtually every letter he wrote during his long life. He also nearly always indicated where he was when he wrote a letter. In this way, readers can track his movements—often alternating seasonally between Roxbury, Connecticut, and Vineyard Haven, Massachusetts—but his extensive travel around the world is also catalogued in these letters. We have dispensed with elaborate abbreviations of archival locations, autograph versus typescript letters, and the like in order to include more of Styron's actual correspondence. Unfortunately, there is no single location in which to view Styron's letters. Our efforts to collect material from libraries (The Harry Ransom Center at the University of Texas at Austin and Yale University's Beinecke Library and Manuscripts and Archives among them) represent a small fraction of the publicly and privately held letters that we solicited, copied, and received in order to represent Styron's correspondence. In other words, you hold in your hands the closest approximation to an archive of this writer's letters. Please enjoy them in the spirit in which they were written and received.

WILLIAM STYRON: A TIMELINE

1925 Born William Clark Styron, Jr., on June 11 in Newport News, in the Tidewater region of Virginia.

1932–37 The Styrons move to Hilton Village, a small community just outside Newport News, in 1932.

1939 Pauline dies on July 20, after years of intense pain.

1940 Starts his first year at Christchurch, a small Episcopal boys' prep school near West Point, Virginia, in September.

1941 Father and Elizabeth Buxton marry and move to Hampton Roads.

1942 Completes year at Davidson College in North Carolina. Transfers to Duke University to join the Marines' V-12 program and enrolls in Professor William Blackburn's creative writing course.

1944–45 Ordered to boot camp at Parris Island, South Carolina (sent to the VD ward with a mistaken diagnosis of syphilis). Transferred to Camp Lejeune, North Carolina, for officer training, then sent to Platoon Commander School at Quantico, Virginia, where he is commissioned a second lieutenant.

1946 After the war ends, Styron returns to Duke University. In summer, signs up as a deckhand on the *Cedar Rapids Victory,* a merchant cattle ship bound for Trieste.

1947 Graduates from Duke and reenlists in the Marine Corps Reserve. Moves to New York City and becomes an assistant editor at Whittlesey House, but is soon fired. Inherits $1000 from his maternal grandmother's estate, which, combined with his GI benefits, allows him to survive without taking another job. Enrolls in a fiction-writing seminar at the New School for Social Research at the invitation of its instructor, Hiram Haydn. Haydn arranges a $250 advance from Crown for Styron's first novel.

1948–49 Briefly returns to Durham before moving back to New York City. Stays rent-free with Sigrid de Lima, a friend from the New School, and her mother, Agnes (Aggie) de Lima, then finds a room in the Flatbush section of Brooklyn, where he meets an Auschwitz survivor named Sophie. Faces money problems as GI benefits run out and accepts an offer to live rent-free with Aggie and Sigrid de Lima at their country residence in Valley Cottage, a village near Nyack, New York, north of the city. Father urges Styron to continue working on his first novel and pledges to send $100 a month until its completion.

1950 Hiram Haydn leaves Crown for Bobbs-Merrill in Indianapolis. Styron negotiates a release from his contract with Crown and follows Haydn.

1951 Recalled by the Marine Corps, but Haydn secures him a deferment. Pushes himself physically and emotionally to write the final one hundred pages of *Lie Down in Darkness* before returning to the service.

Completes an all-night, thirty-three-mile march, and soon afterward is discharged because of a cataract in his right eye.

Lie Down in Darkness published September 10. Invited by Louis D. Rubin, Jr., to meet with graduate students at Johns Hopkins that spring, where he is introduced to Rose Burgunder.

1952 In February, *Lie Down in Darkness* wins the Prix de Rome of the American Academy of Arts and Letters.

Sails to England on the *Île de France* for the British publication of *Lie Down in Darkness,* then on to Paris. Becomes friendly with the American writer Peter Matthiessen, who introduces Styron to his circle of literary expatriates, who will soon found *The Paris Review.*

In Rome, begins to date Rose Burgunder, writes the

manifesto for the first issue of *The Paris Review,* and proposes marriage to Rose.

1953 Marries Rose Burgunder and honeymoons in Ravello, Italy.

1954 The Styrons move back to New York; Styron spends ten days in bed with heart palpitations. The Styrons purchase a large, two-story nineteenth-century frame house in Roxbury, Connecticut.

1955 Hiram Haydn moves to Random House in January and Styron signs a two-book contract with Random House. Daughter Susanna Margaret born February 25.

1956–58 Norman Mailer and his wife move to nearby Bridgewater, Connecticut.
Daughter Paola (Polly) Clark Styron born March 13, 1958.
Mailer accuses Styron of spreading slander about Mailer's wife, Adele, ending their friendship for twenty-five years.

1959 Hiram Haydn resigns from Random House to start a new firm (Atheneum). Styron decides to work with Bob Loomis at Random House.
Son Thomas Haydn Styron born August 4.

1960 *Set This House on Fire* published May 5, 1960. The Styrons spend February and March with James and Gloria Jones in Paris, then travel through Geneva, Milan, and Florence, and arrive to settle in Rome in early May.
James Baldwin moves into the Styrons' guesthouse to work on a novel.

1961 Travels in May to Southampton County, Virginia, with Rose, his father, and a local relative as guide in an attempt to trace the path of slave rebel Nat Turner's revolt.

1962 Travels to Paris for the publication of Coindreau's translation of *Set This House on Fire.*
The Styrons attend a dinner at the White House.
Styron transfers the handling of foreign publishing rights, in May, to the London-based Hope Leresche and Steele agency.
Attends William Faulkner's funeral service in Oxford, Mississippi.

1964 The Styrons decide to purchase a harbor-front house on Martha's Vineyard.

1965 Viking Press publishes Rose's first collection of poetry, *From Summer to Summer.*

1966 Daughter Claire Alexandra (Al) Styron born October 28.

1967 There are prepublication orders of 125,000 copies when *The Confessions of Nat Turner* is published on October 9.

1968 *The Confessions of Nat Turner* wins the Pulitzer Prize for fiction.

Flies to Seattle with Arthur Miller and Jules Feiffer to campaign for Eugene McCarthy in the Washington and Oregon Democratic presidential primaries.

Serves as an honorary pallbearer at the funeral of Robert Kennedy.

Beacon Press in Boston issues *William Styron's Nat Turner: Ten Black Writers Respond,* a collection of essays attacking the novel.

Attends Democratic National Convention in Chicago.

Travels with Rose to the Soviet Union to attend an Afro-Asian authors' conference.

1970 Awarded the Howells Medal.

1971 Father, aged eighty-one, marries Eunice Edmundson, aged seventy-six.

1972 *In the Clap Shack* produced by the Yale Repertory Theatre.

1973 Decides to stop work on Marine novel *The Way of the Warrior* and begin writing *Sophie's Choice: A Memory* after a vivid dream involving Sophie, a Polish Catholic survivor of Auschwitz.

Viking Press publishes *Thieves' Afternoon,* a collection of Rose's poetry.

1974 Styron travels to Europe to visit the death camp at Auschwitz.

1977 James Jones dies of congestive heart failure on May 8, 1977, at age fifty-five.

1978 Stepmother Eunice dies and Styron moves his father to a nursing home near Roxbury where he dies on August 10, 1978.

1979 *Sophie's Choice* is published on June 11, Styron's fifty-fourth birthday, reaching number one on the *New York Times* bestseller list.

1980 *Sophie's Choice* wins the first American Book Award in February 1980.
Styron attends presidential inauguration ceremonies for François Mitterrand in Paris.

1982 Publishes a collection of nonfiction prose entitled *This Quiet Dust and Other Writings.*
Alan Pakula's movie of *Sophie's Choice* is released.

1985 Begins to suffer from clinical depression and considers plans for suicide. Admitted to Yale–New Haven Hospital on December 14. Receives treatment and medication and makes a steady improvement.

1986–90 Speaks about depression at two events in 1989. Meets *Vanity Fair* editor Tina Brown who offers to publish his account.

1990 Publishes *Darkness Visible.*

1990–2000 Speaks frequently on depression to groups of physicians and therapists.

1993 Publishes *A Tidewater Morning: Three Tales from Youth.*

2000–2005 Styron's final years are unproductive, as the results of depression affect his narrative ability. Cancer is discovered.

2006–07 Hospitalized for much of the last year and a half of his life, Styron dies in Martha's Vineyard Hospital on November 1, 2006, and his ashes are buried on the Vineyard.
A memorial service in his honor is held on February 2, 2007, at St. Bartholomew's Church, New York City.

SELECTED LETTERS OF WILLIAM STYRON

cially good. It's the writer's attempt, through fiction, to portray America and its people. Mentions Newport News and Norfolk, and the Northern Neck—to quote: ". . . you'd ride slowly home hating the goddam exhausted land and the drought that wouldn't let the garden grow and the katydids and the dryflies jeering out of the sapling gums and persimmons ghostly with dust along the road and the sickle-shaped beach where the sea nettles stung you when you tried to swim out and the chiggers and the little scraps of talk about what was going on up to the Hague or Warsaw or Pekatone and the phone down at the cottage that kept ringing whenever any farmer's wife along the line took up the receiver to talk about things to any other farmer's wife and all down the line you could hear the receivers click as they all ran to the receiver to listen to what was said. . . ."*

Sounds just like the Northern Neck and Dolph Chowning.† Brings back old memories.—About that story I wrote I was telling you about: It's scheduled to be published in the Christmas issue of the Archive.‡ The Editor said it would have won the prize in their short story contest, but I didn't know anything about it (the contest), so I didn't win. They were going to run another story of mine, entitled "Home Again," but the MS. was lost, and I didn't feel like doing it over. We get three days leave Xmas so I'll see you then. Write soon and give my best to everyone.

Your son, Bill Jr.

P.S. I enjoy Mech. Drawing very much. Take after Pop, eh?!§

* Styron quotes John Dos Passos, "The Camera Eye (21)," *The 42nd Parallel.*

† The Northern Neck of Virginia lies between the Potomac River on the north and the Rappahannock on the south. Randolph Chowning was a friend from Christchurch.

‡ "Where the Spirit Is."

§ Bill, Sr., worked as a mechanical draftsman in the Newport News shipyards.

To William C. Styron, Sr.

March 12, 1944 Duke University

Dear Pop,

I got your letter a few days ago, and I certainly enjoyed it. I was glad you enjoyed my story. Another one of my opuses (or operas, I think, is the plural) is going to appear in the April issue of the Archive. It is, appropriately enough to my faculty for picking primitive subjects, a story about a lynching, and the psychological effect of it on a young boy. The title is Delta Night.*

Dr. Blackburn, in his comment on the story said: "I take great pride in your progress this term. While I don't usually urge undergraduates to make writing their livelihood, you are definitely one to be encouraged . . . you have grown . . . in both strength and wisdom. This story is the strongest you have done."

My studies are coming along pretty well. We've had no tests as yet, so consequently I've gotten no grades. But I'm coming along.

We got paid this week, and I got $45. So I suppose I'm all set financially, for the time being anyhow. Incidentally, I was 45 minutes late coming back from furlough, so I was put on a week's restriction, that is, no liberty at night, having to sign in at the N.C.O. "every hour on the hour." That's O.K., though; I won't spend so much money.

Leon is now at Miami Beach, taking pre-flight training.† I hope he makes out O.K. But I think he will.

* Published as "The Long Dark Road" in the March 1944 issue of *The Archive* and reprinted in *One and Twenty: Duke Narrative and Verse, 1924–1945* (Durham, N.C.: Duke University Press, 1945), which collected the writing of William Blackburn's students. The story is reprinted in West, ed., *William Styron: Letters to My Father.*

† Leon Edwards, a childhood friend of Styron's from Virginia. As Styron wrote to Mattie Russell on November 20, 1980: "Dr. Edwards was killed in a plane crash in 1979 and these letters were sent to me by his widow. I think that some of the letters might be of interest because they were written while I was writing Lie Down in Darkness and Set This House on Fire. Edwards was also trying to write fiction and some of the letters from me are in response to his requests for criticisms. Edwards was an almost exact contemporary of mine, we were in high school together in Virginia, and when he was going through Harvard Medical School I was in a position to lend him money enough to complete his education. Some of the correspondence deals with this matter but I think most of the interest has to do with my own reflections on writing my early work."

Last week-end, four of us went to Danville and had dates at Averett college. We came back Sunday night, starting out at 10:30 hitch-hiking. We got stuck in Yanceyville, N.C. for four hours, and we just barely made reveille at 6:30. I almost froze to death! What a detail!

Am now rooming with Art Katz of Memphis, and Claude Kirk of Montgomery, Ala.* Both are transfers from Emory, and they're good guys.

Give my regards to Eliza. Write soon.

Your son,

Bill, jr.

To William C. Styron, Sr.

April 3, 1944 Duke University

Dear Pop,

Please excuse this stationery, but I'm writing this in Shakespeare class, which is a very boring class, so I reckon you'll understand.

Last weekend John Carson, Chet Stull, and I went up to Danville and dated at Averett college. We had quite a time. I have been dating this girl Doreen Stanley from Queens Village, L.I. She's 18 and very nice looking, intelligent, and her father is Sales Manager for National Distillers, Inc. (Old Grandad, Old Overholt, Wilson's, Black & White, etc.)! In these days of liquor rationing it might not hurt to date the daughter of a whiskey magnate! No kidding, we had a fine time up there. Stayed at a tourist home for $1.00 and ate at the college, which made things very inexpensive.

While I was up at the school, the girls put on a Palm Sunday musical service. It was very good, and I noticed especially a choral piece for women's voices entitled, "Look Homeward, Angel." It was taken from a chapter of the book by Thomas Wolfe and the music was arranged by a gentleman by the name of William Schuman. It was beautiful, and I was very surprised. Specifically, the passage was the one which begins: "A stone, a leaf, an unfound door; of a stone, a leaf, a door. And of all the forgotten faces. Naked and alone we came into exile. In her dark womb we did not know

* Claude Kirk, governor of Florida from 1967 to 1971, was eventually a candidate for the Republican presidential nomination.

our mother's face, etc." It ends beautifully like this: "O waste of loss, in the hot mazes, lost, among bright stars on this most weary, unbright cinder, lost! Remembering speechlessly we seek the great forgotten language, the lost lane-end into heaven, a stone, a leaf, an unfound door. Where? When? . . . O lost, and by the wind grieved, ghost, come back again." Only the girls had to pervert the whole thought of the passage by inserting "O lamb of God" in the last line. That rather irritated me.*

The gym instructor really got rough with us this morning. We had hard calisthenics for forty minutes, which included push-ups, pull-ups, deep knee-bends. When we were all but completely exhausted, we had to climb a 30-foot vertical rope twice. But that wasn't all. Then we had to work out on the parallel bars for ten minutes. I was pretty well pooped out when we finished. But, as they say, "That's where they separate the men from the boys." If you don't completely pass out, I suppose you're a man.

I got a letter from Leon saying that he is now a Qualified Air Cadet. That's what he was aiming for, and he's pretty happy about it. Right now he's in the Base Hospital at Miami recovering from a cold. Nothing serious, he says.

I might have told you before, but I just finished reading Schopenhauer's "Studies in Pessimism." It's not very long, and it's very good, although I don't agree with or understand many of his ideas. I've started on Kant's Basic Thoughts, including "Critique of Pure Reason." I fear that this boy Kant is just a little bit too profound for yours truly. I may, however, be able to struggle through it.

We get paid to-morrow, and I'm really going to need it. I owe about $15, which won't leave me much from the $35, since we'll probably be compelled this month to pay the $5 athletic fee. But, that's the way it goes. "Always Broke" Styron, that's me!

My second "Archive" story will be published this week. You said that you had entered a subscription, so it won't be necessary for me to send you a copy. It's not a bad story, but on the other hand it's not as good a story as I set out to write. I suppose, though, that no story is exactly what the author intended to write.†

* Schuman's *Prelude for Voices* (1939). These are the opening lines of Thomas Wolfe's 1929 novel.

† Styron's "The Long Dark Road."

Is it okay if John Carson comes home with me on furlough? We don't plan to stay home more than two or three days, since we have a big party scheduled up in Urbanna.* This is planning right far ahead, I know (furlough begins 17 June), but I just wanted to know if it meets with your approval. Carson's father is a captain in the Navy and is commander of the U.S.S. Boston, probably based now at Kwajalein atoll. When Pearl Harbor came, he was operations officer for the southwest Pacific area, and sent the submarines and P.T. boats to Bataan to take off MacArthur and his staff. John's lived practically everywhere. He graduated from N.M.M.I., and went two years to the Univ. of New Mexico. Also he's a swell guy.

Well, I'd better close now. Give my love to Eliza, and write soon.

Your son,

Bill, jr.

To William C. Styron, Sr.

July 26, 1944 Duke University

Dear Pop,

Please excuse the long delay in correspondence. I've been rather busy of late. My three English courses have been keeping me on the ball. Not only do we have to read the prescribed text, but we also have to do outside reading and, while interesting, it eats up the time considerably.

I've just finished another story. It's real short, and while it's not nearly as good as I had hoped it would be, it is an incident taken from "early childhood" and might prove of some interest to you.† If I can find a large envelope I'll send it and the other short sketch I was telling you about to you.

I've just about decided not to write any more. Each time I sit down to write I usually have a good idea in mind, but the idea turns up flooie and the story consequently ends up in a lot of drivel.

In reading a biography of Wordsworth, the author mentions that in

* Urbanna, Virginia, was the biggest town anywhere near the Christchurch School.

† "Sun on the River," appeared in the September 1944 *Archive* and is reprinted in *William Styron: Letters to My Father.*

Wordsworth's village there were two thieves, very brutal characters. One was a doting old man of 90, the other was his grandson—aged 3. They would steal slyly hand in hand into the fruit market and stealthily steal all sorts of fruit and candies. Unknown to them, the villagers were watching their every move and, of course, instead of condemning them, looked upon their malefactions with gentleness and pity. As an idea for a story, I don't think this has ever been worked upon and, if I get sufficient incentive, I think I'll try my hand at it. I can think of no more touching or pathetic a scene.*

Things around here are about as usual. Eat, study, sleep.

I'm doing very well in all my subjects. Made a "B" in the last Physics quiz which, I think, will take me off the black list.

I'd better sign off now. Why don't you send me the plot of that story you were telling me about?

Give my love to Eliza.

Your son,

Bill jr.

To William C. Styron, Sr.

July 27, 1944 Duke University

Dear Pop,

I got your letter this morning, and agree with you that the plot has opportunities for greatness, if handled properly. However, there are a few very tough obstacles which must be eliminated. Since Mary, or "Jenny Field," as I have named her, is a female and the central character, and I'll have to handle the narrative from her point of view, it may prove extremely difficult to get the feeling of her character from the introspective male's point of view. Christopher Morley did it excellently in "Kitty Foyle," and I think I can do it too. I've started on the outline, and plan to do it in this manner: Make it a short novel of about 20,000 words (about

* Styron was probably reading George McLean Harper's *William Wordsworth: His Life, Works, and Influence* (London: John Murray, 1916). Wordsworth's "The Two Thieves, or The Last Stage of Avarice" is based on this story.

the length of "Goodbye, Mr. Chips"), dividing it into 10 chapters of approximately 2,000 words each. The story, as I see it, should fall into three parts, namely, (a) Jenny at home in Guinea, (b) her life, and the various conflicts that arise at the hospital, and (c) the finale in the South Pacific.*

But still more complications arise. In a novel of this sort, one must obey the certain rules of technicality which crop up. Not ever having been a nurse, or overseas, I would hesitate to describe life in either place. So I'll have to do some research. First, find out from Elizabeth the following things:

(1) How does a prospective nurse make application for a hospital career in nursing?
(2) What courses do the nurses take, and later, what specific courses would an anesthetist take? How long would all this take?
(3) How would a girl make application for becoming a Navy nurse?
(4) What are some of the duties of the student nurse, and of the Navy nurse?

The rest, I think, I can find out from the library and from my friends at Duke Hospital.

Right now, the plan as a whole seems to be taking good form in my mind, and I think that if I do a good job on it, work hard, it might turn out to be something. However, I won't know until I've finished it. I'll start on the first part, and you send me the information. With careful revision, it should be finished in a month and a half.

Thanks a lot for the idea, and I'll keep in touch with you as to my progress.

Your son,
Bill jr.

Ask Eliza to tell you of any typical class-room incidents which have reflected the general ignorance of a country girl. Please tell her also, that <u>anything</u> she can tell me about nurse training I can use.

* This novel does not survive. Christopher Morley's *Kitty Foyle,* a 1939 bestseller, was narrated by a working-class woman from Philadelphia. James Hilton's 1934 *Goodbye, Mr. Chips* was set at a British boarding school.

*Styron arrived at Parris Island for boot camp in October 1944. He was almost immediately confined to the urinary ward of the base's hospital when his blood falsely tested positive for syphilis. After a stay of more than two weeks, Styron was informed that he actually had trench mouth and was allowed to resume training.**

To William C. Styron, Sr.

November 25, 1944 Parris Island, SC

Dear Pop,

I received your letter today, and was very glad to hear from you. I have not yet gotten the underwear, but I imagine that they will arrive in a day or two.

Today I fired the M1 rifle for the first time, and I am now firmly convinced that it is without a doubt the finest small-bore weapon in the world. Its accuracy and power are unbelievable until you actually fire one. The M1 has a chamber pressure of 32,000 lbs. per sq. inch, and yet it has a very slight recoil. It gives one almost a sense of exhilaration to fire one—the sense of power it gives you is uncanny. It is semi-automatic, and will fire as fast as the trigger is pulled (squeezed, I mean); it fires, extracts, ejects the cartridge, and reloads in 1/40 of a second. Of course by now we've learned the nomenclature and functioning backward and forward, but it is rather complicated. Even as complicated as it is, though, we can field strip completely and reassemble the rifle in less than a minute. Another interesting feature of the weapon is the fact that it not only fires a clip of eight rounds as fast as the trigger is pulled, but automatically ejects the empty clip after the eight rounds are fired. While I've gotten off to an excellent start, I think, in learning my positions, trigger squeeze, windage, etc., it's going to take quite a bit of practice before I can fire expert.

I'm glad you wrote me what you did in your last letter. Frankly, I was very worried when I was in the hospital for fear I had syphilis; and of course I was very relieved when I heard that the positive Kahn came as a

* Styron wrote about his hospital experience in the play *In the Clap Shack* (New York: Random House, 1973) and in the essay "A Case of the Great Pox," *The New Yorker,* September 18, 1995, reprinted in *Havanas in Camelot: Personal Essays* (New York: Random House, 2008).

result of trench mouth. If I had had the disease, I wouldn't have known where it could have come from, for, although I'm not exactly what one could term an angel, I have always taken extreme precaution about what sort of women I went out with. Last night when I first started to write this letter, I wrote a couple of pages attempting to explain my views on the idea of morality. After rereading it, I tore it up because it really makes no difference to you or anyone else what my moral philosophy is. I'm probably not old enough to have such a philosophy. I know this for a fact, though—that the morality which we have in a so-called "moral" society is the weakest leg that civilization has to stand upon. The religion of the Church, which is the basis for morality, is a religion of hypocrisy, and each man should realize that the good life is a life of Good Will, a life of Love and Loneliness (as Thomas Wolfe would say), and not the fanatical adherence to a Book, most of which is a gruesome melange of cruelty and pagan cosmology. The Bible begins with the fantastic story of Adam and Eve, continues through countless bloody anecdotes of "religious" warfare, torture, and human sacrifice, and ends with St. John's laudanum dream of an absurd and impossible Apocalypse. In parts the Bible is a literary masterpiece. Nothing finer has been written than the story of Job and the sermon of Ecclesiastes, and I believe that if Christ was not the son of God, he approached such a divine kinship as nearly as any man ever born. But it is impossible for me to cling to a Faith which attempts, and succeeds in too many cases, in foisting upon the multitude a belief in so much which is utter fantasy. And it is such a religion which, throughout its history of corruption and strife, has promulgated its own standard for morality behind a thin veil of cant and hypocrisy. I have my own personal religion, and I believe that I am as steadfast in it as any one of our Baptist Fundamentalists. I am far from believing with George Santayana that religion is the "opiate of the poor"; but I do believe that an overdose of religious activity, in which people tend to take the syrupy tenets of the preacher and the vindictive dogmatisms of the Old Testament at face value, both deadens the mind and makes life a pretty sterile and joyless affair.*

I have probably not made myself very clear (which makes little difference), and I imagine you are not a little disappointed in knowing that

* Styron misattributes to Santayana the statement of Karl Marx, "Religion is the opium of the people."

your boy, after all those years of Sunday School, has not "turned out right"; but please don't think that I have sunk into the slough of degeneracy. I have never as yet done anything which I was really ashamed of. After the war I'm going to write a book and tell people what I think. Carlyle, I think it was, said that the real preachers are not those who stand behind the pulpit, but who sit behind a writing desk. In the meantime I'm going to keep on thinking, loving Life as much as I can in a world where the value of life is only the value of the lead in a .30 calibre bullet, and loving my fellow man (which the greatest Preacher said was the finest virtue of all).

Well, I hope you don't think what I've said sounds ostentatious for one who has not quite reached his 20th birthday. I might still be a college boy know-nothing with a sophomoric attitude, but I still think quite unreservedly that I have more understanding than quite a few people of my age.

I won't be home for Christmas. I am now in the real Marine Corps, and there is no redundance of furloughs. When and if I get to Quantico, though, I think I'll be able to get home fairly often. I'm almost positive I'll get a furlough before I get shipped overseas.

I'd better close now. Please give Eliza my love, and I certainly hope she's feeling better by now.

Your son,
Bill jr.

To William Blackburn*

November 28, 1944 Parris Island, SC

Dear Professor Blackburn,

I am now in the hospital, so I have plenty of time to write letters.† Now and then they call me to carry out the garbage, but that won't hinder me too much.

* William Blackburn was a renowned literature professor at Duke University who helped create the school's creative writing program. He mentored Styron as well as the writers Mac Hyman, Reynolds Price, Fred Chappell, and Anne Tyler. Styron said of him: "He possessed that subtle, magnetically appealing quality—a kind of invisible rapture—which caused students to respond with like rapture to the fresh and wondrous new world he was trying to reveal to them. . . . He was unquestionably a glorious teacher."

† Styron's stay in Parris Island V.D. Hospital.

I don't know exactly why I'm in here, or what I've got, but it seems that I contracted a case of Vincent's angina (euphemism for trench mouth), which set up some sort of reaction in my blood. I've been in here almost two weeks, and they've done nothing at all. I feel perfectly healthy, and spend most of my time reading Action Comics and well-worn copies of Zane Grey and Agatha Christie. At night I go to the movies with a V-12 from Franklin + Marshall who has the same trouble that I do.

Yesterday I went to the Post Library for the first time. It's a very good library. They have some excellent poetry anthologies, and some fine novels. I checked out Crime and Punishment, and am reading it now.

I have lost my platoon, so I will have to go to the rifle range and the rest of boot camp with another platoon. I won't like that at all, but I suppose it can't be helped.

Bobbie Taeusch wrote and told me that you wanted to cut the "love angle" in my story.* That's perfectly okay with me, and I wish you would make what other corrections you see fit. I can write a story, but have little faculty for criticism; so you make whatever changes you think should be made. Bobbie also said something about the Archive wanting to print the story, which is all right with me, too.

Well, I'd better close now, since they want me to carry out the garbage.

Sincerely,

Bill Styron

To William C. Styron, Sr.

February 14, 1945 Parris Island, SC

Dear Pop,

I received your letter, and letters of recommendation, and also the long letter you wrote me—which came belatedly through the devious channels of the Marine Corps mail system.

I especially enjoyed the letter you wrote me—the one in which you enclosed the letter from Mr. Fleet. Naturally I was very happy to learn that

* Barbara "Bobbie" Taeusch was a classmate of Styron's at Duke, a student of William Blackburn, and one of Styron's first serious girlfriends.

my story was accepted so favorably by the Virginia Writers' Club, and I am only sorry that my inevitable redundance of adjectives kept me from winning the prize. However, it is almost impossible for me to become what you termed swellheaded over any of my so-called literary achievements. Although I'm no scholar, I have read enough to know that my stories are very insignificant compared to what people have written, are writing, and what I myself would one day like to write. Especially during wartime, as I am beginning to find out, the futility of writing, art, of most everything—becomes more apparent. As you said, there is a story around every corner, and I see a million potential stories around me all the time. Now the crux of the situation lies in the fact that, to the writer, war is a gigantic, inexorable, relentlessly terrible panorama which, although at every hand fraught with mists of beauty and pathos, swirls about him so swiftly and chaotically that he is unable to find a tongue to utter his thoughts. And after the war, if he has extricated himself from the whole mess with a sound mind and body, he is usually so terribly cynical and embittered that those golden words turn to dust. To be platitudinous, it changes one's viewpoint immensely. Like Wolfe's Eugene Gant I see "Time, dark time, flowing by me like a river"—and that is all one can say. I intend to write some more, whenever I get a chance. That story that you have an idea for sounds very interesting, and I would like to hear the details.

Whenever I get a chance I'm going to write to Mr. Fleet and thank him for his kind words. I was astounded at the impressive array of judges who liked the story, and until I read Mr. Fleet's letter I had no idea what competition I was up against. I also enjoyed Eliza's letter, and please tell her I will write at length when I find time.

My application for O.C. has not gone through as yet, and I am still in a state of confusion.* This company is due to ship out for California (dread word!) sometime around the 23rd of this month, and I fully expect to ship out with everyone else, unless a miracle happens. I'm sure that, with a little prodding, the application would go through and be accepted (since I passed the physical), but at present it is lying dormant somewhere in the sergeant-major's office—while the hour of departure fast approaches! I

* Officer Candidate School.

don't mind going to the West Coast and points beyond if I am definitely out of O.C., but I fear that all is lost if I get to San Diego without having had any action taken on the application while I was here at Lejeune. If you have any friends who are friends of Forrestal or any of the other Navy-Marine Corps gods, it certainly wouldn't hurt to give them the word, as I am beginning to think that I have been kicked around enough.*

If we are all not restricted to the base this week-end, I will try my very best to get up to see you. It may be the last time for quite awhile, so I will try and get a pass. If I do get off, I'll wire you before-hand, giving time of arrival, etc.

Well, I had better close now. Again, I appreciate the fine letter; and that "pardnership of Styron + Styron" is okay with me! Please write soon, and love to all.

Your son,
Bill

P.S. You should have seen me throwing TNT grenades today. Quite a thrill!

To William Blackburn

May 8, 1945 Quantico, Virginia

Dear Professor Blackburn,

I got your note last Saturday, and was both surprised and pleased to learn that my story had been received so favorably by the judges of the Story contest. Since I was home last weekend, and saw the letter which you had written to my father, I was still more surprised to learn that the story stood among the top ten or so.†

* James V. Forrestal (1892–1949) was Franklin D. Roosevelt's Secretary of the Navy from 1944 to 1947.

† Blackburn replied to Styron, Sr., on January 19, 1945, "I know you are proud of William, especially since, as you say, he has chosen to be so tight-mouthed about his literary efforts. Having seen him come a long way in these efforts, I am proud of him too. He is one of the very few students I've had in the past fifteen years about whom I was pretty safe in saying, 'You can become a writer if you want to be.'"

As you might have noticed from my address, I am at Quantico now, taking a "refresher course" which will ostensibly prepare me for the O.C.S. So far it has proved to be nothing much more than a relief from the atrocities of New River, since the program here is designed more to treat us like gentlemen and future officers, and less like recruits. I am scheduled to enter O.C.S. in about two weeks, and from then on out I can only keep my fingers crossed, and hope I make it.

I have an idea for another story germinating, but I don't know when I'll get a chance to write it down. I also see more and more every day which might go toward that novel, and I hope to come back to Duke after the war and complete it.

Whenever I finish writing the story I have in mind I'll send it to you for criticism, approval, and disposition. Thanks again for all the help you've given me, and I hope to see you sometime before very long—with bars, I hope.

Sincerely,
Bill Styron

Styron was commissioned as a second lieutenant in the U.S. Marine Corps in July 1945. Following the nuclear bombing of Hiroshima and Nagasaki in August, Japan surrendered on September 2, 1945. After commanding a guard platoon on Hart's Island in Long Island Sound, Styron was discharged in December and he returned to Duke in March 1946.

To William C. Styron, Sr.

March 8, 1946 Duke University

Dear Pop,

I just now went down and got the money order, which I appreciate very much. I will attempt to keep track of all my expenditures. For two days I was flat broke, but borrowed a few dollars from a friend of mine, Ben Williamson, who is a medical student here.

My trunk just got here, too. They held it for some time—why, I don't know—down in Durham. So all last week I slept on a bare mattress (which I've done many times before) and used my overcoat for a blanket. I presume that I have a roommate—most of his clothes are on an empty bed and the man at the rooming office told me I had a roommate—but he certainly hasn't showed up yet.

I spent my first night here with Prof. Blackburn, and the next day he helped me make out my course card. He advised me to take the minimum number of subjects, so that I may have time to write on my novel. He's fully expecting me to write one, it seems; and although I want to—and probably will—I don't see <u>now</u> one in the offing. However I'm going to start pitching in and see if I can't finish one in six or eight months.

I'm taking Russian history, Psychology, Geology, and—of course—Composition under Prof. Blackburn.* The Russian course and Psychology both look very interesting, and the Geology—for a science—doesn't look too hard.

Duke is the same old Duke, full of vacuous looking Long Island <u>nouveaux riches</u>, and odd-looking persons, dressed exquisitely in the latest in male + female fashions, who, I surmise, are here because they couldn't get into Princeton or Vassar. It's a shame, I think, that the current situation prevents me from going to Columbia or U.N.C., but I don't suppose it will be too bad here.

I find that I only know two or three people here—mostly medical students whom I knew at Davidson—but, if my present judgment is correct, I don't care to know too many of these noisy oafs.

There are three things which I wish you would try and find for me. First, a desk lamp. Duke, naturally, doesn't provide a study lamp. Also a record player and typewriter. I don't necessarily need a typewriter (for I can't type) but I do need the lamp. If you can also find a second-hand record player combination, it would be fine, for I really feel the need of good music at times.

Write me a letter. Take care of yourself, and give my best to Eliza and Helen.

Your son,
WCS jr

* "Composition" was a seminar in creative writing.

To William C. Styron, Sr.

May 6, 1946 Duke University

Dear Pop,

I am enclosing a notice from the Dean's Office which was sent to all students in reference to entrance here next Fall. As you can see, it will be necessary to pay the $25 fee—which will be refunded to veterans—or else one loses all right to a reservation.

Please send me a check for that amount before May 10. Although it's true I might get into Carolina, I still don't think I'd better take any chances, do you?* Professor Blackburn, anyway, has suggested that I sweat it out here at Duke for another semester—since that's all I'll have to go. He said that the very fact that I dislike Duke might be a greater incentive toward my finishing the "novel," since if I went over to Carolina the atmosphere might be too distracting. I think perhaps he's right.

I got a letter from Crown Publishers today, which is headed by Hiram Haydn, ex-professor of English at W.C.U.N.C. Blackburn wrote him about my projected book, and Mr. Haydn wrote in return that he'd be glad to read it when I finished it. So, with Rinehart, that makes two publishing houses that I know will at least give the ms. consideration.†

I'm not progressing too fast on the ms., but I don't mind since I think it's best to take my time. It'll probably take a year or more, including this summer.

I received the $65 and the clippings, both of which I appreciate very much.

Give my best to Eliza and Helen.

Your son,

Bill jr.

* Styron had hoped to finish his degree at the University of North Carolina in Chapel Hill but graduated from Duke.

† Blackburn sent copies of *One and Twenty* to several editors in New York, including Hiram Haydn, who had taught English at the Women's College of the University of North Carolina in Greensboro. Styron's "Autumn" and "The Long Dark Road" appeared in *One and Twenty.* Styron received letters from John Selby, an editor at Rinehart, and Haydn, who was then an editor at Crown. Haydn became Styron's first New York mentor and the editor of *Lie Down in Darkness,* which was published by Bobbs-Merrill in 1951.

To William C. Styron, Sr.

June 10, 1946 Duke University

Dear Pop,

I received your letter and telegram, both of which I enjoyed very much. In regard to your encouraging telegram, I can only say that I don't know how "gigantic" a stature I can ever realize, but I hope I will always have the assiduousness and will-power to learn, and to work toward doing the very best I can. As each day goes by I acquire more and more introspection into my own make-up, and I know that I have many faults and weaknesses—some of them very bad—but I hope to fight toward conquering these weak spots and foibles to the best of my ability. It's a hard job, but I can succeed.

I have two more exams, and then I leave for New York; but I'll be back on the 26th or 27th. It will certainly be a pleasure to see Aunt Edith again, won't it? It's really been a long time . . .

I don't know what I'm going to do for the remainder of the summer—outside of going to Middlebury—but if I stay at home I fully expect to establish for myself a definite schedule for reading and writing. By establishing such a schedule I'll go at least part of the way toward conquering my chief fault—laziness.

I wish you would send me $25 for the trip before this Friday P.M., as I may need some extra money. I think I'll have enough money anyway, but I would like to have $25 "just in case." In case I don't use it, I'll return it. I'll see you soon. Give my best to everyone.

Your son,

Bill jr.

To William C. Styron, Sr.

October 21, 1946 Duke University

Dear Pop,

It'll be necessary to send in with my application for the Rhodes Scholarship State committee (I passed the local board) (a) a statement certified by you before a notary public that I was born on June 11, 1925, and (b) the names of two citizens who can attest to my character, sobriety, virtue, and all that sort of thing. I don't have to have the statements, but merely the names of two reputable and fairly prominent people who will be willing to write a short panegyric if called upon by the Committee. However, I have to have the application in by November 2nd, so please send these to me as soon as possible. My chances are mighty slim in getting anything out on this deal, but I don't suppose it'll hurt to try.*

I've still got some money left from the check you sent me, but not much. My check from the V.A. will undoubtedly not get here until the first of next month, food still costs $1.50 a day, and Bobbie is coming down on Nov. 2 for the homecoming game. Please send me $15 with the letter, as I fear I shall be in desperate straits before the end of the month. At that, I'll probably have to ask for more if my Veterans' check doesn't come before Bobbie gets here.†

I'm fed up, disgusted, and totally out of sorts with Duke University and formal education in general, for that matter, and I hardly see why I'm taking a crack at this Rhodes scholarship when I'm such an execrable student. Only the fact that this is my last semester keeps me from packing up and leaving.

I've come to the stage when I know what I want to do with my future. I want to write, and that's all, and I need no study of such quaint American writers as Cotton Mather or Philip Freneau—both of whom we are studying in American Lit—to increase my perception or outlook on literature and life. For a person whose sole burning ambition is to write—like myself—college is useless beyond the Sophomore year. By that time he knows that further wisdom comes from reading men like Plato + Montaigne—not Cotton Mather—and from getting out in the world and living. All of the rest of the scholarship in English literature is for pallid, prim and vapid young men who will end up teaching and devoting 30 years of their sterile lives in investigating some miserably obscure facet of the life of a minor Renaissance poet. Sure, scholarship is necessary, but it's

* Styron's mentor, William Blackburn, who had urged Styron to apply, was a Rhodes Scholar and a member of the North Carolina selection committee. See Styron, "Almost a Rhodes Scholar," in the 1993 edition of *This Quiet Dust*.

† Styron finished his degree under the G.I. Bill (Servicemen's Readjustment Act of 1944), which paid college expenses and provided fifty dollars a month in pocket money for unmarried veterans of the war. Styron's checks were issued by the Veterans' Administration ("V.A.").

not for me. I'm going to write, and I'll spend the rest of my days on a cattle-boat or jerking sodas before I'll teach.

So far, though, I'm making good grades and I hope to get out of here soon.

Give my best to everybody,

Your son,

Bill jr

To Robert Penn Warren*

December 11, 1946 Duke University

Dear Mr. Warren,

Dr. William Blackburn, who teaches Creative writing here at Duke University, suggested that I write you in regard to the possibility of my studying writing under you at Minnesota after I graduate in January. Rather than burden you with any manuscripts now, I would like to know first if you would care to read any of my stories, and if you regarded them with favor, if there is any chance of taking your course at Minnesota.

In 1944, I won an Honorable Mention in Story's college contest, and two of my stories were included in One and Twenty, the Duke anthology of student prose and verse. Mr. Peter Taylor came over from W.C.U.N.C. in Greensboro, sitting as guest critic in our class, and completely demolished one of my latest efforts, but remarked that the story was well above the college level.

I would be glad to send you some of my manuscripts, if you are considering admitting new students to your class.

Very Truly Yours,

William C. Styron, Jr.

Styron graduated from Duke in early 1947.

* This letter was written to Warren when he was a member of the Department of English at the University of Minnesota.

To William C. Styron, Sr.

March 2, 1947 Duke University

Dear Pop,

Of making many books there is no end, and much study is a weariness of the flesh.* Therefore, taking a sudden and rather desperate inspiration from Ecclesiastes, and from mine own turbulent mind which for quite some time has been rebelling against the academic cloister—such as one may call a cloister at Duke—I have decided to throw it all up and go elsewhere for my wisdom. In other words—I should be blunt—I'm leaving Duke as soon as I settle my affairs.

There is, I think, little need for rationalization. After four trying years of college I finally have my degree (an end, I think, in itself) and I can only foresee a modicum of knowledge to be gained from three stretched-out and ineffectual months at Duke. I am doing nothing here now but boring myself, drinking beer, and wasting time better wasted somewhere else. Duke, as you know, in all of its aspects, has pained me to a certain degree always, and I have only been happy in this environment through a suspension of reason and through the utmost exertion of will. Consequently, having obtained the much sought-for sheepskin, I see little reason why I should irritate myself any longer. In short, I quite frankly think that I'm wasting my time now in, for the most part, unattractive surroundings and that—though my mental bewilderment and unrest is not contingent upon Duke alone—I should definitely begin to try my luck in another and perhaps more auspicious climate.

So I will be home sometime within a week—will wire you the exact time. I realize, as you do, that my being at home for any length of time is a rather nervous and uncertain business, so I hope you'll believe me when I say that I hope to get a job lined up elsewhere soon. I also hope, though, that it'll be all right if I can plan upon staying at home until I do get straightened out.

This move I am making—though I perhaps, egotistically, exaggerate its import—is not conventional and is, at the same time, an important decision. But it is not impetuous. I have given it good thought.

* Ecclesiastes 12:12.

I'm sorry the bonding company bothered you with their forms but, as usual, I used your name in reference. I don't know why in hell they should worry about me running off with any of this garbage I have to read.

I understand from Bobbie that Mary April is coming up here sometime soon. I think Bobbie has written her, and we'll be sure to have entertainment on hand when she comes. New York is vast, hideous, and strewn with the wrecks of lost and fidgeting souls. It's a trap, venomous, and woe to the person who stays here too long.

I'll try to be a better correspondent in the future. Drop me a line and give my best to Mrs. Blackburn.

As ever,

Bill

P.S. Since I live in a gloomy dung-heap down in the Village—a place which I avoid like the plague—perhaps it would be better for you to write me at the above address.

To William C. Styron, Sr.

August 20, 1947 Whittlesey House

Dear Pop,

I hadn't realized that time passes so fast, for when I looked at the date on your last letter I found that our last communication was nearly three weeks ago. Life is progressing here about the same. New York has been fiercely hot during the past few weeks but has moderated during the last couple of days. The weatherman, however, promises that a two-day heat wave will begin anew tomorrow. I haven't made definite plans yet, but think I might run down to see Bobbie in Washington tomorrow for the week-end. But, since I had planned to see her Labor Day week-end, I don't know if I'll splurge to the extent of seeing her both times. Bill Bowman wants me to go down to Urbanna with him on Labor Day, and I'm considering that, too. I haven't been down to the old place in a long time, now.

New York can get painfully monotonous, especially on Saturday and Sunday, when there's no place especially to go. Most of the people I knew here when I first came up have flown the coop, so I have to more or less shift for myself when it comes to entertainment. But then some wise man said that an educated man is one who can (1) entertain a new idea, (2) entertain his friends, and (3) entertain himself. The last is the hardest to do for me, but with the aid of things like books I am gradually developing to the point that I don't of necessity need people around me all the time—or beer! At the present I'm reading a new novel Under the Volcano, by Malcolm Lowry, which got excellent reviews. I haven't gotten far enough into it to deliver any opinion, but it certainly looks, so far, as if it's really something. The books I've been reading at Whittlesey House have been uniformly bad—or mediocre. I had the pleasure the other day of delivering an opinion on a book by Walter B. Pitkin ("Life Begins at 40") which he sent in as a possibility. It was a manuscript called ON YOUR WAY AT 20, directed toward young boys who, denied college, have to get out on their own. Mr. Scheaffer, the editor, wanted my judgment of the book, and I wrote what I thought—a platitudinous pep-talk, full of the same worship of spurious values which made LIFE BEGINS AT 40 such a success. Mr. Larned, the director, read the report, liked it, and I'm pretty sure that Mr. Pitkin's phony blandishments are doomed as a result of my report, at least as far as Whittlesey is concerned.*

No results on an apartment yet, although Bill Bowman and I have signed up together for an apartment in Peter Cooper Village, Metropolitan Life's new development on the East River.†

They didn't promise us anything over there, but said that we stood a fair chance of getting something before Christmas. I don't think I'm a complete sybarite, but I believe that even a Jesuit would find it gloomy business living in the box I live in. Imagine a room the size of the big bathroom upstairs at home, ill-lighted, decorated with muddy wall-paper, and subjected to a ninety degree temperature all summer, and you'll get an idea of my nocturnal mode of living.

Continuing our genealogical discussion, I would be most happy if you would send me any information or anecdota concerning Beaufort County, the Clarks, Styrons, or anything else that you think might form germina-

* Pitkin's *Life Begins at Forty* was published by Whittlesey House in 1932.

† Metropolitan Life Insurance Company built this enormous complex of low- and middle-income housing in the late 1940s and early 1950s. Styron never lived there.

tive thoughts in my mind and get me started on a saga of Eastern North Carolina. I've got lots of ideas and theories but, like Sinclair Lewis, I'll have to search through records to find a family framework upon which to hang my story.

I see in the papers that the Terminal Leave bonds of veterans may be cashed any time after September 1st. You are holding one for me, I believe, and I wish you would send it to me some time before that date so I may add it to my savings account. It's written out for about $225—with a picture of Carter Glass on it—and I'd rather cash it and add it to my account, since in the form of a bond it doesn't pay interest, as the War Bonds do.*

That's about all the news for now. I'm glad to hear that you are coming up in November, and I'll see that you are properly feted, as they say in the society columns. Tell Eliza that I'm glad she is continuing on with the story, and hope she sends it to me. I'll write her soon.

Your son,

Bill

P.S. Peace of Mind is gratis. After all, we in the publishing business have to get something at discount.

To Tom Greet†

August 22, 1947 Whittlesey House

Dear Tom:

Our dear and mutual friend, William Blackburn, dropped in on me this morning, we had lunch together, and I was pleasantly regaled with the late goings-on at Duke this past semester, amid which it seems that you and Mac and Mr. Davenport have certainly been creditably acquitting yourselves in the literary field.‡ I wish I had your pertinacity.

* Carter Glass (1858–1946), a native of Lynchburg, Virginia, and Secretary of the Treasury under Woodrow Wilson.

† Greet was another writing pupil of William Blackburn at Duke.

‡ Styron refers to Blackburn's students and aspiring writers Mac Hyman and Guy Davenport. Mac Hyman (1923–63) was born in Cordele, Georgia, and was a fellow pupil

Blackburn informed me also that he had taken your manuscript to Diarmuid Russell, spoke very kindly of Mr. Russell, and suggested that I get in touch with him in regard to sending your manuscript over as a possibility for Whittlesey House. I did so, and he told me that, although he had sent the chapters and outline to one publisher, you had not definitely decided whether you wanted the manuscript to go to another publisher—in case the first was not interested—or whether you wanted to do some more work on it first. I'm sure you're your own best critic—as Dr. Baum was wont to say—but should the first publisher not be encouraging (which I hope he won't, for your sake), I do hope you'll remember that I'm interested in your work and that you'll ask Mr. Russell to put Whittlesey House high on the list of publishers next to see the manuscript. When I last saw you, your novel—at that time a short story, I believe—was still in the germinative stage, but it sounded promising and I never did get the chance to see how it turned out. Blackburn is enthused to say the least, and I hope that you and Mr. Russell will arrange it so that we might take a look.

The Professor and I are going down by train together to Washington this afternoon—I for a week-end and he for a bit of scholarship at the Folger Library. I know I'll pick up some wisdom along the way. I hope you'll drop me a line and let me know how you are progressing on the book, and in case you get up to New York any time soon I'll consider it an affront if you don't give me a call.

Best regards,
William Styron
Associate Editor

---

of Blackburn at Duke. His novel *No Time for Sergeants* was published by Random House in 1954. Another novel, *Take Now Thy Son,* was published in 1965. After his untimely death, Professor Blackburn put together a collection of his letters, *Love, Boy: The Letters of Mac Hyman* (Baton Rouge: Louisiana State University Press, 1969). Guy Davenport (1927–2005) was a prolific poet, writer, and translator, a Rhodes Scholar and MacArthur Fellow. He eventually published twenty-two original works of fiction and poetry along with a dozen major translations.

vinced of its youthful truth and passion and genuine loveliness that I can only look upon Guy Davenport with the greatest awe and respect. If Guy doesn't become, within the next decade or so, one of America's best writers, then my faith in whatever grim and fickle god who so capriciously guides the destinies of sad, golden men—men like Guy Davenport—I will be shattered forever. Such poetry, such beauty! I am amazed and thankful, and a bit embarrassed at my effusion. Quite frankly I am unable to say what the book's chances for publication are, since it is not the sort of book, I know, that the average publisher takes to; and since I'm no longer a "publisher" I can't exert even mild pressure and opinion in the right places. But I will commend it as highly as possible to the people I know at Whittlesey House, and will hope for the best. The astute publisher and editor, I know, would accept it per se—with all of its faults—just to get their hands on such a promising talent. I'll do my best.

It is, then—in view of Mr. Davenport's work—with a considerable feeling of inadequacy, that I submit a short story for your appraisal. I am taking Hiram Haydn's writing seminar and this is one of the stories he read in class. He liked it. In fact, he praised it in the most glowing terms, said all sorts of things—including the induction of a dark sort of symbolism which I really didn't intend—which embarrassed me and troubled me and made me very happy. If I didn't know, from having attended other classes, that he is a rather harsh critic, then I would take his words lightly. He thinks the story should be published. My self-critical faculties are very dull, and I would greatly appreciate your letting me know—quite objectively—whether or not you think the story stands a chance, before I try it out on the magazines.*

There will, one day—and I say this with hope and with candor and with, believe me, the utmost sincerity—be a school of writing known, perhaps, as the Blackburnian "school" of writing. It will not be—as in the manner of Ruskin or of Pater or of any of that vast crew of pontificates and precious fathers—a "school" formed out of style or manner or mannerism or substance, but will be—God and the world willing—a group of people

* Styron refers to his story "A Moment in Trieste," which was eventually published in the anthology of New School writers, Don M. Wolfe, ed., *American Vanguard* (New York: Cambridge Publishing Co., 1948), and reprinted in *William Styron: Letters to My Father,* 205–10.

who—talented, gifted perhaps, but "not as great as Chaucer"—shall have derived from the founder of the school a certain grace, a certain wisdom, a certain understanding, without which their meager talents would have been lost. And the product of their search and wonder—an end indeed as perishable as the flowers, or any other thing—will nevertheless have been enriched and ennobled, and the way made more plain, through their having known one man, for a moment, who was gentle, wise, honest and good. Some do not know it—others, who know, will not speak it—and I for one know it, and say this with all certainty and humility.

I would appreciate your giving me an opinion of the story, and hope to hear from you soon.

As ever,
Bill S.

To William C. Styron, Sr.

October 28, 1947 New York

Dear Pop,

I received your letter the other day, and was glad to hear that we are both coming into a little cash.* Your borrowing half of my share is perfectly all right with me—better, in fact, since it assures me, for a time, of a steady income each month. I am now listed with the New York State bureau as a "self-employed" veteran and will be receiving $80 a month from that department which, along with the $60 you send me, will make a tidy $140—about the same as my starting salary at McGraw-Hill.

I was also happy to hear that you are coming to N.Y. next month, and I'll certainly be on hand to give you a big welcome. I wrote Aunt Edith and told her when you are coming, and expressed the hope that she would be here at the same time, so we could all do the town together.

The story I mentioned in my last letter was read in Hiram Haydn's seminar at the New School. Haydn, as I think I told you, is editor of Crown Publishers and also editor of the extremely respectable American

* Styron's maternal grandmother, Belle Abraham, left money in her will to Styron and his father. Styron used this experience for the story of the slave Artiste in *Sophie's Choice*.

Scholar, journal of the Phi Beta Kappa organization. Haydn, who is a fairly harsh critic, said that the story was "terrific," "powerful," and "certainly publishable," all of which delighted me no end. I also sent a copy to Blackburn and Brice, both of whom thought the story was excellent. Brice suggested that I send the story to The New Yorker, which I have done (no answer yet) and then to the various literary quarterlies. The New Yorker is very particular about the names of their authors, and I doubt seriously if they will accept it; but both Blackburn and Brice are convinced that I can get the thing published somewhere so I'm going to keep trying until I get an acceptance.

I'm very glad that you see eye to eye with me about my present attitude concerning my attempts at writing, and about the loss of my job. I realize that I've finally come to grips with myself, and that the job was in reality merely a delaying action. Writing for me is the hardest thing in the world, but also a thing which, once completed, is the most satisfying. I have been reading the letters of Joseph Conrad, and really feel a kinship—if nothing but in spirit—with the late master, for one discovers in the letters that writing, for Conrad, was the most despairing, painful job in the world.* It most definitely is that way for me. But someone—I think it was Henry James—said that only through monstrous travail and agonizing effort can great art be brought forth from those who, like himself (James), are not prodigies or, like Shelley, spontaneous founts of genius. Anything less than unceasing toil will produce nothing or, at best, facility. I am no prodigy but, Fate willing, I think I can produce art. For me it takes much girding up of loins and an almost imbecile faith in my potentials—but I suppose that's part of the satisfaction.

I'd better close now. Give my love to Eliza, and I'll see you soon.

Your son,

Bill jr

* Joseph Conrad (1857–1924) was a Polish-born novelist best known for his novel *Heart of Darkness*. Styron was likely sent Conrad's letters by William Blackburn, who was editing *Joseph Conrad: Letters to William Blackwood and David S. Meldrum* (Durham, N.C.: Duke University Press, 1958).

of money if I write a novel. Of course, since I haven't written anything on the novel he can't offer me a contract right now. But he was so enthusiastic over the stories that he called me down to his office at Crown and told me that he had informed the publishing director (the big shot) at Crown that he had so much faith in my potentialities that he suggested that they break their rule (against giving advance-on-royalties to unknown writers) in my case. The publishing director finally agreed, after a lot of rhetoric by Haydn, so now all I have to do is write the damn novel. I have to write a first chapter and outline and Haydn said he'd do all he could to help me along with it so it would be met with approval by his associates. Of course all this doesn't mean that it's in the bag and I wouldn't like it to be rumored about that Styron has finished the great American novel; but it has inspired me with such confidence that I know I can write a good novel.

It was interesting to hear more about Barbara Bottom's progress through life. Luckily I haven't run into her here in N.Y. yet. Probably wouldn't recognize her if I did. Who's the new man?*

Eliza, have you written anything else in your "spare time"? I still have your story here, which this friend of mine sent to a few magazines. She got some very nice notes back about the story, but no checks. I suppose you're partly right—magazines nowadays (even the good ones) just don't seem to want childhood stories. Do you want me to send it back to you, or would you rather me try again? I'd still like to see some more stuff you've written, as I think it's mighty good.

Thanks again to both of you for your nice presents. Write soon.

Love,

Billy

* Barbara was the daughter of Commander and Mrs. Raymond B. Bottom of Newport News. Her father was the owner of the *Newport News Daily Press.* Styron based the character of Peyton Loftis in *Lie Down in Darkness* in part on Barbara.

To William C. Styron, Sr.

March 31, 1948 New York

Dear Pop,

A much belated letter to let you know that I am still kicking and that everything is coming along all right. The little visit home, though short, was enjoyable and I'm only sorry that I couldn't stay longer. We are still having trouble with our landlady here—though nothing serious—otherwise the scene on the domestic front is okay. An evil brood, landladies!

I'm progressing well on the novel, although frankly it is a mystery to me how I am able to keep going from one section of the story to another. Haydn read the completed portion of the MS in class tonight and I am, to say the least, excited at what he told me (in front of the class) about the novel, to wit: "Although you can't really say anything positively, of course, until the novel is completed, this part seems to me to stand up beside <u>any contemporary American writer</u>." I nearly fell over and, of course, walked home in a daze. He said something about the fact that I have a "tragic sense" of the place and the people I'm writing about and, after class, told me he thought what I had written was "terrific." I needn't have to tell you that I'm terribly encouraged, because I feel sure that Haydn's comments and criticisms are judicious and considered.*

I can't tell you how much this novel means to me. The process of sitting down and writing is pure torture to me, but at the same time I think about the book all the time and am in more or less a suspended state of worry and anxiety if I'm <u>not</u> writing. I worry, too, about the sincerity of my effort; if whether what I'm writing is not so much rhetoric, and it is only in my most now-self-critical mood that I can even come vaguely to realize that what I write does, in truth, have an element of truth in it and is, after all, a more faithful rendering of life than I believe it to be in my moments of doubt.

The world situation is such that I—along, I suppose, with everyone else—really don't know whether a novel, or a symphony, or anything else, is worth the trouble or not. But I suppose that if you relinquish your claim

* Styron was working on *Inheritance of Night,* the early version of *Lie Down in Darkness.*

as an "individual," no matter what your endeavor might be, or in whatever state the world is in, you might as well cease living. So I'll go on writing, hoping that we will survive, and perhaps taking a measure of courage from the fact that in the face of disaster my story might become even more significant.

New York is beginning to wear on my nerves, and now that spring is coming I want to leave. The novelty has worn off; the city, with all its excitement and grandeur, is a terrible place. The tide swarms on; how people manage the pretense of humanity in such a jostling, surly ant-heap is beyond me. The eye bends down from the jutting skyscraper—man's material achievement—to gaze in horror on the pawing mess of Broadway at lunchtime and the greasy, muttering squalor of the interior of a subway car—surely the symbol of man's spiritual decay. I hope I get an offer of an advance on royalties from Crown within the next few weeks; I think I will. And that Eastern Shore deal, if you still want to try and help me out, sounds good indeed.

Do you think that if people learned to love one another, that if the collective human mind could be conditioned to good-will and rich laughter, the resultant effect would be boredom? That mutual hatred, a natural antipathy for his own species, is a predetermined condition of the state of man on earth? Sometimes it seems that way to me.

Haydn's words still ring in my ears. Wish me luck!

Your son,

Bill jr.

P.S. Did you read the reviews of Haydn's The Time Is Noon? Last Sunday's Times and Tribune's were fine, and the daily reviews in the same papers even better. (see enclosed)*

* Styron attached a mixed review from the March 28, 1948, *The New York Times Book Review* as well as more positive ones from the *New York Herald Tribune Weekly Book Review, The New York Times,* and the *Herald Tribune.*

To William Blackburn

May 28, 1948 Cordele, Georgia

Dear Professor Blackburn,

It has been a long time since I have written you and I am ashamed, but I have thought of you often, if that's any consolation at all.

I have been down here on the river with Mac and Gwendolyn for something less than a week and if I could I believe I would stay here forever. It's a wonderful place, isn't it? I think I nearly killed myself during my last bleak neurotic weeks in New York, staying up until dawn and sleeping miserably until the waning hours of afternoon. So, in desperation, I cunningly contrived to escape the city and took the "Southerner" to Atlanta, anxiously pondering a sour sort of guilt as I sat in the barren club car all night; and only when I arrived in Cordele and was installed in my room in this marvelous place on the river did I begin to breathe human breaths again, feel blood and not the city dweller's fetid sluggish fluid flow through my veins once more. In a week I have possessed myself of an incredibly healthy sense of well-being. The Georgia sunlight, I'm sure, contains more vitamins per cubic centimeter than all the synthetic, "niacin"-fortified bread north of Baltimore and for the first time in many months I am positively witless with virility. Mens sana in corpore sano.* The Hymans, of course, are wonderful. They send you their love.

I have signed a contract with Crown for my novel. The advance is $500; $100 now and $400 when I get a substantial amount of the book done. Mr. Haydn is a wonderfully sympathetic and human person and seems to be as enthusiastic about the novel as I am about the possibility of having him as an editor. I understand that you get a cut of the proceeds on the sale of the book, so I am sure we shall both soon be millionaires. The novel, as projected, concerns Newport News and the people there in general; in particular a girl, my age, who comes to no good end. It's all very melodramatic and morbid and tragic and I'm sure it will shake the foundations of the literary world—"cause a flutter in the literary dovecotes," as it were.† I'm already thoroughly dissatisfied with what I've written so far,

* Latin for "a healthy mind in a healthy body."

† An expression meaning to cause a stir in a quiet setting. A dovecote is a small compartment for domesticated pigeons.

even though Mr. Haydn likes it, and I fear that the book as a whole will be the most fearful mélange of stylistic apings and posturings ever seen.

In case you hadn't heard, American Vanguard, the New School anthology, is just off the press. I am represented—"a humble and sad" writer, it says in the introduction—by my Trieste story, a startlingly reactionary piece in a volume made up of inflammatory appeals for social consciousness, solemn fellow-traveler essays, and trouble "messages" by confused innocents. I am sure to be called a "callow armchair liberal" by some squat mustachioed female on the Daily Worker or PM, and am waiting, in a real tizzy, for the reviews to come out. I'm sure the book will sell all of 150 copies.

A Christchurch friend and I are planning a trip to England late in June, although we're still in the planning stage. If we go we'll leave from Montreal on a freighter, having learned that one can secure passage from that port for only $120, which is sure enough reasonable. Should the thing materialize I'd certainly like your advice on what to see, and where. I've always taken the advice you gave me to heart, and I remember your saying, in effect, that I might as well see England, and Europe, now, before life becomes too complicated.

I plan to stay here until around the middle of June and then I'm going to New York and pack up my things and remove myself from that most monstrous travesty of civilization. I don't feel I'm escaping, beaten, because I did make a mild success of my year there. I just heartily believe that anyone who stays there when he doesn't have to is a damn fool. On my way I hope to stop in Durham and I want to see you, if you are going to be there. I wish you'd drop me a short note and let me know. Please give my best to Mrs. Blackburn, and everyone.

As ever,

Bill S.

Styron left New York in July 1948 to live and write in Durham, North Carolina.

To William C. Styron, Sr.

July 11, 1948 814 Sixth Street, Durham, NC*

Dear Pop,

Suzie sent all my stuff—records, books, etc.—down from New York, so I am now prepared to move into the apartment that Bill Switzer and I have rented. The apartment, just in back of the Woman's College Campus, is in the first floor of a private home—two medium sized rooms, kitchen, bath, and large back yard, $40 per month. It is <u>not</u> furnished, and that is the big difficulty; we plan just to buy bare essentials at first—beds, chairs, kitchen utensils—and get the rest later. I'd appreciate it if you would send me a check for $150 as soon as possible, as I figure that is about what it'll take to supplement the money I already have to pay the first month's rent and buy a bed and maybe a lamp or two, besides food.†

Switzer and I have, in the meantime, been staying with Brice. I have done some work on the novel, but I find it pretty rough going. I don't seem to have the innate confidence in myself or my work which I suppose is a part of genius; consequently I am diverted too easily into less favorable channels—like reading <u>Time</u> magazine. Every word I put down seems to be sheer pain, and although I often am a victim of sloppy writing I have nonetheless too much of what I suppose is called artistic integrity to put down something I know is not true or merely a half-truth. Because of that, I suppose my sessions at the desk are doubly painful in that where someone else might put something—some idea or word-picture—to paper merely for the effect, I have to ponder and ponder and reject anything I sincerely believe at the time hints of fraudulence. Even so, I know there are many things in the work I've already accomplished that I didn't mean to say. I think the crux of the issue is merely that I don't know enough yet about people to be writing a novel. But I'm at least giving it my earnest application, and trying hard to put myself on an inflexible schedule. I realize that I'm among the favored few, that there are not many people my age who've been given the sort of encouragement I have and that it would be

* Ashbel Brice's apartment near Duke's East Campus.

† Suzie was one of Styron's girlfriends in New York. Switzer was a friend from Duke, but Styron shared the apartment with Bill Snitger, who worked at a radio station in Durham.

both sinful and weak not to attempt to live up to the faith that has been put in me. I'll have a novel finished next year this time—I hope a good one.

Durham is an ugly town but many of the people I know here are very fine. Last night, for instance, Brice had Frances Gray Patton* over. She's married to a Duke professor of history, is an O. Henry short story prize winner (see "One and Twenty") and is now a regular contributor to The New Yorker. A very charming lady. She lived as a girl in Newport News. Her father was editor of the Daily Press and Times Herald in the early twenties.

Write soon, and please don't forget the check.

Your son,

Bill jr.

To William C. Styron, Sr.

August 3, 1948 Durham, NC

Dear Pop,

It was nice seeing you the other week-end, and I hope you enjoyed it as much as I and the others did. You and Mr. Switzer seemed to have gotten along fine, struck a common chord. Bill said that he hadn't heard his father talk so much in years.

The novel is coming along at about its usual slow but steady turtle's pace. I read part of it to Dr. Blackburn and his class, and he seems to be immensely and sincerely pleased by what I've done so far. It's a tedious and agonizing process and I loathe writing with almost a panic hatred, but as I've said before I'm always restless when I'm not working at it. If ever I become well-known because of my writing, it may honestly be said by whatever person that chooses to tell about me: "he wrote in spite of himself." I know that what I've written so far on this book is good, but that it

* Patton (1906–2000) was one of the first professional writers whom Styron knew socially. Her stories appeared in various magazines, including *The New Yorker, McCall's,* and *Ladies' Home Journal;* her novel *Good Morning, Miss Dove* was published in 1976. Her best short fiction is collected in *Twenty-Eight Stories* (New York: Dodd, Mead, 1969).

is far from maturity or perfection. I've noticed the maturation process taking place in me and I know I've barely started growing. I do hope to get the book finished by next summer, but I just don't know, at the rate I'm going. A man just doesn't realize, I believe, what self-doubt and despair are until he's tried to express himself in a work of art. Perhaps that is a self-conscious and adolescent statement and maybe I use the word "art" too freely, but it's the way I feel now. My moral and intellectual values are as yet far too undeveloped for me to be able to assess the worth of this novel I'm writing in terms of its conception. I hope when I'm finished with it people will read it, and I hope it's at least a good start. Beyond anything, though, I hope that the writing of it will somehow enrich my own mind in that it may teach me perseverance and calm thought and make me more of a man. Writing a novel of course involves a good deal of contemplation—most of it, it is true, false or worthless—but it is my constant hope that this pure fact of contemplation, which wise men so cherish, may lead me into sunnier and wider avenues of the spirit. I don't say that with pretension. I have somehow already felt vague intimations of the satisfaction that can come from working hard, sweating blood, indeed. If I come through it will only be at the price of a great deal of anguish, that price, I suspect, being worth the reward.

To get down to more practical matters, I would like for you to send me $50, if you will, as soon as you can. The first of the month brought a number of bills—telephone, milk, etc—which I'm unable to pay in my present financial status. So if you'll send a check as soon as possible, I'll be greatly obliged.

In the meantime I hope everything goes well with you and that I'll get to see you sometime soon. Regards to all.

Your son

WCS jr

To Elizabeth McKee

October 12, 1948 901 Fifth Street, Durham, NC

Dear Miss McKee:

Here is a carbon of what I have finished, or rather typed, so far on my novel. I hope you will enjoy looking at it, although if you have the sense of miserable failure upon reading it that I have it probably won't make you too happy. There are a few good things in it, but I've found that one never gets around to saying the things he wants to say.

The story, in short, is nothing but that of a modern upper South middle-class family, and the daughter of the family, named Peyton Loftis. I've got no drum to beat, political or otherwise. I just want to give a picture of a way of life that I have known, and of the people therein. I probably have a moral purpose—the late Bliss Perry said that you had to have one—but it hasn't quite yet emerged.* Anyway, Peyton, who is twenty-four and something of a bitch, has just died violently and I must say horribly in New York and is being returned to her home town for a hasty and unpublicized interment. What transpires on the one day of her burial is the burden of the novel. Gradually, through their memories, you get a picture of Peyton and, I hope, of the "way of life" of which I was speaking. If the story seems morbid it's because I'm probably morbid myself, although I've got some good ghastly humor later on. Well, I'll let you read it yourself, and I'd be most happy to hear what you have to say about it. Of course, there are probably incidents in this first part which don't seem to tie together, but I plan to fill them out later on.

Thanks so much for relaying the comments on AUBREY CRUMPLER.† I hope we have success on that one, but if we don't I hope I'll have others for you soon.

Sincerely,
William Styron

* Styron refers to Bliss Perry, *A Study of Prose Fiction* (Boston: Houghton Mifflin, 1902).

† This story does not survive.

Styron was in New York for the holidays and decided he should return to the city in 1949.

To William Blackburn

January 13, 1949 Valley Cottage, NY*

Dear Professor Blackburn,

I want to thank you for the book of folk songs you sent me Christmas. It was indeed thoughtful of you, and you can be assured that it has been well-thumbed already. Now if I can just work up enough courage to learn how to play a guitar, I might turn professional. There's a wonderful old guitar up here, made in 1880, a sort of Stradivarius among guitars, and I'll have only myself to blame if I don't learn how to use the thing. Incidentally, have you heard Leadbelly? I heard an album the other day of his, and went overboard for him. He's the Louisiana negro convict who died just recently. If you can get a couple of records of his—especially "Midnight Special" ("shine your ever-lovin' light on me") and "Irene, Good-night," I think you'll see what I mean.†

Well, half of the novel is all-typed, and Haydn has read it. As I wrote Brice, he thinks it's very fine stuff and gave me an additional advance, which wasn't much but better than nothing. I've sent a carbon to Brice and I'd be honored to have you read it and give me your opinion of it, provided you have time for such a frivolity. I've been so "close" to the novel all these months, that re-reading it gives me a severe sort of expression, so I'd be interested in hearing what you, a spectator, have to say about it. I've begun the second half of the novel, which I hope will progress a bit easier than the first half, now that I've gotten the sights lined up pretty well on all my characters. One thing I'm certain of—I shan't ever attempt such a

* This letter was written from the family home of the de Limas. Agnes ("Aggie") was a progressive journalist, editor, and educator. Agnes and her daughter, Sigrid, befriended Styron at the New School. Sigrid was a girlfriend of Styron's and became a novelist in her own right. Bill dedicated *Lie Down in Darkness* to her.

† The guitarist and ex-convict Huddie William Ledbetter (1888–1949) did not die until the end of the year. The records Styron described were some of Lead Belly's first recordings for Columbia Records in the 1930s.

complicated theme again, until I'm well aware of what I'm doing. But even having plunged so recklessly into this novel, I'm glad I did it. It's been rather a strengthening thing, like swimming up the Colorado, or going into battle.

Sigrid and I both enjoyed seeing you when we were down in Durham. The breakfast you gave us on our departure was very heartening and enabled us to get all the way to Colonial Heights, Va., without hunger pangs. Hope that we can all get together again soon. Sigrid's book is getting promoted with much exciting hoopla and everyone's waiting breathlessly for the reviews which I think are bound to be good ones.* The final coup is the fact that the book has already been accepted in England by Eyre and Spottiswoode where, I understand, Christopher Morley's brother is editor. Isn't that fine?

I hope you had as pleasant a Christmas as I did, and that all is going nicely with you in this first part of the New Year. Thanks again so much for the book. I'll sing "Shenandoah" for you tonight.

As ever,
Bill S.

To William C. Styron, Sr.

March 31, 1949 Durham, NC

Dear Pop,

It was good to get your letter with all the fine encouragement and advice, and I would have written sooner, except for the fact that I've been giving your "proposition"—which was so generous—some serious thought. I know it isn't easy for you to do it, and that's one reason the thing troubled me, but I'll gratefully accept, provided you take to my counter-proposition: that it be in the nature of an informal sort of loan, to be repaid when I've made some money at this writing game. That, of course, is a wild sort of statement, since heaven only knows when I'll make enough to pay it back. But in this miraculous country of ours anything can happen, so it's at least

* Styron refers to Sigrid de Lima's first novel, *Captain's Beach* (New York: Charles Scribner's Sons, 1950).

worth the try. At least be assured of this: that with your backing I won't stop until I've reached the goal. This time it's all or bust, and it's got to be all. And I'm grateful to you for your help, more than you can know.*

Now here's something which you may or may not take to. Between Haydn and myself we have finally—after much talking and letters back and forth—agreed that perhaps the novel I'm now engaged on is worth postponing, in favor of another project less ambiguous in conception, and perhaps less ambitious. This new novel I have worked out in my mind is, unlike the other, concerned with just a few characters (too many characters I fully believe, is the stumbling-block of a first novelist), is concise in its conception, and, best of all, is much shorter, viz., it can be worked out thematically in a more or less predetermined number of pages. It's actually what I should have started on a year ago.†

But all this only leads up to the fact that Haydn and I both think that I'd do better back in New York where, as Haydn puts it, "Uncle Hiram can keep an eye on you." For one thing my work in the last few months seems to have slacked off down here; maybe it's the atmosphere; maybe I need a change of scene. For another thing, sad but true, I guess I do need someone to throw a whip over me, someone like Haydn, until I get to the point of having enough confidence where I can wield the whip myself. At any rate, it'll be the last move for some time for me. I do know that your environment doesn't have too much to do with what you write, but I feel I've exhausted everything that Durham has to offer and that New York, with all its chaos, will be a better place to work off this first novel. The furniture I can keep in safekeeping at Brice's until I have need for it.

Enclosed is Haydn's last letter—after I had written him, agreeing that I should come back to New York as he suggested. It shows, I think, that he has my best interests at heart still, despite my recent defection. I'll probably leave here the last week of April.

Thanks again for your kind offer. I think it'll be best for me all around. It'll give me something added to work for and to live up to. Let me hear from you soon.

Your son,

Bill, jr.

* Styron's father had offered to send him $100 a month.

† This was Styron's imagined novella about his Hart's Island experience.

Styron returned to New York in April and Agnes de Lima helped him find a cheap, temporary apartment in Flatbush, Brooklyn.

To William C. Styron, Sr.

May 2, 1949 1506 Caton Avenue, Brooklyn, NY

Dear Pop,

I am writing this letter from my new home in—you wouldn't believe it—Brooklyn. I arrived in New York a little over a week ago, immediately began hunting around for an apartment, but found that places to live in are still terribly difficult to get, even though I had heard beforehand that things had loosened up somewhat. The last isn't true at all. You'd think that everyone in the country had converged upon New York, and that each was making a concerted effort to get an apartment, room—even an alcove somewhere. I suppose that it all involves some terrifically complicated economic theory, but it still strikes me as being a gigantic sort of fraud—that one has to knock his brains out and pay away his soul to boot to be able to get a roof over his head and a minimum of the necessities of life. I guess it's merely the fact that I'm politically naïve, and that the way to knowledge is mainly through experience—such experience as I am going through now. I suppose, too, that 99% of the radicals, so-called liberals, and Communists are only that way, not through any a priori, bookish idealism, but because they were broke once, or out in the rain, and had to turn to some politico-economic father confessor. Which from my point of view is all the more reason for bucking life as you see it—artistically speaking, that is—or accepting it, or making the most of it—writing about it faithfully, in the long run, and not getting mixed up with the soothsayers. I suppose that if you really catch hell from life—as an untouchable, say, or a sharecropper—your artistic instincts wither, and you become political. That's natural enough. But Americans are political enough as it is. We've got nearly everything, and we still bitch about this and that at every turn.

Which is all by way of saying that though I somehow resent not being able to settle down in a cozy Greenwich Village apartment at $40 a month, I am still glad to be in Brooklyn in a clean and decent place; and although there are no doubt better places in New York I'm not going to get angry and political about it and start joining the Communist party.

Actually I hope I'm not giving the impression that I'm complaining, because this is a pretty nice place by anyone's standards. It's in an old weatherbeaten house overlooking Prospect Park. There are plenty of trees around, plenty of grass, and big windows to look at the grass through. I'm in an apartment on the ground floor—two rooms, bath, kitchen, all furnished, $70 a month—the rent being impossible were it not for the fact that I am—or will be in June—sharing the apartment with Bob Loomis of Duke, who is coming to N.Y. to get a job. Split, the rent will be $9 a week, utilities included, which isn't bad. The apartment is owned by a nice, easygoing woman who seems anxious to please. She's educated, runs a school for backward children down the block.

I've seen Haydn, and I'm ready to go; in fact, I'm more than ready. I've already started the New Novel.

For some reason, although I'm not exactly ecstatic about the world and life in general, I'm very happy. I don't know why that should be, as I've always thought of myself as an exceptionally melancholy person. Maybe the melancholy was merely adolescent, and maybe, though I can't really sense it, I'm growing up, or reaching an "adjustment," as the psychologists say. Whatever it is, it's nice.

It's not love—love of a girl, that is, because I haven't found her yet. It's not the excitement of being in New York, because I've been in New York before and now know how to take with a grain of salt its synthetic stimuli (though I still love New York). Actually I don't know what it is. For the past four or five days I've been alone, not seeing anyone or talking to anyone I know except over the phone. Ordinarily this aloneness would have made me miserable, utterly wretched. But I haven't minded it at all. I haven't drunk hardly anything—a few beers, that's all. And yet I've been quite content, suffused with a sort of pleasant well-being that demanded really nothing strenuous of myself, or of anyone else.

Perhaps it's merely that I've gained a measure of Emerson's self-reliance. Perhaps it's just that, for some reason I can't put my finger on, I feel surer of myself than I ever have before—more confident of my worth and my ultimate success, and less fearful of failure. I used to like to drink by myself. I still do occasionally, but gradually I've found myself stopping after the third beer, because there seems to be none of that fake pleasure in it anymore.

Maybe—again for some reason I haven't quite been able to analyze—I'm finding that life excites me, appeals to me in a way I've never felt before. I still have awful moments of despair, and I guess I always will, but they don't seem to be as overpowering as in the past. I don't take so much pleasure in my despondency any more; I try to throw my bleak moods off—which again perhaps is a sign that I'm growing up.

I don't know how this novel will turn out. Naturally, I hope it's good. But best of all is the fact that I'm not afraid of its being bad, literarily speaking, provided I know I've done my best. In the meantime I'm taking great pleasure in living, and in being alone without being a recluse. At night, after I've worked through the day, I walk up Church Avenue to Flatbush and thence down Flatbush, enjoying every minute of the walk. The faces are all Jewish, all harried and metropolitan, all enormously middle-class; yet as I say it's somehow all of a sudden wonderfully exciting. Maybe it's just forgetting one's self for a minute, not trying to be smug and self-centered and aloof. And I've learned to do finally—at least with far less effort and self-consciousness—something that three or four years ago you told me was one of the touchstones of maturity: being nice to people even when they're not nice to you.

There's something hideously crass and gaudy and meretricious about modern life; not that it hasn't always existed, but that it increases proportionally with time and with Science. God seems to be at times nothing more than Someone playing a neon-colored, television-equipped pinball machine. Yet I've found that although it all revolts me horribly at times, I can take it much more in my stride than I could before. I hate the way people think, especially in America; I'll always hate the stupid and the bat-brained and the petty. But it doesn't seem nearly so important anymore to hate, as try to understand.

Now I can look at two ignorant, slack-jawed, bloodshot men in a bar talking about the horseraces at Jamaica, and I think I can understand. At least I try to understand. That's one of the things, I guess, that Christ wanted one to do. Not that I'm getting religious all of a sudden, but I think He'd approve.

It's incredible how one runs about frantically at times like a rat in a maze, not really knowing right from wrong (and often really not caring), victim of one's own passions and instincts rather than master of one's own soul. I suppose the proper thing to do is just to stop every now and then and say, Where am I heading? Actually, though I'm still much like the psychologist's rat, I find myself asking myself that question almost too often. I suppose the very fact that I realize my indulgence in too much introspection is another sign (I hope) of maturity. Too much brooding is unhealthy and, although I still have my slumps, I've begun to realize that one of the great secrets is striking a balance between thought and action. Between the Romantic and the Classical. Just living healthily. Living, acting, thinking; not just vegetating neurotically, on one hand, or blundering about, on the other hand, like so many people do, like trapped flies. It's a hard balance to strike, but I think it can be done, and that in this exciting-sorrowful age of ours it can make great literature.

Well, I've written more than I had thought. I've got to get up early tomorrow—another innovation!—so I'll close now. I hope everything at home is going along okay, and that you'll write soon.

Your son,

Bill, Jr.

In June, Agnes de Lima offered Styron her weekend home in Valley Cottage. Styron lived there for a year with her daughter, Sigrid.

To William Blackburn

July 23, 1949 Valley Cottage, NY

Dear Professor Blackburn

Since I've hit against shoal water, to quote an original metaphor, in the composition of my novel, I thought that now would be as good a time as any to belatedly apprise you of my recent doings. The momentary pause in the novel is, I assure you, only momentary; each time I finish a section I have a day or two in which I bleakly cast about for the next thing to write about, while at the same time assuring myself that it's a folly, and an outrage to go on any further. I always manage, however, to proceed somehow.

Perhaps you've been informed, but I am now living with friends of mine, the de Limas, at their house in Valley Cottage which is about 25 miles up the Hudson from New York. It's a delightful place to live and to work, and the de Limas—mother and daughter—are among the most exquisite humans who ever lived. Since I've been here—a little over a month—I've completed a good-size short story which I think is quite satisfactory and which is now going the rounds, and I've recommenced steady toil on the Peyton novel—following your advice and others' and my own conscience—and I find it goes remarkably well. Maybe it's just the atmosphere and the delightful and constant stimulation of my friends, but I've never yet hit such a period of steady and agreeable labor. There are also many books here, and also a very fine record player with a big record library, including the Bach B♭ Violin Concerto—the slow movement of which almost paralyzes me each time I hear it. Then too, as a consequence perhaps of all these delights, I've taken to living a somewhat less disorderly life, rising at eight instead of twelve, working all day or as long as my imagination permits, and in the evening playing chess with Sigrid until midnight, at which time I go to bed properly and decently like most humans. Perhaps I will begin writing like Anthony Trollope.* At any rate I am often conscience stricken, wondering what good works I've performed in order to merit such a life.

The actual writing of the novel I still find a fairly agonizing business, but not without its moments of charm and excitement. The big reversal in my plans came when one day I hit upon the idea of dividing the story into four or five sections, each section treating subjectively one of the principal characters, and the final section describing Peyton, the girl, on the day of her death. Thus I can still retain the motif of the story being told during a one-day cycle, and at the same time I have a good, not-too-contrived device for telling various things that happened in the past. The lack of such a device was what stopped me six months ago, though I still don't know what colossal simple-mindedness caused me to fail in thinking of this device in the first place.

So I roll merrily along, trusting that the Gods will let me finish the

* Anthony Trollope (1815–62) was one of the most successful and prolific authors of the Victorian era. He claimed to have written every morning with a watch open at his elbow. After exactly one hour, he would board the train to earn his living as a postal inspector. Although he was widely criticized for his mechanical approach, it turned out that Trollope only claimed to follow such a strictly regimented routine.

book, and will help keep me on the right paths. I have also determined that I'm not going to rush the thing. Most first novels seem to me to have a distinct quality of "spareness" about them; they seem to be rushed, in a mad effort, no doubt, to find print early at any cost. If necessary, I'll take three years to finish this book, but I'll not sacrifice quality for early printing. I'm tired of being prodded on all sides by people who wonder why I haven't finished by now, why I'm not on my second or third book—by people who just don't know really how much thinking and writing and scratching-out it takes to produce something worthy of the name of art. I'm quite serious about this whole business now. Suddenly—after a horde of vacillations—I've waked up to find myself at a realization that I am a writer, come what may; and I've really got to work like hell to become first-rate. Committed to the sea, as the saying goes, I've got to man the pumps.

For the first time, too, I've actually come to the conclusion that I want to write, not just be a "writer." That, I suspect, is a good sign. Each day that goes by I find something else that I really want to say, while becoming gradually more and more secure in my own concept as to just how I want to say it. By that I mean that I've stopped taking the book-reviewers seriously, and the sorry little critics of the Partisan Review, people whom I once thought were soothsayers, but whom I now realize to be little more than spineless, gutless parasites.* Not that I've deserted "artistic" principles; far from that, I'm terribly conscious of them. But my "talking" period is over; now I'm acting.

My work, I hope, will be neither pessimistic nor optimistic, nor will it, I hope, belong to any "school." I'm interested in people and in their eternal dilemma, and if I can give to these artistic substance, I will be satisfied. If I have any "message" I don't know what it is, unless it be that of kindness, which, expressed just like that, may sound rather trite, but which I'm coming to believe in as a principle of considerable importance.

Now then, I hope you will forgive me for having been so tedious, but I thought that you might be interested in knowing that one who profited so in having you as a teacher and friend has been in the process of coming to grips with himself, and is now prepared to do things.

* This is Styron's first mention of his distaste for critics, a major trope in his correspondence over the following fifty years.

How do you like living at 901 Fifth St.?* I understand from Brice and others that my ex-roommate left the place in something of a shambles. I imagine the apartment is pretty hot now, but will be compensated in that matter by the jolly heat you'll get in winter. I haven't heard from Mac Hyman lately, but I intend to write him in a few days and get the news.

Please write and let me know how things go with you. Wish we could have a martini together with Brice and my favorite old manse—814 6th St.

As ever,

Bill S.

To William Canine†

October 6, 1949 Valley Cottage, NY

Dear Bill,

First, allow me to congratulate you, as they say, with great joy upon the coming of Andrew. Next to the red convertible I think he's the finest acquisition you could make. Please tell Emily that I'm proud of her; I can't wait to see how A. stacks up against David, and I'm glad to hear that the newcomer hasn't evoked any nasty jealousy, or "sibling rivalry," as the nasty psychologists call it. Anyway congratulations—probably hard to take in the light of the fact that 18 years from now you'll be buying not one, but two, brand-new Buicks.

Now, on this Thursday, is one of those certain days, after completing something in the book that I like, when I let go and take it easy and contemplate things. The radio is tuned to WNYC-FM, which has a two-hour program of music every afternoon; right now WQXR-FM has a program at noon, then WNYC, then WQXR again and then WABF at five—the best station of them all. So if one wants to, by graceful manipulation of the dial, one can get music all day. Which is nice, but it takes a dreadful

* Blackburn had separated from his first wife.

† William Canine was a member of the "West Durham Literary Society," an ironically named group Styron socialized with during his months in Durham while taking refuge from New York and getting started on *Lie Down in Darkness*.

lot of self-control to keep the radio off while attending to work. Much as I love music—obviously so, I think, a gross form of lust—I find I can't write worth a damn while actually listening, though I can write letters, where you can express yourself freely without too much attention to the strictness of A.C. Jordan. Incidentally, the fall colors are all out now in full dress uniform, so the Pastoral adds sort of a noble grace to the afternoon.

I got a very depressing letter from Brice. His troubles are truly heart-rending, and I hope that they come to a head soon, because if something definite happens it'll take the burden off his shoulders a lot. However, I do hope, too, that nothing violent happens. I think he should give Exie the old bowling-ball group and heave her up to Main Street, but I guess that's asking for too much.

I have what I think must be the equivalent of 100 typewritten pages done on the novel, all of which, due to my tortoise-like "art," will probably stand as they are with no rewriting or retouching. I've been harried and worried to death whether the last couple of chapters were significant, integral, but now that I've completed them I think they're OK and that they'll remain. I was very foolish, I think, to attempt such a difficult story, with all the flashbacks and complications of character; however, it's too late now for regrets, and I have to keep beating my way through the wilderness. Doesn't writing provide an excellent means of soul-searching? You find so much in a character that's actually your self that it's almost embarrassing.

I think we beginning writers tend to worry a thing to death, though. Best thing to do is to sit back often and take it easy and consider your own very minor importance. You can do that too often, of course, but a sudden sense of humor is a great and healthy thing.

I'm awfully glad to hear that your stories are coming along with such success. I'll try and get a copy of the Prairie Schooner sometime when I'm in London (Christ! What am I thinking of: there was an English prof. from the Univ. of Durham, England up here last weekend, a very fine fellow who found 1/3 of the new Boswell MSS.* That's what caused the slip.)

* In the fall of 1949, Lord Talbot de Malahide discovered several thousand pages of unknown manuscripts by James Boswell (1740–95), the eighteenth-century biographer of Samuel Johnson. Yale University eventually purchased the papers for its renowned collection of Boswell materials.

when I'm in N.Y., rather, but if I can't find one I wish you'd send me a copy.

I haven't written any short stories in some time now. One I wrote a few months ago, concerning the Virginia School, is still out.* I thought it was a good story, of its sort—whatever that may be—but I doubt if it'll meet with any success, except perhaps in a little magazine. You know, there's a great conspiracy working against unpublished writers, always has been, I guess. It's entirely obvious to me that the Atlantic and Harper's publish cultivated trash by prissy Englishmen and horrible crap, "folk" stuff in dialect by Kentucky schoolteachers, whereas the little magazines and quarterlies still, by and large, print the quality fiction. If you've got a name you can get by with most anything. Not that it bothers me too much. I've got a lot of patience and I know there'll come a day . . . but it does seem a shame.

I haven't read much of Eudora Welty, but it does seem to me, from what I have read of her short stories, that the stuff is fairly pale.† She doesn't seem to want to commit herself to anything, emotionally or intellectually, either, and thereby commits the crime, as you indicated, of women writers in general—seeing life through pastel-tinted spectacles, lovely in its way but not in clear white focus. Of course, any writer has his own particular distortion of view, but I want my figures, no matter how grotesque, to breathe at least a lot of real air. I think, too, that the Deep-South "school" of writing, outside of Faulkner, tends to go in for a lot of unnecessary baby-talk which, like baby-talk, is charming for a while, but can be overdone. I don't know if you've noticed that, but I think I can point out what I mean sometime.

Well, hell, I still respect greatly the manly art of fiction. I believe, with Forster (did you read the Harper's article?) in Art for Art's Sake, mainly because I'm just not versatile enough a soul to be a scientist or a doctor or an insurance executive, too. I have such a footless and indolent nature that whatever imagination I can summon up has to be channeled into writing,

* "The Enormous Window" was first published in Charles I. Glicksberg, ed., *American Vanguard* (New York: Cambridge Publishing Co., 1950), and reprinted in *William Styron: Letters to My Father.*

† Eudora Welty (1909–2001) was an author best known for writing about the American South. She won a Pulitzer Prize for her 1972 novel *The Optimist's Daughter.*

or else go to waste. It's a rough job but maybe it's worth it, bomb and all, and perhaps, too, we'll both be famous someday and have our pictures on the front of Time, complete with warts and wrinkles and profound symbols hovering in the background.

Best to all, and write soon.

Your,

Bill S.

P.S. I'd appreciate if you'd send me Snitger's new address.

To Elizabeth McKee

November 10, 1949 901 Fifth Street, Durham, NC

Dear Miss McKee:

That story The Enormous Window, which I sent you last summer, I imagine you have withdrawn by now from circulation. If not, I have a possibility for publication. Unfortunately there is no payment involved, but at this stage of the game I am working on the principle that publication most anywhere is better than no publication at all.

Dr. Charles I. Glicksberg of the New School is getting up another volume, second in a series called American Vanguard, devoted to younger writers. I'm fairly sure he'll take The Enormous Window. So, if you'll send the MS. to Mrs. Agnes de Lima, c/o The New School, 66 W. 12th St., she will see that he gets it, and I'd be much obliged. I'd also be interested in hearing what comments, if any, were passed on the story.

The novel is about three-fifths done. With good luck I hope to have it all done before next summer.

Sincerely,

Wm C. Styron

To William Blackburn

January 7, 1950 Valley Cottage, NY

Dear Professor Blackburn,

I have played the two Monteverdi madrigals over and over and I can certainly understand why they are among your chiefest delights. It certainly is dark and tragic and heart-rending music, and I thank you so much for introducing me to it. All these centuries separate us from that soulful composer, but there's no denying that when those frenzied voices shout at the tomb it is a threnody no less poignant and meaningful right now. Mr. Truman just let me know that the State of the Union leaves much to be desired, I turned him off and turned on Monteverdi, figuring that though the latter might not have had the answer his lament was sweeter and more abiding than Harry's. Thank you ever so much for giving me the pleasure.

I'm struggling through to the end of the book and I should, if all goes well, have it done in a month or so. It takes a lot of effort from time to time to avoid the creeping paralysis which seems to be hovering in the air these days, but so far I've come out on top. I'm too close to the end to be vanquished and, anyway, the pressure has given me a real sense of urgency. Like most everyone else I have a fidgety sort of feeling that my hands will be radioactive long before their work is done, but like everyone else I go on anyway. It's really becoming a pretty good book, which I'm glad of, because it makes me go on with increasing courage. I'm practically into the last scene, which is the day of Peyton's death, and I have no doubt that <u>that</u> part will be effective. Then comes the baptism at twilight and that's the last scene of all and will be filled with a valiant, if faintly wistful, hope.

I'm looking forward also to coming to Durham when the book is done—in March maybe, and I'll happily take up your invitation to rest for a few days at Blackburn manor. The place sounds very nice indeed. I hope everything is going well with you and that you aren't finding these days too tough to bear. I don't know <u>why</u> but I somehow think we'll endure; it's hard to get rid of Monteverdi and Mozart, really, or of the people who love them so. Don't you think?

As ever,

Bill S.

To Leon Edwards

January 19, 1950 Valley Cottage, NY

Dear Leon,

It's about time for me to send you an adequate reply to both of your very full and enjoyable letters, so here goes. First, let me say that I'm happy to hear that your life, connubial and scholastic, seems to be proceeding in such a fine and gallant fashion. I do hope, and know, you'll keep up the good work. The Ph.D. Business sounds fine to me—alas! I seem to have missed the main chance long ago, and I have a sneaking suspicion that I should be on your road instead of mine—and I sort of imagine that when the sweating over my eighth unreadable novel, you'll be the head of the Harvard English Department with a shelf full of criticism to your credit, two shelves of novels, and the Nobel prize. I admire your courage and tenacity and direction greatly, you'll never know.

As for me, I just recently finished typing what I hope is the final draft of the first half of my novel, to be known as The Death of Peyton Loftis, and to be published, I hope, in the first part of next year. I'm fairly well along on the second half and hope to have the whole business done by mid-summer, although I suspect it'll really take me until fall, at my rate of speed. What one will behold at the end of all this, I really don't know. I have a feeling that it won't be as good as I think it is in my moments of exaltation, nor really so bad as I believe it to be in my periods of desperation. Let us say that it'll be a very good first novel, and an absolute wonder in the light of who wrote it. Let us wait and see. Hiram Haydn is quite ecstatic about it, says nothing at all needs to be changed, and he gave me some much-needed money, but I think he has some sort of weird fixation on me. At any rate, I feel as good about things at the moment as is possible in one so universally morose, so hooray!

If you are at all like me, this is the way the symptoms of novel-sickness manifest themselves: At first, as I have pointed out, you waver between hysterical joy, and suicidal despondency. Of course, this is common to neurotics in general, but is increased a thousand times in people foolish enough to write a book. On a more minute and casual plane this manic state applies to the slightest word or phrase you venture to put on paper. You ponder a sentence. Perhaps by most critical standards the sentence is good. Perhaps it isn't, but let's say it is in this case. The monstrous thing is still the fact that, being good, it could be better and you know it. The metaphor is concise and handsome but it could be conciser and more handsome. That worries you. Then there's the problem of "pure art." There are a lot of things, thousands of things, you'd just love to put down, but you know you can't or at least shouldn't, because it would hinder the narrative or because it's simply out of place. That worries you, because you wonder if such a beautiful inspiration will occur at another time. This has been a constant bother to me, because my book is complicated enough to begin with, feeble enough in its structure, to be saddled with sheer extraneous prose. Then there's the problem of honesty, which I mentioned to you, I believe, at another time. It's very important to me that I don't try to exceed myself, which I seem to do, nevertheless, each time I put pen to paper. The old incessant upsurge of banalities, pseudo-poetry, emotional excess. A constant threat. I could go on and on: the threat of fame, or lack of it, wondering whether this will be read by important people or not (a very nasty symptom, to be got rid of as soon as your temperature goes down); the impulse to rush, to see yourself in print (also a nasty syndrome, as the psychologists put it); and the final horror: is it really worth all this trouble?

Answer: I guess it is. I seem to be dealing in stock attitudes tonight, but that does seem to be the answer. It's worth it if it's inconceivable to you that you could live out the rest of your years without doing it; so, merely because of that, you do it. Actually, I'm quite happy, really very happy, and all these things are merely a very facile way of getting things off my chest.

The approach of maturity has been for me long-coming. Only recently do I think I've seen the first glimmering signs on the horizon. It's a very pleasant thing, in a way, to know that gradually you can really begin to take stock of your possessions, examine yourself. Because I believe that before maturity itself comes, there is this wayside station—when you begin to question your own motives, when you wonder what ends your coming maturity will be directed toward. It's an almost palpable state for me, and hard to describe! You don't quite possess level judgment, wisdom, and sympathy, yet you know they're at hand, and in my case it's merely wondering what's to be done with them when I've got them. Incidentally, I should like to discriminate between "maturity" and "experience" as related to art. I'm aware that there is such a thing as an ivory-tower, but I believe, too, that the better parts of maturity are merely imagination and contemplation, and that you can subsist forever, artistically, upon the accretions of experience gained during the first twenty-one years of your life. That time limit admittedly is arbitrary, but I do believe, despite edicts to the contrary, that one can settle down to creating at a fairly early age and the earlier the better.

I think the foundations of artistic achievement rest perhaps on your legs, the legs themselves being the real touchstones: despair and joy, talent and hard work. Despair and joy coexist and seem to me to be almost the same. I think perhaps you have to be able to live, in the same minute, the wildest despondency and the giddiest joy, to be able to really create. A sort of synthesis of egotism and humility. Talent itself is obvious; you've got it or you don't, and I think that, given the breaks, hard work can make that talent genius. I don't value genius for itself; I do value what it implies, and in many cases, it seems to me, that genius is merely talent transcended, a sort of self-imposed slavery whereby, through toil and discipline—discipline mainly, so hard for Virginians—and through undeviating effort toward a single goal, you expose yourself for what you are—a man who has grown, a man who has become a man. I happen to think that in this age of tiny, tiny things there are more ignoble objectives than to try to grow through art, no matter what pain it causes one.

Now I've said enough about credos. Every time I write you I seem to want to state a credo. Anyway, I hope you have been an indulgent listener. Despite my probably obsessive worry with what I'm writing, life is fine down here. I haven't been reading as much as I should, but I've managed to get started on the new Putnam translation of Don Quixote, and have read at random a considerable amount of Gide's Journals.* I think Gide is highly overrated as a creative artist, but as a journal-ist he's absolutely first-rate. There seems to be a lot of deadwood in the Journals, but there's much that is stimulating, and I think you'd find them interesting to read, if you haven't already. I just recently re-read Babbitt and thought it was great stuff.† The sophisticates are currently sniffing at Lewis, but of all the writ-

* Samuel Putnam, ed., *Ingenious Gentleman, Don Quixote de la Mancha* (New York: Viking Press, 1949), and Justin O'Brien, ed., *Journals of André Gide* (London: Secker and Warburg, 1948).

† Sinclair Lewis, *Babbitt* (New York: Harcourt, Brace & Co., 1922).

ers of the twenties, including Hemingway, I think he's most likely to survive.

I don't know if I'll get a chance to come to Boston anytime soon, but I'd love to. Incidentally, if you come through New York by any chance, the telephone is NYack 7-1806-W. I dearly look forward to seeing you all before long. In the meantime, don't be overwhelmingly shy that you wait eight months to write me. That's shameful, you'll have to admit. Send me a picture of Geoffrey, if you have one; I hope to God that he looks like Marianne, to whom I send love and greetings.

As ever,

Bill

To William Blackburn

February 23, 1950 Valley Cottage, NY

Dear Professor Blackburn,

I seem to have mailed my last letter to you just before I received yours, but anyway I want to thank you for your nice words of praise and the criticism, too, which was accurate and to-the-point and appreciated. I'm very glad that generally speaking you looked upon the book and found it good, for although I like to feel myself Olympian and aloof from either criticism or praise—in the manner of the grand artiste—I know that I'm really not that at all, but actually just dying to hear a good word spoken, especially from you, whose words are always so just and right. In general I think that so far I've accomplished what I set out to do at the cost of a lot of effort, but worthwhile effort. I think that my next work will be a little easier to write on account of all this present strain and toil. The rhetorical passage about Peyton's beauty, which you mentioned, was already noted by Haydn and by others, including myself, and consequently I plan to change it in the final version. Outside of the choruses, which are grandiose and which I really plan to dispense with eventually, this passage is the only one I'm not satisfied with. Of course, when I read the MS over myself I'm often not satisfied with anything, but that comes only in moments of over-critical and over-reproachful despair; actually, I just don't think I can change very much at all, except for a few minor phrases and the passage I mentioned. My natural bent seems to be rhetorical and in this book I have to fight against the inclination all the time, realizing, as I finally do, that the scope of this particular novel, despite my visions of grandeur, is too limited to allow many "purple patches." However, I'm not a devotee of the Hemingway tight-lipped mumble school, as you know, and eventually when I mature and broaden I expect to use the language on as exalted and elevated a level as I can sustain. I believe that a writer should accommodate language to his own peculiar personality, and mine wants to use great words, evocative words, when the situation demands them. I believe in infinite artistic restraint, but I also believe that the "lean, spare style" of our time can be, and is, just as artificial as the more orotund and high-flown passages in Tom Wolfe. Somewhere there's an in-between and I aim to find it. As for this novel again, my only over-all worry is that Peyton won't emerge, treating her as I do so objectively. But maybe that's what I'm really trying to do: leaving her out, except as a background figure, so that finally in the doomsday monologue (which I plan for the end of the book) she becomes a symbol of suffering and lost youth and all eternal tragic misunderstanding.

Thanks again for the guitar-book. I'll do my best so that next time we meet we can make the music of the spheres. And thanks again for your letter: it means a great deal to me.

As ever,

Bill S.

To William C. Styron, Sr.

April 13, 1950 Valley Cottage, NY

Dear Pop,

Whenever I look at the calendar it always seems that it's this part of the month that I write you, and that I've been most dilatory in writing you anyway. I hope I can beg your indulgence for my neglect, this month at least, for actually what with one thing and another—forging ahead, as the phrase goes, on my novel, and finishing a short story—I look back and find that in weeks I haven't written to anyone at all. Not that that's much of an explanation.

Your advice as to my getting exercise was well taken, and the exercise itself will go into effect as soon as the weather clears. Right now, here at this late date, it's snowing in small flurries outside, though I don't think it'll stick. At any rate, I hope you weren't really concerned over the stomach upset I had, for it cleared itself up in no time at all and I feel fine once more.

The story I mentioned above I just finished a week or so ago, taking time off for a few days from my book, and I do believe it's the best short story I've done to date.* It concerns an "ex-" Southerner's visit to a ramshackle farm in Virginia, where he meets his old uncle, only to be driven off the place with derision and imprecations. It's not a pretentious story: by that I mean that I think I've balanced the intention of the story with the substance of the narrative, and all in all I believe I've managed to carry the thing off with a peculiarly, and successfully, haunting effect. The "haunting" part, I think, derives from the fact that it's based almost fully on a dreamy half-nightmare I had one night, which was so impressive that I didn't go to sleep at all but wrote the outline for the story in the hours before dawn. I've sent it off to my agent, Elizabeth McKee, who is irritatingly slow always in answering my letters to her, so I don't know whether she thinks she can sell it or not. If she can't sell this one then I doubt if she'll be able to sell any of my stories. By this time, though, I've become, if not resigned, then at least accustomed to remaining in literary oblivion. I've lost most of the old frantic desire to get printed. I realize now that most of my stories of the past few years really weren't worth being printed, and it makes me happy, if not especially wild-eyed and desperate for recognition, to see how well I've progressed—as with this latest story. So I just bide my time and keep on writing with the same slow, identical painstakingness that I imagine I'll be employing forty years from now, and am more comfortable in the realization that eventually these things will not only suffer the painful accouchement but will get the smiles, maybe, and the approval that all good fathers' sons should receive.

* This story does not survive.

I also this month completed a chapter of the novel, which leaves me, if my present plan is followed, only two more to go out of a total of six. These last chapters, however, will be somewhat longer than the first. What a baffling, splendid job writing a novel is! With all of the heartaches involved, it's the most rewarding task, in a way, that a person can set himself to. Each paragraph, each page becomes better and better—at least in my case—and it's a wonderful revelation to see how strikingly one's power of expression becomes more forceful and strengthened after the exercise of two hundred pages or so. This novel will be shot through with faults, but when it is finished I will know my own style, I will know how to write.

I have been reading Sandburg's "Lincoln: The War Years," and it's really an astonishing book.* It's heightened my interest in the War Between the States, which I've always had to some extent, and I think that sometime not too long from now, after reading a lot more, I'll walk over the Virginia battlefields: the road to Richmond is full of them: Seven Pines, Gaines' Mill, Malvern Hills, Chickahominy. What a splendid thing it would be to write a vast book about that war, I mean a really great book. Some say (the "intellectuals") that America has never had glory or tragedy, but, with all its stupid confusions of motive, that war was both glorious and tragic, and I daresay that it was the last war in which the Lord God of Hosts hovered over the battlefields.

The papers are still coming and I enjoy them and tell Eliza I appreciate, too, the various and interesting clippings.

Best to all.

Your son

Wm. C. Styron, Jr.

Styron moved back to New York City in June 1950, sharing an apartment with Howard Hoffman, a painter and sculptor.

* Carl Sandburg's *Lincoln: The War Years,* 4 vols. (New York: Harcourt, Brace & Co., 1939) won the Pulitzer Prize for History in 1940.

To William C. Styron, Sr.

June 5, 1950 314 West 88th Street, New York City

Dear Pop,

I suppose you might be surprised to see the change of address above, but I moved down here a few days ago and I expect to be here all summer—a temporary stay, I hope. I think my wonderful stay at the de Limas was destined to come to an end about this time, and although the move was not effected without a certain amount of regret on all sides, it came about with as little pain as possible, and I think it was the only thing to do. I don't know whether I'll go back to Valley Cottage or not—permanently, that is—but even if I don't I'll remember my stay there as about the most pleasant, mutually rewarding of my life. At any rate, before I left I planted corn and tomatoes in the garden up there, and so Sigrid and Mrs. de Lima and I have planned to go back most every weekend to weed and cultivate and pick the crop.

The novel still goes very well, and I have picked out a nice place, I think, to write. It's located between Riverside Drive and West End Avenue, 1½ rooms, which I share with a fellow named Howard Hoffman, kitchen, bath—$8.25 a week, which is very reasonable. The guy I share the place with is a New School student—had an advertisement up on the bulletin board down there. He is a teacher and a sculptor, and seems to be both very intelligent and very nice. So I think I'm all set up until I finish the novel—at which time I intend to move to Sussex County, Va., and raise peanuts, with writing as an avocation.

It has been a long hard road for me—not from a material point of view (there I've been much better set up than most, I know), but in the inner struggle and the quest. I'm still far from my goal, but gradually I'm beginning to see things clearer, and to learn how to relate my art to my life. I'm sure I'm writing better all the time, and that my writing is becoming stronger and more mature. I think that I am becoming more mature, too. It is certainly a manifest truth in this day that what, above all, our people need to have is maturity and strength and an illumination of that spirit which has never died, or never will die—even if it means that in order to write with truth one has to batter his head bloody against a mass of materialism, and hypocrisy, and runaway "progress." Even if it means being "reactionary" to write in the name of Christian charity and the worn-out virtues, I will show them, as powerfully as I can, if I can beat the race with time.

In regard to the money you have been sending me, all I can say is that I would have been just about completely lost without it—and you must know yourself how much it has meant to me. But I don't wish to keep taking it until my novel is written, or for any length of time, if it is more than you can spare. This is all by way of saying that I know the year is up, and more, that you offered to send me the checks, and I wouldn't feel right in accepting still others, especially in the light of the shipbuilding slump and so forth.

You have had faith in me, and it has been a wonderful feeling to know that one is not alone. Even in this day when art is frowned upon still as a not quite healthy profession, a lot of artists are lucky and I'm glad to be one of them. In the long run, despite the sneers and indifference, the artist, the real one, has always been vindicated in the end, except that it takes a long time and some have a more fortunate time than others. Amor Vincit . . .*

No other news except that everything, again, goes well on the writing front and that, at the risk of sounding selfish, is gradually becoming to me the only thing that matters, although the lesson is fairly hard.

Your son,

Bill Jr.

To Sigrid de Lima

June 8, 1950 314 West 88th Street, New York City

Dear Such a Sweet Sweet Baby:

Here it is a very hot (88°) June night and I am writing to my sweet baby because all this time I've been thinking about her and missing her very much. All week I have been writing on my book and today I reached an impasse, but I'm not too worried because I'll conquer it tomorrow and, besides, impasses are to be expected. Loftis is getting ready to do the

* Styron begins to quote "Love conquers all," immortalized by Caravaggio's painting and Chaucer's *Canterbury Tales,* among others.

Kreksing with Dolly, only he doesn't want to really, because he has a thing against violating the sanctity of the house; anyway, he's writing a real hot semi-love letter to Peyton, and I think that somehow he identifies Peyton with Dolly, or vice versa, or something. All I have to do is think of my sweet baby and I can write real good. Really.

Otherwise I haven't been doing much of anything, Last night I went down to see Loomis and we sat around and played Beethoven. He seems much better now, because he has a girl that he's interested in and who appears to be very nice. She's rather unfortunately associated, though, with television, and last Sunday she took us behind the scenes at a television show—The Aldrich Family—and it was really something strange and wonderful. What phoniness and barrenness and toothpaste smiles and general squalor! It's sponsored (The Aldrich Family) by My-T-Fine desserts.

Loomis and I think that poor Brice is going psychopathic or something. His letters get more and more irrational and "secretive" and odd. I think he realizes that all of his old friends are tiring of his eternal pettiness and are beginning to lose interest in him. Anyway, it's very sad.

Your letter was so interesting—about going through the blizzard and everything, and the Frenchman (how old was he!) and the Utica meatpacking papa. Such a sweet baby, I sure do wish I had gone with you in the Vista-Dome and was with you right now in the Pacific place. We could go to the Top of the Mark and you could watch me as I drank Martinis and got ver-ti-gi-nous.

Biggest news is the fact that Haydn is going to become Editor at Bobbs-Merrill, and he had a talk with me about it the other day. It seems that he doesn't want to abscond from Crown with all of his authors, since that is not quite cricket in publishing. So I seem to have two alternatives: stay with Crown, which is the most legal thing, but which I don't want to do, because of the fact that I think they haven't been too generous with me and that only Haydn is responsible for the $250 I have got; the other alternative, as Haydn told me, is to go see Mavis McIntosh, who is Eliz. McKee's partner, and who also is his agent.* He doesn't want to make any

* McIntosh, Robert Penn Warren's agent, helped establish the literary agency McIntosh & Otis, which represented Hiram Haydn, John Steinbeck, John Irving, and many others.

motions himself, so through Mavis (I called her today) I'm going to try to work it so that when Haydn goes to Bobbs-Merrill, I'll go too, and Bobbs-Merrill will reimburse Crown the $250 I've got so far. Also, this move, if it works out, might result in my getting another $250, although I'm not banking too strongly on that. But I surely hope it works out, as I have no love, a priori, for Crown. Incidentally, if you write Aggie* any time before the 21st of June, don't mention this thing about Haydn, because it's supposed to be, for some weird reason, a "trade secret."

The more I think of it, the more I don't think I'll be able to go to Hill and Dorothy's wedding.† I don't know how I'm going to tell them, and I'll have to tell them soon, but I think they'll understand that I just can't afford another trip down there at this time. That last trip just about ruined me, and if I took this one, with the train fare and all both ways, plus "entertainment," I'll be flat busted. Or, as Peyton (Tom) puts it, I just "plain flat can't afford it." God. I hate to let them down, but as I look at it—along with the fact that it'll interrupt my schedule, my "work cycle"—I think the whole thing would be ruinous and catastrophic.

It's really not bad at all up here—although every time I think of V.C.‡ fair my poor heart collapses. This Howard is a very likeable guy, and considering that I came here sight unseen, we're marvelously amiable. Speaking of V.C. fair, I called Aggie yesterday and she said that last week guess who helped her weed the corn—none other than our friend Niel, the Dutchman! Either this weekend or the next I'm going up there and hoe and weed and sweat and everything and think of my sweat baby. Joke!

Please write and tell me about that San Francisco place—everything, and all the places and things you've seen. Everything, because everywhere my sweet baby goes I want to know about it. Write!

Wind is blowing off the river, that flows by Nyack and all those pretty places, and I'm thinking of you.

Love, love, love.
S.B.§

* Agnes de Lima.

† Hill Massie and Dorothy Conway, friends from Durham.

‡ The de Limas' home in Valley Cottage, New York.

§ Styron's abbreviation for "Sweet Baby."

To Sigrid de Lima

July 18, 1950 314 West 88th Street, New York City

Dear Such a Sweet Baby:

Guess what! Bobbs-Merrill is going to give me $1000—count 'em—a thousand dollars for the famous novel Death of Peyton Loftis. Isn't that a lot of dough? Actually, it's not so immense as it sounds because I'm really going to get $500 now ($250 of which I have to pay back to Crown) and the other $500 is promised to me as soon as I deliver the completed MS. At any rate, it still is a very pleasant surprise, and I feel very wealthy and important although, being down to 13¢ and the check not in my hands yet, I'm really most broke.

The book itself is coming along—slow, as usual, but steadily. After considerable back-tracking, side digressions and such, I'm almost to the Charlottesville scene. After that, a switch to the funeral again, then the wedding, then Peyton's day of judgment. Isn't it going to be a long big book?

Howard and I went down to see John Maloney on Sunday night and had a very pleasant evening talking about life and art and the Korean situation.* Maloney still seems to be writing good reviews for the Tribune—his latest in last Sunday's paper, were reviews of Shelby Foote's novel (he's a young Mississippian) and "The Dog-Star" by Donald Windham, from Georgia, I think.

Yesterday afternoon I went to a cocktail party at a friend of Haydn's high in a building over First Avenue, where in the twilight you could see the UN building (a really startling structure: too bad it'll be a 5 + 10¢ store in the next war, or a storehouse) and all of the other beautiful sunlit midtown buildings. It was like Hollywood's idea of a New York cocktail party. Douglas Southall Freeman's daughter was there (she's married to Julius Ochs Adler, Jr., of the Times) and we talked about the old times in Richmond when we were both in prep-school and danced together. Also present was Grey Blake, who played the part of the young suitor in "The Cocktail Party." He's very British, as the phrase goes, but very nice and

* Maloney was a fellow writer and student of Hiram Haydn at the New School. Haydn's recollections of him appear in *Words and Faces* (New York: Harcourt Brace Jovanovich, 1974).

personable and we had a long talk. At the Algonquin he had a room next to Tennessee Williams, who kept him awake all night with his typewriter, and when "Tenn" moved out, in moved Anton Karas (of "The Third Man") with his zither. So Blake moved out. Also at the party was Gwyned, the "career girl" working in an ad-agency, whom Life wrote up a year ago, crying on her boy friend's shoulder, etc.* She's a very spoiled, lovely, silly-looking tomato.

Korea looks bad, but it doesn't do to worry. If one worried one would go batty and get nothing accomplished. Ars longa . . .†

A Kiss for my S.B. (X). Two Kisses (XX) and much love from plain, hot little ol' NYC.

To Sigrid de Lima

July 23, 1950 314 West 88th Street, New York City

Dear Such a Sweet Baby:

It is toward the end of a hot and humid Saturday afternoon, and I have been working—ineffectually enough, on account of the heat, or just maybe a lack of inspiration—and so thought it would be a good enough time to apprise you of what I have been doing recently. Aggie called me up a couple of hours ago and asked me to go to V.C. fair with her and the Maxwells, and it was a considerable temptation, but at the time I thought (mistakenly) that my thoughts were flowing well toward the book. I should have gone, but I hope to go tomorrow, to write a little and look at the corn which Aggie says is now higher than my head. Isn't that miraculous? I had lunch with Aggie on Thursday at the Captain's Table and had a nice talk, and then I went over to the School and saw the beginnings of her fine new, pale blue office on the sixth floor.

Last Thursday, too, I guess it was, I finished the scene between Dolly and Loftis and am now ready to go on to the Charlottesville episode. It's about time, and I would be there quicker, had it not been for the fact that

* Leonard McCombe, "The Private Life of Gwyned-Filling," *Life* (May 3, 1948).

† "Ars longa, vita brevis" are the first two lines of an aphorism by Hippocrates: "Art is long, life is short."

in the Loftis-Dolly sex scene I had to go back, through some compulsion, and describe a Christmas dinner of the year before. The scene is pretty long (the Xmas episode) and it won't surprise you that it bears quite a resemblance to the first-hand Christmas dinner experience which I once told you about. I'm terribly put off about this Charlottesville scene, because I want it to be one of the best ones in the book. It seems to be obstinate in starting, but a couple more days of concentration should put it on the road. I'll feel that when that scene is done, the end, for the first time, will really be in sight.

My check for $500 is due sometime this next week and I'll welcome it with relief. I've been living off nothing at all during the past week or so and I'm tired of poverty and of borrowing. After I sign the contract on Monday, Haydn is going to take it to Indianapolis with him (he's flying to B-M's head office) and I'll get the money by air mail as soon as he can arrange it out there. I haven't seen the contract, but Haydn says that Mavis McIntosh arranged a fine one, so I'm happy. Actually, though, it looks as if the book won't get published until fall of '51, because I really don't think I'll get it finished until Christmas, possibly, even February, and it takes six or seven months to get a book published. Haydn is rather put out by the fact that I won't get it done by this November, because the spring season, for some reason, is a better season to promote a first novel, but I think he also realizes that not only am I a slow worker, but that I won't be satisfied if I rush the job, get sloppy or hasty. My vanity has desired that I get the book published before my 26th birthday, but that's a rather stupid conceit anyway, so what the hell. It's going to be such a good book, I think, really a fine book—with all of its multitude of faults—and it's progressing better and better each day—each day, that is, in which I force myself, with pain and groans, to write. I just hope that this last part won't be so much better than the first that it becomes evident that I was just groping around in the first chapters. However, I'm going to do a little tightening and rewriting in the first chapters anyway. What a long road it is! Nothing in my life has ever seemed so incapable of completion—not that I don't want to complete it (it's exactly the opposite of that), but it's still like carrying knapsacks of unbearable sand through endless woods to a sunlit meadow, the lovely contours of which I can only vaguely imagine.

New York is hot and sluggish, and there is incessant chatter of war. God, what a time we live in! Who cares really for art or beauty or anything like that when one is so inundated by perpetual mementoes of distraction, ugliness, television faces. At a party at Loomis's last night I was surrounded by a real herd of television and radio creatures. It was a veritable shame to hear them talk, and so I got abruptly and impolitely drunk. Surely this Peter Viereck is correct in writing that the real Babbitts of our time are not the hollow-headed businessmen but the intellectual chic: the ones who read Flair, and go to avant-garde movies and think Charlie Chaplin is the new messiah, and believe that the music of Kurt Weill and Burl Ives and South Pacific reach dizzy summits of emotion. Maybe the outfit is headed for extinction, and we do need the Atom bomb. Collier's, incidentally, has a really horrifying article portraying the destruction of N.Y.C. by the Bomb, with a capital B.*

The corn will be ripe when you return, so come back and you and I will eat some, also our tomatoes. We'll also avoid Anna O'Higgins like a plague and if I take my MS up I'll wrap it in windproof cellophane.

Now I must go out and sponge a meal from someone I know, probably Loomis. If Haydn wants to know why I've been writing so slowly, I'll tell him the truth: all I've been able to write about is food.

Much love and hugs from S.B. Kisses from
S.B.

To William Canine

August 8, 1950 Valley Cottage, NY

Dear Bill,

I was happy to get your letter and to read all about life and art in Durham. What with your short stories and the fable (what is a fable? Like Aesop? La Fontaine? It sounds interesting.) you seem to be coming along faithfully and well, and I hope and expect Mr. Fuller (whom, incidentally, I've heard of but don't know) to have them in print for you very soon. From what you write I gather that you have a considerable portion of the novel finished, which is a fine thing, too. Before I go any further I'd like

* "Hiroshima, U.S.A.," *Collier's* (August 5, 1950).

to call your attention, as they say, to both the Houghton Mifflin fellowship and the Saxton Fellowship—you've no doubt heard of them. Why don't you give them a try, since they seem to me to be the best ways in which to place an unfinished MS? Both funds provide a working author with $2400—no strings attached, except the obvious one of literary promise, and the rather natural provision that you give publishing rights to Houghton Mifflin, or to Harper's, with whom the Saxton trust has a somewhat incestuous relationship. You can get application blanks for the HM Literary Fellowship by writing to the HM Company, 2 Park Street, Boston. The Eugene F. Saxton Memorial Trust blanks you can obtain from Harper and Bros., 49 E. 33rd St., NYC.

Now that that's off my chest, I might go on to finer and better things, which brings me to music. The music up here is wonderful. We have a Lafayette FM-AM radio, with all sorts of fine attachments, LP, and I'd imagine one would call the other SP. I'm rapidly beginning to believe that Mozart is the most important man since Shakespeare. Have you heard the Horn Concerto No. 4? Or the Divertimento No. 17? The latter is on Columbia records with the Lener Quartet and the brothers Brain playing the horns. In both pieces the horns give this lovely sense of space and poignancy to the foreground melody, and I get utterly "sent" when I hear them. If I'm not mistaken, the Durham Music Co has the Divertimento. Maybe they're having a 50% reduction sale, and you could pick it up cheap, if you liked it. Yesterday (Sunday) WQXR played all of The Marriage of Figaro from two till five, and from five till eight WABF, a lovely New York FM station, played all of Don Giovanni. It's almost indecent, really, listening to all of this grand stuff, but I don't know what I'd do without music. Somehow I believe that one of the conditions of art—literature—is to approach, like Pater said, the state of music, although I believe, too, that one should have a bit more to say than Pater. At any rate, I wonder whether people without a proper appreciation of music (in the un-snobbish sense) can impose a feeling of poetry upon literature. And without this poetry (I don't mean "poetic prose") I just don't believe that the best literature can be produced. Which all leads back, perhaps, to loving Mozart and Beethoven and Bach and the best of Brahms. Frankly, I don't know much about the rest of them.

I'm glad you mentioned Gide. I've read nothing of his, including the Journals, but from time to time I've planned to do so, because what the reviews have said all seemed so interesting.* The laziness, the boredom, the striving toward a discipline—all these have been mentioned and have intrigued me, as they probably do you, because they seem to strike some common chord. So many people, as I have made bold to say before, seem to think that writing is an act apart and discrete from the author's personality, that one sits down each day and gets such-and-such an amount of words written, and that's that. Well, it's not the case; at least it's not the case with me, and I suspect that it's not the case with any writer except a hack, who undergoes no probings of his mind and doesn't care about halting to consider this or that way of expressing a thought or turning a phrase. It's not a precious pose. This agonizing, in any real writer; most of the writings of any real writer are, I suspect, merely the projections in fictions of his own personality, and he isn't willing to sweat and strain and make it as nearly perfect as he can, then he ain't a real writer, because he's not searching through his mind for the real him, but is just putting down the first old thing that pops into his head. As for this novel, Peyton, that I'm writing, it lacks too much form to begin with for me not to sweat over the inside particulars. Actually, it's coming along very well, but God! You want to put in everything, express so much, but you find that if you try to do this you're deserting the little form and unity you already have. I'll be satisfied if, say about the summer of next year, I've gotten one/fiftieth of what I want to say within my vague and sprawling outline. By that time I should be finished, and I hope it'll be good. It's what I'm living for.

If and when you come to N.Y. in September, don't fail to let me know you're here. I don't know if I'll still be up here or not; I probably will, though. The number is NYack 7-1806-W. We could have a number of rousing good beers, or martinis, if you prefer. I haven't heard from Loomis in a number of weeks; I think he's suffering from a curious sense of guilt or betrayal over Suzie, but it's all right with me if he wants to be such a young child. Tell Brice, if you please, that I'll write him soon, also Snitger, to whom I'm in debt a little. I'm glad he got a better job. Embrace Bennett-Lee for me, and give my best to Emily, Gipp, Cricket, and Byron.

* Styron claimed to have read Gide's journals in a January 19, 1950, letter to Leon Edwards.

Incidentally, did you ever play chess? We play the game often up here, and I'm getting to be something of a gee-whiz. Back to work.

Yours,

Bill S.

P.S.: See the pretty stamps?

To William Blackburn

October 19, 1950 314 West 88th Street, New York City

Dear Prof. Blackburn,

This is just a note to thank you for your letter, which was wonderful. Everyone is just as happy as you are that you had a nice time at Valley Cottage and perhaps, like Gen'l MacArthur, you shall return, soon.

In regard to Lead Belly, I'm glad that you were able to get a copy of "Irene." However, Sigrid and I have had copies made for you, on two 10" unbreakable 78 rpm records, three of the songs which you heard at Valley Cottage: They are "Frankie + Albert," which takes up two sides; "Midnight Special"; and "Take This Hammer." They are a little noisy and since the originals were cracked, the cracks have been reproduced, too, but they sound good just the same. I am wrapping them up and you should get them next week.

The Occasion for this is, of course, the death of Sir Thomas Browne, which took place 268 years ago today.*

As ever,

Bill S.

* Sir Thomas Browne (1605–82), English author whose works include *Hydriotaphia, Urn Burial, or a Discourse of the Sepulchral Urns lately found in Norfolk*—the source of the title *Lie Down in Darkness*. The relevant passage is quoted in Styron's letter of April 17, 1951, to William Blackburn.

To William C. Styron, Sr.

December 6, 1950 314 West 88th Street, New York City

Dear Pop,

A note to let you know that I'm thinking of you, and that I'm hoping everything goes well and you're on your way to a good recovery. Eliza has been keeping me apprised of your progress and at last reports you were doing admirably well. Keep it up and stay in good spirits and I know you'll be in prime working order very soon.

The big news up here recently has involved three things—the Long Island train wreck, the big storms and, of course, the war. The wreck was awful and most people I know out on Long Island are actually paralyzed with fright.* As for the storm, it really did leave havoc in its wake, as they would say in the newspapers. I was up with the de Limas in Valley Cottage that weekend and, while there was no damage to the house, all the lights were gone for three days and also the water, which is worked by an electric pump. It was an amazing journey; riding back down to the city through northern New Jersey there were whole acres in that thickly wooded area where not one tree was left standing. They were all blown down like so much kindling, looking as if a bomb had blasted away at them—an A-bomb—and it was appalling and rather pathetic.†

The really gruesome news here, as elsewhere, is the war.‡ I don't know what's going to happen, and I try—in order to keep my wits about me—not to think about it, and proceed about my work in an orderly fashion. The Marines (so Tommy Peyton, who is now back at Quantico, informs me) will probably not make me join up for a while yet—unless there's a real war—because reserve officers are called up by serial number, and my number is a relatively low one. So that's some temporary consolation, at least.

* Two trains collided on the Long Island Rail Road on November 22, 1950. Seventy-five people were killed and close to one hundred injured. See "Cars Telescoped: Hempstead Train Halts in the Path of One Going to Babylon," *The New York Times,* November 23, 1950.

† A serious storm hit New York on November 25, 1950. See "Floods Rout Many," *The New York Times,* November 26, 1950.

‡ Styron had remained in the Marine Corps Reserve and was eligible for recall in Korea.

The book, finally, I can say, is nearing completion. I'm over the hump and the end is in sight. I've been working very hard on it lately—due to the pressure of the news and monetary considerations—and I don't know whether the book will profit or suffer by my sense of urgency. I surely hope, at least, that it doesn't suffer too much. Not that I'm writing sloppily; I'm just not taking so long to ponder and find the bon mot, the impeccable phrase. Right at this moment Haydn is reading for the first time the second 175 page chunk of the book, which brings me up currently to p. 365. I haven't heard from him yet, but I know he'll like it, and at any rate I'm still writing furiously, with roughly 75–100 more pages to go.

Do take care of yourself, Pop, and try not to be too depressed. Remember that you're only one of a legion of people who've had the same thing, and most of them have recovered handily and are now active and happy. Please try to write me when you can, and give my best to Eliza and everybody.

Your son,
Bill Jr.

To William Canine

February 23, 1951 314 West 88th Street, New York City

Dear Bill,

Got your note and am glad to hear that you are coming up to the fleshpots of the North. You'd of course be welcome to stay with me, except that frankly there's not a shred of anything to lie on in my squalid room. There's a seedy, but clean, hotel called the Colbourne, which sounds like it should be on Fifth Avenue, but which is on Washington Place near Sixth Avenue right off Washington Square. If you'll write next week and tell me just about when you plan to get here I'll reserve a room; which is pretty cheap there, and you'll be all set when you arrive. It's in the heart of the so-called Village, where I spent more of my so-called Nights, and so it would be convenient to what parties are on hand at that time. Just let me know about when you plan to get here. My telephone number, incidentally, is Trafalgar 7-2895 and if there's no answer there I can generally be reached at Walker 5-2041, which is the number of Wanda Montemora,* this girl I know, and at whose apartment I do some of my work. There are good shows at the Metropolitan and at Modern Art; I think it's a fine season to come to the city.

I did receive a call from Cate, indeed. The orders were to report to the 2nd MarDw, whatever that is, CLNC (Camp Lejeune) on March 2nd. I took my physical at the Brooklyn Navy Yard and passed beautifully. I had 70–20 vision in one eye (uncorrectable), but I could have strolled in there with no arms and a case of leukemia and they still would have taken me. However, Haydn got on the phone to HQMC WashDC (Code DF) and contacted a General Jerome, who is head of USMC publicity. Haydn gave him a sad story and the general was sympathetic, so I have been deferred until May 1st. Ample time to finish the book, but hardly enough time to finish the book and celebrate its completion both. You said you thought you'd be raging mad if you got the call. I have no doubt that you would. I was absolutely frantic, planning to turn myself in to the FBI and tell them to take their bloody war and ram it, as we say in the Marines, and other desperate expedients. But now I'm a little calmer and my rage has turned into a greasy sort of bitterness. I think this country—at the moment—is strictly from hunger.

The book will be finished by April 1st and will be published in July. This is the straight scoop. I'm on Peyton's death scene now, page 480-something. The book's too long. The jacket is going to be handsome, with a design by George Salter, who did "Joseph in Egypt" for Knopf. I wish I would be more excited over these trifles, but the Marines have deadened me to every emotion except disgust.

We'll have time to talk when you come. Let me hear from you before.

Yours,

Bill

* Montemora was one of the women Styron used to create Sophie Zawistowski. She was the daughter of the anthropologist Bronislaw Malinowski.

To William C. Styron, Sr.

April 7, 1951 Valley Cottage, NY

Dear Pop,

I'm up in Valley College this weekend with the de Limas—a beautiful spring day (the first this year up here), and listening to Beethoven's Ninth adds a touch of supernatural grandeur. The book was finished over a week ago and since then I've been resting up—as much as I can, since the rest period has involved trips to Westport with Haydn and visits to Bobbs-Merrill for touching up and revision. Fortunately, there hasn't been much of the latter, except for minor changes here and there, and I'm on my way back to regaining the 15 pounds I lost writing the final hundred pages. Now, finished, I can say I'm pretty well pleased with what I've achieved. The book has quite a few flaws but generally speaking I believe that I've accomplished what I set out to do. It's a big novel in size (620 typed pages) but I do think it's big in quality, too. I suspect that if I don't achieve fame from it I'll at least get a certain notoriety, for the last part of the book has pages that are exceedingly frank.* Necessary, though, to my intention. Some people, too, will no doubt think the book is filled with a sense of needless despair. I don't much care what they think; it has plenty of despair in it, but none of it, I think, needless. I've done what the true artist must do: paint life honestly according to his vision. If my vision is, to use a phrase, tragic, the tragedy is not gratuitous, but a part of our monstrously tragic times. The hope offered at the very end of the book is also not gratuitous; I think you'll agree with me when you read it. Title: Lie Down in Darkness.

Outside of my own reactions, the book has really gone over with the rest of the people so far. The ones, that is, including Haydn, who've read the MS. Haydn really does think I'm the best writer living and it does me no harm to hear him say it, although I'm too much the natural pessimist

* Bobbs-Merrill made significant alterations to Peyton Loftis's interior monologue, deleting words and substituting others. See Styron's essay "'I'll Have to Ask Indianapolis—'" in his *Havanas in Camelot: Personal Essays* (New York: Random House, 2008). Arthur D. Casciato examined these cuts in "His Editor's Hand: Hiram Haydn's Changes in *Lie Down in Darkness,*" in Arthur D. Casciato and James L. W. West III, eds., *Critical Essays on William Styron* (Boston: G. K. Hall, 1982).

to let it turn my head. George Salter, the fellow who has done the jacket, has written a note to be sent out by Haydn to the booksellers. Salter is a very snooty guy, according to Haydn, and is not given to insincere tributes; Haydn will send you the note when it's printed and I think you might be pleased by it. The book, incidentally, is finally scheduled to be published on August 20th and you'll get a galley copy long before that, probably sometime in May. So far three very big literary people have promised to read the book and to give a comment, if they like it, for the jacket. They are Robert Penn Warren, Allen Tate, and Van Wyck Brooks.* Haydn also expects comments from the following: Edmund Wilson, Louis Kronenberger, Budd Schulberg, Lionel Trilling, Alfred Kazin, Joseph Wood Krutch, Mark Van Doren, and John P. Marquand. Quite a list, no?† I might even get rich; if so, how about a new Pontiac for you?

I hope it won't disturb you, as I heard that it did, to tell you that I'm marking time, resignedly, for my re-entrance into the Marine Corps.‡ Last time I didn't mean to give an impression of abject anything—terror or despair. I just really felt then (heightened by the sudden shock), as I do now, a sort of disgust with the whole business. One can't feel overjoyed at the prospect of being, in the prime of one's life, militarized indefinitely. Communism and its threat (acknowledged), or the fact that I've already spent three years at it before, with or without combat—these have not so much to do with my disgust as that of being faced with a civilization ap-

* Allen Tate (1899–1979) was a poet and essayist who helped form the Fugitive literary group as well as the Southern Agrarians. Van Wyck Brooks (1886–1963) was a literary critic and biographer best known for *The Flowering of New England, 1815–1865,* which won the National Book Award and the Pulitzer Prize.

† Edmund Wilson (1895–1972) was a writer and literary critic who authored many books, including *Patriotic Gore* (1962). Louis Kronenberger (1904–80) was a writer and critic who wrote and edited dozens of books over his long career. Budd Schulberg (1914–2009) was a screenwriter, television producer, and novelist, best known for his Academy Award–winning screenplay for *On the Waterfront.* Lionel Trilling (1905–75) was a prominent literary critic and major contributor to the *Partisan Review.* Alfred Kazin (1915–98) was a writer and literary critic. Joseph Wood Krutch (1893–1970) was a writer and critic who wrote several important biographies and works of criticism. Mark Van Doren (1894–1972) was a poet, writer, and critic who won the Pulitzer Prize for poetry in 1940. John Phillips Marquand (1893–1960) was a writer best known for his Mr. Moto spy novels who won a Pulitzer Prize in 1938. There were no quotations from any of these on the cover of the first edition of *Lie Down in Darkness.*

‡ Styron used the delay Hiram Haydn arranged to finish *Lie Down in Darkness.*

parently going stark raving mad. I urge you to read a book called 1984 by George Orwell. It pictures beautifully the situation toward which we seem to be headed, and will reach unless people quit their mad lust for power. I despise Soviet Communism in any of its forms, but I equally believe that America is—at the moment, at least—far from guiltless and perhaps even a little criminal in its foreign policy. You understand I'm not speaking as a marine-to-be, but as a citizen. "My country right or wrong; but always my country"—these are fallacies that should have been shattered long ago, in a nation potentially as great in its democratic ideals as this one. I realize that we face a hideous threat, and it's not the Marines or our foreign policy or possibility of combat which I protest so much as, again, being involved in a sort of zombie world where the only music is the sound of marching feet. Please don't let this personal attitude affect you. As usual we aren't taking it lying down; but the young people of today who do any sort of thinking do feel, I can assure you, somehow tricked and cheated. I feel lucky. I've written a book, my words are "graven with an iron pen and lead in the rock forever."* But what about the ones who want to write, and won't have a chance?

You'll get a copy of the jacket and the proofs sometime in May and I hope you enjoy it—especially since you'll have the knowledge that you, mostly, made it possible. Because of more work I won't be able to see you before I go to Lejeune, but I'm sure I'll be able to see you on the weekends and furloughs thereafter.

Your son,
WCS jr

To William Blackburn

April 17, 1951 314 West 88th Street, New York City

Dear Doctor,

I'm glad you like the title. It is, of course, from the old master himself—Chapter V of Urn-Burial: "since our longest sun set at right declensions . . .

* Job 19:23–24. "Oh that my words were now written! Oh that they were printed in a book! That they were graven with an iron pen and lead in the rock for ever!"

and therefore it cannot be long before we lie down in darkness and have our light in ashes. . . ." Since I have Peyton herself say part of the line, just before she jumps from the window, I'm not using it as a quote in the front of the book but merely appropriating it, a la Eliot. I hope Sir Thomas won't turn over pompously in his grave. The quote I'm using as an epigraph is from Finnegans Wake: "Carry me along, taddy, like you done through the toy fair."—the cry to Earwicker from his children, as he hears it in his sleep. I think it fits the book pretty well.

I wrote the last 15,000 words in about two weeks. The most exhausting fortnight I've ever spent, or imagine I ever will spend. I lost fifteen pounds and I'm still in a state of semi-convalescence. I had to become Peyton and kill myself in the first person, and as it worked out I came pretty literally close to it. Luckily, I had Daddy Faith and his baptism to resuscitate me at the end. The book, as I told Brice, runs to over 600 typewritten pages. The last part is very frank and this will no doubt make me notorious and get me censored in Boston. If it turns out that way I will be able, no doubt, to buy you a new Cadillac, although I believe the part which may cause raised eyebrows was written honestly, and with no deliberate intention to shock. Harrison Smith* and J. Donald Adams† will gag over it, but other people will like it—and have liked it already. I only wish I didn't have to go back into the loathed Marine Corps, but I've already resigned myself to the extent that it no longer gives me bad dreams. I'm indeed looking forward to seeing you on the weekends. As I recall from the last war, it's not too long or rough a trip up from New River and no doubt I'll soon meet someone with a convenient automobile to make the journey less a bore. I've stopped for a while my moaning and groaning about the state of the world. I'll no doubt get angry again and soon, but at the moment I'm trying to practice a sort of Matthew Arnoldesque attitude of resignation, in the hope that though things might not measurably improve they may at least not get a hell of a lot worse.‡ I hate in a way to leave New York but

* Along with Jonathan Cape (and later Robert Haas), Harrison Smith was William Faulkner's publisher beginning with *The Sound and the Fury* (1929).

† J. Donald Adams (1891–1968) was a book critic and editor, best known for his edited collections of poetry and prose.

‡ Styron refers to the British poet and literary critic Matthew Arnold (1822–88) and his poem "Resignation."

perhaps there are pleasanter spring fields in Carolina. I'll be leaving on May 1st. If you write me after that, and before you get my Lejeune address, perhaps you'd better write in care of Bobbs-Merrill, 468 4th Avenue. But I hope to hear from you before that.

As ever,
Bill

Styron reported for duty at Camp Lejeune, North Carolina, in May 1951.

To Thomas Peyton III

May 9, 1951 Camp Lejeune, NC

Dear Satan,*

As you can see from the above address, while I don't have it precisely made I have been at least temporarily saved from snoopin and poopin in the swamps. Right now I am assistant 5-3 of the 8th Marines, a job about which I know nothing and care less. They have so many 1st Lieuts. down here that they don't know what to do with them, so they shoved me in here, hoping, I suspect, that I would at least keep out of the way. Mornings at 7:30 I go to Staff Command School, whatever that is, where a bunch of knucklehead Majors from TTU lecture on "high level" policy in Amphibious Tactics.† When they have movies, just as in the old days, and the lights are out, I sleep. Afternoons I come back here and write letters and drink Coca-Colas. Evenings I sulk alone with a bourbon (already, after only a week, I think I've overrun my account) and correct the page-proofs on my book (they are coming in now, beautifully, permanently printed, and these provide my only consolation) and brood over the peculiar fate of our generation which has us tied helplessly to the brute wheel of evil and power.

Anyway, for a time, to more mundane things. How does this new re-

* Styron's nickname for Peyton.
† Texas Tech University.

serve alarm affect your status. Down here it has caused mixed horror and joy. To people like myself who have just come in, the part about one year's service has been very depressing, but of course the boys who came in in August are quite happy. The so-called proposed expansion of the Corps might blast everyone's hopes, but even so the expansion seems to be a long-range proposition and, after all, might not get through Congress.

God, ain't it horrible? You should know even more than I, old buddy, being in your position. I sure hope something good happens to you before you go west, like losing a finger or a toe. It'd be worth it. There ain't no justice, to think that only four months separated your PCS class from mine, and yet by some purely chronological quirk you boys got crapped on this time. At least (so far) most of us have gotten easy jobs. Let me know how you think this new order will affect you. I sho hope something will keep you East and that this whole bloody mess will clear up miraculously and that you and your spouse and me and mine (I'd be half-way married myself this month) could get together on the river somewhere and drink beer by the soul-cleansing gallon. It is possible though I can hardly see how it's probable. If the lunatic fringe of both the Republican and Democratic parties would for Christ's sake just get killed and the sane members get together, and quick, there might be a way to finish off Korea and work for a lasting, final peace. But I doubt it. If we are destroyed, remember that we are destroyed by evil, ignorant, criminal men, not only in Russia but in D.C. A man would be justified using a BAR on about half of Congress.*

I'm tired of thinking about the situation, and I'm more tired of being held captive by the enemy. Maybe I'll rebel, go over the hill, I don't know. At least I know that no men of good will would point a finger at me and cry "shame." My dreams are haunted by visions of a time when you and I were younger and more innocent, a time long before the time when, as the Bible says, violent men raised spears against us.† Let us pray.

Let me know your progress, old boy; keep me well informed, and don't let the bastards get you down. In all the despair I still somehow have a secret place in my heart that says that we will prevail.

Your buddy,
Sty

* Browning automatic rifle.

† 2 Samuel 23:20.

To William C. Styron, Sr.

June 1, 1951 Camp Lejeune, NC

Dear Pop,

I heard from Eliza that you are a little under the weather now. I'm terribly sorry and know how you must feel, lying so quiescent on your back; but also knowing the old spirit, I have no doubt that you will snap back and be in good shape again soon.

If any kind of doubts or wonderings are troubling your ability to get back into shape, please don't worry about me, or let a worry about me hinder your recuperation. I am in the finest of spirits, both mentally and physically, and am making the best of my lot down here in the swamps. I would rather, of course, be elsewhere, but I have found to my absolute surprise—after all these years of living my own life—that the new discipline agrees with me very well. I rise at 7:00, eat three big square meals a day and have a sunburn that even Johnny Weissmuller would envy.* We go out into the field once every two weeks for about two days and although lying on the swampy turf amid all the ticks and chiggers is not exactly my idea of the Waldorf, it nonetheless and undoubtedly gives a certain sense of physical well-being.

I'm getting the last of my proofs now, and they should be in bound pages very soon. Hiram will send you a copy as soon as they come through, which should be within the next three or four weeks. About the book, of course, now that it's over, I am wildly happy. People all over—I understand from my New York Intelligence—are already talking about it, and there's no doubt about it—and modesty has nothing to do with it—that your boy is about to become <u>the</u> sensation, at <u>least</u> of 1951. God knows, I'm not getting swell-headed over the thing—being essentially too aware of the transitoriness of fame—but I don't mind getting all this additional reward, especially after knowing that first and foremost I was honest, that the book represents hours of real sweat and pain, and that I did my level best, in every word of it.

Of course you must know what you've done for me. If it hadn't been for your faith in me, and your gentle and constant encouragement, it would

* Johnny Weissmuller (1904–1984) was an Olympic swimmer and the most famous portrayer of Tarzan in films.

never have been written. There are few enough artists who have gotten encouragement from people at large, much less their parents—toward whom the very fact that they create usually represents a tacit antipathy. But you have been faithful to the very end of my first endeavor, and I appreciate it to the bottom of my heart. We live in a troubled era, there is no doubt of that, and sometimes I wonder if we will all endure. Yet with all my complaint, often, at the times, and at life in general, I somehow know we shall endure and that all this striving is not at all in vain. The very fact that you and I have worked together, no matter with what unspoken understanding, represents a partnership of the spirit, and if that is love, it will prevail—forever and ever. I will write until my knuckles are worn and my brain bewildered, but I will write on and on, and if it can be done by a feckless soul like myself it can be done by the human race: this eternal creation and recreation, even in the face of the bleakest future. You have given me the chance and I'll not let you down. When you read my <u>second</u> book, or play, or whatever it is, it might not be very good, but no matter. Remember that your faith in me has given me the watchword, or something: you have believed in me, so because of that I have believed in myself, and so, having strived, I believe, ceaselessly upward (in the words of Goethe), I can be saved. And so can we all be saved.

My God, it's been a long pull, but, as I say, I'm as happy as it is possible to be. Don't mind the reviews when they come in August—they're going to raise hell with me. But I <u>know</u> that I've written a fine, true book and that it will live for a long time. And I thank you for everything you've done to make it possible.

Soon we come to Little Creek in Norfolk for amphibious training—sometime within the next month—so then I'll be able to see you. I'll give you the exact details very soon. Keep the doormat out and we'll have a fine talk together.

Your son,

Bill, Jr.

P.S. I thought the biography you sent to Duke was fine stuff, if a little embarrassing to read first-hand by the biographee.*

* Styron's father wrote an eight-page biography of his son for the Duke alumni office. It is reprinted in *Letters to My Father*.

To Dorothy Parker*

June 19, 1951 Camp Lejeune, NC

TOP SECRET 8th Marines (Reinf.)
IN THE FIELD

WES/wb-1
Dlt-14
AUTHENTICATED
TIME:191950Q

REGIMENTAL OPERATION} [Begun Tuesday P.M
ORDER 16-51} JOCKSTRAP for civilians]
TASK ORGANIZATION: ME AND YOU

Dearest: I am at present sitting in a tick-ridden bed of pine needles amidst a group of oddly-camouflaged tents surrounded, in the twilight, by a grotesque confusion of bushes and trees. Although I am not suffering hideously and although I have just gorged myself on a huge meal (in the field we eat twice a day, squatting or kneeling, at 6:00 A.M. and 5:30 P.M., so the interim hunger is great) I am definitely not enjoying myself, and the associate boredom and waiting, the total idiocy of the thing, the getting rained on when it rains, the mosquitoes and ticks, the sleeping on the good earth when and if you get a chance to sleep, the not taking of baths—all of these tend to put one in a state of mind which, mildly stated, might be called cranky. There will be tonight and tomorrow and tomorrow night and half of the next day; then all will be over for quite a while, but already I feel like I've been out here for a year.

Then yesterday I got your letter telling me that the weasel of Whittlesey House has pulled another of his fanciful coups and fired you—which made me feel ugly and distressed and more morbid than just the lack of sleep could ever make me—not so much because of his act in itself, because you'd be quitting anyway, but because again we have the tiny little man up to his abysmal, petty tricks. And I feel dreadful about the whole business. Why did he do it? And what weak-minded, mealy-mouthed excuses did he offer? And where do you think you will land another place, and when?

Of course—or perhaps not of course—but anyway a tiny bit of the sad

* Dorothy "Didi" Parker was one of Styron's colleagues at Whittlesey House. She should not be conufsed with the Algonquin Round Table founder of the same name.

feeling I have is simply the fact of your leaving that monstrous green building; perhaps no building on earth should be less capable of evoking nostalgia, but topographically I have thought of you always enthroned in one of those fake mahogany offices, and now I shall have to rearrange all my tender visions.

But, as you say and seem to think, it's all most very likely the best thing (I've always thought Aswell wanted to take you into his scented boudoir), and that pile of money due you certainly sounds worthwhile, God Knows. So I don't know whether to really mourn or what; I think it's just Aswell—who bears a remarkable resemblance, physically and morally, to some of the dangerous little colonels around here—that has sickened me, and the knowledge that somehow, no matter in what slight way, he has managed to hurt you.

Incidentally, and seriously—and I mean it—don't you think it would be a good thing if I wrote to Hiram about you? I don't know what he could do right off, but he knows well of you through me and he would be powerfully interested in you if I wrote, and I would write him a powerful letter. I'm dead serious about this, and Hiram is a man of influence and the fact of the matter is that he would do anything in the world for me that he could—so please think it over and let me know as soon as you can.

God, life is a bloody trial sometimes, isn't it? Right now it's almost ten in the evening and, having risen at 4:30 this morning, I feel that this day never really began, but just existed always. I am sitting in a blackout tent with my two sergeants (they are really fine fellows; the tragic part about war + the military is not—as the so-called sensitive person who has never seen it might think—the fact that one is thrown in among disagreeable people; for most all of the people are pretty decent and good, and grow affectionately together in their common misery) and the tent, being shut up, is stifling and smells of DDT. At midnight I will get off my stool and climb down on the ground in the fashion of some other animal than a human—a dog, perhaps—and sleep the four hours allotted me until H-hour at 4:00 A.M. and then arise, exhausted and scratching. Well actually, I suppose, it could be a lot worse and I've had it worse myself, but because it's happening to me now I feel it with a moderate pang of hurt and degradation and futility, so please excuse a moment's bitching. I've gotten it off my chest.

The main thing, of course, is that I love you and that grows and grows until sometimes I feel I won't be quite able to stand it—if that doesn't sound too silly. Out here in the swamps, separated further from you by this week's chancy business of mail, I feel that an ocean of silence keeps us apart—and the ocean is green—not "our" ocean—with the unhealthy, persistent green of a military forest. They even shame nature in war, soiling what should be grand and exciting by their very presence, their very touch. Anyway, I love you more and more each moment, because each moment allows me to think more about your loveliness and all the things I love about you; and you touched me when you said that when we meet it'll probably be like two strangers who have only heard a lot of each other, because that's no doubt true and we'll likely be absurd for a while—but not for too long. So last night gave me quite an opportunity to think about you, for the first night in the woods is generally a sleepless one for me, and, supine in the weeds, with this damn gasoline lamp roaring in the tent about me, I went through the most fetching fantasies—trying, I suspect, to summon you to accompany me to sleep and dreams: first I thought of you and I walking through Central Park and then of you and I in the Green or perhaps White Mountains, then of you and I slumbering together in a garden full of flowers.

A few days later: well, I was mistaken: we all suffered pretty hideously. Immediately after the above trifle was written, the Colonel came in the tent with plans for a hike. I went to bed at four, woke at six and spent all morning on the radio. Then at noon all hell broke loose; two mortar shells burst into the Sixth Marines lines adjacent to us—strictly an accident (did you read about it in the papers?) but eleven men were killed and twenty-some wounded and I had to guide our own regimental surgeon to the area to give aid. It was terrible. I stood by down there for three or four hours while the wounded were evacuated, and then at eight o'clock in the evening we began a 30-mile forced march back to the base. It went all night, with a ten minute break each hour, and it was sheer hell. A hike doesn't sound like much, probably, but 30 miles is a long way, even for the Marines and I don't believe any of us thought we'd make it, considering the fact that none of us had more than four hours' sleep during the two preceding nights. I have blisters the size of eggs on both feet and I all but collapsed at the finish line and—oh well, I'm frankly just too goddamn tired to bore you about it any longer, though I'll probably regale you over martinis with a complete account of the whole ghastly day.

I had intended to write you much more but I just haven't had enough time, and now I must pack up (it's Friday noon now) and go out to the rifle range for a week. Write me at the same address you have. I want this to get to N.Y. in time for you to read it when you get back on Monday. It ain't much of a letter and I wanted to tell you many more times that I love you. And I do love you, my darling, and for 30 miles the thought of you kept my feet moving ahead, and the thought of you will forever sustain me through worse trials than that. —Bill

To Sigrid de Lima

June 30, 1951 Camp Lejeune, NC

My dearest Such a Sweet Baby,

I'm sorry for taking such a long time to write you this time, but I've never had two weeks in which time was at such a premium and when so many things seemed to be happening. First we went out to the woods and I will tell you about it. We established a bivouac for the regiment (this was Monday before last) in the most trackless wilderness of sand and pines and thorns I've ever seen. It rained constantly and though every now and then I had a tent to shelter me, I still stayed soaked for hours. The first night I got two hours' sleep, in the wet grass, the second night I got 3½ hours sleep, this time a little dryer, though—wrapped up in a poncho. On the third day all hell broke loose. The regiment adjacent to us and working with us on the problem had two mortar shells go off in its line, killing nine men (did you read about it in the papers?) and wounding twenty-odd.* Although it was not our outfit, we of course sent doctors and ambulances and it was my duty to take the regimental surgeon down to the area in a jeep. It was ghastly, and it was just like war, and that's about all there is to say. Then that night the colonel ordered the entire regiment to march the entire 33 miles back to the main base. We marched and marched and marched from 8:30 P.M until 7:00 the following morning, and it was sheer hell. I don't believe anyone has the slightest idea of how far 33 miles

* "Shells Fall Short, Kill 8 Marines, Wound 23 at Camp Lejeune, N.C.," *The New York Times,* June 21, 1951.

are, until one has hiked them, at a set pace (2½ miles per hour) and in 85° heat and with a ten-minute break every hour. Even for the marines this hike was something of a record and only 65% of the regiment made it and I made it all the way in, with blisters on both feet the size of pingpong balls—though why I stuck it out I don't know. I—who have not walked 200 consecutive yards in the last five years. Now if you will add, to the simple fact of the hike, the blisters, the drugged, dead, plodding exhaustion after the no-sleep for the two preceding nights, the memory of the slain marines I'd just seen, the heat and, above all, the futility of it all—you can imagine what a state I, and all the others, was in at the end of the trail. I fell into bed and slept until 5:00 in the afternoon and only now have my feet begun to cease limping.

Then comes better news, or I should say great news. This last Monday we went to the Rifle Range, and there—as I had anticipated—I pulled my trump card. As I told you, I can't see a bloody thing out of my right eye at any distance. So after failing to hit the target at 500 yards I turned into the hospital with a sad story. The results were astonishing. They examined me, found the old cataract, and immediately recommended that I be released to inactive duty—i.e. discharged. This was further corroborated by the Chief Medical Officer of the Camp, who ordered me transferred to the Marine Barracks here for processing to release from active duty. So it looks from here like I'm to really be out of this lousy outfit very soon—and for good. There is still a slim chance that they'll try to delay it or waiver me or something, or take a long time at it—but the chance is slim, I'm certain, and I don't think I'm being too optimistic when I say I think I'll be back in the city fair, permanently, within a month. Now isn't that great news, following the story of my hardship?

Strange, though, I don't feel too overwhelmed. If I get out, it's sheer good fortune and there are too many guys down here still suffering for me to be exclusively happy. I won't forget them and when I'm out I'm going to campaign for them to the very limit, because the misery of the company of the damned, who seem to be faced with endless years of 30-mile hikes and exploding mortars, is sad indeed.

Last night I listened to the Emperor Concerto with this friend of mine, and the music reminded me of V.C. fair. Are you there, with Talluley and the flowers and everything? I hope and trust it won't be long before I'm there, sitting with my Sweet Baby in the warm summer filled evening, listening to the music from the other room and perhaps gnawing on a piece of golden Bantam corn . . . Love to Aggie and all. This weekend I'm going to Durham, where Blackburn is throwing me a cocktail party, and I will wish that you were there.

With all love from,
S.B.

Styron was discharged from the Marine Corps in August 1951.

To William Blackburn

August 22, 1951 West 13th Street, New York City

Dear Doctor,

I'm in New York now, staying with a friend on West 13th street.* I would like to have come to Durum† before I left Lejeune, but I had to go see my father in Newport News (he is much better) and to go to both places would have been a little too much.

Hiram is sending you a copy of the book, fruit of our (your and mine) efforts. I think it's going to go fine. Maxwell Geismar thinks it's the best book he's read this year.‡ Malcolm Cowley§ says the book is "wonderful" and is going to feature it in The New Republic. Harper's Bazaar has got an effete picture and article on me next month. Best, though, is news that

* John Maloney, 117 West Thirteenth Street.

† One of Styron's affectionate spellings for Durham. He also used Durms, especially with Blackburn.

‡ Maxwell Geismar (1909–79): American literary critic and biographer who taught for many years at Sarah Lawrence College; author of a four-volume history of American novelists as well as two biographies, *Henry James and the Jacobites* (1963) and *Mark Twain: An American Prophet* (1970). He also edited literary collections by Ring Lardner, Thomas Wolfe, and Walt Whitman. He praised *Lie Down in Darkness* in print many times, most notably in *American Moderns: From Rebellion to Conformity* (New York: Hill and Wang, 1958).

§ Malcolm Cowley (1898–1989) was a novelist and poet who became especially influential as an editor at Viking Press in the 1940s.

John W. Aldridge, the young critic who just wrote the book damning all the young writers, thinks that my book is terrific and is going to review it in the Times Book Review.* I'm becoming a sensation. Full-page ads everywhere.

I've never been so happy, I guess. And you know how much you helped make it this way. I'll try to come to Durum before long. Tell Brice I'll send him a copy shortly, but that he'll have to read it. And thanks for everything again.

Always yours,
Bill

To William Blackburn

September 13, 1951 West 13th Street, New York City

Dear Doctor,

Thank you so much for your wonderful letter. I hardly think I deserve that kind of praise, but thank you ever for your faith in me, and trust.

I tried to give you a much bigger plug than what finally came out in the Saturday Review profile on me. I told the girl interviewing me that you were the prime mover of my talents; that you are an "instructor" who liked "some" of my work is just her transcription.

The reviews, most of them, have been quite wonderful. You probably saw the Sunday Times and Tribune. The out-of-town reviews have practically all been superlative, with the exception of the Chicago Tribune, which said I needed an editor like Maxwell Perkins. Time Magazine didn't like the book, nor did Lewis Gannett, but these two were more or less to be expected. Otherwise I could hardly ask for a better reception, and the sales already have gone well over 20,000. Hiram got wonderful letters from Budd Schulberg, Robert Gorham Davis, and Allen Tate about the book. Tate is almost certain I can get the $1,000 award of the American Academy of Arts + Letters.

So I feel fine. And maybe still you will be able to share some of that

* Aldridge reviewed *Lie Down in Darkness* in "In a Place Where Love Is a Stranger," *The New York Times Book Review,* September 9, 1951.

feeling when I tell you again that without your pruning and patience it would never have happened.

Yours ever
Bill

To Leon Edwards

January 9, 1952 48 Greenwich Avenue, New York City

Dear Leon,

Due to some mix-up in this almighty, awful postal system we have, I didn't get your letter of December 15 until today, which is two days after the completion of a Christmas tour to Newport News, Durham and Richmond. Nevertheless, I appreciate, retroactively, your holiday invitation and I'm sorry I didn't get to see you again, except that I probably wouldn't have been able to make it anyway, since I hadn't seen Pop for quite a while and felt that I'd better spend Christmas at home, even if it meant step-mother trouble. I really can't say that I had a riotously happy time in N.N.: I have the feeling from the way people acted around me that I'm the Peninsula's most famous writer of pornography, or perhaps infamous or notorious is a better word. I spent a harrowing evening on Christmas Day at the country club, where, lucky me, I ran into the girl—whom I talked to you about—who is the model, roughly, for Peyton. An embarrassing half-hour was had by all. I also called up your mother and was going to arrange to see her, but took ill briefly with too much food and whiskey, so we didn't get together, but I certainly intend to see her next time I'm down. She's my bravest and most vehement supporter on the Peninsula and God likes her for that.

The news about the book is about the same, except for two facts: the reprint contract with Signet Books has come through with a first printing of 200,000 copies, probably in April or May. I don't know how much money I'll get but it's likely to be "sizeable" according to the man at Bobbs. And a large book club in France seems likely to take it, which pleases me, although I had no idea that France even had book clubs.

I'm glad everything seems to be going well with you all, and I hope I'll be able to see you before long. In the meantime give my best to the family and write whenever you get time off from Gray's Anatomy and the Pharmacopeia.

As ever,
Bill

To Edith Crow*

January 11, 1952 48 Greenwich Avenue, New York City

Dear Aunt Edith,

Since you mentioned in your Christmas letter that you are saving clippings about "Lie Down in Darkness," I am sending you in today's mail three reviews which you may or may not have seen, plus an article, syndicated in North Carolina, from the Raleigh paper. I'm clearing out my small collection—Pop has all of them anyway, since he subscribed to a clipping service—and if they are new to you, you can paste them up, or if you have duplicates you can use them to stuff up window-cracks in place of weatherstripping, or something.

I enjoyed your letter very much. However, in answer to your question about what does a celebrity do to celebrate Christmas, the only thing I can say is that I do—if I am a celebrity, which I doubt—just what everyone else does. For one thing, I went down to Newport News, where I spent a very quiet and uneventful four days, then on down to Durham to see my friends over New Year's, finishing up with a weekend in Richmond, with an old pal of mine. I had a very nice time, but it seemed no different from any other Christmas, even though I've been told I'm an Author with a capital A.

Latest particulars about the book are: sales, something over 30,000; reprint, pocket edition by Signet, sometime late this spring, with a first printing of 200,000 (not a whole lot of money in this for me, but lots of readers at 25¢ apiece); foreign rights; translations in French, Spanish, Danish, Swedish, and Norwegian, and a British edition in April. One of the nicest things, really, that I have to look forward to is the fact that, ac-

* Edith Abraham Crow was the only sister of Styron's mother. She lived in Uniontown, Pennsylvania.

cording to pretty safe rumor, I stand to win this year's "Prix de Rome," awarded by the American Academy of Arts and Sciences, for outstanding achievement in creative writing. This is a grant amounting to $3500 with stipulation that the one who gets the award must live in Rome for a year, all transportation being paid for. It's not an absolute certainty yet, but according to reliable sources it's all but in the bag. So, you see, even if Time doesn't like me much, someone does!

Incidentally, did you see the January issue of Mademoiselle, with my homely face in it, all haggard and lined and worn? Well, the fellow who did the accompanying article, Leo Lerman, is a funny little bald headed man with a beard, who is independently wealthy and who has the habit of "collecting" people with "names" and throws big parties, trying to attract as many luminaries as possible. I was invited to one recently, and went, thinking that perhaps I, too, was a big name. You can imagine how I felt, then, being outshone in the celebrity field by Marlene Dietrich, Tennessee Williams, Laurence Olivier and Vivien Leigh, all of whom were very much at the party, too. I met all of them; the Oliviers were very frostily, Britishly pleasant, "hadn't had the pleasuah of ridding my book," but hoped to soon. Tennessee Williams had read it, though, and said he liked it very much, but you could have knocked me over with a pin when Leo took me over to meet la Dietrich and she took my cold clammy hand in hers and said she had not only "rad" "LDID," but "lawved" it! It was pure Elysium, I can tell you that, and the young Stendhals and Flauberts and de Maupassants who pined for the salons of Paris back in the 1850's couldn't have asked for more.

To be serious, though, writing a successful book is not all it's cracked up to be—the aftermath, I mean. If it does anything at all, to tell you the truth, it increases, rather than diminishes, the sense of anxiety and insecurity one had in the process of writing. I don't know why this should be so, unless it puts you in the double position of (a) not knowing, because of all the reams of criticism which have been written, and which you have perhaps foolishly read and taken too seriously, just how good or bad a writer you are, and just how much of the praise or criticism is real or valid, and (b) being faced with the ominous duty of having a "reputation" to uphold, which makes you extremely hesitant and worried about Novel No. 2. Of course, the only answer to this is to get down to work and start writing again, with no thought about critics, because a real writer (and I think I'm that) is only happy, really, when he's writing.

I got a nice letter from Aunt Adelaide and a Christmas card from Cousin Jud; I wish you'd thank him for it for me, and wish him the best for the New Year. I wish you the best, too, and I hope it won't be too long before I'll be able to see you—in Uniontown, I hope, but maybe in New York if you're planning a trip anytime soon.

Love,

Billy

To Louis D. Rubin, Jr.*

January 28, 1952 48 Greenwich Avenue, New York, NY

Dear Louis Rubin

I had a thoroughly enjoyable time in Baltimore last week, enjoyed meeting everyone—they were all most interesting and pleasant—and I want to thank you for making my stay such an amiable one. I hope my first experience at speechifying didn't seem too awkward for those exposed to it, but perhaps in the confusion I managed to let drop a few things that may be of some interest and help.† As you, especially, are undoubtedly aware, there doesn't seem to be much one can really say about fiction writ-

* Southern literary critic, professor, and publisher (b. 1923). Rubin is a cofounder of Algonquin Books as well as the Fellowship of Southern Writers. He taught at Johns Hopkins University (1950–54), Hollins College (1957–67), and the University of North Carolina at Chapel Hill (1967–89). A correspondence and friendship with Styron began when Rubin sent his review of *Lie Down in Darkness,* "What to Do About Chaos," in *The Hopkins Review* (Fall 1951).

† Styron first met Rose Burgunder, his future wife, at this meeting of Rubin's graduate seminar at Johns Hopkins. Rose was working on a master's degree in poetry and criticism. Styron was nervous about his appearance, writing in a letter to Rubin on December 18, 1951: "I'll do my best at a talk to the students, though I'm inexperienced at that sort of thing. I expect I'll make out all right, perhaps with a little prompting from you." Rose recalled of the visit: "Bill was terrible, we all said to each other, nice guy, but not an intellectual." Bill wrote to Rubin on March 26, 1968, declining an invitation to speak at UNC: "I guess I'd better decline. Who knows, though, I may change my mind. If I hadn't done that before, you may remember, I would not have met Rose Burgunder."

ing; if you can relate, as I tried to do, merely some of the particular problems you ran up against as a writer, then I suppose you've been at least entertaining. At any rate, I didn't come armed with any theories and I hope no one was too disappointed. Incidentally, I gave Admiral Ageton's address to my friend at Bobbs Merrill, and I expect he'll be hearing from Louis* in a few days.* I'm sure the admiral can at least expect a full and sympathetic reading.

The train fare which you asked me to report to you was $14.50 round trip. I don't think you should bother about the meals, as I would be eating them no matter where I was.

I hope I'll have the pleasure of coming down to Hopkins again sometime. In the meantime, thanks again for the hospitality and my best regards to Mrs. Rubin, Miss Greenslet, the Messrs. Coleman and Woodward, et al.†

Sincerely,
Bill Styron

* Louis Simpson, whom you know of

To William Blackburn

February 21, 1952 48 Greenwich Avenue, New York City

Dear Doctor:

Brice informed me in his last communication that you were recovering from a strep throat; I hope that by now you have recovered and feel hearty and able to confront John Donne again.

I've tried to figure out a way to get down to Durham before I leave for Europe but since I've made reservations on the Île de France for March 5th

* Arthur A. Ageton (1900–71), rear admiral in the U.S. Navy and later (1954–57) U.S. Ambassador to Paraguay. Louis Simpson (1923–2012), Jamaican-American poet who was an editor for Bobbs-Merrill in 1952.

† Elliott Coleman (1906–80) was a poet who founded the Writing Seminars at Johns Hopkins in 1947. C. Vann Woodward (1908–99) was a renowned American historian who taught at Johns Hopkins (1946–61) and Yale University (1961–77). Woodward and Styron became close friends.

I don't know how I'm going to do it, what with the fact that all the multitudinous details accompanying such a journey are still not taken care of. I plan to land in Southampton on the 11th and to go from there to London where apparently Hamish Hamilton, my English publisher, has a hotel room for me. I expect to kick around England for a month or so, thence to France, and thence to Italy. Good news: Malcolm Cowley, with whom I was at a "Young Writers" forum at Columbia Friday night, told me that I had won the Prix de Rome of the American Academy of Arts and Letters, which means a year's residence, all expenses paid plus transportation, at the American Academy in Rome. This includes room and board and books, encouragement to travel in Italy plus $300 to do it with, plus $1250 as a stipend. It beats the Pulitzer Prize all hollow, or any prize for that matter, and I'm extremely proud and grateful. It doesn't commence until October of this year, but that will mean I'll have the time to knock around France for a few months before going to Rome, and I'll be back in New York or, more preferably, Durum, in November 1953. With a novel under my arm, I trust. The judges for the award were, besides Cowley, Francis Hackett, Van Wyck Brooks, John Hersey, W.H. Auden* and Allen Tate, and the fact that such a high-powered assemblage sat in judgment certainly adds zest to the triumph and takes away the sting of such a trifle as the New Yorker review.

I'll try to write again before I sail but if I don't I'll certainly keep in close touch while I'm in Europe. I think it'll be a great experience and I'm going to set myself toward wisdom and accomplishment. If you write me after the 5th of March you'd better address it c/o Bobbs-Merrill, 468 4th Avenue, N.Y. 16., as I don't know what my address abroad will be. And if you have any people that you think I should look up in England, I wish you'd let me know.

Ever yours,
Bill

* John Richard Hersey (1914–93), Pulitzer Prize–winning writer and journalist and resident of Martha's Vineyard. Wystan Hugh Auden (1907–73) was a poet and one of the greatest writers of the twentieth century.

To Edith Crow

March 13, 1952 London, England

Dear Aunt Edith,

You were too generous in sending the check, which I got through Bobbs-Merrill today, but I appreciate it dearly and have sent it back to my agent in New York for deposit, and I appreciate even as much your very nice letter, which warmed me immensely tonight, when the chill of England seemed to be settling solidly into my bones. I'm sorry, too, that you weren't on hand when the Île de France sailed, but it's probably for the better, because I was pretty confused and unhinged at sailing time. The voyage itself was nice and calm, with excellent food, with mild sunny days, and with Lena Horne,* whom I met through my friend Arthur Laurents, who was also aboard (he directed and wrote the movie "Home of the Brave," and wrote the screenplay for "Snake Pit"). Lena sang for the assembled company and afterwards for a couple of nights Art + Lena + I managed to get paralyzed together in the First Class bar, up in God's country where Lena was staying. I wasn't precisely carried off the ship at Southampton, but I'm still rolling, rather than walking, around London.

I've seen only London but what with all the austerity and the bad food, it's not the most entertaining city on earth. I don't suppose the food ever was good in England, but if there's any one thing that strikes the visitor now it's the indescribably horrible boiled stuff available in the average restaurant: the British are admirable people in their uncomplaining acceptance of leathery shad and brussels sprouts steamed to the consistency of a green wet floormop. Fortunately, I've been shepherded about by my English publisher to some of the better places, where food is good and available in quantity; I think, though, that the average American feels like a heel eating so well at the better places with his dollars, while his poorer brethren gag down a boiled shad which tastes like a well-steamed copy of "Lie Down in Darkness." London, it is true, closes up at 10 P.M. but my editor has taken pains to show me as nice a time as I guess there is to be had. His name is Roger Machell and he lives right around the corner from my hotel, in a nice apartment which Lord Byron used to live in. He's in-

* American singer, actress, and civil rights activist (1917–2011).

dependently wealthy, by English standards, and thoroughly entertaining. He's taken me to La Ronde, the movie which was banned in New York for obscenity or something, though I don't know why because it's tremendously funny, I think, and about as suggestive, really, as "The Bobbsey Twins." He's great friends with Terence Rattigan and Alec Guinness, whom I'm going to meet next week—besides being the publisher of Angela Thirkell and Nancy Mitford. The latter two I haven't read but I expect I'll be appropriately impressed if he trots them out.

The book will be published on March 21st over here and, as I told Pop, I'm a bit regretful that I'm here at the same time, because I'm honestly just as fed up as I can be with having to read reviews. Of course, you don't have to read reviews and for some reason I don't think I'll give the same weight to English reviews as I do American, but there they are nonetheless. What I imagine I'll do is to go up to Durham, where I have a friend in the English Department, and to Oxford, where I have an acquaintance or two, and then head for Paris in the middle of April.

I do want to start to work again and I must say that this sort of travel, though it lessens the opportunity for writing, increases the desire. In a strange land one might not feel exactly lonely, but one feels a sudden strange urge to write, perhaps because the distance touches one with a certain nostalgia and a desire in the heart to say something about all those people and places that have been left behind. At any rate, I hope you'll be seeing something of mine in print soon.

The English mail system is wonderful, but the radio, despite the occasional programs of good music, is dreary; I've heard in the last two hours three talks: "The Moral Politics of Gladstone," "New Developments in Scandinavian Architecture," and "Spring Prospects for Bird-Watching in Surrey." Really.

Do write when you get the time. I'll keep you posted about addresses. Thanks again for your check and the letter and please remember me to Buddy + Aunt Adelaide, whose letter I received yesterday, and to the Parshalls. I'll try to get notes off to all of them very soon.

Love Billy

To Dorothy Parker

March 15, 1952 London, England

Darling Didi—

This will have to be in pencil because I no longer have my Parker '57'—stolen on the day of my sailing—and the ballpoint which what's hername gave me has run out of natural-born ink. I'll buy a good one on Monday.

I got your letter this evening and it was a great joy to hear from you, a joy, however not unmingled with pain (I seem to be getting into the English habit of using double negatives) because reading the letter was like talking to you only having you very far away, unable to kiss you and touch you and hold you in my arms. Anyway, I read it about 10 times and looked at the Harper's picture of myself—it really is pretty lousy, isn't it?—and then read your letter about 10 times more. I love you.

I got your letter just before supper, after a long and fairly exhausting day, but an interesting one. Roger Machell (did you ever meet him? He's a wonderful fellow, full of that marvelous understated British humor which is, I guess, characteristic of the English but which in his particular case seems to possess a warm, even slightly Americanized individuality)—well, I went on an expedition with him in his car to a place in Sussex to fetch back some eggs, which are strictly rationed here, but which he can get for himself through some sinister manipulations with a farm lady he knows who owns chickens. Anyway, we went by a roundabout route through Windsor about 25 miles from here, where we stopped at an inn and had a perfectly atrocious meal. But the day was sunny and mild and afterwards we walked up the hill to Windsor Castle (where King George was buried the other week) and it was a great experience—you feel that old ancestral shiver up the back—to see the walls and battlements and cobblestone streets still solid and standing after nearly a thousand years. It's an enormous place, about the size of Stuyvesant Town in area and although it doesn't have a moat (which all genuine moneyback guarantee castles should have) it's a fine one and commands a magnificent view of all those distant sloping fields and hedgerows you see in an Arthur Rank movie. Right below the castle and less than half a mile across the Thames is Eton, where we went afterwards (Roger is an old Eton boy) and the sense of time there is much the same as you get at Windsor, bare rugged stone walls that enclose grassless courtyards so ugly they're simply beautiful, shaded archways and ancient panelings of wood upon which the boys have whittled things like "A. Worthington April 1761" and "Thomas Lyttle A.D. 1644." My God, just to stand there, watching the boys now alive hustling along in their toppers and tails, and to think of all those who've been there since 1441, touches you with such a sense of mystery and time that you want to break up and cry. I wish you could have been there, just as I wish you had been with me yesterday in Westminster Abbey, where I walked in the afternoon; there you run up upon little niches which say: "Here lies: Edmund Spenser, the sweetest singer among the poets," and step upon the mortal bones of Tennyson and Browning (they're resting chummily side by side), Coleridge, and Congreve and Hardy and Garrick and Ben Jonson ("O rare Ben Jonson," says the inscription) and Christ knows who else, I wonder if they'll let T.S. Eliot in.

At any rate, to shorten the story a bit, the ride from Eton back down into Sussex for the eggs and on up to London was lovely and I repeat, I wish you'd been along, except that it might have been uncomfortable for English cars are as small as a peanut.

My itinerary for the next three weeks is pretty well mapped out. Monday night I'm going to Hamilton's for dinner, Tuesday to Roger's for dinner with Eric Ambler and his wife, Wednesday to dinner with a friend of Hank Simons, Thursday to a play with Roger, and Friday there's to be some sort of publisher's cocktail party, because the book is coming out that day. Saturday this actor I was telling you about, Brian Forbes, and myself are renting a car and are going to tour the south of England for a week—the Cotswolds and down to Cornwall with stops in Somerset and in Lincolnshire, where some of his family lives. Then that week-end—the 29th—I'm going out to Surrey to visit another friend of Hank's, followed by three or four more days in London and then in the first week of April, to la belle France.

London can be heavily depressing if you allow it to be. The English are the only people who seem to be individually wonderful while being collectively half-dead. There is really a great truth in the classic descriptions of the present-day English: of people who seem literally to be gritting their teeth in the midst of the pain of a gray and unlovely way of life—of a world of tiny pieces of bread and tiny martinis, ill-lit roads and rooms, bad paper, bad plumbing, seedy clothes, no eggs, little milk and chilly corridors. It will be an achievement if they aren't utterly warped by the experience—already they seem to be more + more becoming Colonial, in an odd reversed sort of way, in that the French are taking over their cuisine, the Italians are their waiters, and most importantly practically any commodity, gadget, or piece of machinery is an imitation of, or otherwise derivative from, something American. And America is in their speech, their manners, their imitation-Hollywood magazines. Maybe they won't be completely taken over; no, I don't guess they will: they'd come last of all, after the French, the Germans and even the Russians, because the hotel porter just came in the room and when I gave him a sixpence he said, "Thank you, sir," and there was something about him—maybe a visibly stiff upper lip—that precluded his ever paying allegiance to Truman. A great country, only I haven't got guts enough not to want to go to France in just about three weeks.

BBC just signed off, and I must, too, my darling. How I wish you were with me tonight. Tomorrow is my day of Spartan duty, when I start to create again. Wish me well. I love you, darling.

Bill

To Robert Loomis and John J. Maloney*

March 17, 1952 London, England

Dear Bob + John (a joint letter, because Didi wrote me that you two had joined forces at 117); if there's one city on the face of the earth that's deader than Durham, N.C. on a Sunday afternoon, it's London, England. The bars are closed, the stores, the restaurants and I tried for a whole half-hour, vainly, in the middle of Piccadilly Circus, to get a drink of water. However, being the resourceful American that I am, I spent the afternoon in a moderately entertaining fashion, walked over to Buckingham Palace to watch the parading of the guards. The palace is huge, just as in the pictures, and monstrously ugly with an enormous asphalt courtyard, utterly without grass. I didn't see the Queen Mother or Margaret Rose but I saw, for the first time in England, a really beautiful English girl. Then I walked

* Loomis and Maloney were sharing the apartment at 117 West Thirteenth Street.

through Green Park, through crowds of Englishmen and Englishwomen and Englishchildren (I've never seen so many sprats in my life, even in Central Park on a Sunday in June), and on up to Trafalgar Square, where there is an ugly monument to Lord Nelson, with his back turned to the National Gallery; and everything—streets, Lord Nelson, and National Gallery, is covered with more pigeonshit than I've ever seen in my life. The paintings in the National Gallery are marvelous—especially the Rembrandts—but the Gallery itself is a monstrosity; like practically every structure in London, it seems to have been built by a nut. Did you ever see a picture of the Albert Memorial, built by Victoria in honor of her departed consort? I have drawn a picture of it on the other side of this page for your pleasure.

Then back to my hotel for an evening with Gore Vidal's new novel, which is either a brilliant satire or a piece of dull and tawdry exhibitionism—I haven't decided which.*

Actually, this is the first really dull day I've had since I've been in England. Roger Machell, who is Hamish Hamilton's partner, has been most kind. We've had dinner together a number of times and yesterday we went for a long and quite lovely drive through Berkshire and Sussex in search for some black-market eggs. We stopped at Windsor Castle, where the King was lately buried and which, unlike the Albert Memorial, has good sense enough to be a monument of real, almost incredible grandeur. It's enormous and stands on a high hill commanding a magnificent view of hedgerows, the Thames, rolling countryside, and the playing fields of Eton. Later we went down to Eton and saw the boys, who look pink-cheeked and not too happy in their frock-tailed uniforms, and saw the ancient carvings in the walls and on desks: "Alexander Bycroft, Oct. 1652," and such. It seems to have even more of a sense of tradition than Davidson College, and is twice as beautiful.

I won't go into English cooking. I think it's safe to simply say that that part of it which I've tasted so far is unspeakable, loathsome, and I've confined myself to eating in Italian and French and one or two of the better hotel restaurants, where you can get as fine a meal as in New York, though unfortunately at New York prices.

* Gore Vidal (1925–2012) was the author of dozens of fiction and nonfiction works and screenplays. Styron refers to his 1952 novel, *The Judgment of Paris*.

The book is coming out Friday the 21st. If both of you will pardon my sudden excursion into Art, I have traced a reasonable facsimile of the jacket on the back of this page.* I think it's atrocious, but I've been polite with Roger + have not told him.

I'm being well entertained in the evenings. I'm booked up solid this week with dinners at Hamish Hamilton's and elsewhere—one of them to meet Eric Ambler and his wife—and there's going to be a cocktail party in connection with the book on Friday. Next Saturday a guy I met, an actor my age who's a friend of Roger's, named Brian Forbes, and I, are going to hire a car and take a 6-day tour of Southern England—to Somerset and Cornwall and South Wales—and return on the 29th, in time for me to go on a weekend out in Surrey with friends of Hank Simons, and in time for Brian to fly back to Hollywood to his wife, who's an actress named Constance Smith. Ever heard of her? I hadn't. Except that she's in a thing called "Red Skies of Montana" with Richard Widmark and was in "The Mudlark." I expect that after the 29th I'll stay for a few more days and go to France toward the end of the first week in April. I just really can't say that so far I've found London the most fascinating city in the world, though all the stories are true about England being a charming place in the countryside—at least what I've seen of it. My hotel is quite nice, though I have an idea that my bill is going to be very high. It has lots of hot water, modern plumbing and waxed toilet-paper which seems to be an austerity measure though you'd think that waxing it would be more expensive than just going on and let it be absorbent. The radio in my room is generally very fine but pretty erratic—a Haydn and Bach program followed by some asshole talking about steel production in Lincolnshire, or someone singing a terrible thing which seems to be very popular now over here: "As I was strowling down Pic-pic-adilly, the bright mahning air." The English, in spite of such indigenous ditties, seem really to be going quite madly American; all the magazines are Hollywood movie magazines, most of the radio songs are from Broadway, and all the literati read <u>Time</u> and the <u>New Yorker</u>. It's sort of like stepping into a foggy American colonial possession, surrounded by people who look like seedy Vermonters

* Here Styron had rendered the UK cover of *Lie Down in Darkness*. He described the cover in a letter to Elizabeth McKee on March 13, 1952, as "full of drowning Peytons and prancing ostriches."

with bad teeth. But I don't mean actually to be disparaging because all that I've met have been hospitable, communicative, and generous.

I got a card from George and Gerda Rhoads.* They have a tiny apartment in Paris and headcolds, which they maintain they caught over here. But they seem to be doing well. I caught a slight cold myself, on the boat, probably a result of standing at the rail trying to look like a man of mystery. It didn't work, and my sex-life aboard was circumvented, although I did dance with both Lena Horne and Mrs. Gene Kelly. Lena is going with her husband (who is white and wears a goatee) to Copenhagen, and apparently the Kellys are going to make a movie version of "Brigadoon" in Normandy, though it seems a non sequitur, and when I asked if they were going to do "La Gaiete Parisienne" in Dublin, Mrs. Kelly didn't think it was clever at all.

John, please ask Sally to forward all mail from now on which comes in to Hamish Hamilton, as I think I'll be moving from the Staffords soon. Drop me a line and let me know how things are going on—both of you. Give my best to Hiram, Louis, + all.

—Bill

To Dorothy Parker

March 19, 1952 London, England

Dearest little crumpet

I saw T.S. Eliot in the subway this morning. Imagine coming all the way to England and running into the Bard, not at a Cocktail Party, but under Piccadilly Circus. I didn't talk to him—I was too bashful, I guess—but there he was, as large as life (bigger, in fact, than I'd imagined him) with a kindly, sad face and a sort of melancholy stoop. Odd thing was that no one else except myself, and friend Bryan Forbes who was with me, seemed to recognize him at all. Or maybe it isn't odd.

Monday night there was a drunken dinner party at Hamish Hamilton's. Present were the Hamiltons (he has an attractive, vivacious Italian

* George Rhoads (b. 1926), painter, sculptor, and one of the first American origami masters.

wife), a man called Leonard Russell, editor of the Times Literary Supplement, and his wife Dilys Powell who is a film critic. Also a rather voracious woman novelist, Emma Laird by name ("Of Former Love") who invited me to her house in Sussex weekend after next, if I'm still here. I detected a carnal gleam in her eye but if I go—which I doubt, since I think I'll be in France—I don't think I'll have any trouble holding her at arm's length, since I'm bigger than she is. Hamilton is a sort of whimsical, nervous fellow—even more nervous than I am—and the austerity doesn't seem to have had any marked effect on him, since he turned out a marvelous meal, complete with butlers and footmen, and the hangover I had the next day testified to the size of his supply of Scotch.

Last night Roger Machell had a small party complete with Eric Ambler, who seems to me frankly to be one of the less disagreeable brands of jackass. His wife is from Nutley, New Jersey and he has a really terrible propensity for talk and for getting drunk, and we had a long pointless argument about who won the American Civil War, and was McClellan really the bad general everyone made him out to be. The party broke up at 2:00 A.M. and every one was fairly polluted, except myself, of course, who held my liquor like a Virginian. Today had lunch with Roger and Mollie Parker-Downes, who is very likeable except that she, like practically all the London literati, puts terrible emphasis on the value of The New Yorker as a journal of opinion . . .

Bill

To Robert Loomis and John J. Maloney

March 26, 1952* Cornwall, England

Dear John + Bob. The Austin really rolls. We've been to Cambridge and all the way up to Lincolnshire in the north of England, back down to London and then Cornwall, where I am now, in four days. The scenery here is marvelous and I'm staying with a vicar, his insane wife and 90-

* Postcard, "General View, Cadgwith, Helston."

year-old Aunt. Made a horrifying trek at 3:00 A.M. night before last across Dartmoor, but was neither accosted by escaped convicts nor Baskerville hounds.* Saw Stonehenge, which is disappointing, being very small + surrounded by wax paper + apple peels, but saw the Cambridge chapel, Ely Cathedral and a 10th century castle, called Tottenhall, on the Lincoln trip and all are magnificent in their various ways. Tomorrow I'll see Daphne du Maurier's in Devon. God!

To Elizabeth McKee

March 27, 1952 London, England

Dear Lizzie:

I haven't received any communication from you regarding the money I asked for, but I expect it will come in today's or Monday's mail.

We got in from our grand tour last night. Stopped over in Par, Cornwall—which is near the village where we were staying, Porthleven—and were well fed by Daphne de Maurier, who is really quite charming, I guess, and put out a wonderful meal but who makes a terrific fuss about being impoverished, this being all highly incongruous considering the fact that she lives in the most enormous house I've ever seen (about the size of the old Raskob mansion on Riverside Drive, only larger) and that she's #1 on the current list.† Oh to hell with it; life is a mystery. The stay in the vicarage in Cornwall, something straight out of Evelyn Waugh, was hilarious; I'm writing Dorothy all about it and I guess she'll tell you about it.‡ But Cornwall really is lovely: with tremendous, breathtaking seas.

I had lunch with Walter Baxter today, and you may tell Ted that he's really a most likeable chap, rather nervous, quite tall and much older in ap-

* Styron refers to Sir Arthur Conan Doyle's *The Hound of the Baskervilles* (1902).

† Daphne du Maurier (1907–89) was a British author and playwright. She wrote the novels *Rebecca* and *Jamaica Inn* as well as the short stories "The Birds" and "Don't Look Now." Much of her work was adapted for films, most notably by Alfred Hitchcock.

‡ Evelyn Waugh (1903–66) was a prolific British author best known for his novel *Brideshead Revisited* (1945).

pearance than his picture, with slightly graying hair and a small limp, both of which were a result of the war.* I don't think he's queer, at least there's not a hint of the fag in his manner, and my total impression was extremely favorable. I hope he does sell, because I really think his book is quite fine.

I wish you'd do the following for me sometime soon: write to the Director of the Manuscript Division of the Library of Congress and ask him if there's any way I can get ahold of a copy they have of "The Southampton Insurrection" by William S. Drewry (Washington, D.C., 1900). It's the only full account I know of the Nat Turner rebellion, and I'd like to read it.† The reason I mentioned the MS Division director is because he's a friend of Mr. Chambers and he wrote me once asking for the MS of LDID.‡ I forgot his name but Hiram can tell you, and I think that perhaps this fellow—Mears or something like that, I think it is—could get the book, while perhaps it couldn't be gotten through ordinary channels. Also, I'd like one book which might describe life and customs in Virginia in 1830–31. If this involves too much research or trouble on your part, let me know, but I think it can be done pretty easily. I'm really pretty desperate to get started on something and I want to do the Turner thing, in spite of what Hiram says. I'd appreciate it if you could get these two books for me and mail them over before say, sometime in June. I'll have a Paris address by then.

The weekend I'm temporarily staying at the Cavendish Hotel on Jermyn street, which is draughty and unbelievably cold, a great sordid hulk of a building whose only claim to actual eminence is that it is run by an old hag, still living but totally immobile in a wheelchair; the ex-mistress of Edward VII, who gave it to her as propitiation or pay; or perhaps both.

Love

—Bill

* Walter Baxter was a British army commander in Burma and the author of the novel *The Image and the Search* (1953), which was prosecuted in Britain for obscenity.

† This was Styron's first mention of the slave rebel Nat Turner, the subject of his third and most controversial novel, *The Confessions of Nat Turner* (1967). Turner (1800–31) was the leader of the most fully realized slave rebellion in American history, a revolt in Southampton County, Virginia, that led to the murder of fifty-six whites, and probably a hundred blacks killed in reprisal.

‡ David Laurance Chambers was an editor, editor in chief, and eventual president of the Bobbs-Merrill Company.

To Robert Loomis

March 31, 1952 London, England

Dear Bob

Just a short note in reply to your nice letter of the 25th, in which you encouraged me to get over my initial disappointment about England. I guess I sounded more than intentionally gloomy; actually I'm having an awfully good time over here, or as good as the austerity will permit. I suppose you + John got my letter (or card, rather) from Cornwall; that was sent at the tail-end of a really first-rate trip through parts of England with this actor-fellow I met, Brian Forbes, in a new Austin. We were in Cambridge first, then Lincolnshire looking at really magnificent castles + cathedrals. Stayed with a well-to-do farmer and his family who live in the Fen Country (like Holland, dikes [not the Village brand] and canals) on a little river which is the loveliest I've ever seen. They were very gentil and most hospitable.* Then down to Cornwall by way of the moors, where we stayed at an absolutely insane vicarage with the vicar and his wife who looks like Laurette Taylor in The Glass Menagerie (she asked me, "Do they have many flowers in America?" and stoutly maintained that Stalin was a "Jew-boy" and couldn't be over 40), and with their 90-year-old aunt, deaf as a post, who is in favor of Taft. But they were all almost pathetically nice (one has to strain to avoid sounding patronizing about the British these days) and put out some wonderful food and showed us the Cornish coast, which is rocky and bleak and absolutely marvelous, putting either Maine or Point Lobos to shame. On the way back we stopped at Daphne du Maurier's, a friend of Brian's; she seems very nice, would still, I think, be good for a fair-to-middling roll in the hay, and lives in a house that is precisely twice as big as S. Klein's On the Square, which, among other things, makes all her talk to me about being impoverished something of a bore, to say the least. Back in London I almost came down with something, but propped up my hypochondria and went to see Mr. Baxter, who looked down at me in mercy, and seems all in all a most sensitive, excellent fellow, not a bit a fag, and an extremely interesting talker, in a shy, nervous way. Friday, I've been invited to Hamish Hamilton's to

* See Chaucer's *Canterbury Tales*: "He was a verray, parfit, *gentil* knyght . . ."

meet T.S. Eliot's roommate, John Hayward, but I think I'll be out of England by then; besides, I've already seen the Bard himself, in the Piccadilly subway, of all places! I think Calder Willingham,* who's here briefly, and I will take off for Denmark on Friday; why, exactly, I don't know, except that I'll probably never go to Denmark if I don't go now.

I was sorry to hear about your father, but certainly hope he's better now. However, if it'll put you at ease, my father had something of the same thing and is now back at work; they do miracles these days.

How's Bishop's book doing; well, I hope. Haven't gotten Mandel's proofs yet, but I expect them any day.† Best to John + keep me informed. Hamilton will forward any mail. Ever yours, Bill

P.S.: LDID seems to be doing fine, with three lead reviews so far which don't say it's the greatest thing since Tolstoy, but that it's got "something."

To Ernest Lehman‡

April 20, 1952§ Paris, France

Dear Mr. Lehmann,

Thank you very much for your letter, which I received a few days after my arrival in Paris. I'm sorry to say that I don't have any short pieces for you at the moment, but I'd be proud to have you consider one for your program, and I'll certainly send you something as soon as I work up enough energy and will-power to write again. Actually at the moment I'm planning another novel, but I expect to do some short pieces to fill the gaps and I'm flattered to think that I may be able to keep you in mind.

* Calder Willingham (1922–95) was a novelist, playwright, and screenwriter best known for his novels *Eternal Fire* and *Rambling Rose*.

† George Mandel (b. 1920), novelist whose debut, *Flee the Angry Strangers* (New York: Dial, 1952), is considered the first Beat novel.

‡ Ernest Lehman (1915–2005), American screenwriter, who was nominated for six Academy Awards and won an honorary one. In the early 1950s he was working as a freelance writer.

§ Attached to the letter was Styron's completed questionnaire.

The party was great fun and I enjoyed meeting you, along with all the other nice people.

Sincerely,
Wm Styron

1. What do you believe to be Joseph Conrad's permanent place and rank in English letters? When Conrad died, some critics were uncertain of his final position and Virginia Woolf, in particular, doubted whether any of his later novels would survive. On the publication of a new edition of his collected writings, Mr. Richard Curle wrote in "Time and Tide" that Conrad's works now rank among the great classics of the English novel. Which of these views in your opinion, is correct?

Both, in a way. I think that Conrad's earlier great works—Youth, Heart of Darkness, Lord Jim, etc.—do rate with the finest novels written in English (certainly a work like Heart of Darkness is one of the few supreme masterpieces in English prose fiction), but I must agree with Mrs. Woolf in her feeling that much of his later work was thin, that when away from the sea Conrad seemed to be on uncertain ground, that his treatment of sex and society reflected in the main unfelt experience.

2. Do you detect in Conrad's work any oddity, exoticism and strangeness (against the background of the English literary tradition, of course) and if so, do you attribute it to his Polish origin?

No.

3. Has Conrad had any influence on American literature?

Among the comparatively few American writers for whom the forging of a prose style—an individual prose style, that is, in which words sing and weep and celebrate, and are not merely bloodless ciphers—has been a central factor in their writing, Conrad has been, I think, one of the important influences. If I'm not mistaken, Faulkner, Hemingway, and Wolfe have all declared their debt to Conrad.

4. Do you feel that you owe him anything in your development as a writer?

Yes. What writer, what young man is there who has read Youth or Heart of Darkness who has not come away feeling that this is English prose as it should be written, and who—when the lazy desire to go slack or to shun his true emotions sneaks up—has not remembered Conrad's own dark struggle, his faithfulness, and his unremitting honesty—and has then not given his best.

William Styron

To William C. Styron, Sr.

May 1, 1952 Paris, France

Dear Pop,

May-Day in Paris is the day when everything is closed—buses, subways, stores, even the police, and the only people who transact business (outside of the bars) are the vendors of lily-of-the-valley, which seems to have some sort of May Day symbolic significance.* It's a perfect day, then, to write you a letter and tell you briefly what I've been doing since Denmark. I arrived here a couple of weeks ago, after having taken the night train from Copenhagen—a twenty-two hour trip made longer than it ordinarily would have to be because of the number of island channels in Denmark that the train has to traverse—by railroad ferry. The route goes through Germany and Belgium and since most of it's at night I didn't see a whole lot, though I did get a pretty good twilight look at both Hamburg and Bremen. From where I sat both cities looked rich and thriving, but I gather that both are still pretty well smashed up behind view of the railroad tracks.

Paris is just about all they say it is, a beautiful, incomparable place, made more lovely by the springtime. I must say that the atmosphere here, however, is treacherous—so lulling and lazy that one is content to sit for

* The French give sprigs of lily of the valley (*muguet*) to their friends on May Day as a symbol of springtime. Flower vendors and workers' organizations are allowed to sell the flowers on May Day without charging tax.

hours and hours drinking a beer in a café, and to do nothing more, no work, just sit. My French is still pretty sketchy (I should have applied myself more at Davidson and Duke) but already is showing improvement, and I no longer am afraid as I was at first to go into a "Tabac" and order a pack of cigarettes. Through friends in New York and London I've met a lot of very nice and interesting people and so my days and nights are well-filled. Through one of these people, a young writer named Peter Matthiessen* from Connecticut, I got a very large, sunny, comfortable hotel room in a hotel called the Liberia in Montparnasse. It costs only 10,000 francs a month (less than $40) and I've contracted to stay there until around the middle of June, after which time I think I will have had my share of Paris and will head on somewhere else. I also plan to buy this Mr. Matthiessen's 3-year old Fiat car for $500, and this will solve my transportation problems during my Rome stay, although nice as the car is, it doesn't sound nearly as jazzy as the new Pontiac you described, which indeed must be a beauty.

I've finally pretty much decided what to write next—a novel based on Nat Turner's rebellion. The subject fascinates me, and I think I could make a real character out of old Nat. It'll probably take a bit of research, though, and I've written to people in the U.S.—among them Prof. Saunders Redding (whom I saw Christmas, you remember) of Hampton Institute—asking them to pass on any reference material they might have. Perhaps you know of a book or something on Nat Turner and would be willing to get it sent to me somehow. Actually, I'd be extremely interested in anything on life around the Southside–Caroline Border country of Virginia in the 1820–1850 period. If you can get your hands on something on that order without too much trouble I'd appreciate your letting me know. I don't know but whether I'm plunging into something over my depth, but I'm fascinated anyway.†

* American novelist, nonfiction writer, a founder of *The Paris Review,* and environmental activist (b. 1927). Matthiessen's first novel, *Race Rock,* was published by Harper & Brothers in 1954. He was one of Styron's closest friends.

† Haydn edited Redding's book *On Being Negro in America* (New York: Bobbs-Merrill, 1950) and introduced the Hampton Institute professor to Styron. Redding sent Styron a packet of materials, including William Sidney Drewry's *The Southampton Insurrection* (Washington, D.C.: Neal Co., 1900) and Frederick Law Olmsted's *A Journey in the Seaboard Slave States* (1856). For a careful discussion of Styron's use of these two

I hope everything is going well. Best to all and keep your wandering boy posted.

Bill Jr.

The food here, as in Denmark, is magnificent, but I'm provincial enough to still miss Southern fried chicken.

To William Blackburn and Ashbel Brice

May 9, 1952 Paris, France

I got both of your letters on the same day, so hope you will pardon my making this a communal job.

Dear Doctor and Brice—

I have just had a long and involved conversation with my chambermaid regarding the relative prices for postage stamps, for telephone calls, for telegrams, and for messages par pneumatique, and as a result I am heavily exhausted. It was a fairly interesting conversation, and I got the information that I was asking for, but to tell you the truth what I don't know about the French language would fill the Encyclopædia Britannica and a talk with a Frenchman leaves me limp and defeated. Get an American and a Frog together—both nations being lousy linguists and both thinking their language is the only one—and the result is usually the sheerest chaos. I wish I'd studied under Walton, instead of having squeezed through with a "D." Anyway, in order not to give the wrong impression, I want to say that I'm enjoying Paris a lot and have found that springtime in this city is pretty much what everyone always said it is. A balmy sky, sunlight, pretty girls, and perpetual lolling about in the cafes. To a melancholic neurotic like myself, saddled as I am with the burden of Calvin and Knox, this has a strange effect, i.e., it's too goddamn enjoyable to be true.* The unwritten

sources, see Arthur D. Casciato and James L. W. West III, "William Styron and The Southampton Insurrection," *American Literature* 52 (1981).

* John Knox (1514–72) was a Scottish clergyman and leader of the Protestant Reformation.

motto here is obviously live and let live, toujours gai, and it's all definitely hard on a man with a conscience. Not that I'm doing any great soul-searching at the moment, but I must say that it's difficult to sit in one's room and work when so much tempts from the outside.

The contrast with England is striking, to say the least. One learns in Europe the truth of the adage about traveling on one's stomach. I think that if any one thing in England serves to leave a final bad impression it's the unbelievably repellent food; whereas here it's next to impossible to get anything but a superb meal, and for practically nothing—par exemple, last night's repast was an hors d'oeuvres of snails beautifully served up with garlic sauce, a beautifully juicy steak with potatoes and salad, dessert and coffee, and a beautifully amiable check—$1.10. It's better than the Little Acorn, even.*

I fled England a week after my trip to Cornwall and Lincolnshire. I found London both depressing and expensive, but loved the week's journey in the country. The Cornish coast itself is worth a trip to England. I don't know how I did it but I missed going to Oxford and it's the main thing I regret about my entire stay. I did see the best of the wonderful cathedrals though—the Cambridge chapel, Ely, Lincoln, and Salisbury. My favorite is still Ely, which I think is generally ignored because it's on such flat land that it has no commanding approach. But it's so marvelously lofty inside, and the octagonal tower is a gem. I stayed back in London for a week before going to Denmark, and the high point of that week—if you can call it a high point—was a cocktail party which John Lehmann gave for Calder Willingham. The English have a very incestuous literary set and everyone was there—Rosalind Lehmann (John's sister), Philip Toynbee, Peter Quennell, Alan Pryce-Jones, Henry Green, and William Samson, the last so drunk that he had to be poured home in a taxi. I myself got too high to make much sense of the whole affair but I must say that the literary chit-chat floods high at such London soirées and that the propor-

* The Little Acorn was a restaurant in Durham's warehouse district, started in 1940 by Robert Roycroft. In the words of a 1951 write-up, the Little Acorn was "one of the most modernly equipped establishments of its kind in Durham. . . . Private dining rooms [were] maintained for parties and banquets. They specialize[d] in pit-cooked barbecue, brunswick stew, Southern-style fried chicken, and sea foods." See http://endangereddurham.blogspot.com/2008/07/little-acorn-restaurant.html.

tion of fairies per capita is somewhat higher than on Park Avenue at Charles Role's, if that's possible. Incidentally, I got what by British standards are excellent reviews and yesterday learned that the book, hideous jacket and all, is going into a second edition—meaning that I've sold at least 5,000 copies. In substance the reviews were as confused as the American ones—no one comes alive except Loftis, only the soliloquy is any good, everyone comes alive but after all it's so depressing, etc. etc.

Denmark was fine but fairly dull and after a week I was ready to leave. The Danish girls are très amiable, the food wonderful and the only really unfortunate part of my sojourn there was that Calder, who is otherwise a most affable person, bounced a bad check on me to the tune of $50, the bastard. I came down on the night train from Copenhagen, via Hamburg and Bremen, but didn't see much. Then Paris bloomed for me. What a town. I got a wonderful big sunny room at a hotel called the Liberia (makes me feel like one of Andrew Johnson's displaced niggers) for roughly $25 a month, and sort of let the concierge know that I'll be here for a couple of months. It's right around the corner from Le Café Dôme, in Montparnasse, where one is supposed to be impressed by the fact that it's the same café where Hemingway used to hang out. Not too far away are the cafes of St. Germain-des-Prés, the Flore and the Deux Magots made chic by Sartre, and I suppose that there you will find, at literally any hour of the day, the greatest floor show on earth . . . French, American, Arab, Scandinavian, Chinese, masculine, feminine, neuter, and in all shapes and sizes. It makes the San Remo or Marja look as staid as Schrafft's after a Wednesday matinee. I've met some excellent people on my own—so far all American, since I have no way to communicate with the French. Everyone over here is writing a novel and one of them, with whom I've struck up a friendship, is a nice fellow named Peter Matthiessen, who is bright and witty, knows Paris well, and won the Atlantic Monthly "First" contest last year. I also met Sam Goldwyn, Jr., who is a nice guy, and received from him a strange invitation to drive down to Italy with him, but I had to decline on the ground that his set and mine are not likely to see eye to eye.* Through a couple of people in New York I'm supposed to look up

* Samuel Goldwyn, Jr. (b. 1926), is the son of the pioneering film mogul Samuel Goldwyn and the producer of *Mystic Pizza, Master and Commander,* and other films.

Irwin Shaw* and Alice B. Toklas,† but I don't know if I will because, as interesting as it might be to meet them, I am having a perfectly contented time on this side of the river, and I've heard that Shaw is something of a jerk. Oh yes, finally I saw Truman Capote in the Café Flore and he was obviously perfectly furious that no one recognized him.‡ This about covers everything to date and I'll write more soon. As it is, life just drifts along, even though I get nostalgic for Durum at times—Bill

P.S. I'm going to buy a Fiat for $500

To Elizabeth McKee

May 14, 1952 Paris, France

Dear Lizzie,

Thank you for the letter re Nat Turner and so on. I think I told you that I have written Saunders Redding for information but I haven't heard from him as yet. Here is what I wish you would do, though, first try to get hold of the Drewry book somehow. Maybe Columbia has it in its library, or perhaps you can call up one of those outfits that advertise in the Times Book Review and say they can locate any book. I'm willing to pay anything reasonable for a copy, or the loan of one, and I'll let you, with your instinctive feeling for reasonableness, figure out just how much seems to be reasonable. The other two books I wish you'd get for me are the Aptheker book on Negro Slave Revolts which I'd like to read even though it's not exclusively Nat Turner, and the book by Ulrich B. Phillips.§ Charge

* Irwin Shaw (1913–84), playwright, screenwriter, and novelist best known for his novel *The Young Lions* (1948). He and Styron became close friends.

† Along with Gertrude Stein, Alice B. Toklas (1877–1967) hosted a salon in Paris which included some of the most important American writers and French painters.

‡ Truman Capote (1924–84) was a writer best known for his novella *Breakfast at Tiffany's* (1958) and his nonfiction novel *In Cold Blood* (1965). Capote was already an established writer for periodicals and the screen when Styron met him.

§ Herbert Aptheker, *American Negro Slave Revolts* (New York: Columbia, 1942). Aptheker (1915–2003) was a Marxist historian who pioneered the study of slave revolts them both to my account. In the meantime I am going to write to the Virginia State Library and see if they don't have a copy of the Drewry book. No, on the other hand, maybe it would be better if you wrote to the Va. library in Richmond about the Drewry book, simply to avoid any possibility of duplication. I hope this doesn't sound like too much work for you, but I really am anxious to start reading up on my next project. I'm getting more and more worked up over the thing and the way I look at it is—Hiram's caution to the contrary—that a person should write about what excites him the most, and not about what will necessarily and neatly pigeonhole him into a certain métier.* I don't want to be known as the J.P. Marquand of Virginia or the Scott Fitzgerald of Lost Generation II, but simply as a writer who is versatile enough to tackle anything.†

As for the Willingham check, just forget about it for the moment. I'll keep on Calder's tail by mail until he coughs up a check.

I made the mistake of allowing my name to be carried in the Paris Tribune "Who Is Where" lonelyhearts column and have received about a dozen letters from people whom I haven't the vaguest desire to meet. One of them, however, was a very nice note from K.S. Giniger of Prentice-Hall and I guess I'll look him up because he sounds like a nice guy, though I don't know.

I am leading a clean, well-ordered life, but won't be entirely happy until I start writing + working again. Tell Didi I miss her very much, + will

---

and was one of the first professional historians to pay careful attention to Nat Turner. His outspoken communism led to many struggles in the academy. Styron later critiqued the Aptheker volume as a white man's "fantasy" in "Overcome," *The New York Review of Books* (September 26, 1963). Styron's review focused instead on Stanley M. Elkins's *Slavery: A Problem in American Institutional and Intellectual Life* (Chicago: University of Chicago Press, 1959). Styron also refers to Ulrich Bonnell Phillips and his seminal work, *American Negro Slavery* (New York: D. Appleton and Co., 1918). Phillips was a historian at Columbia University who professionalized the study of the South in the 1920s by defending slavery, calling it a system of "gentleness, kind-hearted friendship and mutual loyalty," concepts that guided several generations of historians.

* Haydn wrote Styron on May 15, 1952, warning the author off Turner: "I would hate to see you get involved in subject matter as purple as your own imagination is."

† John Phillip Marquand (1893–1980) was a novelist initially famous for his Mr. Moto spy stories, but Styron cites him here for his nostalgic treatment of the crumbling New England aristocracy. He was also the father of one of Styron's friends, John P. Marquand, Jr.

write today or tomorrow, and also that I'm having dinner with Irwin Shaw, if that's of any interest.

Love + Kisses—Bill

P.S. I hope you sent the other copies of the English edition to the people I listed

To William C. Styron, Sr.

May 20, 1952 Paris, France

Dear Pop,

If I don't forget, I'm enclosing a copy of the review of Lie Down in "Punch," which was sent to me from England.* Excellent reviews in England, I've been told, but not much in regard to sales.

Dorothy wrote me that I was runner-up in a Saturday Review of Literature poll concerning Who Should have Won the Pulitzer Prize. Not bad, all things considered.

Thanks for the list of books on Nat Turner. Things seem to be getting a bit out of hand, however, in my search for background material, since I've written to a couple of other people—namely my agent and Prof. J. Saunders Redding, the Negro professor of English at Hampton Institute—for material, and I'm afraid that all sorts of unnecessary duplications might result. Would it be asking too much to have you either call Mr. Redding (his number is in the Hampton phone book) or talk to him, and in any case get together and figure out just what each of you are going to send? He wrote me that he had a bunch of stuff he was going to send and I don't know just how much of that might be on the list you sent from the State Library. At any rate, I think you'd enjoy very much talking to him—a striking, forceful, but thoroughly affable gentleman whose only

* The review appeared in the April 30, 1952, edition of *Punch* and was a rare positive response from the British critics."The writing," the review noted, "a rare and satisfying mixture of graphic realism and subtle impressionism, reaches a very high standard, and the story loses none of its effectiveness by starting with the dénouement and back-pedalling through numerous day-dreams and recollections. Warmly recommended."

difference from any other human, so far as I can tell, is in the pigmentation of his skin—and I think also that he'd be in a good position to tell you which items on the list are valuable, which ones are not, and which ones, if any, he's already sent me. Pop, don't exert yourself over this thing, but if you find that it's no strain, and that you enjoy doing it—including seeing Mr. Redding, whom I think you'd like—well then that's fine. For my part, I would like to have photostats of practically all the articles on the list, if you can do it without too much trouble. #1 Redding says he's going to get for me. I think you can ignore #7, since I have no particular desire to read a fictionalized account, and #6, which I've already read and is rather slight. #10 is starred as unavailable for loan, so you can forget that; but all the rest look interesting and I'd like to have them if possible. Perhaps Mr. Redding could tell you which ones of the other items are intrinsically valuable and which ones merely repeat.*

Pop, one thing I wish you'd do for me and that is not to bruit it about too much concerning what I'm planning to write about. I don't mind anyone knowing that I'm working, but for some reason I really prefer to be a bit secretive about the nature of the project; could you just say from now on, to people who don't already know, that I'm doing something "historical" on "Virginia in slave times," or something like that?

As for the article in the Michigan Alumni Bulletin, I enjoyed it very much; it was one of the few things Cousins ever said that made any sense.† This idea about "noble themes" does have some truth in it; the only catch is that a writer never must search for noble themes; he creates the noble theme himself. Nat Turner, for instance, is on the surface pretty much a bastard through and through; however I subscribe to the theory that all people, no matter how bad—and that includes the Loftises—have a scrap of nobility in them; it's not the writer's job to particularly exalt humans or make them noble if they're not all noble, but the writer is shirking his duty, and is not much of a writer, if he fails to show that scrap of nobility, the scrap varying in size according to the person. I hope that when I'm through with Nat Turner (and God, I know it's going to be a long, hard job) he will not be either a Great Leader of The Masses, as the stupid, vi-

* The list does not survive.

† Styron's father had sent him a copy of a talk by Norman Cousins, "In Defense of a Writing Career," *Michigan Alumnus Quarterly Review* (Autumn 1950).

cious jackass of a Communist writer might make him out—or a perfectly satanic demagogue, as the surface historical facts present him, but a living human being of great power and great potential who somewhere, in his struggle for freedom and for immortality, lost his way. And that is the human condition and no one is even half-noble unless he deserves it and no one is all noble, even a saint. Which is where Mr. Cousins is wrong.

As for me, I'm healthy, wealthy and happy in the Paris spring and I await your correspondence on Mr. Turner.

Your son,
Bill

To Dorothy Parker

May 25, 1952 Paris, France

. . . I have been doing a rather intellectual round during the past few days. There's a big thing going on over here called "Works of XXth Century" in which leading intellectuals all over the West have been invited to participate. Ken Giniger, the Prentice-Hall guy, is writing an article for the Saturday Review on the series of lectures and concerts and asked me to go along to some of them as his guest. We had excellent seats at a concert of the Boston Symphony under Charles Munch, playing Berlioz and Brahms, and on two afternoons we went to forums involving topics like "Revolt and Communion" and "Artist and Isolation" and speakers like Allen Tate, Auden, and James T. Farrell; I must say the discussions were terrific bores, but I was glad to hear Auden, for instance, who made some sense.* Speakers speak in French and English, depending on their nationality, and we sat at long tables just like the ones at the U.N., and put on ear-sets which were wired for simultaneous translation. This, however, did not minimize the boredom or the stratospheric generalization and abstractions; as an English friend wrote me, "if you were to squeeze my ennui, I should let fall a drop of pure quartz." But I did meet Allen Tate, who said he liked my book, and Auden, who had also been on that Prix de Rome Committee

* James T. Farrell (1904–79) was a novelist best known for his Studs Lonigan trilogy.

and, if anything, gave the impression that he had been one of the dissenting judges but who, withal, was very genial and nice. He reminds me of my Aunt Deborah who, at your every word, is about to raise his hands limply and make a great indrawn laugh and emit a very middle aged and spinsterish "whoops!" James T. ("Call me Jim") Farrell was pretty well plastered but I had a rather lengthy chat with him and he wants me to have an evening with him at the Deux Magots this week. He goes on a bit about trade unions and such, but has a lot of interesting stories to tell. Two of the nicest people I've met in France, through Giniger, are a young couple named Jacques and Colette Duhamel (no relation to Georges) who together run a publishing house called Editions de la Table Ronde and specialize in translating young American writers. She's extremely pregnant at the moment, but I've never seen a woman who could be so lovely while enceinte; they've been very hospitable to me and have invited me to dinner a couple of times, and I plan to return it, in my imitably Southern way, by cooking them some Virginia fried chicken.

Yesterday the Matthiessens and I were driven out into the country by Irwin Shaw and wife in their beautiful convertible to the most absolutely elysian wayside inn that I've ever seen. The day was perfect, balmy and cloudless; you sit in the back, in a garden full of rosebushes and chrysanthemums, and look out over a distant pasture where cows are grazing, and far below the Seine, we started at one-thirty and didn't finish until past five, having consumed langoustine (like small lobster), pâté made of rabbit, steak two inches thick (I give you my word), strawberry shortcake and six bottles of wine. If, in these letters, as it seems, I'm becoming disgusting about food, let me know, but I promise when I see you next to be straight + hard as . . . I love you.

Bill

P.S. Give Lizzie my best, and tell her my father is sending me a lot of stuff on Nat Turner.

To Robert Loomis

May 27, 1952 Paris, France

Dear Bob,

A note to catch you up on my vicissitudes of late. I'm living in Montparnasse in a nest of vice-dens: Le Café Dôme (Hemingway's old hangout), la Rotonde, la Coupole, and shady dive called Le Chaplain, which is the nearest Paris equivalent of Luis' Bar on West 4th Street. Really, this whole area is so reminiscent of Greenwich Village that I want to laugh and cry and scream at the same time: great buck niggers in zoot suits, bearded poets, unwashed little raggedy-assed girls and a whole slew of unsavory people that look like a cross between Toulouse-Lautrec and Marshall Allen. Fortunately I've made the acquaintance of a member of the nice, normal folks and so only part of my day is spent swilling cognac. I miss whiskey, and beer. The French beer tastes like horsepiss and is just about as intoxicating. Most of my spare time (and about all my time is spare) has been spent with a guy named Peter Matthiessen and his wife. He's from Connecticut and won the *Atlantic* "First" Prize last year, and is now writing a novel for Little, Brown. We go over to Irwin Shaw's every now and then and get drunk. Last Saturday the Shaws and the Matthiessens and I drove out in Shaw's beautiful convertible to an inn in the country: it was a gorgeous day and we sat at a table on the lawn and watched the cows graze, while we drank six bottles of wine, ate *langoustine* (small lobsters), sirloin steak two inches thick, and strawberry shortcake so light that it almost blew off the table. Really a productive life I'm leading. Right at the moment I'm not withering away for sex, but I must say the tail was steadier, if you'll pardon the expression, in dear old New York. First contact I made was a beautiful divorcee, aged 26, from the Singer Sewing Machine fortune. She has an alimony of $3000 a month, a white Oldsmobile and a four room apartment, but being American was getting psychoanalyzed and was in general so screwed-up that I drew an utter blank. My most recent work-out has been with an English girl who is a midget; she's a terrifically intelligent girl, good-looking, loves sex, but she's only about four and a half feet tall and it's like making love to a mouse. I think I've flushed her for good, much as I hate to, and am now casting about for a normal French girl who doesn't know a word of English and hasn't ever heard the word Freud. It shouldn't be too hard. You'd think it would be hard to draw a blank in Paris, but there are dry spells like now.

My name was in the Paris Tribune and so a fellow named Giniger from Prentice-Hall called me up and has been taking me around to various events. He doesn't want to lure me away from Bobbs but merely liked my book. We've been to a concert of the Boston Symphony under Munch playing my favorite composers, Berlioz and Brahms, and to a series of forums which comprise part of a big thing called "Work of the 20th Century," which Giniger is covering for the Saturday Review, and in which a lot of bigshot literary names from America have been invited to participate. The thing is a terrific bore, but it's organized along the lines of the U.N. insofar as translation goes, with earphones and hearing Auden come out in French. I met him and Allen Tate and Robert Lowell and Stephen Spender* and James T. Farrell, who must have been just along for the laughs. Farrell invited me to dinner sometime this week; he's a very nice, easy-going guy with a wry sense of humor just like Irwin Shaw, when you're around him you get the impression that writing and all that sort of stuff is a bit sissified.

I must say that my main and practically only regret about Paris so far is that I haven't gotten much work done. I have finally gotten part of the way into my long piece on the Marine Corps but, I don't know, Paris doesn't seem to be particularly good for my inspiration and I can't seem to stay at it. I am determined, though, to finish that thing (I think it'll be long and good enough for either New World Writing or Aldridge and Bourjaily's new magazine)† before I leave Paris (a month from now? two months?) and before I start in on the Nat Turner novel, material for which hard-suffering people are sending me from all points of the globe. Right now I'm trying to re-gain my vision, if that doesn't sound too pretentious; some of the feeling I had, and the music, when I was writing the last part of

* Stephen Spender (1909–95) was an English poet and novelist.

† With John Aldridge, Vance Bourjaily (whom Styron called Raoul Beaujolais, following the example of John Appleton) was an editor of *Discovery.* Bourjaily was also a novelist whose first novel, *The End of My Life* (New York: Charles Scribner's Sons, 1947), was critically acclaimed. According to *Esquire* magazine, "Everyone came to Bourjaily's parties in the early 1950s," and Styron attended enthusiastically alongside Mailer, Jones, actors, literary personalities, and many others. See Bruce Weber, "Vance Bourjaily, Novelist Exploring Postwar America, Dies at 87," *The New York Times,* September 3, 2010.

Peyton's soliloquy. I think when I get that again, which shouldn't be too far off, and combine it with more experience, I'll be able to write a really fine book. And speaking of vision: believe it or not, though it's hard to be lonesome in a place like Paris, it is tremendously easy to have pangs of homesickness. I guess at last I'm just that provincial and there are times, if you'll forgive the banality, when I'd literally pay $20 for a single hamburger from the White Tower and a cold glass of real milk, instead of French milk, which tastes as if it cometh not from the teat but from the asshole. When I consider that I'm going to be over here until probably autumn of next year, I could literally <u>come</u> with chagrin. But lest finally you jump at conclusions and think that I'm not enjoying myself, let me reassure you that such moments of panic are momentary and that, being in the prime of my youth, I would consider it not just a disgrace but a crime against nature not to have the time of my life.

George and Gerda have an apartment not too far from here, but George spends most of his time in a tent out in the country, alone, doing what God only knows. I guess painting. I got drunk once and rode on the ass-end of his motorcycle at 60 miles an hour through Paris with my feet dragging wildly along the cobblestones and I still haven't recovered. Incidentally, they mentioned that you mentioned that Leslie Flatt Belker might be coming over.* If you see her, tell her I will welcome her to Paris with open arms, but that I warn her that she mustn't try any of this psychoanalytical monkey-business with me. Styron welcomes only uncomplexed women into his bed and board. Drop me a line about the New York life and give my best to John, George + Mickey and all.† How's George's book doing? I never did get the galleys.

Love forever—Bill

* Leslie Blatt Felker was a Duke classmate, but she did not earn her degree because of her marriage to Clay Felker (1925–2008), a Duke classmate and later founder of *New York* magazine. After their divorce, she married literary critic and Styron admirer John W. Aldridge, and her third husband was Princeton University population researcher Charles F. Westoff, whom she also divorced. She recalled an unsatisfying sexual encounter with William Faulkner in Leslie Aldridge Westoff's "A Faulkner Flirtation," *The New York Times Magazine,* May 10, 1987.

† George Mandel and Mickey Knox. Knox (b. 1922) was at the time a blacklisted actor living in Rome, and a close friend of (and fervent correspondent with) Norman Mailer and James Jones. See Mickey Knox, *The Good, the Bad, and the Dolce Vita: The Adventures of an Actor in Hollywood, Paris, and Rome* (New York: Nation Books, 2004).

To Dorothy Parker

May 27, 1952 Paris, France

Dearest little omelette aux champignons—I have just spent a harmless, quiet Sunday reading (Prize Stories of 1951, and The Stockade, an unpublished first novel which Little, Brown sent me and reads very well) and writing (a short story about the Marine Corps which I'm just getting well into) and now, before I dash over to the Ritz (to have cocktails with an immensely wealthy young guy I met in England) I figure that it's time to talk to you. When one sojourns in a place for quite a while one's life tends to become crystallized and static and even (to one's self) a bit uninteresting; but now upon reflection I guess there are a few things to note that you'll doubtless find fascinating. First, about my sex life—dead, mort, hopelessly barren at the moment, even in Paris, imagine! I tried desperately to put the big make on a lush little American divorcee who gets an alimony of $3000 a month (the Singer Sewing Machine fortune) and who has a fancy apartment near the Invalides and an obscene stark-white Oldsmobile. But it turns out that she'll endure all sorts of wet grappling but draws the line like a Duke co-ed when it comes to the Real Thing. Imagine that—also imagine me dating a neurotic (she's getting psychoanalyzed) Scarsdale girl in Paris in the month of May. Better I should go back home. So I gave it up as a bad job. Why don't you come over here and save me all these extra-curricular miseries?

So I've just been coasting about for some time on the thin-ice of my frustration; never, however, giving up hope. After all, some people have considered me attractive at times. I see quite a bit of Peter Matthiessen and his wife, as I think I've already told you; the other night we all had dinner with Irwin Shaw and his wife and I must say, in spite of stories to the contrary (probably inspired by jealousy), that I find Shaw a hell of a nice guy—honest, gentle, witty and not at all the sort of Brooklyn wise-guy that he's been made out to be. I got very drunk that evening and had to be revived, at about 5:00 A.M., by great draughts of coffee in the Dôme.

Zeph Stuart (you remember, McDougal Street) is here with her three children in a hotel on the other side of the river, and adds considerably to the atmosphere and fun. Yesterday she, Peter, and I paid a call on an old French guy named Tristan Tzara, who is an acquaintance of Peter's, and who in the '20s was famous as the founder, along with Arp and Miro, of the Dadaist movement—a fabulous old gent who rather wistfully lives off the memories of past grandeur but whose apartment is absolutely crammed with original Picassos (a great friend of his), Miros, Chiricos, Utrillos and practically anyone else you can name. He's a communist, like most left-bank French intellectuals, but withal quite reasonable. Among his bons amis were Joyce and Hemingway, Gertrude Stein, and he was and still is apparently an intimate pal of Malcolm Cowley. He was great fun to talk to. Afterwards I seemed to have gotten myself stuck with a cocktail date with Ken Giniger of Prentice-Hall, who doesn't move me in the least, but we all met at the Ritz and had cocktails ($1.50 per martini) on my publisher, Mr. Enoch of Signet Books, who was passing through with his wife on a trip from India and who seemed pleased enough to meet one of his authors in Paris, though I don't know.

I think the crowd of hangers-on around the cafes still interest me most clinically and as a group. The Americans, I mean. The general impression I had of Americans in Paris, at least before I came, was that they were a highly intellectual bunch, serious and dedicated to the creative act. But to tell you the truth I've never been so disappointed in any one group of people in all my life; outside of a few people here and there like Peter Matthiessen and a few of his friends, these Americans are the most no-good ignorant lot of bums I've ever seen, loafers and fortune-hunters who have absolutely no purpose or visible reason for existence, a perfectly appalling bunch of philistines and know-nothings and creeps, whose only daily act seems to be cadging 60 francs for a sandwich or a beer. None of them have given me personally any hard time or unhappiness, and I avoid them when possible, but I thought you'd be interested in hearing my reactions to our contemporary ambassadors of culture.

Please tell Lizzie to call off her research for the Drewry book, "The Southampton Insurrection," as I've gotten a letter from J. Saunders Redding at Hampton Institute, saying that he'd get it and send it to me. But tell her, too, that I would still very much like to have the other books I wrote her about.

I'd better close now and be off to the other side of the river . . .

Bill

To Elizabeth McKee

May 27, 1952 Paris, France

Dear Lizzie,

I hope Dorothy got you to call off the search for the Drewry book, because I told her to, since Saunders Redding, to whom I wrote, said that he was pretty sure he could get a copy for me from the Hampton Library. As for the Aptheker and the Phillips items, you'd better just send them to me here c/o American Express by ordinary mail, even if it does take longer, since airmail sounds too expensive.

Giniger is one of the most charmless people I've ever met, but he has been nice to me. Took me to a couple of forums in the "Oeuvre du XXme Siècle" series and introduced me to Allen Tate, Auden, Robert Lowell, James T. Farrell, Stephen Spender, all of whom are terrible bores. Glenway Wescott was present, too, an aging pansy with a coterie of elf-like, twittering young men.* I must say the literary life can be nauseating. Even if occasionally interesting.

This thing that I'm writing looks like it might be too long for anything but New World Writing or the book that John Aldridge and Vance Bourjaily (commonly known as Raoul Bojalay) are working up. But they don't pay much, do they? Please call up Arabel Porter or Mac Talley and find out when the closing date for the next New World Writing is.

I'd be glad to get you the bottle of Lanvin's Prétexte and will send it along to you sometime soon with someone who's coming back.† Incidentally, I lost Douglas McKee's address and I don't know what an A.P.I.A. is. Is it American Piepan Intelligence Associates, or the association for the Prevention of Indigent Authors, or what? There are so many initialed agencies over here now that I've lost track, but I would be glad to give him the loot if you'll send his address.

I was wrong about my life being clean and ordered. It is now slightly fingerprinted around the edges and distinctly disordered, but très gai.

Love + Kisses

Your littler 10%er

* Glenway Wescott (1901–87) was a major novelist in the expatriate community in Paris in the 1920s.

† Prétexte was a perfume, now discontinued, by the French house Lanvin.

To James Jones*

May 27, 1952† Paris, France

Dear Jim,

If you think you've got a writing set-up out in Illinois, you should come to Paris. You won't get a *thing* written here, because just as the poets always intimated, the prevalence of cafes, booze, and an incredible assortment of women absolutely precluded anything but what we used to call in the Marines "fiddle f-king around." Sometime this summer I'm going to find a clean, well-lighted place in Italy and start to work. How's everything with you?

Bill Styron

To Elizabeth McKee

June 11, 1952 Paris, France

Dear Lizzie,

I braved through the throngs on the right bank to get your Lanvin's Prétexte, and this is just a note to let you know that I am sending it to you in the hands of a young man named Ormond de Kay, who is leaving on the Île tomorrow, the 12th, and should be in New York early next week.‡ He said that he would call you as soon as feasible. In case he doesn't (unlikely), his address is 142 East 18th St., Phone Gramercy 3-0582. A very likeable guy. He wrote the screenplay for that movie about the Negro doctor in Vermont or New Hampshire—"Lost Boundaries." He is also think-

* James Ramon Jones (1921–77), a novelist best known for his novel *From Here to Eternity* (1951), which established him as a major voice in postwar American literature. He and his wife, Gloria, became very close friends of the Styrons. This is the first correspondence between Styron and Jones; the two met through John P. Marquand, Jr., at a party in Manhattan in the fall of 1951. For more see Willie Morris, *James Jones: A Friendship* (New York: Doubleday, 1978).

† Postcard, "Van Gogh's bedroom in Arles." Styron addressed the postcard to "James Jones 'Author of Catcher in the Rye.'"

‡ Ormonde de Kay (1924–98), writer and editor, who wrote the 1949 film *Lost Boundaries,* as well as several children's books.

ing about writing a novel. The price of the perfume was 3900 fr. Or almost exactly $10.00 which you can take care of. Also, I told de Kay that in exchange for this service I would ask you to give him one of those extra English copies of "LDID," which I hope you'll do. And finally, I am also asking him to deliver, c/o you, a little something for Dorothy, which I'd like you to give her. You may tell her that the design on it is an ancient form of dice game, and that I hope she lays a nickel down for me.

Two things I'd like you to do for me. The first is try to find out through either Willingham's publishers (Vanguard + Dial) or his agent just what Calder's present address is, so I can jig him about the $50 he owes me, long overdue.

The second is this. I don't know why Hiram Haydn manages to get such stupid secretaries, but he does. Lately she has been forwarding mail that comes in for me at Bobbs by merely scratching out the original address and writing "c/o American Express, Paris," on it. Naturally, if only a 3¢ stamp is on the envelope, as is usually the case, the letter gets sent back to the original sender for foreign postage, occasionally a letter comes through with postage due, and two weeks late. Please call either her (her name is Sally something) or Hiram immediately, and ask her to continue putting my letters in a separate envelope, properly addressed to Paris, and sent by air mail. Tell her the air mail rate is 15¢ a letter, roughly, and that I'll pay the postage if necessary, out of my account, but that I don't want to keep having my mail screwed up by her stupidity. Or words to that effect.

No more news since my last letter to Didi—except I'm having a birthday party tonight (my 19th). I'll look for Kathleen Winsor on the 18th.

Love + Kisses
WCS

To Vance Bourjaily

June 13, 1952 Paris, France

Dear Vance,

Anticipating your rude remark, I took my hand off that teat long ago in order to place it on the typewriter, having come to the conclusion that in France arse is longa and vita is brevis which, freely translated, means that there's plenty of tail around but it's not every day you get a chance to pick up a buck through Discovery.* The magazine sounds fine from the prospectus and I should like to think that I might be a charter contributor. Right now I'm in the midst of a long short story which looks as if it might run to as many as 15 or 20,000 words.† I plan to have it finished within a month or so, but what I want to know is when the deadline for manuscripts is. If you could give me an approximate idea as to the latest date, it would put my mind at ease and either spur me to more strenuous effort or in some way help me to adjust my pace. Also, if the story is good enough—which I think it will be—is 20,000 words (at the very most) too much? Please let me know.

Europe is great but I'm provincial enough to miss the New York parties. One also must steer clear of the American girls in Paris—they're all being psychoanalyzed and think that the vagina is meant for wee-wee. Or something. If you know where Calder is, let me know his address, because he pulled a quick one on me in Denmark to the tune of $50 and hasn't made amends. Best to Tina and the Aldridges.

Yours—Bill Styron

To Dorothy Parker

July 19, 1952 Paris, France

Honeybunch darling—the story is, I believe, coming along just dandy and my pretty much night and day work on it is the main reason I haven't written you before this. It is now between 11,000 and 12,000 words, which I figure is about two-thirds complete. It has some really good—fine—things in it so far, and I think it will be even better when it's finished. In fact I think I can say it has some of my best writing in it and will make stories by people like Hemingway and Turgenev pale in comparison. That sounds a bit like what Hemingway would say, doesn't it? No, what I really mean is that it won't have any of the really "cool, gone" (in

* A pun on Hippocrates' aphorism "Art is long, life is short."

† Styron refers to his draft of *The Long March*.

junkie parlance) quality of the best in LDID, but it will be good, "true," powerful and nicely-textured. I do hope I'll be able to finish it within the month, and am determined to do so somehow, because I want the thing if possible to go into Jack Aldridge's and Bourjaily's magazine "Discovery," and Vance wrote me that the outside deadline is August 15th—the very latest, and I'll probably have to get special dispensation to get it in even by that date. Tell Lizzie I'll send the MS as soon as it's finished and typed and that she can wrangle with Vance about rates after he's seen it. Vance said 3¢ a word probably, but of course I wouldn't be averse to 3½ or 4¢ if Lizzie could work it. I really think "Discovery" is a good bet—in the first place because the story will obviously be too long for practically anything else, in the second place because $600 (or more) is pretty good dough, and in the third place because the magazine is not only going to have a large readership but, according to Lew Allen, a friend of Vance's, I'll be in fairly good company—Mailer, Jones, Hortense Calisher, and most likely little Truman.*

The joke, which really isn't a joke, that I forgot to tell you in another letter is more really just a mot. It concerns the remark made by a bright lad concerning a honeymooning couple, the guy a pallid sort of fellow and the gal a kind of frigid-type debutante. Quoth he: "I'll bet you that's going to be like trying to get a marshmallow into a piggy-bank." End of joke. You either like that type of joke or you don't, n'est-ce pas?

I have met Mlle. Bataille, my French agent, who is very nice and who has introduced me to my publishers at Les Éditions Mondiales. I've also met my translator, a man by the name of Michel Arnaud, who is a genial bright sort and has translated Steinbeck, Sinclair Lewis and Upton Sinclair. He's been working on LDID for about three months and is almost finished. The book is scheduled to be published in October sometime and they plan to give it the works. Incidentally I also met—Mrs. Franz Horch.† I've seen her a number of times and I must say that I certainly like her a lot. She's coming back to the U.S. early in September but in the meantime

* Hortense Calisher (1911–2009) was a prolific author nominated for the National Book Award three times. "Little Truman" refers to Truman Capote.

† The Franz J. Horch literary firm was a major manager of foreign rights at the time. The firm became known as the Roslyn Targ Literary Agency in the 1970s.

she asked me to send you, and Lizzie too, her best regards and felicitations.

Social life here is about the same—gay when I'm working at the social life but rather circumscribed at times by the fact that I'm pretty much at work writing most of the time. Zeph Stuart and la Wanda are coming up tomorrow from Milan, so the coming week or so promises to be jolie. Incidentally, you asked if I saw Barbara Taeusch here. She's left now, about two months ago, but I did see her, to answer your question, and the results are just about what you might imagine. What do you imagine?

I have sort of a chore for Lizzie, as usual, which I wish you could communicate to her. I hope it's not asking too much but I think it can be done. Friends of mine here—chiefly Peter Matthiessen, about whom I've written—are starting a magazine which promises to be a very good one, since unlike others they have managed to get quite a bit of backing (one of the backers is the brother of Ali Khan)* and are all set financially besides having a more than ordinarily intelligent editorial approach. It's to be called "The Paris Review" and one of its features each issue will be the photostated copy of a fiction or poetry MS, along with the author's comments. E.M. Forster is going to be in the first issue with part of the MS of an unpublished novel, plus comments, and I've been picked for the second issue. Now what I want Lizzie to do, if she possibly can and it's not too much work, is this: get hold of the MS of LDID, or the specific part that I want, and have that part photostated and sent to me. The MS was in the possession of Mrs. Hannah Josephson at the American Academy of Arts + Letters (in the phone book) but Lizzie can find out where it is now by calling her. Sigrid might have it. At any rate, I would like to have photostated that part of the MS which, in the English (H. Hamilton) edition, begins on page 223 and ends on 224, i.e. the part in the MS which, on P.223, begins with "Helen held her breath. Rain had begun to fall. . . ." And ends, on P.224 with ". . . She kept on crying, loud and unreasoning and anguished, and said, 'No! No!'" If Lizzie could possibly swing this deal

* Prince Sadruddin Aga Khan (1933–2003) had been a classmate of George Plimpton at Harvard and socialized with the *Paris Review* crowd in the 1950s, becoming a close friend of the Styron family. He served as United Nations High Commissioner for Refugees between 1966 and 1978.

I'd appreciate it, and I think it will very much be worthwhile because the magazine will be well-circulated both in the U.S. and in France and could no doubt sell a few books . . .

Bill

P.S. Enclosed is the type of fan letter I've been getting recently. Pop forwarded it to me. It had been addressed to "William Styron (writer?), Newport News, West Virginia."*

To Robert Loomis and John J. Maloney

August, 1952† Saint-Tropez, France

This part of the world is fabuleux, with blue, blue Mediterranean water and fishing with harpoon among the rocks. I've become terribly rugged + haven't had a drink for over a week. I've been staying at a 35 room estate owned by an old woman who starred in René Clair's first movie, now living in a sort of impoverished elegance. In a few days I'm going to a place on the Atlantic + visit with Irwin Shaw (where I'm sure to stay drunk) and then back to Paris for a week or so before I head for Rome. I've sent off a 20,000 word story to E.M. McKee which I expect will appear in the first issue of Jack Aldridge's Discovery and which will settle the Marine Corps situation once + for all. I'm glad I'm over here because if the USMC brass read it they're going to have a shit hemorrhage and send out patrols for me. The tail situation here is flourishing and is probably even better than Westport. Love + Kisses

WCS

* Letter from Geneva Marsh of Ventura, California, who called *Lie Down in Darkness* "the biggest hunk of nothing I've ever had the displeasure to stumble through . . . the most unsatisfactory waste of time I've ever spent."

† Postcard of la Côte d'Azur.

To George Plimpton*

August 16, 1952 Saints-Girons, France

Dear George—

A card from the Provence, a little south of Toulouse, where Doc, Moose & I are spending the night en route from St. Tropez to St. Jean de Luz.† Fine time on the Côte d'Azur, where I fell in love with a 15-year-old girl, alas but am looking forward to more sun + water on the Atlantic. Expect I'll be back in Paris around next weekend, so stand by for a blowout at Le Chaplain. —Bill

To Hiram Haydn

September 7, 1952 Paris, France

Dear Hiram,

I got your letter and thank you for your detailed comments and advice. Day before yesterday I got a letter from Elizabeth, who told me about all the confusion the story seems to have caused. Being so far away, and not having gotten your letter yet, I was not sure what the confusion was about, and so wrote her a hasty and what might have seemed a peevish note, telling her to take it easy, but now I'm more in the clear as to what is going on.

I will follow your letter point by point and try to give you my ideas on the various matters. First I should like to say that I'm of course very glad that you, John and Louis like the MS. I could feel blessed by no better approval. I also feel that I am aware of the various shortcomings of the MS which you mentioned. As a result, I think I would most certainly be willing to try to clarify certain things (the "slightly unsatisfied feeling" the reader might have at the end, for instance); although I'm not sure that I know how to go about making such changes, or whether I'd be successful if I tried. My approach to my own writing is such that when I've finished

* George Plimpton (1927–2003): journalist, writer, and longtime editor in chief of *The Paris Review,* which he helped found.

† H. L. "Doc" Humes (1926–92): a founder of *The Paris Review* and the author of two novels. His girlfriend at the time was nicknamed "Moose."

something I feel that I've literally finished, and that in spite of excellent criticism (and warranted criticism) I hardly feel up to changing it all around again. This might be laziness—I don't think I really have a bull-headed, proprietary sense which says "this is perfect and not a word will be changed"—but I think that it would be nearer the truth to say that my execution so closely coincides with my conception that afterwards, when it's all over, I just sort of feel that any major tinkering will . . . [Incomplete letter.]

To Louis D. Rubin, Jr.

September 8, 1952 Paris, France

Dear Louis Rubin:

I'm glad to hear that you're at work on a novel. I can both sympathize and wish you the best of success with it. I'm also happy to learn that Bob Hazel has had his work accepted by World, which someone had already informed me.*

As for doing the reviews you mentioned, I'm afraid I'll have to decline, and my reasons are two. The first is that I've tried reviewing and I'm simply no good at it. I get terribly wordy and rather emotional. The second, and more important, reason is that I'm somehow rather averse to criticizing my contemporaries. Not that they don't need criticizing, some of them, but I'm afraid that for a writer to start talking in print about another writer, a contemporary, is in a way sort of sticking his neck out. I write something nasty about Shelby Foote,† then he writes something nasty about me, and first thing you know we've become squabbling critics rather than writers of books. I hope you understand my position, because if I did undertake to write reviews there would be no journal I'd rather write for than the Hopkins.

* Robert Hazel (1921–93), poet and novelist, author of *The Lost Year* (1953) and *A Field Full of People* (1954).

† Shelby Foote (1916–2005), historian and novelist, authored the multivolume *The Civil War: A Narrative*. He became especially well known for his starring role in Ken Burns's 1990 PBS documentary *The Civil War*.

Paris has been very pleasant, and I've even managed to get some work done, but soon I'm off to Rome. Hope all goes well with you and the Review, in spite of J. Donald Adams.*

Sincerely
Wm Styron

To Dorothy Parker

September 8, 1952 Paris, France

Darlingest Didi,

Right now it's cold and rainy in Paris, and I miss you and I love you. I've put off writing you for this long because of your rather enigmatic letter about that which "I ought to have done years ago" and "I can't gather my strength from outside myself," and so I've rather imagined that you would just as soon not get any letters from me for a while. Is that right? If so, I understand perfectly, but at the same time I did want to write you this and tell you that I understand. I hope it doesn't disturb you, because if there's anyone on earth I don't want disturbed or discomfited, and want to be happy, it's you, my darling. And if you don't write me for a while, I understand, too, but please, baby, make all this quick, for I yearn for the sound of your voice, no matter if it's in ink and second-hand.

As for me, I'm back in Paris once more after a long and for the most part delightful voyage to the ends of France. I sent the long story off from St. Tropez, hoping that it would get into the first issue of Discovery, but it got such close and lengthy examination by E. McKee and Hiram that I'm afraid it's going to end up in the Rocky Mountain Review, if that. Perhaps by the time you get this something will have been done about it. I hope so. At any rate, St. Tropez was marvelous, with the sea deliciously just like you described your own sea off Long Island, with wine, and with women. It wasn't love but at least I got my ashes hauled, as they say. Incidentally, some day I'd like to write you a long pornographic letter describing my fantasies about making love to you, which I have 10 times a day, but that

* J. Donald Adams, literary critic and editor of *The New York Times Book Review.*

would no doubt disturb the rather delicate equilibrium you're in at the moment, I guess.

Anyway, from St. Tropez we drove to St. Jean de Luz on the Atlantic where, with the Matthiessens and with Irwin Shaw, I weathered, with the help of a pile of martinis, four or five days of absolutely foul weather. Finally it cleared up and we did a lot of fine surf-swimming at Biarritz, went to a bull-fight in Bayonne with Art Buchwald of the Herald-Tribune, who wrote a very funny piece on it afterwards, and then—last week—came back to Paris, finding all much the same, but lamenting the fact that you hadn't been along to be with on the sand.* I love you.

I'm making now slow preparations to go to Rome but they seem to be hindered almost impossibly by the continuing night life here in the City of Light. What I like to call the Elsa Maxwell circuit holds me in thrall.† Last night I went to a birthday dinner for Sammy Goldwyn, Jr., given by his father at a sordid little Nedick's-type dive called Joseph's where the entrees alone usually run to about $7. I had coq au vin, crêpes suzettes, champagne, and Mrs. William Paley, on my left, who is a tasty dish herself but not nearly so good as the coq.‡ Darryl Zanuck was across from me and we had a fierce and regrettable fight over Chambers's Witness, which I've just finished reading and consider one of the vilest, most unwholesome documents I've ever read.§ Zanuck is apparently a mile to the right of Msgr. Sheen, and so the discussion, especially since I was loaded to the ears with martinis, was a bit heated.¶ I also somehow alienated Goldwyn, Sr., by saying Ike was a platitudinous ass and learned that Goldwyn is

* Art Buchwald (1925–2007), American humorist and longtime summer resident of Martha's Vineyard, where he was a close friend of the Styrons.

† Elsa Maxwell (1893–1963) was a gossip columnist and author best known for hosting high society parties.

‡ Mrs. William Paley (1915–78) was born Barbara Cushing. She was the CBS television founder's second wife.

§ Darryl F. Zanuck (1902–79) was a producer, writer, and studio executive and winner of three Academy Awards. Styron refers to Whittaker Chambers (1901–61), the Communist turncoat, Soviet spy, and winner of the Presidential Medal of Freedom. Chambers testified against Alger Hiss and wrote a scathing anti-Communist account of the trial and his life in the bestselling and influential 1952 autobiography *Witness.*

¶ Fulton John Sheen (1895–1979) was a conservative archbishop in the American Catholic Church known for his radio program *The Catholic Hour.*

head of the Ike-for-Emperor movement in California. I'll never get into the pictures that way.

You must read Witness, if you haven't already; it's an obscene, infuriating book but engrossing, perhaps, because of this—in the same way that a lot of revolting things are fascinating. Someday I'd love to be able to do a J'Accuse against Chambers, in the same way Zola did against the French government in the Dreyfus case. The more you read the book the more you become convinced that Hiss, though probably guilty, was nonetheless the dupe of one of the most frightfully, psychotically vengeful men in history.

I must close now, dearest. I hope things are going well with you, and that you do find within yourself the courage you need. But always remember that I'm ready to give you more courage if you need it and that I love you, always more than anything on earth.

Your

Bill

John P. Marquand, Jr.*

September 17, 1952 Paris, France

Dear old Jack,

"Skinhead," which is what Cass calls his old man, was over here the other day on some sort of crazy joy-ride with T.K. Finletter, and he told me about your receiving 25 G's from the Post for "The Second Happiest Day."† I wanted to hurry to be the 500th person to congratulate you so here it is—congratulations mille fois. It really was great news; with that dough you'll be able to organize a rival boot camp in competition with old Jim

* As noted earlier, John's father was the novelist John P. Marquand. When John, Jr., wrote *The Second Happiest Day* (1953), he published under the nom de plume John Philips. He was part of the *Paris Review* circle, serving as an advisory editor and contributor.

† Marquand Jr. won the *New York Post*'s emerging writer prize, worth $25,000. Cass Canfield (1897–1986) was a publishing executive, and the longtime president of Harper & Brothers.

Jones, only far better furnished and with all of the trappings of elegant depravity. At least you and no doubt Miss Bailey will be able to swing a trip to Europe; why don't you come over?* Incidentally and of even more importance, to me, than the dough, I'm very interested in seeing the book when it comes out. Do you think you could manage to send me a set of proofs, or at least an advance copy? Everyone here who's seen it—Cass Canfield père and fils, among others—have great things to say about it, and so I think the least favor you could do for an old buddy is to see that I get a first look.

Furthermore, I want to thank you, shamefully and very belatedly, for the fine letter you wrote me this summer. I can't tell you how much I appreciated it then and how the impression of it still lingers. After all the postal abuse I got (and still get every now and then) from illiterate morons in places like Modesto, Calif., complaining about my degeneracy, I can tell you that a letter like yours was a great thing and I'm not shitting you when I say that I'll treasure it.

Life in Paris has been fine but has become monotonously the same during the past few weeks and I'm looking forward to Rome toward the end of the month. Cass and I have gotten drunk with a rather dangerous regularity recently, and the new vogue, originated by Cass, has become a sort of blackface toward the end of the evening, whereby with the aid of a burnt piece of cork everyone is transformed into Groucho Marx, glasses are thrown into the street, and Franco-American relations become utterly dissolved. On my part I think this footlessness arises from the fact that for the past month or so I did no work. I had a fine trip to St. Tropez and then to St. Jean de Luz (which Michael no doubt told you about) but with nothing to do now in Paris, and no project to concentrate on, the place has become something of a drag. I hope to get busy in Rome. I wrote a 22,000 word story this summer which apparently now is in the first mitts of John W. Aldridge for consideration for Discovery, but I have a lingering hope that somehow it'll turn up in Harper's, in spite of its great length. Oh well—hell, the literary life is sure a pain in the ass, isn't it? I'm of the opin-

* Pidey Bailey married Peter Gimbel (1927–87), heir to the Gimbels department store chain, before marrying Sidney Lumet (1924–2011), the director of such films as *12 Angry Men, Dog Day Afternoon,* and *Network,* and also a producer and screenwriter.

ion that if you have an agent, as I do, you're lucky if your stuff gets into Women's Wear Daily.

Look, old Jack, do try and get over here this fall or winter. I can assure you from experience that there are happier things than being in New York when your book is published. After October 1st I'll be at the Accademia Americana, Porto San Pancrazio Rome, so drop me a line then if not before. Tell Appleton to keep his elbow straight and give him and all the boys in the back room at Harper's, including Mike and Jack Fischer, my best and love to M. Bailey.

All the best, Bill

To Elizabeth McKee

September 25, 1952 Paris, France

Dear Lizzie,

Thanks for the cable and for the letter about the story, which I received today. I was happy to hear that Discovery took the story and that they liked it; no, $725 doesn't seem too small at all—outside of LDID it's the first thing I've ever written which I got paid for, and $725 seems good for that kind of starter.

There are two small but important items I want to mention here. First is the title of the story. On reflection, the title "Like Prisoners Walking" seems a bit flowery—a couple of other people here who read the story are of the same opinion. Instead, I think something like THE LONG MARCH is more direct and apropos, so I wish you would get in touch with Vance or Aldridge or whoever has the MS and tell them I want the title changed to THE LONG MARCH. I hope it's not too late to make the change. Secondly, on reading over my handwritten MS I noticed a misusage of a word. This occurs on what must be the third or fourth page of the typewritten copy and it's in the passage where I describe Culver's home-life in New York. I had written "a cat which he deigned to call by name." This is the wrong usage of "deign"; and implies that Culver condescended to call the cat by name. What I meant was that Culver wouldn't call the cat by name and so the phrase should read "a cat which he did not deign to call by name." I wish you'd have this changed in the MS. Incidentally will I get galley proofs of the story to check over before publication? I hope so because though I don't think I'm especially prissy about my stuff, I like to be on the lookout for those important mistakes which occur in even the best-edited copy.

Now, as for the contract, that sounds fine with me. However, I've already promised my friend Annie Brierre, who wrote the enclosed interview, first crack at the story for possible publication in the weekly magazine she works for—Les Nouvelles Littéraires—and told her that I would arrange to have a copy of Discovery sent to her when it comes out. So that's all taken care of. By the way, there's a lotta garbled stuff in that interview (I didn't tell her I was in Korea for seven months, or even one month), but you know the French and their flair for drama.

As for sending me the contract to sign, that brings me to the fact that sometime next week, probably Tuesday or Wednesday, I'm leaving for Rome. My address will be ACCADEMIA AMERICANA, PORTO SAN PANCRAZIO, Rome, but since I'm not absolutely sure whether this is the best address or not you can check by calling Miss May T. Williams at the American Academy in Rome office at 101 Park Avenue. The number is in the phone book. At any rate, if you have anything to send me before the middle of next week you might as well send it to the American Express here in Paris, with whom I will leave my Rome address and who are supposed to be very efficient about forwarding mail.

That's about all. I'm about as devoid of news as you are, except to say that life is pleasant still here, but unexciting, and I'm looking forward to things picking up down in Italy. Best to all.

Love,

Bill

To Vance Bourjaily

September 29, 1952 Paris, France

Dear Vance,

Thank you very much for your letter. I'm at present in a state of grim confusion about getting to Rome (I don't know if I'm expected at the Academy, there's a foul-up on train reservations, I've got to get money changed, etc—you know how it is) so I think you'll understand if this letter is brief and to the point.

First, I checked carefully over your list of emendations and corrections and agree with you on all of them, without exception. They all make perfect sense to me, and I'm glad you took a priori liberty in making the changes. Since you're so strapped for time I won't plead for copies of the galley proofs, but will trust you at your word about checking over it carefully yourself, which I know you will. The change in the first paragraph from "Flit-gun" to "hose" is Haydn's correction, but he told me about it as a suggestion and it's fine with me. I can't think of anything else.

The magazine sounds like it's shaping up fine, and I'm as proud to be in it as you say you are to have The Long March. Of course, I'll be interested in all developments and I hope you'll keep me posted from time to time. I'll have a short list of addresses, later on, of people to whom I wish you'd have copies sent. My address, as of a few days from now, will be c/o Accademia Americana, Porta San Pancrazia, Rome. I've heard nothing of or from the people there, or their representatives in New York, since I first got word of winning the prize last March—and all this in spite of letters I've written—so I'm beginning to wonder if it's all not a great big yuk on me. At any rate, I think the above address will do and I hope you keep in touch. Best to Tina, Aldridge and Company and all the characters you run into.

Best,

Bill

Styron arrived in Rome in October 1952 and began living at the American Academy.

To John P. Marquand, Jr.

October 8, 1952 Rome, Italy

Dear Jack,

This will be I think a rather uninspired letter, in comparison to your very lively one, because the three days I've spent in Rome have resulted in nothing but a beautiful cold in chest and head—the second in six weeks. It must be psychosomatic or something, or perhaps because the only person I've seen to talk to has been Truman Capote, whom I ran into in the Excelsior Bar.

The Academy is really some joint, a beautiful place, totally inhabited by the queerest group of egg-heads you ever laid eyes on. I suspect that most of them will be very nice once I get to know them, but it's a bit out of my frame of reference to be set down amidst a bunch of people which, to the myopic last one of them, almost, is made up of nothing but archaelogists. Your proposed trip with your uncle to Greece and points south already begins to appeal to me, anything that steers clear of archaeology, and although I can't say yet for sure whether I'll be able to go with you or not, I think I can safely say that the chances are that I can and will. I hope that this doesn't sound too indefinite. I want to do another long story this month, aimed shamelessly at something like Harper's Bazaar, or any chic place that will pay me a pot of dough, and if I get that done by the time you arrive—which I think I shall be able to—then it's off we go to the flesh-pots of Smyrna. I wish I could be more conclusive, but I hope this will do for an answer.

It's good to hear that you're finally coming to Europe, even without Mrs. Bloomingdale, or whatever the hell she calls herself by now. I suppose it was a grim sort of summer for you, but I always am a sucker for platitudes and maintain that it's all probably working out for the best. I trust that by the time you get this letter you will have shaken the burden of grief, or whatever shoddy emotion you've been feeling, from your shoulders and have begun to live high off Ben Hibbs's $ $ $ $.

I left everyone in Paris in good and characteristic shape—Cass high as a kite and the Matthiessens only a bit more sober, due to the fact that they're expecting a bundle from heaven and don't want it to arrive bleary-eyed and reeling. I caught this cold on the Rome Express and arrived in Rome in a feeble state and mumbling broken Italian. Since the Academy is sort of in the suburbs of Rome I've spent more money in taxis than I did the whole time I was in Paris. I've really begun a dreary regime and have become a typical Amurrican, refusing to go to see the Colosseum or any of the celebrated wrecks around here, but staying safely within the confines of the Excelsior Bar where they speak English, have Truman Capote, and sell martinis at 60¢ apiece. Could anything be more shocking? I'm really not much of a traveler, my baggage being my own neuroses and a hacking cough, which weigh me down too heavily, even if I were in the Garden of Eden. However, by the time you heave on the scene I have no doubt that my perspective will have altered and I'll be a hardy voyageur, ready for hashish in Haifa and belly-dancers in Baghdad. Let me know how things progress with you and in the meantime I'll try to clear my conscience with Art.

Best,

Bill

To William C. Styron, Sr.

October 27, 1952 Rome, Italy

Dear Pop,

Thanks for the piece by Mr. Jebb, which I liked, and for your earlier letter. The reason I haven't written more promptly is because I've just recently finished a week's trip by car—along with some other members of the Academy—to Florence, Siena, Ravenna, Urbino and Assisi. It was an excellent trip, lasting about a week, and thoroughly illuminating because my companions were all either painters or, better yet, art historians who gave me first-hand scholarship and information about the Art (with a capital A) we were seeing. I think, Art-wise, I was most impressed by the Medici tombs in Florence and by the Ravenna mosaics, which date from the middle of the Dark Ages and shine today in all their glory. As far as towns go I think I was particularly struck by Urbino, which is pitched on the top of a mountain and is filled with winding, steep streets and the nicest people in all of Italy. Assisi, on the other hand, is a tourist trap, filled with knick-knacks and holy pilgrims from places like Munich and Brussels.

Back at the Academy now, I've somewhat settled down. I wish I had a photograph of the place, but I'll try and get one for you soon. It's really a lovely place, a real palace, and big enough so that no one gets in anyone else's way. The painters, sculptors, and architects all get enormous studios which would cost a four-figure sum in New York, and each of which commands a marvelous view of Rome down below. I myself, not needing so much space, have to be content with two huge connecting rooms, excellently furnished, with large ceiling-high windows and a view of the Academy courtyard below, where there is a fountain surrounded by four beautiful cedar trees. We eat in a sort of community dining hall. The food is good Italo-American style, but as in Paris I generally, except for lunch, prefer to eat down in Rome where there are of course excellent restaurants. The keynote here, somewhat like Rabelais' Abbey of Thélème, is "Do What You Will" and there is no more routine here, or regulations, than in a hotel. That suits me fine. Of course I've already met some very amiable and interesting people, yet in spite of the slightly community aspects of the place, it doesn't look to me as if there will be any trouble in keeping out of each other's way, nor, on the other hand, as if there will be any lack of parties and bon camaraderie when the occasion demands. I have also met an absolutely beautiful girl, American, named Rose, with whom I get along right well, and who has an apartment on the other side of Rome, which will obviously necessitate my buying a car pronto.* It won't be a Fiat, but either a German Volkswagen (an excellent car) or an English Austin, either of which will cost around $1300 but which cost I can get back substantially in re-sale before I come back to the U.S.A. One thing just leads to another. A young man just must have a girl, and that always—even, or I should say especially in Europe—brings up the question of wheels.

The election of course is a big topic over here, too, although perhaps not so intensely emotional as in the U.S. Everyone seems to be rooting for Stevenson and I hope he gets elected, too. The only reading matter avail-

* After finishing her master's degree, Rose took a year off to travel and study in Europe. Louis Rubin wrote to tell her that Styron had won the Prix de Rome and was at the American Academy. Rose left a note in Styron's mailbox there and they made a date to meet in the bar of the Hotel Excelsior.

able is Time and the Herald-Tribune and it seems to me that even in those arch-Republican journals it cannot be disguised just what a prime jackass Eisenhower has made of himself. If he had come out just once and roundly condemned McCarthy he might have had a chance with the not-after-all-so-dumb voter. But by the time you get this letter I suppose all the issues will be coming to a head.

As soon as I get this car situation straightened out, I'm going to settle down for a spell of work. I have ideas for three or four more long stories, which will help me financially, and in the meantime I suppose I will have thought up something for a new novel. I suspect that my long story "Long March" will be the strongest piece in the forthcoming issue of Discovery, which I'll have sent to you in December or January. Meanwhile, I've gotten a proof of the jacket of the jumbo, economy-sized 50¢ Signet Double Volume, which will appear in every Walgreen drugstore in November, in which a wan, sad, half-clad Peyton is seen on the verge of climbing into bed with one of the most unsavory-looking Italians you ever saw. Sic Transit Gloria Literati, but it will sell 250,000 copies and my stock will soar in Peoria. Best to all. In Italia Ego. Yet, American to the bone, I think often of home.

Your son,
Bill

To John P. C. Train*

November 6, 1952 Rome, Italy

Dear John:

I think that I was probably a very poor person to write a preface; judging from the edited copy which I got back, there were about three and a half lines of copy which seemed acceptable.† Being new at the preface-

* John P. C. Train (b. 1928) is an investment adviser and author. A college friend of George Plimpton, Train was the first managing editor of *The Paris Review*.

† Styron's first attempt at an introduction for *The Paris Review*'s debut issue was harshly criticized by Marquand, Plimpton, and Matthiessen.

writing game, I am completely amenable to suggestions, and thank you for your comments, which in most cases seem to me to be reasonable enough; however, I would really quite frankly like to know where the line is which separates the rather dogmatic approach to the preface and the more informal approach of that "letter" which you suggest. In other words: I wrote a rather formal preface, a good part of which has been so completely altered or grammatically changed as to make it not "my" preface any longer, but someone else's. This seems perfectly logical to me because, since all the editors have slightly varying points of view, and I used throughout the word "editors," meaning "all of us," some drastic tailoring has to be done in order to have my original beautiful prose conformed to a sort of median opinion of all the editors. However, in this case, what is finally left will apparently still appear above my name, and I don't think I would want that too much, simply because the end result is not what I wrote.

As an alternative, then, you seem to suggest a letter to the reader. Before writing that I would like to ask you what you think should be in the letter. Again, I would like to avoid having you suggest what I should say. I think the letter idea is a good one, and one which finally solves the pompous manifesto, however I think you would agree with me that such a letter—if it is at all to possess the informality of tone implicit in a letter—has to be left intact pretty much completely, excluding, of course, two or three proofreaders' marks. When I ask you, then, what you think should be in the letter, I am really asking: don't you think it should be no more and no less than any friendly piece of correspondence from one so-called thinking person to another, or group of others? I have written one on the following pages which incorporates some of your counter suggestions. I do hope that it won't be altered, since if it is it will lose its point.

As for your comments on my original preface, I do not agree with all of them, but since both my ideas and your comments upon them end up pretty much being matters of opinion, I can't readily say that I shared them (and I'm not being harsh) "very interesting." I did not, however, mean to imply that decadence, defeat, and decay in our literature is merely a fancy of the critics. I myself, like you, do think the times are serious, and I think that our literature is full of a concomitant despair; I only meant to say (and I no doubt simply didn't say it clearly enough) that the shallow critics (call them "book reviewers") assail modern writing, poetry for its "decadence," "defeat," "decay," without honestly juxtaposing the despair of the literature against the despair of the times.

At any rate, the letter follows on the next pages, and I hope you and PM and GP and the others will find it suitable. As for your commentary, I found it an excellent + perceptive piece and liked it very much, perhaps one reason being that your moderate attitude toward the expatriate literary life thoroughly concurs with mine.

Tell Peter that I got his letter (and also George's letter) and will write them soon. Sending along the MS page which Peter asked for.

Yours, ob'd servant
Bill

To Elizabeth McKee

November 14, 1952 Rome, Italy

Dear Lizzie:

Your letter was received last Monday, just a few minutes before I and a few other members of the Academy went for a three-day tour to Naples, Pompeii and Ravello, so I delayed writing until now. Business first then I'll tell you about the trip.

First, the money from the bank was sent to the address I wrote down, as I requested, so the car deal is taken care of. They also sent $400 here to Rome; however, they neglected to tell me what branch or affiliate in Rome I can pick the money up at. I suspect that since the form letter I received has "any branch, affiliate or correspondent" at its head, it means just that, and I will be notified by the branch here that the money has arrived. But in the meantime, just to be safe, I wish you'd call up NCB and ask them what branch or bank here the money was sent to. I won't be needing the money for a couple of weeks or so, so there's no real hurry, but I wish you'd find out that address for me so that I'll know where to go in case I'm not notified.

About the taxes: the accountant didn't tell me how much I should lay aside for next March. Perhaps you'd better call him up and find out what the scoop is. As you know he has power of attorney to write out checks to the Bureau of Internal Revenue (although no other power), and if he advises that I owe a certain amount to Mr. Eisenhower (or whatever crook is chosen as the new Secty of the Treasury) then I guess we'd better take his word for it. Incidentally, when does the $8000 or so start coming in from the New American Library? I hope you will arrange somehow to have that paid to me in a way which will also cut down on the tax-bite, but no doubt the accountant can give you advice on this. Also, just for general information, the money which I get from the American Academy is non-taxable and I wish you'd tell the accountant.

As for the mis-spelt Argentine edition, please send one to my father; one to Sigrid de Lima, 282 West Fourth St. N.Y.C.; one to Prof. Wm. Blackburn 6177 College Station, Durham N.C.; and one by slow boat to myself.

As for talking to Cyrily Abels about the Mademoiselle piece, I think that's a fine idea, especially the fact that you think you can get more money than the $500 she mentioned. Tell her that I wrote you that by now I feel—or will feel in a month or so—acquainted enough with Italy to do the superficial little piece (don't mention that) that they no doubt want filled with all sorts of chic references to people like Little Truman and writers and painters and the slanting amber light over Sorrento, and that you understand they want to order a piece (at say, about at least half again the sum they originally mentioned) and that I'd be willing to do it, just let me know, through you, and I'll have it down presto, providing they don't hack it to bits.

I'm really beginning to get my feet on the ground here in Rome and am going to start work as soon as I can get out from under a pile of letters that need answering. John Fischer airmailed me galleys of Jack Marquand, Jr.'s new book, "The Second Happiest Day," under the pseudonym John Phillips, which I've got to read, but which I don't know whether I'll like, from a brief look already, well enough to comment on. Jack Fischer + Jack Marquand are both great guys and it'll be embarrassing if I don't like it, but since the book got $25,000 from Satevepost and is the Feb BOMC selection, I don't think they'll miss a blurb from me. Anyway, it's another thing I have to do. The trip to Naples and environs was really wonderfully pleasant but while everyone else went out to poke around in the dust and ruins at Palestrum, I stayed in Ravello (the place where, unaccountably, Wagner wrote Parsifal) and just looked. It is indeed the most bewitchingly beautiful place on earth, with incredible vistas of sea and hills, and I've set my mind on living there next spring and summer, even at the risk of writing something as tedious as Parsifal.

Love, Bill

P.S. I received galleys from Discovery, fortunately, because I caught about 10 misprints.

To Robert Loomis

November 21, 1952 Rome, Italy

Dear Bob,

It was good hearing from you again, though I think, come to think of it, that I was amiss—or is it remiss?—anyway I was glad to hear that everything seems to be sliding along in N.Y. with what seems to be a minimum of friction, especially glad that you and Gloria are hitting it off so well. If your prediction comes true I must say it will certainly be odd to see R.D.L. in a state of nuptial whatever-you-may-call-it, but I want to offer you, anyway, my premature congratulations.

I'm just recovering from the post-election depression, so that I feel up to catching you up on all the latest news. As for the election itself, I think reactions to it may best be summed up in a cryptic note my father sent me, dated Nov. 5th: "Once in France, where Thomas Carlyle was asked the population of England, he replied: '25,000,000, mostly fools.'" It has depressed all of us over here, but perhaps Mr. Dulles won't fuck up things too much.

As for me, I've been here for a little over six weeks, have not done any work, but have been struggling with the adjustment-period which seems inevitable to me when I travel around foreign places. I'm just beginning to like Rome, and Italy, and even the Academy—which is a bit harder to like. My stay in Paris ended up pleasantly, it's really a great and wonderful city once you get to know it, and as you may know I even found that I could work there, though I don't think the $725 for 23,000 words, which I got from Raoul Beaujolais, is exactly a lucrative deal. Anyway, it's a great place, I can understand why the Rhoads are not happy there, though. They wouldn't be happy anywhere, because what with their incredible parsimony (there's a difference between parsimony and frugality) and their really frightening concentration on saving four francs, they don't have enough time to muster the joie de vivre to be happy anywhere. Myself, my equanimity in Paris was only shaken, in its latter days, once—when I was set upon by that conniving little prick-teaser . . . who lured me to her suite in the Hôtel Crillon one drunken, hazy dawn, stripped naked as a jaybird, and then at the decisive juncture shut up her jewel-box tight like a clam. The trouble with her—while she does have a certain charm that I think magazines like Glamour call "fey"—is that she is still living back in dear old Bassett house, and until she realizes she's out in a world of men and women, and not of pimply sophomores slurping up milkshakes at the Dope Shop, she's going to be forever flitting about from one . . . to another, wondering why she's so dissatisfied and unhappy.*

Rome is wonderful in that department. I've happened upon a beautiful dark-haired girl,† American (no language barrier) who has an apartment half-way across town; this has necessitated my buying a car—a practically brand-new Austin which runs like a charm. She and I are planning to drive up to Paris in it around Christmas time and then perhaps fly to England for the holidays. To keep my conscience clear for this junket, however, I'd have to do some work before then; I should be able to do a short story in the intervening month. For some reason time seems to pass with horrifying speed these days, and I seem to spend what should be my best writing time fidgeting and contemplating my thumbs—all of which I rationalize away as a Necessary Period of Adjustment. Actually, though, I have done a lot of traveling the six weeks I've been here—Florence, Siena, Ravenna, and Assisi in the North, and Naples, Pompeii and Ravello in the south; it was all quite fine and the South, especially Ravello (an impossibly beautiful town on the sea, with cliffs, clouds, bottle green water and golden light, where I'd like to spend spring and summer next year) was especially exciting. I avoid the Ruins and Monuments and look at the scenery; in the South it's absolutely crazy with people and movement, unlike France, which is lovely, but cold and even moribund in the countryside. At any rate, I've gotten the traveling out of my system for a time and perhaps will be able to do some work. All I've been able to do this week,

* Bassett House was one of the women's dormitories at Duke.

† Rose Burgunder.

though, is read Jack Marquand's book, the proofs of which Fischer sent me.* I think it's a good book, ably told story, and lots of witty interludes, but unfortunately it didn't get me excited enough to want to comment on it. No comments needed, perhaps, since it's BOMC's choice at $25,000. I guess I'll see Jack down here in a few weeks.

The Academy is a fine place to work (I have two huge connecting rooms with lots of light) but not the greatest place on earth to live. Three or four of the people are fine, and I've made some pals, but most of them, though agreeable enough, are terrible bores—archaeologists and classicists, whatever that is. Most of my evenings I spend in Rome, which has a fine nightlife; I've seen quite a bit of Truman,† who has a wonderful apartment and a pet crow named Lola. I think he's a fine, generous and entertaining little guy. Leo Lerman's coming to Rome soon, so we'll all probably have a blowout.

Drop me a line when you can and give my best to John, Gloria, John Selby if you see him, et all.

Bill

To John P. Marquand, Jr.

November 25, 1952 Rome, Italy

Dear Old Jack,

I hope this will get to you in good shape, as I wanted to let you know right off and first hand how much I enjoyed your book, the proofs of which Jack Fischer airmailed to me just last week. I wanted to say first, unequivocally, that I think it's really a terrific job and I stand in real awe of your achievement. It's a real novel, big and vital and superbly written—and when I say "real" novel I mean that it leaves you with a sense of lives lived, love loved and all the rest—and it's not simply one of those thin, pallid little abortions which first novels usually are, written by people who neither have anything to say nor any ability to say it. I'm sure you should have no worry anymore about riding to a literary heaven on your old man's

* *The Second Happiest Day.*
† Truman Capote.

coattails—because in this book you've patently demonstrated a very considerable achievement and it's clear from the outset that you are the proud possessor of a genuine and individual gift. Besides obviously having had the last say on the people about whom you've written, you should glory in the additional fact that you've also written about them with an enormous wit, tenderness and perception that hasn't been seen since the days when old F. Scott was around; if I were you I'd be very very happy, and I congratulate you on a simply stunning performance. Here endeth the first lesson.

I trust you are finding Paris gay and entertaining—you deserve it, and I hope you and Matthiessen unleash a celebration that hasn't been rivaled since the return of Louis Philippe. I'm still poking around, trying to get to work and though I'm not sure whether I'll be able to go on the near-eastern junket with you right now, I will welcome you to Rome at any time and will present you with whiskey, hospitality, rides in my new automobile, and a brand-new self-starting 14-carat good-looking woman whom you may couple with on balmy Roman nights. Paris is dandy, but Rome is home, so come on down and try it on for size.

Best,

Bill

P.S. It's not true about me and T.C.,* but he's going to be absolutely livid with envy when "The Second Happiest Day" is published.

To Robert Loomis

January 24, 1953 Rome, Italy

Dear Bob,

I've settled down enough after my long and arduous trip to Paris to be able to keep you up on recent developments, such as they are. The trip itself was great fun. We—myself and this composer and his wife and my girl

* Styron refers to humorous rumors that he and Truman Capote were romantically involved.

Rose (she's from Baltimore, beautiful, and I'm getting very serious about the whole matter)—drove up in this nice English Austin I've bought. We went up by way of the Riviera, which was warm and sunny, and came back via a pass through the Alps, which was cold as hell and clogged by the worst snowstorm in 24 years. We were stuck in the snow for five hours, with visions of starvations, avalanches and the like, but were finally hauled out by a couple of English-speaking Italian horses. I don't recommend driving around Europe in the middle of winter. But the holidays in Paris were festive. I saw a lot of Marquand and Tom Guinzburg and we all stayed appropriately polluted, except for a three-day spell during which Rose and I flew to England and stayed sober in London for a whole night.*

Life at the Academy is about the same, which is to say that it's fairly tolerable an existence as long as one steers clear of the aging spinster archaeologists and the rest of the bores. I eat practically all my meals out, preferring musical trattorias to the long institutional table where these freaks mumble about Etruscan iconography between mouthfuls of spaghetti. There's a story about one young novice archaeologist, female, was digging around some Roman ruins and came across the big bent prick of Jove or Apollo or someone, and promptly identified it as a knee. But there are lovely people here, too—my composer friend and wife, a wonderful fellow, an art historian named Cooke who drinks like a whale and can tell you more about Piero della Francesca than Berenson, and a great fellow named Robert White (Stanford White's grandson) who also is a close friend of the Canfields and knows Marquand.† All in all—in spite of the predominantly tedious oafs—it's a good place to work. I'm getting started soon on something Big and Significant. Which for some reason reminds me, in case you're interested, that if someone were to ask me finally what I thought my most significant impression, culturally speaking, of the difference between Europe and America, I would say an almost complete lack of chatter about psychoanalysis and the ills of the brain. It struck me like a brick just the other day: I haven't seen hide nor hair of a head-feeler

* Thomas Henry Guinzburg (1926–2010), editor and publisher as well as cofounder of *The Paris Review.* He succeeded his father as president of Viking Press.

† Robert and Claire White were two of Styron's closest friends in Italy. The couple partly inspired Cass and Poppy Kinsolving in *Set This House on Fire.*

since I've been over here and when someone mentions Freud it's as if he had spoken of some obscure entomologist, so little is one's consciousness in the psyche. You might mention this to some of your ulcerous acquaintances, and tell them I recommend that they come to Italy for the Cure.

I don't know what got me off on that item. Maybe because I was thinking, god knows why, of Brice, who wrote me a monstrously long letter recently, which was an identical transcript of an earlier, just as lengthy letter he had written, describing his trip to New York, all the sex that went on in the room adjacent to his at the YMCA, the boys who tried to pick him up at Mary's, etc. Poor Brice, so infinitely small is his tiny little mind that he can write two letters, weighing half a pound each, and containing the exact, trivial contents.

Have you seen a copy of "Discovery" yet? I haven't, but E. McKee said she was going to airmail me a copy. Incidentally, if it wouldn't be too much trouble, and if the thing is reviewed at all, I'd appreciate your clipping anything you see about it and sending them to me. I see Time magazine each week, but that's about all. Marquand, by the way, is presumably due here in Rome at his publication time; I think he wants me to salve his wounds, if there are any, or something. He says he really wants to be in Kenya hunting lions when the book comes, but is now a little leery of the Mau-Mau, so I expect he'll hunt movie starlets here at the Hotel Excelsior.

Tonight Alexei Haieff (he won the N.Y. Critics Award in music) is giving a party and Truman will be there and so will I. I'm beginning to suspect my self, and that I'm in the wrong set. Best to John and your doll and all the gang at the office.

Love + Kisses—Bill

To Hiram Haydn

February 27, 1953 Rome, Italy

Dear Hiram:

Thanks for the clipping from the Post on Long March. I've gotten quite a few letters from people about the story, all favorable, and so in the last analysis, as my old headmaster used to say interminably, I suppose "Discovery" wasn't too bad a lodging for the piece.

I'm certainly happy to hear that you're coming to Europe this summer. I've already more or less gotten my plans fixed up for the summer, and so you and Mary must come to vist me at Ravello, which is the fantastic town I think I've described to you, perched above Amalfi and filled with lemon trees, donkeys, crazy streets and at the moment, unfortunately, a bunch of movie stars, who with their cameras and equipment and attending publicity will no doubt spoil the place for the next seven generations. However this awful piece, starring Humphrey Bogart and Jennifer Jones and written by Truman Capote (whom I saw this past weekend when I was down there scouting for a place to live, and who told me that he "jes writes one crazy scene one day and they film it the next day. It's all crazy.") won't be out for another year or so, the movie stars and their accompanying rabble of seedy-looking beslacked and sodden characters from Beverly Hills will be gone by May, and Ravello this summer will still retain its incomparable beauty . . . Rose and I are going to share it with another couple. A great guy named Bob White, who is a sculptor and the grandson, incidentally, of Stanford White who built the Academy, and his wife. It won't matter which one we take because each has a magnificent view, from eight to ten rooms, kitchens and plumbing and terraces and gardens and private groves of lemon trees. God Almighty. And none of them cost over $150 a month, including servants. So this here is an invitation to come down and stay as long as you like.

Incidentally, and to change the subject slightly, I am somewhat peeved by a letter (a form-letter which I received from D. Wolfe and addressed "Dear Author") which informed me that that Trieste piece I wrote when I was in your class had been chosen to be included in a new anthology that Permabooks is bringing out. You no doubt know of the project.* What I would like to know from you is whether you think it's arrogant of me to be somewhat unhappy over the fact that Wolfe didn't ask my permission first before including me in. I think I would have given permission all right, provided they append a note or date it anterior to LDID or something, but as it comes out now it will doubtless appear to be something I dashed off this past winter. This whole situation is not important, I realize, in the great scheme of things, and I'm glad to lend my name to some-

* Styron refers to Don M. Wolfe, editor of *Discovery*.

thing which might help New School writers; but the Trieste piece of prose (although for having been some six years ago I'm not ashamed of it), and I am all in all rather dispirited by the prospect of having people who read this Permabook thing thinking: "ah hah! see what I told you about Styron." If it is made clear that it's an early job, that's best—there's no indication of such in Wolfe's letter and I'm inclined to think that any . . . [Incomplete letter.]

To William C. Styron, Sr.

March 3, 1953 Rome, Italy

Dear Pop,

My story "Long March" seems to be evoking some favorable responses, although there certainly has been a paucity of reviews. Some Hollywood agent liked it enough to send it around to all the studios (though he said there's fat chance, not only being anti-war but anti-Marine, which in the U.S. is like being anti-Mom), and the editor of Perspectives, the magazine which the Ford Foundation distributes all over the world, called Miss McKee to say that he loved the story but it was too long to reprint. And at the moment I'm in receipt of a letter from Norman Mailer ("The Naked and the Dead") who tells me "as a modest estimate it's certainly as good an 80 pages as any American has written since the war."* I'm very touched by that, since Mailer of all my contemporaries is the writer I surely most admire. No need for you to think all this turns my head, as you cautioned. Along those lines Mailer added a word of criticism, implying I suppose that I should have perhaps a slightly more swollen head. "The tendency in you to invent your story, and manner your style, struck me as coming pos-

* The first correspondence exchanged between Mailer and Styron was Mailer's very generous and engaged letter of February 26, 1953, reprinted in *The New York Review of Books* (February 26, 2009). Mailer called Styron's *Long March* "just terrific, how good I'm almost embarrassed to say, but as a modest estimate it's certainly as good an eighty pages as any American has written since the war." Mailer continued with "one humble criticism": "I wonder if you realize how good you are." Mailer identified a "manner" in Styron's prose which reveals "a certain covert doubt of your strengths as a writer . . . which I suppose is like saying, 'You, neurotic—stop being neurotic!'"

sibly from a certain covert doubt of your strengths as a writer, and you're too good to doubt yourself."

Meanwhile, I seem to have struck a slight snag in my work and have done really nothing of any value since Christmas. I'm not actually worried at this impasse, however, though my inactivity irritates me and seems to make much of life weary, flat, stale and unprofitable, or whatever the hell it was that Hamlet said.* I'm only really happy when I'm working. This I've finally realized in looking back over the periods when I was engaged in writing, those periods which seemed at the time so painful and full of drudgery and toil; actually upon a sort of Proustian type of reflection I can see that they—those hours of concentration, and slow scribbling—they are the moments of true delight. So, if only in a therapeutic vein, I intend to start into work again soon. The Nat Turner thing, for the moment, lies idle; Lord knows when I'll wrestle with that, perhaps not for years.

I hope you got my recent card. Since then I've been to Ravello—that town of magnificent and craggy beauty on the Amalfi coast. We drove down just for a couple of days, a young lady from Baltimore of whom I'm very fond and a sculptor named Robert White and his wife—superb people, he's the grandson of Stanford White, the architect who had a hand in building the Academy and of whom, of course, much has been written. Riding in Italy, especially around Naples, is a blood curdling experience, what with the absolute unconcern the natives have for any motorized vehicle and what with the incredible procession, still, of carts and wagons. However, the highways here seem to be much safer than in the U.S., perhaps because of necessity drivers appear to be more cautious and wary. In Ravello we stayed a day and two nights in a villa of an old Countess, a friend of the Whites, and I'm afraid I could never describe either the munificent, regal quality of the place or the breathtaking view of precipitous rocks and cerulean blue water over 1,000 feet straight down below. On our scouting expedition we explored half a dozen or so villas which we hope to occupy this summer, finally settling on one which has nine beds, two baths, a view of course, terraces, gardens, a private grove of lemon trees, and a couple of servants thrown in. All for what amounts to about

* *Hamlet,* 1.2.133: "How weary, stale, flat and unprofitable seem to me all the uses of this world!"

$170 a month. Divided among three or four people this is peanuts. I hope to send you some pictures of it soon. Speaking of pictures, the only sour note in Ravello last weekend was the presence of Humphrey Bogart and Jennifer Jones and an entourage of Hollywood creatures, on location for a movie which will no doubt provide enough publicity as to spoil the place for the next 50 generations.* O tempore, O mores!† But they won't be there this summer. Hope all goes well at home, and drop me a line soon.

Your son,

Bill

To Norman Mailer‡

March 4, 1953 Rome, Italy

Dear Norman:

Your letter, of course, certainly flattered me—elated me, indeed, about as much, or more, as any compliment I've ever received, and we won't turn this into a mutual admiration society by my wondering if you know how much or often certain shades and nuances from <u>Naked</u> have crept into, from time to time, my own work. However, they have, much and often—I don't know how visibly—and we'll let it go at that.

I appreciate, too, your comments concerning certain things which I do to my prose every now and then which seem to reveal that I don't know how good I am. As for that, I think you may be right, having suspected it from time to time myself; but I think I'm arriving at a point which more and more I'm conscious of the mannerisms, and therefore tend to avoid them and go instead more directly to the point. It's a hell of a hard process, but I take to it more instinctively than the other way around: the brawny method, like a big guy bellowing his way through a crowd. I wonder, for instance, to paraphrase your comment, if Jim Jones knows how really <u>bad</u> he is. I don't know why I single him out, but really dreadful stuff like that

* *Beat the Devil* (1953) starred Humphrey Bogart, Jennifer Jones, and Peter Lorre. John Huston directed Truman Capote's script.

† Cicero's oration against Verres: "Oh the times! Oh the customs!"

‡ Styron's first letter to Norman Mailer.

piece in the second New World Writing* seems to me to be indicative of the method of a writer who is so dazzled by the vision of his own strength, so earnestly wanting to think deep and write strong, that the result is an achingly conspicuous gaucherie with no significance for either writer or reader. Of course there's a middle ground in prose, between the tenuous, mannered web of the young lady writers, both male and female, who, whether they have or haven't anything to say, can't just quite squeeze it out—and the Older Boys, who always say what they have to say too loudly, too often, and not carefully enough. All this of course is cliché. But it's simply remarkable to me how so few writers who call themselves serious are unaware of the simple fact that a piece of prose, complex or written in the simplest, most unpoetic language, is akin nonetheless to poetry in that it's supposed to move men—to laughter or tears, at least to something—and it will very rarely do this unless it approaches this queer middle ground, where the reader can marvel at the excellence of the style and the power of the thing being said, without being really conscious of either. You feel that these boys are never really initially moved by the thing they want to say, or, if they are moved, rush in with flailing arms and without ever having considered the various wheres and whens and whys with which to move the reader. I suppose it would be impossible to explain to someone like Jim Jones where this middle ground is; you've been solidly encamped there ever since Naked, even in Barbary Shore which had strange and wonderful stretches.† I swear, I can hardly read any of our contemporaries. I'm either deafened by them, or find them practicing onanism in the corner.

At any rate, apologizing for this chatter, I want to thank you again, Norm, for your letter. I can't tell you how it pleased me. I would like to hear from you from time to time, and hope you'll drop me a line whenever you feel in the mood. I'll be in Ravello this summer, surrounded by lemon trees and an almost overpowering quaintness, and if you come to Italy, by any chance, I hope you'll give me a visit. Best, Bill

* James Jones, "None Sing So Wildly," *New World Writing: Second Mentor Selection* (New York: New American Library, 1952).

† Mailer's first two novels, *The Naked and the Dead* (New York: Rinehart, 1948) and *Barbary Shore* (New York: Rinehart, 1951).

To John P. Marquand, Jr.

March 9, 1953 Rome, Italy

Dear Jack:

I suppose that by now you're somewhere in the darker recesses of the mysterious East, smoking hashish, wrapped in a burnous, and in general acting like some character out of Paul Bowles.* But when this reaches you, it's to acknowledge your letter and to tell you that as usual you are welcome at Rose's and my poor hearth when you come back to Rome. Also, it's meant to prevail upon you, if you will, to spend some time with us down in Ravello this June. The Whites, Rose and I all drove down there weekend last to size the joint up and not only sized it up but were so smitten by the place that we're going to take a villa, with terraces, a magnificent view, and a private grove of lemon trees. After the beauties of Greece this is all no doubt old hat to you, but I can assure you that there's enough second-rate wop beauty down there to satisfy even a world-traveler, Micky Yelke–type character like yourself. So far, and by remote control we've persuaded the Matthiessens to spend June there and there's more than enough room for you, too, if you'd like to come. I think it would be a fine way in which to terminate the old European whirl.

I still haven't done any work, and am content these days to read only Time magazine, a pleasure which, however, I've cut down to only two re-readings per issue. My clots seem to have disappeared; I expect them back at any time, though. We've seen neither hide nor hair of Guinzburg and have five or six letters waiting for him, among them yours. I suspect that he and Buffington are outdoing even you in the Paul Bowles motif and are trekking in some abysmal, sex-ridden caravan through Tunisia—which is where he was the last I heard from him.

At any rate, both Rose and I are looking forward to seeing you when you come back to Rome, and hope you'll consider Ravello.

Best,

Bill

* Paul Bowles (1910–99), composer and novelist. His novel *The Sheltering Sky* (1949) was a major success. In 1947, Bowles settled in Tangier, where he lived for the rest of his life.

P.S. Matthiessen was here for a couple of days after you left, very smug in his W.C.T.U. kick, I must say, but he'll probably outlive us all by two decades.

To Robert Loomis

March 16, 1953 Rome, Italy

Dear Bob,

I wrote to Sigrid for Mac Hyman's address, and I'm writing you for it, too. Not that she'd fail to send it, but just in case that she didn't know his address, while you might. It's been a long time since I've had any news of old Mac; I hope he's not torturing himself as usual and this time will come to grips with the unsettling problem of living in the big city, and writing.

Your last letter was very amusing, especially the strange sort of Old Will–Rare Ben Jonson business that's going on at that place I seem never to have heard of: what's it called, the White Horse?* It sounds perfectly horrible, especially with that fine team of Raoul Beaujolais and Harry Eimerl. To tell you truth, I think the whole lot of them, including and especially Leslie Flatt Belker, are a bunch of literary dead-beats. It's a miracle to me that with Raoul Beaujolais running things Discovery ever got out at all and I thank E. McKee for insisting that he send me galley proofs of my story, for if I hadn't gone over them carefully, the piece, with its swarms of mistakes and typos, would have read like a Swedish Army manual. As it is, the thing has at least five errors. Thanks for the reviews, incidentally; the book certainly doesn't look as if it'll compete with Marilyn Monroe in popularity. Speaking of this dreadful rash of magazines, you probably know from John that that horrible ass Don M. Wolfe is up to his old tricks again. I've been burning up the mails with protestations and cries, but apparently all is lost, and this Cross Currents, or whatever it's called, especially in its introduction, with its picture of Sigrid and me in

* The White Horse Tavern is a Greenwich Village bar that was frequented by Dylan Thomas, Bob Dylan, Norman Mailer, James Baldwin, Hunter Thompson, and Jack Kerouac.

blue jeans and boondockers, bravely hammering at our typewriters, is as fearsome as the yearbook of Elon College. I'd love to hear Handel on the subject; according to Elizabeth both he and John are frothing at the mouth.

Rome has been dark and rainy and I've been utterly paralyzed and unable to write a line. It's no great spiritual crisis or anything like that; it's just a damnably annoying inability to get passionate enough or excited enough about anything to want to sit down and do anything about it. So I'm perfectly in sympathy with you when you mention retyping chapter heads and character lists; I haven't been able even to do that, but am praying that the advent of spring will give me strength. The maid here points her finger at me and giggles, every day calling me uomo vecchio, which means old man; I think that she thinks that with my sallow skin and melancholy attitude, I'm not long for this world. It's probably simply too much spaghetti. But the social life is still pretty entertaining: last week I drove down to Ravello to shop for a villa for this summer. A wonderful place. I ran into Truman C., who is writing the script for a movie which is being shot there. Humphrey Bogart, Jennifer Jones, and Zsa Zsa Gabor all over the place, looking very wan and dispirited, as if they all wished they were a million miles from the wops and back in the pool at Palm Springs. Truman makes, he was quick to inform me, $500 a week, and is rooming with John Huston, though I must say that combo leads to spine-chilling speculations. I found a villa, incidentally, with a private grove of lemon trees, a couple of servants whose obsequiousness would make Uncle Remus look like a Prussian, and with more rooms than I can count. I certainly wish it were possible for you and Gloria, John, Mandel, and the whole crew to come over and spend the summer.

I trust that everything is going O.K. at Rinehart and that you are staying reasonably sober. Mrs. Luce is undoubtedly going to cut off my pipeline to the embassy whiskey supply, but I can make do, if I have to, with the good Chianti. Best to all, and give me the latest news when you get a chance.

Yrs In the Bond. Bill

To Maxwell Geismar

March 24, 1953 Rome, Italy

Dear Max:

I got word just recently from my friends in Paris that you had done a job on Discovery in The Nation.* I hope you had a good word to say for my story, because the Geismar-Nation combination is certainly one in which a writer wants a bit of praise. I wonder if you would do me a favor and send me a clipping of that review, if there's one easily available. That story took me a couple of months last summer in Paris to write, and when it was done I certainly felt that I had gotten something off my chest. I don't think Discovery, from the copy I've seen, will win too many honors, but my story was much too long and too heavily laden with 4-letter words to be published elsewhere. All in all, though, I can't complain because I suppose these pocketbook ventures have pretty wide readership.

Since finishing that story, unhappily, I've done practically nothing and this fact seems to be making neurotic inroads upon my personality. (I used to snicker when I read about the anguish writers had whenever they found themselves bone-dry, but I snicker no longer.) It's hell the way these days go by with nothing accomplished and, seemingly, with nothing to anticipate in the future. I am as inspiration-less as a newt. And yet there's something in me which absolutely refuses to allow myself to sit down and turn out some sort of automatic drivel. Nothing is more tedious in this world than to read anything that's second-rate, and practically all second-rate stuff (and there's so much of it) comes, it seems to me, from a writer writing something without having anything particular to say, feeling that perhaps if he isn't constantly in print he won't become rich and famous. Of course, a lot of second-rate stuff comes merely from second-rate writers. At any rate, here I am high and dry in Italy, sweating it out; maybe you have a few words of psychiatric advice, gleaned from your many researches among the diseases of writers.

Otherwise, all is fine, and Italy is blossoming out all over with spring. It's really a great land, and my stay here has been enhanced by a lot of travel, all of it in a little Austin which I bought, which has squeaky brakes.

* Maxwell Geismar, "The End of Something," *The Nation,* March 14, 1953.

The Academy itself, of course, is frightful, being populated by myopic archaeologists, bone-pickers, and other spinsters, but it's a convenient headquarters and they do a nice job on my laundry. This summer I'm renting a villa down in Ravello, which is a place of fantastic beauty, and then I suppose I'll head back to the States next fall—in order to be able to keep in sociological touch with Eisenhower land. By that time I'll probably have such a tan that I'll be excluded under the McCarran act.

I really would like to see that Nation piece, Max, and any advice you might have about total paralysis would be greatly valued. Meanwhile, here's hoping that all goes well with you, and Ann, to whom also I send warmest greetings.

Bill Styron

P.S. I hope you won't let my remark about critics, in The Paris Review, disaffect you. I love the good ones.

To William Blackburn

Spring, 1953* Paris, France

I am the one on the right eating a sandwich and that is Barbara on the left with bubble-gum on her chin.

Bill

And we're looking down on all the Parisians and laughing

Bobbie

And Paris in the spring is toujours gai, just like they say

Bobbie and Bill†

* On postcard of gargoyles at Notre Dame Cathedral.

† Styron was in Paris with Bobbie Taeusch during the brief period when he and Rose had broken up after an intense courtship from October through December 1952.

To William C. Styron, Sr.

April 8, 1953 Rome, Italy

Dear Pop,

I am enclosing two items which may be of interest to you: (a) a clipping from last week's Newsweek, which you may or may not have seen (I've asked E. McKee, incidentally, to send you a copy of The Paris Review) and (b) a recent picture taken at a party.* Reading from left to right the characters are Samuel Barber, the famous American composer who is visiting here; young Elliott Braxton, who came to Rome and is now gone, but with whom I had long talks about Newport News and vicinity; a young lady named Mrs. Marge Allen who with her husband lives here in Rome; yours truly, who somehow here looks sick and disheveled, but who is actually the picture of health and whose sour appearance in the photograph can only be blamed upon the light and bad Italian gin; another composer, Alexei Haieff, who just won the N.Y. Critics' Award for the best musical composition of 1952; a young lady from Baltimore named Rose Burgunder, accent on the second syllable; and Tom Guinzburg, a good friend who is the managing editor of The Paris Review and whose father owns the Viking Press.†

I think it will probably interest you further that I am going to get myself married to the girl named Rose, second from right. I won't go into a lot of sentimental double-talk about how I think she's the most wonderful girl in the world—because I do—but suffice it to say that she's the girl from whose presence I get the greatest sense of well-being and fulfillment that I've ever had, and for whom I have the greatest affection, and I'm happy to think that you will see why, when you meet her. I imagine we will get married sometime in May, here in Rome. Incidental to this, I wonder if it would be possible for you to prevail upon Aunt Edith to send

* The first issue of *The Paris Review* had just been published. Styron enclosed a clipping from *Newsweek* mentioning Styron's "Letter to the Editor." See "Advance-Guard Advance," *Newsweek* (March 30, 1953).

† Samuel Barber (1910–81) was already well known in the 1950s for his *Adagio for Strings*. Originally written as the second movement of String Quartet Op. 11 (1936), his orchestral adaptation was first performed in 1938. Elliott Braxton was a native of Newport News. Alexei Haieff (1914–94) was a pianist and composer who created the music for George Balanchine's *Divertimento* (1944).

me, by registered air express, that fine engagement ring which, I gather, reposes in some safe-deposit box up in Uniontown. I remember your having often mentioned this to me, and you know of course that I would be greatly honored to be able to give it to Rose. I would appreciate it, and be greatly indebted to you, if you could arrange this as soon as possible.*

Needless to say, I'm delighted at the fact that you have a European trip in prospect, and am looking forward to being able to extend you and Elizabeth the hospitality of Ravello. Just let me know in advance your itinerary and all that, so that I'll be able to stock up on gas coupons and drive you both around this miraculous land. It's a trip, I'm sure, which you won't regret.

No further news. I wrote to Mrs. Ferguson and received a nice note in reply from Isobel. My writing project at the moment seems to be confined to an article for a symposium in The Nation, on "What I Believe," to appear later this spring.† It's a stern order, that sort of thing, to state one's philosophy in "25 words or less." Perhaps, though, it will give me the impetus for another long short story which has been slowly germinating in the back of my mind.

Best to all, and write soon.

Your son,
Bill

P.S. "LDID" has been accepted for translation in the German, which makes 7 languages in all.

To John P. Marquand, Jr.

April 17, 1953 Rome, Italy

Dear Jack:

I received your telegram, and I must say that Rose and I feel that there would be nothing more delightful than to play Byron with you for a while,

* This was the ring that Styron's father gave to his mother when they became engaged in 1919.

† "The Prevalence of Wonders," *The Nation*, 176 (May 1953).

and we were especially intrigued by the line which said a special tour was being arranged, or would be arranged, "in our honor," which conjured up visions of open, bullet-proof sedans, police escorts, and jonquils being thrown into our faces by a frantic populace. It would indeed be nice. But we have talked this thing over and have decided that in view of the fact that we will probably be getting married within the next few weeks, and that Rose's brother and wife are expected at any moment, it would put a strain on our nervous resources to come, at least my nervous resources, already depleted by a soggy, constant drunkenness brought on in part by the prospect of marriage, by insomnia, by clots, and by a general spiritual enervation resulting from the realization that already, going on 28, I am a wash-up as a writer and fit only to do the "Recent & Readable" part of the book section in Time. In other words, I will be going through a crisis this spring and although I don't doubt that Greece is an excellent place to weather such a storm, I hope you can understand my position. I hope also, by the way, that when you finish diddling your Greek lady-in-waiting you will come back to Rome in time to take part in the shoddy ceremony which is due to be enacted in the city hall. That will be some time toward the end of this month, no doubt, or the first week or so in May.

Meanwhile Guinzburg has gathered his clots together and has gone back to Paris after a long stay here—which he alternated between the Academy and the Condons. He was the picture of health as he took off for Nice; I still haven't gotten my tire.

None of the charter subscribers have received copies of The Paris Review and are kicking like hell. I don't know who's responsible for this fuck-up. Did you see the big spread on the rag two weeks ago in Newsweek?

The Matthiessens have given birth to a big manchild named Luke. We talked to them on the phone and they said it was as easy as pie. They've decided to come to Ravello in June. Why don't you, too?

You've been selling quite handsomely, according to the Times best-seller list—this you no doubt know. I never got above No. 7, but of course I had that prick Salinger as competition. Pretty soon you'll have more money than Bing Crosby. Lots of people reading it in Rome, according to the Lion Bookshop.

Irwin Shaw is living here, ensconced in the most hideous apartment in Parioli. He promises me a wedding shindig, so you'd better be here for the blowout.

In the meantime most of the creeps have crept away from the academy for their spring bone-hunt, leaving it clean except for a couple of seedy art historians and myself, who is struggling manfully with his destiny, and who, along with Rose, is looking forward to seeing you again sometime soon.

Best—
WCS.

To William C. Styron, Sr.

May 6, 1953 Rome, Italy

Dear Pop,

After incredibly complicated dealings with the Italian bureaucracy, Rose and I were married on Monday afternoon (the 4th) in truly gala style, at the Campidoglio, which is Rome's city hall. It was a very nice ceremony, unlike the equivalent in an American city, I'm sure, since the little room where it was performed was covered with wonderful crimson brocade and the officiating judge (in Rome the marrying judgeship is a high civic honor and our man, Signor Marconi, is Italy's Samuel Goldwyn) was dressed in a beautiful green and red sash. On hand for the ceremony were a few Academy friends, Irwin Shaw and his wife, Jack Marquand, who came from Athens especially for the wedding, and Peter Matthiessen and Tom Guinzburg (my Paris Review friends), who flew down from Paris, also especially. Afterwards, the Shaws had a big reception for us in their apartment, with cake and champagne, and after that we had a big dinner in a restaurant, with fettuccini and chicken alla diavolo. It was just fine. Best man was Bob White, whom I've mentioned; and his wife wrote a poem which she sang at the reception to a special tune written by Frank Wigglesworth, who accompanied her on a recorder. This sounds extremely corny, but I assure you it couldn't have been more touching, to be surrounded by so many fine friends. No honeymoon, since it won't be long before we decamp for Ravello.

Because of my matrimonial involvements (I've also bought four tailored suits) I haven't had much time to write, but I did go to the American Express, as you requested, and was told very definitely that it would be far better if you arranged the travel from Havre to Italy through their New York or Washington office, rather than go through the procedure of lots of complicated air mail letters to you from Rome or Paris. I really think this would be much better. As a matter of fact, Rose's family, who do a lot of traveling, use a very good travel agent in Baltimore. The woman, whose name is Miss Ethel C. Einstein, runs the Metropolitan Tourist Agency (North Charles St.) and is a very influential person, apparently, in the travel field. She is also a personal friend of Mrs. Burgunder, Rose's mother. I suggest that you write this lady, tell her who you are, and include information on where you want to go, how long you want to stay, how much you want to pay, etc. I have a feeling that she'll fix you up much better than American Express.*

That's about all for now. Hope everything goes well, and I'm certainly looking forward to seeing you this summer.

Your son,

Bill . . .

To Robert Loomis

May 18, 1953 Rome, Italy

Dear Bob,

Thanks many times for your felicatory letter upon my nuptials. I suppose that by now John has received my letter describing the wedding day activities and has filled you in on the details. Both your and John's letters have amused me greatly (John's was really an encyclopedia of a letter) and it has only been the pre-wedding confusion, which involves, among other things, buying rings, flowers, new suits (4), struggling with the fantastic Italian bureaucracy, that has kept me from writing you all sooner. I can't understand, though, why this event should top your list of unlikely happenings. I am now practically 28 years old, I have two faintly healthy gonads, and Rose, to me, is an enormously appealing girl. Practically everybody that both you and I know (and presumably including yourself)

* The Styrons decided instead to travel to South America.

is either (a) married, (b) has been married, or (c) going to get married. I don't know what qualities of potential celibacy I've ever exhibited to make you believe I'd stay a bachelor all my life. As Jack Marquand wrote me, marriage is no doubt not particularly desirable but it is nonetheless inevitable; and the fact of the matter is that it seems to me far more desirable than I ever thought it would be, and I hope you will take it in a spirit of good old fraternal Phi Delt advice when I suggest that you certainly won't go wrong in taking the plunge yourself, providing you have the right girl—and from what I've heard and seen you seem to have the right girl. This is not the talk of the man in the trap who wants to get all of his buddies trapped, too. Marriage must have its points, or else so many people wouldn't get into it. I think people like you and I, being of the so-called artistic temperament, have felt perhaps too much that this matrimonial business encroaches on our personal freedom; this attitude is perfectly valid, of course, and only becomes selfish and, to my way of thinking, wrong, when one's interest has been for so long, in simply fucking that they allow this interest to warp their outlook when the right girl comes along. I don't mean to sound priggish or All-American, and I probably sound confused. What I'm trying to say is this, and I'll shut up: that (a) fucking is wonderful and even marriage doesn't put a halt, alas, to a desire to get into a million new women, but an endless round of fornications and "affairs" is, at our advanced age, both wearing on the mind and body, and infantile; (b) that if you're lucky and I think I am, the girl you marry far from even trying to impinge upon your intellectual and artistic independence will indeed go so far out of her way to let you alone that it's almost embarrassing, so that you have to whistle, from time to time, for her to come back. Besides, if you're lucky, you simply like to be with her. End of lesson.

I didn't mean to go on at such length; I just wanted to unload upon you some first impressions, I guess. Meanwhile, in a couple weeks we're going down to Ravello for the summer and I trust that by September I'll have written solidly and true, as Papa would say, and that when I get back to New York I'll have both a MS to show off in the way of a "novella"* and the beginnings of a novel, besides a pretty wife. Let me hear how your

* The novella Styron refers to is his story about the Hart's Island prison. The piece was eventually published as "Blankenship" in a special Styron issue of *Papers on Language and*

Gloria business is developing. I got a long, wistful letter from Suzie the other day; for God's sake see if you can't fix her up with a nice big man!

Yrs in the bond,
Bill

To Norman Mailer

June 1, 1953 Rome, Italy

Dear Norman:

I note that you began your last letter: "I've been kind of depressed lately," and by way of preface to this letter I should say that I've been both depressed and elated since you last heard from me—elated at having just married a most admirable girl (perhaps you've gotten an announcement) and depressed because for roughly your own sort of reasons—an inability to get going again at this writing game. To complicate the situation, a few days ago, barreling down the Autostrada in an effort to catch up with Irwin Shaw's Ford convertible (we had been on a two-car picnic at Angio) I smacked into a motorscooter going full tilt and glued an Italian all over the front end of my car.* The guy was made of brick and will survive with nothing more than lacerations, and fortunately for the legal end of the thing it was his own fault (he was a moron, for one thing, and for another had been driving with a glass eye) but such incidents always leave me spookily aware of just how vulnerable we all are. Perhaps they're valuable as such from an ah-tistic point of view, but I doubt it.

At any rate, having descended from my earlier manic phase, I can easily appreciate your present difficulties. In waiting for my car to recover from its wounds (which were much more grievous than the Italian's) so that we can go to Ravello, I've been futilely trying to get started on something—another novelette, I think—and the complications arising from the thing certainly support that old saw about the more you go along in writing the

Literature 23 (Fall 1987). It also appears in William Styron, *The Suicide Run: Five Tales of the Marine Corps,* ed. James L. W. West III (New York: Random House, 2009).

* This incident inspired the collision between Peter Leverett and Luciano di Lieto in *Set This House on Fire.*

more difficult it gets. I admire your tenacity; at least in this book you're doing you seem to be plunging ahead. As for me, if I don't feel that my very first page is a real sockeroo then I tend to give up in anguish—which is an attitude that is fatal and will, if anything, if I don't snap out of it, be my downfall. It certainly justifies your earlier comment about a peculiar tendency I have to invent and manner the style; indeed, I'm beginning to see that everything I write and my whole timorous approach to writing is of the same rough pattern of my day-to-day life—that being one of caution, trepidation and cowardly fears. No self-confidence. How do you beat it? Perhaps I'll change some as I get older but it seems to me that life (and I wonder how closely it parallels the experience of other men) is a long gray depression interrupted by moments of high hilarity. No wonder Time magazine is forever complaining about young writers re-writing their own tangled neuroses. However, I should add (in a brief flicker of exaltation, and bugger Time) that any writer worth 10¢ has written out of nothing much more than his own neuroses; and I have no doubt that this summer—prompted by the absence of whiskey (most of us drink too much), a set of tennis each day, and wife who will rout me out of my slothful, womb-like sleeping habits sometime before noon—I'll do that novelette somehow, cautious and fearful as it may turn out to be when it's finished. Incidentally, while I think of it, I'm flattered about your supposition about reading my book; I reread part of it for the first time again not long ago, and while I'm certainly not ashamed of lots of it, I can realize why quite a few of the critics took it to task, for much of it is dreadfully self-indulgent, and cluttered up with all these fears and cautions I have. Not that I'm going to start writing big, hopeful books for Harrison Smith, but there seems to me now to be far too much agonizing in it: Anyway, I shouldn't feel timid about reading it if I were you, who, as I said before, are one of the tiny number of contemporary writers who have a solid, unshakable, recognizable style. By the way, these lousy war novels still seem to be coming out, don't they? "Battle Cry." "By a man who loves the Marines." Jesus!*

Your problem of point-of-view confronts me, too. You're right about the 3d person and the world-view, yet I should think that after so effectively

* Leon Uris, *Battle Cry* (New York: Putnam, 1953).

achieving a welding of the two in Naked that it shouldn't be too rough on you now. I know too, though, how one's attitudes change. Me, I've never been successful with 1st person, mostly for the reasons you describe. One gets to love-scenes, for instance, and if the "I" happens to be the hero-narrator, as is often the case, the result is: "I took her in my arms and felt her responsive belly scalding mine; she looked at me with adoration and desire and with a tremendous whimper of love said 'Darling Bill,' and slid onto my pulsating pecker." Which seems self-centered. Anyway, Norm, I shouldn't worry about the "fundamental poverty of imagination" you assign to yourself; that's the kind of talk I indulge in. Keep at it, and let me hear how things are going. My address after the 10th will be c/o Hotel Palumbo, Ravello (Salerno) Italy. Best to you, and to all.

Bill

To Mac Hyman

August 15, 1953 Ravello, Italy

Dear Mac:

It certainly was good to hear from you again. Every now and then I'd get a word or two from Sigrid or Bob Loomis or someone about you, but the information was rather sketchy and so I'm mighty glad to hear from you first hand. Glad you got out of the USAF. For me, anything military is only about two yards removed from hell, and since, as you probably know, I was back in the Marines in '51, I can feel the relief you must have felt on getting out.

Externally, I am living the rich, full life, something like J.B. Duke in his later years. Rose and I have an 11th century palace which has been completely modernized, with tiled floors, chromium plated john, garden, private grove of lemon trees, and an incredible sort of panorama overlooking the area. It costs $100 a month and we have a full-time maid who slaves like a Cordele nigra and costs us about $25 a month. I have a car, a new English Austin heavily carapaced with birdshit, so we can drive down to the beach at Amalfi almost anytime we want. Internally, however, I am living a very different kind of life—often I think sort of like St. Sebastian when that 35th arrow was shot into him. The reason behind this is the same reason I can so easily sympathize with what you said in your letter—"not being able to break out of this goddamned whirlpool of living." The fact is—and I really mean it—that I often wonder whether it would not have been better to go unpublished than to be in the state I am now, which is a state of feeling that I've written all I can and that anything else I write will be the sheerest sort of manufactured crap, without meaning or conviction. Of course, I'm not recommending you to stay unpublished—and I know you won't—and I'm not trying to say that I wasn't crazy to be published when I wasn't published. I'm merely saying that I used to think (before I was published) that it was a pose, all that business about the tortures a person goes through trying to get something written after having had a successful first novel. As it stands, here I am: living the short happy life of Alfred Gwyne Vanderbilt, 2½ years since the last word of "Lie Down in Darkness" was written and with only one piece (the story in Discovery) written since then. Of course, I can rationalize by saying that of that time 7 months were spent in the Marines, when perhaps I could hardly be expected to write, and that, after all, a person's time in Europe should be spent in "education" and "discovery," but that's so much hooey. The fact of the matter is that I've doped off to a monumental degree and every day that goes by I'm getting older and older and with nothing done to show for it. My main flaw (and it seems to me to be a goddam big one) is a sort of total paralysis of will, and I envy those who can write and write and write, and I shudder when I think that time will no doubt find me an old, old man with one novel and a novelette to my credit.

All this probably doesn't interest you in the least, but what it narrows down to is this, if it'll give you any comfort—that is, if you need any comfort. What I mean is that I think that any writer who ever lived, who was any good at all, has had long long periods of precisely the same sort of strain and struggle that both you and I are going through; I only comfort myself (and God knows it seems like forlorn comfort at times) that it seems to be true that often such periods of doubt and thrashing around eventually produce the best work. They often eventually produce the best work because it is during such periods of struggle (when one is long unpublished or goes through long periods of tortured sterility) that a writer really suffers. A lot of crap has been written about suffering, and the value of it, and in about two seconds I'll shut up, but every now and then, even in the midst of my most dried-up, sterile depressions, I have a crazy confused moment of joy in the knowledge that anything good I ever did seemed at one time or another impossible of attaining, that it was a hard struggle in getting it out, that it seemed at times to be crushed under the weight of my doubts about it, but if it happened to be good at all it was because of the doubts, and perhaps a little suffering. End of quotation.

Well, now that I've deluded myself a little more, I'm free to tell you that no doubt Rose and I will be coming back to the U.S. sometime early this December. At first when I got over here I hated Europe with a passion, but now I've gotten to like it right well, and I can't say that I'm actually panting to get with the New York psychiatric set again. Funny thing, over here you never hear the words "psychotic," "trauma," "frustration," and this time I think I'm going to get as fed up as you with that city. But as much as I like Italy, I can't be an expatriate forever (I will have been over nearly two years) so I'll have to come back to the States and since most everyone I know is in N.Y. I'll probably settle down there, at least for a few months. Will you be up around there in the winter? If so, we with our healthy, manly, robust attitude toward life could probably together take some of the curse off all the horrible cocktail Freudian chit chat. I've not changed much, except I'm thinner and have three new suits. I've started in on another novelette, based on that naval prison I was at in N.Y., but don't know how far I'll go on it before coming back to the U.S. If it's anything like my present mood toward literature (real boredom, sometimes) it'll no doubt go down the drain, like everything else.

Give my best to Gwen and your folks, and let me hear from you. Hope you have luck with the novel and sell more copies than Jim Jones. So far as I know, I'll be here until around December 1st, so this will be my address.

All the best.
Bill

To Norman Mailer

August 25, 1953 Ravello, Italy

Dear Norman:

From time to time this summer I've thought of sending you picturesque postcards from this place, with select views of our "gorgeous panorama" (it is gorgeous, in spite of the advertising) but someone (Vance?) wrote that you had taken off so I held off until I got your address. It's good to hear that you're in Mexico, and I hope that by now you're finding it more "congenial," and I <u>certainly</u> hope that you're not degenerating—which you said you might do. Did you ever read Lowry's <u>Under the Volcano</u>, by the way? (There's a nice study of soul-sickness against a tropical background.) I say that it's good to hear that you're in Mexico only because if you're like me a change of scene—especially a change from the New York scene—is mighty therapeutic. Now that I've made this big tour of Europe I feel that I'll hardly even be able to stay rooted in one spot—especially an American spot—for any great length of time. That's the way I feel now anyway; and already I'm pretty much dreading having to go back to New York, which we plan to do early in December.

Yet I think there's something sick, too, in being what they call an "exile"—if not sick, then unnatural—and I say this because I think that anyone at all sensitively attuned to his surroundings (the "ah-tist") just can't jump feet first into an entirely new culture without suffering all sorts of traumas. Suffering, indeed, so much—from a sense of alienation and isolation and strangeness—that his opposite—that is a suave, bearded gent who becomes more French than the French, more Italian than the Italians—becomes, for me at least, an immediate object of suspicion, in his greasy and painless adaptability. Perhaps I'm just jealous of these other birds—for, after all, I find it hard to get along with strangers, "the people," even in the dear old U.S.A.—but I can't help but think that some sort of personal—not moral—integrity is lost when one immerses one's self so totally and swiftly into an alien way of life. I no doubt sound like one of those British Colonials you mentioned, and I don't mean to at all. Perhaps I only realize that in some subliminal way I'm really an "exile" at heart, and so I'm self-consciously withdrawn and [unknown] of from life over here only as a means of self-preservation. At any rate, it's something of a problem with me, and along these lines I certainly know what you mean by contrasts of wealth and poverty. I suspect that this part of Italy is not so poor as most of Mexico, but it's plenty poor nevertheless. We live in a fantastic sort of duplex apartment which is part of a made-over 11th century palace. Past our windows all day long go these terrible emaciated women—already in their twenties looking old and dried out—laboring ferociously under great piles of brush which they use to bed down the cattle. What we pay in rent for two months, which at $200 is pitifully cheap for what our accommodations are, is about what these girls are worth as work-horses for an entire year. What can you do? Give them your money? Write a novel titled "The Brush Bearers" (becomes a tremendous bestseller in the States, M-G-M contract etc, etc.)? No, frankly, in spite of the relative lack of certain tensions here in this palace, there are particular sprung-up European pretensions which I've acquired that will make me welcome in a way the new tensions of N.Y.C.

My book came out in France recently and the other day someone sent me a review from "L'Observateur," a line of which might interest you: "Ce qu'il nous montre vaut tout un mal américain: celui de la 'frustration': le mot qui revient aussi souvent chez Styron que chez Norman Mailer, Paul Bowles et quantité d'autres."* What interests me most about this is not so much the frustration angle but that our frustration should be considered in the same league with old Paul-baby's. But the French have a queer way of equating all things American; they have a terrible hate on now for Americans, partly justified I should certainly think, but really about 8/10 is pure deathly insecurity. They find it intolerable that along with our Coca-Colas and moneymaking movies and Chevrolets we should also be winning Nobel Prizes. Considering the chaos there as of this moment, it's hard not to dislike the French as much as they do us; but obviously something much deeper + tragic is at work, and maybe in another 50 years, if we're here, we'll judge them and ourselves in an entirely different light.

It was interesting to get an inside view of the Jones story. I remember meeting him that night (we went out with you and Clift to a bar) at Vance's and he did strike me as someone worth knowing better, but unfor-

* The review of the French edition of *Lie Down in Darkness—Un lit de ténèbres* (Éditions Mondiales, 1953): "For he shows us above all an American evil: that of 'frustration': a word which recurs as often in Styron as in Norman Mailer, Paul Bowles and many others."

tunately my impressions of that night remain febrile and somewhat clouded by alcohol.* I'm glad you like him so well, because (and I don't mean this facetiously) his, quote, mercurial career so far impresses me as one which, unless it keeps roaring forever mercurially forward, will be mighty unfortunate, and he'll need a pile of cushioning well-wishers and friends. I don't mean this meanly at all, because there was enough in his book which excited me and which I so honestly admired that I would like to see him repeat over and over again and do better.

As for my literary struggles, I've finally cracked—just barely cracked—the beginnings of a novella or short novel or something, and I'm at least far enough out of the darkness so that I'm regaining my appetite. I have begun to love my predilection for psychosomatic colds, and am no longer dangerously suicidal. For some reason until just recently I had no idea of the despair of a life of creation; maybe it means I'm a real live artist. Anyway, it's true for me that writing and writing is the only way to ward off the mental—what they call in Virginia—hootenanies, and a million fears. It's a negative way of doing things, but maybe a lot of so-called art is simply the positive product of interior and negative horrors. Meantime, I hope that novel is roaring on golden wings. Remember Flaubert—"talent is a long patience"—if you and I and the rest could get a hammer-lock on patience I think we'd be a lot better off.† Anyway, best to you and Adele.‡ Will you be in N.Y. this winter? Write me here; we'll be here until around December 1st.

As ever,

Bill

* Styron met James Jones and the actor Montgomery Clift at a party in New York given by Vance Bourjaily. Clift's encounter with Jim Jones at that party led to one of the actor's signature roles, as Prewitt in the film of Jones's *From Here to Eternity*.

† Gustave Flaubert (1821–80): "Talent is a long patience, and originality an effort of will and intense observation."

‡ Adele Morales was Norman Mailer's second wife. Their relationship ended after Mailer stabbed her with a penknife at a party. She wrote a memoir about the relationship, *The Last Party: Scenes from My Life with Norman Mailer* (New York: Barricade, 1997).

To George Plimpton

September 18, 1953 Ravello, Italy

Dear George:

Last night I did something which I only do once or twice in a generation: I stayed up all night with a bottle of Schenley's and watched the dawn. That sort of thing is a perverse, masochistic business and at around 9 A.M. I was entertaining the idea of writing two or three novels before I went to bed, but oblivion closed in an hour later, and I just woke up. It is now almost sunset. This is mainly by way of saying that if this letter doesn't have a Chesterfieldian elegance + grace you will at least have been apprised of the reason.

My main reason for writing this letter is one-fold, I have been forced down certain channels of contemplation by a recent communiqué from John ("The Second Happiest Day") Phillips, to use current journalese. Primarily, I was interested in his remarks about a Hemingway issue of PR; and I think at this point and without further ado I can shoulder my burden as advisory editor of the snappiest little mag on the Rive Gauche and say that I think it's a great idea. Peter and THG apparently (according to Marquand) are not so enthusiastic about the proposition; as for me I think that if you really have enough interesting, fresh material in the offing (it must be interesting, fresh, original, and there must be quite a bit of it) then it might be one of the literary coups of all time. As Marquand said, print the word Hemingway in neon all over each page and both covers. Anything goes. I must admit that such an issue would slightly compromise my Ringing Assertion in the first preface about printing new talent; but this thing, if it's at all as good as Marquand makes out, sounds too good to be missed and will put PR in the same league with transition, Broom, Time, Fortune, and other top-notchers. Anyway, you have my full support if that means anything, and I hope you'll get snapping soon and also let me know how things develop.

Rose and I are having a lovely time down here with our Gorgeous Panorama, rosé wine, flies and other items. We extend to you a cordial invitation to join us anytime this autumn; as you may have heard from Peter, Ravello really is delicious and it would be a great pleasure to have you here if you can manage a short vacation (you can fly from Paris to Naples). Meanwhile I'm writing a long novelette which, when it's finished, should have some of the pace of Death in Venice and a little of The Red Badge of Courage surface savvy. Thanks, incidentally, for the nice remarks in the U.S. Lives PR. It renews my faith in American literature. Also, thank Mr. Mathieu, if you see him, for sending me the issue. Let me hear from you when you get the chance.

Best—
Bill

P.S. The No. 3 PR is easily the best yet. Like movies, it seems to be getting better and better.

To John P. Marquand, Jr.

November 11, 1953 Ravello, Italy

Dear old Jack baby:

I am long overdue answering your last letter from Paris, which was enjoyed and appreciated by Rose and me, but I hope you will realize that the torpor is due to that acedia, that sin of sloth which was the bane and affliction of the medieval monks, and which has from time to time seized all great artists, especially Baudelaire (this is some bullshit I picked up from a recent issue of the Partisan Review, which Rose's mother providentially airmailed to me, and which has allowed my great prose efforts to come to a screeching halt). Anyway, a recent letter from the Matthiessens has informed me that you've taken up residence on their end of the island, which confuses me about your present address and your present activities. I hope you haven't altogether deserted the City, because Rose and I are coming there soon and hope to see your bright-eyed, puffy, dissolute face again.

We are arriving on the Independence on Dec. 22d and there has been some loose talk among ourselves and the Matthiessens about an extravagant dinner that night at Pavillon or Voisin or some other crazy place. I hope of all things that you've been apprised of this scheme, because you're expected to be on hand. Anyway, you can bet your boots that, although anticipating seeing all those friendly faces again, I am beginning to get distinct nervous twitches about coming back, and in fact am still unable to dig up any reasons as to why I'm coming back, unless it's to re-establish my roots or some such crap like that that writers are supposed to do. The Italians have gone temporarily insane and are marching about in mobs smashing Austins and other English cars during this Trieste crisis; but I still love Italy, our wonderful house here still costs only $60 a month, fall + winter, and most of the time I am utterly unable to figure out a reason for returning, unless it's to get psychoanalyzed. As to your question, where are we going to live in New York, since mainly Rose has never spent any time in New York, except for brief visits, and it's something that everyone should do for at least one winter and it will be fun for me to show her around all the smoky joints and more fun for her. Meanwhile, we are holding on to this place, and no doubt we'll beat a rapid retreat here next summer, + expect you for a prolonged visit.

My work is fitful. I'm writing a novelette and a short story simultaneously, which sounds good and creative, but my enthusiasm for both of the things waxes and wanes so erratically that they don't proceed very fast. I wrote an article on the European radio for Harper's, which they reluctantly accepted and with the proviso that they be allowed to cut it down by half and rewrite it completely. This is not good for the ego, nor for the bank account, since they're paying only $150, but as Irwin once said, no magazine is happy unless they can remove the gonads from a writer's work. Sometimes I feel that I should go into the advertising business, so that my talent for pace and surface savvy may be experienced untrammeled. Tell Guinzburg if you see him that I thank him for sending me Augie March and that I think this Bellow fellow could stand a bit more surface savvy. It's been a long time since a book has bored me so, though Peter wrote me that it was the greatest thing since Crime and Punishment, and so maybe I've just lost all my literary feeling. Incidentally, when you see the Matthiessens next, tell them that I'll be writing them soon, so that we can work out places for our pre-Xmas get-together well in advance.

I hope that by now you've found your daemon. Max Geismar tried to send me one by parcel post, but I told him mine was hanging around and showed up now and then.* An American, Baltimore fellow, and his wife have moved into the big apartment above us. He has a wonderful electric

* Styron refers to "daemon" in the Aristotelian sense (from the *Eudemian Ethics*): a spiritual guide or muse.

train which I play with and Rose spends most of each day making paper dolls for their little girl. So you can see how my literary desires have succumbed completely to an infantile regression. Hope we can straighten our common ailments out by talking them over over a beer in some low Village dive.

Irwin and Marian are, I think, still in St. Jean but I have not heard from them in some time. I got a note from Annie Brierre, my Nouvelles Littéraires friend in Paris, who admires your book immensely and said you had given her an interview for her sheet. Have you seen it? Also heard from George Plimpton, who is hot for the Hemingway issue, as am I, in spite of all my early proclamations. I'm a two-faced, commercial bastard and am on the verge of selling out to Selznick. Looking forward to seeing you, as is Rose.

Bill

To Norman Mailer

November 15, 1953 Ravello, Italy

Dear Norman:

I don't know why it is, but you could write to me until you were blue in the face, describing in monstrous, frightening detail the ordeal of being in New York again after a period abroad, and it still wouldn't sink in. As for me, I sense exactly the feelings you described to me in your last letter—the depression, the cocktail parties, the yak yak yak, and all the rest—and though I know I'll be similarly afflicted after precisely 10 days in N.Y.C. I nonetheless, like you did in Mexico, feel that I have to get back. So I'm packing my bags, my trophies and medals and souvenirs, and am due to arrive in the North River on December 22nd. God alone knows why. It's cheap here, and beautiful, and I'm leading the good contented life. My writing, while it isn't of the quality to make the shade of Tolstoy bite his nails in envy, is nevertheless proceeding apace, and I should be satisfied. But no. That old compulsion takes me back to soot and subways and pale rheumy faces, psychoanalytic chatter and hangovers and discontent, indigestion and "literary competition." I can see it all coming with wonderful clarity and yet I'm coming, and if you can tell me why I'll give you a gold-plated typewriter for Xmas. I suppose, though, that in the end it's just that simple fact that New York, of all places on earth, is the most totally fascinating and "complete," and with the place, you've got to come back and get booster shots periodically, even if it hurts. That, coupled with the plain truth that one—at least I—can't remain expatriate forever. Then, too, in spite of everything, in spite of my immense love for this country, being here too long gets finally to be like eating 20 chocolate sundaes in a row; it begins to cloy, and a drowsy stillness numbs my senses, and I want to get shut of Italy completely for a while, at least—and get back to a place riotous with 100% Anglo-Saxon neurotic symptoms and the high excitement of puritanical moral conflict.* Where the traffic is regulated, the milk is tested for TB, and all those amenities which make this life worthwhile.

One thing honestly I'll never regret leaving though, is the American Academy—a place which regrettably occupied more of my time than it should have; an archaeologist's haven, full of gravediggers and bone-pickers and the morbid students of dead alphabets, and a place which a writer should avoid at any cost.

I had another letter the other day from Lew Allen; I agree with you—he's one fine boy.† He's so damned honest and self-effacing and genuine. I don't know if he can write or not but I certainly wish him well. I don't know what the precise connection is, but when I think of a guy like him and then of that talentless, self-promoting, spineless slob you mentioned, Gore Vidal, I want to go on a book-burning pogrom. I haven't read that piece in New World Writing yet, but I can imagine; I wouldn't think, however, that it's very important in the scheme of things.

I'm really very glad that Calder has made such a splash on Broadway. I would have sent him congratulations and a request for two seats on the aisle except that my last letter to him of many months ago in which I mentioned the money he owed me was so pointedly ignored that I felt

* Styron is loosely paraphrasing Keats's "Ode to a Nightingale": "a drowsy numbness pains / My sense, as though of hemlock I had drunk."

† Lewis M. Allen (1922–2003), a playwright and producer who produced *Annie* on Broadway with Mike Nichols. Styron and Allen met as two Virginians in New York and became very close friends. Allen married Jay Presson, a very successful screenwriter, who happened to be the first person to hold Styron's first daughter, Susanna.

another letter would embarrass both of us. According to Lew, Calder's touched everybody in N.Y. for money except Barney Baruch,[*] only it's too bad that with Calder his perpetual debts have the effect of estranging him with some people. Lew says that without these debts he wouldn't be the writer he is, though that's a statement which may be taken in two distinct opposite ways. Anyway, I wish him the best, including a Mercedes-Benz, and if you see him I wish you'd congratulate him for me, as a fellow creditor.

Speaking of Broadway, have you ever had the notion of writing a play? I know that when Lillian Hellman was in Rome (she came to our wedding reception) she said that she had worked for a while on a dramatization of Naked, but I wonder if you yourself have thought of the idea.[†] There's a saying that prose writers are notoriously bad playwrights, but there's certainly no rule, and I'd certainly love to try my hand at the thing. My trouble, though, is that I know hardly anything about the theatre or the art of playwriting and I wouldn't even know how to start. What I'd like to do at first would be to collaborate with someone who knew some of the fundamentals, and then maybe go it alone afterwards for other plays. Or does collaboration bisect one's "unity"—one's vanity? Anyway, the whole thing interests me. I've been reading Ibsen for the first time, and Shakespeare again—and one of my projects when I get back this winter is to see as many plays as possible.[‡]

I hope to see you around Christmas time, when I hope you'll have that first draft polished off. Rose and I will probably stay in N.Y. for two or three days when we first get back and then go to Baltimore and Virginia for a week or so and come back around New Year's. Do you have a telephone number? If so, I'll give you a ring; if not, I'll probably see you at Vance's—I think I remember him writing something about a party Christmas Eve, which sounds like as good a place as any to get on the greased slide.

* Bernard Baruch (1870–1965), enormously successful financier who advised Presidents Woodrow Wilson and Franklin D. Roosevelt.

† Lillian Hellman (1905–84) was an author of numerous plays and screenplays, and was nominated for an Academy Award for *The Little Foxes* (1941).

‡ Rose Styron on January 31, 2011: "It's interesting that he said this, because he hated the theater."

Anyway, I'm looking forward to seeing you on my return to purgatory, as is Rose who, incidentally, bought a copy of the Weybright edition of Naked in Rome and read it a few weeks ago and wants me to convey to you the fact that she thinks it's the very best since the war, and even better than that, Gore Vidal notwithstanding.

All the best,
Bill

To George Plimpton

December 1, 1953 Ravello, Italy

Dear George:

Herewith the interview, revised and expanded.* I think that in the future it might be a good idea for you to get a tape-recorder for these darn things, because it's a bitch of a job for the interviewee to edit his own words. Now you will note that I did not completely eliminate all the first part; as a matter of fact I retained the bulk of it, but made quite a few changes and emendations. I think it's better now, certainly printable. Besides all the additions, you will notice I made a few eliminations. I cut out a few of the cuss-words, which were all too abundant. I cut out the cracks against little Truman and Anthony West, who God knows deserves them, but they seemed a little in poor taste.† I also tempered my criticism of Faulkner. I have tried to keep the tone impersonal and conversational throughout, and I think that I've succeeded.

You will notice, too, that I've taken your suggestion and have added quite a bit toward the end. I hope you will find the questions—some of which are yours—and answers suitable; at least the piece is considerably lengthened, and I've gotten off my chest a few things I've wanted to say.

* This is the interview of Styron by Peter Matthiessen and George Plimpton that would appear in *The Paris Review* 5 (Spring 1954), later republished in Malcolm Cowley, ed., *Writers at Work: The Paris Review Interviews* (New York: Viking, 1958).

† Truman Capote and Anthony West. West (1914–87) was a British author best known for the biography of his father, *H. G. Wells: Aspects of a Life* (New York: Random House, 1984).

One important thing is that I think you must somehow invent a little atmosphere to surround the piece. It's mighty bare without any stage directions, and I think if you place the thing right where the original interview started, in the Café Select, or some equivalent, it will provide a suitably bibulous background.

You are of course at liberty to edit any of this, by excision, but I hope you won't find it necessary to put new words in my mouth, important ones, anyway. I am enclosing a sheet of MS from Long March, I really want you to return it, though, when you're finished with it, to the New York address which I'll give below. I'm also enclosing a pretty photo for Billy. Please tell him to make my hair a little flatter on top and to give me a tie. I look like a muskrat trader.

I wish you'd acknowledge this by the quickest means possible; fast airmail should do it. The reason is I'm packing up my traps and lines and setting sail with Rose on Dec. 13th from Naples, back to the land of Borden's milk and Arrow shirts. Why I still don't know—I'll probably be in Paris again by March—but the spaghetti is beginning to pall, much as I love it here, and Italy is getting chilly. Marquand and the Matthiessens, however, have promised to be on the dock to ease our arrival, to take us to Voisin, and to help us with the native tongue. My address in New York, since we'll probably be sleeping under the New York Central tracks, is c/o my agent, Elizabeth McKee, 30 E. 60th.

Best regards to Billy and Jane, and hope to hear from you about this soon.

All the best,
Bill

P.S. I changed the question "Do you feel yourself in competition with other writers?" to "Do you feel yourself to be, etc." Since the first question is fairly pornographic.

The Styrons left Naples for New York on December 22, 1953.

To Robert and Claire White

March 15, 1954 231 East 76th Street, New York, NY

Caro Roberto + Clara Bianco,

It was very fine to hear from you all, and your letter somehow stirred me out of my lethargy; this is the second letter of any kind that I've written to anyone since our return to the land of the free and the home of the brave. We were both sad and happy to hear about your staying over for another year—sad because we won't be seeing you this summer, but of course very happy that the gods looked down and shelled out the dough for another year of sunny profit on the Gianicolo. Actually, maybe we'll see you sooner than you imagine, for we are already fed up enough with the U.S.A. to be planning to come to Italy again in the spring of '55 and live for the rest of our natural born lives in Ravello. Ravello—which we saw in that movie last night—"Beat the Devil," which Truman wrote and we saw being filmed down there; it's a dreadful movie, really, but we wouldn't have missed it for anything, because even though they completely ignore most of the scenery there are a lot of shots of the crotille of the Congalone where we lived, and old Humphrey Bogart coming down the stairs and smooching with Jennifer Jones in front of our door and there was even a shot of Saverio—the portiere of the Palumbo, whom we liked so much—lugging one of Bogart's suitcases. God, we got homesick.

Actually, we don't have it too bad, for benighted New Yorkers. We have a nice apartment on 76th Street, which we've painted up pretty, and have hung Bobby's "Vespa" sketch on one wall, and Anne Wigglesworth's nude on another wall. It makes quite an impression on the visitors. I have bought the largest hi-fidelity record player in New York and piles of records and so we have music and whiskey all the time at night and get weepy and sentimental listening to Mozart and looking at Bobby's Vespa and wish the hell we were back in Italy where we belong. Incidentally, I am not in bed with funny books and peanut butter sandwiches, though I'll have to admit that when I got off the Independence I was so nervous and upset that I was in bed for 1 day with what my fine doctor diagnosed as post-Ravello despondency. The symptoms were watering eyes, heart palpitation and a desire to jump out of the window. I'm now healthy again, though, and resigned to my destiny and all the symptoms have disappeared—except for the same thing Bobby has, buzzing in the ears, which my doctor informed me is harmless, being generally an affliction of sculptors and writers and other jittery nuts. He says it almost never means anything like a brain tumor, though of course that's what I was sure I had.

I have begun Novel No. 2, which will be laid in Ravello and Rome mainly, with maybe a side-glimpse at Paris and New York.* It's going to be about two young guys who were friends—a good guy and a perfect bastard, and it ends up with the good guy pushing the perfect bastard off the drop at the Villa Cimbrone. Also the bastard ropes one of the local girls in Scala (the girl whom the guy who is good is in love with). It is very complicated and very tragic and I will work on it for probably ten years and it will sell exactly 726 copies. We know a girl in this same apartment building, upstairs, and that's where I do my writing, because she works during the day. That's where I'm writing this. I have a wonderful view of a clothesline and a row of garbage cans, and I have written so far on the novel about 4,000 words, all crap.

Irwin Shaw was over here from Switzerland just recently to collect $100,000 for the movie rights to "The Young Lions" and we gave a party for him in our apartment. The Matthiessens came, and all of Irwin's pals—who are a shady bunch and more or less connected with the radio or TV or movies. There were a lot of freeloaders, too—we invited 20 and in came 55 and I bought 10 bottles of Scotch. Charles Addams came—the cartoon man in The New Yorker—and he poured salt in people's drinks. Very funny. I think I'll become a Trappist.

Peter and Patsy have a nice house in East Hampton, which we visited a weekend ago. Peter's book is coming out in two weeks and he's sort of disgruntled because Harper's isn't plugging the book, which is true. Marquand wanders fitfully about, searching for his daemon. Guinzburg is going with a beautiful girl named Francine du Plessy, whose father owns Vogue, but I don't think he's making out too well, since apparently she's the girl who is destined to wed Blair Fuller when he comes back from Ubangi-land.† We saw Bernard Perlin the other night between the acts at

* *Set This House on Fire,* which Styron would complete in 1959.

† Francine du Plessix (b. 1930) is a Pulitzer Prize–nominated writer and literary critic best known for her essays in *The New Yorker.* She married the painter Cleve Gray (1918–2004) in 1957.

a play; he was with some curious-looking people, who appeared sexually unhinged, but he reports that all is well with him.

The next issue of The Paris Review is going to feature 30 pages of funny drawings, made in the guest books of Paris restaurants, by Picasso, Matisse, Dufy, Braque, Utrillo and practically anyone you can think of. There's a very good chance that Life magaine will use part of the piece, which would be great for the Review. I hope you see it.

Rest content that you are where you are rather than in the land of Chlorophyll and Odo-ro-no. We miss you all very much and mourn each day that we are not all together drinking chianti again. But perhaps that time will come sooner than we think. Meanwhile keep us informed, give our love to Fran and Anne (tell them we'll write), to Sebastiano, Steph and Christian, and be sure to brush your teeth with Gleem, contains GL-70, the antienzyme factor.

Love + XXXXXXXX Bill

To William Blackburn

June 17, 1954 231 East 76th Street, New York, NY

Dear Doctor:

I seem to have a writer's block to end all writer's blocks and as a result I have found it nearly as difficult—if not more so—to write a letter as to write rich, beautiful fiction. Hence my long absence from the post.

I have wondered a number of times since I last saw you here in N.Y. just how Duke and Durms were treating you after the rich delights of Europe. Like me I suspect you have found much to be desired in the American landscape. Outside of good old Borden's milk and a rapport with the language, I have rediscovered nothing in Amurka that would not send me back hopping straight to the bosom of the Amalfi coast.

Rose and I are ensconced in a dismally modern apartment opposite a noisy excavation project that looks like Warsaw in 1945. The sole advantage of the building is that in it, on a top floor, lives a friend whose apartment I use to work in during the day. It is quiet and cooler, but so far during this long, long season it has produced nothing in the way of prose that will be remembered in future centuries. I am fairly well along into a new novel, but the thing is weak, halting, and insipid—a bit like the stuff Michael Arlen used to write. It has a sort of archness of tone and a perversity of emotion and a paucity of intellect that should make it sell well in places like Scarsdale and Webster Groves, Mo., among the Clay Felker set. Incidentally, had you heard that the ex–Mrs. Felker, nee Leslie Blatt, has set up housekeeping with the spokesman of the Lost Generation No. 2, Mr. John W. Aldridge, who left wife and four children in Vermont for her tarnished embraces? It shows you can't keep a good girl down, from Duke.

I would try to keep you abreast of local happenings, but I suspect that you've gotten most of it from Alex, who Loomis told me has gone south for the summer, or part of it. Rose and I plan to stay in town through June and July—why I don't know, except to allow me if possible to break the back of this new book, as the saying goes—and then I guess we'll move for a month or so out to the end of Long Island, for the waters. I pine for Ravello each day but I suspect that it will be sometime before we become expatriate again.

Hope all goes well with you and that you're bearing up under the Durham summer. Or are you at the beach now? Best to Brice and cheers from both of us.

As ever Bill

P.S. There's a chance we might drive down to Florida in August or Sept., and if so will plan on a stop in Durham.

To Norman Mailer

July 19, 1954 231 East 76th Street, New York, NY

Dear Norman:

First, let me explain that the uncommon delay in my correspondence results not out of any reluctance to write you about "The Deer Park," but simply from a neurotic procrastination coupled with an unwillingness to spend a scanty 15 minutes or so writing you a "Hiya, how's everything in Mexico" note, when what I really want to do is send you something lengthy, thought-out and considered—like what I hope this will be.

I'll try, then, to dig in on the book without further ado. I read it a couple of days after you left and although it's of course not quite so fresh in my mind as it was then, I took quite a few notes on it and have done considerable pondering in the meanwhile. First of all, I think it's a fine, big book in the sense that it's a major attempt to re-create a distinct milieu—an important one and one deeply representative of all the shabby materialism and corruption which are, after all, the real roots of our national existence. As a picture of this milieu, the book seems to me to be both honest and brilliant. It is also a depressing book, really depressing, in its manifest candor, and I'm afraid there aren't going to be many people who will like it. The chapter toward the end, for instance, which reveals Teppis in all his gruesome horror is, I'm convinced, the most brilliantly scathing assault on a Hollywood demi-God that has yet been written; the blow-job is just right, the perfect symbolic admixture of impotence and cruelty.* But it is just this sort of unrelenting honesty, as you must know, that is going to make the critics howl. The sex throughout the book is painful—painful as sex can only be when it has become a meaningless sensation. It is that way I know that you meant it, and it gives a tone to the book of unalleviated and leaden anxiety. Anxiety runs through the book like a dark river—the true torturous anxiety—and gives to the book this deep sense of depression, which is totally divorced from purely literary concerns. This I think the critics are going to miss—they're going to flay you alive for indulging yourself in sensations when in fact it is the piling up of sensation after meaningless sensation, of lovelessness and debauchery, which gives such a meaning to the novel as a whole. Truly, modern life is golden-filled with golden girls like Lulu Meyers in resplendent Jaguars—but set in a wasteland of endless corruption and despair. A real Desert d'Or. But you're going to be criticized for not being "gayer," lighter about it.

Outside of Teppis (who really, I suppose, figures in a relatively minor role) your best character is Eitel. His final corruption is complete, and you portray his finish with power and a great deal of sympathy. Even he is depressing though, for since he is the only really "nice" character in the book one hopes desperately for his triumph and is deeply depressed by his

* These lines, appearing on page 277 of the Rinehart proofs sent to Styron, are reproduced at the end of "Fourth Advertisement for Myself: The Last Draft of The Deer Park," in Norman Mailer, *Advertisements for Myself* (New York: G. P. Putnam's Sons, 1959).

finale. It really is an appalling picture you paint, appalling and truthful, and the book, I suppose, is so unpleasant—and so fascinating—to read, because the truth is so appalling. It is the apotheosis of total vacuum. Yet out of that vacuum I wouldn't doubt but that you've created the most piercing study of Hollywood that's been written. I only personally wish I "liked" the book more, that for all of these glittering creatures which you've skewered with such real art and insight I felt more heartbreak.

Some minor things: The party at the beginning is wonderful—the dialogue there is as good as any I know. Sergius doesn't quite come off as a character (as someone else—I think Loomis—pointed out) and I wonder whether really that's at all important, and whether that should worry you, if it does at all. It seems to me that first person narrators rarely if ever come off, and perhaps it's better that they don't but remain (like Nick Carraway in The Great Gatsby) shadowy and unobtrusively in the background, even though they participate in some of the action. At any rate although Sergius did seem elusive to me, I reflected while reading that it didn't seem to bother me much—perhaps because I came to accept him pretty much merely as a window through which to observe Eitel and Lulu and the rest. You worked some sort of magic, too, in the transitions, so that I found that I accepted motivations and actions even when Sergius wasn't on hand to observe them. The curious thing about first-rate writers is that they can ignore the iron-clad conventions and rules and get by with it.

Here, then, is my final pompous verdict: you've written a book like sour wine, a lethal draught bitter and unlikable, but one which was written with a fine and growing art, and about which I think you can feel proud. It doesn't have the fire of "Naked" but I think has primer and maturer insights. It is not an appealing book, but neither does it compromise, and for that alone you should be awarded a medal. If lacking the large universe of "Naked," it doesn't have "Naked"'s impact, it is also a book which burns with a different, somehow keener light. I don't like the book, but I admire the hell out of it, and I suppose that's all I have to say for the moment—or until I can talk to you face to face. What is really important is that the book is a solid one, with a deep sense of morality.

So I haven't written you all this before because I seem to finally have become gripped by the creeping paralysis which has taken hold of me within the past year or so, and which has extended even to letter-writing. My mornings (12 noon +) are agony, and the daily Angst is hell. I look forward each day with the same hopeless ardor that a monk must envision paradise to the time when I'm free of this thing that constricts me, to the time when I'm "liberated" enough to be able to sit down and write 25 consecutive words without fear and trembling. It must be my liver, though it might be the heat—which has been terrible—and withal, no doubt, booze is heavily to blame. Anyway, it can't last too much longer, for I'll simply have to throw it all up and become a druggist or something. One thing, Rose is going to have a baby (I hope it's a baby) next March and that might have the quality of snapping me out of my neurotic antics. It is strange, too, how on the weekends, when we go to see people in L.I. or in Conn., a sheer euphoria takes hold of me. I'm self-analytical enough to realize that my murderous anxiety mornings here in the city is because I'm faced with the ridiculous responsibility of creating a masterpiece, whereas the weekends have me gaily unburdened.

After you left, Maloney went temporarily off his rocker, drunkenly attempted suicide with his seconal, and ended up for a week in Bellevue.* He's all right now, but is going to lose his job, and God knows where he'll eventually end up—the Bowery, probably. We are all by now sorely tempted to go on and let him slide down to limbo. We had supper with Larry and Barbara last night—a pleasant time. I read his novel finally; it's really got some good things in it, though awfully spotty.

Say Hello to Lew Allen for me, will you? I owe him a letter from way back. His matador girlfriend got a lot of space recently in the N.Y. paper.

Ars longa. I think we perhaps flagellate ourselves too much. I hope my little critique made some sense to you; at any rate, believe me when I say that everything I said was as honest as I know how. Rose sends her love to both of you and requests that at one time or another you pick an orchid for auld lang syne. Catch me up on everything when you get time.

As ever, Bill

* Bellevue was at the time a psychiatric hospital.

To Norman Mailer

September 28, 1954 [Roxbury, CT]*

Dear Norm

I am writing this from Roxbury, Conn., where Rose and I have set up housekeeping for the past couple of weeks in my agent's house while she is in California.† It has been a fairly depressing time, since I started out with high hopes of getting a lot of work done, only to come down with bronchitis, which necessitated my taking aureomycin, which in turn acts violently and horribly upon the system, and seems to reduce the "liver functioning" to nil. At any rate, I've recovered somewhat by now, and it might interest you to know that we have bought a big house near-by, a real New England dwelling with an orchard and 11 acres and a dammed-up spring which makes a swimming pool.‡ I've been alternately elated and appalled by this place, the hideous responsibilities it presents, but having spent a footless and transient existence so far I am hoping that the place will give me some mild sense of rootedness and permanence. It's 2½ hours from New York, distant enough to give a feeling of isolation and to be removed from the dreary station-wagon community belt, but close enough so that the delights, such as they are, of Manhattan are not too difficult of access. We plan to move in sometime in November or December, and we are hoping that you and Adele and your daughter will favor us with many a weekend; I think you might like the joint.

Since you heard from me I have finally come to the point where I think I can hazard the statement that my next novel is under way. I never thought that a project could be so hellishly difficult or seem to stretch out so aimlessly and vainly toward the farthest limits of the future, but I am embarked, at least, and can begin to hold . . . I remember your once asking me if it was to be a "major effort"; I don't know what I said in reply, only now I'm beginning to realize that it is a major effort—major

* Styron wrote his New York address, 231 East 76th Street, New York, NY, because they had not yet moved in to Rucum Road.

† Elizabeth McKee had a house in Litchfield County.

‡ Friends eventually dubbed the house Styron's Acres, and Styron lived there until his death, in 2006. Rose Styron sold the property in 2011.

in the sense that it has become impossible for me to write anything without making it a supreme try at a supreme expression. I don't want to sound pretentious; it's only that I'm so unprolific, frightened, and paralyzed most of the time that, once I do start writing, I feel that I owe it to myself to give it my all. The technical problems of this one are not minimized, or enhanced either, by the fact that it's written in the first person, which, as you once mentioned, rather severely limits what you can do and makes it hard to end up with that quality of richness which you get in the third-person, omniscient narrative. But this one "feels" like a first-person story, and I'm following my instincts. And, incidentally, I took great heart from your encouragement, which reminded me to struggle along while I've got "lead in me pencil." I think probably the saddest thing in life is to reach a certain age and look back and think of all the wasted, ruined time.

I got a letter from Vance two or three weeks ago, asking me if I would read his novel.* I sent him back a note saying I would, but heard nothing after that. Has Vance gone coo-coo? I think your remarks about him were most apt—and also about Tina, who seems to wear better with time. I think Vance's main trouble, which you described as "gloating over his petty triumphs," is simply a sort of dreadful self-centeredness which severely restricts his outlooks and intercourse with others, and which might be mildly tolerable if he were at all talented, but which in his daze makes him only seem pompous and a bit ridiculous. I suppose he's too old to be put wise.

I saw in the Times that "Naked" is being made into a movie.† I certainly hope it's a good one, and I hope you'll take me to the premiere so that I can wear my tux and ride in a Cadillac . . . also that "Rebel Without A Cause" was bought by Warners and is coming out next year? Rose and I were out at East Hampton in August and on the way back stopped in to see the Lindners at Peconic.‡ We had a fine time except for the presence of

* Vance Bourjaily, *The Violated* (New York: Dial, 1958).

† "Gregory Acquires 'Naked and Dead,'" *The New York Times,* August 20, 1954.

‡ Robert Lindner, *Rebel Without a Cause: The Hypnoanalysis of a Criminal Psychopath* (New York: Grune and Stratton, 1944) was the source of the film's title but none of its content. Peconic is a town on the North Shore of Long Island.

a horrible person named Chandler Brossard, of whom Bob, so he says, is one of the three friends Chandler has left in the U.S.A.*

Parts of The Deer Park still keep coming back to me. It's amazing how solid a book it is, in the sense that its effect hangs on, even if you don't particularly want it to. I think this is because there is in the book an unremitting determination to be truthful, and that beautifully distinguishes it from most of the novels which are coming out these days, the writers of which have become so bewilderingly entangled in the dishonesty and million-dollar-hokum of contemporary American life that they've lost their point of view entirely, so that their slickly cynical distortions are accepted as realism and truth. Most every form of expression in America is now keenly attuned to the second-rate, if not third-rate (Michener, Rodgers + Hammerstein, "Mr. Roberts," "Teahouse of the August Moon," "Battle Cry," Dr. Norman Vincent Peale, etc.) and God Knows how we will find our way out of the wilderness.† Mediocrity which succeeds is the norm and, as Louis Kronenberger says, "personality" replaces "character."‡ Let us hope that posterity, at least, will redeem us.

Rose and I are looking forward to your return in the cold New York autumn, and send our fondest to you and Adele. Please give my best to Lew Allen and our love to all the brave bulls. And also let us know when you expect to arrive.

As ever,
Bill

* Chandler Brossard (1922–93), prolific journalist and writer whose first novel, *Who Walk in Darkness* (New York: James Laughlin, 1952), documented life in 1940s Greenwich Village.

† James A. Michener's first blockbuster, *Tales of the South Pacific* (New York: Macmillan, 1947), won a Pulitzer and was turned into the Rodgers and Hammerstein musical *South Pacific,* which won ten Tony awards and a Pulitzer. *Mr. Roberts* was a comic production starring Henry Fonda, who appeared in the Broadway role and the film. *The Teahouse of the August Moon* was another comedy, appearing on Broadway in 1952 and as a film in 1956 starring Marlon Brando. Leon Uris's *Battle Cry* was made into a film in 1955 starring Van Heflin and Raymond Massey. Norman Vincent Peale (1898–1993) was a Protestant minister and radio personality. He is best known for his book *The Power of Positive Thinking* (New York: Prentice-Hall, 1952), which spent 186 weeks on the *New York Times* best seller list.

‡ Louis Kronenberger (1904–80), author of *Company Manners: A Cultural Inquiry into American Life* (New York: Bobbs-Merrill, 1954).

The Styrons purchased their farmhouse and eleven acres in Roxbury, Connecticut, in October 1954.

To Mac Hyman

February 2, 1955 Roxbury, CT

Dear Mac:

Deep congratulations on coming through on siring a man-child. I knew you could do it if you worked at it long enough. This way you'll be able to keep some of the wealth in the family, instead of seeing it go to some adventurer who one day will be cruising after the girls. Tell Gwen I'm right proud of her, too. As for Rose, the new recruit for the Young Communist League hasn't yet arrived, but we expect it within 3 or 4 weeks. I hope it's a girl, because I hear (whether rightly or wrongly) that they're a lot less fuss and bother. Anyway, with a girl I won't have to take her camping or teach her to build fires or any of that sort of rugged stuff.

I think I know what you mean about pulling up stakes and moving to new ground. Although we have a very fine place up here in Conn., it's already making me uneasy, and I have a feeling that before too long the size of the place, and all the possessions that go along with it, will be giving me a pain in the ass. There's a lot to be said about marital bliss, but there's no doubt that it also clutters up life a lot. With all the worldly goods we seem to acquire every day I sometimes get the feeling of a man walking around in 30 lb diver's shoes. But I guess that's man's fate on earth, and there's not a hell of a lot that can be done, except possibly write about it and even that isn't a big consolation.

I'm glad your oil well is still booming. Incidentally I know Ed Trzcinski, the Stalag 17 man; I met him in Rome, a very nice guy, and I think he'll do well by the play.* As for getting sort of fed up with all the post-publishing crap and talk that attends a successful book, I think that's natural; there are a lot of bullshitters in the world and they can make life miserable. It is obviously better, though, to be in a position where these

* Edmund Trzcinski (1921–96), playwright best known for his drama *Stalag 17*, written with Donald Bevan, and made into the Billy Wilder film of the same name in 1953.

things happen, than to have none at all, as is most often the case, and that, too, is a sizeable consolation. I think it will all pretty much fade away in your mind when you start on Opus #2 for if you are at all like me you will suffer such contortions on your second book as to make your first one seem like something that happened to someone else. Actually it's been a solid year just getting started on my first chapter—thinking and moaning and suffering every day—and the only really joyful thing in my life within the past month or so is that finally I seem to have seen the light, the first chapter and the whole book are taking shape. Actually you may have no trouble at all, and if so you can consider yourself fortunate. But if you do have trouble I'd like to offer you the small contentment of knowing that there are others who have been in the same boat. God Knows, writing can be a pleasant and rewarding thing when it's moving along well; but the business of first trying to figure out how to give order, shape, and movement to the things you want to say can be distilled hell.

Rose and I are moving back to N.Y. on Feb. 7th for two months while she has a baby. We have a large apt. at 430 East 57 St., where you can reach me after that date. I hope maybe you can make it up to the big city for a few days in February. If things are going well with Rose you're certainly welcome to stay with us, and if I know Rose things will be going well with her. Our phone no. is MUrrayhill 8-9299, so give us a ring if you come up. We'll have a party and I'll fix you up with a nice hangover like the last one you had, plus maybe a hot number I know in the chorus line at the Copacabana (you think I'm kidding?).

Give my best to Blackburn when you see him and tell him I'll write him at length when I get this maternity business in the groove.

All the best,

Bill

Susanna Styron was born on February 25, 1955.

To William Blackburn

April 20, 1955 Roxbury, CT

Dear Doctor:

Now that I have given birth to a child (a girl child named Susanna), now that the gray, grimy winter's lying-in in New York is over, now that I have moved 2½ tons of equipment out to the permanent home, now that spring has begun a tentative foray into my life, and now that I've made the first successful stab toward conquering a sort of incipient and dreary alcoholism into which for seven or eight months I was threatening to fall, now that my Presbyterian conscience has finally asserted itself and I have begun the attack on another masterpiece of 20th Century prose—now that all these are out of the way, I feel that I can sit down and write you a rational sort of letter, along with tendering you my apologies for having been silent so long.

The girl child is quite handsome, I think, although she is so far completely inarticulate and has all of the moist habits of one so young. It could not have been an easier process for Rose, who went through her <u>accouchement</u> with the practiced grace of Mrs. Dionne. We are now all installed in our pseudo-farm in Roxbury, which is in real honest-to-God country about 2 hours from New York. I say pseudo, because my efforts along agricultural lines have so far been limited to the planting of a few early radishes and onions around our back door, but with spring in evidence it is a lovely place and we hope that someday before long you will see it. We have a sort of swimming-pool—this will be my damnation as a writer, but I don't care, and about eight acres of untarnished woodland to trample in or on. Also a television set (it came with the house), a huge stone fire-place, and all sorts of other bourgeois comforts.

I had been told that the second novel often posed quite a problem, but I had no idea that it could actually lead one to toy with the idea of suicide. However, as I say, I've passed the hour of crisis with a hair's breadth to spare, and am at least "embarked." I honestly believe sometime that I should have concentrated on business administration at Duke. These are really ridiculous times for the writing of fiction. A fifth-rate entertainer on TV has more tangible and satisfactory rewards than a novelist. I know in a sense that sounds ridiculous (tell Mac when you see him that I'll write him soon) but it's more than half-way true. I suppose the only answer—

without wishing to sound pretentious—is to write with the idea that you're writing for the generations unborn and not for Lewis Gannett.

Hiram, as you probably know, is now top banana at Random House and the difference between it and Bobbs-Merrill is like the difference between the Little Acorn and the Tour d'Argent. For one thing, Hiram has already persuaded Bennett Cerf to publish LDID in the paperback Modern Library, which is beginning to appear; for another, I have started to feel like an author, rather than someone who published a book.* I went to lunch a few weeks ago with Hiram and the maître himself, Mr. Faulkner of Oxford, and the conversation, while not exactly glittering, was worthwhile. Mr. Faulkner had one whiskey sour; he allowed as how he was glad to be going to the Ky. Derby under the auspices of Mr. Luce's Sports Illustrated. They were sending him down in a chauffeured limousine, and since he had never ridden so far in a chauffeured limousine before, he thought that would be a right nice experience. As for Mr. Capote, his writing reminded Mr. Faulkner of a "big flea." He didn't elaborate. I got the impression that Mr. Faulkner had begun to like the New York whirl right well.

Rose and I both hope you will be up this way before too long. I suppose Connecticut country living is a cliché, but it's also very pleasant. Anyway, as I say, this is real country and not the kind of suburbia that New Yorker dreams are built on. Say hello to Mac for me, and Brice, and let me know sometime how things are on the Durham scene.

As ever,

Bill

* Bennett Cerf (1898–1971) was a publisher and cofounder of Random House.

To Henry Miller*

June 27, 1955 Roxbury, CT

Dear Mr. Miller,

I am very happy to be able to recommend Ravello to you. It is a spectacular place, a thousand feet almost straight up above Amalfi, with a broad and noble view of the sea and the adjoining peaks and hills. People who know have told me that in a way it is not too unlike your country around Monterey, except of course that it faces a much more tranquil body of water (though still very dramatic) and that it is not the U.S.A. but Italy. Anyway, my wife and I lived there for nearly eight months and thought it was great, and we are waiting for the day when we are able to go back there. From all the Ravello lore I have been able to store up I have noticed that some extremely sophisticated people have tended to criticize it as being too "stagy" in atmosphere, with too many vertical and upsetting plunges and slants—perhaps post-card-like, in the way that the Alps are—but this is a theory I never was able to appreciate. I simply think that it is one of the loveliest places a person could choose to be in.

Ischia I visited only for an hour or so, so I'm unable to say what it would be like for living. Positano I saw more of—it's only half an hour or so from Ravello, down the shore drive—but I never cared for it at all. It's right on the sea, which Ravello isn't, but the beach itself is lousy and, more importantly, the town has become terribly chic and as far as I can see has attracted all sorts of boring riff-raff, American, Swedish, Italian, and otherwise. It would certainly be no warmer than Ravello in the Fall or Spring, and I think duller and not nearly so beautiful.

Since heat seems to be one of your first considerations, I'd advise against living in Ravello in the dead of Winter—January or February, say, or March. But from what I've been able to tell, almost any part of the Mediterranean is likely to be chilly at that time of the year, except for Sicily and maybe parts of the Riviera. My wife and I were in Ravello from April until late December, though, and although at the beginning and the end it got

* Henry Miller (1891–1980), novelist, travel writer, and painter, best known for his controversial novel *Tropic of Cancer* (Paris: Obelisk Press, 1934). At the end of the letter, Styron compliments Miller for *The Colossus of Maroussi* (San Francisco: Colt Press, 1941), a reflection on a year Miller spent in Greece with the writer Lawrence Durrell.

a little brisk at times, there was no point where we were ever really uncomfortable. We lived in a villa which, like most of those in southern Italy, had no central heating. There are two or three hotels and pensiones, however, which are heated, and so I think that if you avoided the dead of winter you would be quite comfortable.

In terms of relative inexpensiveness Ravello is fine (at most ½ as expensive as France, I'd think). Our villa, which comprised two floors—a huge vaulted living room upstairs, also a large kitchen; downstairs, two comfortable bedrooms, modern bathroom, plenty of closet space—cost us $60 a month. During July and August the rent went up to $100, but since this was the vacation season it was understandable, and we were glad to pay it, in view of what we got away with the rest of the time. We also had a really excellent cook who doubled as maid and laundress, who worked eight to ten hours a day, and whom we paid $25 a month, and relatively without guilt, since most of her cohorts in town got a little more than half that amount.

Our padrone also runs the best hotel in town, and I'd like to give you his name and suggest that you write him, because he should be able to dig up for you (especially in the off-months of Fall and Spring) a really good place to live; at the very least, I think he would give you advantageous rates at his hotel (a first-class establishment) if you decided to live there for any length of time. He is a fine, tragic man, a Swiss-Italian who married an English woman and who has three fabulously beautiful children. I'm sure he's the only hotel-keeper of Swiss blood whose heart still dominates his desire for a dollar. At any rate he's an excellent, good man, and I suggest you write him. (In English) The name and address: PASQUALE VUILLEUMIER, HOTEL PALUMBO, RAVELLO (SALERNO), ITALY. Pasquale is also somewhat absent-minded, so that if you write him and he should fail to answer after reasonable time, let me know and I'll jog him up.

Well, I hope this has been of some help. Ravello is not the place to go, I think, if you're in search of the same kind of constant diversion you find in seaside places. It has a tranquility, a kind of austerity with color and beauty, if that's possible, which I found wonderfully healthful to the soul after a year or so of places like St. Tropez and Cannes and St. Jean-de-Luz and other Coney Islands. It is frankly a resort town, and makes its money that way, but it is not garish, it is not a clip-joint, and I like to think of it as a place which still holds out against noise-makers, exhibitionists, press-agents, and other heathens. To my mind, the beauty of the place is incomparable, but the pace is gentle, the people are pleasant, and the tone civilized.

If there is anything else you'd like to know about Ravello, I'd be glad to let you know. I love to promote the town; I only hope it doesn't finally get over-promoted and filled up, like any Elysium you can name, with lunatics.

Sincerely yours
William Styron

P.S. No, I'm not Greek, though it has that sound. The name's a corrupted form of the original English, which ended in "-ring."

P.P.S. "The Colossus of Maroussi" was a really superb book. Ravello is not far from Paestum, incidentally, where the glory of Greece is marvelously enshrined.

To Peter Matthiessen

December 16, 1955 Baltimore, MD

Merry Xmas to Patsy and Peter and Lucas and Leary from Susanna Styron (age 9 Mos.)

Dear Peter:

Merry Xmas. Tragedy of tragedies. I just lost my cigarette Denicotea, which I bought in London and have had for nearly four years.* My nerves are all on edge. I write this from Baltimore, where we are convalescing from Rose's appendix, extracted at Johns Hopkins by the world's most famous surgeon (I had never heard of him) in 8½ minutes. She is doing fine now and we are heading to Roxbury day after tomorrow.

I recall drunkenly telling you that I would write you and tell you what

* A Denicotea is a German-made cigarette holder with disposable filters.

I thought of it, along with New Year's plans.* Delighted. First, before I say the con things, I want to say how impressed I am by the fusion of your style and your narrative power. You've achieved an ease, in the last sense, which you didn't have in Race Rock, and by that I think I mean simply that, artistically, you've become much more sure of yourself, and as a result the scenes flow naturally, one into the other without that kind of shaky lack of authority which in places marred Race Rock. Furthermore, I'm really tremendously impressed by what I think are really Dostoievski-like glimmerings of characterization-cum scene—like that of the appalling Marat conducting Sand, Virgil-like, through the lower depths of Paris, a trek in which the reader becomes involved, not only because you've so beautifully established Marat's identity at the outset (again, the initial business with Marat in the bookstore is wonderful, Dostoievskish in its strangely rational, acceptable grotesquerie) but because you have at the same time such a fine sense of place—the hellish abbatoir, for instance, and the dismal potter's field. Moreover, the ability you've developed to resurrect the nuances and overtones of a scene by one or two beautifully exact, extraneous observations (I'm thinking here, for instance, of the business with Sand in bed and Lise, half-sensual, half-repellant, gobbling croissants) is quite wonderful and something, so far as I can see, that is uniquely your own.

What do I see wrong with the book? I think my final disappointment lies not so much in any inherent, particular, and specific flaw as in the fact that you simply missed so many opportunities to flesh it out, give it substance, transform what was the marvelous suggestion of a scene into something which could be a dramatic powerhouse. I think or had the feeling that in every single scene a fine, pure imagination was at work but at the same time I felt terribly let down that this same imagination did not let itself go, prolong itself, take advantage of itself and fill out the crannies and corners. I'm thinking, for example, of the love-scene between Lise and Jacobi, which seemed an outline of a love-scene rather than the real stuff. And of course I'm not saying that you should have made it either sloppy or clinical. I think I simply mean (and I really say this with the profoundest respect for that real great talent glimmering throughout the book) that

* Matthiessen's new novel, *Partisans* (New York: Viking, 1955). *Race Rock* (1954) was his first novel.

there's a hurried quality, as if it were written by a man who for some reason or another failed to realize the richness, the pregnancy, of his most promising and exciting scenes. Here endeth the lesson. I'd knock the piss out of anyone who said this to me (for my condescension by now must be sickening), but I think—such is my faith in your imagination, which you really haven't let loose—that if you were to sit down and, say, over a period of two or three or even four years really suffer over a scene and let it loose, you could make us all look like Harold Bell Wright. Shit you not. I don't think I've ever read a novel which, so skeletal as it seemed to me, impelled me to such famous conclusions.

Because of Rose's incision I doubt if we'll be able to go further than to Sodom for New Year's but as of this date Guinzburg informs me that interesting things are brewing in town that night. I guess we'll be there for something or other, and Rose and I fondly and fully expect you to be there, too.

B.S.

To Hiram Haydn

April 20, 1956 Roxbury, CT

Dear Hiram:

I have thought it over and I think the best thing to put on the cover of the book is "The Long March," a short novel by W.S. I think this because (a) in actuality, it is a short novel, and (b) to put simply a story by might discourage a potential buyer, besides making people wonder, perhaps, why on earth a "story" should be out between covers in a separate book. I don't like "novella" because it sounds a bit too fancy to me; "novelette," unfortunately, has gotten to mean the longer stuff you read in magazines like The Ladies' Home Journal and Redbook. So, I think a short novel is both most honest and accurate.

As for the reviews, if I remember rightly the ones in both the Times + Tribune were written by queers and I got rather short shrift, or at least just a kind of ho-hum praise. Max Geismar reviewed it, I think, in The Nation and said some very nice things about it. But as for the exact quotes, I can't give you them and so perhaps the best thing for you to do is to check with

Pocket Books, Inc. I think Robert Kotlowitz is the one to talk to, if he's still working there. I also now remember that I got glowing mention in The Commonweal, if you want to use that.

As for the inside blurb copy, I just don't know what to say, except that I would like it to be brief and have dignity. I remember that when the piece first appeared, N. Mailer wrote me that he thought it was probably the "best 100 or so pages written since the war," and maybe you'd like to have him repeat it for a blurb, if he's so inclined and still thinks so.*

I'm sorry I can't be of great help, but maybe these few notes will give you an idea or two. Hope to see you soon, when spring comes, if it ever does.

Benediction qui venit in nomine etc. etc.†
Bill

To Peter Matthiessen

May 15, 1956 Roxbury, CT

Dear Peter:

Here is a story which I like very, very much and which, in my august position of advisory editor, I am advising to be published in the Review.‡ It is a sort of Southern Engines of Hygeria, but has a great deal of humor, I think, besides being very warm and poignant. Let me know whether or not you agree. It may, however, be too long. The Virginia Quarterly Review, according to the author, would have taken it if he had reduced the length by 3 or 4,000 words, but this he didn't want to do. What do you think?

The author is a North Carolinian, presently a Rhodes Scholar, and was

* Styron is quoting Mailer's first letter to him, February 26, 1953. Mailer actually wrote: "I think it's just terrific, how good I'm almost embarrassed to say, but as a modest estimate it's certainly as good an eighty pages as any American has written since the war, and really I think it's much more than that."

† A pun on a line from the Christian prayer known as the Sanctus. The actual line is *Benedictus qui venit in nomine Domini* (Blessed is he who comes in the name of the Lord).

‡ An unknown story by Reynolds Price. Price (1933–2011) was a novelist, poet, dramatist, essayist, and professor at Duke University.

a student under Wm. Blackburn at Duke, which is how I came to know about him. If you don't decide to take it, please send it back to Diarmuid Russell. Love to Patsy and all the young ones. I hope you're having a better winter than we are in Conn. I'm planting lichen in the vegetable garden and have seeded the lawn with tundra.

All yours,
BS

To John P. Marquand, Jr.

July 4, 1956 Roxbury, CT

Dear Marq,

Since this is the night of Independence Day, I thought it not remiss to let you know—you who seems to be callously lacking in any proper respect for the country which nurtured you—that all is well with the Republic. Are you in Spain? I don't know what kind of news you've been getting. Eisenhower has been force-fed through the asshole for lo these many weeks, and the Trib reported with some joy today that he got his first hopefully albeit feebly licks in with his mashie at Gettysburg. An acquaintance of mine in advertising, who has a pipeline to BBD+O, swears that they are going to run the poor bastard even if they have to call in a taxidermist. Two airplanes crashed in a kind of Huxleyesque rapture of horror over the Grand Canyon, claiming 128 lives (come back by boat). A middle-aged man in Miami Beach had a stroke while sunbathing and lay paralyzed beneath the blazing sun for 2½ days until someone on a church picnic discovered his mute and helpless condition. He died of second-degree burns. Nixon is in the Philippines, spreading sunshine to the gooks. Foster has been out in the corn country, Iowa or someplace like that, receiving Le D's and sowing seeds of disaster. The country is in the hands of morons, juvenile rapists, water skiers, and a pimply crooner whom thank God you've been spared the ordeal of seeing named Elvis Presley. In our pathetic and lovely little hometown of Roxbury this past week there was consummated the wretched alliance of Marilyn Monroe and an ex-playwright named Arthur Miller, bringing to these tranquil glens and glades a gawking procession of shortshirted, Pontiac-ensconced, growling cretins such as you would never have imagined, and leaving dead around an oak tree not ½ mile from this house the lady correspondent from Paris-Match, who cracked up chasing the couple.* Malcolm Bray, the rat-faced real estate agent who sold us our place and who also doubles as town constable, told us with Rotarian pride that land values hereabouts have skyrocketed since the event. I wouldn't be surprised. At any rate, I am too sad about everything to go on any more about what's new with the U.S.A.

Rose and I were both vastly entertained by your letter, especially by the account of Mr. Aldrich's goodwill ambassador who put the whammy on Steve Spender. However, you must have been mistaken, in that such a palpable arse could not have come from Virginia.

You chose the wrong time, of course, to dissociate yourself from The Paris Review. It has been quoted at length in all the journals throughout the land, Luce papers included, and to belong on its masthead is definitely a cachet of honor second only to being on that old ladies' magazine, The New Yorker. I think you'll eventually regret the move when the literary history of our time is written and the name Phillips is not connected with the gallant little organ. Plimpton, whom I saw recently at a gala fete given at the St. Regis for our millionaire friend, Irwin Shaw, told me that he was very upset by your move and suspects that the only reason you left us is because you are on the verge of doing a literary hatchet job on your erstwhile Paris pals. Is there a patina of truth to this observation?

Here at random are some more items which may be of interest to one who has chosen in the most démodé fashion possible to expatriate himself from the finest and most progressive nation on earth (speaking of things démodé, I hope you have let Michael and Lee† know that what they're up to is not only terribly non-U, in spite of the obvious paradox, but dangerous as well, and that I should not like to be on hand to see them in some Socialist turnbail some years hence, being hauled to the gibbet at the Marble Arch): being now in the Random House fold I am great pals with not

* The playwright and essayist Arthur Miller (1915–2005) was a neighbor of the Styrons in Connecticut, and they later became close friends. Miller married Marilyn Monroe on June 29, 1956, and they divorced in 1961.

† Michael Temple Canfield and Lee Radziwill (née Caroline Lee Bouvier).

only old Ben Cerf but his pals, too: old Arlene Francis and old Buddy Schulberg and old Mossy Hart and swell old Colesy Porter and Dickie Rodgers and sweet, wry-witted Stevie Allen.* We all get together at Ben's place in Mt. Kisco and go swimming and play charades and that sort of thing and then I get on the phone and call up old Joe Fox in Crowfields and taunt him about the fun I'm having with all my swell celebrity friends. I'm a pretty good man with a tongue in the right place: as a result of my efforts, The Long March is coming out in the Modern Library this Sept. You are wrong, however, about LM being acted by Brando + Lancaster. I wouldn't have them. It is to be filmed next spring in Florida by a guy named Coe that Joe works for and Fox is to be the grand panjandrum and unit manager. I thought if you + Suay got back in time, we could all go down there and suck on tangerines and watch the cameras spin. Or dolly in, as we say in the business. I have written 400 rather faltering pages on my newest effort, and the end is still not in sight. With all my cinema commitments my literary emotions have of course suffered a kind of anemia. Who wants a Nobel prize when you can pal around with people like Gore Vidal and Peter Viertel and Niven Busch and "Gadge" Kazan and Edmund Purdom?† I have taken to smoking black Brazilian cigars, so that my lips have become wet and lubricious.

Now as to the questions in your last letter:

Guinzburg and his now-recovered spouse are reported by Denton

* Arlene Francis (1907–2001) was an American actress, radio talk show host, and game show panelist. Moss Hart (1904–61) was a playwright and theater director. Cole Porter (1891–1964) was a composer and the writer of many memorable Broadway musical scores and popular songs. Richard Charles Rodgers (1902–79) was a composer of more than nine hundred songs and forty-three Broadway musicals, best known for his songwriting partnerships with Lorenz Hart and Oscar Hammerstein. Steve Allen (1921–2000) was a television personality and the first host of *The Tonight Show*.

† Peter Viertel (1920–2007) was an author and screenwriter whose work included such notable films as *The African Queen* (1951). Niven Busch (1903–91) was an author and screenwriter best known as the co-writer of the screenplay for *The Postman Always Rings Twice* (1946). Elia "Gadge" Kazan (1909–2003) was one of the most important directors in the history of Broadway and Hollywood, and was infamous for his testimony as a friendly witness before the House Committee on Un-American Activities. Kazan earned his nickname in college—"Gadge" or "Gadg," short for "gadget"—because he was compact and useful. Edmund Purdom (1926–2009) was a British actor.

Walker as making "goo-goo eyes" in the Hauvyn, a fashionable bistro. I see Guinzo every now and then. His clots are better but he is still surly.

Peter is still in Gansett, exposing his best friends to 6" blowfish for $15 a head.

Appleton was up here for a recent week-end and was a wonderful guest until—I hate to say it—he came to a climax and left a ghastly mark like the track of a snail down the front of the dress of a woman named Mrs. Theodore Murkland.

The swimming pool is, to use Connecticut patois, as cold as a welldigger's ass; the tomato crop withering.

John Aldridge's fixation in the firmament is, if I may mix a metaphor, at a rather low ebb, his last book (in which I received nice praise) having been rent from limb to limb by all respectable critics, without exception, as the work of a maundering, confused, second-rate young man with delusions of glory. They wanted to buy a home up near here, but Rose + I conspired to chase them away.

Rose and I are anxiously awaiting your return to these shores with your blushing bride and have waiting here in Roxbury—besides Susanna, who has suddenly become appallingly talkative—all sorts of booze, Smithfield hams, good American milk and all sorts of other goodies which should make you regret that you ever sojourned so long among the wops and spicks and other types scarcely human. Set aside one of your earliest weekends and we'll have a wonderful bleary time of it.

Give my love to Suay

All the best

Stybo

P.S. Very much enjoyed your article in <u>Harper's</u>.* It really gave me a new perspective on the situation, to quote Eric Sevareid.

* John Phillips, "What Is the Matter with Mary Jane? The Tragicomedy of Cyprus," *Harper's Magazine,* June 1956.

To Herbert Weinstock*

July 26, 1956 Roxbury, CT

Dear Mr. Weinstock,

I must apologize for not having written you sooner about The Lost Steps.† I asked Henry Carlisle to tell you what I thought about it, but he must have forgotten.

The fact is that I read with great interest, and that I liked it in a strange way but that I found it so overpoweringly exotic and curious that, in the end, I just don't know what my opinion is. I read it much as if I were tasting some new tropical fruit whose flavor was quite unique and wonderful but which I had to turn down in the end for the good old stand-by orange. In other words, I liked it but it was too off-beat for my own particular taste in fiction, and as a result I don't feel competent to give you a statement. I also found that my interest flagged about two-thirds of the way through, which is probably not so much the fault of the book as, again, my own particular taste.

Thanks for sending me the book—I am sorry about the delay—and I hope my feeling about it won't deter you from sending my way anything else of special interest in the future.

Yours sincerely,
William Styron

* Herbert Weinstock, executive editor at Alfred A. Knopf in the 1950s.

† *The Lost Steps* (*Los pasos perdidos*) (New York: Knopf, 1956) was a novel by Alejo Carpentier, a Cuban writer and supporter of Castro's revolution. Weinstock initially thought Carpentier's novel was "unreadable," but did not want to lose the author to another publisher. He solicited blurbs from Styron, Ralph Ellison, Lionel Trilling, and Robert Penn Warren, among others. Only Ellison, Trilling, and Styron responded.

To Louis D. Rubin, Jr.

October 15, 1956 Roxbury, CT

Dear Louis,

I'm afraid I don't have anything on hand right now for publication in The Provincial. I am up to my neck in this new novel I'm writing, a process which is as usual so painful & irksome to me that it leaves me soured on all writing in general. I very well might have something later on, however, and I'll of course be proud to see it in The Provincial. I thought your first issue was most attractive; it seems literary yet refreshingly unpedantic, and I'm looking forward to seeing it expand in size. I liked the Lardner piece very much. I hope you won't take it as a minor compliment, either, that the whole thing is handsomely printed and proof-read; after my experience with The Paris Review I know this is no mean accomplishment.

I shouldn't worry too much about Aldridge if I were you. As grateful as I might be for the sweet things he's said about me, I am also aware that about many things he is rather grotesquely opinionated and one-sided, and goes off half-cocked about 50% of the time. It's too bad, since quite often his judgments are astute enough. To hell with all such critics anyway—a difficult thing to say for me, incidentally, since Aldridge (& wife), out of I suspect some bizarre desire to be near the only writer he loves, has bought a house 5 minutes away from us here in Roxbury—the same house which provided the nuptial surroundings for that strangely & frantically opportunistic dramatist, Mr. Arthur Miller, and that sexually endowed barrel of pineapple Jello, Miss Mmmmarilyn Monroe. Perhaps he'll become a better critic with all those carnal ghosts lurking about the house.

Rose tells me to tell you that a friend of ours from Charleston, W.Va., a writer named Mary Lee Settle, is earnestly in need of a fellowship, and will probably be writing you for information about the Sewanee deal. Perhaps you would be kind enough to oblige her. She's really quite talented, I think, greatly in need of support, and a bear for work. You may have seen or heard of her last novel, O Beulah Land, which got quite superior reviews everywhere.*

As I say, I hope I'll be able to send you something later on. In the meantime, congratulations on what looks like a really auspicious start at something first-rate. Rose joins me in sending all the best to you & Eva.

As ever

Bill

The Random House edition of The Long March *was published on October 29, 1956.*

To Elizabeth McKee

December 4, 1956 2707 Lawina Road, Baltimore, MD

Dear Elizabeth

Here are some hollyhock seeds which Pop + Elizabeth Styron, who are visiting up here for a few days, asked me to deliver to you! Plant them in the spring, next to a wall.

I hope you received the letter from the Hollywood-type agent + are making profitable contact. Let me know if anything develops.

Susanna is wonderful, brilliant, articulate (I'll swear she can write every word perfectly of "Mary had a little lamb") but she breaks my heart because she won't say a word to me at all + turns up her nose at all paternal advances.

Love + XXX Bill

* Mary Lee Settle (1918–2005) was best known for her historical novels about West Virginia. *O Beulah Land* (1956) began the series.

To William Blackburn

December 8, 1956 2707 Lawina Road, Baltimore, MD

Dear Doctor:

Just a note from the in-law bailiwick in Baltimore to let you know that I got your note and I'm glad that all goes well. Rose and Susanna and I have been here for a week and expect to spend a week more, before going back to the Connecticut glades for Xmas. I don't expect that we can make it down to Durum this season, but I hope we can perhaps visit you sometime in the spring. Reason: we have been invited to spend two weeks or more next March or April in a friend's house at Cocoa Beach, Fla. Also, from what I can make out, "The Long March" will be filmed in the swamps of that part of Florida at around the same time. The producer is an amiable gent who evinces a remarkable respect for the opus per se, and has said that he would like me to be on hand for the production. I have no great illusions that the movie is going to be any work of art, but I have been told that this fellow's attitude is unheard of, miraculous, and incomparable, so the chances are that I might take advantage of it and go down and lend my pennyworth of inspiration to the venture. One way or another, I hope we'll be able to stop off and see you. Last Saturday (Dec. 1) Jim Brown, the agent, gave a party for Mac Hyman in N.Y., which we went to, and we rode as far as Baltimore on the train next day with Mac + Gwen. Mac seems to be in great shape and I'm hoping to drop in on Cordele, too, if this trip really materializes, which it ought to.

The new novel is proceeding apace, despite shoals and snags and misadventures of one sort or another. One thing that it is impossible to do is accuse Styron of excessive speed. But I have 550-600 yellow sheets done, all fairly clean and with little rewriting to be done, and I pray that next year this time will find me close to the end of the accursed thing. I find the whole business abominably, sweatily tiresome. I loathe writing with what amounts to a kind of phobia, and I suppose that it's only a sort of perverse masochism that keeps me at it. I have developed, in my old age, an exhausting pessimism about all things literary; this is not a pose, Doctor, because I have examined it from all angles and only come up with a perpetual wonder over the fact that I have chosen to engage my mind and spirit in an activity which gives me so little satisfaction. The extraordinary thing, however, is how with this attitude I can go on writing things which seem to me quite good. It might seem strange, but it is as if in my hatred of the act of writing I had to prove myself supremely superior to it by turning out stuff that is, at least by my own standards, always of a high order. And I suppose that's why I write so slowly, approaching the wretched work each day as maybe a sculptor does when confronted with a 20-ton block of granite to give meaning to, with a paring knife for a weapon. Right now I don't know how this book is going to end up. It couldn't be more totally different from LDID. It is told in the first person. The narrator is a glib wisecracker. The book abruptly breaks off mid-way and is told by an entirely different character, third-person. How out of this mess I am to fashion the noble tragedy which glimmers ever and anon before my eye, I still do not know. And maybe it will all be a terrific botch. But I do know that at least it will have a few fine things in it—these I have written already—so it simply cannot be a real disaster. Furthermore, I have a secret, tiny feeling that in spite of all my fears it will be the best thing I have written, which is a strange thing to say, if not idiotic, by one who has just stated his (excuse me while I find the phrase) "exhausting pessimism about all things literary." Finally, I am simply exasperated by all of this stale, left-over adulation of people like Hemingway. If literature is to be viable and worth a damn it's got to be perpetually renewed, and I'm determined that this book will be an important factor in the renewing process, or else I'll pull a severe Sherwood Anderson and go into the paint business.

LDID, incidentally, is coming out next month in the Compass paperback editions, published by Viking at $1.25. Maybe at that price you can drum up some trade at the Duke bookstore.

Rose sends her fond regards and joins me in saying that she looks forward to seeing you before long. If you should come to N.Y. before then, don't forget to call us. Meanwhile I hope you have a gorgeous Yuletide.

As ever,

Bill

P.S. The paper today brought me one bright item of hope—about Bob Goheen, the new president of Princeton.* He was at the Academy in Rome when I was there and a more elegant nice gentleman you could not hope

* Robert Francis Goheen (1919–2008), classics scholar, president of Princeton University (1957–72), and U.S. Ambassador to India (1977–80).

to know. I would say he bears the same relation to Edens or Manchester as St. John does to Norman Vincent Peale.

To Elizabeth McKee

March 7, 1957 Cocoa Beach, FL

Dear Elizabeth:

I got your communication with the various attached letters. I'm not very optimistic either about Bob Arthur* doing anything inspired, but I don't see much else to do except to string along with whatever Coe has up his sleeve. I wrote him just now and told him essentially that: that I was sorry, too, but that I was interested in seeing how the next version turned out, etc., and my prayers went with the project and so on. Just a nice letter. There's not much else to do as far as I see but to wait and hope.

I wrote to De Liso and told him that I was interested—which I am—but that it would be at least a month before I would be able to do anything about it. If he really does corral Bellow, Jones, Mailer, etc., it might be an interesting book.

It went down to 45° here today, but we've had some lovely hot days and the prediction is for more. We're leaving here around the 14th and, with a stopover in Virginia, we should arrive in Roxbury around the 21st or so. I rode down the Inland Waterway with Mac Hyman on his Chris-Craft: 160 miles of clear cruising until, 10 miles from here, we ran aground on a mudbank and had to have the Coast Guard pull us off. No damage; Susanna + Rose are fine. Susanna is a regular duck in the surf, but can't decide really whether she loves it or loathes it. The work is coming along well. Any news from Padula? Best to all.

Love + XXX
Bill

* Robert Arthur (1909–86), screenwriter and producer.

To Maxwell Geismar

April 29, 1957 Roxbury, CT

Dear Max,

Was going to tell Ann—during the phallic interlude of the other night—why I thought you were my most perceptive critic (which, of course, means the most perceptive critic around), but somehow I forgot what I was going to say. Anyway, it's this: you were the only person who wrote anything about "LDID" who found any humor in the book. There is humor in it, by God, and I think you'll find humor in the one I'm writing now. Most critics are such solemn jackasses, really. Jonesy, incidentally, thought both you and Anne were the most, to use his own picturesque mot.

Hope you have (or have had already) great success at Brandeis.

Ever yours,
Bill

P.S. Ask Ann what she thinks of International Cellulose Products, Inc., mfrs. of "Tampax," "Midol" & other aids to ladies. I suspect that this would be akin to Exposition, Horizon, & other vanity houses, though I really don't know.

To Mac Hyman

April 29, 1957* Roxbury, CT

Dear Mac—

Blackburn wrote that our misadventures on the Inland Waterway even got into the papers, why I don't know, but with all the facts wrong. Any-

* Styron discovered the original of this letter, which had been returned to him after Hyman's death, when William Blackburn collected Hyman's correspondence. He wrote to Blackburn on June 8, 1964, in frustration: "I looked in vain through my letters for communications from Mac. Not a solitary one showed up, though I'll look again. I think the simple fact of the matter is that whenever Mac and I got in touch it was almost invariably by telephone. This of course is the curse of our age, and I suspect a lot of interesting chatty stuff has been lost to posterity because it was uttered over the phone rather than

way, it was a fine day, except for the last business, and even that wasn't too bad, I guess (from what I heard when I went back to the canal the next day), since there didn't seem to be any big damage to the boat. Was this accurate information? One guy said that when you steamed away the next day, everything was shipshape. I hope so. The people from Rome were still there with your cleat stuck in their transom, but they didn't seem to be all that disgruntled, so I suppose that the only real damage all the way around was the ignominy of running aground in the first place. In assigning the fault there, I see it purely and simply this way: it was clearly your fault. I, of course, was at the wheel (I do take it into account that it was graceful of you to say, as you did at the canal, that we were "changing over"), and I was, to be sure, somewhat drunk from the Jack Daniel's I'd been swilling down ever since Mosquito Lagoon, and as a result I was at least 20° off course. As even the most uninformed person knows, however, it is the captain of any craft who is in the end responsible for the behavior of the people aboard, including drunkenness, and so I can hardly see how you can avoid the burden of blame. I should think that from now on you will be a lot more careful about who you let steer that tub of yours; after the next wreck you have you might not be so lucky, and the Coast Guard board of inquiry is not going to politely ask who was doing the steering, etc.: they're simply going to get you.

Anyway, it was a fine trip, even with the disaster, which I hope you haven't let overshadow all the rest. I would be glad to help reimburse you for that cleat, incidentally; actually, when I come to think of it, we're damn lucky that one of us wasn't buried with it rammed halfway down his throat.

I hope that the writing is coming along well, and that you'll be able to take some time off before too long and come up this way. We've got a lot of room now that the other house is fixed up and if you feel the need for a change of scene or anything like that you're welcome to stay here and work or relax or do anything you want.

I'm at page 590 of this great bloated overwritten monster I'm working on. I'm sick of it, and there's no end in sight. If you ever begin to feel dis-

---

written down more or less imperishably. I have another batch of letters stored away elsewhere, and when I can get my hands on them I'll look to see if any of them are Mac's and let you know—though I rather doubt that any will show up."

couraged, maybe you can at least take a small bit of comfort in the fact that there's one other writer who's just as sour about it all. Or more so.

Thanks for the warm Ga. Hospitality and the wonderful boat trip which will forever live in my memory, in spite of its demonstration of man's inherent fallibility. By which I mean that I think that it's damn close to criminal that the Army Engineers or whoever's responsible is not made to dredge a wider channel out of Hanlover Canal, about 800 yds. at least, and that furthermore it seems to me utterly ridiculous that by now the Chris-Craft people haven't developed a small, cheap, foolproof sounding device for the bottoms of their goddamn boats. It seems to me that when they expect you to stay sober and on top of that pay attention to the buoys + the rules of the road + all that sort of crap they've pretty nearly taken all the fun out of it. I hope you agree.

Bill

To Maxwell Geismar

May 14, 1957 Roxbury, CT

Dear Max—

I'm glad you got an agent, and thanks for passing on the wise sentiments of Mr. Jack Jones. I'm not at all certain that Rose will receive his MS, but I've tipped her off about it and she will have an eye out when and if it comes, and so will I.

Latest source of despondency is an essay in "Dissent" by some new critic named Richard Chase. It was actually a review of Aldridge's "In Search of Heresy," attacking him for a "middlebrow," and saying that it was typical of J.W.A. that he should condemn such "low-middlebrow" books as "Marjorie Morningstar" while defending such books as "Lie Down in Darkness," which he called a "middlebrow novel with highbrow flourishes of rhetoric." It wasn't so much the jab at me that was so depressing, since I've received worse, in such middlebrow journals as Time and The New Yorker, but the whole appalling, snobbish, mean-spirited, frightened-of-life tenor of the article. I've never read much "New" criticism, but if this guy is at all representative of the school—and I gather he is—then I can really see at long last that the situation is dangerous. Perhaps it only takes a personal reference to bring it home; since the New critics have not paid any attention to me I suppose I can assume that this is the general feeling they have about my work. But as I say much more important than this was the whole small and petty, small-hearted, niggardly, undertaker atmosphere this guy's writing generates. Who is this guy anyway, with his cheap mean little chatter about the "highbrow" (by which I suppose he means New criticism) being the only attitude in art that is worthwhile? Why doesn't someone tip this dreary person off, along with all the rest of them, and point out that practically any fine novel ever written was middlebrow, written for the common middlebrow reader who had, presumably, warm blood in his veins and not, as in Chase's case, embalming fluid. Does this guy consider Tolstoy "highbrow," or Balzac, or for that matter Hemingway or Scott Fitzgerald or Tom Wolfe? To hell with him anyway. It seems to me that the writer of heart, intelligence, good-will, and talent is in a terrible limbo at the moment—between the mass moron on one hand and on the other hand the frightened, grubby-souled little academic, like this Chase, who would turn literature into a kind of desolating calculus, or would level it horizontally to approximate the wasteland of his own spirit. At any rate, Max, outside of the good auspices of yourself and only one or two others, I think I can say that if I ever become famous and if Lie Down lasts for a while it won't be because I got any boost from the so-called "pros" of literature, the New critics. I am looking forward to the day when my hair is crowned with laurel and a New critic starts jumping belatedly on the band-wagon and I am able to tromp on his fingers and say, "Get your dirty hands off." I'll do it, too.

Well, that's that for today.

Biliously yours,

B.

To Maxwell Geismar

June 26, 1957 Roxbury, CT

Dear Max:

Congratulations! Or is it best wishes? I ask the last only because as I write this my Susanna is scrambling all over my shoulders and is saying such a lot of precocious things that I am stricken chill with the notion that her day, too, is not far off. Rose and I would love to come to the fiesta, but unfortunately we have guests lined up for that week-end and won't be able to make it. Please kiss the bride for us, though; we'll be there in our hearts.

I am up to p. 703 (this is a quantitative age, which is why I'm so quick with figures). Your last letter bolstered my spirit some. There are bastards on the right and left of us—the mob and the university creeps—and sometimes I wonder which is worse. Have you looked at this new anthology "Mass Culture"?* It's spotty but there are some really brilliant essays in it, especially one by someone named van den Haag whose view is so gloomy as to make one want to weep but whose analysis of mob culture is so brilliant as to be spellbinding and in an odd way strengthening.† One finally gets from this book such a grim + apocalyptic view of modern times that in a curious way it's almost a cathartic and the duty of the writer—if there is any longer such a thing as duty—seems forlornly and rather splendidly noble. Read it.

I hope Rose and I will see you all before long. We are going to Nantucket for a while in August, but there's plenty of free time before and after, and among other things I should like to engage Anne in a conversation regarding Eisenhower's gonads and other pharmaceutical subjects.

Love and kisses to bride and all Geismars.

Bill

To Leon Edwards

August 29, 1957 Roxbury, CT

Dear Leon,

Your recent and much-enjoyed letter recalled to mind what a lousy correspondent I am. Forgive the lapse, if you can, and chalk it up not to indolence but to the fact that, as a writing man, so called, the day's end leaves me fed up with words as they are writ—even such amiable, non-

* Bernard Rosenberg and David Manning White, eds., *Mass Culture: The Popular Arts in America* (1957).

† Ernest van den Haag, "Of Happiness and of Despair We Have No Measure."

professional ones as I might write you. I have just this month handed in 90,000—100,000 words of my next literary experiment to my publishers and, being still not much more than mid-way in the book, have for the past few weeks taken the sort of complete vacation that you seem deservedly to be taking down in San Antone. I'm all for it the easy life, that is; it clears the mind of too much seriousness and allows one to get a half-way decent perspective on life—not as she is lived by the bottled-up self but by other people, too. At the same time, the grass is always greener, etc., as the saying goes. I for one certainly curse myself for taking up the writer's craft, or profession, or art, or whatever. It's a miserable trade, cowardly and neurosis-producing. Some Protestant ethic in me keeps nagging at me that it's not a fit job for a MAN and that I should be out healing the world's wounds like you are doing, but it's too late to go back, of course, and I can only keep grinding away. All this is merely in response to a statement in one of your last letters to the effect that you were still seized by the itch to write; my advice is to stay the hell away from it. It will do nothing but fill your life with nightmares.

However, all these disclaimers aside, I think I'm writing a good book. It's absolutely totally different from LDID in theme and subject matter so that I will either be praised for "versatility" or condemned for getting out of my depth—probably the latter, but either way it doesn't matter. You end up writing what you have to the most. At the same time writing a long novel, as I am doing, has an overpowering effect on the psyche. There's so much of it, there are so many things to keep straight, so much that you want to put into but for artistic considerations can't, so much that's almost bound to fall short of your lofty aims that, if you're at all serious, you end up existing in a perpetual state of sweat and melancholy and quasi-alcoholism. In effect, it's a perfect symbol of one's own strengths and weaknesses as a human, and I can only console myself with the rather feeble notion that perhaps, after all, that is all a novel is supposed to be.

We are now living like the Massah himself in the "big" house, which we have fixed up to resemble something that falls between House + Garden and The Saturday Evening Post. We have also acquired a huge Newfoundland dog weighing 150 lbs. who for some reason is named Tugwell. You mentioned in your letter that you were reporting back to Boston next January so you must right now make plans to stop by on your way and pay us a visit. One thing we have is a surfeit of rooms, so do try to come. I have no intention whatever of approaching your disturbing fecundity, but just to show that I'm keeping my hand, or something, in I want you to know that Rose is expecting another in March. We have already nearly given Pop apoplexy by promising to name it, if a boy, Harry Flood Byrd Styron.*

Tomorrow we're heading toward your country for Labor Day—to Newburyport, for several sessions on the beach with the Marquands. I'll give a Hail Mary as we pass Newton Centre. It is sad to see summer draw to a close, and we often could wish that Roxbury were more in the general latitude of San Antonio. At the same time I'm usually pretty happy to be up here in this frosty climate—too much sun breeds a soft mind and softer books, I always say. Don't forget about us on your way back. Rose joins me in all sorts of love to Marianne and the Kids.

As ever

Bill

To Maxwell Geismar

October 2, 1957 Roxbury, CT

Dear Max—

Thanks for your letter, which was fine, although I don't really know what the postmistress will say about the "Artist Extraordinary" cachet on the envelope. It's tough enough being an artist in this country, anyway, without advertising the un-American fact. But thank you for the compliment.

The essay sounds nice—or more than that—and I'm grateful for it, and I hope you'll send me a copy of the book when it comes out. I think I've told you before that I'm not so removed in interest from the critical scene not to be touched and flattered by your espousal of my cause—whatever that might be. Outside of Aldridge, you're the only critic (I'm not talking about the newspaper boys) who has ever paid the slightest bit of attention to me, or anyone of my colleagues, for that matter. What the

* Styron refers to Harry F. Byrd, Sr. (1887–1966), a governor of and senator from Virginia, whose political machine dominated state politics for most of the twentieth century. Styron and his father both abhorred Byrd's politics.

hell did Hemingway, Fitzgerald + Co. have to scream about and call themselves the Lost Generation? In terms of any literary recognition or acceptance this (our) generation is about as lost as you can get. As an attitude generally prevailing, I call your attention to the review several weeks ago in The N.Y. Times by one Du Bois, of a book called "Best Short Stories of World War II," in which The Long March is included.* He roundly damned all 20 stories—Mailer, Burns, Shaw, Jones, et al.—and finished up by calling The Long March "this slightly hysterical piece." In other words, the general tone—outside of the review's essential ignorance—was that the generation post World War II was simply not worth a damn. Du Bois, of course, is simply and patently a stupid person, but what is so depressing is how representative such a review seems to be of the thinking of those who would judge the literary group which has emerged since the war. Hemingway and Fitzgerald and that gang, it seems to me, had the least claim to being lost of any people I know. They were read, they were celebrated, they were appreciated. And we are roundly damned at every turn. I hope the tincture of self-pity here is not too strong. I don't mean it to be. I simply think that all this is true, and that is why people like yourself are rare and valuable. Perhaps around 1980, with your help, people will wake up to the fact that we were writing our literature after all.

Someone gave me the galleys of Jones' new book, and I'm sorry to say that I have to agree with you, and even more: I think it is very close to a catastrophe. In "Eternity" he was writing the real McCoy. Here most of the stuff sounds like the work of a not-too-bright literary 15-year-old, and it really grieves me, because it will simply be another turkey for the Du Boises to fall upon and say, "See about this generation? I told you so!" But maybe the experience (and I can't possibly foresee anything but mayhem in the book pages) will sober Jonesey (he has been outrageously cocky) and he'll go on to write a good #3.

I've turned in 650 pages of my next one to Hiram, with about 400 or so to go, which should occupy me for another year. Christ! it takes a long time to do a good job. I think Hiram is enthusiastic. Personally, I think

* William Du Bois, "Books of the Times," *The New York Times*, September 14, 1957.

it's better than LDID, but then I'm not a critic. Hope it won't be too long before we get together.

Bill

P.S. In response to your wonderment about writing Jones, tell him frankly what you think of it. Flattery, as the saying goes, will get you nowhere. BS

To William C. Styron, Sr.

November 9, 1957 Roxbury, CT

Dear Pop—

I was indeed sorry to hear about your little set-to with the hospital, but was mighty happy to hear that you pulled through in good shape. With the feeling that some of your distress might have been occasioned by the criminal sort of bills that TV repairmen seem to be in the habit of sending these days—and that goes for auto mechanics, too—I am sending the enclosed check (written as you can see on my Nipps checkwriter, the use of which I am getting quite adept at) with the hopes that it will help ease some of the autumnal strain. American gadgetry has gotten into a preposterous mess. As I told you before, I think, our Bendix washer went into the sick decline to the tune of $115 for repairs, an amount which could have almost purchased a new washer. The man had the gall to send me another bill the other day for $15 more, at which I balked finally, writing him a letter to the effect that I felt under no obligation—morally, legally, or otherwise—to pay any more, that he could sue me if he wished, but that he would not get a penny more from me. After a point one can not be bled further. I have not heard from him, and don't think I will.

Everybody is well up here, and we are crossing our fingers in regard to the flu. About a week ago Susanna had a fever of 104°, but to show you how sturdy the little scamp is the fever went down to almost normal the next day, and she had not a sniffle nor a complication, and within 48 hours was bedeviling the life out of us, as usual, with her chatter and her dollies and had spread several hundred poker chips the length and the breadth of the house. So I think we can be sure that if anyone suffers badly from this

Asian malady it will not be our darling daughter. Rose is well + thriving. She is going in Monday to see Alan Guttmacher about the new heir or heiress—a routine thing. We will of course be satisfied with whatever the Lord chooses to bless us with but we are both secretly hoping that it will not have quite the high-octane charge that was built into Susanna—though it probably will.

As I think I told you, the book is coming along quite well. I think I'm over the hump now; at least the end seems a possibility and not just a misty improbable vision. It is the most difficult thing I have ever had to do in my life and since I'm putting so much into it, and since deep down I feel that when it is done it will be one of the finest novels in a long time, I think it is only fitting to tell you that it will be dedicated jointly to Rose and to yourself, who are the two people who, as they say, are the most.

Rose sends her love to you + Elizabeth, as do I, and joins me in hoping that the autumn brings fair skies and sunny days.

Bill

To Maxwell Geismar

November 23, 1957 Roxbury, CT

Dear Max:

I don't know if you saw this, but it is something said by Albert Camus in a wonderful interview in the current Reporter: "Like so many men today, I am tired of criticism, denigration and meanness—in short, of nihilism. We must condemn what deserves condemnation; it should be done with vigor and then put aside. But what still deserves to be praised should be exalted at length. After all, it is for this that I am an artist, because even when what the artist creates is a denial, it still affirms something and pays homage to the miserable, magnificent life we live."

I think you mistook my last letter. No honest man wants the limelight; this is for movie actors, quizmasters, people of the caliber of Charles Van Doren, and other such pallid creeps.* A writer who is worth anything

* Charles Van Doren (b. 1926) is a writer and editor who was involved in the 1950s scandal surrounding the television quiz show *Twenty-One.*

wants, however, like Dylan Thomas, to be known, and in order to be known look at Thomas—look at the excruciating posture he had to put himself in in order to get the recognition which should have been his due anyway: it killed him. This is an extreme case, of course, but the symptoms are the same. What I'm getting at is that a writer these days has to compete like he never did before. Was there ever a time when a serious artist had to contend with attention with the wretched likes of a Paddy Chayefsky? This sounds silly in a way, perhaps, and I have enough residual respect for the human race—though I sometimes wonder why—to realize that art eventually triumphs and all that crap; nevertheless, the feeling that one is writing in a vacuum sometimes gets overpowering. Look at your pal Griffin; I recently read Devil, and while I don't perhaps share your complete enthusiasm for the book, it was a damn good job, but in spite of the NAL reprint and your critical support and so on did it get 1/10th of the attention it deserved?* No, the assholes were all reading The Caine Mutiny or some such tripe.

But I'm tired of complaining and I'm not going to do any more for a while. I can only reiterate, though, that like Camus I am tired of criticism, denigration and meanness. This book I'm writing—I have gotten to about p. 800 in the monster, and am at a point, over the hump, so to speak, where I can clearly see its virtues and defects. The defects, I think, are minor, or at least are outweighed by the virtues, which is as much as I can ask, I suppose. I have had the notion off and on that it might be too long, but I am now able to see that it encompasses its longness, and that makes it all right. What is most important, though, is that I think it's going to be a better book than Darkness—it is less of a "novelistic" novel in that it is less confined, spreads out more, and I simply have more to say.

Trouble with Darkness, I think—in spite of the fact that it was a good book and all—was that it wasn't intellectually attuned to that dreaded word Zeitgeist, that though it was a fine job for a novice it was still more arty than art; in short, it was a book which had almost everything except a really solid apprehension of the present in relation to the past. This book I think lacks some of the youthful zest and lyricism of Darkness and it has the grave and limiting but necessary defect of having the whole first half

* John Howard Griffin, *The Devil Rides Outside* (Fort Worth, Tex.: Smiths, Inc., 1952).

told in the first person; but it is a bigger book in every other respect. The book is really the reason why I say I'm not going to do any more complaining for a while, since all the things I hate most are getting pretty well taken care of in the story. I don't mean that it's a polemical book or anything stupid like that. I think it will serve however as an antidote to a lot of smug shallow contemporary American thinking. As a matter of fact, the whole thing is fairly Anti- or un-American all the way around. Also anti-Catholic, anti-criticism, anti-denigration, anti-meanness, anti-nihilism. *Time* will hate it, the New Critics will ignore it, people instead of reading it will burn holes in their heads looking at *What's My Line?* But it will be a good book. Rose will read it, you and Anne will read it, and it will be banned by the Archbishop of Detroit. What more could a writer ask? Want to know the title? *Set This House on Fire*. From a sermon by John Donne.

In this same essay Camus says: "I hate self-satisfied virtue. I hate the despicable morality of the world, and I hate it because, just like cynicism, it ends by depriving man of hope and preventing him from assuming responsibility for his own life with all its terrible burden of crimes and grandeur." There could not be a more eloquent statement against the rotten hypocrisy which is the modern American way and therefore the way of the world. I just hope this book of mine is able to help reaffirm that statement. It is a tough road to go, but it has to be worth it or else we are all worth nothing at all. That is not ego speaking, it is faith.

I hope we can get together before too long. I realize as you say that you have more to complain about than I do, "being the obscurest critic in America," which however is not true. If my feelings hold any water, though, let me say this: you will be un-obscure and you will endure simply because you are about the only critic I know who does not secretly loathe and despise the creative act. You have no envy. You are not an insane little prurient groper who hates both life and art. You will endure. It is embarrassing for a novelist to say this to a critic, I suppose, but it is true.

Love from all the Loftises,
Bill
Milton.

To Robert C. Snider*

January 29, 1958 Roxbury, CT

Dear Bob,

I have tried to write you several times since receiving your nice Christmas card, but for one reason or another always got hung up. Maybe if I try pen instead of Royal Portable I'll have better success.

First, let me congratulate you upon your fine looking wife and boy. Second, let me felicitate you upon your appearance; the passing years have done little to efface what I remember as always being a slightly jaded optimism—good combination—and unlike myself and most of my contemporaries you seem to have taken on only a few ounces of avoirdupois around the jowls. Third, may I express my happiness at your professorship, especially at a place like Chicago; I always felt that, in spite of all the odds, there was one person in the F.M.F. who was destined to become something other than a plumber or a golf pro or a used-car salesman—and that man, of course, was you. What are you teaching, by the way? Chaucer? Socio-dynamics? Sanitary engineering? I'm in the dark.

The U.S.M.C., of course, laid a trauma upon my soul from which I am only gradually emerging to this day. To be sure, I had them—or they had me—twice, since I was called back in 1951, spending the whole time (10 months) at Camp Lejeune, where with that wonderful irony that happens only in life and not in books I was assigned to an outfit which made its headquarters in the identical building we both suffered in during the regime of Lt. Perry. Did you ever put a tracer on that bastard? He could not possibly survive in civilized society, except behind bars, and I've often yearned to know what institution he was eventually committed to. Anyway, pleading blindness and psychosis both, I got out, quickly got myself a discharge, and in this age of miracles finally consider myself safe and invulnerable. But it took a lot of sweat along the way.

We have a nice old 18th century farmhouse here in the Berkshire foothills and a swimming pool (Connecticut-type, which means that it gets fouled up with algae and salamanders, and is box-, rather than kidney-shaped) and a place to play croquet and a lot of mice in the attic. For the

* A friend from the Marine Corps.

East Coast, we are in the middle of nowhere, which suits me just fine. The we is my wife, Rose from Baltimore, and daughter Susanna, age 3, though we, I guess, are what you might call a quasi-four, since another is on the way and is due early in March. There are just enough people around within spitting distance—mainly literary queers—to keep the solitude from being oppressive, and we manage to get to N.Y. (85 min) often enough to retain the tremendous veneer of culture and sophistication we are so celebrated for here on the Atlantic Seaboard. So it is not too bad; it seems to snow a lot, and often seems as cold as it must get in Jamestown, N.D., but you've got to live somewhere.

To fill you in on my whereabouts since the Marine bondage, as briefly as I can: I got out of Duke in '47 and went to N.Y. and became the most unsuccessful editor that McGraw-Hill ever had. After this debacle I decided that there was only one thing left to do and that was to redeem myself by writing a book that would expose McGraw-Hill. Well, this didn't turn out very well as a leitmotif, but I did hole up in Nyack, N.Y., and wrote a spook-ridden, guilt-laden, desperate novel about Virginia which, as you probably know, came out in 1951. After that I bummed around in Paris for a year or so, and got a fellowship to the American Academy in Rome, where I went for a most unprofitable year—except for the exposure to Italy and for meeting Rose there. We were married, amid much panoply, at Michelangelo's Campidoglio. When we came back we spent a year in New York—a total waste of time—and since early 1955 we've been holed up here in Roxbury. Probably the most unexciting career a youngish writer has had since the days of Walter Pater.

At present I am under contract to Random House for a novel, and am 800+ monstrous pages along toward the end. I don't think it will ever end, although now I am so far up to my ears in it that I don't really care. What with sputniks, Lawrence Welk, critics and God knows what else, the novel seems to me a fairly useless form of expression, as is "art" increasingly in general, but I have made my bed and will try to fit into it somehow. I can always console myself with the fact that there are worse things to be doing—and there really are: working for B.B.D. & O., for instance, or working one's self up the ladder in the United States Marine Corps. Or writing for television. In the meantime, parts of this novel really aren't half bad. It's laid in Italy and is full of murder and rape and all sorts of romantic trash, and will appeal mainly to the discontented middle-class matrons who make up the bulk of our reading population anyway, but parts of it are really O.K. and the hero—a true enfant du siècle, full of all sorts of morbid longings—is, I think, a very successful creation.

Someday I want to get down on paper those Marine Corps days of ours. They were really too unheroic and sordid to be very valuable as fiction, but as some sort of reminiscence they could be a lot of fun. That psychopath Perry, for one, would make a nice vignette of some kind, as would our scroungings-around in Washington. I recall that you had a luscious little blonde creature, very acquiescent, whose name I forget, while I was stuck with a WAC radio operator, a skinny redheaded Mormon from Utah named Iris Sparks. I've always held that against you, Snider.

In answer to your query, am I ever in the Midwest, the answer is never yet, except on somber nights when the miracle of television carries me as far west as Chicago (I have never in fact been west of Pittsburgh), but this is not to discount the notion that I might come in the future. If I do, I will certainly get in touch with you. Meanwhile, do you ever come east? If you do, please let me know in advance, because we have plenty of room and would like nothing better to put you and yours at ease in Roxbury. Let me hear from you.

All the best,
Bill

P.S. It occurs to me now, if I'm not mistaken, that you were not directly under Lt. Perry, but were merely in the same squadroom where we less fortunate slobs hung out. No matter. Surely you must remember him anyway. Frog-faced fellow with hornrims, and a soul and spirit that would shame a jackal. Sometimes I still dream about him and wake up screaming, rigid with outrage.

To Leon Edwards

February 3, 1958 Roxbury, CT

Dear Leon:

The accompanying clipping, from the N.N. Daily Press of Jan. 31, which Pop sent me, should incline you to believe that there is after all in our universe a divine justice.* 150 days in the Denbigh jail, eating collards and fatback with the Negroes I'm sure our Milton despises, should certainly cancel out all the meannesses of the past. I hope therefore that you will shed a tear over this document—as I did—rather than give rein to your baser impulses and laugh like hell (which I really did). Pop assures me that this is the original M. Adams† and no cheap counterfeit, and adds that Raymond "is keeping his head above water," which somehow redresses the balance in a way for which I'm glad. As Pop continues so justly: "with their antecedents, it's no wonder the whole tribe didn't spend time in jail." Which leaves only one question. Who is Mrs. Virginia Toler? It has a good white trash ring, that name, but the sad thing about newspapers is the way they skimp the whole appalling scene—crazy Milton, spittle-mouthed, yelling obscenities, advancing on the poor woman with a brick (this does not seem to be a sex case), while Virginia herself, howling for protection from the monstrous apparition, wakes up all of Ferguson Park and brings forth a horde of welders, drugstore clerks, and deputy sheriffs to the rescue. At least that is the way I envision it, probably unfairly.

Outside of what a series of barium X-rays proved to be a case of "duodenitis" (I cannot find this term in Merck's manual), I am doing O.K., for a writer. I have just this day passed page 850 on my accursed manuscript, and the end is still not in sight. I will not bore you with a description of the agonies this book has caused me. I have heard it said that out of suffering great things come, and I certainly hope so, since to me at least it would be a colossal irony if all that came out of it was an exacerbated duo-

* The clipping reads: "A total of 150 days in jail was assessed against Milton Adams, whose address was given as 5971 Jefferson Ave. He had appealed from a conviction in Warwick Municipal Court of assaulting Mrs. Virginia Toler, 217 Court A, Ferguson Park, Dec. 28. He was found guilty on the assault charge and was fined $50 and given 90 days in jail. He had been convicted in Municipal Court on two charges, one an ABC violation and another on a charge of creating a nuisance. He received 30 days on each charge, the jail terms being suspended. When he appeared in Municipal Court on the assault charge the suspension of the two previous sentences was revoked. Judge Armistead ruled yesterday his terms would run consecutively. Adams was not in court at the time of trial yesterday. He was not represented by counsel. Judge Armistead directed that a capias be issued for him and he was arrested in the afternoon and taken to Denbigh jail."

† Milton Adams lived in Hilton Village, Virginia, and was a bit older than Styron. His father ran the dive bar that is fictionalized in Styron's story "A Tidewater Morning."

denum. I am taking probanthine, also Alka-Seltzer and several other panaceas, and they all seem to help some, but probably the major effect of this disease (which in turn, I'm sure, is caused by the wretched novel) has been to curtail my drinking which—since booze is such a remarkable tranquilizer—is a curse, but also—since I have always tended to drink too much—is no doubt a blessing. Doubtless some day I will have to call upon you to perform that sub-total insertion of my gizzard I've read so much about.

Our offspring is due in March and for that month we will be in New York, since Rose's doctor is at Mt. Sinai. Then I expect that we'll come back to Roxbury and start cultivating our garden again. I hope that it won't be too long after that that we will all be able to get together again. We procrastinate entirely too much along that line—renewing old sweet and mournful memories and such—and before you know it we'll all be a bunch of doddering old idiots with nothing to talk about at all—not even the Adamses. Along the felony line I rather expect Pete Preston to be next, for some especially grotesque and fumbling excursion into sodomy, or maybe Mole Howell (our coeval that is, the one that had underarm problems), though for nothing much more than some kind of inept larceny. I imagine I'm being cruel with these wicked prejudgments, but I didn't mean to be. It's just that my memories of Newport News have all gone sour; even the slight nostalgia I had once has all worn off, so that there is a kind of grey blank where my childhood was, and all I can remember is Hopkins Street on a September morning, and all the Downses issuing forth from their lair, and it raining like hell.

All my best to Marianne and the children. Keep up the good work that your last letter reported, and drop a line when you can.

Ever thy Bill

To Louis D. Rubin, Jr.

February 4, 1958 Roxbury, CT

Dear Louis:

Many thanks for your kind invitation and for all the news of various and sundry—the happiest of which, of course, is Eva's July 4th issue.* Rose joins me in warm and patriotic congratulations. Also I'm glad that you are feeling a bit more at ease at Hollins than in Richmond. I always thought that as a town Richmond was pretty much a dreary pain in the butt, frankly, and I'm glad you're enjoying the fresher air of the hills.

As for your invitation, I am of course flattered—as I was with your invite some years ago to Baltimore, and its happy results—but this time, even in view of the possibility that some more happy results will ensue, I feel I've got to turn you down, and I will try to tell you why as honestly as I can.

In the first place, let me say that whatever my remarks vis-à-vis academics and critics, they do not apply to you. No one was kinder or more generous to me than yourself and thus I am inclined to look upon you as a more or less remarkable and sympathetic anomaly in the dreary groves of academe. Besides, you are a genuinely creative person, which removes you from the herd. So kindly count yourself out of this discussion.

What I am getting at, though, is this: after long and painful and sometimes despairing consideration (despairing because basically I am not an enemy of the ideals of teaching) I have come to the conclusion that the young American writer—the writer, that is, of some guts and independence and vitality, and I modestly include myself—has no greater enemy than the academic critic or scholar such as would be represented at your meeting. To my mind they are the scum of the earth. Want to know why? Because in the whole history of our literature never has a group of people retreated in such a cowardly fashion from the times, from their contemporaries, from life and from books. Never has a group of people so scamped its responsibilities to its coevals (fancy word), turning its back on writers who, beset with enough troubles anyway—TV and mass culture and Christ knows what all, needed a little support more than ever before, and

* Eva Rubin's due date.

who in the end have come to feel about as unwanted as it is possible to get. Let me quote from Alfred Kazin* out of this week's Reporter: "Serious critics in this country write only in behalf of literature that came to fruition in the 1920's. This is what they mean by 'modern literature,' and in its name they shut the door to the young, the new, the 'crude,' the unfamous, the unheard. . . . It is 'modern literature' alone that gives background to critics like Leslie Fiedler . . . who complains that young novelists are always a terrible bore and that he would rather go to the movies. 'Modern literature' is a terrible tyrant. The 1920's died several world cataclysms back. It is time that we stopped worshipping Joyce and Eliot and Hemingway and made a place for the young." End of quote. This of Kazin's is from a review of The Living Novel, a symposium of which—as Kazin himself points out—the prevailing note is self-pity. The last thing on earth I want to do is to sound self-pitying, yet if I were to take you up on your invitation I would have to look out upon that bland safe sea of Faulkner-Fitzgerald-Kafka faces and say, "Why haven't you paid any attention to me?" Pretty please? And I'll be damned if I'll do that.

Indeed, it's damned hard to approach this subject without sounding self-pitying, try as one might to avoid the tone. No writer worth anything writes, or has ever written, for the benefit or approbation of the academic critic, yet I'll bet there are few writers whose work hasn't blossomed a bit in that atmosphere where they felt they were, for better or for worse, at least being taken seriously, making an impression of some sort. The generation of the 20's—so-called Lost—really had it made. Yet not one of them, to my mind, except Faulkner, ever wrote a novel as fine as The Naked and the Dead, which to this day is regularly being put down as obscene or clumsy or crude—all as if everyone was embarrassed over the initial naive enthusiasm it was received with. Or, worse than that, the book is hardly even mentioned at all any more. As for those few of my coevals who are taken seriously, I've gotten so used to picking up the Sewanee or the Kenyon or whatever and seeing long solemn essays on Robie Macauley or Peter Taylor or Andrew Lytle or Caroline Gordon or God knows what all—not to mention such monstrosities as the one by James Gordon Cozzens or whatever his name is—that it takes an act of

* American writer and literary critic (1915–98).

supreme will for me to come back down to earth and remember that I, too, am a writer and some day might be as good as Robie Macauley.* I scarcely have to mention that to my fairly accurate knowledge I never once have profaned the pages, by mention or reference, of a literary quarterly—except in The Hopkins and by unowho.*

But enough of this revolting self-pity. The fact of the matter, when you come right down to it, is that with only a long novella and a single novel under my belt I should hardly expect to be treated like Count Leo Tolstoy. As Kazin says in the same review: "Alas, nowadays American writers want everything they can get from society." Meaning, I gather, critical praise and popular success and fame and money. Even power, I suppose. We're all bitch-goddessed up by the idea of success.† As for myself, I should be contented (and really am, when I ponder it calmly) with the physical facts of my existence, which allow me to write what I want and at my own pace. I would be a cad to ask for more. Yet, getting back to the same issue, and speaking maybe for some of my contemporaries who haven't had my luck, it does seem to be a depressing fact that at a time when really good writing tends to get lost in the great deafening shuffle there have been so few critics who have cared or dared to come to the aid of a baffled public, and have tried to separate the good from the indifferent or the merely bad. If there had been, I'll bet such writers as Shelby Foote, who wrote in "Ride Out" one of the best short novels I've ever read, would not have turned as he has to Civil War history—which might be good but it's not "creation"; if there had been, such shallow trash as Françoise Sagan would have fouled out as she should have; if there had been several of these estimable and vocal critics, as there were back in the golden twenties, maybe—but honestly, there's hardly any use in belaboring the point.‡ The academics have

* Robie Macauley (1919–95) was a senior editor at *Playboy* and Houghton Mifflin, as well as the author of two novels and a volume of short stories. James Gould Cozzens's *By Love Possessed* (New York: Harcourt, 1957) was a bestseller. Styron used the term *unowho* (or *unuhoo,* in later years), to refer to God.

† Styron is paraphrasing a September 11, 1906, letter from the renowned psychologist and philosopher William James (1842–1910) to the British writer H. G. Wells (1866–1946) in which James famously wrote, "the moral flabbiness born of the exclusive worship of the bitch-goddess SUCCESS. That—with the squalid cash interpretation put on the word success—is our national disease."

‡ "Ride Out" appeared in Foote's 1954 collection *Jordan County: A Landscape in Narrative* (New York: Dial Press).

done a great job of sandbagging the spirit of literature, at least in this generation. I hope they choke on their Joyce and their Hemingway and even old man Faulkner, too.

So at your meeting I would be telling them all this, and I couldn't tell them without shedding at least one single pearly self-pitying tear. Ergo, all self-respect gone while the Ulysses-exegesists snickered up their academic sleeves. No, I just couldn't do it. I'd feel like a whore in church and shaking, as they say down home, like a preacher with the clap. What right would I, a mere writer, have to tell a group of littérateurs what place the modern young writer stood in society? I'd have to say no place at all, as far as I could see, and that if they were looking for a culprit look around them. It would be very unpleasant.

But I hope this won't deter you from getting in touch with us when you come Nawth. In private I don't talk about such matters at all, and can't cry over literature. As a matter of fact, I've just passed p. 850 in a novel which threatens to outdo even Jim Jones in quantity, and I hope to have it done when the summer's over.

All the best to Eva and yourself,
Bill

* the most intelligent review I ever received, by the way.*

Paola Styron was born on March 13, 1958.

* Rubin's review of *Lie Down in Darkness* from *The Hopkins Review*, Fall 1951.

To Norman Mailer

March 17, 1958* Roxbury, CT

Norman:

I don't know who your sick and pitiable "reliable source" is (how much he must hate and envy me, or maybe you, but above all hate himself), but you might have him or her get in touch with me some day and repeat his allegations to my face. Your letter was so mean and contemptible, so revealing of some other attitude toward me aside from my alleged slander, but most importantly, so utterly false, that it does not deserve even this much of a reply.†

B.S.

* This letter was written in response to (and on top of) Mailer's letter of March 12, 1958, where he quoted "a reliable source" that Styron had "been passing a few atrocious remarks" about Mailer's wife Adele. Citing past instances of Styron besmirching other women, Mailer invites Styron "to a fight in which I expect to stomp out of you a fat amount of your yellow and treacherous shit."

† At the urging of Rose (who had just given birth to Polly) and Jim and Gloria Jones, Styron decided not to send this annotated response.

1) I suggest that this "reliable source"—and I thought you above this type of shady allusion, Norman—is either a person with a warped and perverted imagination or simply an outrageous liar. I have no idea how close he or she is to me but, as a curator of paradoxes, you must be aware that closeness is no guarantee for the preservation of decency, and the fact that you have obviously not asked yourself whether this person simply does not hate and envy me, or you, or both of us—and above all himself—is one of the saddest parts of your letter.

2) "Atrocious remarks." An unmitigated lie. Or, depending on your definition of atrocious, simply a lie. You force me to explain myself in some detail. I would be less than frank if I told you that Adele was my favorite person in the world. At the same time, I am honestly fond of her, and I do not defame the character of people I care for. The fact remains, though, that she does seem to be able to handle her liquor very well, and that at parties she becomes aggressive and [unknown] beyond the ordinary limits of what people call fun. If you think that this fact cheers me or gives me any malicious delight, rather than pain, you are dead wrong. And I have remarked about this, in company with more than a few others who have felt the same pain. I have however passed no "atrocious" remarks at any place or time, and if you wish to fight me on this point you will morally have to battle several dozen others who share my regret and my sentiments.

3) The venomous tone of your letter leads me to believe that, quite to the contrary, you wish to believe it more than anything in the world.

4) This is odd. The only woman I can remember slandering in your presence, the wife of a young critic, richly deserved the slander, and I remembered that you did not hesitate to join merrily in the slander, adding your own sage judgments.

5) Your delicate style, which would be degrading to you even if I were guilty of the monstrous things you allege against me, leaves me in little doubt that something is, and must have been, eating you that has nothing to do with the "viciousness" you so meanly and falsely saddle me with.

Mailer's response on March 27 invited Styron to repeat his defense "face-to-face" or Mailer would know that Styron's account was "a crock of shit." This would be their last correspondence for more than twenty years. Styron admitted in a letter from April 2, 1980, that Mailer's version of events was essentially correct.

To Mrs. Thomas P. Peyton, Jr.

June 1, 1958 Roxbury, CT

Dear Mama Peyton,

Many thanks for your sweet letter. I don't really know how that article happened. There was a girl named Betty Tyler who called me up from Bridgeport. She used to work on the Richmond T.D., and now works in the Bridgeport paper. Anyway, she heard I lived in Roxbury, and so she came up and did an interview with me for Bridgeport and, since she still had Richmond connections, she sent the same article down there to Va. It really wasn't too bad an article, actually, but I wish she'd left out the part of it which said I got drunk on weekends. Well, the fact of the matter is I do get drunk on weekends, but it's not the sort of thing you go around publishing in the newspapers. I only wish old Tommy and old Charlie were around more often so I could get drunk (mildly drunk, that is) with them. I certainly do miss those boys, just as I miss all the sweet old Peytons. Many times in the past few years I have thought about the wonderful times we used to have in Crozet, and the wonderful eating—quail and stuffed lettuce, and one Thanksgiving dinner I still recall as the best meal I ever had—and I long for the time to come when we can all get together again.

Styanna knows all her letters and numbers and is mean as hell, but we sure like having her around. Polly is extremely young, as you know, and we are not on speaking terms yet; however, I don't think it will be too long before she starts taking over the house like Suzanna did.

If you can send me Satan's address, please do, or better yet tell him to write me. I have heard through the grapevine that he is going great guns in Charleston and I have no doubt that he will be running the company before very long. I would dearly love to see him again. He is the best old friend I ever had.

In the meantime, Rose, Styanna, Polly and I are having a good time in our Connecticut retreat. I hope to have this novel finished by the end of the year—at which point we plan to cruise down to Virginia and maybe we can all have a reunion. I will sleep until noon, Satan can go out and shoot some birds, and we will sing songs en masse after dinner.

Give my best to old man Tom Peyton, and tell him I am surviving, God knows how, in Yankeeland. I must be charmed.

Love to everyone,
Sty.

To Elizabeth McKee

August 8, 1958* 75 Main Street, Nantucket, MA

Dear Elizabeth:

Everything up here is dandy, except for occasional fog and airplane crackups that disturb the even tenor of our days. Rose + Susanna are sun-drenched and flourishing and they send their love to you all.

While on the Vineyard I saw a lot of Lillian Hellman and she wants me to write a play for her production company, Devon Productions.† She is ready to give me an advance + contract. I told her I'd be delighted to give it a try, but of course I had to finish the novel first. She understood that, of course, and asked me to ask you to get in touch with her partner so that you could talk over terms and so forth. Will you do this? I think he is expecting your call. His name is Lester Ostermen, Devon Prod., 55 W. 54th St., Judson 6-5570.

* Postcard of the *Mayflower II,* a full-scale replica of the original *Mayflower.*

† Bill, Rose, and Susanna Styron visited Martha's Vineyard for the first time that August, at the invitation of Hiram Haydn.

Will be back around Labor Day, sound and brown, I hope. Take care of Roxbury.

XXX Bill

To Louis D. Rubin, Jr.

October 24, 1958 Roxbury, CT

Dear Louis:

It seems to me that not too long ago I wrote you an extremely ill-tempered letter telling you why I despised all the critic swine and so forth and that you wrote me a much more well-tempered letter back, pointing out how my spleen was misdirected and it all made pretty good sense to me—so much so that only a sense of embarrassment at having gone off half-cocked must have prevented me from writing back right away. I still hate the critic swine—and you know the type I mean—but maybe now with a little more sympathy, at least understanding; that was a fine letter, and I'm glad you pointed out a few things to me about which I was rather pig-headed and blind. Anyway, we got your letter and are both very happy that your Robert is flourishing and has a big mouth. As an old hand at this racket, bub, let me tell you that the first 3 months are the EASIEST, then it gets worse—everything gets worse before it gets better—and that there are moments in the mid-watches of the night when a razor or the oven look mighty enticing, I'll tell you; then all of a sudden, around the time that they are almost grown-up, they start to behave and act human, then you can knock the shit out of them. Tell Eva she's got a lot to look forward to.

The other thing I was interested to hear was about the Hispano-Virginia don, Señor Salamanca, who has apparently done the commonwealth up brown.* Since my own new book will probably exceed even his in length, or grossness, I can only applaud his good American stick-to-itiveness, I think it's called. But, man, that dialogue. I'll lay you even money right

* J. R. Salamanca, *The Lost Country* (New York: Simon & Schuster, 1958), was set in Virginia and adapted for the Elvis Presley vehicle *Wild in the Country* (1961).

now that MGM has bought it for a juicy sum. People like Salamanca always have it made. . . . Speaking of which, I don't know whether you saw it or even heard about it, but "The Long March" was on TV recently—a total disaster from beginning to end, with my tragic little tale being turned into a paean to the Marine Corps, the lead actor dead drunk, gumming his lines, everything appallingly grim and tasteless for 1-½ hours.* Well, I more than expected this even before it happened, happily collected my CBS loot, and really couldn't have cared less how it turned out. But let me tell you a small but sad sequel to the whole thing. Just yesterday comes this letter from the headmaster of Christchurch School, my old alma mater, telling me that it was so fine and dramatic, that program, and how he sat breathless watching it, and all the boys thought it was just the greatest thing ever, and finally how happy he was that I'd really made the big time and from now on out Christchurch had its EYES ON ME. Well, I could have almost wept, thinking of this Bright Young Educator down there on the Rappahannock—entrusted with the guidance of 125 nubile young boys—who, if I wrote twelve masterpieces to equal Tolstoy wouldn't bat an eye or give me the time of day but who, having seen a cheap piece of quackery on TV which is a travesty of the original, comes all over himself telling me how great I am. Do you want to know what I did? I sent him a large check (CBS money) and a pompous letter telling him to buy some books for the library, if they still had one, and letting him know that I had no fear for American education as long as the likes of him were in the saddle.

Well, maybe the written word is dying, I don't know. Anyway, remembering my mean letter to you about the critics, I reflected that the critics were still probably not the writer's friend, but that here was the REAL enemy—young headmasters, young so-called educated people, teachers, frauds and cretins everywhere who are supposed to know, supposed to be educators, leaders, but who really have no more concept of culture or history or of the humanities than some country sheriff's poor harelip daughter. You don't expect the clods or illiterates to dig you or even care; it's when people like my headmaster buddy cheer you for the wrong thing that you begin to think that you're living in a vacuum, or a madhouse.

* The CBS adaptation of *The Long March*. Styron wrote a disparaging piece about the experience, "If You Write for Television . . . ," *New Republic* (April 6, 1959).

Well, to hell with it. I'm very glad to hear that your novel is coming along. Curious, although practically all of my book is set in Italy, the framework which supplies the story and the flashbacks is all laid in Charleston, S.C. Which makes it difficult, since my knowledge of Charleston is limited to about three visits of 24 hours each. However, I have solved the problem by having the two major characters—who are trying mutually to recollect what went on in Italy—sit fishing in a skiff in the Ashley river, from which they never move. Describing rivers is easy. However, I know nothing about Charleston fish so I wrote to the Chamber of Commerce and they sent me a flashy pamphlet which set me straight—spot, croakers, and channel bass.

Rose and I don't know yet where we're going to be between Christmas and New Year's—it will be either here or Baltimore—but I hope we can get together during that time. If it's Balto. maybe you can stop by on your way up to or down from N.Y.; if here, I should think surely we could get together somehow, either in N.Y., or perhaps we could entice you up to the country. Our vines have tender grapes, the children raise hell, but we call it home. We would like to see you.

Give Eva our best. As Kerouac says: "Like I mean, you gotta swing with it."

Yours,

Bill

PS I was re-reading The Web and the Rock the other day (part of it) and it becomes more and more apparent that this was the most tragic writer as Writer who ever lived.* Such power and majesty he has still, for me, such a torrent of pure grandeur, and, in the end, such godawful CRAP.

* Thomas Wolfe, *The Web and the Rock* (New York: Harper & Brothers, 1939).

To James and Gloria Jones

January 20, 1959 Roxbury, CT

(You must understand I have not placed these items in any particular order. Actually I would put you above Mikoyan, though several cuts above Herbert Hoover.)*

Dear Jim and Gloria:

Rose + I figured that, though you must undoubtedly subscribe to the Enquirer, you probably don't get the Air Mail edition, so I am rushing these clips off to you tout de suite, so that you may know that you are still keeping the best of company. I have written to J.J. Miller, who of course runs the whole show, telling him your correct address (if it isn't, you won't get this), and I hope you will appreciate that fact. Incidentally, Gloria, when you really get pissed-off with Jim you can come live with Rose + me.

We've read a lot of the reviews of The Pistol, and are very pleased that it seems to be getting more judicious treatment than Running.† Most of the ones I've seen have treated it with the greatest respect, which it very much deserves. It is, as I think I told you several thousand years ago (when was it, last March?), quite a wonderful job, and I'm glad that the critics are at least basically acknowledging that fact. Why we give a God damn what the reviewers think is something which, in the long run, escapes me, but we do, even though they're all practically scoundrels and nitwits. Anyway, to repeat, I'm happy that The Pistol is receiving (at least partially) its just measure.

We enjoyed your various postcards from exotic shores and envied you both until we were each the color of pea soup. Cannes! The Italian Riviera! Paris! To hell with both of you. As I write the temperature outside is 18° and our monstrous dog, Tugwell, has just vomited all over the living-

* Styron pasted in several items and the header from the *National Enquirer: The World's Liveliest Paper:* One paragraph about Russia's deputy premier Anastas Mikoyan meeting escorts in New York City, another about Herbert Hoover and a "curvey cutie." And: "James Jones, the 'From Here to Eternity' author, is holed up in an apartment at 17 Rue du Cirque, working diligently on a new tome. Mrs. Jones reports that her husband is 'not very pleasant' to live with while he's embroiled in writing. 'A lesser woman would have left him,' she states bitterly."

† James Jones's third novel, *The Pistol* (New York: Charles Scribner's Sons, 1959).

room rug. Do you call this living? We wish we could join you at the Lapérouse, but unfortunately we can't, until I finish this novel, which I'm still writing on, as I was last March, and which I expect to be doing until I'm a dreary old man, scrofulous, incontinent, and a ward of the State.* Actually, I hoped and prayed that I'd have it all done by now, but the deeper I get into it the more horribly complex and endless it seems to get. Though I'm being somewhat melodramatic, really. If I keep a steady hand I should have it all done in a matter of a few months. The trouble is keeping that steady hand. Though sometimes I tell myself that I know it's a fine book, most of the time it seems a big gross idiotic pain in the ass. In the meantime, time skips by and I develop a big fat gut and everybody seems to be looking at television.

Speaking of which, The Long March was on television last fall (Playhouse 90) and it was turned into an absolutely incredibly delicate abortion†: Jack ("Mannie") Carson drunk, blowing his lines, Sterling Hayden as the Colonel striving valiantly with lines no one, least of all me, could conceive of, a chorus line of cuties, Inez and Pearl and Roberta, a lot of dames I never heard of, a triumphant mountain climb at the end, the Marine Corps supreme, beautiful, inviolate, etc. Thank God you're in France.

If you have time to send a letter, do so; otherwise, don't send these terrible, glittering, sexy, seductive, abominable postcards with angle shots of sun and sea and European poontang which makes me wish you'd drop dead. But in spite of all my gloom, there's a fairly good chance that we'll make it to Europe by summer. We want to go back to Ravello and if we go we plan to ease through Paris and give you a hard time as a couple of visiting firemen.

The children are fine. Polly is an incredible production, fat as a pig and with an ingratiating moronic grin; Susanna stuck a safety pin (closed, thank God) up her vagina, but we got it out O.K., and where she goes from here is anybody's guess. They send their love, as does Rose, and I too—

Truly yours always

Billy

* Lapérouse is a venerable Parisian restaurant overlooking the Seine.

† Styron used this same descriptor, "abortion," for Mason Flagg's account of Alonzo's movie in *Set This House on Fire*.

To Mac Hyman

February 4, 1959 Roxbury, CT

Dear Mac:

This is just a short note to tell you that though I was extremely tempted by your invitation to go to Castro-land, I have had recently a lot of second thoughts. Man, they shoot you down there! Anyway, as soon as I finish up this economy-sized novel of mine, maybe we can join forces, you and I, and go to some nice civilized place like the Belgian Congo (they're having just a small revolution there) and shoot crocodiles and sip up a few rum Collinses.

I thoroughly enjoyed your boat piece in Esquire. It was really funny all the way through and, having had one nautical experience with you anyway, that only made it that much better. Speaking of Esquire, they are running a longish hunk of my novel next June, so you might take a look at it, though I have more than a few qualms about pre-publication of parts of novels: I mean, taken out of context, the stuff often just doesn't make too much sense. Anyway, they don't pay too badly (though not too good, either) so what the hell: I figure you can't really lose.

Are you going to make the New York run anytime soon? If so, let me know, so that we can get the great room squared away and lay in a few cases of Rheingold. I'll tell you one thing: by now I am so sick and tired of writing that I get spots before my eyes everytime I sit down at a desk. Wouldn't it have been great to have lived in those days when everyone sat around and talked about how exquisitely wonderful it was? So come on up and we'll sit around and talk about—boats, maybe, and sex, and writing.

Best to Gwen + your family

Bill

To William Blackburn

February 4, 1959* Roxbury, CT

Dear Doctor

So belatedly that I fear I am past hope, I want to thank you for your fine Conrad book, which I read with enormous interest, and also to tell you that, despite my silence, I am still alive and kicking.† I was sorry to learn from your last note that you had suffered an indisposition. I hope everything goes well now. But mainly I wanted to congratulate you on the Conrad; the letters are really worth having (he was one of the last who knew how to write them). Perhaps it is only because they are so good that kept me from writing you for so long! Even when he was talking about money (and money did seem to be on his brain) his letters are alive. I love that line: "Perhaps true literature is something like a disease which one feels in one's bones, sinews, and joints." And I love the letter to Blackwood about "Thackeray's penny worth of mediocre fact," followed by his creed—character living through action. It is a really valuable book, and I was delighted, incidentally, to see that it was accorded proper treatment in the Times Book Review.

I am staggering numbly and blindly through the last pages of my own mammoth economy-size novel. It will be the most blissful day of my life when it is finished. Then I will write nothing but short pieces—none of them any larger than a postage stamp. The newly-vamped Esquire, by the way, which has pretensions to something called quality, is going to run a longish excerpt from the first part of the book this coming June. The piece will, I fear, do very little to communicate the real quality of the book, but the reaction in itself is not too bad and I got $1,000 for it (I sound like Conrad), and perhaps there is an outside chance that it will whet one or two readers' appetites for the book itself. We shall see.

I trust you are still planning on the big Duke jubilee in April, as I have

* Styron attached a note (and presumably a British review) dated February 9, 1959: "Dear Doctor—I suppose it's only the direct insecurity that motivates my sending you these little plugs for myself, but I did want you to see that, possibly, I am finally being accepted in the Old Country. Would you return it, please, whenever you get a chance to write. Ever, Bill"

† Blackburn's edited collection of Conrad's letters.

it on my calendar. Will I have to make any formal speech? I sincerely hope not, although I won't balk at making a few introductory comments. I have for some reason never gotten over a kind of childish stage-fright. Perhaps a year or two of honest teaching would have cured that. At any rate, I am looking forward to Carolina in the spring. The climate up here is fit for muskrats and the birds.

All the best,
Bill

To Rust Hills*

February 9, 1959 Roxbury, CT

P.P.S. One typo I've noticed (my fault): on p. 38, line 18, please change the word "But" to "Bent."

Dear Mr. Hills,

Naturally one never gets everything worked out right in a telephone conversation. Since talking to you today I have had these minor afterthoughts about MS. On page 106–107, regarding your query about the construction of Line 8, I have consulted Fowler and find that he views this sort of thing as one of those cases where you just have to throw up your hands and say O.K., technically it is not right but let it stand.* So maybe we'd better let it stand. Another thing—pp. 114, 115—it is of course a good thing to throw out the references to the Kinsolvings, which you had marked. Please cut. Finally—p. 105—(and this is also something I wish to delete in the book MS) please change the name S.J. Perelman [note in margin: "P.S. besides, Gibbs is dead, so no problem for Esquire about invasion of privacy. Mainly, they're sweet as she is, I have conceived of Rosemarie as one of those people who think of the New Yorker as a sophisticated Holy Bible, sweet as 'it' is."] to Wolcott Gibbs. This is exceedingly minor,

* Lawrence Rust Hills (1924–2008), renowned fiction editor for *Esquire* magazine off and on from the 1950s through the 1990s. He was famed for being able to excerpt famous writers' novels (such as Styron's *Sophie's Choice*) and make the pieces seem like standalone short stories.

meant only as a small swipe at New Yorker–worshippers, but I don't in any way wish to malign Perelman, whom I admire, while I couldn't care less about Gibbs.

Only one other thing, I gather from the fact that you're going to run my photograph and so forth you will have at least some kind of explanatory text to run along with it. I don't know whether you have any intention at all of using any kind of critical reference, but in case you do, I have one for you which I received the other day which pleased me immensely. (This is the author blowing his own horn.) It was from the London Observer of Feb. 1, and the critic was Philip Toynbee, who I gather is one of the best in the Old Country.* At any rate, the quote was embedded in a review of Faulkner's collected stories, in which he was discussing the fact that Faulkner was not only the first but "by far the best" of the "Southern school" of American writing. The quote is this: "William Styron's Lie Down in Darkness is the only other novel of this school which seems to me to be on a comparable level of achievement." Actually, I really don't consider myself of the Southern school, whatever that is, but I think the comment was a handsome one, and I rather immodestly hand it on to you, and won't feel in the slightest miffed if you don't use it.

Many thanks for your excellent help and comment, and I hope we will all be mutually pleased by the June issue of Esquire.

Sincerely,
William Styron.

* Fowler's pitch seems to be that in a case like this the phrase "or merely the struggles of the day" has sufficient "rhythmical weight" to override the more grammatical "he." (If I flop as a writer, I can always get a job as a grammarian.)

* Theodore Philip Toynbee (1916–81), prolific British writer and critic.

To James and Gloria Jones

March 24, 1959 Roxbury, CT

Dear James and Moss:

In the past six weeks I have been scouring the N.Y. Enquirer and all the other gossip sheets, including Leonard Lyons,* for news of you but found nothing, so I've decided to venture a communication in order that I may, perhaps, find out how you are first-hand. Your last letter was greatly enjoyed. The apartment sounds fabulous and you cannot know how much we envy you. Especially since we are at present concerned with such problems as: the spring running dry (this can cause a big stink in the house, but we finally got it fixed); Susanna filling up all the milk bottles, put out for collection, with jellybeans; the Plymouth V-8 station wagon catching a case of the clap, or whatever the hell else it is that causes it to use a quart of oil every 100 miles; the washing machine getting clogged with grease and running all over the kitchen floor; the maid sulky because we don't call her "ma'am." You people don't really know how lucky you are. Also, you may be interested to know that the both of us, caught up in the grip of overpowering lust one winter night, got exceedingly careless, and we are going to have Scion #3 next August. I don't know what possesses me to do such a thing; I am not a Catholic and it is certainly not (since I am secure in my virility) ego-gratification: it must be madness. Any way, I hope the two of you will for Christ sake get started along the same lines so I won't feel like a complete fool about this thing. The worst thing, of course, is that it cuts out any hope of a trip to Europe this summer, you will just have to do the Portofino bit by your own selves, and we will curse you every minute. We are going to Martha's Vineyard. Shit, do you really think He does care for us at all?

About your liver ailment: forget it. All French doctors, I found out when I was in Paris, think that my ailment is caused by, and any overindulgence is detrimental to, le foie. You must put fear out of your mind, and resume drinking right away. I really mean this. I know a guy who received the same edict from the doctors, and stopped drinking, and very shortly he died. I am quite serious, James; to be temperate in France is

* Leonard Lyons had a column in the *New York Post* entitled "The Lyons Den," which covered entertainment gossip.

moral and spiritual suicide, and never mind what Montaigne said in regard to wine.* I know what I am talking about.

One of the things I wanted to tell you is that there is very shortly coming to Paris for the first time in his life a friend of mine, a writer named Edwin Gilbert and his wife, who live not far from here.† You are probably chewing my ass out this very minute for the presumption, but I told him that if he sent you a pneu sometime you would be delighted to see him and show him all the fleshpots. For God sake don't feel obliged on my account, but he's a very nice guy and so is his wife, and I think you would like them, and I know they would be tickled to meet you and Moss. He wrote Native Stone and Silver Spoon, both big best sellers. His latest is called The Hourglass (Lippincott) and it should sell a million. Norman knows him well, too, incidentally.

Speaking of Norman, about whom you asked, I have not seen him since I saw you last, and still don't much care to. He has moved back to New York—the Village, of course—and I hear very little about him. I am quite serious when I say that I think he has flipped his lid, or is gradually flipping it (there are a lot of other stories), and it is all very sad, but it is something I'd rather talk to you about than write about.

My own personal professional-type news is very scanty, except that I'm gradually edging up on the grand climax of my book, and am about to pee my pants with excitement over the fact that it might soon be finished, after four long years. It is about 825 typescript pages with maybe 100 more to go, which falls somewhat short of War and Peace, but it isn't bad and I'm not really that competitive. The MS got into the hands of the people at ESQUIRE, from whence it came back sort of smeared with Coca-Cola stains and burgers, but for a very stiff fee they are going to run about 20,000 words of the book, starting in the June issue and featuring it and all (they took a very glamorous picture of me, impaled upon a Gramercy Park fence railing), so since I imagine it will be good publicity I am not

* Michel de Montaigne (1533–92), one of the most important essayists of the Renaissance period. Styron probably refers to Montaigne's essay "Of Drunkenness," in which he made many observations on wine, among them: "Plato forbids children wine till eighteen years of age, and to get drunk till forty; but, after forty, gives them leave to please themselves."

† Edwin Gilbert wrote many bestsellers, including *Native Stone* (New York: Doubleday, 1956) and *Silver Spoon* (New York: Lippincott, 1957).

complaining.[*] Did you read in TIME about Hiram Haydn starting his own publishing house? Much as I care for Hiram I guess I will have to stay at Random House, for this book at least.[†] Anyway, without being cynical, it puts me in a good situation re Random House. I got a love letter from Bennett Cerf the other day, telling me he'd just die to have me stay, etc.[‡] So I got him over the old sawhorse. This is probably the bitchiest sort of talk, but I figure that if you work your ass off over a book it's good to see the publishers scramble for you. There are few enough delights for a writer these days. N'est-ce pas?

I've heard some very fine things, incidentally, about THE PISTOL recently—nothing official, that is, but from various people I've run into. In other words, it's being read, which is the main thing and all that counts. I hope you're still staggering along somehow and keeping at it. I don't know exactly why I say this but I think writing in general is very subtly enjoying some sort of renaissance and is due for a real breakthrough soon. I think people are just really fed up to the teeth with TV, Kirk Douglas, Norman Vincent Peale, and other such imposters, and are ready for the real scoop. I don't mean tomorrow, but soon. It can't be any other way, I

* *Esquire* published the excerpts "Set This House on Fire" (June 1959) and "Home from St. Andrews" (May 1960).

† Haydn left Random House in March 1959 for a new venture, Atheneum Publishers, which he founded with Simon Bessie and Alfred A. Knopf, Jr. Hiram assumed that Bill would join him. Among other minor squabbles with Haydn was one over Vladimir Nabokov's *Lolita:* Bill had brought it to Random House, and Haydn found the book offensive and humorless, while Bennett Cerf, the head of Random House, wanted to publish it. Styron wrote about the conflict over *Lolita* in "The Book on Lolita," *The New Yorker* (September 4, 1995). Hiram and Rose had a huge dustup over it, but Random House didn't take the novel. In *Words and Faces,* Haydn described the parting: "Styron made a decision that he must have found difficult. Moreover, there was never any question of his being ungrateful; there is strong evidence to prove the reverse. Part of his reasoning was that he had twice gone with me to a different publishing house; if he did this a third time, it would only confirm the opinion he had often been exposed to—that he couldn't make his way without me. Add his liking for Cerf and Loomis, and the strength of Random House—and I think his decision was a sound, logical one. Today we get together over a rowdy game of croquet now and then, but it took quite a while for the hurt to heal."

‡ Bennett Cerf admired Styron's writing and liked him personally. Cerf wrote Styron on March 17, 1959, "We were proud to add you to the Random House list, and we will make every possible effort to keep you there. In a single sentence, I would like to be your publisher for the rest of my life."

figure, else everybody will have to slit their throats—and I don't mean just writers.

Now that we have started on this correspondence, send me a billet-doux sometime. Susanna, Polly, and Rose send their dearest best to both of you and ask me to tell you that they won't be too upset if in the midst of Martha's Vineyard I just fly over by myself and take a piss in the Seine from your balcony.

Ever yours,
Billy

To George Plimpton

May 11, 1959 Roxbury, CT

Dear George:

I hate to be a pain in the ass about this thing.* Your own comments—and Peter's—were most sensible and also very sympathetic. I don't think I would be nearly so adamant about my position in this matter had it not been for Train's puerile and pedantic and really quite insulting remarks.† I was told by you and Peter not to take Train seriously. Yet on second thought, it comes to this: if he is not to be taken seriously in a matter like this he seems hardly in any position to be an editor of the magazine—a serious business, or so I've always thought.

So I must repeat: I am perfectly willing to make the one or two major changes you + Peter suggested but I must insist that I cannot let the piece be published if any of Train's changes are heeded (with the one or two exceptions, the grammatical errors listed below). I am sorry to have to put it that way, but if you want the piece you will either have to want it as I substantially wrote it, or get Train to write it for you. To my mind Train is and always has been an arrogant and supercilious little prick—but I've told you that before. If I felt that except in one or two minor points Train was right about this piece I would have the grace to admit it. But in every

* The excerpt from *Set This House on Fire,* which ran in *The Paris Review* 22 (Autumn–Winter, 1959–60).

† John Train, editor at *The Paris Review.*

basic criticism he is simply wrong. Therefore, I hope you see my position in the matter.

. . . If you've got any questions about this please give me a ring and I'll be glad to iron out any details. I'll be coming in town no doubt in a week or two and hope to see you. Meanwhile, watch the burbling.

All the best + say hello to Bob
Bill

To John P. Marquand, Jr.

June 10, 1959 Roxbury, CT

June 10, tomorrow I'll be 34 sob!

Dear Marchand

Many thanks for your splendid vote of confidence in the Esquire piece; I'm deeply grateful since I respect your opinion as I do few others. I don't know but whether you aren't a bit premature, though, since the rest of the book upon recent re-reading seems solemn, pretentious and windy beyond all countenance. However, I am working hard to salvage something out of the wreckage before the Vineyard and Mrs. Tynan set in. I am very much looking forward to the beach. My esteem for John Welch has gone up 1005%. Love to Sue and the miraculously redeemed bush baby.

B.S.

I have a terrible feeling that Normie is going to show up on the Vineyard, along with several other hippy studs.

To Claire White

June 14, 1959 Roxbury, CT

Dear Claire,

Thanks so much for all the spooky, ritualistic, Catholic information, which I really do need to get on properly with this godforsaken novel I'm writing now. It is already something that I've used to fine effect (how I could have thought that Ash Wednesday came in Holy Week I'll never know) and if the book sells 100,000 copies, as I passionately am certain, it will all be due to you.

I think you know it, but let me repeat—we are expecting all of you for the Fourth of July. Rose says come any time after the First, and she adds that Stephanie can stay here in the "big house" (plantation talk), and if you want to you + Bobby can take your repose with the other two (excuse me, three) in what we are pompous enough to call the cottage. Anyway, we're looking forward to seeing you all, and though it's sad to me that due to your condition we probably won't have much sexy nude swimming together I console myself with the notion that perhaps I can use you for a float.

Kiss Bobby for me + tell him we have his Lambretta picture hung up in the new living room, which he'll see.

Love + XXX
Bill

Thomas Styron was born August 4, 1959.

To James Jones

September 15, 1959 Roxbury, CT

Dear James:

I just talked on the phone with Tom Guinzburg, who is at this moment unfortunately languishing in Harkness Pavilion with a thrombosis in his leg. It is something he has had for a long time, on and off, and I gather it isn't gravely serious—there are drugs now to loosen the clot—but he said if I wrote you to say hello. So hello. He also said that he had seen you holding court in front of Doney's with a bunch of your usual sycophants and worshippers and free-loaders, and that both you and Moss looked fine.*

* Ristorante Doney is located on the Via Vittorio Veneto in Rome.

Though I don't particularly envy you an entourage made up in any part of Ed Trzcinski or however the hell you spell it, I do envy you in general—Rome, Portofino, etc.—and I'd give a gonad, both of them, to be over there right now.

I will not try to apologize for not writing in so long (I do still love you), except to say that in the interim since your last letter I have, consecutively, had a young son (Thomas, born August 4) and a novel (tentative title: Veronica and Her Uncle Max, brought to a close only a week ago). The former is now eight pounds, red, ugly, and has a huge cock; all I can say about the second is that it is 961 ms. pages long and, whatever its worth, it is my baby and I love it. It will be out in the spring. So before you curse me for my silence, please take all this into account and realize that I have really been beset, and that I haven't been tooling around all over Europe ruining my liver and living like King Farouk.* Though I have been, God knows, doing no good to my liver here; I thought I'd taper off bourbon now that the strain is mostly over, but no, I booze it up all that much more, part of some sort of semi-mystical act, I suppose, to convince myself that the book really is as good as Stendhal—which it isn't—but at least as good, say, as Sloan Wilson and Herm Wouk.† What a pile of crud, unmitigated crud, this writing dodge is. I thought I would get a big bang out of finishing this book, but all I have is a feeling of exhaustion, and a sense of extreme foreboding as I wait for the Prescotts to devour me and the highbrows to ignore me and the public, as usual, to not buy me (current total sale of Modern Library Long March: 4,523; that is not a misprint; I hear Leon Uris' latest excresence has just topped a cool million copies).‡

Well, I'm going to stop whining for a minute, and tell you that otherwise everything has been pretty good. We spent part of the summer on

* King Farouk I (1920–65) of Egypt was notorious for his glamorous lifestyle on the Continent.

† Sloan Wilson (1920–2003), author of *The Man in the Gray Flannel Suit* (New York: Simon & Schuster, 1955), which was a bestseller. Herman Wouk (b. 1915) is perhaps best known for his novel *The Caine Mutiny* (New York: Doubleday, 1951), which won the Pulitzer Prize in 1952.

‡ Orville Prescott (1907–96) was the main critic of fiction for *The New York Times* for nearly twenty-five years. Leon Uris, a frequent target of Styron's envy and ire, had a number one bestseller in 1959 with *Exodus*.

Martha's Vineyard, where we were neighbors of Lillian Hellman's; I don't know if you know her or not, but she is a fine lady, and a great friend to the younger literary generation. She's a staunch admirer of your work, incidentally. We were also neighbors of Elaine Tynan,[*] who is indeed a somewhat different story than Lillian. I gather you two were living it up in Germany with Kenneth while we two had the decided burden of the distaff half; she is straight out of Scott Fitzgerald, though without some of the dew and freshness, and is possessed of what I can only describe as a kind of morbid carnality. She drops names like pennies, and perhaps it sums her up to say that she is the only person I have ever seen drop with an immense glow of self-satisfaction the name of George Axelrod.[†] We had a very full summer.

Rose and I definitely plan to come to Europe next year—probably in the spring, if we can swing it to leave one or two of the kids with Gran'ma—and hope to make it to Paris first. As an old Paris hand I do not feel like a visiting fireman, and I trust you will treat us with the proper respect. Are you still going to be there then? I do hope so, as both Rose and I have missed seeing you all. We'll tell you when to lay in a supply of Old Forestry.[‡]

I have not seen hide nor hair of Norman, except to hear that he has coming out soon an anthology of his work called Advertisements for Myself, a characteristically self-effacing title, which includes a 75,000 word essay, heretofore unpublished, about the problems facing a man who wishes to become a "major" writer in our time. The sad, sad thing is that Norman could be a major writer, but I don't see how he can be one if all his energy is thrown into crap like this. Who gives a damn about the problems of becoming a major writer? Nobody. Except maybe a few other writers. The only way to become a major writer is to write books.

Incidentally, God knows why, but I have become literary adviser to

* Elaine Dundy (1921–2008), actress and author of novels, biographies, and plays. She was married at the time to the actor and critic Kenneth Tynan; they divorced in 1964.

† George Axelrod (1922–2003), screenwriter, playwright, producer, and director, is best known for his play *The Seven Year Itch* and for his movie adaptations of Truman Capote's *Breakfast at Tiffany's* and Richard Condon's *The Manchurian Candidate*.

‡ Old Forester bourbon.

Harper & Brothers. I realize that this is in the best tradition—Eliot, Graham Greene, Moravia, etc.—but I can't help but feel slightly creepy about it all. Like I should start wearing a bowler hat and umbrella. Anyway, if you have any loose manuscripts hanging around . . .

Look, James, tell Moss that I think of her with hard despondent lust at all hours. I really miss that girl. I miss you too, and I hope that this one time you will forgive me for my lapse in correspondence. I will certainly do better, much better, from now on out. Swallow your pride, you bastard, and send me a letter.

Love,

B.S.

I hope this gets to the address Guinzburg gave me.

To Edgar Hatcher

September 23, 1959* Roxbury, CT

Dear Hatcher:

I appreciate and was greatly tickled by the seminal intelligence you sent me, which puts my mind at ease about a great many nagging worries I have had about certain obese women in my past.† I have sent the piece on to Tom Guinzburg, who needs it, since he is at present recuperating from phlebitis at Harkness Pavilion.

If I can stay sober long enough, my book will be totally complete within a week or ten days. There is a very minor character in the book whom I have taken the liberty of naming after you.‡ He is quite an old man and

* Hatcher supplied this letter to William Blackburn for Mac Hyman's collected letters. As Hatcher explained on November 11, 1965, "Unhappily, Mac and I never wrote to each other . . . I do have one surviving note from Styron, a xerox of which I enclose."

† Hatcher had attached a clipping from the *Journal of the American Medical Association* on the "Fat Content of Semen," August 1, 1959.

‡ "I was, of course, tickled to have him use my name in his book," Hatcher wrote Blackburn, "although I threatened to use his name as the hero of my (mythical) novel about a sodomite."

his name is Vice-Admiral Sir Edgar A. Hatcher. He is retired and, though vacationing in Italy, his permanent address is Southsea, Hampshire—which is something of the equivalent of La Jolla, where our decrepit seadogs go to die. I was casting about for the perfect name for a British Admiral, and yours simply struck me as being without parallel. If you are offended, or feel that in the future you will wish to sue for invasion etc., let me know so that I can strike it out of the galleys. This Hatcher was once third sea lord of the Royal Navy, in charge of submarines.

When are you all coming up here? The weather is good.

B.S.

To William Cole*

December 1, 1959 Roxbury, CT

Dear Bill:

Now that I have perused Capote's and Avedon's OBSERVATIONS which you so kindly sent me I am somewhat inclined to agree with your own acerb observations when I saw you last.† Some of the pictures are really quite striking, and every now and then Truman has a sharp thing to say, but there is such a desperate air of vogue and chichi over the whole venture that it all tends to try one's patience before long. But thank you for sending it; it will adorn my coffee table, and give to our Connecticut homestead a proper air of swank. Incidentally, you might let your copy-editing department know, if they care, that in Truman's prose I found at least five typos and misspellings (especially mistakes in the Italian) after only ten minutes quick skimming.

Thank you mainly for your own book. Just from the little bit of dipping into it I have done already I can tell that it is a lovely anthology, and I plan to take it with me when I go to Europe this winter. I am glad you

* William Rossa Cole (1919–2000) was best known as an editor and anthologist. He was an editor for Simon & Schuster and Viking and a columnist for the *Saturday Review*.

† Richard Avedon and Truman Capote, *Observations* (New York: Simon & Schuster, 1959), featured Avedon's photographs of artists, writers, and celebrities, and Capote's text.

put in Hoffenstein and especially Walker Gibson's circus ship poem which I read when it first appeared and have looked for vainly since.*

My novel, SET THIS HOUSE ON FIRE, will be in bound books—so I am told—by the latter part of March. I'm sure Jean Ennis will send you a copy and I hope you like it.†

All the best,
Bill Styron

PS. It has now occurred to me, after reading the fine section in your book titled "Primitive," that someday you might want to do an anthology of gruesome verse. Accordingly, I am enclosing the words to an old hymn which was included in an anthology done by an English friend of mine. I think it has real style, and I have copied out a few stanzas for you.‡ The entire poem may be found in Hymns as Poetry, compiled by Tom Ingram and Douglas Newton (London: Constable & Co., Ltd., 1956).

To James Jones

December 7, 1959 Roxbury, CT

Dear Jim:

You're no doubt as surprised to be getting a reply so soon to your letter as I am to write it. I might as well tell you that what it's prompted by mainly is the fact that Rose and I have begun to definitely make plans to come over your way, and no doubt you will see us, grinning from ear to ear and dressed like visiting firemen, as we stand on your doorstep sometime early in February. My book is completely finished (I'm going over the galleys at the moment) and it is mainly the fact that I've been up here in Roxbury for the four-plus years that it has taken me to write the thing that

* Walker Gibson's poem "To the memory of the circus ship Euzkera, lost in the Caribbean Sea, 1 September 1948" (*The New Yorker,* November 6, 1948) was based on a true incident.

† Jean Ennis, director of publicity at Random House.

‡ Styron enclosed the same Moravian hymn he had sent William Blackburn in March 1956.

makes me now want to take off from here and get away from the American scene for a good long while. It must be a fairly natural reaction; anyway, though this doesn't mean a permanent move, it does mean that I am wanting to spend six or seven months in Europe, so as I say Rose and I will come over and scout around for a place toward the end of Jan., or early Feb. We may stay in Paris, we may not—I've got my eye on something around Lake Como or the Ticino part of southern Switzerland—but anyway this will be a scouting trip, then I expect I will stay over while Rose goes back to Baltimore and collects our proliferant brood of offspring and comes back and settles down with me wherever it is we plan to stay. However, we definitely expect to use Paris as a command-post, as Hemingway would put it, so I imagine you will be seeing us more often than is decent or healthy for a while.

Rose and I are both delighted about Moss' condition, which is another reason for this letter, and we want to tell you that we too have our fingers crossed and hope that everything goes well this time.* As a father of three I can now attest to the fact that though the traffic-pattern around the house often gets a little congested, and it is sometimes hard on the nerve-ends, there is nothing like one or two of the little monsters to give a kind of roundness to one's life. If this sounds a little fatuous it is only because most basic truths are fatuous, and difficult to express freshly. Anyhow, I think you will discover this for yourself, and we wish you all the best.

As I say, the book is all done. It should run to about 500 printed pages, and everybody at Random seems to like it very much; they are showing their faith in it by a first printing of 30,000 copies, which naturally pleases me: I only hope they aren't going to get stung. At any rate, now that I can see it in galleys some of my confidence in it comes back after weeks of rather grim depression. There is an authority in the fact of print which tends to make one feel that it was somehow all preordained, and perhaps pretty good after all. I've even gotten to the point where I am no longer so foolishly worried about the treatment the book is going to endure at the hands of the critics. What the hell I say, I've done my best. If it's really a good book then all the little maggots can't harm it in terms of its ultimate value; if it deserves their attacks then it deserves it. The book is not going

* Gloria Jones was pregnant with their daughter Kaylie Ann Jones, born August 5, 1960.

to be published until June, when I'll be in Europe somewhere, and perhaps I'll have the distant and frosty objectivity, this time, not even to read what they say about it . . . perhaps, I doubt it.

Norman's book got very good coverage and mixed reviews, some saying it was all crap, others saying just what Norman says: that he is the most powerful and amazing writer of the generation. Maybe you will have read it by now. It doesn't make a bit of difference one way or the other, but I think we come off rather well among his contemporaries ("competitors"), in spite of the fact that you've "sold out badly" and that I have "oiled every literary lever and power" to advance myself. There is a terrible air of paranoia and self-destruction all through the book, and the most intelligent thing that was said about it was in some review which pointed out the tragedy of a man with such genuine talent ranting and raving so wildly instead of employing that energy in the construction of a work of art.

I'll try to keep in touch and let you know when we'll be turning up there. Drop me a line if you find the time. You sound as if you feel you've found something good and strong in this new work of yours and I'd love to look at it, if you'll let me, when it's done. These are singularly crappy times for writing, but you've got it, I know, and I've got some of it, I'm pretty sure (Mailer's got it, too, if he'd quit writhing in agony over recognition), and maybe someday in the 22d century they'll put our pictures on a set of postage stamps. Wouldn't that be something to strive for?

Rose sends her love to you and Moss and the conceptus (a horrible word, but I can think of nothing more beautiful) and I hope it won't be too long before we'll have a fine à l'eau.*

As ever,

B.S.

* *Fine à l'eau:* cognac and water.

To Robert Brown*

January 8, 1960 Roxbury, CT

Dear Bob:

I have no quarrel with most of your premises about my premises; indeed, I thought (I'm having trouble with my h's†) your letter was an excellent one, and I'm at least glad that my introduction—with all your disagreements—provoked you into writing me. Actually, I think writers of fiction like myself shouldn't write discursive essays at all; their brains don't operate right, and their prejudices and peeves tend to get out of hand.

Basically, I think I'm a lot more sympathetic to critics and criticism than most writers I know. I have read an amount of criticism, in college and out, and have profited by it. Good criticism is a creative act; some criticism is infinitely better than nine-tenths of the so-called "creative writing" that is being produced nowadays. I don't think that even the best criticism will be as good or as valuable as say, <u>MOBY-DICK</u> or <u>HUCKLEBERRY FINN</u> but that's begging the question; the point is not only as I said in the introduction that "it is not necessarily a shameful act for a writer of fiction to read criticism" but that a writer will be denying himself something very good and illuminating if he does not at one time or another avail himself of the <u>best</u> that criticism has to offer.

This said, I would like to uncloak myself, and in a somewhat autobiographical way tell you why I still feel that criticism has a long way to go in this country before it becomes half-way responsible. I will have to talk about myself, and I hope it will not embarrass either of us too much.

One of the functions of criticism, I think you will agree, the function that sets it apart from the Prescotts and that sort of trash, lies in its requisite that it separate the real cream from the crud, that it informs the small body of honest, serious, seeking readers that such and such a work or writer is <u>really</u> good, as distinct from the rest of second- and third-raters who are daily touted as geniuses in the press. This is what Edmund Wil-

* Brown was an editor at *Esquire.*

† The key was evidently malfunctioning—the *H/h* is barely legible throughout the letter.

son did for Hemingway and Fitzgerald, what Mencken* did for Dreiser and Sherwood Anderson, and there are countless other examples in France and England; this was the time when in your phrase, quite rightly, the critic was the writer's "best and only ally and friend."† You go on: "he pays serious attention to what the writer writes holding that it is rich, unique, valuable, interesting, important, complex, difficult," etc., and all that is very good. Now I don't know what you personally think of LIE DOWN IN DARKNESS. I assume that you may have some regard for my work to write me such a complex and interesting letter. But now I will tell you about the career of LDID, letting the self-pity fall where it may.

It came out in 1951, and due to the good offices of an editor and publisher who had faith in the book it received considerable journalistic attention. It got fine reviews in the Sunday book pages; embarrassingly enough, even Prescott half-liked it, and though Time Magazine and The New Yorker shrugged it off as another magnolia-and-moonlight potboiler, there were a lot of very fine and intelligent reviews from the provinces. It was even a moderate best-seller for a while, and then it dropped out of sight. Well, I thought all this was swell enough, but being university-bred myself and not ashamed of it, I began to wonder when I would get really serious attention. I mean I began to say to myself that all this middlebrow attention was very good, but now—how about the serious audience? How about the old Kenyon and old Partisan and the old Hudson and all the rest? Who was going to tout this book onto the college readers—the serious young people in college or just out who after all make up one of the major parts of a serious writer's audience? When were the people I had been taught to respect—the critics, the Edmund Wilsons of the era—when were these boys going to loosen up and put a laurel or two on my fevered brow? I should not have bothered to fret so. Because with one single exception—the short-lived Hopkins Review—I got not a solitary notice anywhere . . . nor to my knowledge have I gotten a solitary notice

* H. L. Mencken (1880–1956) was a journalist and critic of American life and culture. One of the most popular and widely syndicated American writers before World War II, Mencken became especially notorious for his coverage of the Scopes trial of 1925.

† Theodore Dreiser (1871–1945) was a novelist best known for *Sister Carrie* (1900) and *An American Tragedy* (1925). Sherwood Anderson (1876–1941) was a novelist best known for his short story collection *Winesburg, Ohio.*

to this day. I used to read them avidly, these literary journals: there was a lot of stuff about the wry, sly talent of Miss Mary McCarthy,* or Truman Capote, or such giants as Peter Taylor and the artful Robie Macauley, but not a breath about me. Yes, there was indeed one mention: this was from the illustrious Richard Chase, who in a single line damned my work as "a middlebrow novel with highbrow flourishes of rhetoric." So be it, I thought; maybe it was just that, after all the Critic knows best. So just kept on writing.

Well, for several years after publication the fortunes of LDID declined. To be sure, every now and then I would get a breathless note from a club matron in Palmyra, Ohio, telling me how fine she thought my work was, but this would only give me a feeling of Weltschmerz and fatigue; and though I knew I had a small group of fans—cultists, you might say—most people who might have heard of LDID had, in fact, not heard of it (or The Long March either) and I saw the zooming ascent of the talents of James Jones and Salinger and John Updike, but looked upon these ascents with some equanimity, knowing that I was simply not in their league (had not Chase, that "best ally and friend," told me so?).† Anyway, I still kept on writing, and then about two or three years ago I noticed a really singular and astonishing change. I found that despite the total indifference of the learned critics, despite the fact that I did not have a Wilson or a Mencken, my book was actually being read—that people were somehow stumbling upon it (and The Long March, too) and reading it and passing the word on, and reading it in considerable numbers. I found that at a party, instead of shyly standing in a corner and being introduced to someone who then would ask me what my "line" was, I would actually be known before I even got to the goddam party; that someone would actually come up to me and say they had read my work and tell me how much they liked it. Naturally, all this strange new interest necessitated a revival of the printed page itself, and your friend and mine, Thomas Guinzburg,

* Mary McCarthy (1912–89) was an author, critic, and political activist. Best known for her memoir *Memories of a Catholic Girlhood* (1957) and novel *The Group* (1962), McCarthy also became somewhat infamous for her feud with Lillian Hellman.

† John Updike (1932–2009) was a novelist and critic best known for his Rabbit novels. Updike won the Pulitzer Prize twice, published twenty-three novels, and contributed regularly to *The New Yorker* and *The New York Review of Books*.

reprinted it at Viking. This edition has now undergone the astonishing phenomenon (for fiction in "quality" paperback) of a second printing, and now, mirabile dictu,* I find that LDID is on the required reading lists at close to ninety colleges and universities throughout the length and breadth of this great land. With no more attention from those best and only allies and friends of the writer than you could stick up the ass of a flea, I find that my book has become some sort of modern classic; I find that in England Philip Toynbee, who until a year ago had never heard of the book (how could he? surely his American critical cousins would never have sicked him onto such a middlebrow book), reads LDID and writes of it in the Observer that it is the only book since Faulkner's early work that is on a comparable level of achievement. I find, in short, that after a long period of utterly needless neglect and indifference on the part of those whose duty it was presumably to pay attention to important writing (at last belatedly I know I'm better than the fustian creeps and homunculi they were writing about all those years) my work has simply vindicated itself. Which of course is as it should be.

I know that this letter sounds terribly self-centered, and I also know that it doesn't come to grips with some of the more specialized and cogent observations you made about criticism in your letter. To practically all of them I say amen, and I hope you will believe me when I say I have no war with criticism per se. But if, as I believe to be true, one of the important functions of criticism is not only to explicate the whiteness of Melville's whale but also to apprehend and pay serious attention to the literature of one's own time, then I personally feel that I do not owe to contemporary criticism a plug farthing. I think that contemporary literature is blighted not so much by the Prescotts and J. Donald Assholes (though they are bad enough) but by the cliquishness and myopia of the Trillings and the Chases and the deadly young squirts like Podhoretz and such actual haters of books as Leslie Fiedler, who wish the novel to be dead.† That is why such introductions to anthologies as I write are apt to be cranky, and I

* Wonderful to relate (from Virgil's *Aeneid*).

† In addition to Orville Prescott of *The New York Times,* Styron refers to J. Donald Adams (1891–1968), a literary critic who wrote for *The New Republic* and *The New York Times*. Norman Podhoretz (b. 1930) is a neoconservative writer known for his work for

hope you understand. I hope I have not been too immodest. I am all too well aware of the limitations and faults in my own work, and in retrospect I cannot claim for that first book of mine anything that isn't there. But I do think that it has proved on its own hook its own value, which seems to be a fairly lasting value; unlike most books published since the war, mine still lives, but if it had been up to any imprimatur from modern criticism to keep it alive, rather than the slow accumulating enthusiasm of readers, it would now be as dead as the dodo. Incidentally, I am all for symbols.

Yours,
Bill

PS Rose and I are giving a party at Cass and Sidney's on Jan. 29th, a Friday, from 9:30 PM on. Why don't you come? I think Rudd,* of "THE FISHERS," will be there.

PPS. I'm having Random House send you a copy of "Set This House on Fire" in March. It is not an obscure work, but it cannot be made explicit to an idiot, thank God, and I think you might like it.—B.S.

To Elizabeth McKee

February 22, 1960 Hotel Lotti, Paris, France

Dear Elizabeth:

I received this letter today from our friend Giblin and am sending it on to you so that you may communicate with him.† I am writing him to tell him that it is all right with me if he and his group want to put on the play

---

Commentary magazine. Leslie Aaron Fiedler (1917–2003) was a literary critic best known for his book *Love and Death in the American Novel* (1960).

* Hughes Rudd.

† James Cross Giblin (b. 1933) worked on a stage adaptation of *Lie Down in Darkness* (for the Broadway producer Edward Pakula), which was never produced. Giblin was writing in the hopes of staging a free performance at "a loft workshop on West 17th Street."

but that the final word would have to be with you and Cy because of the possible legal complications, etc.* But do get in touch with him and let him know one way or the other.

Paris is a ball and the kids are eating it up. It is, God Knows, so expensive as to stagger the mind but I am trusting that between you and me and STHOF we shall be able to remove some of the ominous pall from this problem. We've seen a lot of Jim + Gloria Jones, also the Gilberts—the latter about as wildly chic and parisien and expatriate as you could manage to get. I don't know just how long we are going to stay. There's a far-out chance we may get an apartment and stay here until summer, but more probably we will be going to Italy in a week or so.

The Kids and Rose all send their love to you and Ted, as do I, and please keep in touch with your benighted client.

Love,

Bill

P.S. Let us know your plans for Europe as they develop.

To Lew Allen

March 6, 1960 Hotel Principe e Savoia, Milan, Italy

Dear Lewie:

This will be a somewhat shortish note, as we just got off the train from Geneva and are kind of worn out after a long albeit spectacular trip through the Alps. However, the Hotel Principe e Savoia is not too unlike the Sheraton-Hilton in Cincinnati and I have beside me a double Scotch so at least I should make sense.

Mainly I wanted to tell you that I am pleased about the news concerning the movie and Radwitz (is my spelling right?). I got your letter in Paris and it all seemed to me very optimistic this time. Youngstein I know has

* Charles "Cy" Rembar (1915–2000), an intellectual property attorney who happened to be Norman Mailer's cousin.

for a long time been a hot personal admirer of LDID and I think that it is a good sign that he is for the picture, since I have little doubt that he will wish to make a good picture rather than a film a la Jerry Wald. So all I can say now is that I hope things continue to progress in the near future in the way we want them to.

I suspect that you may wish to keep me informed, so maybe I should tell you that after the 11th of March we will be staying in Rome at the Hotel Majestic, Via Veneto. We'll be there a week or so, I imagine, in the meantime trying to find an apartment for our terrifying and proliferant brood. This trip has been so shockingly expensive that I am reduced nightly to warm, bitter tears, but in spite of all it has been tremendous and sometimes hair-raising fun. We have come close to losing both Polly and Susanna in at least three train stations, and in Geneva, Polly very nearly fell off the fifth floor terrace of the Hotel de la Paix. We have 18 pieces of baggage which considerably cramps a train compartment, especially when, as between Paris and Geneva, we got our reservations mangled and had to share the compartment—spilled milk, shitty diapers and all—with two exceedingly unfriendly Swiss businessmen.

The Gilberts showed us around Paris' mauve and elegiac streets, but for some reason Paris is no longer the great thing it used to be. Most of the Americans are either deadbeats, beatniks*, or remittance men of one sort or another, and though the social life is incessant it seems to lack any real fun or reality. The exception is Jim and Gloria Jones whom we saw a lot of, exhaustingly. They are great folks and are in love with Paris and have just bought a $34,000 apartment on the Île St. Louis. Jim is hard at work on a new novel, parts of which he read to us, and which seems to me very good indeed.

I hope you'll let me know how things are going. As I say, we'll be at the Majestic in Rome until around the 20th. After that, Bob Loomis or Elizabeth will know my address. Tell Jay that Susanna pines daily for Brooke, and we all hope you come to Europe soon.

xxx

Bill

* Speaking of beatniks, I went to a jazz-poetry reading on the Left Bank, and afterwards, completely unawares, had my picture taken for L'Express

with Gregory Corso and William Burroughs.* I look like an advertising man, Corso like a madman, and Burroughs like a mean, elderly dike.

To Robert and Claire White

March 6, 1960 Hotel Principe e Savoia, Milan, Italy

Dear Bobby + Claire,

Traveling as we do like the Archduke Otto and entourage, we get little chance to mingle with the natives or brush up on the local patois, but there is one compensation for it all: we pay through the ass. We have just landed in Pittsburgh from Geneva and are ensconced for the night in a hotel that outdoes any American hostelry you can name for sheer brass, vulgarity, and assy bad taste. The Venetian blinds go up and down when you push a button, and the various servants' bells go off like a pin-ball machine registering tilt. Milan is a hell of a city and I pine for tomorrow when our ludicrous safari of 6 (did you know we have a maid?) pushes off for Rome by way of Florence. I thought Paris had become Americanized, then I thought Geneva was the nadir, but you haven't really seen the effects of the good old U.S.A. until you visit the bar of the Hotel Principe e Savoia and see several Milanese Rotarians buttering up a Cincinnati soap tycoon over a Very Dry martini.

In Paris, Bobby, I saw a copy of the new Paris Review and was appalled to see that they didn't have your drawings illustrating the excerpt from my book. I immediately sought out the Paris editor, a little shithead of about 20 named Nelson Aldrich (I suspect he's one of your cousins, since he's kin to the Astors), who told me that, yes, he had seen your drawings and had liked them but that he had a friend who needed the commission, etc.† A long sad tale which didn't move me a bit. I gave this kid hell, telling him

* Gregory Corso (1930–2001) was a poet and the youngest of the Beat Generation inner circle. William S. Burroughs (1914–97) was a novelist, poet, and central figure of the Beat Generation, best known for his novel *Naked Lunch* (1959).

† Nelson W. Aldrich, Jr. (b. 1935), served as Paris editor of *The Paris Review* and edited the oral biography of George Plimpton, *George, Being George* (New York: Random House, 2008).

that I had explicitly wanted your drawings, but of course it was too late. At any rate, I wanted you to know how aggravated I was by this typically stupid Paris Review maneuver and how much I regret the fact that they weren't included. I have been on the verge of quitting the miserable little rag for a long time, and now I think I have good reason.

Anyway, we are going on to Rome and will be at the Hotel Majestic for a week or so while we hunt up a big outrageous Parioli-style apartment. I expect to be hobnobbing only with movie stars, diplomats, Counts, monsignors, and other assorted trash, but perhaps if we can prevail upon you all to come to Rome we could have a wonderful time. So come! My book should have left the manufacturer in a couple of weeks and I've told Random House to send you one. If there's any slip-up write R.D. Loomis at Random and tell him I told him to send you one. Rose and the kids are fine and all send love + kisses to you all. Love B.S.

To James and Gloria Jones

March, 1960 Hotel de la Ville, Rome, Italy

Dear James + Moss:

Well, the last of the big spenders has really just about gone completely through his National City Bank travelers' checks, having stayed in more exorbitant hotels than he ever cares to count or remember. We are now at this big inn in Rome and have already been billed $25.00 for the upholstery they (the kids) ruined with butter, minestrone, and modeling clay. If this traveling doesn't stop soon I'm going to go flat-and-straight out of my mind. Right now we are looking for an apartment and we seem to have several good leads; they don't appear to be hard to get and, from the examples I've seen, some really rather sumptuous ones are available at not too high a price. In spite of all the miseries of hotel living I'm getting a really big boost out of Rome and so is Rose. It is of course totally different from Paris and has its lacks, but what a really spectacular place it is, after all! The light and the buildings—they're all still here, and it's as if the city didn't mind it a bit when I left here seven years ago. We haven't been here long enough to tell the calibre of the social life but I am trusting that it will be somewhat less hectic than in Paris. Rose and I really had a ball in

Paris, seeing you and Gloria especially, but I think a few more 4 A.M. soirees with those Left Bank cats would have left me limp as an old tampax. Both of us hope you will come down here for a visit soon. Get on a jet in Paris and you'll be here in less than two hours. Rose asked me to tell you that her mother is arriving here on Mr 31, staying with the ambassador, and then on April first she is leaving for Greece and won't be back until April 17. But anytime you want to come will be fine with us. We'll line up a hotel for you and by that time we will be in socially to the hilt with various counts and countesses, movie no-counts, diplomats, and all sorts of other trash, so you may expect to have a good time. We do hope you'll try to make it.

I've gotten several advance comments on my new book which are so ambiguous as to tend to depress me far more than if they had been violently unfavorable. John W. Aldridge doesn't much care for it, I gather, but Max Geismar thinks it's swell, though not as good as "Darkness." This pre-publication period is a depressing drag and sometimes I really know it would have been better to go with B.B.D.+O.* Besides, what does it all mean? What does it all mean?

Hope you will write soon (this address, but it will be forwarded) and we'll see you. The kids are fine and send slobbery love to all.

Bill

To Mrs. Franz J. Horch

March 12, 1960 Hotel de la Ville, Rome, Italy

Dear Maria,

I got your letter yesterday, and appreciated it, and want to take the opportunity now to tell you how I feel vis-à-vis the French publishers. As you well know, I was first offered a proposition by Robert Laffont, when at that moment I was told by an acquaintance, Annie Brierre who works for Plon, that Plon would very much like the book. So I sent back the Laffont contract and signed a contract with Plon for publication of The Long

* The advertising firm Batten, Barton, Durstine & Osborn (BBDO).

March and an option on Set This House on Fire. However, when I got to Paris I discovered several malheureux facts. First, through Mme. Brierre, that the readers at Plon were far from unanimous in their enthusiasm for the book. Second, that they wished to publish the book only after making extensive cuts. Third (this acquired by talking to people who know French publishing well), that Plon was notoriously slow in publishing, even to the extent of violating the time limit in contracts (Bellow's Augie March, for instance, was not published until five years after acceptance). Naturally all this made me very unhappy, and in the meantime I met Jean Rosenthal of Laffont, who had wanted to publish the book in the first place. He was still most enthusiastic about the possibility of Laffont publishing the book, and I was so impressed by his attitude (a verbal promise, for instance, that Laffont would make no cuts at all) that I could not help but wish that I had not changed my mind and signed with Plon.

Naturally, I don't want any cuts made in my book and I am most disappointed with Plon's entire attitude toward the book. Further, after getting your letter, I am extremely opposed to Plon's really outrageously binding option clauses. So I have written Mlle. Bataille in Paris, telling her that as much as I regret causing all this trouble I hope she will do everything she can to prevent Plon from taking the book. Possibly she will have to be adamant about not allowing cuts, or perhaps she will have to set a prohibitively high price on the book. At any rate, I hope Laffont gets the book, as I think they are in every way more capable, more enthusiastic, more everything. There is of course the possibility that Laffont will refuse the book after reading it, but I do think that this is a slim possibility indeed, and in any case Gallimard or someone else would doubtless take it eventually.

I hope this is not too confusing, and now I dearly wish I had signed with Laffont at first, but I think you can understand how completely in the dark I was about Plon. But I wanted you to know the situation. Are you coming to Europe this year?

All the best,

Bill Styron

To Elizabeth McKee

March 12, 1960 Hotel de la Ville, Rome, Italy

Dear Elizabeth:

I got your letter yesterday at the Majestic, which is on the Via Veneto and exceedingly noisy it is too. So we have moved here, where we'll be for another week or so, I imagine. I have arranged, however, to collect any mail which you may already have sent to me c/o the Majestic or Mrs. Zellerbach. We expect to get an apartment soon. This hotel traveling a la the Duke of Windsor is straining my bank account fearfully.

I read the letter to you from Mark Hamilton and as far as I can see it looks very good. So you may tell Mark Hamilton that I accept Jamie's offer. Actually, I was pleasantly surprised at the £1,000 advance. That's $2,800 and will pay for quite a few hotel rooms. Indeed, I thought that for England the whole proposition was quite O.K. In Paris I saw the Hamilton catalogue and though to be sure they were jumping the gun, the stuff they wrote about the book made it appear that this time they may get off their asses and go all out for S.T.H.O.F. So bully.

I've run into a few complications with my French publishers. Plon wants extensive cuts and naturally I don't want any made, but I'm putting the whole thing in the hands of Franz Horch + Mlle. Bataille in Paris.

Write me here with any news, good, bad or indifferent, and I'll let you know later my final address. Rose + the kids are fine + send love. B.

To Jean Rosenthal

March 13, 1960 Hotel de la Ville, Rome, Italy

Dear Mr. Rosenthal,

I thought you might like to know that recently, while I was in Geneva, I wrote to Mlle. Bataille, telling her that I hoped she would take every measure possible to see to it that Plon did not publish Set This House on Fire, and that you should get a chance to see the book as soon as it could be arranged. In a very few days there should be bound copies available in New York, and I have instructed my editor at Random House that you receive a copy by airmail at once. I need not describe again to you my extreme disappointment with Plon. Also, since I saw you my agent in New York sent me a copy of Plon's contractual terms and they seem to me—as to my agent—almost ludicrously unacceptable, tying me up by option for not just my next book but the next three, etc. Also, they still definitely wish to make extensive cuts. Needless to say, I was most impressed by your own attitude toward such matters as mutilating a book in this manner, so I do hope you like the book and will decide to publish it.

I will be here for another week or so, but after that should you care to get in touch with me you may send any communication here and it will be forwarded to my permanent address in Rome. It was a pleasure meeting you in Paris and I hope we shall see each other again.

Sincerely,

Wm Styron

To Maxwell Geismar

April 4, 1960 Via San Teodoro, 28, Rome, Italy

Dear Max:

Though I suspect that my erstwhile pal, Norman Mailer, would consider a letter like this simply another example of literary politicking, I wanted to write and tell you how really pleased I was by your reaction to SET THIS HOUSE ON FIRE. Bob Loomis delightedly sent me your quote and I think I can say without qualification or sentimentality that it touched me like nothing in a long time to see how you responded to the book, and how you understood it. Though I'm all too well aware that the book has its faults, in my better moods I believe in this work, and think it will eventually get its just due and recognition; you have been one of the very few people who professionally has cared for my work, and has spoken up for me, so I would like to think that this new book—and your understanding of it and belief in it—will eventually prove to be vindication for both of us. Loomis tells me that John Aldridge didn't particularly go for the book, having gotten hung up on, of all things, "Mason's repressed homosexuality," an infinitesimal factor in the book which here perhaps reveals a lot more about the secret life of Aldridge than it does about Mason, or the book. Naturally, and as usual, I am looking forward to being ignored by the Partisan highbrows, etc. In an age when horrifying anal fantasies like The Naked Lunch are all the rage, I have no doubt that the schoolmasters will find this book of mine too broad, too "social," in short, too full of life. But most of the time I find myself feeling so much faith in the book that it really doesn't matter. I can only sense a certain kinship with Stendhal and say to myself: "My work is there. Try to move it, you bastards, try in vain."

We have the whole gang over here in a nice apartment overlooking the Forum. The reason I am here is mainly to get away from Roxbury for a while—from the scene of my wrestling for so long with Cass and Mason—and to get a breath of fresh air, a momentary new slant on things. Loving Italy as much as I do, I am no expatriate, and I have no doubt that we will be back in the U.S. toward the end of this summer. The book will be published around the first of June and I am of course going to be very interested in seeing how it goes. It would be fine if Fate ordains that you review it for the Times, but those things as we both well know are in the hands of God + Francis Brown. Give my very best to Ann. Rose sends love, as do I, and I hope you'll let me hear from you.

All the best, Bill

To John P. Marquand, Jr.

April 4, 1960 Via San Teodoro, 28, Rome, Italy

Dear John

Bennett Cerf–baby just the other day sent me a package containing three copies of my new book. To be sure, the package came first class airmail, but nonetheless it may be an indication of the colossal size of this work of fiction when I tell you that I counted the postage and found that it totaled $28.80. I am being utterly serious when I tell you that, hefting this mammoth excrescence of mine, I have never been so utterly bereft and depressed in all my life. Who, in God's name, is in this day and age going to sit down and read 507 pages of haggard, neurotic outpouring when they can go see Tony Curtis or learn to water-ski or fly to the Bahamas or read something slim and jazzy by John Updike? How and why do we make the fatal mistakes we make? Please, John, I implore you—this book you're completing, for your own sake and for the sake of literature, try to keep it down to a manageable size: 350 pgs. is about tops. If you'll just do that, I won't even nag at you to finish it. I have never been so disconsolate over anything in my life as the concrete proof, between hard covers, of my own appalling logorrhea.

But now I am so heartbroken over the whole thing I don't even want to talk about it, but instead will try to forget it by telling you about more mundane and credible matters, chief among them that we are now settled in Rome in a chic, hideously expensive apartment owned by Prince Paolo di Borghese, whose wife Marcella is a sort of mouthpiece for Revlon's quality line of cosmetics. He is a fat little guy, totally impoverished, who makes a living off of renting this apartment to American fly-by-nights like myself; he is of course several miles to the right of Louis XIV and it might amuse you to know that previous tenants were John Wayne, Rock Hudson, Van Heflin, Jayne Mansfield and Mickey Hargitay—all of whom I presume nodded off to sleep, as I do, over such books in his library as Mussolini's memoirs and tracts like "Il Destino d'Italia: Monarchista o Fascista?" But there is a maid named Virginia and a boy from Capri named Paolino who cooks fine spaghetti, and everything has been all right so far except that Susanna has knocked over and broken a $500 Della Robbia vase.

We saw a lot of Jim + Gloria Jones in Paris. They were in great form. Gloria is successfully pregnant and they have bought an enormous new apartment on the Île St. Louis, where I presume they intend to stay for the rest of their natural lives. They both speak an extraordinary brand of French, well larded with shits and fucks, but they make themselves understood easily enough and they both know everyone in Paris. It might interest you to know, by the way, that while in Paris I attended a jazz-poetry session presided over by Gregory Corso. All the international hip set was there and afterwards I fell into company with Bill Burroughs. He is an absolutely astonishing personage, with the grim mad face of Savonarola and a hideously tailored 1925 shit-colored overcoat and scarf to match and a gray fedora pulled down tight around his ears. He reminded me of nothing so much as a mean old Lesbian and is a fantastic reactionary, very prim and tight lipped and proper who spoke of our present Republican administration as that "dirty group of Reds." I thought he was kidding but he was not; he is as mad as a hatter and after the jazz session a photographer from Paris Presse buttonholed Corso, Burroughs, and myself and took our picture (in front a charcuterie), later captioned—so help me God—"Les 'Beats' à Paris." I'll send you a copy if you don't believe me.

I have no idea, really, why I am in Rome, unless it's only because I felt that after four years solitary confinement in my megalomaniac-dreams of a novel I had to get away, escape the great Eisenhower glut for a while, and regain my bearings. So far we've had a pretty good time of it, with no dearth of social life, but I'm astonished even more than I was six years ago at how utterly alike in so many ways Italy and America are. The fucking noise and traffic here are so appalling that New York seems like Roxbury by comparison. Macho-men have taken over, chaos reigns everywhere, and I quite honestly often long for Connecticut—to which we shall doubtless return at the end of the summer. We've seen quite a bit of Blair + Nina (who seem to hobnob quite a bit with ducal Italians) and though we only saw the Sims' once we expect to see them again when they come back from England. She reminds me so much of Suay it's almost spooky.

We've heard from Lillian and understand the play is a great success, which is fine. Kiss Suay for me and the Bush-baby and say hello to the other cats—Harry Hines, Normie, Artie, etc., and drop me a line.

Stybo

To William C. Styron, Sr.

April 17, 1960 Via San Teodoro, 28, Rome, Italy

P.S. Did you read that the two main American Olympic track hopefuls are the Styron twins from Louisiana? I wish them well but am beginning to wonder if they're white.

Dear Pop:

Well, it is Easter and as usual it rains in Rome on Easter so I'm taking this chance to drop you a short line. Tonight Rose is throwing a party for some people—the Fullers, whom we knew in New York, and their parents (he is Cass Canfield, Sr., who is president of Harper + Bros., and in effect my boss since I have become Harper's "literary advisor"), and a Count Alvise di Robilant who is married to, of all things, a girl from Lynchburg who went to Randolph-Macon, and Peter Ustinov, the actor, and his wife.* Since "Virginia Gentleman" costs more than one-third less than it does in Connecticut this party should not tax our resources too greatly: thank heaven for Roman whiskey. Spring has finally arrived in full force in Italy, as have the German tourists; we can hear them twenty-four hours a day beneath our window as they clump through the Forum. The kids seem to be flourishing in this climate. Susanna has begun to chatter in Italian, with the aggravating perfection of accent that children have which their parents never achieve. Polly speaks of "latte" instead of "milk" and even, believe it or not, "frigerifico" instead of "refrigerator" and as for Thomas I imagine he will start out speaking no English at all. We rented a television set, which the children watch at dinnertime just like they do in Roxbury. The cartoons are the same—Donald Duck, Bugs Bunny, etc.—but all the voices are of course dubbed into Italian, and the kids get a big kick out of all this, understanding everything much better than their papa. The apartment itself is quite nice, with a balcony which looks out up toward the Palatine hill and the tiny little ancient church of San Teodoro—the oldest church in Rome (about the 2d century A.D.). We are enjoying ourselves peacefully and I expect we will be here through most of the summer. We might, however, go to somewhere near the sea in July and August . . . perhaps Ravello. In any case we are fairly certain that we will take advantage of the reservations we have, and come back to the U.S. on the "U.S." in September. Perhaps, first thing, you will be able to visit us in Roxbury or Baltimore. I think the kids miss their grandparents very much.

I expect that by now you have received a copy of the book from Random House. As you can see, you are one of the dedicatees. I received several copies the other day by air from N.Y., and I agree with Bennett Cerf, who wrote me that he thought that it was one of the handsomest books that Random or anyone else had ever published. Anyway, they are going all out to put the book over with a bang (pub. date is June 3d) and the advance rumor throughout the trade is that it might do extremely well. Keep your fingers crossed.

Rose and the kids all join in sending love to you all in Port Warwick.

Billy

* Sir Peter Alexander Ustinov (1921–2004), beloved British character actor and prolific author.

Set This House on Fire *was published May 4, 1960—the Styrons' seventh wedding anniversary.*

To Mr. Thompson

May 12, 1960 Via San Teodoro, 28, Rome, Italy

Dear Mr. Thompson:

Thank you for sending me a copy of the Book-of-the-Month Club News, containing Gilbert Highet's perceptive review of Set This House on Fire.*

The only thing I know about Gilbert Highet (save for the fact that I always confuse him with Dr. Ashley Montagu) is that one night, driving up the Saw Mill River Parkway, I heard him lecturing over WQXR, about The Aeneid. Poor peasant that I was, I was terribly grateful when, during the first minute of this talk, I was told that The Aeneid meant "a story about a man named Aeneas." I near about drove into a ditch.

Many thanks again.

Ever sincerely yours,
William Styron

To James Jones

May 17, 1960 Via San Teodoro, 28, Rome, Italy

Dear Jim:

Under separate cover there will arrive a statement which four of us writers in Rome have prepared about the Chessman case.† I think when you

* Highet's review praised Styron's "remarkable talents" even as he called attention to the novel's "preternatural interest in sexual depravity. . . . It is a tribute to Mr. Styron's skill with his language and his gift for manipulating people that he carries you on, over waves of nausea, to the last word of his long and complex novel."

† The Chessman case was a landmark execution for the anti–death penalty movement, and the first such case in which Styron involved himself. Caryl Chessman was a career criminal convicted of several rapes in California. He was sentenced to death, many

read it you will understand why we wrote it. If you agree with our position we want both you and Gil to sign it, and do all of us the additional favor and service of sending the statement to one of the influential French newspapers—we have all thought of Figaro Littéraire, in the hope that they will run it as a letter. Writers swing a hell of a lot of weight, of course, in France and Italy, and we thought a statement like this, coming from writers, might help clear the air. If you agree, and if you sign, would you send it to one of the influential journals? A large Italian weekly has agreed to run it here in Rome as a letter, so if you sign will you cable me your willingness to allow us to add your name to the Italian copy, and also Gil's?

This is a hurried note, but I hope it makes sense. I think this is a good point, when the hysteria has died down somewhat yet when the affair is still fresh in the public mind, to state the American intellectual's position. I hope you agree. Right now I'm frantically working on the British edition of my book, so pardon the haste.* There were so many fucks, pricks, horse-shits, and the like in STHOF that the fucking English printers refused to touch it. You should be getting the American, un-bowdlerized edition from Random House any day now and I hope you read it, you bastard. Love to you and Moss from the both of us and hope that Jones, Jr. is coming along fine.†

Ever,

Bill

---

thought illegitimately, and executed on May 2, 1960. In addition to Styron, the statement was signed by Blair Fuller, Ben Johnson, Philip Roth, and Wallace Stegner.

* The British edition of *Set This House on Fire* (London: Hamish Hamilton, February 16, 1961). To comply with British obscenity statutes, the book was printed in the Netherlands.

† Gloria was pregnant with Kaylie.

To Elizabeth McKee

May 31, 1960 Via San Teodoro, 28, Rome, Italy

Dear Elizabeth:

After our rather tortuous phone call I came to Rome and found your letter and am writing right away to let you know my feelings about everything. God Knows, as you say, it is complicated.

The man from Gallimard, who flew from Paris to see me, pointed out that Gallimard did have prior claims on STHOF. He showed me a letter dating back to spring of 1958 which he sent to Hiram (he also showed me Hiram's reply); this letter was referred to you and Mavis, and what happened to it after that I have no way of telling. He sent other letters to you and Maria Horch, and he showed me copies of these also. So to some extent Gallimard can claim priority.

On the other hand, this morning I got a phone call from Paris, from Jean Rosenthal of Robert Laffont (while we were in Ravello, I was told, they called every day) and Rosenthal pointed out that, though it may be true that Gallimard made early inquiries, they nonetheless refused to accept a "package deal" which included The Long March when it was offered to them. Laffont accepted this package deal, and it was my own horrible mistake to change over to Plon. So at the moment we are back where we started, with the exception that now Gallimard is banging at the door. Basically I think that the deal that Gallimard offers is infinitely preferable to any of the others, but I do somewhat feel that it would be screwing Laffont to once again pull out on them—I'm mixing my metaphors terribly, but you see what I mean.

After so much turmoil over this thing, what I am now going to do is to place this whole situation in the hands of you, Maria Horch and Mlle. Bataille. Among the three of you, God Knows, you should be able to work this dreadful contretemps out. I don't mean to be crass, but this is precisely what agents are for and this is how they are supposed to make their living. My mistake was to yield to that dreadful woman, Annie Brierre, and get involved with Plon. But now I am washing my hands of any personal contact with any more of these awful Frenchmen, and I expect you to act as my liaison officer and to get things straightened out. It is probably my fault that things are in such a mess, but the mess is not inextricable, and I want you to make Maria Horch and Mlle Bataille earn their percentage by now taking the responsibility of choice off my shoulders. If I get any more phone calls from Paris and any more monstrous little Frenchmen parking on my doorstep I'm simply going to have to take the extreme measure of refusing to have the book published in France, by anybody.

As for the book itself, the advance stuff about it is really very fine. I'm on the cover of the Saturday Review and the accompanying review by Granville Hicks is as lovely as you could wish.* The A.P. review is excellent, also Edmund Fuller in, I think, the Chicago Tribune. I don't know yet about any of the really major reviews (Times, Trib, etc.) but I've got my fingers crossed; meanwhile, I've been inundated by letters from people who have read the book in advance, and all of them are mad for the thing—Lael Wertenbaker, for instance, wrote me from Hawaii, saying it was the finest she'd ever read, etc. I think it's going to be big.

I'm as sorry as you that our European contact has to be business mainly, but when we get back to Roxbury we shall all relax. The kids had a wonderful time in Ravello–Sambuco, as did we, and they send their love. Rose does too, and I, and let me hear from you soon.

Bill

To Maxwell Geismar

June 20, 1960 Via San Teodoro, 28, Rome, Italy

Dear Max:

Well, I received the lovely review of STHOF and it certainly did a lot to take the curse off the terrific lambasting I've received of late. I couldn't have asked for a more keen and sensible appraisal of what I was trying to do in the book. Perhaps someday I will be an honored, instead of a dishonored, author; I'll probably write my memoirs, and you may be sure that there will be a chapter on Max Geismar, who was about the only one to keep the faith. Your paragraph about my being a "Russian" writer was es-

* Granville Hicks, *Saturday Review,* June 4, 1960.

pecially good, I thought, but the whole thing was good, unassailable, fine, and I am grateful to you for it.

The reviews were really appalling, weren't they? Time and The New Yorker I could ignore (though even they revealed themselves in the amount of space they took to flail me) but all I could think about that silly prick Mizener was that he was angry because I had not written "The Golden Bowl."* The others were just impossible; Hutchens obtuse, Prescott an hysterical old woman (though it will probably sell books) and 99% of the major reviews stupid, uncomprehending or just plain silly. Ironically, all the major Chicago and West Coast reviews were fantastic raves, and I suppose I should masochistically say that these people are soft, or bought, or something, but so many of them, like yours, were simply so intelligent, so well thought-out, hit upon so many things in the book that the others missed, that I cannot help but think that the major literary injustice and imbalance in America is the complete reliance put upon the four or five major N.Y. media. Well, as my friend George Mandel wrote—fuck them all.

It turns out that Mailer is a false prophet. He said that I wrote a phony big book and I would be "made" in the mass media the most important writer of my generation. In reality, I wrote just what he shuddered to think I would do—a true book—and now I shall have to become the most important writer by the hard route—by living down all the cheap but powerful Time–New Yorker shit, and by having S.T.H.O.F. achieve its reputation in the same way "Darkness" did—slowly but steadily and with the immeasurable help of M. Geismar. I'm certain to be even more written off by the academics as a total loss (most of them won't even read the book) but so what? All of the really important writers have been attacked in this way. As someone wrote me, people like Mizener simply do not believe that men die of hideous diseases or kill one another, so in the long reaction their point of view is of no importance whatever. The book is going to be with

* Donald Malcolm's long review of *Set This House on Fire* in the June 4, 1960, *New Yorker* was highly negative. Malcolm's closing line was that "one begins intensely not to care" for either the plot or the characters in the novel. However, Malcolm's review was not as severe as Arthur Mizener's "Some People of Our Time" in the June 5, 1960, *New York Times Book Review*. After a sustained critique of the book's "melodramatic" characters, method, and plot, Mizener maintained that *Set This House on Fire* proved the falsity of Styron's "promise" as a writer. Styron never forgot Mizener's review.

us for a long, long time—this I know as much as I have known anything in my life.

So many thanks again, Max, and write me a letter soon.

As ever,

Bill

To William C. Styron, Sr.

June 23, 1960 Via San Teodoro, 28, Rome, Italy

Dear Pop:

Well, a prophet has never had much honor in his own land.

About three weeks ago, just before STHOF was published, I received a letter from a man named Prof. Maurice Edgar Coindreau. A Frenchman, he has taught French at Princeton for over 30 years, and for a very long time has been chief literary advisor to Gallimard, which is the largest and most influential French publishing house. He is also probably the best-known and most respected translator of American books, having done all of Faulkner and Hemingway and Steinbeck, and having been enormously important in introducing these writers to the French public. In other words, he is a man of great intelligence and stature. In his letter to me he said this: "Your new novel is one of the most powerful books I have read in years. It is not only beautifully put together, with an uncanny sense of unbearable suspense, but the psychological analysis is as keen as it is fascinating. This book will stand as a masterpiece of modern American fiction." Coindreau is going to translate the book into French—though I should add that at the time he wrote the letter he had no professional connection with the book, and his sentiments may be taken as totally objective.

I only mention this because I wanted you to know that, though STHOF has been lambasted in a way few novels ever have, I am utterly certain that Coindreau's opinion (and the opinion of others like him) will eventually win out. As a very fine poet I know, Louis Simpson, wrote me: "Of course, this adverse reaction is a sign that you are marked out to be one of the few important writers of the age. There has not been a major novelist of this century who has not been at some point attacked in a similar way. The violence of the attack is in itself an indication of the vitality and truth in the book." I could go on and on in describing similar reactions from people whose opinion I respect, but I think that probably you can see how, after a lot of initial gloom which I frankly confess bugged me for more than a few days, I am now completely confident in the stature of the book: it will endure beyond a doubt. And my gloom has become cheer.

Either way, the attack on the book has certainly sent people running to the bookstores. I have been getting elated messages from Bennett Cerf, who tells me that at last report sales are already over 20,000 copies, with re-orders running to as many as 467 a day. It will be a curious irony to see this book, so roundly damned by the middlebrow press, bought by the thousands by people who were told to stay away. So it turns out that the old saw is right: the truth really hurts. And when a Prescott belabors that truth his shrill cries of shock and pain may cause more people to seek out the truth than if he had kept his silly mouth shut. It may take some time for the truth in this book to sink in, but I know that it will eventually make its profound mark as well as I know anything in my life.

Meanwhile, Rome is sunny, hot, and great fun for all of us, especially our little tadpoles. July 1 we are taking a house up in Ansedonia, near Orbetello, and in August we are going to the Dolomites, then to Havre and home by way of Switzerland and Paris. We shall certainly look forward to seeing you in Roxbury in September.

Incidentally, I don't know if you knew that STHOF was a selection of the Book Find Club and that Max Geismar wrote a fine review in their magazine. Have you seen it?

Buona fortuna
Bill

To Donald Harington*

June 30, 1960 Via San Teodoro, 28, Rome, Italy

Dear Mr. Harington,

It was good to get your excellent, complex, and most understanding letter.† It came at a time when I had had a surfeit of abusive or stupid or malicious reviews, or all three, and it indeed shored up my flagging spirits to know that at least one reader understood what I was trying to do in the book. No book of any stature, to my knowledge, was ever lambasted so thoroughly and hysterically, and I am at a loss to explain the fury of the assault, unless it was a matter of a sort of By Love Possessed‡ in reverse, or unless, as you point out, I cut so deep into the consciousness of Prescott, Malcolm, Mizener and their small ilk that screams of outrage were the only possible result. I'm inclined to think it is the latter, and I'm glad you believe so too. Receiving a letter like yours, I am made to believe that there are other intelligent and life-sized human beings around who will eventually appreciate the book; without having received it, I might have been more doubtful, and I am very grateful to you for taking the time and the trouble to express your feelings at such rich length. Fortunately, the eventual value and influence of a book does not rest upon the opinions of

* Harington (1936–2009), novelist and nonfiction writer, was born and reared in Little Rock, Arkansas. Trained as an art historian at the University of Arkansas and Harvard University, Harington was an assistant professor at Bennett College in Millbrook, New York, when he first wrote to Styron. After reading *Set This House on Fire,* Harington wrote a detailed appreciation to Styron on June 4, 1960. This letter began a forty-year correspondence, which Harington collected and bound in 1986 for Styron's archive at Duke University.

† Harington wrote: "I have read everything by Faulkner . . . everything by Fitzgerald, most everything by Steinbeck, Dos Passos, Wolfe, Farrell, and even Erskine Caldwell, everything by the young moderns: Agee, Salinger, Jones, Mailer, McCullers, Capote, et. al., and I have read your two earlier books; and among all the thick and thin, sick and well, glad and sad volumes in this mountain of American literature, I have never read a finer novel than STHOF. It is the most, to say the least." Writing that it was sure to be deemed "controversial," Harington echoed many of Styron's own complaints: "I am beginning to grow tired of book reviewers who get a tight hard-on themselves from passages in a book and, feeling shamed afterwards, denounce the book." "I want to write them and tell them off, but I remember what you said in your Paris Review interview about critics, and I remember your saying it's the reader and not the critic who means something to you, and I decided to write to you instead of Prescott or Malcolm."

‡ James Gould Cozzens's immensely popular and critically well-received novel (1957).

mean-spirited little people getting, as you so aptly put it, their "sweet detumescent revenge." Its value rests in the understanding of people like yourself, and I appreciate the warmth and good-will which impelled you to write me.

Sincerely,
William Styron.

To John P. Marquand, Jr.

July 22, 1960 Via San Teodoro, 28, Rome, Italy

Dear John:

I read the news of your father's death in the Rome paper, and also several people sent me clippings from the U.S.; and I did want you to know how sorry I am. He was a grand old guy and I know you will miss him. But how fine to go, when you go, in your sleep—which is what, after all, our little lives are surrounded with. No distress, no horrors, no degrading pain—just sleep. He deserved it, and all that one now can say is that we are indeed sad to see him go. Rose told me to tell you how sorry she is, too, and also my father, who was a great fan of his. No matter how one rationalizes it, it is a horrible wrench, and all the fatuities—time cures all wounds, etc.—are of little help. But anyway, I did want you to know that we were thinking of you all this time.

We are leaving Rome, mercifully before the Olympics, on August 7th and going to Bolzano, Switzerland, Paris and London before coming back to the land of the big PX in mid-September. I will be rather happy to get back and try to resume my somewhat splintered writing career after the most grisly reviews since "The Passing of the Third Floor Back" and "Tall Grows the Eel-grass" by Ella Wheeler Wilcox.* I did get one good review, however, in Amarillo, Texas, and I cherish it like an amulet, and someday, if you ask, I may show it to you. How is your book going? I hope you are

* Wilcox (1850–1919) was an author and poet, most famous for her poem "Solitude," and the line "Laugh, and the world laughs with you; Weep, and you weep alone." Her work frequently appears in anthologies of bad poetry.

persevering, since some one among us must eventually get across to the bastards.

Rose sends all her best to you and Sue, as do I. And say hello to Lillian; with love to all of you—B.S.

P.S. It looks as if your friend and mine, the Irishman from Palm Beach, is going to make it.*

To John P. Marquand, Jr.

Summer, 1960 Klosters, Switzerland

Dear one + John

Got your letter here in the celebrated Klosters, where we are living it up with Irwin and his group, including "Pete" Viertel and "Deb" Kerr, "Art" Buchwald, "God" Liberawn, "Vera" Zorina and a host of lesser lights like ourselves. We will be back in the middle of Sept. and are anxious to see the waning summer on the Vineyard and catch some last sailfishing. We leave tomorrow for Paris via Basel and then will be in England for 10 days, including a trip to Dublin with Philip Roth + frau. I am already exhausted at the prospect. In case you communicate, our address is Hotel Washington, Curzon St., London W.1. Love + see you soon.

Bill

To John P. Marquand, Jr.

August 24, 1960 Ireland

Dear JP:

Received your letter in London and indeed enjoyed it and am looking forward to seeing you all (as is Rose) when we return. Your note to The New Yorker kid was a gasser, to use a Humes-ism, and I greatly appreciate

* John F. Kennedy.

it. Dublin is a crashing horror of a city, with the shade of Joyce inundated by a spinechilling amalgam of S.S. Kresge, hamburgers, Pat Boone, atrocious food, ugly girls, malnourished men, and the Son of Tarzan at the corner flickers. We are here with Phil Roth and proceed to Wales tomorrow, which I suspect will be just as gruesome. See you soon and love to Suay.

B.S.

To William Blackburn

October 8, 1960 Roxbury, CT

Dear Doctor:

Your note of October 4 was really very confusing to me, since I never received the cable you mentioned. Knowing Italy as I do, not receiving the cable is not surprising; most of the telegrams and such I ever sent from Rome either never arrived or arrived late. However, I still can't understand your letter, and I don't know what you mean when you say that in time I will forgive you, you hope. Not that there is anything for which I should forgive you, but there is nothing that I would not forgive you—you know that. I have the feeling that you were upset that I have not written you—and for that, of course, I hope you can forgive me. I can only offer in simple explanation the fact (and I mean this) that the last letter you sent me, from Florence (which I received in Paris), I stupidly and infamously lost, so that I did not know your address; you mentioned something about coming back in October, which seemed a short time, and I knew I would contact you then. If this is the reason for your (to me) enigmatic and forever lost cable, I do hope you will forgive me and understand. If there is another reason, I trust that somehow you will make it all clear to me when you return—or before.

Most cryptic in your letter was your remark that you should have added something about the critics be damned. Naturally, I can't understand what context this comment was offered in, but universally speaking I couldn't agree with you more. Writers shouldn't read critics but invariably do, and now I have been clobbered all around the country with such passion and venom that my mind is numb. In critical print, I am a slob, worse than a failure; and yesterday there came to me a horrible little magazine called Critique, from the Univ. of Minn., with three essays on me and three on Saul Bellow (he gets straight A's) which rakes me over the coals in a way that would make your toes curl up. I am a cheap Hollywood sellout, vicious, sexy, titillating, altogether on the level of Mickey Spillane* and Grace Metalious.† And so now I know who the enemy is: it is the Academy, the same Academy which took the life of Fenton,‡ whom I never knew, but who wrote about the only good thing about STHOF that I've received. I don't know, doctor, sometimes it hardly seems worthwhile, but long ago it was you who taught me something very real about the meaning of fortitude, so I shall damn the critics with you and keep on writing. One amusing footnote: critics be damned, I am still admired in the innerest of sanctums. I have been invited to give something called the Dinsmore Trust Lecture in Philosophical Theology at the Yale University Divinity School—subject, Good and Evil in Contemporary Literature. There is rugged irony in this.

Whatever I have done forgive me. But please don't let too much time pass before clearing up the mystery. And do come see us when you land in New York. I am as ever your damned, derelict, but ever hopeful and devoted.

Bill

* Frank Morrison Spillane (1918–2006) was an author of numerous bestselling crime novels, best known for his Mike Hammer series.

† Grace Metalious (1924–64) was an author best known for her controversial and bestselling novel *Peyton Place* (1956), which sold over 30 million copies.

‡ Charles A. Fenton (1919–60) was an author and a college professor best known for *The Apprenticeship of Ernest Hemingway* (1954) and *Stephen Vincent Benét: The Life and Times of an American Man of Letters* (1958). His laudatory review "William Styron and the Age of the Slob" (*The South Atlantic Quarterly,* Autumn 1960), applauded Styron's novel for capturing "the national mood."

To John P. Marquand, Jr.

Fall, 1960 Roxbury, CT

Dear John:

Perhaps as my apologist you would like to do the same job on this fellow as you did on the New Yorker boy, though now, in spite of the N.Y. Mirror tone of this exposé, I am really beginning to acquire such honest self-doubts as to my place in the scheme of things that I wonder whether your protest to Ms. Malcolm was not sentimental & ill-advised. The enclosed is from a U. of Minn. Rag called "Critique," containing 3 essays on me (all attacks) & 3 on Saul Bellow, all blowjobs.* I don't know, thus was it always. So you will finish your book & this is what will happen to you. We had a lovely time up there. Enclosing check for phone calls. Love to Sue & Sarah & BB & even Ponto.

BS.

PS. Tugwell e morto.

Hope we see you for election eve.

* The three pieces were by Robert Gorham Davis, "Styron and the Students," David L. Stevenson, "Styron and the Fiction of the Fifties," and Richard Foster, "An Orgy of Commerce: William Styron's *Set This House on Fire,*" *Critique: Studies in Modern Fiction* 3 (Summer 1960). Foster's piece concluded that "we must be willing to throw a writer like Mr. Styron back into the hopper of anonymity and make him at last prove his claim to the amount of attention he has had from us undeserved. And we must do this not only in the interest of the writer's soul, but in the interest of our own as well." Styron wrote beneath the comment: "The little prick who edits this mag sent me 5 copies, and had the gall to write: 'A liberal supply of this issue is available to send to your friends.' BS."

To Louis D. Rubin, Jr.

January 24, 1961 Roxbury, CT

Dear Louis:

I received the copy of the Sewanee, for which many thanks.* For so long a time I have been accustomed to hearing nothing but howls of execration about the book, that to read what you say comes as a most pleasant and bracing antidote, and naturally I think you are righter than the others. The last wholesale onslaught upon the book (which you may have seen) came not from the slick mags but from the very heart of the Academy itself, in a little quarterly called Critique, which contained three essays (all unfavorable) on the book, including one piece by someone named Foster which was so rabidly down on the book that the tone became almost psychotic—so furious, as a matter of fact, that I could not help but believe that the book held a perverse and lascivious sexual attraction for the man which in some way he was trying to exorcise. At any rate, the book has been catching hell from all sides. I really do feel initiated into the same purgatory which, I console myself, was endured by Melville, Faulkner, Fitzgerald & Co.; but one can put up with this sort of crap only so long, so it was with all the more satisfaction that I read your essay. Aside from its being a shrewd and honest appraisal, it will I suspect be read by a number of people who might quite justifiably have been put off the book by such rankly dishonest swine as Mizener & the jerk on The New Yorker, and these people will go ahead and read the book, and your purpose will be served. We do seem to live in an absolutely impossible time insofar as decent appraisal and literary integrity are concerned. I never wanted any sappy, slavish praise; I only wanted a few people to say that here was a book which—whatever its faults—had solid virtues and deserved to be read, but almost no one seemed to be willing to own up to that—why, I don't really know, except that it seems that the literary cult and coterie are flourishing in and out of the Academy to a degree I had never imagined.

It is good to hear that your novel is on the brink of publication this year, and of course I will be eager to read it.† I will also be happy to offer

* Louis Rubin, "An Artist in Bonds," *The Sewanee Review,* Winter 1961. The piece was an assessment of Styron's work, focusing mainly on *Set This House on Fire.*

† Louis Rubin, *The Golden Weather* (New York: Atheneum, 1961).

you my comments, for what they're worth, if you would like. I know that Hiram thinks it's wonderful, and that's a great sign already. However, if it's as good as I think it's going to be, dear Louis, you will have to grow accustomed to a lot of abuse. That seems to be the way the cookie crumbles in the quality lit. biz.

As for my own recent work, I am at present worn out from having given a stern lecture at, of all places, the Yale Divinity School, and am now preparing to do a film script of Set This House on Fire, which a French movie company has optioned. I do not know whether this is going from the sublime to the ridiculous or vice versa, but in any case I hope soon to resume my misadventures in literature with an honest to God novella about which I've been thinking for a long time.

I'm still sorry that circumstances prevented my coming to your aid a few months ago—I certainly would have if I could have—but I hope it won't be too long before we get together in one way or another. Best to you all from us, and let me know when and if you're coming to the snowbound north.

As ever,

Bill

To William Blackburn

January 24, 1961 Roxbury, CT

Dear Doctor:

I received your delightful telegram last night about the Sewanee review, and I do appreciate it, and I wish you would tell the other two signatories (who have been most faithful to me) how pleased I was.* It was a good and honest appraisal, I thought (I received a copy just yesterday), and though I've by now become completely inured to every type of hostility and meanness (so much so that in a sluggish, masochistic way I've come to actually suspect any good word that is said about the book), it really is refreshing to read the words of someone who feels that the book might have some worth, after all. And, as I say, it was good to get your concurring telegram.

* Rubin's piece on *Set This House on Fire*.

After all these months, though, the bitterness has pretty much worn off. I know what the book is. It is a good book, and it will be read for a long time to come, after the barriers so meticulously set up by the small, the blind and the envious have been broken down. I have come to understand recently that the book really did crucify a lot of people; that it wasn't any inherent structural fault, or aesthetic fault of any kind, that got people so angry and stirred up; it was, rather, that something in the book itself (its "message," for want of a better word) was too strong a mouthful for them to get down, much less digest. Book reviewers, after all, are a soggy lot, and have a weak stomach for evil, and now that I look back on it I can see that I should have expected nothing better than I got. Incidentally, I don't know whether I told you or not, but the reaction abroad has been somewhat different, and perhaps indicates the validity of the "message": the book has been contracted for publication in every western European language (with the single exception of Dutch, where everyone reads English, but including such odd ones as Portuguese and Finnish) and my agent tells me that the advances paid in France and Germany are the highest ever for a "serious" novel. This might strike a rather commercial note, but at this point I don't give a good God damn.

I am sorry to have missed you as you came back to these shores, but I hope it won't be too long before we can get together. You may find it difficult to believe but just the other day I gave a lecture on certain aspects of Good and Evil to a class in Philosophical Theology at the Yale Divinity School. It was wildly received by the milling throng present, especially inasmuch as I told them a little less Christian forbearance and love and a lot more sex and disorganized, negative, hateful thinking would create a truly productive society. So far as I know, it will be published in a forthcoming issue of the Yale Review, and I think it settles the problem of Good, Evil, and Manicheanism once and for all.

Incidentally, I read Reynolds Price's stories,* and I think they really achieve something unique and fine; I told the Guggenheim people so, but what they do about it is Fate. As a poet friend of mine, Louis Simpson, wrote in a letter: "One must respect one's self and accrue virtue. Everything else is in the lap of the gods."

* *The Names and Faces of Heroes* (New York: Atheneum, 1963).

Many thanks again for the telegram, and I hope all goes well with you until we meet again.

Ever yours,
Bill

To William C. Styron, Sr.

February 24, 1961 Roxbury, CT

Dear Pop,

Well, the snow has begun to melt, and it looks as if the worst of the horrible winter is over, although I am knocking on wood. After all, we have had blizzards up here as late as the beginning of April. Nonetheless, I am hoping for the best. At least our various minor and major catastrophes attendant upon the weather seem to have slackened off, and I have only one more to look forward to—Susanna's birthday party, tomorrow, with 18 squalling children, horns, melted ice cream, and total bedlam.

Perhaps you remember my interest in old Nat Turner's rebellion some years ago, when you sent me various photostated items which I carefully put away and kept. Well now the interest has returned, I have re-read all the literature (including the books which were sent me long ago from Hampton Institute); only now the whole project seems to shape up much more as a movie than as a book. By movie I mean a good movie, not one of these Hollywood flashy colored numbers; and now that a few Americans, at least, are attempting to make serious, good films, it seems the subject is pertinent now as it never was—the black man raging against the white—and if done properly (meaning done as I see it in my mind's eye) it would make a violent, moving film. Very few "historical" movies made in the U.S. have ever been good, because they tend to be cheap and romantic; the story of Nat, however, could be full of raw truth very meaningful to our time. . . . I have elicited a lot of real interest in this movie from several people whom I know and trust who are closely connected with the industry but are not "Hollywood" types, and it is a matter now of getting the story down on paper in outline form before doing the script. I by no means intend to abandon my other writing, but I have great feelings for the movies (at their best) as an art form, and I think something really fine can be done with this story of Nat and his rampage. All you have to do is read about Lumumba and what's happening in the Congo to see how significant Nat's story is, how contemporaneous and universal.*

What I am leading up to is this. I think Rose talked to you about bringing Susanna and Polly down to Newport News sometime this spring and all of us paying you a visit. This sounds fine to me anyway, because we'd love to see you, besides getting south for a change. Meanwhile, I have looked at various maps, and it occurs to me that Southampton County and Courtland and Drewryville—where Nat's rebellion took place—couldn't be more than about an hour and a half from Newport News. I have always wanted to trace the route of Nat's warpath—at least that part of it that can be traced—and, moreover, see whatever original houses and buildings are left standing, and in general get a "feel" of the exact landscape. Naturally I have a superficial sense of what it's like, having been through country like it many times when on our way to Washington, N.C., years ago; but the feeling tends to fade after some years, and I would like to re-experience the countryside, if only for a day. If you are game for this, what I'd like to do is make a trip with you down there one day, starting early in the morning, and just snoop around for four or five hours. One or two of the houses he raided may still be there; certainly the sites are marked. The revolt was in August, and our visit would be in the spring, but this wouldn't matter. Another thing, just a shot in the dark: perhaps you know someone from Courtland or Drewryville (or know someone who knows someone) or that general Southampton area who, let us say, still lives down there, and who might have some Turner lore, and whom we might look up. But this is just an eventuality, and since the sense of history is all but dead in our country, I doubt if such a person exists; they are probably all listening to Lawrence Welk.

In any case, I thought it would be interesting to mention the possibility of this excursion to you. I think it would be a lot of fun, and very enlightening, too, provided we knew what to look for first. We'll be letting you know soon just when we plan to come down with the kids. In the mean-

* Patrice Émery Lumumba (1925–61) was the first legally elected prime minister of the Republic of the Congo, after helping his country win independence from Belgium in June 1960. Twelve weeks later, he would be deposed, arrested, imprisoned, and finally executed by a Belgian firing squad.

while I am writing to the state library in Richmond and various other sources in regard to the manner in which to go about what would be called, in the de luxe magazines, a Tour of the Turner Country, and will keep you informed of the results. Love to you both.

Bill jr

PS The bulky letter you forwarded to me from the University of Virginia was an invitation to give the annual Peter Rushton Lecture in Contemporary Literature at the Alderman Library, next year. It sounded very distinguished, since some of the past lecturers have been Robert Penn Warren, Archibald MacLeish, W.H. Auden, Malcolm Cowley, Stephen Spender, and James Thurber, but I turned it down in the honest belief that I need no such fancy feather in my bedraggled cap.* I thanked them kindly, but told them I had more important rows to hoe. I was not in the least arrogant, and it occurred to me as I wrote them that for a man whose career (if the reviews were any touchstone) had ended with his last book I still hadn't done too badly in the eyes of my fellow Virginians, and I thanked them for thinking of me.

To Rust Hills

May 1, 1961 Roxbury, CT

Dear Mr. Hills,

Thank you for your letter about my various projects. Elizabeth McKee is quite accurate if she told you that I am doing the Nat Turner thing instead of the novellas, which I have temporarily put aside. However, it looks as if the Turner work will develop into a shortish (possibly 60,000 words) but still full-scale novel instead of a novella-length story. So I think that Esquire's interest would be in excerpting a piece or two from the work, as you did from my last novel. I will certainly keep you posted, for as you know I have a high regard for Esquire (you have courage, which is more

* Archibald MacLeish (1892–1982) was a poet and Librarian of Congress who received three Pulitzer Prizes. James Thurber (1894–1961) was an author and cartoonist best known for his contributions to *The New Yorker*.

than can be said for, let us say, The New Yorker). As for it being historical, I hope you will not think me presumptuous if I say that I do not think this work will be any more "historical," in the pejorative sense, than the plays of Shakespeare or War and Peace. "Historical fiction" has received a bad name, and for good reason, most of it having been costume melodrama to titillate the ladies. But it seems to me that if a serious writer can bring his imagination to play upon a historical event, and does it well, the resulting insight and illumination are just as valid as if he had been dealing with contemporary themes. Anyway, in this case we shall see . . .

Thanks, incidentally, for your comments about The Long March. Philip Rahv is including it in an anthology called Great American Short Novels, which starts with Melville and ends with me, so I feel that in a sense it has "arrived."[*] I agree with you about Seize the Day. I think it is Bellow's best work, and truly superb.

Sincerely,

William Styron

To Leon Edwards

September 11, 1961 Box 1242, Vineyard Haven, MA

Dear Leon:

Since you and Marianne are immersed in the world of the "world's most foremost ass-hound" I thought you'd like to see this review, by a friend of mine—Stanley Kauffmann[†]—which I believe wraps up Miller[‡] once and for all—also wraps up Karl Shapiro,[§] for that matter.

We've been up here on Martha's Vineyard since the first of August and plan to go back to Roxbury in a few days. I've been working mildly at a new novel, but have spent most of my time on several columns for Esquire.

* Philip Rahv, ed., *Eight Great American Short Novels* (New York: Berkley Books, 1963).

† Stanley Kauffmann, "Across the Great Divide," *The New Republic* (February 20, 1961).

‡ Kauffmann's review is highly critical of Arthur Miller.

§ Karl Jay Shapiro (1913–2000) was a poet and essayist, winner of the Pulitzer Prize (1945) and the Bollingen Prize (1969).

Don't fail to get the November issue, which has my thoughts on Beverly Aadland, Errol Flynn's 15-year-old mistress.* I think it will be on the news stands in mid-October.

I'll write at greater length soon. Meanwhile, fond wishes to all of you.

Bill

To Robert Loomis

November 9, 1961 Roxbury, CT

Dear Bob:

Not, I'll swear, because of any premonition, but because the indomitable Mrs. Pilpel† (who really impresses me in many ways) tells me I'm an idiot not to (especially in the light of all my forthcoming movie loot), I'm at the moment on the verge of drawing up my last will and testament, in preparation for bliss eternal. This is a morbid subject but, as Harriet tells me, and I think quite rightly, it should not be; after all, Shirley Temple had her will drawn up at the age of four. And there is always the chance, in Roxbury, of being run down by a maddened cow.

At any rate, what this note is about is to ask you if you would be willing to become my literary executor, and to have that fact stated in the will. What this means is simply that, when I join the angelic host, you will be responsible for preventing all sorts of lunatics from turning "The Long March" into a musical with Chubby Checker playing Captain Mannix. I don't know whether you wish to take on this awesome responsibility, and I think it is presumptuous of me even to ask, but I think you know my work better than anyone else, and this and other more personal, affection-

* Styron reviewed Florence Aadland's *The Big Love* (New York: Lancer, 1961), an account of her daughter Beverly's affair with Errol Flynn, in "Mrs. Aadland's Little Girl, Beverly," *Esquire,* November 1961. Some credit Styron with helping turn the book into a cult classic. Aadland addressed Styron in a letter she sent to the editors of *Esquire* on October 24, 1961, after seeing the review, to say that she did not "know how to begin to thank you. I am on cloud nine after reading your article in *Esquire*. . . . For you to find in our book the things that were truly in my heart . . . words fail me, I can only say thank you again."

† Harriet Pilpel (1913–81), a literary lawyer.

ate considerations cause me to think of you very much first. I wish you would think it over, at any rate, for old time's sake. According to Mrs P., the burden is not usually very heavy and your function is really extra-legal and advisory; and I think in the end you could derive great pleasure from telling Dore Schary* to go screw himself.

The enclosure is self-explanatory.† It is somehow so awful that the mind boggles.

—B.

To James Jones

January 22, 1962 Roxbury, CT

Jones:

Sources closer to you than you may realize have told me that you have been making atrocious remarks about my cat.‡ Ordinarily, I would not have believed these rumors, but recalling the way you have talked about cats in the past, I would not put it beneath you at all. Let me tell you something, Jimmy-boy. What you say has a way of getting back to me. If I hear that you have said one more thing about my cat, I am going to invite you to a fight in which I expect to beat out of you a fat amount of your yellow and treacherous shit.

Bill

PS: Enclosed check is to pay for $10 each borrowed by me and Gerry. I'd forget otherwise. See you Thurs.

* Isador Schary (1905–80), screenwriter (of *Boys Town* among other films) and movie producer, who became head of MGM Pictures after ousting founder Louis B. Mayer.

† The clipping concerned Styron and Loomis's friend John Maloney, who was "accused of stabbing a woman writer during a quarrel" and charged with felonious assault.

‡ Styron was parodying Norman Mailer's threatening note of March 12, 1958. Not surprisingly, Styron used that episode in *Set This House on Fire* for Mason Flagg's threats to the narrator Peter Leverett: "You wait here, Petesy boy, because when I come back I expect to stomp out of you a fat amount of your yellow and treacherous shit." Alexandra Styron refers to Flagg as "the avatar of Daddy's revenge" following Mailer's *Advertisements for Myself,* in Alexandra Styron, *Reading My Father: A Memoir* (New York: Scribner, 2011).

To Leon Edwards

February 5, 1962 Roxbury, CT

Dear Leon:

Next Thursday the 13th, Rose and I are sailing on the maiden voyage of the jolly S.S. France for Le Havre, thence to Paris, where—with side trips—we plan to be for a month or so. The reasons for this trip are rather frivolous. My French publisher is bringing out Set This House on Fire and has invited me to be on hand. My German publisher (I've heard that I'm very BIG in the land of Auschwitz and Buchenwald) has also invited me for a visit, and I am supposed to give a lecture or two in Frankfurt or Berlin, and to appear on the Kraut television. My shame over this latter visitation would ordinarily be enough to drive me into the deepest anguish, save for the fact that I've already bought a Mercedes-Benz sportscar, thus being in the position of the famous murderer Judd Gray (he conspired with his paramour to kill her husband, ca. 1927), of whom it was said that once he had committed adultery (he was also a Presbyterian Sunday School teacher) his sense of sin was so great that the crime of murder seemed only a logical extension of his malfeasance. At any rate, it looks as if it might be a good trip. The France on its maiden voyage, so I've heard, promises to be a remarkably vulgar affair, with press agents, free booze, and international floozies (informally, I'm supposed to write it up for Esquire, so the passage is free)—but once we get off the boat I intend to hole up in the French alps, at the home of a couple Rose and I know, and there try to do some work on the Nat Turner novel which I've been sweating over for so long.

In case one of the planes I will be flying on later should go down over Silesia, and I should join bliss eternal, I want to inform you that I have made you the recipient, in my recently drawn-up will, of the note sum of $10,750.* Already I find this subject both grisly and rather embarrassing,

* Edwards had asked Styron for a loan to help him pay for medical school, and Styron agreed to lend Edwards money. As he wrote on August 31, 1955, "Your promissory note(s) seem fine to me, and I feel a great smug sense of power in having you so firmly clenched by your financial balls. You'd better watch your step, buddy. To be honest, I couldn't be more satisfied with the arrangement, not more pleased that I have been able to help out.

but my lawyer told me that I should tell you this—for the record, so to speak. My motives are both more generous than they might appear, and I shall try to explain. In the first place, disabuse yourself of the notion that I am well off enough—or that my estate, morbid word, would be large enough—to leave you this REAL sum, much as I would like to leave it—and to about only two other people who deserve it, besides yourself. To put it simply, in my mortal state I hope that you will be in a position someday to pay the note back. Dead as a smelt, however, as I surely will be if that kraut pilot makes a misstep coming into the Tempelhof airport, I will not need $10,750; and since Rose, who is well provided for, will not need it either, I and my lawyer figured that this would be the best way, under such circumstances, for you to be disencumbered of any posthumous debt to me. Furthermore, as it stands, you see, this loan is in the legal sense a sort of a gift: that is, it is money upon which I have already paid taxes and which, if paid back while I am alive, is tax-free. Under law, however (at least in N.Y. & Conn. which have the worst estate taxes in the union) a note is like a liquid asset: if my estate collects from you when the note comes due (which, as I have explained, I do not want them to do, nor does Rose), the estate will have to pay taxes on it—something like a horrifying 50%, too. I think you will agree that we don't want all of that money to go to the govmint, the motherfuckers. When, then, Jesus forbid soon, I have become but clay, my estate will bring you the glad tidings that in my generosity I have left you $10,750. Choking back a sob, you will present your copy of your note to me in the same amount (my lawyer will also have a copy of the note in his safe), and it will be thereupon agreed that nobody owes nobody nothing. The government doesn't get a nickel, you owe nothing, and they will sing an extra psalm for me in the hereafter. I hope all this is clear. My lawyer, incidentally, tells me that this sort

---

One thing I want to tell you, though, in all candor. When I told you over the telephone that I thought I'd be able to swing the whole $16 G, or whatever it is thereabouts, it was with more sanguinity than realism. Actually, I still hope to be able to lend you the annual installment each year as you have outlined it. As far as I can see, I'm well-enough fixed to do it. What I hope you will realize, though, is simply that although I'm filthy rich I have very little Rockefeller blood in my veins, and only one or two piddling little oil-wells, and there is always the chance that next year or the year after will not find me so well-heeled. This is the result of being a writer."

of thing goes on all the time. As for myself, the very subject depresses me hopelessly, and I don't want to say anything more about it.*

I hope we shall be able to get together again soon, when (and if) I get back from Europe—did I gather from your Xmas card that you are going back to Walter Reed? If possible, I am never again going to spend a winter in Connecticut. Post-nasal drip, chronic bronchitis, and general sullenness have been my lot for two months. The children are all fine, though I think Susanna is coming down with measles. Small World Dep't: it turns out that your first cousin, Betty Lou Holland, in whose father's N.Y. apartment you and I slept our first night ever in New York, has gotten herself married to a friend of mine named Cordier, a Frenchman who has taken on an option on Set This House on Fire for the movies. I saw them the other night. They look the picture of wedded bliss, and though Betty Lou is a curious amalgam of both you and Bozo, I find her hauntingly sexy.

Love to Marianne and the kids.

Bill

* My lawyer pointed out that the foregoing knowledge could be an incentive to murder, but I told him that you were a decent chap.

To Myrick Land*

February 8, 1962 Roxbury, CT

Dear Mr Land:

Your book sounds interesting and I wish you success with it, but I really don't want to go into anything about Mailer and me, save perhaps to reflect on the fact that both Mailer's honesty and his gift for prophecy are contained in his statement which you quote in paragraph 4: "For Styron has spent years oiling every literary lever . . . and there are medals waiting for him in the mass-media." As anyone who read the reviews of Set This House on Fire can recall, the medals were made of solid lead. As for the

* Land (1922–88) wrote a book on literary feuds, *The Fine Art of Literary Mayhem* (New York: Holt, Rinehart and Winston, 1963), which included a section on Mailer and Styron with quotations from this letter.

rest, any "feud" which exists has always, for some queer reason, seemed far more important to Mailer than it has to me.

Sincerely,
William Styron

P.S. Feel free to quote the above in part or in toto.

To Louis D. Rubin, Jr.

March 10, 1962 Grand Hôtel de la Ville, Rome, Italy

After this date: Hotel Lotti, rue Castiglione, Paris

Dear Louis—

Many thanks for your letter. Yes, I will certainly agree to come to Hollins, provided I don't have to make a formal speech but can either (a) read from my work and/or (b) engage in a kind of colloquy with you, as I did that time at Hopkins. Speeches scare me and I'm no good at them. If this is O.K., let me know.

It might provide an interesting footnote to your piece on me to mark the fact that Set This House on Fire has, in French translation, achieved the biggest success (both critical and popular) of any American novel in France since the war. It even astonishes me. It is selling by the thousands, there have been new printings every week, and overnight I have become literally the best-known American writer in France since Faulkner. What the secret of all this is, is mystifying, except I imagine that the book contains just enough nasty but honest knocks at the U.S. to satisfy the fainting French spirit. But you have never heard such praise. L'Express, front page (equivalent to the Times Book Review): "the most intelligent and optimistic of the great American tragedies."* Robert Kanters (the Edmund Wilson of France) in Figaro: "a great book which may not be a work of

* *L'Express,* March 8, 1962. An interiew with Madeleine Chapsal also appeared in the same issue, reprinted in *Quinze Écrivains: Entretiens* (Paris: René Julliard, 1963) and in James L. W. West III, ed., *Conversations with William Styron* (Jackson: University Press of Mississippi, 1985).

genius but is certainly the product of the highest talent" etc. I am really left quite numb and had to flee Paris for fear of being plastiqué like Sartre and Malraux. At any rate, vengeance is truly sweet and I shall be overjoyed when the news seeps back to the American super-literati and super-patriots, as it most certainly will.

I'll be looking forward to seeing you in Hollins next year, if not before. Hope the book goes well. Naturally, I'll be interested in seeing it, even if I don't agree. But I expect I will.

Best to you and Eva,
Bill

To William C. Styron, Sr.

March 24, 1962 Hotel Lotti, Paris, France

Dear Pop:

I have been traveling at such a great pace these past weeks that I've hardly had time to sit down, much less write. The Book, in France, is now a matter of history. It received the greatest reception of any American novel since the war. "A masterpiece," "one of the great American tragedies," "written with an almost supernatural power to impart life, like God the father," "a miraculous achievement." Those were some of the quotes. The most severe criticism I received was in one of the journals, which said that it wasn't quite a masterpiece, but still a literary work of the highest order. So at last I feel pretty much vindicated after the mauling I took from the American critics. The book is selling very well indeed. I allowed myself to go on a television program (something I'd never do in the U.S.) and since there is only one channel in France (state-owned) I was seen by every Frenchman with a TV set. As a result of all this, Gallimard the publisher is planning to reissue the translation of Lie Down in Darkness. It is quite astounding the seriousness with which the French take a novelist, who in the U.S. ranks somewhere below a local politician, and certainly below a preacher or a doctor. Here he is without doubt Numero #1, as with the Chinese.

Rose and I are both getting dizzied with travel. The trip to Rome by jet

Caravella (1 hr 40 min) was spectacular but not nearly so spectacular as the Rome–Geneva flight, with the light sparking on Mt. Blanc at 15,000 ft. Tomorrow we go to Frankfurt, and all next week I will be giving readings to the Krauts, in Frankfurt, Berlin and Munich. I will tell you about Dachau, which I intend to see. My publishers, the Fischers, were Thomas Mann's publishers, and are extraordinarily kind, gentle, and intelligent people. They are Jewish and were evicted by Hitler at around the book-burning era of 1937–38. They went to Vienna, and were forced to flee during the Anschluss. They then came to the U.S. via Sweden and Russia under the aegis of Thomas Mann, who was then living in California. They became American citizens, have a house in Greenwich, Conn. and now run the biggest and best publishing house in Germany. Really extremely civilized people (they make no bones about deploring their fellow countrymen) and Rose and I will be glad to see them. Rose is flying back to N.Y. on March 31st from Frankfurt, and I'm coming back to Paris for two or three weeks to work on my book about Nat Turner. Then I shall return to Roxbury spring and the kiddies. I expect to stay here at the Lotti during that time, though a French friend offered me the use of an elegant 12-room apartment which I found hard to resist, save for the fact that it is simply too huge for one all alone.

Selma says the kids are flourishing and I know you enjoyed seeing them in Baltimore. I hope we'll be able to see you in the spring. Love to both of you from both of us.

Bill

To Robert Loomis

April 3, 1962 Hotel Lotti, Paris, France

Dear Bob: As of this Thursday "Set This House on Fire" is the #3 best-seller in France. There is only one list (in L'Express) of 10 books and it includes both fiction and non-fiction, so this is something of a rare phenomenon, especially since there are only two other fiction works on the list (one of them Salinger's "Nine Stories," #6 or 7, I believe). I have even outstripped Shirer's "Third Reich." The man at the French-American cultural center who gave me the advance news, and who seems to have firm knowledge in such matters, said that he was fully confident that next month (the list is publicized only monthly, incidentally) it would be #1; and he added that so far as he knew this had not happened to an American novel since the war. The reviews continue to be fantastic. I've been trying to get a copy of the review in Le Monde, which of course is the French counterpart of The N.Y. Times. They ordinarily don't give much space to novels, especially foreign ones, but as Romain Gary pointed out to me they treated the book more as a news story, and the article is long and laudatory in the extreme. I'll send it to you soon.

I've finally gotten to work on Nat Turner and it is proceeding well. I'm going to stay here alone for about three weeks, returning to Rox. on April 21st. The German trip was very tiring but fascinating, and I suspect I'll never again do so much flying. Frankfurt is a sheer drag, resembling Bridgeport, but Berlin is an amazing place to see, especially the other side of the famous wall in East Berlin, where the world suddenly turns unutterably gray and dismal. There everything remains in complete devastation, and any rosy concept of Communism has to be abandoned in East Berlin. I had great audiences everywhere (in Berlin they had to pipe the proceedings by loudspeaker to the overflow in the lobby) and it is really touching to see how all these young people really dig American lit. I had to go all the way to Munich, incidentally, to finally meet my neighbor Arthur Miller, and flew with him and his wife from Munich to Paris.

Drop me a line. I know Rose would love some company in Roxbury, so why don't you arrange a week-end while I'm gone?

Love to all, especially Gloria Margerainelle Loomis and Fat Di.

B.

To Rose Styron

April 5, 1962 Hotel Lotti, Paris, France

Dearest Mouse: Enclosed are what may be three items of interest: the best-seller list from L'Express, which came out today; the expert review in Le Monde, which I finally got hold of; and Romain Gary's "attack" on

Southern writers in Candide.* The sub-head of the last piece, as you can no doubt tell, reads: "Stop your eternal groaning over the poor Negro, Mr. Faulkner. Cease so exquisitely cultivating your guilt Mr. Styron." But the tone is rather light-hearted and all in all it's a rather clever piece. . . . While I think of it, I may as well mention the other enclosure—the authorization forms for income tax which Ader sent me and which I think he's already written you about. I hadn't realized it would be so enormous—over $15,000 for both last year and this year—so maybe to be on the safe side you should get in touch with John Motz and have them transfer at least $10,000 to the Baltimore checking account, and then write out those two checks accordingly. Anyway, as you know, it has to be postmarked no later than April 15th.

I loved getting your letter and learning about the smooth trip and about all the dear little mice. They sound wonderful and I know they really flipped when they saw you, + vice versa. I long to see them but it will be even more fun to see them in the Roxbury spring. Speaking of which, "April in Paris" is a fraudulent phrase, as I have never seen the weather here quite so dreary, wet, chill, and dismal. I am hoping that it will let up, but my hopes are not too high. I have been on the verge of a cold, but Cordiel touted me onto Vitamin C which I've been taking in quantities and which so far has staved off a major attack.

T. Capote called me this morning and we had lunch at the Ritz and as usual his communication was one long malicious delight. His malice ranged from Mailer to Salinger to Jamie Hamilton to Jackie Kennedy and I enjoyed every second of it. He took special pains to tell me to send my fond regards to you—he remembers you with great affection. He has with him a hideous English bulldog named Charlie whom he spoils outrageously and feeds pâté from the table. I also saw in the lobby of the Ritz your friend and mine Connie Bessie, and we're going to get together sometime. Paris is getting to be about as exotic as Grand Central Station.

Tonight I'm making my last public appearance—the lecture at the French-American cultural center. I somehow dread it—these things are getting to be a drag—but I guess I'll pull through all right. Jim and Moss

* Romain Gary, "L'ONU n'existe pas," *Le Nouveau Candide* (December 21–27, 1960).

are going along for support and afterwards there is to be a small dinner chez Jacques Faro. So I suppose it could be worse.

I miss you and all the mice enormously. Are Ethel and Terry O.K.? Give them my fond regards. And also Gerry, of course. Kisses all around, and much love from your own

W.S.

To Rose Styron

April 9, 1962 Hôtel Lotti, Paris, France

Dearest Mouse: It was lovely talking to you both times and hearing all the kiddies' voices and surprising and delightful, also, to hear Red Warren's unique Kentucky accent from 3,000 miles.* I miss you all very much and though I am indeed profiting greatly, I think, from three weeks by myself, I will be happy to come home to Roxbury. As it is, I plan to take the 11:00 P.M. Air France flight from Orly on the 21st and will arrive at Idlewild at 3:30 P.M. or thereabouts. If you would like to meet me I will be happy and we can go back to Roxbury the same afternoon. I've received a couple of your letters since Sunday's phone call and enjoyed them both. As for the Mercedes, why don't you go ahead and have them re-paint it at the St. Denis Body Shop—whatever color you choose. As for your item #2, you might as well go ahead and pay the Roxbury town tax. If, as you say, we have around $10,000 in Baltimore and if Motz put in $10,000 more, we should have an adequate amount for the immediate future, including payment of all taxes. Item #3: I should think $50 to the Rumsey Development fund should be enough. Item #4: tell Mr. Sanderson that I just can't make the Suffield Academy writer's thing.† Incidentally, I wish you would also ask him if he got a letter from Eliz. McKee, telling him that I couldn't participate. The reason I want you to do this is because, when you and I were first here at the Lotti and Eliz. was forwarding my mail, she included a letter from Sanderson about the same thing. I wrote her back, asking her

* "Red" was Robert Penn Warren's nickname.

† Paul G. Sanderson, Jr., ran a literary event called the Suffield Writer's Conference. He asked Styron to participate nearly every year for a decade.

to write him, saying no. It would seem possible now that Eliz. failed to write him, as I had asked. If this is so, it certainly would be another reason for me to quit her, and that's why I'm asking you to ask Sanderson.

Apparently, while STHOF has been making the big stir in Paris, The Long March begins a belated ovation in London. Truman Capote called me excitedly this morning from the Ritz, saying, "Honey, haven't you seen the reviews?" I said I hadn't, whereupon he told me that yesterday (Sunday) he had read the reviews of The Long March in the Observer and the Sunday Times, and added: "They're the most fantastic reviews I've ever seen, sweetie, why you're the biggest thing in London since King Kong." I haven't seen them as yet, but Truman is going to pass them on to me, and I'll send them to you. The enclosed review from The Spectator was sent to me by Jamie Hamilton. Aside from the gibberish at the beginning about "moody gravy" and "burdensome obligations," it certainly is what might be called a rave review. Somehow though, withal, I still regard the British with a jaundiced eye, and have very little respect for their critical opinions, pro or con.

Tonight Jim and Moss are giving me some kind of party. Mary McCarthy is to be there and Truman, and my "date" is to be that nice faggot John Ashbery, so feel no qualms.* I think it will be fun. A session of bitching between Truman and Mary McCarthy should be a spectacle to be witnessed about once in 50 years.

All my love to the little mice and save great hunks for yourself, for I miss you. And say great hellos to Ethel, Terry, Jerry, et al.

Much love,

B.

To Rose Styron

April 16, 1962 Hotel Lotti, Paris, France

Dearest Mouse: Since I see by the calendar that this is Monday, and since you probably won't get this until Thursday, this is probably the last letter

* John Ashbery (b. 1927) is a poet who won the Pulitzer Prize for *Self-Portrait in a Convex Mirror* (1975).

I'll be writing. (Incidentally, I hope you'll be forwarding no more mail to me after receiving this.) I received both your letters this A.M. and enjoyed them both immensely. They breathe Roxbury and I can't wait to get there and smell the spring. It was also lovely talking to you and the pumpkinheads yesterday, despite the evil weather both here and there. About the call from Mr. Hadley of the State Dept., tell them I wouldn't mind seeing the Hollander, provided I don't have to travel anywhere to see him. I'm utterly tired of traveling, but will have no objection to meeting him on my home turf. You might keep in mind, by the way, that I have to speak to Dick Lewis' class at Yale on the morning of the 24th, but any other time will be O.K. Meanwhile, my last week here—aside from afternoons with Nat Turner, which keeps me busy—promises to be full. Cordier is giving a dinner for me on Wednesday night at La Grande Severine, the chi-chi restaurant which Maurice Girodias owns. Jules Dassin is going to be there (with the sultry Greek, of course) and other assorted movie cats. Tomorrow night dinner with Paul Jenkins, Thursday night with Abe Rattner + wife + the Joneses, and Friday night some kind of a party chez the uncle of Jean Stein vanden Heuvel, who is passing through with her husband en route to Warsaw, of all places. A busy week, as the French say. The book is still going at a great clip. I got a letter from Maurice Coindreau in Sweet Briar (he sends his regards to you) who said that the greatest review yet was in a journal called Democratic 62 (I haven't seen it) which said that the book was the most revolutionary foreign book to appear in France since Ulysses. So there, Arthur Mizener. These have been good weeks for me but I'm truly anxious to get home. I have only one question about my arrival. How on earth are you going to get the entire gang into the Mercedes?

Love to you and all the chicks.

B.

To William Blackburn

May 2, 1962 Roxbury, CT

Dear Professor: —I had a curious experience last Sunday night, and I thought you might be interested in hearing about it. It does not seem to me quite real, but I shall try to convey my impressions of the event. While

I was in France, Rose received an invitation which went: "The President and Mrs. Kennedy request the company of Mr. and Mrs. Styron at dinner, April 29th, in honor of Nobel Prize winners." Since, aside from James Baldwin,* I was the only "younger" writer invited to the affair, you can imagine that I was somewhat baffled, if pleased, by the summons (I have also learned that it is considered unpardonable to decline such an invitation—not that I was about to). Anyway, we went, accompanied by Van Wyck Brooks, who was exceedingly nervous, and by Baldwin, a fact which made us both feel somewhat like Huck and Jim. There was plenty of booze, and at the pre-dinner festivities I found myself wedged between Linus Pauling and President Stratton of M.I.T., getting very drunk indeed (I was taking antibiotics for an earache, and I have since discovered that this accelerates the action of alcohol by roughly 100%).† At 8:20 Jack and Jackie came into the East Room, preceded by flags, and to the sound of "Hail to the Chief." The receiving line was formed alphabetically (I am always at the end of such lines), and as I staggered past our hosts, I hear Jackie say to me: "Hi there! You're a friend of John and Sue's (Marquand)!" I am not being irrelevant—nothing was irrelevant about that evening—since it then occurred to me that perhaps I had been invited because I was a friend of John and Sue's; but then, why not John and Sue too? At any rate, we went in to dine, and I found myself at Mrs. Robert Kennedy's table, flanked by the wives of two Nobel prize winning biochemists and physicists, and within whispering distance of, on the right, President Pusey of Harvard and, on the left, J. Robert Oppenheimer, also Ralph Bunche, who I think sensed that I was of Southern origin and therefore paid me no never mind.‡ Oppenheimer was utterly charming, and I am

* This was Styron's first mention of James Baldwin (1924–87), the author, notably, of *Go Tell It on the Mountain* (1953), *Notes of a Native Son* (1955), and *The Fire Next Time* (1963), who lived in the Styrons' guesthouse during the winter of 1961. Styron recalled the experience in "James Baldwin: His Voice Remembered," *The New York Times*, December 20, 1987, reprinted in *Havanas in Camelot*.

† Linus Pauling (1901–94) was a chemist and peace activist and the only person besides Marie Curie to win Nobel Prizes in two different fields. Julius Stratton (1901–94) was an electrical engineer who was president of MIT between 1959 and 1966.

‡ Nathan Pusey (1907–2001) was president of Harvard University from 1953 to 1971. Julius Robert Oppenheimer (1904–67) was a theoretical physicist often called the father of the atomic bomb. Ralph Bunche (1903–71) was a political scientist and diplomat who won the Nobel Peace Prize in 1950.

here to report that Pusey is one of the crashing knuckleheads of all time. The dinner was splendid, including the wine, which because of the achromycin I was taking fogged me up to the point of incomprehensibility. After dinner there was a boring reading by Fredric March of a garbled and wretched piece of an unpublished Hemingway manuscript; it was done in semi-darkness, and most of the Nobel prize winners—many of whom are over 70—nodded off to sleep. That was the end of the evening—or so I thought. Just as I, with all the rest, was preparing blearily to make my departure, I was accosted by an Army major in full dress (they are all over the place and act as a kind of chaperone) who said (I will swear to this on a stack of bibles): "The President would like you and Mrs. Styron to join him upstairs in his private quarters." In my drunken state it then flashed over me meanly: "Aha! It's just as I suspected. The son of a bitch is after my wife." Anyway, we went upstairs in the private elevator, to the tootling of the Marine Corps band, and entered Kennedy's drawing room. Those selected for this special treat numbered only six: Rose and myself, Mr. and Mrs. Lionel Trilling, Robert Frost, and Fredric March.* A motley crew indeed. I was sitting in the presidential rocking chair when His Excellency entered. The obvious parallel is an obscure poet lolling on the throne of Louis XIV. Rose tells me that when we rose to greet him I was so blind out of my skull that I simply sank back into the rocking chair. Kennedy took this with remarkable (and democratic) grace: he sat down on a couch and began talking with Robert Frost (it turns out that it wasn't Rose at all he was after, or perhaps not). Diana Trilling had the look of a woman who had just been struck a glancing but telling blow by a sledgehammer; Lionel was nervous, but reasonably urbane. One had the feeling (though I confess I shared the feeling to some degree) that for Diana, at least, it was all a dream. Presently then the Palace Guard came in: Pierre Salinger, Bobby and Ethel, one of the other sisters, the simple-minded brother-in-law who runs the peace corps, etc.† I spent most of the hour talking with

* Along with her husband, Diana Trilling (1905–96) was a prominent literary critic and contributor to the *Partisan Review*. Robert Frost (1874–1963), American poet. Fredric March (1897–1975), stage and film actor who won two Best Actor Academy Awards for *Dr. Jekyll and Mr. Hyde* (1932) and *The Best Years of Our Lives* (1946).

† Pierre Salinger (1925–2004) served as White House press secretary under John F. Kennedy and Lyndon B. Johnson, and was later a prominent ABC news correspondent. Robert F. Kennedy (1925–68) was a Democratic senator from New York and U.S. At-

Jackie, who I must say has a great deal of charm, and I treasure her promise to take us out on the presidential yacht when we are across the Sound from Hyannisport this summer. At about midnight, turned once again into a pumpkin or whatever it was Cinderella turned into, this phase of the party broke up; we bade our host and hostess adieu, and were conveyed in the limousine of the Attorney General (he reminds me of nothing so much as a young lion cub, hot-eyed and panting) to the home of Arthur Schlesinger in Georgetown, and there from Schlesinger himself, an affable agent, I learned why I had been so honored this evening. It turns out, according to Schlesinger, that Set This House on Fire is, and has been for some time, the most "controversial" book that the intellectuals at the White House have been reading.* Some of them hate it, some of them love it passionately, but it causes constant and violent arguments, and they have just wanted to get a look at the instigator. Never underestimate the power of the written word. At any rate, it was a jolly time, but in case you feel I have been overly detailed, I would like to say that I just wanted to get it down in writing; it's not just like every Sunday dinner, after all.

I don't know if you got my cable from Rome or not, announcing what happened to STHOF ("La Proie des flammes") in France. Quite simply, it made the biggest splash there of any American novel since Faulkner. The reviews were unanimously overflowing with praise, almost embarrassingly so; they were all so sanguine that I began to get suspicious and even hankered for a small word of disfavor. L'Express, for instance, which next to Le Monde is the most important paper, called the book "the most optimistic and intelligent of the great American tragedies." Le Monde itself, in a rather unprecedented full page review which was more like a news story, simply called it "a very great book, a vast allegory of the American condition." As a result of all this, the book last month was #3 on L'Express's monthly best seller list (a compendium of all books, fiction and non-

---

torney General (1961–64). Robert was assassinated during the 1968 presidential campaign. He was survived by his wife, Ethel (b. 1928). The "simple-minded brother-in-law" was Robert Sargent Shriver, Jr. (1915–2011), who helped found the Peace Corps. He was married to John F. Kennedy's sister Eunice.

* This was Styron's first encounter with Arthur Schlesinger, Jr. (1917–2007), an American historian who served as the unofficial chronicler of John F. Kennedy's administration and taught at the Graduate Center at the City University of New York (1966–94). Schlesinger and Styron became great friends in the ensuing years.

fiction) and is expected to be #1 this month—something which has happened to no American book, fiction or non-fiction, in the 12 years L'Express has been running, and something which happened to only one other non-French book—Dr. Zhivago. Guy Schoeller, who runs Hachette which in turn owns Gallimard, my publisher, said he was fully confident that by the end of the year (sales are somewhat slower in France) the book will have sold between 70–80,000 copies. This would be the equivalent in America of a quarter of a million (Bennett Cerf just told me that the Random House edition sold something less than 18,000, which is a reflection on something). After having been treated by the American critics as a somewhat more clumsy Richard Ruark, I expect you can understand how I feel zestily vindicated. I wish there were some way I could rub Arthur Mizener's nose in it all, but I suspect this victory is its own reward.

Do you think you could come visit us at the Vineyard again this summer? We don't have the same house, unfortunately, and we would have to put you up in a place nearby, but we would love to have you. Try to make it. I will have a larger sailboat, a more comfortable one so there will be no risk of spilling overboard in the channel. I'm delighted, while I think about it, over the reception Reynolds Price's book has been getting; it certainly deserves it, and Hiram told me that it is selling well, which means the most important thing—readers.

Let me hear from you soon.

As ever,
Bill

PS: I think the boy in Hartford is going to escape the electric chair. There has been a tremendous ruckus up there since that article.* Again, never underestimate the power of the written word, learned at the Blackburnian knee.

* Styron refers to his first piece on the death row inmate he helped to save from execution, "The Death-in-Life of Benjamin Reid," *Esquire* (February 1962).

To Elizabeth McKee

May 6, 1962 Roxbury, CT

Dear Elizabeth: This is going to be an extraordinarily difficult letter for me to write, since I might as well say at the outset that it is to inform you that I am leaving the Agency. I have the deepest and warmest feeling for you personally, as you must well know, and that makes it all the tougher for me.

Primarily, the difficulty for me stems not so much from the Agency itself, or from your management of my literary affairs, but from my foreign rights, which I sincerely believe have been badly mishandled. This occurred to me for the first time the year before last when both Plon and Robert Laffont in France were haggling over Set This House on Fire. At that time, you will recall, I was in Ravello and you were in Milan. It was about the first time I really had had a crisis over any of my books, and I called you on the phone to ask you to straighten it out for me. About halfway through the conversation I was interrupted—and rather brusquely, too, I might add—by Ted, who informed me that you were going to the opera. And that was the end of that. By great luck, several days after that Gallimard stepped in from the outside and saved the situation nicely, but I was left with the distinct feeling that had that not happened I would have been left to cope with the Plon-Laffont difficulty myself. And at that time it not unnaturally occurred to me that I was paying a whopping 20% of my foreign rights income to people who not only were not helping me a bit but were actually impeding my progress. Recently, when I was in Frankfurt, Mrs. Fischer told me something else which jarred me. She said that after Lie Down in Darkness came out she wrote repeatedly to your office, asking what the German rights situation was, and received no answer. I know this must be true, because she offered to show me copies of the letters. At any rate, the upshot was that I was published by a lousy little house in Geneva and was wretchedly translated to boot. I have no idea who was to blame in this matter of the letters—I rather suspect it was the Horch office—but in any event it couldn't have been handled worse.

The success of Set This House in France (I hardly need emphasize that I handled personally all negotiations with Gallimard) has certainly made me aware of the importance of foreign rights; in fact, since I've already sold more copies in France than any of my books sold in their original editions in the U.S., I feel that my foreign rights are even more important than my domestic affairs. In Paris I met a lady, who shall remain nameless (not Mrs. Bradley), who when I told her I had no translations in Holland, Israel, Poland, Yugoslavia, etc., was astounded. She handles, incidentally, foreign rights for American writers, and said that she could sell the rights to all of my work in the countries just named within a week. I believe her, as she has done just this for two writers I know very well. She was further surprised that neither you nor Horch had made any attempt to sell my Esquire piece on capital punishment, which she had just read, and which she said she was positive she could sell the rights for in 15 languages.

I am writing Horch—Roz Siegel, that is—telling them that I am terminating my relationship with them at this date. I won't go into any details with Roz, and trust you will eventually tell her why. I could not feel more certain that my foreign rights have been badly handled.

As for my relationship with McIntosh-McKee, I am not nearly so dissatisfied; in fact, in most respects I think everything has worked out extremely well. At the same time, I honestly no longer feel the need for an agent. As I have gone along in my literary career, I realize that I am primarily a novelist, working for long stretches on one book, and my relationship with my publishers (especially Random House) is and has always been eminently satisfactory. In other words, with all due respect to you as an agent, I simply do not need you to get $5,000 more out of Bennett Cerf. He is all too happy to give it to me freely at any time. Such few articles as I write and will continue to write for, let us say, Esquire, are articles they are pleased to get out of me, and you have not had to "sell" them. Surely you are aware of this, and I simply cannot see the plain reasonableness of paying the Agency 10% for doing in the end so little work. To be sure, I will be the first to admit that you have done a considerable amount of work for me. I am aware of all the inquiries you have handled and of all the foolish people you have steered off my track, but I cannot help asking myself if the 10% of the money, say, that I made last year—the Agency's commission being around $3,000, in round-figure terms of my income, that is—is equitable in regard to the services rendered.

Further, I am not at all satisfied with Famous Artists. Abramson is an amiable but total oaf, and Harriet Pilpel has informed me that the contracts they have been drawing up have been near-disastrous. Fortunately, Pilpel saved the day, but again I have to ask myself why I am associated with these characters, people like Abramson. To be sure none of my books have been the hottest thing around in terms of the movies, so this aspect has been difficult all around. Yet now, after seeing what Greenbaum, Wolff & Ernst did to my advantage in those contracts, I would far rather have her simply act as my lawyer—I am speaking of Harriet—have her actually draw up the contract and pay her the large but in the end reasonable fee she would ask, than to have a big commission go to an outfit like Famous Artists. These are simple economic facts, and I'm sure you must be aware of the reasonableness of my argument.

Finally, of course, you still in a sense remain my agent. For naturally anything to do with any of my past work (except future foreign rights) will be handled through the Agency. I expect our professional relationship to continue much as it did in the past; because I am such a slow worker, and because all my past works seem still to have so much "Life," I am sure business will continue to come to me through the Agency. Anything in regard to any of my future work, including "Nat Turner," I will handle on my own. The Agency will also collect commissions on the English Penguin edition of The Long March, which John Dodds* wrote me about, and will collect commissions with Horch and Heath on foreign rights already sold. All future movie rights and all future foreign rights I will also handle on my own. It doesn't seem nearly so awful as it might have been, does it? At least, that's the way I feel.

In the end, in case you were silly enough to entertain the notion that there is or was anything personal in all this, or that I bore you any kind of resentment whatever, kindly put it out of your mind.† To me you are still one of the prized and valued people I know anywhere, and I shall care very deeply for you always. Enjoy your trip and come back soon to Roxbury.

Love

Bill

* John Dodds was Styron's lawyer.

† In a telephone conversation between McKee and Harriet Pilpel on June 25, 1962, McKee reported that she "was so hurt—so personally hurt" by Styron's letter.

To Hope Leresche*

May 11, 1962 Roxbury, CT

Dear Miss (or is it Mrs?) Leresche:

Maybe you will remember me from a pleasant evening at James Jones'. I am writing you to tell you that I have terminated my association with both my general agent and my agent for foreign rights, Franz J. Horch Associates of New York. I have done this for the several reasons we discussed that night—mainly the fact that I don't believe Horch has displayed much initiative in selling my work—and I wonder if you are still willing to take me on as a client for foreign rights. Rather conveniently, in an effort to justify their good works, Horch sent me a list (complete) of the contracts they have concluded for me. The most important one—the Gallimard contract for SET THIS HOUSE ON FIRE—I negotiated myself, as I told you. Perhaps you've seen this month's French Vogue, an article by François Nourrissier who said, quite accurately, that La Proie des flammes is the most successful American novel to be published in France since LOLITA. At any rate, I thought you'd like to see this list so that, in case you decide to take me on, you can determine what gaps there are in my foreign rights. Incidentally, since I am breaking off with my general agent, McKee-McIntosh, this means that I will be breaking off with their corresponding agent in England, which is Heath, so I presume that this means you will become my agent for England, too.

I think we spoke of the Esquire article I did on capital punishment. It has since caused a big commotion here, and it looks as if the condemned boy I wrote about may be reprieved—have his sentence commuted to life, that is. You said that you felt this article might very well be of interest to readers in various countries.† I would be glad to have copies of the article made available to you if you think you can use them.

* Hope Leresche ran her own literary agency in London, Hope Leresche and Steele. Leresche handled Styron's foreign rights after his split with Elizabeth McKee. Leresche played a significant role in his becoming a writer of international reputation.

† "I think it is crazy," Leresche wrote Styron, "that this has not at least been offered in England and elsewhere."

At any rate, if you are agreeable to becoming my English and foreign rights agent for all my future work and past work not already contracted for, I hope you will let me know.*

Sincerely,
William Styron

To George Plimpton

May 22, 1962 Roxbury, CT

Dear George:

Many thanks for your note about the Century.† I expect to see Red Warren this Friday night and will bring the matter up, although he is leaving for France for the summer sometime next week.

The party at your place, forever hereinafter to be known as "the Jones Affair," was certainly a historic blowout, and I hope the damage wasn't too awful. Anyway, send along the bill at your convenience. I can stand the trauma, being most grateful to you for the use of the premises.

Hope to see you soon. We are making the Vineyard scene as of July First. What are the chances of your paying us a visit up there during the sullen summer months?

Ever yours
B.

* Leresche assured Styron, "I shall make every personal effort to further the interest of your work."

† Plimpton had nominated Styron for membership in the Century Association, an exclusive club in New York City founded in 1829 by editor and poet William Cullen Bryant.

To Hope Leresche

May 23, 1962 Roxbury, CT

Dear Miss Leresche:

As a kind of addendum to my letter of yesterday (which I hope you've received by now), I thought I might write a small précis to you about my work, so that perhaps you may be better equipped to talk about it when it comes to dealing with the various people you will be dealing with. I am speaking rather subjectively—a writer is always the last person to know where he himself "stands"—but nonetheless I thought it might be useful to record these observations.

For example, I would suspect rather strongly that at the moment my reputation in America rests largely upon my first novel, LIE DOWN IN DARKNESS. Since it was published in 1951, it has achieved a low but steady renown, and though, for instance, it is nowhere near so well known as THE CATCHER IN THE RYE, it is the only novel which even approaches Salinger's book in terms of "adoptions" in college English courses. I'm of course speaking of novels by the younger or post-war U.S. writers. It is still fully in print in three editions (the original hardback, one "quality" reprint, and one cheap reprint—the last now in its fifth printing), and there is a steady and large demand for it, especially among college students. In a recent poll, for instance taken among a large group of college English teachers, asked to name the twelve U.S. literary classics of the last twenty years (this was published in the Saturday Review), LIE DOWN IN DARKNESS was one of the four novels named (the other were poems or plays)—the other novels being CATCHER IN THE RYE, Warren's ALL THE KING'S MEN, and Hemingway's THE OLD MAN AND THE SEA. In terms of a final literary judgment, of course, this means little, but it does indicate the book's rather remarkable and enduring popularity. (Forgive me if I seem to be blowing my own horn, but I'm trying to provide a practical guide for you.)

Abroad, LIE DOWN IN DARKNESS is practically unknown, although as you can see it was published in England and in over half a dozen languages. In England the reviews were better than average, generally speaking, but somehow I had the feeling that the book never quite caught on; as Roger Machell once pointed out, it was never even reviewed in several of the most important papers, and the sales were quite small. In

France, the book was adequately translated, but was badly published by Del Duca, and made no noise at all. In Germany (so I am told by a few people who read German) it was hideously translated, published in Switzerland (vis-à-vis Germany this is supposed to be limbo), and made even less noise than it did in France. To this day, I have not the slightest inkling what DARKNESS did in the other countries—Sweden, Spain, etc.—but I doubt that it could have been much. Of course, even abroad DARKNESS is a book with which the intellectual in-group (I'm not being snide) is acquainted; and to those to whom contemporary literature is a passionate matter the book is fairly well known. Compared to its relative fame in America the book is just beginning to achieve a foreign reputation. Because of SET THIS HOUSE ON FIRE, Gallimard is planning to bring out a new edition of the book, buying the rights from Del Duca—at least I have a contract to this effect. And in Germany, the book is a belated book-club selection, and Fischer is going to doctor the translation and bring it out in their paperback series. So much for LIE DOWN IN DARKNESS.

The most important part of the history, to date, of SET THIS HOUSE ON FIRE you know yourself—which is the fact that in France it has set all records, critical and otherwise, for American novels, at least those published in the last fifteen years or so. The German reception has been comparable, if not quite so ornate or grand. At the same time, unlike DARKNESS, STHOF achieved what is doubtless a record in America for overwhelmingly malevolent reviews—also in England, I might add (despite the delicious little blurbs that Jamie Hamilton published on the jacket of THE LONG MARCH) the prevalent attitude was that of the guy in the Observer, who spent five columns denouncing this "thoroughly bad novel."

Thus you get your queer cultural anomalies. In England I am doubtless best known for THE LONG MARCH, which is little-known in America and as yet unpublished (though forthcoming) in France, and at the same time vaguely recalled as the writer who wrote those dreary and cumbersome novels, LIE DOWN IN DARKNESS and SET THIS HOUSE ON FIRE. In America I am known as the writer of an early masterpiece, LIE DOWN IN DARKNESS, who badly betrayed his talent in a clumsy second work, SET THIS HOUSE ON FIRE. In France I am known as the authentic genius who created an incomparable chef d'oeuvre, SET THIS

HOUSE ON FIRE, after an obscure and fledgling attempt called LIE DOWN IN DARKNESS.

Re-reading what I have just written, I don't know of what possible practical use this can be to you, except to confuse you perhaps. I realize that I have overstated my dilemma in many respects, and over-generalized, because there are many people both here and abroad who are interested in my entire work per se, and do not view my work in terms of these blacks and whites, but consider the faults and virtues of all that I have done as all of an eventual piece—and that is how it should be. In any case, I am most pleased about your enthusiasm, and have set down these random, introverted, probably warped reflections to use as you will or wish.

Best regards,
W.S.

To William Blackburn

July 11, 1962 Vineyard Haven, MA

Dear Doctor:

I'm delighted to hear that you're coming and will be on the lookout for you at the dock in Vineyard Haven on July 26th. The 4:45 train to Wood's Hole is scheduled to connect with the 5:00 ferry, which arrives in V.H. at 5:45. So I'll be there. In the unlikely event that there should be a foul-up, keep in mind that our number is Vineyard Haven 625 (also listed in information under my name) and that our house is the Kennedy House on Hatch Road.

I have had an exhausting four days, having flown down to Oxford, Miss. to cover Faulkner's funeral for Life magazine. It was quite an ordeal, mainly the plane travel which involved a lot of charter flights hither and yon, and an endless flight back home to Roxbury by way of Nashville, Cincinnati and Pittsburgh, of all God forsaken places. Anyway, the piece will be out in next week's Life and you might want to take a look at it.*

Had you decided to come earlier you would have had a presidential

* William Styron, "As He Lay Dead, a Bitter Grief," *Life* (July 20, 1962), collected in *This Quiet Dust.*

treat, for on Sunday night next His Supreme Grace and wife are coming over from Hyannis to take us out on the good ship Honey Fitz.* I don't know exactly what kind of fixation Our Leader has on me (I still think it has something to do with Rose), but anyway I'm willing to string along with it so long as he pays for the groceries.

See you soon!

To William C. Styron, Sr.

July 21, 1962 Roxbury, CT

Dear Pop: Last Sunday's excursion with the Kennedys was very pleasant indeed. The Marquands and Rose and I were met at noon at the Edgartown Yacht Club by a Navy launch manned by two sailors and a Mr. Hill of the Secret Service. We were told that this boat would meet the Patrick J. (the Honey Fitz's little sister) off Cape Pogue, which is the eastern tip of the Vineyard; and on the way out the radio was full of such talk as: "Magnet to Rockfish. We will rendezvous at Charlie-2 Area at 1245 hours. Magnet to Rockfish: you'd better be shipshape. Lancer (the Secret Service code name for Kennedy) will want to see your boat in shipshape condition." That sort of talk. It was a gray choppy day, but rainless though a little cool and we floundered around in Charlie-2 area for about a half hour until the Patrick J. approached. It's a cruiser of about 45 feet and as we came near we saw two guys up on the forward cabin, bareheaded and dressed in Navy flight jacket. One of them waved and as we got closer we saw that it was none other than the President of the United States his self. We came alongside and saw that aside from Jack and Jackie and Caroline there were only two other guests aboard—JFK's sister Jean and her husband Steven Smith. The boat itself was manned by an affable, aging Navy commander, a Secret Service agent and three or four Filipino messboys. We put on these flight jackets (as I say, it was rather cool) and sat at anchor drinking Bloody Marys. I spent about 15 minutes helping Jackie fix her miniature camera and in the meantime the conversation had turned to politics, Vir-

* President and Mrs. Kennedy had invited the Styrons for a cruise in Edgartown harbor.

ginia politics in particular. The name Byrd came up, and when I said that this was a name which made my own father nearly apoplectic with outrage, JFK laughed and said he could understand, all right—if there was ever an obstructionist and an "old buzzard" in the Democratic party it was Harry Byrd. I had a long talk with Jackie. She is utterly charming and is reading STHOF, finds it especially fascinating because she is going to spend the month of August in Ravello, in a villa not far from where Rose and I lived. We were sitting around a big table in the open cockpit and occasionally she would put her feet up in JFK's lap and wiggle her toes, just like you'd imagine the wife of the President to do. Lunch was served, rather dreary Navy officers' chow—eggs in aspic and a tasteless salad of some kind—but the hot dogs were good, even if the beer which was served with it had become unaccountably frozen, much to the humiliation of the messboys. It began to get a little rough and every now and then a plate would slide to the deck, also the Flamenco records which were stacked by a record player between Jack and Jackie. There was a rather good cake for dessert, which for some reason was placed in front of me and I had the honor of serving the President a slice (he is always served first, protocol), using my forefinger and thumb. The conversation became literary and although I don't think JFK has really much profound understanding of literature at all (his tastes are rather square and conventional; he liked Leon Uris' Battle Cry), he has a remarkable interest in literary matters, as he does in other matters; his mind is wide-ranging and fantastically filled with facts, not a profound mind but an enormously sharp one, and when he asks you a question and you answer him you feel that he is listening to every word you say. In this respect I think he resembles Teddy Roosevelt like no one else. A very vital and magnetic man, whether you agree with him or not. Toward late afternoon the Patrick J. took us back into the Edgartown harbor. We picked up Caroline (who had been taken ashore swimming with her little cousin while we ate) and she came aboard shivering her teeth out, a cute kid, as they say, with Irish written all over her. By this time, word had gotten around and the harbor was jammed with boats filled with people trying to get a look at their Excellencies, but the two outriding Coast Guard picket boats kept them from being run over by the Patrick J. and each other. We were about to pull into the Edgartown Yacht Club (membership composed of the blackest of black Wall Street Republicans) when all of a sudden JFK called to the Captain: "Better not put in there. Go to the town dock." And he said in an aside to me: "There's not a Democrat within three miles of heah. They'd resent it for weeks." Thus I saw, even in such a minor matter as docking a boat, the constant politicking that goes on in the Presidential mind. At any rate, it was a jolly voyage and a good time was had by all.*

I'll write again more when I get a chance. I'm doing a follow-up article on Benjamin Reid for Esquire (his sentence was commuted to life imprisonment) and I have to meet an early deadline. Prof. Blackburn is coming up for a few days' visit this week.

The kids are all fine and send love to Grandma and Grandpop. Susanna is learning to sail and Polly, of all things, is learning to ride horseback.

Love to all,
Bill

To James and Gloria Jones

October 3, 1962 Roxbury, CT

Dear James + Moss:

I ran across the enclosed photo in a magazine and it so touched me with nostalgia that I thought I'd send it on to you.†

I saw where The Thin Red Line has hit #12 on the best seller list and is obviously on its way up. I thought that generally speaking, except for one or two pissants, the reviews were really pretty good. As usual, very few of them were actually intelligent but I would feel very pleased by the overall favorable tone. Time, of course, was predictable; so far as I know, they haven't given a good review to any important writer since at least 1945. As for Geismar, Rose and I saw him not long ago and he was still bubbling

* Styron's essay "Havanas in Camelot" narrated this encounter and was the lead piece in the collection of the same name.

† Styron attached his article "The Paris Review," which appeared in *Harper's Bazaar* (August 1953).

with real enthusiasm for the book; all in all, I think he did the best job, insofar as a book review means anything in the long run.* Most importantly, though, I've heard a lot of really fine private talk about the book, from people I generally respect, and that is infinitely more important than any reviews, pro or con. So if I were you, I'd rest easy in case you aren't already.

After moving into our new pied-à-terre on 61st street, the other night, I pulled your cheap trick and went to P.J. Clarke's, planning only to have a couple of snorts, but got ensnared in the clutches of Danny himself—a nice guy, I must say—who so kept plying me with free booze that I didn't leave until 5:30 A.M. Davis Grubb was there, and Trezynski—naturally—and Jones Harris who, at risk I'm sure of alienating you, I find one of the most dreadful little pricks I've ever encountered.† It was the height of the mess in Mississippi, which is bad enough God Knows, but on top of that I had to have this hysterical little cocksucker screaming at me because I'm a Southerner and presumably responsible for everything that goes on south of the Potomac river.‡ I came very close to punching his little demi-fag's-teeth out. Forgive me, since I know he's a pal of yours, but his charm eludes me. Anyway, Davis was in fine form and it was otherwise a very pleasant evening, but it will be my own death sentence if I start going there often during my nights in town, riding home at dawn with Trezynski, or however you spell it, locked in my hot embrace . . .

Love,

B.

* Geismar's fondness for Styron extended to Jones; he was one of the few critics who applauded Jones's novel. *The New York Times Book Review* (November 9, 1962).

† P. J. Clarke's, owned at the time by Daniel Lavezzo, Jr., provided the model for the setting of Billy Wilder's *The Lost Weekend* (1945). Davis Grubb (1919–80) was a novelist and story writer. His first novel, *The Night of the Hunter,* was a best seller. Jones Harris was the son of Broadway producer Jed Harris and actress Ruth Gordon and was a networking socialite.

‡ A reference to the race riots that followed James Meredith's enrollment at the University of Mississippi on September 30, 1962.

To C. Vann Woodward

December 9, 1962 Roxbury, CT

Dear Vann:

The enclosed photostat is from an old book on Virginia—exact date uncertain but I suspect between 1840 and 1850.* Jerusalem (where Nat was tried and hanged) had its name changed to Courtland in the 1880s. Don't bother to send this back, since the excerpt from Nat's confession simply duplicates a full copy which I already have. I'm pretty sure that the pure facts in Nat's "Confession" are accurate, but as you can see there is a very phony and manufactured quality about the way of telling. I hardly think Nat would have said "gratify our thirst for blood."

I hope you find that book at Yale. In case you've forgotten, the title is "The Southampton Insurrection" by William S. Drewry (Washington D.C., 1900). I think you will find its fin de siècle attitudes toward the Negro quite fascinating.

Best regards
Bill Styron

To James Jones

December 27, 1962 Milford, CT

Bennett Cerf knows what it all means but he won't tell us.

Bill, Rose, Susanna, Polly, Tom

* Attached to this letter were four pages of photostats from a nineteenth-century Virginia history book.

To C. Vann Woodward

January 16, 1963 Roxbury, CT

Dear Vann:

Many thanks for letting me read this book, which I did at one long day-long sitting.* Mainly because it is inscribed, I am hastening to send it back to you. I shouldn't want anything to happen to it.

All in all, I think it's a splendid job. Every now and then I must confess I got a little hung up on some of the more recondite psychoanalytic allusions, but this was more than overbalanced by Erikson's own almost intuitive insights. In terms of Nat Turner the effect is, as you surmised, quite startling. Read for instance the paragraph I have marked on p. 66 (I have left your margins otherwise intact): if you substitute the word "master" for "father" and think of the passage in terms of a rebellious slave rather than Luther, then Erikson's last phrase—"a deadly combination"—has connotations which send a chill up the spine.

At any rate, my very great thanks. I'm sorry you couldn't make it this week-end, but either Rose or I will be in touch again very soon.

Best regards,
Bill

* Erik Erikson, *Young Man Luther: A Study in Psychoanalysis and History* (New York: Norton, 1962): "I have so far mentioned two trends in the relationship between Hans and Martin: 1) the father's driving economic ambition, which was threatened by something (maybe even murder) done in the past, and by a feeling close to murder which he always carried inside; and 2) the concentration of the father's ambition on his oldest son, whom he treated with alternate periods of violent harshness and of habituating the son to himself in a manner which may well have been somewhat sentimental—a deadly combination."

To Robert Penn Warren

January 22, 1963 Roxbury, CT

Dear Red:

Thanks for the communication about the National Institute.* If it's O.K. with you, I'll sort of gradually ease up on it, and assemble some quotable quotes from the thick-headed critics. So far as I know, they've never said anything nice about me in England (seriously), but as for France—quelle merveille! Anyway, I'll try to get them arranged, and I do appreciate your thinking about me in this way.

Yours in Christ,
B.

PS: The poems were truly fine. Rose, indeed, was so bemused and impressed that she stayed up half the night writing a poem of her own.

To James Jones

April 22, 1963 Roxbury, CT

Dear James:

Mainly on account of the fact that I've got to get Nat Turner done, and I write so exceedingly slow, I've decided to forgo Plimpton's invitation to Lago di Como, although the prospect of being there with you would be very pleasant. I had great fantasies of dallying with Moss on the poop deck of a little barca while you were bubbling away somewhere in the depths of the lake. But art comes before pleasure, and so I have regretfully and manfully made this decision. Is there any chance you will be coming through New York on your way to the Caribbean, or on your way back. We'd like to get a chance to see you.

I was at an awful sort of literary festival at Princeton this past weekend, full of pimply sophomores and dew-snatched little girls from Vassar waiting for the Answer. Why I do this sort of thing is beyond me. I also

* Warren was trying to get Styron admitted to the National Academy of Arts and Letters (formerly known as the American Institute of Arts and Letters).

saw Mailer at a party. We didn't speak but at one point he sort of jostled me, and muttered "Excuse me"—a pointless bit of 10-year-old childish hostility. Fuck him.

There is a guy I grew up with in Virginia, my age, who is a surgeon in the Army at, I believe, Orleans. His name is Leon Edwards, he's very well read and bright, most simpatico, and I think you would get along very well with him. He's only been in France six or eight months, I think he's a major now, and he's only in the Army because they've footed the bill for his surgical training ever since he left Harvard. Anyway, I've taken the liberty of telling him to get in touch with you. Ordinarily I wouldn't sic strangers on you but this guy is, I think, someone rather special—his wife's fine too—and I hope you get together. I expect he'll be in France for another year at least.

Love to all your gang, and let me hear from you if you come over to this continent by way of New York or vicinity.

Love,

B.

Ps: Schwartz's Calliope record has come through, and they did a fine job, very handsome too.* You should be getting yours soon.

To John Dodds

May 8, 1963 Roxbury, CT

Dear John:

I know full well that in California the accent is on youth, and the most callow stripling is granted powers which in a saner, sager age were reserved only for the mature; nonetheless, I think that for these Hollywood lawyers to expect the signatures of my children is a bit much—and probably even illegal. Susanna, just turned eight, could manage some sort of ragged scrawl, I guess, but I have grave doubts about Polly, who if you give her a six by eight sheet of cardboard can get a semblance of her first name down

* Styron refers to a Calliope Records LP of him reading a section of *Lie Down in Darkness:* Calliope CAL 12 (1963).

in orange crayon, but the orthography of "Styron" is still beyond her. As for old Tom, now three, he can make a splendid runny mess with a melting Popsicle, but I'm afraid that the manipulation of anything so complicated as a fountain pen exceeds his present capabilities. Kindly convey to Henry Jaffe Enterprises, Inc., this information, stressing the fact that though they are Connecticut children, and consequently retarded by California standards, their father is all the more determined not to submit them to such a ludicrous ordeal. And that is that.

I can make hardly more sense of the second letter about sending notices and payments to a specified address. Will you try to figure this out, and let me know what kind of letter they want me to sign.

All the best,
Bill

To James Jones

June 6, 1963 Roxbury, CT

Dear James: Perhaps the following communication won't interest you in the slightest, but I thought I'd tell you nonetheless.

This afternoon I got a phone call from Gay Talese (the N.Y. Times fellow who rents me my N.Y. apartment, and who writes a lot for Esquire); his tone was of high dudgeon and outrage.* He told me that he had gotten an advance look at the forthcoming July issue of Esquire, which has our interview, also another nobly-conceived dissection of his fellow writers by Mailer.† Apparently this time Mailer has stooped to an all-time low, even for one who has been flopping around in the gutter as long as Norman. The Thin Red Line according to Talese comes off relatively clean and

* Gay Talese (b. 1932) helped invent literary nonfiction and the New Journalism. His books include *The Bridge* (1964), *The Kingdom and the Power* (1969), and *Thy Neighbor's Wife* (1981). He and his wife, Nan, rented an apartment to the Styrons very briefly in the 1960s.

† Norman Mailer, "Some Children of the Goddess: Norman Mailer vs. Nine Writers," *Esquire* (July 1963). Mailer's piece appeared immediately before a conversation between Styron and James Jones, "Two Writers Talk It Over," reprinted in James L. W. West III, ed., *Conversations with William Styron* (Oxford: University Press of Mississippi, 1985).

unspattered: you are no longer "the world's worst writer of prose," or something like that, and the book in the end is highly praised, if most grudgingly. The bulk of Mailer's hatred is reserved for me. An all-out, slavering attack on Set This House on Fire: but Talese said the thing that bugged and horrified him the most was the personal venom, which has to do with both you and me. I am paraphrasing Talese's paraphrase of the article, but the gist is this: during the time Norman lived up here in Connecticut, and we saw something of each other, I spent a great deal of time ridiculing Some Came Running, running the book down in general and poking fun at it. Well, maybe I did. I was quite nervous about you in those days—not knowing you, for one thing—and besides being exceedingly envious of someone who had muscled through with such prodigious energy that second-novel barrier. My wife Rose, the wife, who is so honest about such matters, is not at all sure: she distinctly recalls Mailer's hatred and envy of you (she has always been one of the greatest fans of Running) and remembers a two-hour argument with Mailer in the kitchen . . . in which she defended the book vainly against Mailer's snarls and sneers. All this, if I'm not mistaken, took place during the time before I got to know you at all well, and after Mailer had written you whatever swinish thing it was he wrote you, and was still in a dreadful stew about you.

I had not intended to make this letter even this long. I want to make a couple of points though. My wife Rose, the student of human nature (and by God she really is), has always felt that Mailer's pent-up homosexuality has always been directed at you, you being the cock-object, or maybe he likes to take it up the ass, who knows; anyway, I believe this is true and I also believe now that the real reason for him having written me that dreadful letter five years ago was that you and I were becoming friends, and he was insanely jealous. This is awful stuff to talk about, but we are dealing with a lunatic. At any rate I'm convinced that this jealousy, combined with a bitter envy of both of our talents, has been at the root of his hatred.

Talese said that, to him at least, the article looked like a foolish attempt to break up a friendship, and that the whole thing looked especially grotesque in the light of our mutual interview in the same issue. Also, according to him, what seemed to bug Mailer was the reference in The Thin Red Line to "Styron's Acres," hence his loathsome little faggoty reference to the time many years ago when we sat around "Styron's Acres" ridiculing Running.

All I wanted this letter to do is to take some of the curse off reading such foulness in print, cold, for the first time, as you will when you get a copy of the magazine. My feelings about Mailer are too low to have him demean me into a position of having to protest my enormous admiration for your talent and great affection for yourself. So, love to you and Moss and my young mistress Kaylie.

B.

PS: I am having to prove, through endless documentation, to some God damned Swiss insurance company that the God damned Mercedes really lives no longer in France, but gradually we are straightening the matter out.

To Lew Allen

June 11, 1963 Roxbury, CT

Dear Lewie: I write you this after midnight, in the grisly first hour of my 38th year, though I'm not asking you to sympathize with me. Actually, all I wanted to say was that I thought Flies a simply splendid movie. I saw it when Al showed it to the Rumsey kids and was deeply affected by it. I'll wait until I see you next to blurt out all the details of my enthusiasm, but I do think you really did yourself and Golding and everyone who cares for good films proud.* I'll never forget that touching Piggy, and that kids' choir singing the Kyrie is an absolute triumph. Other things, too, which I'll talk to you about, but meanwhile it was swell and I also hope you make beaucoup $$$$$.

—Wm.

* Styron refers to the film of William Golding's novel *Lord of the Flies*, produced by Allen, directed by Peter Brook, and released in 1963.

To Rust Hills

June 11, 1963 Roxbury, CT

Dear Rust,

About a week ago, quite a few days subsequent to my talk with Byron Dobell* about doing a popular music column for Esquire, I had a conversation with a girl at the University of Connecticut, who lives near here and who had taken copious notes on Mailer's speech up there a month or more ago. The first part of this speech is in Esquire this month; according to this student, the piece in Esquire—which I read—is a literal transcription of what Mailer read at Storrs, and therefore it is logical to assume that the second part will be more or less a literal copy, too: at least I am going on this assumption. Having spoken at the University myself a few weeks after Mailer, I was hardly left ignorant of the substance of this speech/article. I know he attacks Set This House on Fire with great gusto and style, all of which rather pleased and tickled me, inasmuch as at least part of the book is an assault on everything Mailer represents. (The French, I might add, have been the first to point this out, for although they don't know Mailer from Adam they know all too well and from deadly experience the effects of his perennial philosophy, and that is why I know—from far right to far left—they have dug the book.) So I needed no more proof than that Mailer had leveled an onslaught against the book to reinforce my feeling that I had hit him where he lived. Therefore, although it is never really pleasant to have your work attacked, from whatever source, I could not really feel unhappy that Mailer was lambasting the book, and could even welcome his sneers.

Until I had talked to this student, however, I had not realized that the article carries a lot of disgusting and poisonous baggage about myself, and "Styron's Acres," and Jim Jones—all written, so far as I can gather from the girl's notes, in Mailer's most engaging Westbrook Pegler cum Joe McCarthy style, and serving no other effect than to try and humiliate and disgrace me personally and to undermine my friendship with Jones. I have not read the article as yet, so perhaps I am off base; the girl, however, who

* Dobell (b. 1927) was an influential editor at *Esquire, New York,* and *American Heritage* before devoting himself to painting.

is a combination of fresh young naivete and stony shrewdness, said: "He sounded like a vicious little faggot."*

You may wonder where this prolix introduction is leading. At first I must admit that my indignation at Esquire was quite intense, but it quickly wore off. My respect for free speech—and all the pious banalities attending thereupon—is so great that my initial reaction, which was and in a way still is one of revulsion, was tempered by a kind of grudging admiration that Esquire should allow a convicted wife-stabber and, to my mind, moral imbecile so captiously and naggingly to lucubrate on the conduct of others. I intend no reply to Mailer, personal or in print, for unless I am mistaken or have been misled, Mailer is now spinning out the kind of rope whereby men hang themselves. Nor do I have any final complaint against Esquire, which I don't think I need say has my considerable respect. But the fact is that I simply cannot write for a magazine, and retain my self-esteem, when I am exposed to this kind of personal abuse and viciousness. Therefore, I wish you would let it be known, with all good-will possible, that I will not be available as a contributor so long as Mailer is writing for Esquire. I'm sorry that this happened just at the moment when the project that Byron Dobell and I were working out seemed so interesting and exciting; but I suspect it won't be forever.

I've written you this, instead of someone else at Esquire, only because I feel that I know you well enough that I could lay these matters on the line. I think you will understand because I think, if you were in my position, you would do the same thing.

All the best to you and Penny,

Yours,

Bill

P.S. Just by way of respect to Esquire, perhaps you'd pass the following copy of the letter I got today to Arnold or other interested parties at the Magazine.—B

* Mailer's column, "The Big Bite," had begun appearing in *Esquire* in November 1962, and Styron refers to "Some Children of the Goddess."

PPS: The "divided verdict" allows one jury to determine guilt; but another jury is allowed to examine the prisoner's background, mentality, etc. in order to fix sentences. Much freer of prejudice.

To Robert Penn Warren

July 19, 1963 Roxbury, CT

Dear Red: Just a line to let you know that I have made very good use of the Visit of Lafayette to the seminary material which you got them to send me from Lexington.* It fits in superbly: I've used two entire poems, changing Lafayette to Governor Floyd of Va. visiting a similar seminary in Nat Turner country, and I'm indeed very happy that you sent it my way.

Have been thinking about FLOOD.† It has a real resonance; the fact that it still lingers in my mind so powerfully convinces me how really splendidly effective the work is. I hope the final re-writing is coming along. We're off to the Vineyard Aug. 1. Hope to see you before long. Love to Eleanor and the kids.—B

To William Blackburn

August 7, 1963 Box 948, Edgartown, MA

Dear Professor:

I have stopped smoking (well into my second week) and only now have attained enough self-command to be able to pick up a pen and write a letter.‡ Actually, it is not as horrible as I thought it might be and don't give it a second thought except once in a while trying to work and when social-

* Styron had written Warren on April 17, 1963, considering it "a great favor if you could have these people send me the material on the young female seminarian of the 1820's you were telling me about Sunday."

† Robert Penn Warren's novel-in-progress, *Flood: A Romance of Our Time,* was published by Random House in 1964.

‡ "He quit and took up candy," Rose Styron recalls. Styron recalled this process while reviewing Ruth Brecher, Edward Brecher, et al., *The Consumers Union Report on Smoking*

izing at night. It surely is time: eating is once again a delight with the taste buds restored.

Shocking about Mac.* I received your telegram and send belated thanks. For a while I thought I might try to make the funeral but was so near to completing a part of the new book that it seemed a prodigious wrench and I figured Mac would have understood. At any rate, I suppose like everyone I was stunned. It is just not the right age or time to go.

We are in Edgartown this year rather than Vineyard Haven, but with a similar house + view of the water. While in my non-smoking trauma I have taken a vacation from work but expect to get back to business soon. Two hundred pages done on Nat Turner, and I think they are good. We'll be here until Sept 15th. If you can see your way clear to spending some time with us we'd be delighted as always.

Ever yours,

B.S.

To James Jones

August 22, 1963 Edgartown, MA

Dear James:

We're up here again on the Vineyard, and will be here until September 15th. I wish you and Moss could have seen it last year, as by American standards it is quite a wonderful place to spend a summer. Broad beaches, lousy food (at least dining out) but the best fishing on the East Coast—yesterday I caught 15 bluefish in less than three hours. There is a rather pleasant bunch up here, most of whom you know, I think: Lillian Hellman, the Marquands, Mike Nichols and his new wife, who is quite a dish.†

---

and the Public Interest, in "The Habit," *The New York Review of Books,* December 26, 1963. The piece is collected in *This Quiet Dust.*

* Mac Hyman died suddenly.

† Mike Nichols (b. 1931) is a film, stage, and television director best known for directing *The Graduate* (1968), for which he won an Academy Award. Styron refers to Nichols's second wife, Margo Callas.

Well, maybe you'll make it up here next summer. Not Dalmatia, but not half bad.

You may have seen the enclosed Esquire thing from the most recent issue but I'm sending it anyway. What I'm now really finally convinced about is that, aside from the faggot thing about you in terms of me that he has, he is quite simply obsessed about the fact that I made him a minor figure in SET THIS HOUSE, and a rather nasty figure at that.* Otherwise I cannot figure his obsessive desire to run down the book as he does—in this desperate, clawing way which goes a lot further than simply aggressive criticism. I think if you read the enclosed closely you'll see what I mean. Well anyway, as you say, he is a teapot tempest, and none of this really matters save for the irritation it causes one like an irrepressible flea. I'll certainly be looking forward to your Comments from a Penitent Novelist, where I'm sure you have slapped the flea down.

I'll also be looking forward to the childhood and youth pieces which you're doing. I've thought of doing the same thing† myself after I'm done with the present book. It makes a good change of pace, I think, and certainly a lot of the best writers have felt the same—Tolstoy, Mark Twain, Balzac, and God knows who else. As for me at the moment, I've finished a big hunk of the book—somewhere between a half and a third—and I've got that nice feeling one gets when a real hunk is finished. I've also stopped smoking, it's been a month yesterday; it was getting at my goddam throat in the most horrible way—an inflammation which probably won't be fully cleared up for several months, and the doctor told me to stop or ELSE. It seems that they've discovered conclusively that, among other horrors, smoking eventually destroys the cilia which are the little hairs in the nasopharyngal area that inhibit the entry of bacteria and microorganisms. When these cilia are gone your throat is simply a wreck—as mine is now—and almost everyone suffering from this condition runs a low-grade infection. Fortunately the cilia seem to regenerate themselves after a matter of months, and one gets back into shape but in the meantime: Défense

* There are elements of Mailer in the *Set This House on Fire* characters Mason Flagg and Harvey Glansner. The latter hews most closely to Styron's oft-voiced critiques of Mailer.

† Styron would not turn to this project until the next decade, in *A Tidewater Morning: Three Tales from Youth* (New York: Random House, 1993).

de Fumer . . . I might say, however, to my really astonishing surprise the cessation of smoking is far less an ordeal than I had thought. After a month (only the first couple of days are at all tough) one has only a vague desire for a butt after breakfast and a somewhat stronger desire late at night when everybody else is smoking. But I think it is far easier to stop than any addicted smoker really thinks it is—not completely easy, but easy nonetheless, and I'm just telling you this in case something might force you into stopping sometime.

There's a fair-to-excellent chance that we might make the Paris scene late in the fall. I'm homesick in a sentimental way for the place, as I've always been. We'll let you know when and if we come. Meanwhile, take care, and great love to all your gang from us.

B.

To Berton Roueché*

August 30, 1963 Edgartown, MA

Dear Berton:

I very much enjoyed reading your article on déjà vu in The New Yorker. Just by coincidence and at about the same time I was reading C.G. Jung's Memories, Dreams, Reflections which was published this year and which on p. 254 has a remarkable description of the phenomenon which Jung experienced traveling in Kenya in 1925. He sees a Negro on a cliff, with a spear, and this reminds him of some prior experience, etc. It all obviously ties in with Jung's theories of "The Collective Unconscious" and I thought you might be interested in case you haven't seen it already.

Saluti,

B.S.

* Berton Roueché (1910–94) was the medical writer for *The New Yorker* for nearly fifty years. He was also the author of twenty books.

To William Blackburn

December 18, 1963 Roxbury, CT

Dear Professore:

Just a Yuletide greeting. The season, however, is still somehow touched by melancholy, and one of the abiding wonders to me is the powerful hold Kennedy had on one's imagination.

Here is an instructive anecdote. Exactly two weeks to the day before Kennedy was murdered, Rose and I were in New York and were invited to a party which the President was to attend.* Rose and I were late-comers, which is to say that we were invited in rather an impromptu fashion, at the last moment, and were not dressed in fancy evening clothes like the others, but had on our casual country duds. We arrived late, a little bit before midnight, and as we descended the stairs of this very elegant Fifth Avenue duplex, the first person I saw, out of the entire crowd of 75 or more, was the President, talking to some girl and laughing heartily at what I guess was a joke. Perhaps it was the informal way I was dressed, but anyway it was my intention at that moment to sidle past Kennedy and take up as inconspicuous a position as possible—after all, though I had met him a couple of times and though I had spent an afternoon with him and Jackie a long summer ago, I couldn't claim even what might be called a casual acquaintance. But as I tried to maneuver myself and Rose out of the way, I caught his eye, or he caught my eye, or something; at any rate, he bore down upon us like long lost friends. "How did they get <u>you</u> here?" he said. (I'm quoting exactly.) "They had a hard enough time getting me here!" I didn't know quite what he meant by this, until upon quick reflection I realized that the crowd assembled wasn't quite his style—a mass of rather idiotic show people, not the amusing ones, but the boring ones, and in the distance I could see Porfirio Rubirosa, with whom Kennedy could have had nothing in common at all.

Anyway, I murmured something polite and appropriate, and he said: "Where did I see you quoted the other day? Was it the <u>Times</u>?" and I suppose again I said something harmless and appropriate, but almost immediately he was asking: "How is that book of yours coming along?" Now it

* President Kennedy was assassinated on November 22, 1963.

had been almost a year and a half since I had been on that boat ride with Jack and Jackie, and I had forgotten that I had even mentioned to him then Nat Turner, which I had not even started but just planned, but here he was all these many months later, asking me about the damned thing. And so we talked about it; he asked me something about historical sources, and what research I had used, and what approach I was going to use to tell the story, and of course that started me off, the flood-gates were opened, and we chattered happily about Negro slavery for a full ten minutes, the conversation finally getting around to the present revolt, just the three of us standing there amid a swirling mass of showgirls. It was all quite bizarre, but how much it tells about what kind of man Kennedy was! His eagerness, his honest curiosity, the real interest, the quality of caring! An hour or so later, just before he left the party, he passed me and shook hands and said good-night, casting a wry glance at Rubirosa or someone like him, and said to me: "If you can't get a story out of this kind of party, you're no writer." And Rose said she could feel his hand warm on her shoulder, as he told her good-night and said, "Take care." Famous last words.

Anyway, he is gone, and I suspect that in the great sweep of history he will be measured as somewhat less than the colossus he has seemed to be as the result of his martyrdom. But no matter. No one we have had since Jefferson, certainly, would have literally homed in on a writer as he did that night, and cared and asked questions, and made a writer feel that writing and the republic of letters was an important part of the other Republic, and figured large in the scheme of things. He was, as my father said on the day of his death, better than America ever deserved. I do sorely miss him.

Perhaps by now you have received The N.Y. Review of Books with my anti-smoking diatribe.* On the day of Kennedy's death Life magazine asked me to compose an elegy of some sort, but I was so shattered that I couldn't make it—and ended up writing about the sorrows of nicotine.

Merry Xmas to all in Durms,
W.S.

* Styron had given Blackburn a subscription to *The New York Review of Books,* which he called "an improvement over the N.Y. Times Book Review."

To Donald Harington

January 10, 1964 Roxbury, CT

Dear Don:

I was sorry that you were unable to make it down here, but I fully understand your baby-sitting difficulties, and hope you all will come instead sometime before too long. Almost anytime from now on will be fine with us, if you can give us a few days' notice. Santa Claus brought me a marvelous gift in the form of a 16 mm sound movie projector so we are literally holed in for the winter, each week-end bringing us such delights as "The Informer," "Diary of a Country Priest," "Gold of Naples," and others of the same class.* I once thought that the summum bonum in life would be to have your own movies at home like a Hollywood Tycoon and now that that has arrived I will, in such beatitude, probably stop both reading and writing.

I will, however, save the time to read The Cherry Pit which I am most eager to see. I hope you will arrange to have a copy sent to me, of the MS or whatever, as soon as it is feasible. I have not talked directly to Loomis about it recently, but I have been led by grapevine comments to believe that you have written something very special—therefore my anticipation is running high. About writing "blocks"—I think you must learn to expect them every now and then.† For instance, after a steady run on Nat Turner from the fall of 1962 until fall of this past year, I succumbed to an awful slump (not helped any by Kennedy's death) and have literally only this week managed to start to extricate myself from the mire. I've had these empty periods all my life, and I don't think I'll ever get over them; I console myself with the notion that possibly, they serve as some sort of necessary psychic relief—a moment to restore the brain cells—but this may be a rationalization on my part. At any rate I wouldn't suffer over

* The films: John Ford's *The Informer* (1935), Robert Bresson's *Diary of a Country Priest* (1951), and Vittorio De Sica's *Gold of Naples* (1954).

† Harington's planned visit in December 1963 was postponed. In his letter to Styron on January 6, 1964, Harington wrote: "One of the prime motives behind my wish for the visit was, frankly, that I might get some advice from you on the various personal means for licking that hideous thing called Writer's Block, but my current bout with this incapacitating and insidious disease seems to have cured itself."

them too much but more or less roll with the punch—as you yourself can see, they always eventually go away.

Your observations on Mailer and his "novel" in Esquire amused me greatly.* I was tempted myself to write them a letter, applauding their decision to invade the periodical field heretofore occupied by True Confessions and Agony, but decided not to. Really, the best comment was by someone who said that it all read like Noel Coward trying to write in the style of Mickey Spillane. Horribly enough, another person I know who has seen further installments at Esquire says that the "book" gets progressively worse—which is both easy and hard to believe. Anyway, it is a disturbing sight to see the way Esquire is exploiting his paranoiac misery.

I hope you and your wife venture down this way before long. As I say, we'll be here most of the time—so just let us know.

Bill

To Donald Harington

January 15, 1964 Roxbury, CT

Dear Don:

I thought you might like to have a copy of my current favorite history book† (see quote on back). For me it was quite an eye-opener and I think

* Harington's letter included a long critique of Norman Mailer's *The American Dream,* a novel published in serial form in *Esquire* throughout 1964, before being issued by Dial Press in 1965. Mailer's attempt to write under the same monthly deadlines as Dickens for serialization prompted Harington to say, "obviously a clinical example of free association writing by some poor Bellevue patient trapped in the advanced throes of chronic pathological delusional paranoia."

† Styron enclosed a copy of Stanley Elkins's *Slavery.* Elkins argued that "the typical plantation slave [was] docile but irresponsible, loyal but lazy, humble but chronically given to lying and stealing." Elkins made American slavery a system of such intense domination that blacks could only respond with shameful personal habits and petty resistance, where the slave's "relationship with his master was one of utter dependence and childlike attachment." The book remains very controversial among American historians; it was harshly criticized in the 1950s and 1960s for its almost complete lack of research or evidence. See David Donald, "Stanley Elkins, *Slavery,*" *The American Historical Review* 65, no. 4 (July 1960): 921–22, and Oscar Handlin, "Stanley Elkins, *Slavery,*" *The New England Quarterly* 34, no. 2 (June 1961): 253–55.

it will become a classic, in spite of the critics who cried "rape" because of Elkins daring to call the Negro Sambo. Anyway, read it and see what you think.

—B.

To Robert Loomis

February 24, 1964 Roxbury, CT

Dear Bob:

Here is a real dream I had last night: I was at Dunhill's but the display booths were all empty and flyspecked. The salesman poked around in the back of the shop and finally he came back and said oh so ruefully: "Well I found a couple of old 10 cent White Owls for you."

Actually it was a nightmare but doesn't it have snob appeal?

XXX

B

To James and Gloria Jones

March 16, 1964* Monterey, CA

Swinging on the West Coast with Terry Southern.† Have done some rather impossible things such as having dinner in San Francisco with Shirley Temple.‡ Love

Bill + Rose

* Postcard of Midway Point, 17-Mile Drive, Monterey Peninsula, California.

† Terry Southern (1924–95) was an author and screenwriter best known for his satirical writing and the memorable dialogue in films such as *Dr. Strangelove* and *Easy Rider*. Styron remembered Southern in his essay "Transcontinental with Tex," *The Paris Review* (Spring 1996), also collected in *Havanas in Camelot*.

‡ Shirley Jane Temple (b. 1928) was one of American cinema's first child superstars, starring in films like *Bright Eyes, Curly Top,* and *Heidi*.

To James Jones

March 25, 1964 Roxbury, CT

Dear James:

. . . I heard of your knee accident all the way out in San Francisco, of all places, from that columnist fellow Herb Caen who got the news, I believe, from Bill Saroyan who got it in turn from God knows who.* It must have been really very painful, and I hope it is no more serious than what you've described. Me, I stay off skis. I've been going up to Vermont with Red Warren and there Rose skis, or tries to, while I go snow-shoeing through the woods with Red. It's at least great exercise, though I don't recommend it for pure fun. Anyway, I hope that by now you are on the mend. Why don't you take up something else for recreation? They say screwing is terrific.

Although our bought house on Martha's Vineyard is involved in some kind of litigation—too boring to go into here—I think we will most certainly get our hands on it by the middle of June at the latest.† It is truly a fabulous place, and you and your gang are hereby tendered an invitation to come and stay as long as you like. The Vineyard is really the greatest place you can imagine in the summer—lots of boating and fishing, and swimming practically off the front porch. There is really nothing like a wide American beach, and much as I love France and Italy, a summer by the sea in either country is not my idea of bliss. The Vineyard is still wonderfully uncrowded, easy to get to (there are seven or eight flights daily from New York and Boston), and the people who go there just happen to be for the most part people I like. Lillian has bought a big boat—a cabin cruiser—and I will have to run it for her. There is a marvelous uninhabited island called Naushon we go to, with a great primitive cove, quite silent and still, which oddly enough is reminiscent of Tahiti, and there you can fish and swim or just lie in the sun and get drunk. Anyway, I think

* Herbert Caen (1916–97) was a Pulitzer Prize–winning journalist for the *San Francisco Chronicle*. William Saroyan (1908–81) was a dramatist and author who won a Pulitzer Prize as well as an Academy Award.

† The purchase of the Styrons' home in Vineyard Haven was a terrible ordeal involving a rival buyer who pursued the house through successive lawsuits and appeals (all the way to the Supreme Court of Massachusetts); the legal complications were resolved only in 1966.

you and Moss and Kaylie would have a ball up there, so I implore you to make plans to join us up there in June and stay as long as you like. We will have more than enough room, inasmuch as our dwelling is supplied with a fancy little guest cottage with its own kitchen and everything, and we literally abut upon the little yacht club which will take the kids off our hands all day long. Just let us know when you plan to come.

I was in Washington briefly after the California trip and saw Dick Goodwin,[*] who sent his best to you all. At the moment it is a secret, but it will probably be out by the time you get this, namely, that Dick was asked by Johnson to come to the White House and write his speeches and act as general adviser. I have the feeling that Dick will be running the country yet—a kind of swarthy Harry Hopkins[†]—and we could be in worse hands.

I have a lot of funny jokes to tell you when you come over. The funniest joke of all is Mailer's "novel" in Esquire;[‡] someone aptly said that they hadn't read anything so improbable since the old days of Spicy Detective.

I'm enclosing a love-letter which was here when I arrived back.[§] Love to all of you and stay in touch.

Bill

To James and Gloria Jones

April 25, 1964 Roxbury, CT

Dear James and Moss:

We are delighted to pieces that you are coming. Please send the candelabra and we will take it up to the Vineyard.

Would you also try to bring me a box of Havana cigars—Montecristos or Corona Coronas or Romeo y Julieta—since they are unobtainable here after Castro. You will have to smuggle them in but everyone has been

* Richard Goodwin (b. 1931), adviser to President Kennedy and special assistant to President Lyndon Johnson. He was a summer neighbor on Martha's Vineyard.

† Harry Hopkins (1890–1946) Secretary of Commerce under FDR.

‡ Norman Mailer, *An American Dream* (New York: Dial, 1965).

§ Unknown.

doing it and if you get caught you won't get more than 5 or 6 months in jail. Let us know when you come. Love, —B.

To Robert Penn Warren

July 19, 1964 Vineyard Haven, MA

Dear Red:

This might interest you.* The Sheriff mentioned here is Charlie Capps, who was my roommate for the year and a half I was at Davidson College. He was a bon vivant at 17 and one cold winter day we went to Charlotte, got drunk and found a motheaten South Carolina whore at a place called the Green Hotel. It was my first time but old hat to Charlie, who first got laid with a little colored girl when he was 12.

O tempore, O mores!

The Styrons purchased their home in Vineyard Haven, Massachusetts, in August 1964.

To Hope Leresche

September 5, 1964 Vineyard Haven, MA

Dear Mrs. Leresche:

Thank you very much for your letter. I will certainly be looking forward to receiving the Danish edition.

You may know by now that I had a visit recently from Tom Maschler

* Enclosure, David Halberstam, "Rights Workers Embitter Delta," *New York Times* (July 19, 1964). The article describes the civil rights turmoil in Cleveland, Mississippi. Sheriff Capps asked Halberstam, "What would happen if 200 of us went up to Harlem to tell the Southern side of the story? Why there wouldn't be enough police up there in the city to protect us. Yet these people come down here."

of Jonathan Cape.* He is a most impressive fellow and we got along together wonderfully. He read part of the new book of mine and registered a real kind of enthusiasm, adding of course that he was anxious to become my publisher, and would do every thing in his power to communicate his own excitement in England. As you know, I do very much want to get away from Hamilton. I recently got a curious message from someone at Hamilton—I forget the name, I think in charge of publicity—saying that while "going through their files" they had discovered to their great surprise that they were lacking autobiographical material on me and photographs. I didn't take any action, but it didn't occur to me until a few days later that since I was first published by Hamilton in 1951, and they had never asked me for such material before, it had taken them an awful long time to getting around to it. You may think me petty to be annoyed over a trifle like this, but I think it is something that no publisher who had really cared would do. At any rate, I want to get away from Hamilton and tie up with Cape, if this is possible, and if you think it is possible I will leave the rest up to you. Naturally, there is no great hurry on this. Indeed, it would probably be wiser to wait until this book is finished. However, I want to reiterate my great enthusiasm for Maschler. I actually felt he had understood my work, and that is more than I could ever say for Hamilton, who is terribly nice and all, but . . .

I'll be interested in hearing what you have to say about all this. I'll be up here on this island until around the middle of this month, but a letter either to here or Roxbury will be forwarded.

Sincerely,

And best wishes—W.S.

* Tom Maschler, British publisher and writer, was the head of Jonathan Cape Publishers. In addition to discovering many notable writers and authoring a memoir, *Publisher* (2007), Maschler is most notable for playing a central role in creating Britain's Booker Prize for Fiction in 1968.

To Hamish Hamilton

October 10, 1964* Roxbury, CT

Dear Jamie:

Hope Leresche in London just recently forwarded a letter to her from James Eastwell, which hardly seems even to be from Mr. Eastwell, inasmuch as it was signed by his typist. At any rate, Mrs. Leresche sent the letter on to me because it was an inquiry, wanting to know whether I would like to acquire some of the 700 copies of THE LONG MARCH which you have decided to dispose of as "remainders". At the 1$. a copy

* Styron forwarded this letter to Hope Leresche with a note: "This is a copy of the letter I have just sent to H.H., with your changes, which seemed to me to be perfect. Many thanks! B.S." Those changes—noted in a letter from Leresche on October 7, 1964, began with giving the publisher "too many loopholes through which they can wriggle." Leresche also suggested an entire paragraph of the letter which might "awake in their minds . . . a new and ardent desire to keep you on their list because they begin to perceive where they have gone wrong and what indeed is your true value." The paragraph she suggested omitting followed ". . . spasmodic interest in me." Styron wrote: "Such matters would be less than trivial for me if I didn't quite honestly feel that there was something basically wrong and awry in my connection with the firm. Permit me for a second to blow my own horn a little; it is only necessary to something I am leading up to. I don't suppose I have to tell you what my reputation is here in America; like all writers I have had my slumps and have been bitterly attacked, but I honestly believe that any census taking into account the leading five writers in America would include me. In France, I don't think that anyone but Salinger is better known than myself, and from reports that come back from Paris I'm even getting the edge on Salinger (see Yves Berger's article in The New York Times Book Review last June). I have a similar reputation in Germany, and it is growing. SET THIS HOUSE ON FIRE is going to be published soon in Italy by Einaudi to what I gather will be great fanfare (they have taken exquisite pains in getting an excellent translation). But enough of this—which embarrasses me. The point is that in England, of all places—the country which by tradition and culture and language I should hope to find the most receptive audience outside my own—I am virtually a non-entity. I know this to be true simply because there are too many sympathetic witnesses to the fact: Englishmen whom I have spoken to, who care very much for my work, who are dismayed by the fact that I am so little appreciated or known in Britain. Whole long essays and articles on modern American writing (such as one not too long ago in the Times Lit Sup) which mentions all sorts of writers, including a lot of egregious hacks, but never once utter my name. What's the reason for this? Certainly I am aware that it partially must be due to factors beyond anyone's control: the bad reviews that SET THIS HOUSE ON FIRE got in England, for instance, were merely echoes of the irrationally bad reviews the book got here. The book has already begun to be re-assessed here, and to be found a good one; it was good from the beginning in France. No one can be held responsible for this kind of hostility."

which Mr. Eastwell says you expect to obtain, I calculate your total gain at a little less than a hundred dollars, which doesn't seem to me to be a lot for a good book. Naturally there is not necessarily any opprobrium attached to the idea of remaindering, per se: stuck with an overstock of an expensive book (let us say, 6,000 copies of a $5 novel), publishers have even remaindered Nobel Prize winners. But it is not even the fact that you have decided to make a pitiful ninety-eight dollars off me which so disturbs me; it is the fact that nothing of mine that you have published ever seems to "go."

I have for a long time now wondered if this failure is not due, quite simply, to the fact that my books do not suit your imprint or go well under it; and I feel very strongly a general lack of interest in my work and in its promotion. This summer, for instance, I received a letter from some other functionary whose name I don't recollect, saying that he or she had been through their files recently and had discovered, to their surprise, that there was no biographical information on me available and no photographs. I suppose this person meant recent material and recent photographs (though I cannot recollect the firm ever having asked for photographs before); even so, I'm afraid that, however inadvertently, there was an awful belated tone to that letter, as if someone was just coming around to a kind of spasmodic interest in me.

With all due respect to the very real kindnesses paid me by yourself and good people like Roger Machell, I'm afraid I've never felt the actual surge of enthusiasm I've felt from my other publishers about my work; and this indifference has not been an imagined thing but has been a very real hurt to me—especially in the light of the more than friendly relations we have always had.

Now that you are going to remainder THE LONG MARCH, I feel overwhelmingly that I would like our connection to come to an end. I am a loss to you and, frankly, I should be most unhappy to think that I am faced with the same anxieties when my next book is ready to be published. I am therefore asking you to release me from my option and to leave me to be free when the time comes to find another publisher in England.*

* Leresche wrote Styron on December 3, 1964, "I was delighted to receive from you the note from Hamish Hamilton releasing you from your contract with them."

Please understand the extreme difficulty and pain it has caused me to write this letter, and I hope you will accept the great respect I still hold for you.

Sincerely,
William Styron

PS: On reflection, I have decided to buy myself the 700 copies of THE LONG MARCH, and Hope Leresche & Steele will complete arrangements with your office for this.

To James and Gloria Jones

November, 1964 Mexico City, Mexico

GREAT NEWS ABOUT AMBROSE!*

Dear James + Moss:
Rose and I are living it up in the sin city of the Western Hemisphere—it shuts up tight at midnight. On to Yucatan with Lillian Hellman and other mutual pals.

Love,
Billy S.

To Hope Leresche

January 14, 1965 Roxbury, CT

Dear Mrs. Leresche:
I called John Dodds after receiving your letter, and he said that he would try to get the Harper's article to you as soon as possible—either a

* Ambrose was the Joneses' adopted son; he later changed his name to Jamie. The Joneses met him in Jamaica in 1962 and, after many delays from the French government, finally completed the adoption.

copy of the typescript or, if available, tear sheets from the magazine.* The article is close to 10,000 words, which I hope is not too long for British or European magazines. I would not want to see it heavily abridged. I am quite proud of this essay, because it deals with a fascinating historical matter (Nat Turner's revolt, of course) which no one has heard of except myself, who knows everything about it there is to know. At any rate, Harper's is most enthusiastic about it, and I hope you too will like it and be able to find publication for it over there.

As for the novel, there are 204 typewritten pages available, and I will try to get a copy to you very soon. All of the copies are now at various places, being read for magazines (one copy is in Chicago), reprint rights, movies, etc., but as soon as one becomes available (probably less than two weeks) John Dodds will send you one. I am beginning to have the faint suspicion that this book may be a little too "American" for English tastes (the whole thing is told from the point of view of a Negro slave in the year 1831), but we'll see.

I am snowed in here in this subarctic region but I expect to warm up next week. I was invited down to Washington to attend the inauguration of President Johnson, which will be exciting but nothing like your Coronation. Rather boisterous and noisy, I'm afraid, and filled with drunk Texans in big hats. A far cry from J.F. Kennedy.

Best wishes and a happy New Year.
Sincerely,
Wm Styron

To Hope Leresche

January 21, 1965 Roxbury, CT

Dear Mrs. Leresche: Day before yesterday I was at the White House getting dressed for the Inaugural Do, when Bennett Cerf telephoned from New York all out of breath to say that New American Library—our best

* Styron refers to his meditation on contemporary race relations and the Nat Turner rebellion, "This Quiet Dust," *Harper's Magazine* 230 (April 1965). Collected in *This Quiet Dust.*

mass paperback house—had offered $100,000 for the rights to my coming novel. The combination of my surroundings and the amount made me a bit giddy, but it is true: does it sound as big in pounds, 28,000? Anyway, I wanted to send this news off to you as quickly as possible, as it obviously won't hurt your negotiations in England. I am still somewhat benumbed, but rather intoxicated, too!

All best—
WS.

I have written to the fellow in Prague. Thanks.

To Robert Penn Warren

February 19, 1965 Roxbury, CT

Dear Prof:

I spoke to Lillian today, and apparently I have been passed over by the Institute again, this time in favor of Messrs. Nemerov, Kazin, Lattimore among others.* It is getting so that my desperation at being left out of the company of such literary titans as Glenway Wescott, William Maxwell and Kay Boyle is feeding so savagely at my liver that I don't know how I'll be able to stand it.† At any rate, I wanted to tell you that, as honestly appreciative as I am for your nomination and support, I also feel that it must be getting as embarrassing for you as it is for me, and therefore I want to ask you please not to put my name up again. I am probably—as you once said—making it more important than it really is; nonetheless, I do find this rejection a little embarrassing, and I figure twice is quite enough. I do thank you, though, for your loyalty and your gesture.

Lillian said she suspected that the reason was that the voting musicians,

* Howard Nemerov (1920–91) was a poet who won the National Book Award, Pulitzer Prize, and Bollingen Prize. Richmond Lattimore (1906–84) was a poet and translator best known for his translations of the *Iliad* and the *Odyssey.*

† Kay Boyle (1902–92) was a prolific author best known for *Being Geniuses Together* (1968), an important memoir of Paris in the 1920s. William Maxwell (1908–2000) was a novelist and longtime editor at *The New Yorker.*

architects, etc., don't know beans about "quality lit." and therefore vote for the safe, the well-established, or the recent best-sellers. This may or may not be so, but if it is, then maybe that is all the more reason for thinking that it is not the club for me. At any rate, if nominatated or elected in the future—even unbeknownst to me—I shall, like Cal Coolidge, firmly decline the honor.

We are looking forward to another Vermont visit—with work, this time, also snow-shoeing—; Rose and Eleanor have already talked about it, but of course we'll be seeing you before then.

Yrs. in Jesus,
—B.

To William Blackburn

March 30, 1965 Roxbury, CT

Dear Professor:

About a week ago, Theodore Roethke's widow wrote me, asking if I could locate a letter or two she knew Ted had written me from Seattle before he died. I found one of them, and while I was going through the great mass of correspondence I seem to have accumulated, I found to my great surprise these two letters from Mac, mainly because during these last years we always spoke to each other by telephone—the invention which is in the process of killing off all literary correspondence.* At any rate, I was on the verge of sending them to you when I got your nice letter yesterday. These letters were written to me just after I got back from Italy in 1954, during the time I lived in New York before moving to Roxbury. The earlier one must have been written right after Random House had decided to publish No Time for Sergeants, while the later one—in July—was written after the Book of the Month Club had taken the book and it seemed headed for a great success. As I recollect, we saw quite a bit of Mac during that winter and spring. He was alone in New York, and would often come to the apartment for dinner, and later we would go out on the town, in the

* Theodore Roethke (1908–63), American poet. He and his wife, Beatrice, took over the Styrons' lease in Rome.

Village or elsewhere. Anyway, here they are and feel free to make use of them as you wish.

I am still working away at Nat Turner, and the book doesn't get any easier as I go along. I am rather ashamed to tell you that Random House has already sold the paperback rights to New American Library for $100,000, which will do one of two things to me: (a) totally corrupt me, or (b) cause me to finish it immediately out of shame and necessity. Anyway, I'll keep you posted. Is there any chance of your getting up this way this spring or in June? We'll be here for the next few months and it would be good to see you again.

Yrs as ever,

—B.

To Donald Harington

April 8, 1965 Roxbury, CT

Dear Don:

Regrettably, Rose strained her back on the night before the morning we were due to go to Vermont—and I'm afraid that is the reason you didn't hear from us. Perhaps another time we'll be able to do it.

I've been leading what the French call the High Life (pronounced Heej Leef), going to New York more often than is good for me and ending up at 5:30 A.M. in dingy bars dancing with Jacqueline Kennedy. Honest Injun. I'm afraid that both I and the Widow Kennedy were quite stoned and when I asked her if she wished to dance the Fug she replied: "Oh no, I don't like those dances which have no bodily contact." So we ended up glued together, brow against sweaty brow. Alas, however, she was swept off into the morning in the embrace of a better, luckier man.

Don't fret over your book. It's a fine one—although I do know how you may be suffering from pre-publication jitters . . .

To William Blackburn

June 2, 1965 Roxbury, CT

Dear Professor:

I greatly enjoyed seeing you duly credited by the Times Lit Sup, and sent the editorial along to my father who was also delighted. I was rather surprised, however, to see my name linked with yours for in England, at least, as I think I have told you, I have always had a rather mediocre reputation, with both sales and critical esteem next to zero. At any rate, it was good to see you mentioned in such a flattering way and it probably created a lot of much-deserved envy around Dooks.

In a little over a week I will attain the venerable age of 40, a troubling anniversary which I approach with mixed feelings. Actually one shouldn't worry too much about age, I suppose—as you once remarked, it is Time which is the mystery—and the fact that the novel I am working on seems to be going well does a lot to allay my trepidation. I think it was Lillian Hellman's great friend and mentor, the psychiatrist Gregory Zilboorg,* who had made a study of the matter and pointed out that the decade between 40 and 50 and even the decade after should be the most productive in a man's life. It is a nice thought anyway. I have the highest hopes for old Nat Turner. I think I am in almost perfect control of a subject which demands and is getting whatever good balance of intellect and emotion I possess, and if I don't blow it up in the last part of the book I think it will really be something for the world to see. I regret that the pace is so slow and laborious but that is something I cannot help.

As is not the case in Albion, in France (I say this with complete immodesty) I am along with Salinger the best-known living American writer, a fact which tickles me deeply, and already it has been announced in the French press that I am arriving in Paris on June 23d. I hope this doesn't offend you. At any rate, I am taking a little time off from the book and am going to stay with Jim Jones in Paris, with a side trip down the Loire and to Pamplona, and will be back on Martha's Vineyard around the middle

* Gregory Zilboorg (1890–1959), psychoanalyst and historian of psychiatry who helped popularize psychiatry, partly through his writing and partly through his eminent clientele.

of July. If there is any way you can pay a summer visit to the Island, you are as usual quadruply welcome.

As ever,
Bill

To Manager of WTOP*

June 9, 1965 Roxbury, CT

Dear Sir:

Thank you for sending me a copy of your editorial on Robert Lowell's protest.†

What you do not seem to realize is that, in an age of publicity, Mr. Lowell's boycott of culture was the only public protest he could make. Suppose he had made his protest "poetically," as you put it. Would that have made the front page of The New York Times, and the newspapers of England and France?

Sincerely,
W Styron

To James and Gloria Jones

June 14, 1965 Roxbury, CT

Dear Moss; and dear James & Kaylie & Jamie:

The flight is Pan American #118 which arrives at Orly at 9:40 in the evening on Wednesday, June 23d.

Gerry Murphy won't be flying with us. The sad news about Gerry is

* Frank Wilson was the manager of WTOP, a radio station owned by *The Washington Post*.

† American poet Robert Lowell (1917–77) boycotted the White House Festival of the American Arts because he objected to President Johnson's foreign policy decisions. Wilson criticized Lowell for his "monolithic view of human activity."

that her fiancé, who for so many long years it took to get him hooked, was killed last Monday in a Marine training accident in California. Apparently they were coming down a mountain and a guy slipped and fell into a swift-running river and Gerry's boy jumped in to save him, but both of them were washed out of sight. Isn't that the damndest thing to happen to poor Gerry after all these spinster years?

But the good news is that we are coming with joy at the prospect of Paris and doing the trip with all of you & can barely wait for Biarritz and Pamplona and all the rest.

Oh, I forgot to tell you—Virginia and Ed Gilbert are coming back too; meeting us toward the end of the month in the Loire country and going down to Biarritz in a car they've rented. They have a house there too, also tickets to the Feria in Pamplona. They said they were sure you wouldn't mind if they horned in just a bit. Gil sold his last book AMERICAN CHROME to Paramount for a mint, which is the reason they can swing it. Gil wants to do research for a bullfighting novel to be called SPANISH GNOME. It's all about a very tiny short matador but very brave, etc. They'll also be driving back to Paris with us.

The above is a nightmare I had last night. Please forget it.

Love to all, see you bientôt,

Bill

To Robert and Claire White

July 3, 1965* Biarritz, France

We have et our way through France with the Joneses by way of the Chateux country + Périgueux (Truffleville) and are now ensconced in this pleasure-dome where all is modified bliss. Ran into—guess-who—Duncan Longcope, living in a ratty hotel where we stayed. He sends regards. We are going out tonight with Frank Sinatra. I am the 12th most famous American in France. Love to all—Billie S.

* Postcard of a castle in Biarritz.

To Bonnie Cone*

August 9, 1965 Vineyard Haven, MA

Dear Miss Cone:

In 1943, when I was a student in the Marine V-12 program at Duke, you taught me mathematics—a subject at which I am no more adept now than I was then. I was a terrible student and I recall that I spent most of my time in your class reading Dos Passos and Thomas Wolfe. At eighteen I was a passionate reader and determined to become a writer someday. On one occasion I recall that my non-interest in math was so intense and my concentration upon some novel or other so deep that you called me down in class and, quite rightly, put me on report. I was quite angry at this totally justified punishment, but I remember that there was something about you that commanded the greatest respect, and I also recall that we had a lively and friendly argument. I said that I was going to be a writer come hell or high water and I remember you said with great good humor that you hoped I would succeed in my ambition, adding that when my first novel came out you hoped I would send a copy to your home in (I'll never forget the name) Lodge, South Carolina. Well, it has been more than a few years since that book came out, and I always intended to send you a copy but for all sorts of procrastinating reasons I never got around to it.

As I told Mrs. Whisenant over the telephone not too long ago, I read all about your great achievement in Charlotte in Time magazine—a kind of miracle, really, since it is a magazine I try to avoid (even though they had the good sense to recognize you) but couldn't avoid in this instance since it was my only reading material during a July plane flight from Madrid to New York.† All the memories of you and our brief and curious and (for me, at least) unforgettable association at Duke came rushing back, and I decided at last that I would make sure that you got a copy of Lie Down in Darkness. Ordinarily it might seem too late to send you a book published 14 years ago, but I take a little pride in the fact that in a small way the book has become some sort of classic, and I hope you will receive it in

* Bonnie Ethel Cone (1907–2003) was instrumental in transforming Charlotte College into the University of North Carolina–Charlotte.

† Cone was featured in the July 16, 1965, issue of *Time.*

good spirit from a non-mathematician who, however, has never forgotten you and who holds you and your achievement in Charlotte in the greatest admiration.

Ever sincerely yours,
William Styron

To James and Gloria Jones

August 12, 1965 Vineyard Haven, MA

Having just re-read this letter on the morning after, I hesitate to send it but find it in all major respects absolutely true, and I feel that if it had a title it should perhaps be called: NOTES OF A WAIF ASTRAY IN THE 20th CENTURY.

Dear James + Moss:

Well, there has been a good deal of high excitement around old Vineyard Haven since last we met, so much of a constant buzz in fact that it is a wonder how anyone gets any work done.

First, the widow Kennedy came over for the weekend all sleek and tan in a Bikini, with Caroline and John, Jr., and eight—count 'em—eight Secret Service men in tow, all of them very polite but bulging with .45s, plus two Coast Guardsmen in a turbo-jet 45 mph speedboat for Jackie's water-skiing. Well, we water skied a bit and told dirty jokes (I have the honor of telling the widow K. what a dildo is; she was thereupon horrified to learn that you had one secreted away in Paris; if you had just shown me the dildo like I asked I wouldn't have told her) and we swam around quite a bit on the ocean beach and I rubbed a good deal of Sea n' Ski foam on the widow's thighs. Rose had to undress John, Jr., at one point and she reports that he has an enormous schlong, twice as big as Tommy's. I hate to make it sound like such a sexy weekend, it really wasn't, but anyway we had a very good time and our baby sitter got laid by one of the Secret Service. We are going over to the widow's at Newport later in the month, that's the way we swing, very much like Biarritz, and as I say I really don't know how I get any work done.

Dick Goodwin is up here in a cottage and last week the President called him up and said he wanted him down in D.C. that same day to write the speech for the Voting Rights bill. Dick asked me along and they sent up the Vice-President's Jet Star for the two of us and it took us back to Washington in 50 minutes . . . I rode in the Presidential motorcade from the White House to the Capitol (THIS IS NO SHIT, REPEAT, NO SHIT) in a limousine which was originally intended for Dick and myself but which, since the President at the last minute asked Dick to ride with him in his car, was occupied by me, tout seul. I am not being facetious when I say that eventually I became scared half out of my wits when I realized that without Dick to vouch for me I was the only person in that entire motorcade (which included Humphrey, the entire Cabinet and the Joint Chiefs of Staff) who was totally unknown to the Secret Service and indeed I really did almost get arrested at the Capitol when the motorcade stopped and I tried to worm my way into the procession to the Rotunda; the President's bodyguard is a mean-looking killer from Georgia poetically named Rufus Youngblood and I'll swear he was about to give me a Karate stroke to the neck when by the sheerest miracle, blurting out my name in a strangled gasp, I was saved by the new Secretary of Health, Education, and Welfare, Mr. Gardner, to whom Dick had fortunately introduced me a half-hour before. Oh shit, what a scene. Anyway, the old Jet Star was waiting at Andrews A.F.B.—I still almost come when I am saluted by a Captain, which is the ritual on these planes—and we made it back the same day in time for croquet and beer.

Finally, as an anticlimax, Sinatra's boat put into the harbor here (it is incidentally not true that the Widow K. boarded the yacht) and I thought that somehow we would be free of that particular business, except for the fact that my daughter Susanna, the half-Jewish idiot swimmer, lured by the misty scent of sex and glamour, took it into her head to swim the ½ mile through choppy seas out to the place in the harbor where the yacht was moored. Sinatra saved her, half-drowned, called her "sweetheart," took her aboard and dried her off and sent her back to shore in a launch.* This was bad enough in itself; however, it was also in the N.Y. Herald

* Mia Farrow, then nineteen, brought Susanna back to shore; this was the first time the Styrons met Farrow, who became a lifelong friend.

Tribune along with a picture, the whole story scandalously implying that I was some sort of degenerate pimp for Susanna. I am going to put that child in an institution. . . .

I'll probably be going to Russia for the State Department for a few weeks in December and will make it a stipulation that I stop to see you all in Paris. Much love to Kaylie + Jamie + Kate + all the girls. (Also my friend Mimi)

Love to you all,
Bill

To Robert Loomis

September 30, 1965 Roxbury, CT

Caro Roberto: The reading I gave at V.H. to you was a great help, because your advice was completely right about that part in which Nat overhears the conversation between his Massahs and the two ministers.* I have drastically cut the section down so that it is less than ½ as long and much more pointed but with the same despair on Nat's part at the end at knowing he is a slave. I really think it is very good now and that as you rightly pointed out it was all a matter of emphasis. Not that I have been tempted too much in such a direction, but I simply must at all costs (and have so far) avoid the pitfall of over-explaining certain technical and historical facts out of fear that the reader might not be properly oriented. All that business wherein Marse Samuel explains to the ministers the mystique of the plantation was precisely just such a trap, and I can't tell you how delighted I was to read this bit to you and have you point out the exact weakness. Anyway, I've fixed that up real nice, as they say, and have forged ahead to what I think is other good stuff. The book is taking fine shape now.

Someone in Washington sent me BOOK WEEK which would have come out in N.Y. except for the strike. Apparently there was a nationwide poll among critics etc., on Great Writing of the last 20 years and LDID came in 12th Greatest—not too bad out of the many thousands—and it

* Styron refers to his practice of reading aloud to Bob Loomis from manuscripts in progress.

would really have pleased me save for the fact that the same list showed Saul Bellow as having written four out of the 20 most beautiful novels during the same period. What egregious shit.

There is a really fine new cigar at Dunhill's named Belinda. Very rich & no more expensive than their other exorbitant smokes.

Maybe we'll see you this week-end via the Carlisles. Give a call.

Yrs in Jesus

WS.

To William Blackburn

November 12, 1965 Roxbury, CT

Dear Professor:

The enclosed clipping from the front page of The N.Y. Times will explain why my trip to Moscow was cancelled—or at least postponed. It was a rather bad disappointment—I had expected to spend a week or so in Paris on the way and a similar period in Rome on returning—but it does have its bright side in the fact that it will allow me to progress in the current book without interruption. And I've been told that I will be first on the list when and if the exchange program begins again. And so it goes . . .

I've been invited to spend some time next spring as a visiting scribbler to the University of Virginia and also to take the post of writer-in-residence—a six month thing—held by Mr. William Faulkner first, then Katherine Anne Porter, Dos Passos, + Stephen Spender.* So I may be closer to Durham in the near future. However, I have not made up my mind—anything which tends to greatly interrupt my work I try to avoid—and may possibly put the whole thing off until another year like '67 or '68 when, God be praised and God willing, the endless (not in length but in time) Nat Turner will be finished and done with. But I will let you know.

Your Prof. Warddropper sounds remarkably like his name. Do give him a good boot in the tail for me.

Have you read the new second volume of Camus' Notebooks? If you

* Katherine Anne Porter (1890–1980) was a Pulitzer Prize–winning writer best known for her 1962 novel *Ship of Fools* and her many short stories.

get a copy, do look up the wonderful quotation on the last page beginning "If I were to die unknown to the world . . ." which I am using as an epigraph to Nat Turner. But mainly look up the book because the whole thing is so good—a lovely man. How he would have laughed at Norman Mailer.

Hope all goes well with you. Give my best to my friends at Dook.

As ever in Jesus' name,
W.S.

To James Jones

November 23, 1965 Roxbury, CT

. . . Dear James:

I hope you will be thoughtful enough to bring me back from Paris a box of H. Upmann Petit Coronas. I know that there is an inordinate risk involved and that you may get a 2-year stretch at Leavenworth but it <u>will</u> be a test of your friendship. Right now I'm down to the last three short and frazzled Montecristos I bought in Biarritz.

Anyway, Rose and I will be absolutely delighted for you all to stay with us on the Vineyard. We have, as you may know, a guest house up there and there are all sorts of living combinations we can work out—me and Kaylie in one house, along with Moss; you and my man Terry in the other, etc. At any rate, we are tickled to pieces that you all are coming. There's plenty of room, really, and we can discuss the details when you arrive. I imagine that we will be going up there for the summer around the middle of June and will stay until mid-September. So anytime between those dates is fine with us and stay as long as you like. I think it'll be great fun. We can take a lot of trips to the deserted Elizabeth Islands and lay around in the sun and drink and smoke cigars and look at the adorable teen-age girls at the yacht club. It will be a ball, as they say . . .

The blackout didn't affect me.* We were "out" for only 15 minutes be-

* There was a widespread power outage on November 4, 1965.

fore they got the local waterfall going—we were the luckiest area in 5 states.

Prof. Rubin is coming over fairly soon to talk about you and vice versa. An odd chap. He wants to "play tennis" with Rose, but I told him that Rose will be in Boston and I'd give him 5 hours to talk about you—take it or leave it. Since I've gotten published in Romania I figure my time is worth about $50 an hour, so with this kind of debt over your head maybe you'll bring me two boxes of cigars.

Keep in touch about your arrival. A big smooch to Moss + Kaylie + a firm handshake to Jamie.

Love to all,
Bill

To Carlos Fuentes

December 6, 1965 Roxbury, CT

Alas, Carlos, sad news! The Russians evidently decided that we American writers were peddling dangerous bourgeois ideas, for only a week or so ago they cancelled my invitation—just after Rose had bought a sable coat for the Moscow winter! I should sue! Anyway, we're not coming, at least this year, and will miss you. Please convey my respects to Betty di Robilant and give me a call if you come back through N.Y. I loved Aura—deft + beautiful.* Saluti! B.S.

* Fuentes had sent Styron a copy when Farrar, Straus and Giroux published the novel in the United States in 1965. Styron wrote him, "Many thanks for the handsome book and also the nice inscription. It goes on a shelf next to another treasure—an inscribed copy of [Albert Camus's] La Peste" (Styron to Fuentes, undated, 1965).

To William Blackburn

January 12, 1966 Roxbury, CT

Dear Professor:

I hope you will not consider me churlish or ungenerous when I balk at your publishing that letter of mine.* I've read it over carefully, and while it seems from this vantage point to be honest enough and well-intentioned, I just don't see what purpose is really served by publishing it. In the first place, your book is to be a book of Mac's letters, not mine. Second and more importantly, I have very definite feelings about publishing letters in general (you may recall the long review I did of Fitzgerald's letters in The N.Y. Review of Books; at any rate, I have given the matter some professional thought).† Quite frankly, I feel that the publication of personal letters—as distinct from "public" letters, correspondence to newspapers, etc.—while the writer is still alive has somewhat the quality of gratuitous exposure; to be honest, when I read that letter of mine which you sent and thought of it appearing in print, I felt terribly naked all of a sudden. Certainly as I say the letter has nothing in its content to be really embarrassed about—an earnest youth worrying about his future, etc. Nonetheless, it was not written for public display and since I'm still quite alive (or feel myself to be so from time to time) I would quite simply not want to see these very private meanderings in print.

When a writer is dead, certainly that becomes a different matter. Presumably then there evolves enough interest in the writer's private self that the very publication of his correspondence wipes out the element of gratuitousness. Fitzgerald is an example; the mythology surrounding his name generates enough excitement to make valid the publication of his most casual squiggle. Besides, being quite dead, he can hardly feel the sensation of nakedness. And when I myself am dead and someone wants to put my letters together, I couldn't care less one way or another. But being alive, I have quite strong feelings about this—the only word is again, I'm afraid,

* William Styron to Mac Hyman, April 29, 1957.

† William Styron, "An Elegy for F. Scott Fitzgerald," *The New York Review of Books* (November 28, 1963), collected in *This Quiet Dust*. Contrary to Styron's characterization to Blackburn, the review essay calls Andrew Turnbull's *The Letters of F. Scott Fitzgerald* (New York: Charles Scribner's Sons, 1963) "a fascinating" book.

exposure—and so I really would not want you to include the letter in the book.

The footnote you asked me to comment on sounds perfectly fine to me, though I wish I could cast more light on just what J.P. Marquand said to the BOMC board. If I'm not mistaken I got the news from John Marquand, Jr. I am going to be seeing him soon and I'll ask him if he can recollect any of the details; if he can, I'll certainly send them on to you as soon as I can. We think our powers of recollection are fabulous, but faced with such matters it is amazing how little our memories really stand up.

Yours ever,

Bill

To Donald Harington

January 17, 1966 Roxbury, CT

Dear Don:

Having come back from Jamaica, where I enjoyed and sunned myself in the company of the damndest, fruitiest, emptiest group of English lords and ladies I've ever seen (the English are really the <u>bottom</u> of the heap), I returned to find that the house (the big house) has been invaded by the damndest and fruitiest plague of rats you can imagine. It took me some time to divine the reason, but it's basically simple. The Seltzer farm atop the hill, it may interest you to learn, has gone out of business—at least for the moment—and all the cattle and equipment sold. So all those barn rats up there, suddenly abandoned, homed in on the Styron spread like a bunch of Bowery bums heading for the Salvation Army. Fortunately there is something called "d-Con," a lethal poison, which has been able to cope with the problem, and they are being diminished, but until you've had a real invasion like this you don't know what it must be like to live in the slums of Calcutta.

This is my main problem for the moment. Otherwise all in Roxbury is fairly serene. I've re-read your letter of November and I'm able to sympathize with your plaint as I was back then. Surely the only thing more unsettling and traumatic than to be reviewed hatefully and unfairly and maliciously is to be reviewed either sparsely, as you have, or not at all. I really think Random House is at fault in this; they sit on the book—but that does happen from time to time, and the only thing you can do now is to lament the fact. In consolation I can only say that your experience is really not unique in the history of first novels by writers of great gifts; I am thinking now of a whole horde of writers and their first books (just Americans), ranging from Hawthorne and Fanshawe down through Anderson and Windy MacPherson's Son to Daddy-O himself—I mean Faulkner and his earliest works, Soldier's Pay and Mosquitoes. Unless I am terribly mistaken—and I don't think I am—all these writers and those works were almost totally ignored, and quite as crushingly as The Cherry Pit. The incidence of writers who have scored smashingly with their first work must at the very least be no larger than the other way around, and I suspect you are in very good company, melancholy as that company is. Even as I say all this, I am aware of course that it is in the nature of a consolation; but I have given it thought and I do mean it, and I hope you won't let the experience even partially diminish the determination to keep on writing. Gollancz's faith is bracing, I think—he's no fool—and most of the rest of us are folks who thought and still think you have great talent.[*]

As for J. Dodds, I wouldn't give it a second thought if I were you, since the simple fact is that at the time of that party he was secretly getting ready to quit the agent business anyway.[†] I suppose you know that he kicked over the agency and is now vice-president at G.P. Putnam's. It surely had nothing about it personal, nothing to do with you. I was as shocked as you were to learn he had quit, mainly because he had been for me a truly excellent agent and I felt his departure severely. Von Auw, incidentally, is reputed to be top-notch, so consider yourself in good hands.[‡]

I will soon have two-thirds of Nat Turner or thereabouts finished and as soon as I get it copied on Arthur Miller's Thermoplex machine and then typed up I will send it to you for your appraisal and sage counsel. I blow

* Gollancz was a major British publisher throughout the twentieth century.

† Harington and Styron's agent, who quit without telling either of his clients.

‡ Ivan von Auw, a prominent literary agent who worked for the Harold Ober agency from 1938 to 1973. He represented Pearl Buck, James M. Cain, Agatha Christie, Agnes de Mille, John Gunther, Langston Hughes, Oscar Lewis, Ross MacDonald, Muriel Spark, Dylan Thomas, and others.

hot and cold on the bastard—as I do with everything I've written—at one moment certain it has things in it as good as anything being done now, and at other moments thinking it's the kind of pretentious junk that little pricks like that guy on The New Yorker will (justifiably, this time) have a field day with. Ah well, see for yourself, I'll try to get it to you in the next month or so, and hope you will be kind with it.

Take care of yourself and trust in Jesus.

Yrs Faithfully
Bill

To William Blackburn

February, 1966* Roxbury, CT

I shall certainly not expect to see your shining face at this event, which I am told is a Godawful bore. However, I did want to apprise you of my election to this august body, which was adorned by Mark Twain, Eugene O'Neill + Faulkner and was shunned (doubtless wisely) by Hemingway, Mencken and Edmund Wilson. I only can hope that this does not mean my premature fossilization among the Alexandrian poets and ancient architects, but I think at least it is interesting that my personal statistician has uncovered the fact that I am the only live graduate of Duke to be honored and maybe the only graduate period. Could this astonishing albeit very unimportant fact be true?

* Styron enclosed the announcement of his election to the American Academy of Arts and Letters and the National Institute of Arts and Letters on May 25, 1966.

To James and Gloria Jones

February 28, 1966 Roxbury, CT

Dear James and Moss:

The enclosed clipping will describe what I've been up to lately, politically.* It was an incredible evening, with a huge crowd of peace-lovers sweating in the armpits—and that was the trouble, it was preaching to the faithful and the already-converted, but anyway I don't think it could have done any harm, and if it got noticed in the foreign press (which has the mistaken notion that intellectual opinion in the US&A cuts a lot of ice) then so much the better. Brother Norman was there, as you can see, but we managed to keep out of each other's way, though I accidentally got close enough to notice the fact that, aside from his obesity, he has a case of mean malevolent halitosis.†

We received Moss' snotty little postcard, which made us guilty, and also the letter about your being surprised in the act of coitus by Louis Malle and Marlene Dietrich.‡ What you never explained was whether you disengaged yourself enough to put down the telephone and ask them over for a drink. Such items are important. We never get such kind of calls up here. We hear from the school principal every now and then, and Tom Guinzburg calls every now and then, wanting a date with Rose, but that's just about it. . . .

I've been working my ass off on this novel (every time Jim sends word about having finished his 45th chapter it sends me into spasms of productivity), and am now very close to what is loosely called the home stretch. I have had to fuck around with the plot quite a bit, and change the setting to Kansas and bring in a quadruple shotgun murder,§ but basically I've kept the integrity of the book intact and it should sell quite a few copies.

That was an absolutely lovely time in Jamaica and we have missed you

* Unknown attachment.

† Norman Mailer.

‡ Louis Malle (1932–95) was a French film director, screenwriter, and producer. He won the Academy Award for Best Documentary in 1956. Marlene Dietrich (1901–92) was one of the best-known actresses of her generation, renowned for her glamour and good looks.

§ Styron refers to Truman Capote's *In Cold Blood,* published just a month earlier to great acclaim and commercial success.

very much. We can't wait for your sojourn with us at Martha's Vineyard. After three years of legal shenanigans, the house became ours today and this is a sort of celebration. Please keep us informed about your arrival in June, etc. It seems a long time off, but God how time passes.

We've done very little socializing recently, mainly, because of the book. We did go to one party at Steve Smith's in N.Y. (JFK's brother-in-law); the whole clan was there, Bobby, Teddy, Jackie etc., and someone made a perfectly horrible and true remark about Jackie: "She is the most interesting 16-year-old in America."* I had a long talk with Bobby, and God knows it's hard to believe but I think he is shaping up as a kind of fantastic committed liberal politician who just might be the one who will get us out of Viet Nam. I don't mean to say that I'm completely sold on him yet, but he's certainly come a long way and is weirdly impressive.

Rose told me to tell you what she has written to Jerry what's her name Gibbs at Bonwit Teller and that you should get the refill for your toilet tissue dispenser very soon directly from the store. If you don't, let her know.

A final note: Professor Herbert Ruhm called me up the other night from that veterinarian's school over in New York State to tell me that he has been fired. I told him that I couldn't care less and that as for you (he was worried about your reaction), you would probably be delighted. Then I told him to fuck off and he cried a whole lot. These academic creeps are the fucking limit.

We miss you. Keep in touch. Say hello to Mimi, Kaylie, Jamie and all the gang.

Love, Bill

* Stephen E. Smith (1927–90) was the husband of Jean Kennedy Smith.

To James and Gloria Jones

March 16, 1966 New Milford, CT

Rose enceinte la quatrième fois les hivers de Connecticut sont terriblement froids*

Bill

To Donald Harington

March 24, 1966 Roxbury, CT

Dear Don:

. . . I don't want to get your hopes up prematurely, but I've put you up for a grant of some kind with a worthy, well-known outfit (whose name I can't divulge) and they might come through with some loot. I say "might" simply because there is no certainty at all but we can both pray to Jesus for his aid. Also, I am about to enter Valhalla as a junior member of the National Institute of Arts and Letters, which really means a form of permanent embalmment with 80-year old classical architects and arthritic painters who were once disciples of Childe Hassam and Winslow Homer.† However, I have been told by those who are in the know that the Institute does have the singular advantage of possessing a lot of money, which is doled out at intervals rather freely to people like yourself. The sole object in becoming a member, then, is to recommend artists and writers for largesse and so as soon as I can worm my way into the inner circle I am going to try to get some of that lucre on the first train to Putney, V-T. All of these machinations will take some time, as you may imagine, so don't expect any miracles right away.

Your test in class about Set This House on Fire I found wonderfully amusing but it does seem authentic and revealing. The book has gone re-

* "Rose pregnant the fourth time the winters of Connecticut are terribly cold."

† Frederick Childe Hassam (1859–1935), American impressionist painter and a founding member of the influential artists' group The Ten. Winslow Homer (1836–1910), the preeminent American landscape painter and printmaker in the nineteenth century.

cently into a third edition in Germany, which pleases me, and helps corroborate your test.

I still have a few pages to go before completing the 2/3ds mark on Nat but expect to have it typed up before too long. I'll send you a copy. There is a small excerpt in the current Paris Review which you may have seen.* After the recent Supreme Court decision I've been busy taking all the "hells" and "damns" out of the manuscript.†

Keep cool with Jesus.

Yrs Bill

To Donald Harington

April 22, 1966 Roxbury, CT

Dear Don:

Your letter on Nat was very valuable to me. In case, God forbid, that you ever decide to cease being a writer of fiction you could surely take up the trade of critic and beat everyone now working in the field by a mile or more. Speaking of critics, while I think of it Bob Loomis called the other day to say that he had seen an advance copy of the Herald Tribune Book Week, in which John Aldridge's new collection of criticism is reviewed by Robie Macauley.‡ It seems that that Playboy essay on me which you read (and I didn't) is included in the book, and Macauley really takes out after Aldridge because of the piece, using it as example of critical revisionism and sloppiness at its worst. That tickles me, because it only goes to show how personal animosity and jealousy in a critic will get found out after all.

* Styron published the "Virginia: 1831" section of the novel in *The Paris Review* 9 (Winter 1966): 13–45.

† Styron refers to the Supreme Court decision of March 21, 1966, *Memoirs v. Massachusetts,* which tried to clarify the early obscenity decision of *Roth v. United States* (1957). The *Memoirs* case concerned John Cleland's novel *Fanny Hill, or, Memoirs of a Woman of Pleasure* (1749) and failed to resolve what was or was not obscene.

‡ John W. Aldridge's *Time to Murder and Create: The Contemporary Novel in Crisis* (New York: David McKay, 1966) contains the essay "William Styron and the Derivative Imagination." Also see Aldridge, "Highbrow Authors and Middlebrow Books," *Playboy* (April 1964).

But to get back to your letter—it was fine, really excellent and I appreciate it. Appreciate it not because it scratched my back or buttered me up but because it did neither of these things and was an honest, pointed and above all deeply understanding critique of the book. No one I know could have as well comprehended what I am trying to say in this work, and it gave me a great glow of hope when I saw that you, whose judgment and sensibility I have come to trust so well, had absorbed the plan and the structure and the spirit and had been affected by the story. Also I'm grateful to you for two other things—the words of criticism which were absolutely just (I shall certainly eliminate that bothersome occasional trait of Nat referring to the reader as "you," also I will clear up the question of Rev. Eppes being bugger or buggee, and other such matters as you brought up), but even more importantly the way in which you have so clearly seen how all of this background stuff prefigures as necessity in the killing of Margaret Whitehead. Your theory about I love you, but I am forbidden to put it into you, etc. seems so sound as to provide an almost miraculous solution to Part III, and I would be indebted to you for that if for nothing else. Doubtless I would have arrived at it through toil, but how much nicer it is to have the obvious stated so simply, as you have done. It leaves me free to address myself to 1000 other technical matters.

So mille mercis, mille fois. And, so I go to stick a sword in Margaret's belly while you get on with Mr. Pike. Keep in touch.

Yrs ever,

Bill

To James and Gloria Jones

April 27, 1966 Roxbury, CT

Dear James and Moss:

I am sending you the enclosed book so that you will know exactly what we are up to in the Old Country these days.* I was thinking that maybe if you all stay here long enough this year we could start a wife-swapping club

* Unknown.

and have a lot of fun with some of the attractive people we know in common. This volume goes a bit beyond Drs. Phyllis and Eberhart Kornholer, as I think you will, especially in areas of oral and anal sex, in which I am especially interested. Speaking of this field, the dernier cri in the book world at the moment is a tome called Human Sexual Response by two St. Louis doctors who spent 12 years photographing people fucking with wire attached to their heads.* I have just read it (it is outselling even Kinsey in whatever year it was that Kinsey came out)† and it is extremely valuable if for no other reason than that it once and for all makes it clear that it does not matter how big the penis looks when flaccid because when a hard-on occurs practically all penises are exactly the same size—6" give or take ¼ of an inch or so. I can't tell you how relieved this makes me after 40 years because I remember in the Marines seeing all those big limp cocks and feeling so inferior in the light of what I thought they must be in a state of what the doctors call tumescence. Now I'm put at ease, and you should all be too, Jim, and thank God for American science.

We are looking forward enormously to seeing you all when you arrive this summer after your wonderful tour through the Antilles. We are going up to the Vineyard House around June 20 so any time you arrive will be fine with us. Dick Goodwin has a house very close by and we're buying a boat together, something to take a lot of people a long way with a cargo of booze, so we can have some splendid picnics on those islands I told you about once.‡

Stay in touch and give our love to all our Paris friends.

Love,

Bill

P.S. You may have seen the enclosed book. If so, pass it on to Girodias.§

* William H. Masters and Virginia E. Johnson, *Human Sexual Response* (Boston: Little, Brown, 1966).

† Alfred C. Kinsey et al., *Sexual Behavior in the Human Male* (Philadelphia, W. B. Saunders Co., 1948).

‡ The Elizabeth Islands.

§ Maurice Girodias (1919–90) was the founder of the Olympia Press in Paris.

Styron was inducted into the American Academy of Arts and Letters and the National Institute of Arts and Letters on May 25, 1966.

To Mike Mewshaw*

May 30, 1966† Roxbury, CT

Dear Mike,

Never feel self-conscious—which you seem to be worried about being. That was a good letter you wrote me and I'm grateful for it. Aside from Slim,‡ whose beauty takes precedence over almost anything mortal, your presence and guidance was the most cheering thing that happened to me during my somewhat wasted visit to the University and I do want to thank you for the attention—even if somewhat belatedly. The entire trip was made golden by your company (also by Slim's; forgive me if I seem not to be able to get her out of my mind); you took the curse off a lot of those academics—so much that I can even forgive you for having used me as a subject for scholarly study.

I was quite serious about you letting me see your novel when it gets to the end or toward the end. Early fall would be a good time to let me read it. God willing, I will have gotten to the end of my own by then and will have a nice big open generous mind which, however, will retain enough critical objectivity so that you will be subjected to the most earnest critical scrutiny. Then we shall go to Mexico (with Slim, of course), and wallow in those pleasures and depravities while Random House gets the presses cranking and turns you, overnight, into a Capote-style billionaire.

* Michael Mewshaw (b. 1943) is the author of eleven novels and eight books of nonfiction, and best known for his novel *Year of the Gun* (1984). He wrote his master's thesis and doctoral dissertation on William Styron.

† Mewshaw published this letter (with lengthy commentary) in his memoir, *Do I Owe You Something? A Memoir of the Literary Life* (Baton Rouge: Louisiana State University Press, 2003).

‡ Mewshaw's wife, Linda.

My most profound thanks again for your hospitality. Keep in touch and never give up the faith.

Ever yours,

Bill (not Mr.) Styron

To Donald Harington

June 7, 1966 Roxbury, CT

Dear Don:

It is of course dandy that old John D. gave you all that dough, but the interesting mysteries behind the donation might give you another kind of charge.*

What happened is this. Along about March something, the Rockefeller boys wrote me asking if I would nominate some worthy writer for an unspecified amount of loot. Naturally I thought of you and wrote a hymn of praise, also recommending at the same time (get this) Malcolm Cowley, whom I had just seen and who asked me if I would recommend him for the thing inasmuch as he was putting together a volume of his own poetry. (Cowley didn't get a grant.) They also asked for another reference and I put down the name of Loomis, and he sent a very nice letter about you.

Well sir, I forgot about the whole thing (or put it out of my mind, as you have to do with these Tom Swifts and their Enormous Trust Funds) until two weekends ago. For some reason I wasn't violently optimistic about your chances mainly because I knew there was a lot of politicking and logrolling and inside operating in a thing like this, and also because I knew that you would simply have, with an incredible gravy-train endowment like this, an enormous amount of competition—every little scribbler who had wrote out a third-rate short story from Maine to Oregon trying to get his mitts on some of that dough. On the other hand, I knew who the judges were, all friends or at least acquaintances of mine: Robert "Cal" Lowell, Robert Penn "Red" Warren, Saul "Saul" Bellow, and Stanley

* Styron's letter of March 24, 1966, explained that Harington might receive a Rockefeller grant.

"Stan" Kunitz.* I figured that they were all stout-hearted and wise men and might know a good thing when they saw it.

However, as I say, I put it out of my mind. Then two weekends ago there came to visit at my country home here in the green Litchfield hills my good friend "Cal" Lowell and his wife the Boss-Lady intellectual of New York, Elizabeth "Lizzie" Hardwick. Well, "Cal" and I were chewing the fat one night about various things—Russian poetry, John Donne, mortality, pussy, literature as a Way of Life and so on, and we got onto Southern fiction. "Cal" and I agreed that the Jewboys had done a good job recently fiction-wise, but "Cal" also averred that by no means should Southern writing be sold short yet (as so many of the Jewboy critics, among them Alfred "Al" Kazin and Norman "Slim" Podhoretz, seem anxious to do) and used as an example to back up his claim a novel he had just read for the Rockefeller Committee called THE CHERRY PIT by a young Arkansan named, as he recollected, Harington. It was a terrific novel, he had thought, and not only that the other members of the committee—"Red" and "Saul" and "Stan"—had thought it terrific too. Did I know the book? As a matter of fact, the committee had all thought so highly of the novel that it had been among their first five choices—high praise considering the fact that there were 20 grants in all and that the committee had winnowed these 20 finalists from a field which had been close to 200 writers and poets. So that is how I learned that the choo-choo would be coming up to Putney.

This little episode is simply intended to illustrate a great 18th-century truth, namely, that excellence will in the end find its reward and that though fate may at the outset deal harshly with a good book like PIT it will not be put down forever but like a glittering fish will pop to surface, puffing and flopping and a little out of breath, a little behind the big slick commercial blowfish and carp, but dazzling those rare wise watchful Izaak Waltons waiting patiently on the bank.† What I have described to you should (even if it cannot totally erase from your spirit the memory of the "non-reception" of your "non-book," as you put it with justifiable bitterness) make you aware of how really impressive (in the direct, transitive meaning of the word—to impress) your talent was in that book, and how

* Stanley Kunitz (1905–2006) was a poet who won the National Book Award in 1995.
† Izaak Walton (1593–1683), English writer and author of *The Compleat Angler* (1653).

it shone through to people it was worth shining through to, and how you should go on to THE FINE ARKANSAS GENTLEMAN with confidence and faith in your gifts. And of course that $7,200 U.S. don't hurt much either.

So that is the saga of D. Harington and the Rockefellers. It should make you rest easier in the cool of the evening.

Yours in Nelson and Winthrop's sweet name,
Irving Howe

To Robert Penn Warren

June 30, 1966 Vineyard Haven, MA

Dear Folks

This is a memento of our party at Willie Morris' last spring, in case you haven't seen it.* It was published in The Texas Observer, Austin. We are all happily ensconced at the beach and I am trying to get the book finished this summer in my snappy little studio behind the big house, a kind of slave quarters I should say. We miss seeing you but at the same time envy your sweet situation on the Île. Do you see any of the nudists? Please inform, as I am tired of reading Playboy for edification. All sorts of people are here this summer: Goodwin has a house next door, and of course Lillian is here, "Dean" Brustein, Phil Roth, Jules Feiffer and even, God help us, John Updike, who is arriving soon.† I think I'll move to Nantucket or

* Willie Morris (1934–99) was a writer, editor, and longtime friend to Styron. In 1967, Morris was made the youngest editor in chief ever at *Harper's Magazine.* Styron attached Larry L. King, "The Ole Country Boys," *Texas Observer,* June 24, 1966, a kind of glass-menagerie treatment of the Southern expatriates living in New York and Connecticut: Willie Morris, Styron, C. Vann Woodward, and Robert Penn Warren. "Red Warren was born in Kentucky," King wrote. "Bill Styron grew up in the Tidewater Country of Virginia. Vann Woodward in Arkansas. Ole Country Boys. Take away their Pulitzers, Rolls-Royces, and legions of adoring fans, and they are just the same as you and me." Lawrence Leo King (b. 1929), American novelist, journalist, playwright, and coauthor of the Broadway musical *The Best Little Whorehouse in Texas,* was a featured writer at *Harper's* throughout the 1960s and 1970s.

† Richard Goodwin, Lillian Hellman, Robert Brustein, Philip Roth, Jules Feiffer, and John Updike. Robert Sanford Brustein (b. 1927) has been a theater critic, producer, play-

Port-Cros where the literary gumbo isn't quite so thick. Oh, I forgot to tell you, Bennett and Phyllis* are due to arrive next month in Frank Sinatra's jet—with Frank. You need not mention our acquaintance if you so choose.

Love, B.

To James Jones

September 3, 1966 Vineyard Haven, MA

Dear James: I thought you might like to know that ETERNITY, along with DARKNESS, was included in a book called 100 Great American Novels, a kind of book of synopses subtitled "The masterpieces of American fiction in one portable volume," published by New American Library.† It also has Melville, Hawthorne, Papa and Faulkner. This means that for 95¢ the students can now avoid reading our work. I am sending you some plastic bottle stoppers by separate mail. Unfortunately, I could only find four. Goodwin did steal those cigars, and is on my shitlist forever. WIDOW-MAKER just arrived and I'm looking forward to a good read after Labor Day when the creeps depart.

Love to Moss and Kids.

—B

P.S. I'll be back in Rox. Sept. 15th

---

wright, and educator. He founded the Yale Repertory Theatre and American Repertory Theater. He was dean of the Yale School of Drama from 1966 to 1979.

* Bennett and Phyllis Cerf.

† A mass market paperback published by Signet in 1966, edited by Albert H. Morehead, Harold J. Blum, and others.

To Donald Harington

September 12, 1966 Vineyard Haven, MA

Dear Don:

I wanted to drop you a note before I return to Rox., which will be this coming Thursday. I hope we'll be able to get together this fall. I also hope your Pike-Arrington chronicle proceeds apace. I have had very good work this summer, despite social distractions; in fact it has been the best summer for writing I can remember, having written exactly 100 pages from the point the book broke off when you were reading it. For me, prodigal proflicity. I have only now to develop the relationship between Nat and Margaret Whitehead and so the insurrection itself (which I'm going to make fairly brief, in order to tone down all the bloodshed) and I'll be practically done. So if God is willing (and He told me He would be willing if I was good) I will have the whole thing done late this fall or early winter. It has near about killed me, and I'm beginning to feel as black as Stokely Carmichael.

Thanks for the leads on the various historical volumes.* I have read all but James's THE OLD DOMINION, which I think, however, I will eschew until I finish writing this book. By now I've got the whole thing so firmly fixed in my head that I'm a little leery of any further outside influence.

Good news about your selling a piece to Esquire.† I'll be looking forward to it. It is still a very good podium upon which to establish your further presence to the great reading public—far better, say, than Playboy or one of those jerkoff magazines. The orgasmic reception of GILES GOAT-BOY is an example of our present-day fashion for unreadability (I was happy however to see a reviewer in The New Republic call it a "750

* In a letter of August 1966, Harington had recommended several books to Styron on the subject of Turner and "the Southampton incident": G. P. R. James's 1856 novel *The Old Dominion; or The Southampton Massacre: A Novel* (New York: Harper & Brothers, 1856), Arna Bontemps's novel about Gabriel Prosser's slave rebellion, *Black Thunder* (New York: Macmillan, 1936), and Harriet Beecher Stowe's *Dred: A Tale of the Great Dismal Swamp* (Boston: Phillips, Sampson and Co., 1856).

† Donald Harington, "A Second Career," *Esquire* (January 1967).

page snooze") and more of your stuff in print will help redress the balance.*

Take care of yourself and keep Vermont green.

Yrs in the name of Unohoo,
B.S.

Speaking of Unohoo, I finally saw the St. Matthew movie and thought it remarkably effective.†

To Robert Penn Warren

September 19, 1966 Roxbury, CT

Monsieur Robert Penn Warren

I was about ready to call Albert to see if he had your new address when, behold, your letter came with all of its pleasant description of sun and sea and Gabriel & Rosanna nautical activity. My envy of you at the moment is so intense that my back teeth ache—as once I heard Jim Jones describe his emotions when jarred by the sight of a particularly Bikini-unclad blonde by the pool at Biarritz. The south of France is still all magic for me in my recollections, and you make it all too real to be quite bearable. We all had a great summer at the Vineyard—much too social as usual, but fine nonetheless. As you no doubt know, it was otherwise a typically insane summer in the American commonwealth what with several particularly untidy mass murders and Lyndon amok at the mouth, the more intolerable hypocrisy about Vietnam, but somehow we struggled through cheerfully and are now back here in the pleasant late summer awaiting the birth of Leo or Irving or whatever the hell our next born will be called. Your god-daughter is opting for the name Myron, which in full context will be euphonious at least.

Don't worry about our being left out as dedicatees to that fine poem in <u>Encounter</u>. I have been shafted so many times by the English that I can

* John Barth's *Giles Goat-Boy; or The Revised New Syllabus* (Garden City, N.Y.: Doubleday, 1966) was a satirical novel about American campus culture.

† Pier Paolo Pasolini, dir., *The Gospel According to St. Matthew* (1964).

only assume that it is simply another example of their assiness. No matter. The poem you sent, "Internal Injuries," is just wonderful, I think. All that close, almost unbearably intense observation, that terrible urban stink and clutter, combined with your usual wrenching historical grab at the whole tragedy. I think especially of touches like zinnias down South being called nigger-flowers, and the "nigger, nigger burning bright" verses, the plane overhead, the subtle irony of being run over by a spick. And the whole scene is wonderfully summed up in the 7th section—"We love you, we truly do"—; it's a truly fine piece of sustained emotion. I have read the poem several times now and it grows on each re-reading which I believe is the acid test.

I am planning to make my escape from here once Rose can abandon offspring #4 temporarily and once the book is finally done, which should simultaneously be sometime early next year. So haul out the Pernod and stand by. I had a very, very good summer in terms of writing—got over 100 pages done cold and to my satisfaction, and am now headed in toward that final bloody climax that I've had to circle around for so long during the rest of the book. But it is coming along well still, and steadily, and I foresee no real blocks or difficulties. I am beginning, after this immersion in negritude, to feel almost as black as Stokely Carmichael. Partisan Review is running a short excerpt in their next issue and I'll send it to you; the piece is so much a little vignette (unlike anything else in the book) that I think you might like reading it even though I suspect you (like me) are not too hot on reading excerpts.*

Give Eleanor and the kids a big embrace from all of us here, including your god-daughter who in shiny boot and snap-brimmed patent leather cap, combined with shorter skirt, is suddenly the disgrace of Litchfield County. Stay in touch and toast the sea for us now and then, and the mountains, and France.

À bientôt,

Bill

* William Styron, "Runaway," *Partisan Review* 33 (Fall 1966).

To C. Vann Woodward

September 25, 1966 Roxbury, CT

Dear Vann:

I thought your dissertation on Messrs. Genovese and Aptheker was just great, and I thank you for sending it to me.* It was wide-ranging and witty and plain ordinary engrossing, and I wish I had been there when you gave the talk, in order to see the reaction among the brethren. One really startlingly original insight—to me, at least—was the proliferation of black leaders, like Carmichael, coming from places like Trinidad and the historical ground and responsibility for this, and why their point of view really doesn't work here in the U.S. I've been brooding over something like this for a long time, especially after reading Red Warren's piece on Carmichael,† but totally missed the historical reason, which you've now made clear. I think this is an enormously important point, and I do hope you elaborate on it, in a loud voice, soon.

Let us talk more before long. I think Rose has a plan going to get you all up here early in October. Maybe she's been in touch already, but if not she will. Yesterday reached p. 500 in the true and authentic revelations of the life of Hon. Nathaniel Turner, Bart., so am feeling rather heady. I had a real good summer's work and am fairly confident I can polish off the rest (another 50–75 pages or so) by early winter.

See you soon,
Bill

* Styron referred to Woodward's unpublished essay "Genovese, Aptheker, and Heresy." Eugene Dominic Genovese (1930–2012) was an American historian known for his Marxist approach and his Bancroft Prize–winning work on slavery, *Roll, Jordan, Roll: The World the Slaves Made* (1974).

† Robert Penn Warren, *Who Speaks for the Negro?* (New York: Random House, 1965).

To James Jones

October 2, 1966 Roxbury, CT

Dear James:

An unspeakable case of the influenza shits, from which I still haven't fully recovered, allowed me ample time off from Nat Turner and enough of a jaundiced point of view to read WIDOW-MAKER with both the leisure and detachment I wanted and needed. I finished it yesterday, quite wrung out and excited, and decided to write you now and without delay, while it was all still fresh in my mind. I presume of course that my opinion is wished-for, if not exactly asked for, else you wouldn't have strained Delacorte's budget to the extent of the $2.76 it took to send it to me by the post. Don Fine must be sweating over that item.*

In many ways I think it is easily your most paradoxical book; I am not being intentionally obscure in saying that. What I mean simply is that of all of your works none shows you more at your absolutely glittering best while at the same time reveals your flaws and excesses. First your glittering best, and I mean that: none of your books has displayed a finer hand at that old essential—pure narrative. It is, as you must be aware, an immensely long book, but there was not a moment when after laying it down (usually to take a shit) I was not ready to pounce upon it eagerly again. Your sense of pacing is uncanny, and in terms of simply narrative drive you are at the top of your form (Rose concurs with me in this, incidentally, and she has trouble being satisfied, orgasmically, with narrative; she read it straight through as I did with constant anticipation). Secondly, and just as importantly, your characters are totally compelling and believable, in many ways as fine as you've ever done: the book should stand alone upon the wonderful creation of Lucky herself. Despite the fact that I am acquainted with her prototype, she is nonetheless a really wonderful broad, a true woman, deliciously portrayed. Others too are great—Bonham especially. For me he is perfectly delineated: the lonely American Male, in capitals, wrapped up in his heroic and frustrated and impotent existence, seeking Manhood. A truly remarkable creation. Grant is perfectly real to

* Several of Styron's compliments are bracketed by publisher Donald I. Fine to use as pull quotes for Jones's publicity.

me too (although in certain areas not very sympathetic to me) as are the minor characters: Rene, the abominable Orloffski, Hunt, Ben, and Irma Unowho, and the wonderful little sideplay Jamaica niggers, perfectly anatomized. For some reason Carol didn't, in her monstrousness, get through to me—I think only because she reminds me of my stepmother.

Another place where you are absolutely spectacular, of course, is in the underwater scenes. All of them are fantastically good, breathtaking, but for some reason the ones that stick out the most remarkably for me are the retrieval of the two niggers from the river (that panties bit was superb), the time when Ron gets caught in the net, and the time or memory when Bonham goes out and kills him that shark. They are gems in themselves, and recur still over and over in my mind.

Finally, you have pinned down beautifully the thing you told me you were after in the book: this terrible wrench and anguish men have, especially American men, over their <u>maleness</u>. I think you have dramatized it superbly, especially in the inter-relationship between Grant and Bonham (and to some extent later with Grointon, though there the heterosexual jealousy takes over); and God knows after that hectic, desperate, wonderfully described voyage to the Nelson Islands, the reader stands in perfect awe of your ability to smell out all the hideous little motivations and counter-motivations, sexual and otherwise, that make men into the kind of half-monsters that they are. In fact, I have an idea that <u>WIDOW-MAKER</u> might become <u>the</u> definitive work on the hell of masculine identity.

There is so much fine in the book that I hesitate to niggle about the lapses. I think for one thing (and I speak as a believer in spaciousness in the novel) that it is considerably too long—many too many maneuverings of people around hotel lobbies and bars and in and out of rooms and such, which could have been done in a line or two rather than the paragraphs you took; too much dogged palavering over, for instance, the details of the financing of the <u>Naiad</u>, and goings and comings of Sam Finer, and quite a few bar scenes that are repetitious and could have been left out entirely. And also many random paragraphs here and there which simply didn't—to my mind—have to be there; repetition again. As I say, I believe in scope and length among the Novel's chief virtues; but as your good friend and reader I think that if you apply ruthless and microscopic attention to eliminating in the galleys as many superfluous details and scenes as you can (shrinking certain purely transitional paragraphs to a laconic sentence or two, for instance), you can reduce the book's length by 200 pages and I passionately believe it will gain in force and intensity. At any rate, that is my humble opinion.

There are certain substantive things in the book which, because you saw them that way and because you may be right, I can't ask you to tamper with but still bother me—fit matters for a personal discussion rather than a letter perhaps. Lucky is such an adorable creation, so filled with insight and sympathy and understanding, that I find it somewhat hard to believe that this sweetie, once she heard the truth from Ron about Ron's past relations with Carol, would remain so bitter and antagonistic toward Ron, at least for so long. Perhaps for a night or a day, in a funk so to speak. But for a girl who has up until this moment been portrayed as such a paradigm of warmth and understanding to be so unremittingly resentful and intolerant is a little hard for me to accept. Just as I find it hard to accept (even within the framework of the dependency-type personality you have established Ron as having, with Carol before), or if not hard to accept then irritating, that Ron would be so insanely jealous over the possibility (not the fact) that Lucky stepped out on him with Grointon. My own reaction was, Well, so what? So he stuck it in her once, he won't do it again. In the meantime the universe and the beautiful underwater world still exist. But all of this, as I say, is substantive and has to do less with the aesthetic of your book than with a particular moral hang-up which seems to posit absolute purity and decency on the one hand and absolute treachery and evil on the other, either one depending upon whether one has inserted a throbbing piece of flesh into a more or less throbbing orifice, or whether one hasn't. My honest feeling was that Ron had gotten himself into such an insane state over this matter that, although I didn't know for sure whether Lucky had fucked Grointon, I kind of wished she had.

But all of this does not diminish in the slightest my basic admiration for what you've achieved. Despite my reservations (which I expect you to reject anyway) I think you've produced a really prodigious work of the imagination, broadly intelligent, filled with uncanny insights about men and manliness (and also about women and screwing), and containing some of the best passages about the sea written since J. Conrad left Warsaw to become a cabin boy.* I should think that these facts should fill you with some satisfaction and allow you to go to bed at night and tickle (Lucky's) pussy with a sense of fine mission finely achieved.

I hope you will write me a post card when my book is finished. Love to all and give a stroke to Lucky for old Bill.

B.S.

To C. Vann Woodward

October 26, 1966 Roxbury, CT

Dear Vann:

I think that "The Second Reconstruction" is just splendid, and I certainly don't think that you need have any worries about either pedantic tendencies or gaucheries about the White Negro.† Indeed, your remarks about the hipness and chicness of Negro attitudes among hip white people are among the best I've ever read. It is in a sense, of course, a pessimistic essay, but I don't think that you should be concerned that some new political pronouncement after the election is going to substantially alter the truth of your viewpoint. You have summed up beautifully the quality of the impasse, and of course the historical perspective you have brought to it gives it an enormous added authority. It is a powerful and disturbing piece and I have no criticism at all except the minor suggestion that you add to your list of defectors from the cause one of the most significant groups: I am thinking of the college kids for whom, according to Monday's N.Y. Times, the civil rights movement is a dead turkey. I am simply thinking that perhaps somewhere in the second paragraph on p. 11 you could add a single short sentence adding the campus young people to the

* Joseph Conrad left Warsaw when he was four years old in 1861 and became a seaman at sixteen.

† Styron refers to Woodward's unpublished essay, "The Second Reconstruction in Retrospect" (1966). Styron also refers to Norman Mailer's essay "The White Negro: Superficial Reflections on the Hipster," originally published in the Summer 1957 issue of *Dissent,* and separately by City Lights Publishers, then collected in *Advertisements for Myself* (1959).

groups who have joined in the "great stillness." It is a truly fine piece, and the sooner it appears the better.

I also greatly enjoyed the adroit decapitation you did on Dwight Lowell Dumond* (do you think his middle name had anything to do with his self-righteous ardor?); the reference to Rousseau is perfectly apt.† Also, the observations on the Underground Railroad are fascinating. I'm going to get hold of that book if I can. I'm beginning to think that all of antebellum history was one big pipedream. Who knows, maybe even Garrison was the figment of someone's imagination.

The November 29th visit with Genovese sounds fine, and I've put it down on the book. Also, I've gotten a letter from J.M. Dabbs,‡ who would like to get together with you and me around November 7th. I certainly am amenable to come to New Haven around that time so anything you set up with him will be O.K. with me. Will you let me know what you work out with him?

Yours, sadly, in the backlash,

Bill

To James Jones

October 28, 1966 New Milford, CT

Une jeune fille 3 kilos Love Bill and Rose.§

* Dwight Lowell Dumond (1895–1976) was a renowned American historian and pioneering scholar of abolitionism and slavery, best known for *Antislavery Origins of the Civil War in the United States* (1959).

† Styron refers to Woodward's essay "The Antislavery Myth," *American Scholar* (Spring 1962), collected in *The Future of the Past* (1989). In that essay, Woodward calls Dumond "a modern primitive, a Henri Rousseau of historiography."

‡ James M. Dabbs, Jr. (1937–2004), was a professor of psychology at Georgia State University. Dabbs earned his Ph.D. from Yale University and is best known for his book *Heroes, Rogues, and Lovers: Testosterone and Behavior* (2000).

§ Alexandra Styron was born on October 28, 1966.

To Robert Penn Warren

November 11, 1966 Roxbury, CT

You must read the following message as a short story, without peeking at the ending. You will recall, first of all, the story I told you about my roommate at Davidson College, Charlie Capps, who went on to greater things and became the High Sheriff of Bolivar County, Miss. This story resembles that but exceeds it somehow, and makes me wonder if my youthful roommate background is not somehow strangely blessed, or cursed.

As you know, the other night on TV we witnessed one of the weirdest finales of any national election in recent history. Well around 7 PM—when by way of the new electronic marvels that announce the winners, accurately by God, 10 minutes after the polls close, on the basis of early returns, and make you feel that you are living in 1984—I turned on the set and by pure coincidence saw the smiling victorious face of one of my old roommates. (His face had been preceded by that of Lester Maddox, also smiling, winner of the disputed but probably sure governorship of Georgia.) I near about dropped off the davenport. Anyway, this roommate was my roommate at Duke for 8 months when we were in the Marine V-12 together. Really charming guy—a native of Montgomery who had been transferred to Duke from Emory. I shared a room with him and a Jewish boy from Memphis named Arthur Katz. We had a great time together, boozed it up a lot and went off whoring in Raleigh, and one time—together with a couple of girls from Wilmington, N.C.—had the nearest thing to an orgy I ever encountered. This fellow was bright and engaging, a good student, charming, generous, and I honestly missed him after we shipped out of Duke and went our separate ways in the Marines.

After I had become what they call a Writer, I began to get an occasional very nice letter from him, pleasant and congratulatory and in good tone. He obviously had moved ahead. He was in his mid-thirties (my age at the time) but was already the president of a Life Insurance company down south. He invited Rose and me to come and see him, implying without being ostentatious that he had a pretty good place to make us feel at home in. Then about three years ago I actually ran into him, in the lobby of the Hotel Savoy-Hilton in New York. Great hellos and hollers and all that. He was in NY on business, up from the South. We had several drinks together, terribly pleasant, and planned to hit the town together, as they say, to recapture all the old times, but for one reason or another it fell through. Anyway, during the brief time I saw him I got the impression of an up-and-coming, very unstuffy rich young businessman from Down South that either of us would like to have adorn our living room. Literate without being bookish, all that, knew Warren, Faulkner, Styron, not the whole Canon but enough, all that bullshit.

The short story is coming to an end. The man's name is Claude Kirk, Jr., and he has just been elected the governor of the sovereign state of Florida. I would say that his politics, such as they are (He ran like the rightist in Md. on the platform of "Every man's home his castle," and the Times reported him as winking at old ladies in parking lots during the campaign and promising $3 billion of state goodies on a $1.5 billion budget) is somewhere between Willie Stark and Lester Maddox. Actually, it occurs to me that he is the new Willie Stark, all Duke U. and Brooks & Warren and very much in and sophisticated, lit., etc., and several miles to the right of Mussolini. Some of the things he said in his campaign would curl the hair of a man inured to Vardaman and Maddox. Not because they were the words of a redneck, but precisely because they were so Duke U. and suave. Anyway, that's the end of the short story. I think that before you return from France I will have taken me a little edifying trip to Tallahassee. An essay on Old Roommates.

Our new offspring is just beautiful, and Tommy is meaner than hell about her. On the first day after she was born, when his grandmother called up to ask what he wanted her to bring him, he said quite slowly and deliberately, "Some wire . . . and some . . . batteries . . . and some nails . . . and some heavy weights." I really think he was building an electric chair for the baby in the cellar.*

The book marches toward an end. We plan a spring (early spring) visit to the Alpes Maritimes.

Love to all the Warrens,
Bill

* As Styron later noted: "I was certain he was building a torture device for his new baby sister. But in fact, after a long and sinister silence, he emerged with a wondrous artifact: a wooden bird with metal wings, a gift for Alexandra, and tribute to the fact that even he, after all his isolated maleness, wished to celebrate the arrival of another sister, my new daughter." See West, *William Styron: A Life* (New York: Random House, 1998), 370.

PS: Not that I want to push my weight around about food but tell Eleanor that we have just finished a bushel of Chincoteague oysters.

To Robert White

November 18, 1966* Roxbury, CT

Lyndon B. Johnson's Postal Regulations Forbid Me Signing Anything But A Cryptic: W.S.

To James Jones

December 9, 1966 Roxbury, CT

Dear James:

. . . Fine called me the other day to ask if I would let him quote from my letter to you (a copy of which he sent me) for purposes of plugging, advertising and other forms of commerce. I thought it over for a good while and decided not to, for the following two reasons which I hope will not offend you.

a) Most importantly, I honestly don't think it looks good for two writers who are as well-known as friends as we are to give each other such a scratch on the back in public. I meant every favorable thing I said about the book, and more, and am willing to stand by more words, but I simply think that it lacks style and grace for me to plug you, and I would feel exactly the same if the positions were reversed. My feeling about this is reinforced by

b) the fact that you shouldn't and don't need such a plug. The book is a powerful and original piece of work, you are a famous and venerated and well-established writer; therefore, for me to give you such a plug would seem under the circumstances to be at best superfluous and at worst a

* The postcard image was of a woman's knees, and Styron had drawn train tracks leading in between them.

form of special pleading. The book should—and will—be able to stand by its own self.

I have no criticism of your criticism of my criticism except to say that your howls of dismay won't budge me an inch from my stand about some minor misgivings about what to me is a major and powerful work. I certainly didn't make my criticisms lightly or facetiously, and the fact that you call me "off my nut" and "full of shit" doesn't change my belief that—in terms of the two or three matters I brought up—you were not in the book artistically consistent. You may be right and I may, of course, be utterly wrong, but I don't think so, and I wouldn't have been honest if I hadn't told you what I thought. For me the two things I mentioned didn't come through convincingly, that's all. Otherwise, I think it's a tremendously powerful piece of fiction, and I'll stand by every favorable thing I've said to you about it and every passionate feeling I have for it.

Rose went to T. Capote's masqued ball which was the shriek of New York, but I didn't, being too involved in my own creative writing.* She got rubbed by a couple of masqued faggots, and danced with Henry Ford, but that's about all.† Andy Warhol was there in his own face.

We had a fine time with Monique and Jean-François, both in N.Y. and up here where they spent part of Thanksgiving week-end, but I guess you all have heard the gossip by now. Great folks, I think, even if they are French. . . .

I hope you understand about my reluctance to quote from my letter. Again, I think the book is an absolute knockout, as they used to say in the twenties, and you should be relaxing serenely on your laurels.

Merry Christmas to all etc. . . .

Bill

* Truman Capote held a masquerade ball, the Black and White Ball, on November 28, 1966. The party was the most desirable social event of the year and only five hundred people were invited.

† Henry Ford II (1917–87), grandson of the founder of Ford Motor Company.

To Donald Harington

December 24, 1966 Roxbury, CT

Dear Don:

Just a brisk, brief note on Christmas Eve to wish you all a verrie merrie Xmas and all that bullshit. Our house has turned into a hideous materialistic gang-bang of a Gehanna worthy of the wildest dreams of a Byzantine Santa Claus with tons of junk, candy canes, and all sorts of obscene trash littering the premises from basement to attic. You may read in the Putney Bugle of all sorts of wild, demented, violent acts coming out of our Roxbury homestead. My latest ploy is just before bedtime to tell wonderful Yuletide stories to the kiddies about Santa turning at midnight into a hideous man-eating bat and the sugarplum fairies being humped by His reindeer.

My lousy record as a correspondent may be laid to the fact that I have exhausted myself trying to finish Nat so it will be delivered to the Crystal Palace on Madison Avenue sometime in January.* I will do better after all this is over. I figure that maybe this is my last novel. They take too much out of me to be commensurate with the spiritual rewards. Stick maybe to short stories—that was a damn lovely one of yours in Esquire, incidentally—but even the worth of shorties is a moot point.

I'll try to take you up on that kind invitation to visit, after this monster is laid to rest. Maybe you could find me a Vt. Snowbank to die in.

I hope you're over your Mammoth Writer's Block. Take it from an old hand: they'll keep coming but you'll always get over each one.

Merry Christmas to all and to all a good night,

Yrs in Kris
Kringle
Bill

* Styron refers to the old Random House building.

To Mr. Bean*

January 13, 1967 Roxbury, CT

Dear Mr. Bean:

I am old-fashioned enough so that most of my faith still comes from the poetry and passion of the Bible. So that when I recall the words—

> God is our refuge and strength, a very present help in trouble
> Therefore will not we fear, though the earth be removed, and
> though the mountains be carried into the midst of the sea—

I am moved to a belief in the eternal, in which one's death is only a necessary part of the great design.

Warmest regards,
William Styron

To Don Congdon†

January 21, 1967 Roxbury, CT

Dear Don:

This is just to let you know THE CONFESSIONS OF NAT TURNER is finished and that I am delivering the manuscript to Bob Loomis at Random House sometime during the middle of the coming week—the 25th or 26th probably. Bob will be making Xerox copies and I'm sure he'll give you one as soon as they are available. You may be interested to know that Life magazine is very eager to see the manuscript with the view in mind to break a precedent (except for Hemingway's OLD MAN) and run fiction, in this case an excerpt as long as 7,000 words. The girl up there who is handling this matter, and who approached me about it, is an old friend named Jozefa Stuart, and she'll be the one for you to talk to. Harper's also

* A male schoolteacher in Maine, dying of cancer, who wrote to Styron to ask for some words of faith.

† Don Congdon (1918–2009), literary agent best known for representing Ray Bradbury, William Shirer, and David Sedaris. Bradbury dedicated *Fahrenheit 451* to Congdon.

is definitely planning to run a really big amount (45–50,000 words) coinciding with the publication of the book next fall. I don't know yet how that will conflict with Life. Perhaps that will become one of your pleasant problems.

Anyway, the book is done and I'm off to the Bahamas around February 3d, feeling somewhat like Manchester* at his poorest. Call me up here before then if you need any more information.

Yours,

Bill

To Carlos Fuentes

January 28, 1967 Roxbury, CT

Dear Carlos:

Many thanks for your New Year's greeting card which just arrived by slow boat. It came at a propitious moment, since I have just finished Nat Turner and am passionately ready for a vacation. I hope I'll be able to see you when I make my European landfall; right now, I tentatively plan to arrive in Paris around March 1st. Will you be there? I noticed that your card was from Courmayeur,† but I seem to have lost your Paris address. If by the time I send this I haven't found it, it will go c/o Mexican Embassy in Rome, and I'll hope it gets to you.

I expect that I'll stay in Paris a week or ten days, then Rose will be coming over to join me, along with a couple of my multitudinous offspring, and we'll go down to Rome for a while—though I prefer Paris at that time of the year. I don't think I'll try Moscow now, although Yevtushenko who was here a few weeks ago almost broke my arm trying to get me to go. Basically, I think it's simply a matter of eating Russian pickles when I could be having coq au vin. . . .

* Styron is likely referring to William Manchester (1922–2004), the author and biographer, best known for *Goodbye, Darkness: A Memoir of the Pacific War* (1980), which partly chronicles his serious wounds during the campaign on Okinawa.

† A town in northern Italy at the foot of Mont Blanc.

I'm looking forward to the Richeburg. Please turn out the Viet Cong flags at Orly, and if you get this letter before I write the Joneses tell them that Beelly's coming.

Abrazos,

Bill

PS. I didn't see the Lukács article, but if you've got a copy of La Quinzaine littéraire please save it for me.*

To Robert Penn Warren

February 21, 1967 Roxbury, CT

Dear Red:

After many bumblings about, much confusion and Angst attending upon the completion of Nat, I have finally crystallized my head into some semblance of sanity and have decided to accompany the Warrens to Cairo—instead of copping out, as Rose I think told you I was doing in her last letter to you. Those pharaohs and things really seem irresistible, especially in the company of you all, so I have among other things written to Mr. Rodenbeck at the Univ. of Cairo to put me down too as a cultural emissary. I hope you will pardon my shilly-shallying and procrastination, but believe me it was book-end madness.

We won't be able to come to Magagnosc, I'm afraid, but if it's all right we'll be meeting you in Rome on March 22nd or anytime after. Rose tells me to tell you that our hangout there is to be the Hotel de la Ville (next to the Hassler, you'll recall) and that is where you'll be able to get in touch with us. Then we'll all take off for Cairo and the old Nile. I'm leaving here for Paris next Wednesday, March 1, and my address there will be c/o James Jones, 10 Quai d'Orléans, 4e. The telephone no. there is DANton 18-50 and you should be able to call with ease if you want to get in touch about

* Styron refers to György Lukács (1885–1971), Hungarian Marxist philosopher and literary critic. Styron also refers to an interview that Naim Kattan conducted with Lukács that appeared in *La Quinzaine littéraire* in December 1966.

the trip. And maybe I'll be able to come to Magagnosc after all, if I can take off from the nit-picking last work on the MS. Rose will be coming over 8 or 9 days after I do.

Your poems which I read in leisurely fashion on a gorgeous Bahamian beach are still continuing to be the best and most beautiful you have ever done. I was enormously moved by them and I hope you will allow me to talk with you at length about them when I see you. The Valery poem strikes me as especially great, but all are wonderful and I treasure them.* More about them anon.

Thanks for mentioning Marc Ratner to me.† He has already gotten in touch with me about the book he is doing on me, and I have written him back saying that Random House would send him galleys of Nat when available.

First reactions to Nat are fine, not the least financially—the Book-of-the-Month Club just paid $150,000 for the book and that is quite a hunk of cash to earn off a slave's black back. I hear it's the highest they have paid for a novel. Anyway the book no longer feels a part of me, and I'll be glad when this last minute nit-picking is done.

Best love to all and will see you soon,

Bill

To Hope Leresche

February 21, 1967 Roxbury, CT

Dear Hope:

First news first. The Book-of-the-Month Club, which of course is our most prestigious book club, has just bought The Confessions of Nat Turner for $150,000! This according to my sources at Random House is the largest sum they have ever paid for a novel (as distinct from non-fiction). Interestingly enough too, in order to get the book they had to

* Ambroise-Paul-Toussaint-Jules Valéry (1871–1945) was a French poet and philosopher.

† Marc L. Ratner's *William Styron* (New York: Twayne Publishers, 1972) was the first study of Styron to be published.

outbid the Literary Guild, whose offer of $100,000 was the highest they had ever made for a novel until then. Am I right in assuming this might be intriguing grist for Tom Maschler's mill? Needless to say, I am both flabbergasted and delighted and I just wanted you to know.

I got your letter and noted the number of galleys that you wanted, and of course will have Random House send them to you as soon as they are ready; this should be in six weeks or so. Publication date is not definite, but it will probably be in late September or early October.

On March 1st (next Wednesday) I am flying to Paris and will be staying for a couple of weeks with Jim Jones; I can be reached there. I am taking with me a Xerox copy of the edited and corrected manuscript for Michel Mohrt to read at Gallimard.* This is the only thing I've done in terms of foreign publication and I hope it meets with your approval. It is mainly for Gallimard's general perusal; naturally I will want them to print from the corrected final galleys. They are eager to get it translated, however, and publish simultaneously with the American edition, and this is OK with me.

Perhaps I'll be able to come to England for a brief visit while I'm staying with Jim; if not, is there a chance that you might be coming to Paris? In any case, let us stay in touch. I hope I don't sound presumptuous when I say that everybody in whom I have any confidence here feels that the book is going to be very big indeed, and I mean everywhere.

All best wishes,
Bill S.

* Michel Mohrt (1914–2011), editor, writer, historian of French literature, and longtime editor at Éditions Gallimard.

To C. Vann Woodward

April, 1967 Egypt

Dear Vann:

Traveling up the Nile to Aswan with the Warrens on an old paddle-wheeler that looks like the Robert E. Lee.* Scenery is magnificent, the ruins unbelievable, the food somewhat deficient in everything except flies. Rose and I will be staying in Italy until early May. Our address is Hotel de la Ville, Via Sistina, Rome. Hope you had a good trip to Grenada.

Love to Glenn,

All best. Bill S.

To Robert Penn Warren

May 24, 1967 Roxbury, CT

Dear Red:

Well, we had a fine trip back to the land of the big PX, I sitting next to the most suave and elegant Italian I have ever met, a gentleman who had been (I observed) reading William James and who fell into discourse with me about chamber music. When he got off the plane in Lisbon he handed me his card, which revealed him to be the Italian manager of the Coca-Cola Export Corporation. He sure was a thousand miles from Babbitt.

That was a lovely week-end in Magagnosc, all too brief however, and the kids still talk about it over the breakfast honey I bought for 9 francs in that wonderful citadel on the hilltop. They talk about other things too—the Nile and Esna and roguish camel drivers. Surely it all was the greatest trip that anyone ever took. Rose went down to the Yale hospital and they checked her over and found that her leg was doing fine.† It developed however that the accident caused a minor dislocation of the jaw—nothing serious but one necessitating the use of a support at night while she sleeps for several weeks. One bright note: the lawyer in Rome writes that the mo-

* Styron wrote about this trip in "William Styron's Nile Diary," *Geo* 3 (September 1981). Collected in *This Quiet Dust.*

† Rose had hurt her leg.

torscooter culprit does have money of sorts and will pay for most of Salvater Mundi, which wasn't cheap. Which reminds me, how is Eleanor's indisposition doing?

The galleys of Nat are out, and if you haven't received your copy from Random by now you should get it imminently. I have no word about reviews except that Francis Brown of the Times liked the book very, very much (a good omen?) and that our friend Vann Woodward is going to do a piece on it for, of all places, The New Republic.* I wish the damn thing were out and published and over with.

We are off to the Vineyard around June 23 and hope you all will join us for some Atlantic sun when you come back from Port-Cros. Keep in touch, and give a warm embrace to all the family, including Lilly.

As ever,

Bill

To James and Gloria Jones

May 24, 1967 Roxbury, CT

Dear James and Moss: Well, me and Rose are finally back in Connecticut, after having flown from Nice to New York via Barcelona and Lisbon. My seat mate was Jim Clark, the racing driver, and I learned a lot of things about automobiles that I never knew before.† Now back in Roxbury, me and Rose have been playing a lot of tennis on our fine new court. Rose is still limping a little from her accident so I manage to beat her quite handily; otherwise I'd be up shit creek. Actually, Rose had her leg checked out at Yale hospital, and while they said that it would have been far better if the Guinea doctors had left the bruise alone and not operated, she was making a perfect recovery and everything (aside from a tiny scar) will be well.

* C. Vann Woodward, "Confessions of a Rebel: 1831," *The New Republic*, October 7, 1967.

† James Clark (1936–68), British Formula One racing driver from Scotland. He won two World Championships in 1963 and 1965. He was killed in a Formula Two race in Hockenheim, Germany, on April 7, 1968.

I see by the paper that GTTW-M is on the best-seller list, which pleased us all.* Everybody I know was upset by the nasty treatment the book got and at the same time I've heard some wonderful remarks about the book which pretty much give the lie to the critic-pricks. For one thing, the guy that owns the bookstore nearby in Washington, Conn., told me that he felt it was easily one of your strongest works and likewise the best novel he had read this year by far. He's something of a cynic about books, too, and coming from him the comment is high praise indeed. I also saw Gene Baro at a party up in the neighborhood and he corroborated my own observation that, critics be damned, the general reader was reading the book and very much digging it.

I've got no news on my own lit. scene except to say that the galleys have come in and the book looks good. Hope Leresche has managed to wangle a nice big fat advance out of the Gallimard kikes, so that's a help, and there is going to be an advance piece on the book in McCall's next August—a magazine that goes to suburban matrons but which apparently sells books.† Also Random House has projected a first printing of 75,000, which rather alarms me because I have a feeling that, despite all the good advance signs, the book may just fall flat on its face. But then that's their tough luck, not mine.

We are staying here until around June 23rd and then are going to the Vineyard. What are you all up to this summer, especially with the Greek mess?‡ We sure had a lovely time with you all doing Keblens, Basel, etc., and let's do it again some time. I'll probably be over in the fall, at which point I'll get you to alert all the troops. Rose sends love to all as do I.

Bill

P.S. N. Mailer has a novel (on Lyndon Johnson) coming out the same week in OCT. as mine!!§

* James Jones, *Go to the Widow-Maker* (New York: Delacorte, 1967).

† William Styron, "The Oldest America," *McCall's* 95 (July 1968). Collected in *This Quiet Dust.*

‡ Styron refers to the Greek military coup that began on April 21, 1967. Four colonels in the Greek army took control of the country, beginning a seven-year period of military rule.

§ Styron is likely referring to Norman Mailer's *The Armies of the Night,* which was not published until 1968. This nonfiction novel went on to win the National Book Award and

To Robert Loomis

June 9, 1967 Roxbury, CT

Dear Bob:

I thought I would pass on to you what Bob Silvers* said about the book in a letter; it pleases me because it is almost the first expression of an understanding of what I myself thought I was trying to achieve.

"It seemed to me magnificent and marvelous, the best novel by an American in a great many years and one that will be read always. It is the kind of book that one cannot bear to break off reading and that leaves you sad because you will never have the chance to read it that way again. What it does is make one great part of the country's history horribly and beautifully real in a way that had never seemed possible; and after one reads it one feels that one possesses and is possessed by a consciousness that has been lying in wait and now has come terrifyingly into the open, never to leave. So it seems to me we are all lucky that you wrote this book."

B.S.

P.S. The jacket for Nat is perfect in my recollection. Don't change a jot or a tittle!

To Robert Penn Warren

June 20, 1967 Roxbury, CT

Dear Red:

I'm delighted that you liked Nat and needless to say I will treasure your letter, which is as fine an appreciation of the work as I might ask. I do profoundly appreciate all you said, and I mean that.

The turn-down by Life does probably mean that they are going to run a piece of the book—at least that's what my agent seems to believe. There

---

the Pulitzer Prize. Mailer's novel *Why Are We in Vietnam?* was published in 1967, but is not about Lyndon Johnson.

* Robert Silvers (b. 1929), editor of *The New York Review of Books* since 1963.

is also the chance that they got someone else before you put in your bid, but this seems a little less likely.

I thought I had pretty much exhausted my biography in that letter but with fainting heart will try again.* As for the Okinawa bit, I was not actually in combat there but was on my way there as a newly-commissioned Lieutenant in the Marines when the bomb dropped on Hiroshima; as a result, I am not quite as guilt-obsessed about Hiroshima as some people I know. As for writers that I re-read, I have (among the novelists) re-read Dostoievski and Conrad considerably, Faulkner to a lesser extent, and periodically re-read Huckleberry Finn and Moby-Dick. I'm a great fan of Orwell. Most re-reading I do, however, is probably in poetry—the Elizabethans, John Donne, and among the more modern poets Emily Dickinson, Yeats, Wallace Stevens, R.P. Warren—whose newest poems, especially ones like "Île de Port Cros: What Happened," are among the finest done by a modern poet. Also I have read much of the Bible as literature, which I was saturated in as a youth in Virginia, also later on in college (fundamentalist Presbyterian). It must have been at the New School (which you queried me about, and which I attended in the late 40's) that the Bible merged with a vague social consciousness, producing a cat like Nat Turner. Also music has been an integral part of my work. Without the rhythms and architecture and spirit of Bach, Telemann, Mozart, Handel, Beethoven I doubt that I should ever have gotten a line written. I live a fairly uncomplicated life. Did I quote you the motto from Flaubert I have had tacked for years near my desk? "Be regular and orderly in your life, like a bourgeois, so that you may be violent and original in your works." Suits me to a tee.

Two days from now we are going to the Island so my address until mid-Sept. will be Vineyard Haven, Mass. We hope you will all pay a jolly visit as soon as you return from where the slow fig's purple sloth swells.† All love to all

Yrs ever,

Bill

* Robert Penn Warren used this information for "William Styron," *Book-of-the-Month Club News* (October 1967).

† Styron refers to Warren's poem "Where the Slow Figs Purple Sloth," which appears in John Burt, ed., *Selected Poems of Robert Penn Warren* (Baton Rouge: Louisiana State University Press, 2001).

To Robert Penn Warren

June 20, 1967 Roxbury, CT

Dear Red:

In re your questions from Munich:

1. My blood is Scotch-Irish and Welsh on my mother's side, Yorkshire English on my father's side by way of the Danish conquest. The name was originally Danish—Styring. My mother was from western Pennsylvania, my father from Tidewater Va. and N.C. region. I had grandfathers and uncles on both the Union and Confederate sides of the War between the States.

2. In regard to my connections with the Southern past, I got a big dose of it as a boy. My paternal grandmother was an old lady in her upper eighties in the late Thirties, but she had been born in the ante-bellum South, was born and raised in Beaufort County, N.C., a tobacco and cotton area on the Pamlico River. I never knew my grandfather (father's father) but he had served as a courier during the War in one of the N.C. regiments. Was at Chancellorsville. My grandmother used to tell me about the two little slave girls which she herself had owned as a little girl just before the War. She told me how much she loved them and how well she treated them. One of the slave girls was named, so help me, Drusilla. As a boy I spent much time with this old grandmother of mine. Mainly during the summers I spent much time amid the small-town life of the Tidewater Va. and N.C. region, having all sorts of cousins spread about there. I went to a rural high school about ten miles up the James River from Newport News at a time when there was still a rural atmosphere in the area. I never actually lived on a farm or anything like that (I was raised in a village) but there was still enough real country around for me to get a lot of it in my bones.

3. I wish I could be more informative about the germ of the style and method I used in <u>NAT</u>, but I'm a bit vague. The "Confessions" might have had something to do with it, but it seems that I recall one day thinking (with the vision of Nat in the jail cell in my mind) that the only possible way to tell the story was from Nat's viewpoint. I also noticed that few if

any books by white men had ever been written from this black viewpoint, and—come to think of it—maybe this very fact caused me to try it, caused me to risk it.

4. "Fact-novel." I would hazard the guess that for some unknown reason there is a spirit in the literary air which is tending toward an interest in what actually happened vs. purely imagined experience, and somehow NAT falls into this category. It is an actual happening about actual people to which, however, I have had to bring considerable imagination to bear. The subject of Nat Turner is furthermore a lucky one in that so very little is known about Nat outside of the details of the revolt. Conversely, as I think I've said in talking to you, I doubt that anyone could write a very interesting novel (as distinct from biography) about John Brown, simply because of the plethora of known facts about the man. Nat Turner is just dim and unknown enough in history to make him fascinating as a subject for fiction.

5. & 6. As I may have told you, you can learn all there is to know about Nat Turner during a day's leisurely reading. There is only the "Confessions" and Drewry's book of 1900—The Southampton Insurrection. I have, however, read a great amount about the period, and I doubt if there is an important book on the ante-bellum South, especially connected with slavery, that I have missed. I've also read many plantation records; and the unpublished U. Va. Ph.D. thesis (which I showed you) on Gen. John Hartwell Cocke, upon whom I modeled Nat's Marse Samuel, was especially valuable.*

The weather here on the Vineyard is sparkling. And we miss you all. Love to all and come home soon.

Bill

* Boyd Martin Coyner, "General John Hartwell Cocke of Bremo: Agriculture and Slavery in the Ante-Bellum South," unpublished PhD dissertation, University of Virginia, 1961.

To Robert Penn Warren

June 26, 1967 Vineyard Haven, MA

Here is more info, as requested:

Nat Turner, according to his own "Confessions," was born October 1, 1800 (same year and month, if I'm not mistaken, as John Brown). No one knows exactly where he was born, but it was somewhere in Southampton County, Va.

It is flat, typical Tidewater country with pinewoods and fields interrupted here and there by swampy lowlands with stands of cypress and gum and juniper. In Nat's time, tobacco had all but vanished due to overcultivation, and the farmers turned to cotton, which grows well there but not in the vast Mississippi-Delta-like quantities to make it a valuable money crop. In a kind of desperation they also turned to the cultivation of apples, and found a reasonably good market for cider and brandy in places like Richmond and Norfolk. Then too, of course, there were many pigs (Southampton hams were famous) which flourished off the abundant acorns of the region.

I grew up about 30 to 35 miles away, to the northeast, on the other side of the James River in an area almost exactly the same in its general topography. I lived near a city (Newport News) but as I pointed out in my last letter the little village where I grew up had a thoroughly rural tone. It has completely changed now, of course; World War II and the growth of industry saw to that. But I think it would be safe to say that whatever smell I have for Nat's landscape derives from a familiarity with the same sort of landscape I grew up with as a boy: cornfields, swampy lowlands, pinewoods, etc. Curiously, all U.S. climatic and topographical maps—those which depict rainfall, average temperatures, length of growing season, etc.—include this little bulge in southeastern Va. in a general region which extends from east Texas through the deep South and up through the Carolina lowlands to its terminating point near Norfolk (cotton, for instance, won't grow north of Norfolk). Thus I would say that with certain variations the Southampton region and my own along the James are not too different from the piney woods and flat lands you so perfectly described in the Louisiana of <u>All the King's Men</u>. And you have a strangle-hold on <u>that</u> kind of country.

I hope this is helpful. I've learned that Jimmy Baldwin is doing a long essay-review on Nat for The Atlantic Monthly.* Après moi, le déluge.

À bientot,

Bill

To Don Congdon

June 29, 1967 Vineyard Haven, MA

Dear Don:

I have sent both letters on to Tom Maschler with a stern note telling him to get Cape moving on the BOMC rights nuisance. They should know better, but I think this will get action.

As for the movie offers on Nat Turner, I really do not care to start any negotiations until the book is published and even after that. As I think I told you before, I have had in the past so many annoying and ridiculous inquiries, half-assed options and mendacious propositions about my various books—none of which amounted to 10 cents—that this time I think I can remain completely aloof and call my own shots. As I also told you, truthfully, I have no urgent need for the money, and while I am not totally oblivious to the charms of cash, I simply do not care to bite on any offer that comes my way. In this case, especially, I do not want my book turned into some ghastly soap opera with Sidney Poitier and Lena Horne. If, on the other hand, there comes to your attention some proposition which seems to include the possibility of integrity and taste as part of the deal, I would certainly not be averse to at least talking things over with whomever makes the offer. I like films as a medium and while I know that it is extremely difficult for the writer of a book to have any say-so in its transformation to the screen, nonetheless I want to be able to go as far as possible in that direction, and am completely indifferent to any purely commercial proposition.

* This piece never materialized.

Hope you will have a fine summer and that we can get together face to face for a chat before too long.

Yours—

Bill

To Claire White

June 30, 1967 Vineyard Haven, MA

Dear Claire:

Cold and gloomy up here today, but I'm glad you liked the section of the book. The South was like that, I'm convinced beyond doubt, and even much worse down in places like Alabama. Compared to the Deep South, Virginia was paradise.

I don't understand how my treatment of religion in the part you read is "Freudian," but I think when you read the other parts of the book (there are three main parts, and the one you read is the center one, #2) you will see that Nat is certainly religious, and that his religion is the guiding motif for all that he does, including killing 60 people. You must understand that, even at the age of 18, like so many Negroes who came after him, Nat's religion was not your familiar religion of the Gospels but that of the cruel rhetoric of the Old Testament, and that the Bible was, indeed, often no more than a lofty grammar—as you succinctly put it—to such people. But Nat in his final days does find the Real Thing, as I think you will see when you read the entire book.

Tell Bobby that I am looking forward eagerly to seeing his illustrations. Harper's is going to promote this issue, according to Willie, as they have no other and it is sure to be read by lots of people. Bob Loomis tells me also that the bookstore orders are already 52,000 copies, which is some sort of record for Random House, and that one bookstore in Chicago, Brentano's I believe, has alone ordered 3,500. So we'll see . . .

Come pay us a visit. It can't stay gray forever. And thanks for what you said about the book.

Love and kisses,

—B.

* Tell Bobby I have a few camels up here for him to show.

To Mike Mewshaw

July 22, 1967* Vineyard Haven, MA

Dear Mike:

I have just gotten back your manuscript from my friend, whose opinion lit.-wise I respect, and indeed I am sorry to have taken so long—my reasons being that the ms. arrived while I was in Europe and languished there for a full month before I returned, the other—more important—being that I have until only the past few weeks been able to disentangle myself from the final details attendant upon the publication of Nat Turner; proof-reading, changes, additional proof-reading for the long section that is going to appear in the Sept. Harper's, etc. So now, in the clear, I have finished the ms., and my friend too, and we seem to agree on all major points.

The first and best point is that you are quite obviously a writer, that is, you know how to write, and for you words are not lumpish things to fling on the paper but units of the thought-process to be used meticulously, imaginatively, and with care. You are excellent at rendering mood, have a really fine eye and instinct for nature and the weather, and I was continually impressed, really impressed, by your uncanny gift for dialogue. Your ear here is really magnificent; all that tough idiomatic 20th century speech comes through perfectly, without a single hitch—not just the speech itself,

* Mewshaw reprinted this letter in his memoir and reflected on its influence on his career: "Disappointed as I was that he didn't like the novel, and although I questioned how much encouragement to draw from his comments, I realized something remarkable had occurred. It wasn't just that Styron believed I was 'quite obviously a writer' and would 'do the big thing in the fullness of time.' It was that he had done more than skim the manuscript and respond with polite evasions and tepid good wishes. He identified its flaws as well as its few strengths, and took the time to discuss what I could do to grow as a writer. What moved me most—and does so every time I reread the letter—was Styron's generosity of spirit, his collegiality and readiness to assume an obligation to a neophyte for no better reason than that we both, though vastly different in talent and temperament and age, were committed to writing.

"The letter reveals volumes about William Styron—the seriousness and integrity he has always brought to his fiction, the kindness and concern he has shown lost souls, no matter whether they languished in jail, on death row, or in the Laocoon coils of their own unrealized ambitions. It also proves, if such proof is required, that he wasn't the spoiled rich boy and literary networker his critics accused him of being."

either, but speech in connection with other speech, the dramatic interrelationship of people talking—as on a stage. All that is truly first-rate.

I wish I could say that with all my admiration for your quite obvious gift I felt that this novel succeeds as a book, but I have too many reservations about it to say that I think it does. For one thing, I think, there is something about the theme (in other words, what the writer is trying to say) that bugs me. Your story is about a young man named Chris, who, fleeing a rather unhappy relationship with a girl in the U.S., takes off and sets up housekeeping with four or five oddly-assorted fellow-Americans of both sexes on a West Indian island. The story alternates between flashbacks about his connection with the very pregnant girl, whom he loves, and his present situation with Ted and Gerald and Marty and Simone. What frankly troubles and perplexes me about your story, however, is that very little really happens; there is very little development either in terms of plot (I hate to use that old-fashioned word) or character. There is a lot of drinking, a lot of talk (quite good and accurate, as I've said) about screwing and booze, some action on the water, but I'm never really certain just where the story is leading us. To be quite blunt, I honestly don't understand what the significance of all this is. None of the characters change, that is, nothing in the process of the story happens to change them or to allow the reader to perceive new insights as to what makes people tick. Ted is noisy and raucous in the beginning, loudly entangled in his complicated relationships with Marty and Simone, and he remains that to the very end. Chris himself undergoes no development either, so far as I can see; he rather listlessly observes the shenanigans of his fellow housemates, screws Marty, has a spell in jail, broods about his knocked-up girl, gets the mild hots for Karen, but nothing else really happens to him; neither he nor we—the readers—are in any way changed. There seems to be little dramatic tension in the story. Nothing really happens, as I say; I hate to be repetitious and abuse that word, but it is the only phrase I know how to use to describe my feeling that you have not so much constructed a novel with shifting moods, new insight into character, and a schema of dramatic tensions as a long and I'm afraid too-often monotonous record of loud and drunken conversations between or among, rather, a group of not very interesting people. In short, I honestly can't figure out what the novel is all about.

It especially makes me unhappy to say all of this when, as I've already stated, you have so obviously a writer's real gifts: keen ear for talk, skill at description, and a gutsy sense of the way people yammer at and exacerbate each other when they are confined together as these people are. But honestly, and to repeat, I just don't think you have in this book discovered a theme: which is to say that possibly you have not thought out that striking and original thing in yourself that is absolutely imperative to have as a writer if you are to arrest the attention of 20th-century Americans already so distracted by The Vietnam War, television, pot, LSD, pornography and 10,000 other delights.

I hate to be in the magisterial position of telling a young writer what I think is wrong with his work; after all, it is all too clear that I may be wrong too. But you asked for my opinion and I gave it, and I hope it won't create too wrong an effect. The important thing to me is that you are a writer, with all the fine potential that that single word implies. Just as important is the fact that you are still very young, and have so much opportunity to do the big thing in the fullness of time. I frankly don't think that you have found yourself—your true voice—in this book, but I have no doubt that you will before very long. I would not have gone on at such length about your work if I did not have faith in what will come from you in the future.

In case that it is any comfort to you, I might report that (although at your age I had not produced a novel) I had an equivalent amount of pages of short stories that now I am glad I put away upon the shelf.

Best of luck always. I have no doubt that you will overcome.

Yours ever,

Bill Styron

PS: I'm sending the copy of the ms. back under separate cover.

and best to Slim

To Arthur Schlesinger, Jr.

July 29, 1967 Vineyard Haven, MA

Dear Arthur:

I feel flattered all out of shape by your fine review, and I do appreciate your sending it to me.* Aside from the praise—which is always nice—what I think I liked most about the review was the way you connected Nat with Frantz Fanon, who of course is a 20th-century Nat Turner.† I will be lucky to get any reviews with half the perception you compressed into that brief space.

As to why I did not include the incident about Nat running away, I indeed thought about it but found that it would not fit into the narrative.‡ So instead I put in the part about Hark running away, which seemed to say the same thing. I have the feeling that a lot of M.A. candidates will be kept busy figuring out just where and when I stuck to or departed from the original "Confessions."

Again, many thanks for the fine and understanding review. Both Rose and I will be looking forward to seeing you up here sometime this summer.

As ever,

Bill

P.S. I have just been reading Fanon and find him very scary.§

•

* Arthur Schlesinger, Jr., "The Confessions of Nat Turner, 'Finest American Novel in Years,'" *Vogue* 150 (October 1, 1967).

† Frantz Fanon (1925–61) was a Martinique-born French psychiatrist and writer who supported Algerian independence and helped conceptualize postcolonialism.

‡ Schlesinger wrote Styron on July 27, 1967, telling him that *Confessions* "is a marvelous book." On the *Vogue* review, he added, "I would wish that I had had more space (and a different audience)." He continued: "I would be curious to know sometime why you decided not to use the episode described in the 'Confessions' when, apparently in 1825, Nat ran away from an overseer 'and after remaining in the woods thirty days, I returned, to the astonishment of the Negroes on the plantation, who thought I had made my escape to some other part of the country, as my father had done before. . . . And the Negroes found fault, and murmured against me, saying that if they had my sense they would not serve any master in the world.' This seemed to me to yield an interesting insight both into Nat and the general slave mood."

§ Styron is likely referring to the 1967 translation of Fanon's *Black Skin, White Masks.*

To Robert Loomis

September 4, 1967 Vineyard Haven, MA

Dear Bob:

Philip Rahv showed me the first line of his review in The N.Y. Review of Books which reads, verbatim, as follows:

"This is a first-rate novel, the best that William Styron has written and the best by an American writer that has appeared in some years."*

If you want to use this in that jumbo Times daily ad, however, you should make sure to check dates inasmuch as Philip's review might come after the book has been published. But since it is assured, perhaps you could use some sort of line like "from a forthcoming review in The New York Review of Books." I leave it up to you.

B

The Confessions of Nat Turner *was published by Random House on October 9, 1967.*

To Pamela Marke†

November 6, 1967‡ Paris, France

Dear Miss Marke:

The books I would give Susanna for the Utopian Society on that distant planet might be:

* Philip Rahv, "Through the Midst of Jerusalem," *The New York Review of Books* (October 26, 1967).

† Marke was an editor at *The New York Times Book Review.*

‡ Styron's response, along with one from his eldest daughter, Susanna, was published in "Books to Send to a Distant Planet," *The New York Times Book Review,* December 3, 1967.

1st—A one-volume edition of the complete Greek drama, for its tragedy and laughter;

2nd—A revised edition of HOYLE'S GAMES, for the necessary bulwark against ennui;

3rd—(and I'm at a loss here) Either the U.S. ARMY SURVIVAL MANUAL or Rombauer & Becker's NEW JOY OF COOKING, each of which explains with precision certain techniques fundamental to existence, if not to the elegant life.

Sincerely,
William Styron

To William Blackburn

November 29, 1967 Roxbury, CT

Dear Professor:

Unfortunately, it looks as if I will be unable to get down to the affair in Greensboro, and hence that means that I also would be unable to participate in anything at Duke on the 12th of February (although your surmise is accurate: I've heard nothing from the Duke people either, so I don't suppose I would have been invited anyway). I do hope to get down to Durham before too long on a private visit, though. I have tentative plans to go to Cuba early in January on some sort of writers' junket sponsored by a thawing-out Castro and I'm hoping that maybe on the way back I could stop both in Durham and in Va. But all this is pretty tentative.

Thanks for the kind words about Nat. It seems to be doing extremely well; Mr. Cerf told me the other day that sales are approaching 100,000 which is, as they say, real fine for a book only published six weeks. I don't know if I told you that the book was sold to the movies for a record amount, $600,000, most of which goes to pursue the war in Vietnam but still enough to keep me in sour mash for the next couple of years. These are commercial items of news, but I cannot help but find them fascinating nonetheless. I don't know if you saw the recent review by George Steiner or the one in the Nov. Commentary by John Thompson; along with Rahv's piece in the NY Review they comprise the most intelligent appraisals of the book so far.* Many of the others have been favorable enough though rather stupid.

I hope you will tell Bill Hamilton that, grateful as I am for the gesture, I would really not want an honorary degree from Duke. I was about to say any institution, but this would not be quite truthful for in fact I was just awarded something called the Doctor of Humanities degree by Wilberforce University in Ohio.† Lest I sound inconsistent, I must add that Wilberforce (unless you didn't know, which I didn't) is the oldest Negro college in the USA; the president of the school had read Nat and had been impressed, and to have turned down the degree (plus an invitation to deliver the Fall Convocation address) would have seemed a studied slight on my part. Besides, I was very touched by this particular honor, its context, etc. But otherwise I simply do not believe in honorary degrees—from Duke or Yale or Princeton or wherever, at least for a writer. There is a formal, burlesque quality about such degrees that Mencken used to poke such fun at, and I'm rather in agreement with him. It has, you understand, nothing at all in particular to do with my feelings about Duke; it is rather a matter of general principle, and I hope you can get the word slyly to Bill Hamilton and that he will understand.

I hope all goes well with you and that you are relaxed and happy with the lighter schedule. I'll be calling or writing you in the near future about (in fond hope) a flying visit to Durms.

All best to you.

Yrs ever

—B.S.

* George Steiner, "The Fire Last Time," *The New Yorker* (November 25, 1967); John Thompson, "William Styron," *Commentary,* vol. 44, no. 5 (November 1967).

† Styron was awarded the degree by Wilberforce on November 21, 1967. He recounted the experience in "Nat Turner Revisited," *American Heritage* (October 1992).

To Lew Allen

December 27, 1967 Roxbury, CT

Dear Lewie + Jay:

The Bodyscope and the Love plaque were the only lovely gifts I received out of all the tons of execrable junk that descended on me this Yuletide. They are both truly an inspiration and are hanging now, of course in my downstairs narcissistic bathroom.* I will ever be grateful for this remembrance, especially the Bodyscope which, whenever I enter the sanctuary, is always mysteriously turned to either "male" or "female genitalia."

Love + happy New Year.
—B

"Nat" has just hit 115,000—all white customers.

To Robert Penn Warren

January 13, 1968 Roxbury, CT

Dear Red:

I have nothing but the highest regard for the way you have touted my daughter and your god-daughter on to Milton Academy and I only hope she doesn't end up caught with pot or LSD or something that might besmirch your reputation.

The poem on Audubon is truly fine, one of your loveliest. I'd love to see the others on him. We must get together soon since it has been all too long.

Your Russian translator's name is Victor Golishev, Tishinskaia Sq. 6, Apt. 11, Moscow D-56, U.S.S.R. I'm sure he would be tickled pink, as they say, if you dropped him a note.

À bientôt,
Bill

* The bathroom in the Styron home where many of Bill's awards were displayed.

To James Jones

January 17, 1968 Roxbury, CT

Dear Jim:

This is what may happen to you, too, if you incur Max Geismar's displeasure.* He wrote this in a shabby little Stalinist organ called Minority of One. Watch out, you may be next! Love to all—B.

To James and Gloria Jones

[Unknown] 1968† English Harbour, Antigua, West Indies

Dear James and Moss:

Me and Rose are cruising with Mike Nichols on Joe Levine's 95-foot Jewish cocktail yacht complete with wall-to-wall carpeting in the bathrooms, shocking pink toilet seats, tape recorders in every room and a free blowjob every day before breakfast (you have to pay 25¢ for that, though). Down to Guadeloupe tomorrow where we hope to pick up a few French groceries. Get this: I have an acting part in Mike's movie version of "Catch-22."‡ If you want a part too, let me know; I think you might be a sadistic officer like me. Moss could be either a nurse or a whore.

I see Widow-Maker is high on the paperback lists in N.Y. Thornton Wilder§ won the National Book Award; I guess us young squirts just don't have the stuff.

—À bientôt Bill

* In "Styron's Golem" (*The Minority of One,* December 1967), Geismar wrote, "It has already been decreed, for example, by all these interlocking cultural institutions—from the publishers and the Book Clubs to the critics and *The New York Times* reviewers—that William Styron's *Confessions of Nat Turner,* a rich and ripe if not fruity product of the Plantation School of Southern Liberals, is to be *the* book of the year . . . only a Virginia gentleman who has grown up with the Southern Negro and who speaks his language can dare to penetrate his servile heart."

† Postcard is inscribed "Aboard the Rosalie L."

‡ The film was released in 1970; Styron did not appear in the final cut.

§ Thornton Niven Wilder (1897–1975), American playwright and novelist. His novel *The Eighth Day* (1967) won the National Book Award.

To Mike Mewshaw

April 6, 1968 Roxbury, CT

Dear Mike:

I'm awful sorry not to have answered your kind letter about Nat Turner sooner—I appreciated your words enormously; I've been abominably busy of late, having had to go to Hollywood to "consult," whatever that means, on the film version of the book (that is some scene) and then, recently to Milwaukee to look in on McCarthy at the Wisconsin primaries (I'm a delegate with Arthur Miller to the Conn. convention, both of us for McCarthy).*

I'm delighted you got the Fulbright and I'm sure that you will swing in Paris; it still is one of my favorite places, and I've never found it anti-American, really, at all; the French are just a bit individualistically chilly and aloof (although by no means all of them) and Americans want people to slobber all over them like dogs. I've made a note to write to Jim Jones about you and to make the proper introduction; I think you'll like him and Gloria a lot. But since you aren't leaving for France until next fall it may be best for you to refresh my memory on this matter later on this summer; certainly it'll be fresher in his memory if I write to him about you more or less around the time you plan to arrive in Paris.

My agent, like Donadio, is not taking on anyone new at the moment, but she may change her program this summer; I'll let you know.† In the meantime, I'll sniff the situation in New York and see if I can come up with some other agent for you.

Nat has just passed 150,000 copies, which of course pleases me. I never thought it would do that good. I envy you the Va. weather, but it'll be here soon too. My best to old Slim.

PS: I've re-read your fine analysis of Nat and find it very insightful.

Yrs ever

Bill

* Eugene McCarthy (1916–2005) was a U.S senator who sought the Democratic Party presidential nomination in 1968 on an anti–Vietnam War platform.

† Candida Donadio (1930–2001), literary agent with McIntosh and McKee before founding her own agency in 1969. Donadio represented Peter Matthiessen, Joseph Heller, and Philip Roth, among others.

Also I'm sorry about not responding to the invitation to come to Va. this spring. Somehow I just lost track of it and all of a sudden spring was here and it was too late.

To Hope Leresche

April 18, 1968 Roxbury, CT

Dear Hope:

Thanks so much for the very informative letter and news of the nice amount of money coming in from all over.

I really don't know if I can make it to London, due to a crowded schedule over here. Just <u>possibly</u> I may be able to come to London between the seventh of May and the fourteenth, but I really can't be more definite than that at the moment. The book over here has slipped from its #1 spot on the list but is still doing well and I think has passed 160,000 or thereabouts. There is a lot of agitation among the left-wing Negroes here, who have concluded that <u>Nat Turner</u> is distorted history and racist and all that; they've kicked up a minor tempest in Hollywood, threatening to boycott the film version and picket, but I think it will blow over. Martin Luther King read the book just before his death, and admired it very much. We are going to get an endorsement to that effect from his widow, which I think will pretty much squelch the opposition. A Negro playwright, Louis Peterson, is doing the screenplay and is off to a good start. I was out in Hollywood a few weeks ago and was much impressed by the director (with whom I did a rough treatment), Norman Jewison—his last film, <u>In the Heat of the Night</u>, you may have seen won the Academy Award.

The Cape edition arrived safe and sound and is very handsome; my thanks. Also thanks for news of the varied publicity the book will be getting. I hope it will do well.

Faithfully,

<u>Bill</u>

To William Blackburn

April 19, 1968 Roxbury, CT

Dear Professor:

I am 6'0", weigh a svelte 167#, and have a head size of 7 1/4". I hope they outfit me in something fancy.*

By June I will be able to show you an amazing book, published by Beacon Press, called William Styron's Nat Turner: Ten Negro Writers Respond. I've read the galleys and it is one long hysterical polemic from beginning to end: I'm a racist, a distorter of history, a defamer of black people, a traducer of the heroic image of "our" Nat Turner. The whole thing is a wildly contradictory diatribe, damning me for making Nat too brutal, at the same time too timorous. The whole thing utterly failing to understand the purposes of literature. Incidentally, you might look up the current issue of the Nation for an exchange of letters between me and Herbert Aptheker, the Communist theologian, in regard to the question of Nat. I think I did a fairly good job of rebutting his dreary charges. The colored folk are on the verge of losing all the decent allies they ever had.

I'll be there to lunch after the Commencement and am looking forward eagerly to the whole week-end—as does Rose.

Yours ever,

Bill

To Louis D. Rubin, Jr.

May 1, 1968 Roxbury, CT

Dear Louis:

A long time ago I might have gotten very upset by Gilman's piece, but it is so obviously the work of a pompous literary politician rather than a critic that it left me fairly indifferent.† It is also so appallingly subliterate in terms of such simple things as grammar that it vitiated itself before it

* Styron received an honorary doctorate from Duke in the spring of 1968.

† Richard Gilman, "Nat Turner Revisited," *The New Republic* (April 27, 1968).

even got started. I think the worst thing about it, though, was its terrible naivete—that is, his allying himself with the Black Power people who are calling the book distorted, perverted, historically inaccurate, etc. He apparently does not have enough real critical competence to understand even the basic essentials about the inter-relationship of history and literature, the artist's freedom to deal as he likes with historical matters, and so on. By Gilman's implied criteria, a book like War and Peace would be an irresponsible fraud. But it is a poor piece of writing and the kind of thing that will necessarily rebound upon him sooner or later.

It was good of you to trouble to write the letter, you made some excellent points, and if Gilman reads it—which I expect he will—I rather imagine he will be squirming. Thanks for sending me the copy.

I'm looking forward to my trip to Durham on June 1 and to seeing you all.

Best,

Bill

Styron was notified that he had won the Pulitzer Prize for fiction.

To Arthur Schlesinger, Jr.

May 15, 1968 Roxbury, CT

Dear Arthur:

I see by today's Times that Praeger and Dutton have agreed not to publish Solzhenitsyn's book, so it looks as if that problem is taken care of.*

I regret we missed (by a few minutes) getting together in Roxbury the other day but I'm looking forward to a tête-à-tête before too long. The

* Schlesinger had written Styron on May 13 asking him to join George Kennan in signing a letter protesting the international publication of Aleksandr Solzhenitsyn's writings, which they felt would mute their impact in the Soviet Union.

Black Panthers are after me but Gene Genovese is going to cook their goose in a forthcoming N.Y. Review of Books piece.*

As ever,

Bill

To Dr. Fredric Wertham†

June 18, 1968 Roxbury, CT

Dear Dr. Wertham:

I have before me a transcript of a section of Newsfront, a television program on which you appeared on the night of June 5th, and during which you made several remarks about my novel, The Confessions of Nat Turner. I did not see this program but several people reported to me, in some chagrin and distress, that you said what the transcript does indeed verify. Your words, among others, were "Now all the intellectuals and reviewers, they praise this book The Confessions of Nat Turner—that's an invitation for lynching and I have talked to many people about it who have read it. I have gone over it—this is—we teach the people to lynch. We tell them this is a good thing."

Ordinarily I would not respond to your words, nor to anything written or spoken about my book, but I found it especially disturbing in the aftermath of the Kennedy assassination that you should choose to speak in this way about my work and link it—by implication at least—to the atmosphere of violence which surrounds us and which I deplore as vehemently as you do. From what you said, I cannot tell whether you have read The Confessions of Nat Turner or not—if not, I suggest that you do. But if you have read the book I find it even more upsetting that an authority of your reputation should find within its pages "an invitation for lynching." Inasmuch as no responsible literary critic (and this includes presumably the

* Eugene D. Genovese, "The Nat Turner Case," *The New York Review of Books* (September 12, 1968).

† Wertham (1895–1981) was a psychiatrist who became rather infamous for his crusade against violent imagery in the mass media, and particularly comic books.

distinguished body that awarded the book the Pulitzer Prize) discovered any such incitement to violence in the novel, I find your charge reckless and without foundation.

For years you have distinguished yourself by your sound and well-reasoned attacks on the proliferation of senseless violence in the mass media. I find it all the more painful, therefore, to have to deplore your totally unsubstantiated charge about a work of literature. There is some violence in The Confessions of Nat Turner but it is certainly but a single facet of the work as a whole and in no way dominates the book; nor is the violence purely gratuitous, any more than the violence is gratuitous in the works of Sophocles or of Shakespeare and the Elizabethans (indeed it is far less gratuitous than, let us say, some of Webster) or the novels of Dostoievski.

I am as appalled as you are by the senseless violence on television and the movies, in comic books and other forms of the mass media. But I think that an authority of your distinction is completely overstepping the bounds of his influence, or at least of good judgment, in so facilely equating a book which has been universally judged in terms of the canons of art with that gutter pornography which does in truth comprise "an invitation for lynching." If psychiatrists like yourself seemingly relinquish the desire or the ability—perhaps both—to discriminate between literature and trash and under the aegis of television, with its enormous influence, fall into the habit of damning literature for that strain of violence which has been an integral part of narrative art ever since Homer, then you run the risk of not only a woeful philistinism but the even greater danger of falling into the posture of advocating what should or should not be in a book. This is a danger as ominous as the violence you deplore.

I knew Senator Kennedy and stood vigil beside his coffin in St. Patrick's Cathedral. He was an early and profound admirer of The Confessions of Nat Turner, and I am sure he would not have appreciated your totally unwarranted remarks about the book. It is largely because the remarks you made about the novel came during the grave and inflammatory hours following his death that I attach such significance to them, and write you now, asking that you elaborate upon or explain what you mean by this very serious charge. The spoken word is of course quite often not a very accurate means of communication, and it may be that the various people who heard you and spoke to me about it have misconstrued your remarks, just as I may have misread the rather disconnected transcript I have at hand. This constitutes all the more reason why I must request most seriously that you explain in just what fashion The Confessions of Nat Turner comprises an "invitation for lynching."

Very truly yours,
William Styron

To James and Gloria Jones

June 19, 1968 Roxbury, CT

Dear James and Moss:

. . . We have been thinking a lot about you during the recent troubles and figured that you had escaped harm, otherwise it would be in the newspapers.*

I went out to Oregon and California to campaign for McCarthy with Arthur Miller, Cal Lowell and Jules Feiffer. We of course won in Oregon but then as soon as I got back here Kennedy was murdered. A ghastly time. I stood vigil at his coffin in St. Patrick's cathedral (along with, of all people, Gen. Maxwell Taylor the super-hawk and Mortimer Caplin, the Director of the Internal Revenue Service; they both had their eye on me, I felt); and then went to the funeral mass the next day. It was a terrible time. I think the world has gone totally cuckoo.†

We are very glad to hear that you are coming over. Give me a call as soon as you arrive; we will be in Vineyard Haven then, tel. 693-2535, also listed in Vineyard Haven information. Anytime you can come up for a visit will be perfect for me. Don't fail to keep in touch. The U.S. + A. is in bad trouble and maybe no worse than anywhere else, so maybe you'll find it pleasant this summer, even in Pottsville.‡ I hope so.

We all send much love—
Bill

* Styron refers to the riots that began in May of 1968 and continued through Bastille Day.

† General Taylor (1901–87) was appointed to the Joint Chiefs of Staff by John F. Kennedy in October 1962. Mortimer Caplin (b. 1916) was U.S. Commissioner of Internal Revenue (1961–64).

‡ Pottsville, Pennsylvania, was Gloria's hometown.

To William Blackburn

June 25, 1968 Roxbury, CT

Dear Professor:

Before taking off for the Vineyard, I wanted to thank you (on Rose's behalf too) for the splendid hospitality you and Roma offered us during our all-too-brief stay in Durms. We had a lovely time, your house is truly charming, and please tell Roma how much we appreciate all she did for us. It was good seeing the old gang again, smelling the Proustian scent of tobacco, and revisiting the old scenes.

The days after our departure from Duke were pretty hectic, what with the Kennedy monstrosity and all that.* The day after it happened I got a call from George Plimpton (who had wrestled the gun out of the assassin's hand) asking me to stand vigil by the coffin in St. Patrick's, so I did (in heat hotter than that in Durham), an unbelievable scene with solemn and/or hysterical mourners filing by; the funeral the next day was also most impressive though it filled me with devastating gloom. What a weird and tragic country we live in.

I hope our paths will intersect up here before too long. It was good seeing you again and meeting Roma at last. My very best to her, and Rose joins in sending warm greetings to you and all.

As ever,

Bill S., D. Lit.

To Larry L. King

June 29, 1968 Vineyard Haven, MA

Dear Larry,

I thank you for your card about the crazy professor who was putting down my black boy on television. His name is Doctor Fredric Wertham—a self-professed expert on violence who has made a living for 20 years

* The assassination of Robert F. Kennedy.

lambasting Comic books.* Several other people mentioned that program to me and I have registered a very stiff protest.

I love your piece on Nashville in Harper's.† I think you captured the whole scene beautifully, and I am sending the article to all my friends for whom country music is the cup of life.

I hope things are not too rugged for you at the moment. I am thinking of you, and I trust that, in due time, we shall be able to lay hold of some wet goods with Willie and The Boys.

I also belatedly read your piece on Faulkner—a first-rate job, I thought, enormously evocative, very touching, at the end especially.‡ I hope Holiday realizes how lucky they are to get an article as good as this.

Take care of yourself. I hope to see you soon.

All best wishes,
Bill

To Eugene Genovese§

July 2, 1968 Vineyard Haven, MA

Dear Gene:

I got the review today and just wanted to send you a brief note to tell you that I think it's absolutely brilliant. Although you pulverized them, you did it with a certain gentility that I admire and I send my heartiest bravos.

I think it's going to be an important essay over and above what it says about my book. You hit the nail on the head in the last two paragraphs, and your words to the effect that the book needs to be taken with profound seriousness is dead on target.

* See Styron's letter of June 18, 1968.

† Larry L. King, "The Grand Ole Opry," *Harper's Magazine* (July 1968).

‡ Larry L. King, "Requiem for Faulkner's Home Town," *Holiday* (March 1969).

§ This is the only extant letter from Styron to Genovese, a rare typescript from a short period where Styron typed his outgoing mail. Genovese destroyed all of his correspondence in the 1990s.

I will have more to say to you later about this splendid review, and I cannot help but feel that Silvers will be enormously enthusiastic about the light that you have cast on the psyche of part of the contemporary black intelligentsia.

Bravo for you, again. Hope to see you soon.

Aguri,

Bill

To Mr. Jim Wiggins

July 30, 1968 Vineyard Haven, MA

Dear Mr. Wiggins:

Mr. Styron would like to thank you for your letter, and for your interest in obtaining a signed photograph of him.

Unfortunately, it is not his practice to send out photographs of himself, and he hopes that you will understand that he cannot make an exception, at this time.

In the meantime, you have his warmest regards, and again, his thanks.

Most sincerely,

Secretary to William Styron*

To John Updike

August 13, 1968 Vineyard Haven, MA

Dear John,

Sorry not to have made it to the beach the other night. My enthusiasm for N.Y. alas tends towards zero, or below, and I have informed Plimpton of our common reluctance. Hope to see you at the Friday night McCarthy Mini-Gala, or whatever it's called. Yours, B.S.

* Styron never employed a secretary, but frequently used the ruse to get rid of various inquiries.

To Robert Penn Warren

August 26, 1968 Essex Inn, Chicago, IL

Dear Red:

I enjoyed your letter, which I received before coming out here to the convention; I'm covering the ghastly event for The N.Y. Review of Books and have credentials and all that but am so appalled by the scene that by the time you get this I may have packed up and gone back to the Vineyard.* I came out here last Tuesday to be a "challenging" McCarthy delegate from Conn., presenting myself with 3 others before the Credentials Committee—all in unbelievably 95° heat and the whole try unsuccessful. Then I flew back for a few days to the Vineyard, thence on Saturday to Washington to fly in to Chicago (with Cal Lowell) on McCarthy's plane. More travel than I ever thought I would do in a single week.

This place is a raving lunatic asylum—thousands and thousands of people jammed into hotel lobbies and rooms and bars, the whole scene rimmed by more police in baby blue shirts than you could ever imagine and of course the hippies. Big demonstration just now outside my window, which overlooks the park in front of the Conrad Hilton, where most of the action is. A brutal, crazy scene really—America at its best and worst—and I hope I bear up under the assault. But good weather now.

Good to hear about the progress on both of your novels and about the children. I'll be back on the Vineyard around Thursday of this week and we'll stay until the 14th of Sept., I believe. It will be lovely to see you again in Conn.

Thanks for your kind words about my 10 black critics. Kindly keep an eye out for the next N.Y. Review of Books, which has a devastating review of the volume by Gene Genovese.

Love to all and à bientôt

Bill

* Styron was covering the Democratic National Convention. His article, "In the Jungle," *The New York Review of Books* (September 26, 1968), was collected in *This Quiet Dust.*

To James and Gloria Jones

September 25, 1968 Tashkent, Uzbekistan, U.S.S.R.

Dear James and Moss: Me and my wife are enjoying ourselves here in Central Asia. The Uzbek S.S.R. is a little like Oz, with a lady president, wild tribesmen in the streets, the city very clean and modern though, and better fruits and melons than France even. We have seen a lot of Yevtushenko and tomorrow go to Samarkand and then to Siberia (Lake Baikal), afterwards Moscow and Leningrad.* We are leaving Russia by way of Finland and will try to call you from Helsinki on Oct. 7th. Flying to Paris on Oct. 8th. Hope you don't mind if me and my frau Rose stay with you for a few days.

Love, Bill

or get a hotel room if you're complet

To Publisher, The Beacon Press

October 22, 1968 Roxbury, CT

Dear Sir:

I returned from a long trip abroad to discover that Beacon Press—in an advertisement for William Styron's Nat Turner: Ten Black Writers Respond in both The New Republic and The New York Review of Books—has used the following line: "Black critics reply to Styron's bestseller with rage and contempt for its racist bias, factual distortion, and the increase in mistrust it has engendered."

While it may be legitimate to express sentiments like these in a critical essay or essays, it is quite another matter when such a statement is employed without corroboration in a public advertisement, worded so as to leave the distinct impression that the accusation is true. At the very least it violates all ethical standards of book advertising; in actuality it is a scandalous falsehood.

* Yevgeny Aleksandrovich Yevtushenko (b. 1933), Russian poet and filmmaker who gained great acclaim in Russia and abroad beginning in the 1950s.

This is to notify you that if in the future any such advertisement is repeated in any manner whatever in public print I shall not hesitate to prosecute Beacon Press for libel to the fullest extent of which I am capable.

Yours truly,

William Styron

Unless I can receive some immediate assurance that this advertisement with its present wording will not be repeated in the future, I will have to take steps to make sure that I am protected from such unfair misrepresentation.

To Arthur Schlesinger, Jr.

November 11, 1968 Roxbury, CT

Dear Arthur: Thanks for the clip from the Pilot. I had read Thomas Merton's piece—a disgraceful display of white liberal guilt and piety.* I have sent that clipping and your fine nationalism essay to the archives at Duke University, which is accumulating a mass of material about the "controversy" that in volume almost approaches the to-do over The Origin of Species.

As ever, Bill

To William Blackburn

November 14, 1968 Roxbury, CT

Dear Professor:

Under separate cover I'm sending you a tape recording of an interview I did last summer (by telephone from the Vineyard) with Mike Wallace for his CBS network radio show—the other participant being my per-

* Thomas Merton, "Who Is Nat Turner?" *Katallagete* (Spring 1968). Merton (1915–68), a Catholic monk, wrote nearly seventy books.

petual bête noire, the nigra actor Ossie Davis.* I never heard the original show or the tape but it was broadcast and thought it might be an interesting if aural contribution to the bibliography over the Nat Turner controversy, which still continues, and which, as someone has said, has approached in volume and passion the uproar over The Origin of Species.

A bug laid me low after coming back from Russia but not enough to prevent me from going, last week, to New Orleans, where with Vann Woodward, R. P. Warren + Ralph Ellison, I was on a panel before 1,500 members of the Southern Historical Assoc.† I was also heckled, as usual, by Black Power representatives—imagine!—in New Orleans—but acquitted myself with restrained rage. Am now holed in here for a while to do the piece on Russia for The N.Y. Review.

How go things in Durms? Rose joins in sending fond regards to you and Roma.

As ever,

B.S.

To Willie Morris

December, 1968‡ Roxbury, CT

Naturally, Willie, it has occurred to me that you also "as a leader, are in a position to know and recommend exceptional individuals." Should this

* Ossie Davis (1917–2005) was an Emmy Award–winning stage, film, and television actor known for his social activism.

† The panel, "The Uses of History in Fiction," was a discussion among Styron, Ralph Ellison, Robert Penn Warren, and C. Vann Woodward at the Southern Historical Association meeting in New Orleans on November 6, 1968. The transcript was published in *The Southern Literary Journal* (Spring 1969) and in James L. W. West III, ed., *Conversations with William Styron.*

‡ Styron's note appears on a copy of a letter of December 2, 1968, to Styron from "President Richard M. Nixon." Willie Morris was very fond of playing pranks on Styron and had found some vaguely authentic looking letterhead with a letter asking Styron to "recommend exceptional individuals." Morris's Nixon wanted "the best minds in America to meet the challenges of this rapidly changing world. To find them, I ask for your active participation and assistance."

politician come your way, I would indeed appreciate your writing me in for, say, oh, Governor of the Virgin Islands, a federal post.

Thanks,

Bill

To Yale W. Richmond*

December 13, 1968 Roxbury, CT

Dear Mr. Richmond:

Thank you for sending me the Aptheker review of The Confessions of Nat Turner from "Literaturnaya Gazetta." I have shown the piece to a friend of mine who knows Russian, and although she did not break down the essay in detail she told me enough about it to make it clear that this was a translation of an attack on the book published here some months ago. If you have followed the controversy surrounding the book—which you doubtless have—you may realize that it is an almost totally illogical and propagandistic attack, and although I am sorry that the article had to be published so prominently in the Soviet Union I am really terribly weary of the whole matter and put my trust in the belief that the work will ultimately survive such slanders. Too bad that Russian readers have not been able to read (at least in translation) the piece in the September 12, 1968 issue of The New York Review of Books by Prof. Eugene Genovese—a Marxist who is also a much better historian than Aptheker—which very cleanly and reasonably demolishes all the incredible charges which have been laid against Nat Turner. Anyway, thank you again for sending the piece along. And needless to say I would be grateful to you if you would be so kind as to send me anything of a similar nature on the subject which might come to your attention.

Sincerely,

William Styron

* Richmond was the Counselor for Cultural Affairs at the U.S. Embassy in Moscow.

Styron began work on his never-finished novel, The Way of the Warrior, *in 1969.*

To James and Gloria Jones

April 16, 1969 Roxbury, CT

Dear James and Moss:

I had a particularly fine time with you all in Paris and I thank you bottomlessly for—once again—putting up with horny Uncle Bill. I had a minor crise at Orly with Annie* when I ran into that Swedish girl (Jessie's friend) who suggested that when I come back to Paris "we do something together," whatever that means. Like John Marquand suggested, I'd better cut it off, and hang around the post office like those old geezers in baseball caps. I've tried saltpeter but it just makes my balls itch.

I'm enclosing this excellent piece from the new Atlantic.† It's what some of us have been thinking and saying for a long time and it's fascinating that such an article could come from a Marine Corps general.

I've seen quite a bit of Henry Hyde‡ who sends his best. Do try to come over here this summer and be my guest. I'll furnish all the hash.

Love from everybody,
Bill

* Annie Brierre, an editor at Gallimard.

† General David M. Schoup, "The New American Militarism," *The Atlantic Monthly,* April 1969. The article caused quite a stir, blaming the Vietnam War largely on "pervasive American militarism and inter-service rivalry." See Howard Jablon, *David M. Schoup: A Warrior Against War* (Lanham, MD: Rowman and Littlefield, 2005), 109.

‡ Henry Hyde (1915–97) was a lawyer and American spy who played an essential role in the D-Day landing. See Joseph Persico, *Piercing the Reich* (1997), and Anthony Brown, *The Last Hero: Wild Bill Donovan* (1982).

To Lillian Hellman

June 5, 1969 Roxbury, CT

Dear Lil,

I finished reading An Unfinished Woman early yesterday.* I read it slowly: for some reason it was a book one could not simply breeze through, despite the clarity and ease (and wit) of the style, and I want to say how moved and how impressed I was by all the life, love, joy, pain, and honest truth you have compressed into those eloquent pages. Usually an account like this, anecdotal in nature, ends up being just that: a series of anecdotes which may or may not be memorable. But through some artful process—the art, I should hasten to say, of a fine story-teller—you have made of the remembrance an illuminating and coherent whole, full of wonderful resonances. It is all beautifully proportioned and balanced and the tone is just right—ironic without being cynical and with a detachment that is never once undermined by your honest concern for all the people—decent, indecent and in between—whose paths crossed yours during those crazy years.

Your sense of place is as obviously vivid and exact as is your ability to recapture a person. I was as much at home with your fine portraits of Liveright and Hemingway and various minor Spaniards and Russians (none of whom of course I knew), and with Hammett and Dottie Parker (whom I knew a little) and with Raya and Helena and Elena (whom I knew more) as I was instantly at home with your lovely evocative scenes of Pleasantville and Southern California (though lovely is not the word, you did it up as nightmarishly as Pep West†) and Spain during that war . . . where it is a wonder you didn't lay your bones.‡ Your sketch of Madjanek, for instance,

* Hellman's first memoir, published in 1969.

† Nathanael West (1903–40), American novelist and screenwriter, author of *Miss Lonelyhearts* and *The Day of the Locust*.

‡ Styron refers to Dashiell Hammett (1894–1961), a writer known for his novels *The Maltese Falcon, The Thin Man,* and *Red Harvest,* and Dorothy Parker (1893–1967), a writer and satirist known for her contributions to *The New Yorker* and as a founder of the Algonquin Round Table. Dorothy is not to be confused with Didi Parker, Styron's coworker and correspondent of the late 1940s and early 1950s. The Russian-born Raya Orlova was a close friend of Hellman who translated many of her plays. Helena Golisheva and Elena Levin were other Russian friends.

is superb precisely for the very reason that you saw fit to leave so much of its horror out. But there is also so much of the book that is truly slyly hilarious and wisely and deliciously knowledgeable about all the poor fucked-up people who pass our way, without ever once being knowing, which is a different, lesser thing.

My congratulations and love for such a good-spirited, compassionate, exhilarating book.

Bill

To James and Gloria Jones

June 8, 1969 Roxbury, CT

Dear James + Moss:

. . . Everything O.K. here. Henry Hyde just made me $500,000 in RCA stock by way of Random House so I thank you for putting us together. Now all I have to figure out is how to get out of hock to Henry.

I hate to spring another stranger on you—but this guy is very nice. Name is Richard Yates, wrote a fine first novel called Revolutionary Road several years ago and is an all-round swell cat.* He and his wife will probably turn up in Paris in July and if you're there I hope you'll give them a drink if they call you. Though I imagine you'll be in the provinces. He has been teaching in the writing program at the Univ. of Iowa.

Love to all

Bill

Life is a big put-on. I am beginning to detest almost everything—especially (continued in next letter)†

* Styron called *Revolutionary Road* "a deft, ironic, beautiful novel that deserves to be a classic." Yates (1926–92) wrote a screenplay of *Lie Down in Darkness* in 1962.

† Styron wrote a nearly identical letter to Jones on June 24, calling Yates "a capital fellow." He also mentioned Henry Hyde procuring "a 2-book contract with Random House for 11,500 shares of RCA stock—worth a cool $500,000. I'm glad you got us together."

To William Blackburn

September 28, 1969 Roxbury, CT

Dear Professor:

I finally got around to reading the essays in the South Atlantic Quarterly and while, like you, I wonder why they bothered to publish them for the edification of all 35 of the quarterly's readers, I found them innocuous enough.* Actually, the most favorable one was by the Duke history professor; it was a poor essay in every respect—rudimentary and badly written—but for the most part was on my side. Too bad he didn't make a little better sense. The one by Nash Burger (lately of The N.Y. Times Book Review) was rather pathetic, putting me down in the most ignorant and clumsy way, saying that I betrayed the nobleness of the Old South and comparing me most unfavorably with Stark Young and So Red the Rose.† The nastiest of the three was by the English teacher at, I believe, Hunter College. But I have belatedly discovered that there are certain people on the fringes of literature and the arts who react like a maddened alligator to anyone who is at all successful, and this fellow betrayed himself from the beginning by a terrible lurking envy. Such characters almost always give themselves away in a review by frantically summoning up critics who have also attacked the work at hand—in this case he quoted Richard Gilman and Stanley Kauffmann—and the final effect was one of ineptitude and irrational thinking, and I'm sure he did himself and the SAQ more harm than he did me. Besides, I am by now probably the most adept writer in America at dodging brickbats, and so the essays caused me very little bother.

I was of course very flattered at your proposal that a collection—with you at the helm—be made of my letters. But after the soberest thought I've come to believe that there is something embarrassing and even inappropriate about letters being published while their author is still alive. Certainly I have heard of very few precedents—if any—of volumes of letters of writers being done while the writer is still kicking and, in my

* A special issue on William Styron: *South Atlantic Quarterly* 68 (1969).

† Young's 1934 novel about Civil War Mississippi is considered a classic of the moonlight-and-magnolias school.

case, if I can permit myself a hope, still possessed of enough stamina to go along for a few decades more.

The brief note you wrote me later made me think that you too had had second thoughts about this matter. Certainly the idea is an interesting one, and there may indeed be quite a few readers who have cared for my work who would be intrigued by reading some of these early epistles. But there is something really awfully private about any kind of letter. The death of a person certainly renders that privacy no longer so inviolate (even so I notice that Mencken, for instance, has forbidden certain of his letters to be published until 1991), and when the worms have gotten after me I really don't care too much whether anything I wrote in a letter is revealed. Meanwhile, I'd just prefer them to yellow nicely at Duke and to ultimately be a pasture for some graduate student—probably black, female, and filled with vengeance.

Teddy Kennedy appeared on my lawn up at the Vineyard last Saturday—you could have knocked me over with a splinter from the Chappaquiddick bridge. He had sailed over with wife Joan from Hyannis and simply popped in for a 2-hour visit then disappeared as mysteriously as he had come. Surprisingly, he looked in fantastic good shape, and I could not avoid feeling that he would be Our Man for sure in 1972—except for that incident.

My step-mother died three weeks ago, and my father is coming up here for a long visit. Says he is rooted in Newport News and doesn't want to live with us permanently. He took her death with amazing strong spirit.

Hope all goes well with you, and that glaucoma you mentioned is well under control. Rose joins in sending our best to Roma and yourself.

As ever,

B.S.

To Harry Levin*

December 9, 1969 Roxbury, CT

Dear Harry:

Thank you for sending me your fascinating study on what I suppose has become the non-novel novel. Your reference to Nat Turner was greatly appreciated, since after all the brickbats I have received from the black brethren it is good to see your straightforward appreciation of the book as a novel rather than propaganda or anti-Negro or whatever. As always, your insights were subtle, astute and eloquent. My thanks again and I hope we can have an evening together before too long.

Sincerely,
Bill

To William Blackburn

February 5, 1970 Roxbury, CT

Dear Professor:

I did indeed receive the Mac Hyman letters and thought it was a truly fine and fascinating book—as Max Steele said, it does read like a novel. I also read Guy's excellent review in the Times and thought he acquitted himself very gracefully. I've lent my copy to Arthur Miller, who's very taken by Mac and his letters.

Best—Bill

* Harry Tuchman Levin (1912–94), American literary critic and scholar of modernism and comparative literature at Harvard University.

To Louis D. Rubin, Jr.

May 11, 1970 Roxbury, CT

Dear Louis:

I have only one or two reservations about George Core's essay on Nat Turner, which I think is the best single piece that has been written on the book.* You might be interested in knowing that Nat has received the Howells Medal (given once every 5 years) of the American Academy of Arts & Letters.† Faulkner & Eudora Welty won it, so the South still struggles along.

Best,

Bill

Styron received the Howells Medal for Fiction on May 26, 1970, from the American Academy of Arts and Letters.

To William Blackburn

December 3, 1970 Roxbury, CT

Dear Professor:

Those were really masterful photographs you did of Rose and me. It is true that I lack objectivity about this matter but the comments we have received from detached observers have been unanimously glowing. Thank

* George Core, "*The Confessions of Nat Turner* and the Burden of the Past," *The Southern Literary Journal* (Spring 1970).

† When Styron donated the physical Howells medal to Duke University on February 3, 1971, he wrote, "The medal is made largely of gold and worth, I am told, in the neighborhood of $400. Therefore it is not only not invaluable but probably not even irreplaceable, so it should be treated only with the same good care I'm sure you give to the rest of your material down there. I am told that if someone were to steal it he could only get about $125 at a pawn shop, so I do not think you should be overly concerned about its security. Actually, I would think it might make you a nice paperweight, and I would be delighted to think that you might use it as such."

you so much for sending them up here. If I haven't aged too much by then I intend to put the one of me on my next book jacket.

We still talk of the lovely time we had with you and Roma in Quebec. Everything from the weather to the people was superlative. It's odd how, as soon as we departed, all hell seemed to break loose in that tranquil appearing country. I hope I can visit you all again up there sometime. My memories of Magog are very warm.

In a weak moment I told the Archive boys that I would appear at the next W. Blackburn festival in the spring. I've been asked also to say a few sage words at Randolph-Macon College in Ashland, Va., so I've timed the two together—Randolph Macon on April 14th, Dooks on the 15th. I trust you will allow me to buy you and Roma a sumptuous dinner at the Little Acorn. I will be looking forward to this jaunt, not the least because it is still winter here at that time of year and it will be nice to smell the Carolina spring.

My father, as you may have heard, is planning at the age of 81 to take unto himself a wife; the ceremony is slated for Goldsboro in the middle of January.* She—who is 76—calls him "Dynamite" and he refers to her as "this girl I've been seeing." If there's any way I can pop over from Goldsboro I'll do so and let you know beforehand.

Meanwhile, blessed thanks again for the fine pictures and best love to Roma.

As ever,
Bill

* William C. Styron, Sr., married Eunice Edmondson, one of his former sweethearts, in January 1971.

To Jim and Gloria Jones

February 2, 1971 Roxbury, CT

Dear Jim and Moss:

This joke stationery was given to me at Christmas by Le Roi Jones.* We are announcing our engagement on Valentine's Day.

It seems that everyone has received an advance copy of Jim's book but me.† Why am I out in the cold. I read the fine excerpts in Esquire and Harper's and thought it truly fine stuff, Jim—some of your best writing with a technically controlled narrative drive. It's so good I guess I'll have to finish it even if I have to buy a copy. . . .

My work has been going O.K. but unspeakably slow as usual. I wish I could unplug the dam. But I do rather like what I've done so far and that's a consolation.

I really miss Paris. This is the longest I've been away from there (nearly 2 years) since 1958. Tell Annie I miss her too.

There's a whole long essay in a literary magazine called "Against Styron."‡ I guess I've arrived at last.

Don't ever accept an invitation to be judge of the National Book Award. Since we turned down "Love Story" I've heard about nothing else—a whole editorial in *The Washington Post* damning the judges, especially me.§ What a fucking country we live in. Connecticut is about to institute

* Stationery produced by Leo Carty for Anton Studios that Styron used ironically for correspondence to friends and family. The front has a portrait of a skinny, balding African American man. The front of the card reads: "Nat Turner: POWER OF SELF DETERMINATION." On the back of the card appears a brief biography: "NAT TURNER (1800–1831) Born in Southampton County, Virginia, Turner believed that God had appointed him a leader of his people. In February 1831, he led one of the first successful slave revolts, killing fifty-five white people. Turner was captured and hung but his fight for freedom will never be forgotten."

† James Jones, *The Merry Month of May* (New York: Delacorte, 1971), was a novel set during the 1968 student protests in Paris.

‡ The essay appears in Mark Spilka, ed., *Novel: A Forum on Fiction,* vol. 4, no. 2 (Winter 1971).

§ Styron referred to Erich Segal's immensely popular novel *Love Story* (1970). Styron attached a piece, "Not Literature," from the *Los Angeles Times,* January 23, 1971, in which he was quoted on the controversy: "[*Love Story*] is a banal book which simply doesn't qualify as literature. Simply by being on the list it would have demeaned the other books." The other judges for the 1971 award were author John Cheever, Maurice Dolbler (literary a state income tax (up to ¼ of the federal tax) so I guess I'll be moving over there soon.

Give my best to all the creeps.

Love,

Bill

To Donald Gallinger*

February 10, 1971 Roxbury, CT

Dear Mr. Gallinger—

Many thanks for your very warm and thoughtful letter. I wish I could answer your questions in detail but it has always been my practice to let that be the work of the critics, who are always eager to explain a writer's work. In regard to Nat Turner, however, I will say that the Negroes' reaction was racist: a writer, black or white, must be able to write about any human being of whatever color.

Sincerely

Wm Styron

editor of *The Providence Journal and Evening Bulletin*), John Leonard (editor of *The New York Times Book Review*), and critic and novelist Marya Mannes.

* Donald Gallinger (b. 1953) was seventeen years old when he wrote to Styron about *The Confessions of Nat Turner*. Inspired by Styron's reply and by a friendly postcard from John Updike ("I think you read me very well"), Gallinger eventually became a published writer. His novel *The Master Planets* (2008) examines the effects of a Polish woman's actions during World War II on her American family decades later.

To C. Vann Woodward

February 22, 1971 Roxbury, CT

Dear Vann:

In regard to your reply to Mr. Stuckey's attack on you, all I can say is that your patience, forbearance and good will are truly staggering if not monumental, and I don't know how you do it.*

In regard to Stuckey's attack on the historians who have defended me, his statement that they implied everywhere "that Styron knows more than anyone else about how slaves perceived their experiences" is pretty pathetic since none of them—not Gene, not Duberman—would ever have been so foolish as to say any such thing. It is typical of the hyperbole and hysteria that every black intellectual has used when trying to lambaste me, and tends to undercut their already feeble position even more. Stuckey just doesn't make the grade.

A lovely time the other night. Hope for more soon.

Right on!
Bill

To Philip Nobile†

June 9, 1971 Vineyard Haven, MA

Dear Mr. Nobile:

There were no hard feelings or differences of opinion involved in the fact that I have more or less stopped writing for The New York Review. It is simply because, although I am not averse to writing an occasional critical piece, criticism doesn't really interest me too much and that is why my

* Sterling Stuckey, "Twilight of Our Past: Reflections on the Origins of Black History," in John A. Williams and Charles F. Harris, eds., *Amistad 2: Writings on Black History and Culture* (New York: Random House, 1971).

† Nobile was an editor at *The New York Review of Books.* He wrote an account of the early days at the publication, in which he included portions of this letter from Styron. See *Intellectual Skywriting: Literary Politics and the New York Review of Books* (New York: Charterhouse, 1974).

work has not recently appeared there. Although I find the Review often long-winded and boring, I think it is an invaluable publication and wouldn't do without it.

On purely personal grounds I am especially appreciative of the fact that the Review published the historian Eugene D. Genovese's defense of The Confessions of Nat Turner against the black writers who attacked it, exposing their hysteric foolishness and paranoia for what it was. It was a bang-up job, and I don't know of many other publications which would have given the piece so much space, or in whose pages the essay would have received such serious and valuable attention.

Sincerely,

William Styron

To Don Congdon

June 30, 1971 Vineyard Haven, MA

Dear Don,

There are a few things that I wanted to outline to you about the movie script which I didn't go into over the telephone.

In the first place, neither I nor my collaborator John Marquand feel as I do, say, about the script of Nat Turner. There I felt that the whole thing was so much under the domination of Wolper and his accomplices that I couldn't really care less about how the movie turned out so long as I got that payment which you managed painfully to worm out of Wolper every January.* But with this new script we have a very proprietary feeling, a feeling based on the wish that this turn out to be as fine a movie as can be produced.† Had we not had this feeling, we would not have inaugurated the project. Nor would we have proceeded all on our own and upon complete speculation to finish it. Consequently we simply do not want to sell the script to the highest bidder and thereby lose control of the property.

* David Lloyd Wolper (1928–2010), an American television and film producer with a long list of credits, most notably the miniseries *Roots*.

† William Styron and John Phillips, "Dead!" *Esquire* (December 1973).

We want to participate in the production to the fullest extent possible in order that our vision of the story remain intact. This is what I do hope you keep in mind during negotiations for the property.

While it is at this point, to say the least, premature to consider casting, you should know that concerning an actress to play the part of Ruth Snyder we have a very positive idea. We have written the part from start to finish around a particular actress, Dorothy Tristan, whom we both know well.* We hold her talents in high regard. We haven't written a line for Ruth that we aren't sure she can deliver splendidly. Indeed our identification of the actress with the part is so strong that it becomes difficult to imagine Ruth being played by anyone else. We mean to make the strongest possible pitch for Dorothy.

Also I should tell you in greater detail the reasons for our very strong interest in Aram Avakian as producer. Avakian wants to buy an option on this screenplay. In order to insure our continued involvement in the project and our ability to influence the film to its final result, we believe we will not have a better opportunity than he has offered us. The most attractive aspect of Avakian's proposal is that he, I and my collaborator will have in effect a tripartite control over the production. Our influence upon it is assured by the fact that decisions over content will be arrived at by majority vote between the three of us. And Avakian guarantees us against any "cut off" clause which could remove us from participation as screenwriters. I imagine we would be hard put to get such support from any other producer.

Avakian does not consider that these assurances to me and John Marquand in any way deter his mounting of a production with the major film companies with which he has dealt and is currently dealing. Principal among these are Paramount and United Artists, and secondarily Warner's and Universal. (None of us considers that the contact we have already established with Columbia Pictures mitigates the points I make above.) And Avakian accepts and welcomes these provisions, because he believes they will make his position stronger.

* Dorothy Tristan (b. 1942), actress, appeared in *Klute* (1971) and *Down and Out in Beverly Hills* (1986) among other films, and was married for fifteen years to American film editor and director Aram A. Avakian (1926–87), who was in Paris when *The Paris Review* was founded and socialized frequently with Styron, Plimpton, and Marquand.

More important is that we have the utmost confidence in Avakian and respect him for his talents. Already he has been of considerable assistance to us in the research and development of the screenplay. In that process we learned, to our satisfaction, that he shares our vision of the film and that he is determined to protect its integrity.

We are so seriously considering this arrangement with Avakian that I am anxious for your opinion. At your early convenience, I can arrange for Al Avakian to talk to you.

Sincerely,
Bill

To Philip Roth

July 27, 1971 Vineyard Haven, MA

Dear Philip:

I ever so much enjoyed seeing you up here, and I have a confession to make. I adore your mustache and have had a single incredible fantasy: suppose I was a girl and you were going down on me with that mustache. What would it be like? Please destroy this letter.

The other purpose of this letter. Our friend Dean Brustein was passed over this past year at the august Academy or Institute or whatever it is we belong to. I was not surprised since it is a tough thing I gather to elect critics and such, as opposed to so-called creative artists. Someone told me that Marianne Moore proposed a critic named Morton Dauwen Zabel 14 times and he never got elected.* Maybe it was his name. Anyway, I think we should keep trying. As you may remember, at your suggestion I nominated Bob last year and you were the seconder. There seems to be no rule as such, but an informal practice seems to be that in succeeding years the roles are reversed and one of the seconders becomes the nominator. I suppose this is to avoid monotony or a smell of the obvious. Anyway, I wonder if you would care to nominate Bob this year and write a modest little blurb for him.* I

* Marianne Moore (1887–1972), American modernist poet and writer. Morton Dauwen Zabel (1901–64), author of *Craft and Character: Texts, Method, and Vocation in Modern Fiction* (1957).

think that eventually he will surely make it if we are persistent enough. I enclose the nomination form. Then next year we can start on other critics. What do you think of John Simon? Richard Gilman? Clay Felker?*

I really love your mustache but must now go to bed. Please write soon.

Your admirer,

B.S.

* I of course will second him. (It has to be in no later than October First.)

To Philip Roth

September 4, 1971 Vineyard Haven, MA

Dear Philip:

Your letter arrived in the same mail yesterday as your MS of the Nixon book† from Jason,‡ and I appreciate both. I've not yet started on the MS but intend to do so soon, and you will receive my reactions. As for the review, I have my doubts as to whether I will be able to do it, and this has nothing at all to do with whether I like it—which I expect I shall—or maybe not like it so much, as with the fact that I still feel so far behind on this Marine novel that I don't know if I'll be able to borrow the time to do it. God damned reviews and essays—as you yourself know, they take as much out of good writers as anything else they write. For example, I worked so hard on the Calley review (and did this only because I have been fathomlessly fascinated with Calley and the grotesque response he has evoked) that I began to get the illusion that it was taking me months.§

* John Simon (b. 1925), American author and literary and drama critic. Richard Gilman (1923–2006), American literary and drama critic.

† Philip Roth, *Our Gang (Starring Tricky and His Friends)* (New York: Random House, 1971).

‡ Jason Epstein (b. 1928), American editor and publisher, hired by Bennett Cerf at Random House. In addition to editing such notable authors as Norman Mailer, Philip Roth, and Vladimir Nabokov, Epstein was also a cofounder of *The New York Review of Books.*

§ William Styron, untitled review of Richard Hammer, *The Court-Martial of Lt. Calley,* and John Sack, *Lieutenant Calley: His Own Story, The New York Times Book Review* (September 12, 1971). Collected in *This Quiet Dust.*

(As a matter of fact, it did take me more than a week, plus four days reading.) So, it will have nothing to do with my response to your book, one way or the other, if I don't review it. On the other hand, I would very much like to review almost anything you wrote (About very few other writers can William Styron Make That Statement) and you may very well find me, enmeshed in the toils and agony of criticism, doing it. And I hope for the Times.

Your letter on Marriott was just fine, proving to me once again that writers, real writers (and a few oddballs like Rahv) are the only respectably penetrating critics.* Just about everything you said was dead on target, and I am really grateful to you for the almost uncanny wisdom of a couple of your observations. For example, your bit about the narrator's attitude toward sex, and to his girl Laurel. It is one of the real hazards of excerpting in a magazine that parts of a piece may look contiguous or connecting when they really aren't. For reasons of space, and also to emphasize and play up the Colonel, Esquire left out quite a long episode, which comes before the Jeeter business, where the narrator (hereinafter known as "I") literally courts suicide every weekend by driving at mad speed to N.Y. with his friend Lacy for the sole purpose of fucking Laurel for about 18 hours without stop.† It not only contains the sex you find missing, it is—given the corollary theme of doom and the possibility of death—fairly sex-obsessed, and it is one of my favorite parts so far. It will probably be published separately somewhere else before long. But what so truly impresses me about you as writer-critic (I don't think a Kazin would have caught it) is your ability to so unerringly sense an aesthetic gap, a subtle vacuum in the narrative—and even to point out just where it should be filled. Fortunately, in the actual book it is filled.

You even sensed the bit about the reference to the "obscene bulletin" from Laurel. Because Laurel is eliminated from the Esquire excerpt, the editors thought—wisely in this case, I thought—that the obscene letter from her would be obtrusive, and so it is the only passage (as distinct from a separate episode) that has been removed from the excerpt. But it is

* Styron refers to the main character in his *Way of the Warrior*. This "episode" was published as "The Suicide Run," *American Poetry Review* 3 (May/June 1974), later collected in *The Suicide Run*.

† "Marriott, the Marine," *Esquire* 76 (September 1971). Collected in *The Suicide Run*.

broadly sexual, a long fantasy of how she dreams of sucking his (excuse me, "my") prick, and I think helps satisfy that missing element you so sensitively detect. As a matter of fact, there are several more of these letters—a kind of motif—all lewd, and I had as much fun writing them as you must have had with parts of Portnoy.

There are a couple of places, though, where I did not anticipate you, and for which I find your remarks especially valuable. The vision of myself in bed fantasizing a sodomistic relationship and incest between the two Jeeters is a brilliant idea, and I'm certainly going to go back in the final draft and play with it, to strain a metaphor. The other place where I think you may have accurately divined a weakness is in the playing down of the truly idealistic side of my writer-self, with the consequent overemphasis on the theme of success. I'm not sure whether in the course of the remaining narrative I hadn't been planning to do what you suggest anyway; but in any case your feeling about this lack, at this point in the story, is I feel absolutely right, and I'm grateful to you for expressing it, because I think it will spur me to subtly alter that part of the portrait.

So, fine. It was truly good stuff you wrote, encouraging me for the really remarkable reasons you mentioned, and which I think only two writers, interchanging intuitions, could absorb or appreciate.

Now to finish the motherfucker. Meanwhile, I will be addressing myself to OUR GANG, and with anticipation. And we must do New York together more than once this fall and winter, although the city has begun to sadden me beyond measure. After the funeral mass with you the other day, Loomis and I went to a porno film on 6th Ave.—the first hard-core flick, in living color, I've seen. I maintained about a 5/8ths erection throughout but two hours of all those throbbing cocks and slippery pink vaginas made me feel like Cato must have felt in the Roman mire, and I came out blinking into the bright light of 6th Ave. feeling very downcast about the future of Fun City or any of us.

Keep the faith

Bill

To Jack Zajac*

September 25, 1971 Vineyard Haven, MA

Dear Jack:

I held off writing you because I was awaiting final word on the African thing. Alas, it has had to be postponed, mainly due to the fact that our leader, Myles Turner, who would be essential to the trip, recently had a kidney operation in Arusha, Tanzania, and would be in no shape to go now.† This doesn't mean, however, that the trip is forever off; as a matter of fact, we're already re-cranking up new plans for a safari in the same place as early as next February, when the weather should even be better than October. So do not lose hope altogether by any means, and I can assure you that if there is any possibility of getting you onto the trip I will do my damndest to help do it.

Received your libidinous letter from Greece, which I shared with Rose and others, and also the flies which Tom is using joyously on our little stream down in Connecticut. Finally, I want to say how much I appreciate the dashing bush jacket, which is truly a groovy thing and in this slightly chilly autumn weather has caused me to set something of a fashion here on Martha's Vineyard. Needless to say, it will accompany me to Nairobi.

Little else to report at the moment except to say that to my utter amazement I find myself in the midst of writing a play, my first. I don't know if it's going to work, but I love doing it, since it is about my experiences on the V.D. ward of a Naval Hospital during WW II, and concerns such characters as an evil, moralistic urologist named Dr. Glanz and will have lots of dripping tools and the first full-scale short-arm inspection ever seen on the American stage. I hope you will come to the opening if, God willing, there is an opening—no pun intended.

Rose is in Rox., while I labor here on the island. She tells me that your sculpture looks marvelous in the new big living room, and I'm anxious to

* Jack Zajac (b. 1929). An American artist known for his sculptures in bronze and marble, as well as his figurative paintings, Zajac received a Guggenheim Fellowship and the Rome Prize. He was an Artist in Residence at the American Academy in Rome when Styron was there for the Prix de Rome.

† Turner (1921–84) was warden of the Serengeti National Park in Tanzania from 1956 to 1972. He wrote an autobiography, *My Serengeti Years,* about his efforts to manage the park.

see it. Susanna is in school in Lugano, incidentally, and I hope she'll look you all up when she comes to Rome sometime later. Meanwhile, I'll keep you informed as to my own trek to Europe, which I hope will take place soon, after I finish my dramatic sojourn in the clap shack.* On this note, I send fond greetings to you all.

B—

To Philip Roth

September 25, 1971 Vineyard Haven, MA

Dear Philip:

I have read OUR GANG and I think it is not only mostly hilarious but also a very important satirical document about a man who desperately needs this kind of treatment. It's uncanny, I think, how well you've caught the tone of those droning evasions and fatuous half-truths put forth as "explanations." Also your little extravaganzas are dead on target: the football skull session with the "spiritual coach," etc., is worth the price of admission in itself. Indeed, each piece is, separately, so funny that I think you're going to come in for a kind of criticism that you haven't received before; namely, that this is the kind of book which really should not be read at one sitting, continuously, but should be savored at random and perhaps even haphazardly. That is the only criticism that I have, as a matter of fact: laughter is a difficult thing to sustain in one's self for any great length of time, and this is a book which demands to be sampled. My friend Art Buchwald gave me a collection of his columns this summer. Most of the time, Art is an extremely funny man, but I noticed that in re-reading the columns in book form I was unable to go straight through. I think your book might have the same problem, which has to do with format rather than substance; but after all this comes down to being a voluntary matter on the part of the reader, and perhaps not ultimately important. What I really want to say is that it is a marvelously droll and

* Styron's play *In the Clap Shack* was produced by the Yale Repertory Theatre, and published by Random House in book form in 1973. See Melvin J. Friedman, "*In the Clap Shack:* William Styron's Neglected Play," *The Southern Quarterly* 33, nos. 2–3, Winter–Spring 1995.

trenchant book—an important exercise in political satire—and I trust it's a winner in every respect.

My own feelings about reviewing the book are rimmed round by the fact that I've just embarked, to my utter astonishment, on a play—doing something that I've never done before, not only the play itself but interrupting my Marriott novel to get it done. This play is about my infamous adventures in the clap shack during WWII, and it took off with such surprising speed and feeling of assurance (perhaps unwarranted but assurance nonetheless) that it has preoccupied me entirely for the last ten days. Rather than interrupt the thought processes, I'd better stick with it, and that is the real reason why I would be reluctant to do the review. It might not be much compensation, but I'd be delighted to contribute a quote or anything of that nature—perhaps Jason would get in touch with me about it.

Anyway, it's a hell of a good book. You've removed Tricky's clothes to let us see, in a kind of reverse-Emperor's parable, what we've suspected all along: there's Nothing underneath. So, many congratulations.

Bill

To Susanna Styron*

September 26, 1971 Vineyard Haven, MA

Dear Sue:

We certainly did enjoy your wonderful letter, written under a Lugano fig tree. I had great fun reading of your trials and adventures and am very, very happy that you are so happy. Pasta, as you well know, is a great temptation, and in that Italian-speaking part of the country a plate of fettucine must be truly superb (the Acapulco Gold of pasta); so I am especially glad and proud that you are resisting the temptation to go hog wild and turn yourself into a continental version of Rebecca Stuart.

Since the school recommends a car, I see no reason why you shouldn't get one right away. I do think, however, you should confine your driving

* Susanna had graduated from high school at the age of sixteen and spent the next year traveling around Europe while attending Franklin College in Switzerland.

to Lugano and immediate environs, at least for the next few months. As you know, I owe you an automobile, so it is entirely up to you what kind to get. A Rolls-Royce would be pretentious, an Alfa-Romeo is too fast. Any of those smaller cars you mentioned would be fine, but please try to keep the price down to a reasonable level by getting the straight, unadorned model which is not cluttered up with a lot of extras. Let me know what you decide and I will have the funds transferred to your bank there.

We certainly miss you, and speaking for myself, I just ache every time I walk by the little house on my way into town and realize that you aren't there but are 10 light-years away. But we'll see each other before too long, even though the African trip was postponed—really mean postponed, too, rather than cancelled, because we still have definite plans to do the trip next year, perhaps as early as February. Guess what? I'm writing a play—a morbid, sad play about a military hospital during World War II. Anyway, it's going very well and quite fast and if I'm lucky I'll have it done by the end of October—at which point I expect to take a vacation and come to Europe. Naturally, I'll come to Lugano and pay you a visit, and you can drive me around the country in that car I will have bought you. Parenthesis: Please always drive carefully; from past knowledge I know that the Italians, even if they be Italian-Swiss, are like Teddy Kennedy after a long night's party, so you must constantly keep an eye not only on the road but on the other maniac. Do be careful.

Please do let me know soon about how the school goes, and how you like it, etc. I have a sneaking feeling that you're not going to find it like Harvard, but as you are well aware the most important thing for you at the moment is simply to be located in the heart of Europe with the opportunity to spend this extra year learning Italian and perfecting your French and seeing the continent. You shouldn't take too lightly, however, what Franklin has to offer, because I also have a feeling that, even if it's a new school just feeling its way, it may have some very valuable things to give and you shouldn't overlook them. But also, have a good time; having a good time is, I've noticed, an activity at which generally speaking you're very proficient—and that's all to the good. And don't forget reading, but I think that's already in your blood.

Well, I really miss you awfully, but it does my weary heart good to at least know that you're contented. Don't forget to write. Mummy comes up on week-ends, and I imagine I'll be here for several more weeks, so you'll know where to write. John Marquand said for me to give you an epistolary hug, which I do.

Much love,
Daddy

To Susanna Styron

October 12, 1971 Vineyard Haven, MA

Dear Sue (Cara figlia mia):

Two pieces of good news I've received in the past couple of days. The first probably won't interest you too much since it has to do with my taxes. Anyway I got the bill for my Vineyard Haven tax for this year and found they had been reduced by $800. Isn't that extraordinary? It has to do with re-evaluation and other complex things, and the fact that we on the waterfront had been paying a larger share of tax than we should have for many years; but the important thing, as far as you're concerned, is that it will make it a whole lot easier for me to pay for that new car of yours. So hooray for the new V.H. taxes.

Item No. 2: Paul Newman and Joanne Woodward, through their company, have bought JPM's and my script, DEAD!—A Love Story for $125,000.* Isn't that something? The news just came the other day. Actually, it's only an option arrangement with a percentage down payment, but that is the usual thing in the movie business nowadays, and my agent, Don Congdon, is very optimistic about them actually doing the movie. More importantly, though, is the general feeling that they are going to try to do an honest movie with respect for the script itself. I talked to Newman over the phone, and he was very enthusiastic, giving me all sorts of assurances that the movie would be made in a way that honored the tragicomic nuances of the script, etc., and maybe I'm a sucker but I truly believed him. Now with your newly acquired cinematic expertise, you will have to be hired on this project as an advisor in some sort of capacity. Wouldn't it be exciting if sometime next year when you are back in this

* The screenplay was never produced.

land and the movie is being made (the bucolic scenes around Roxbury), you could be taken on in some sort of groovy, integral capacity.

So there is something to think about. In the meantime, I want to say that I really love your letters, with their splendidly detailed account of your goings-on, your new apartment, your encounter with Proust (I greatly approve of this), and all the other exciting things that are happening to you. How I envy you, and with what amazement I think back on my own self at 16, and realize that I wasn't half as grown-up as you are now, and would have been paralyzed with anxiety and embarrassment when faced with trying to do and accomplish 1-10th of what you are doing.

I love and cherish your descriptions of Pascal Tone and his Hemingwayesque panache, also your sketches of the other Franklin characters.* By now, I'm sure that you and your beloved Mom will have thoroughly "done" the Lugano scene, and I can't wait for her to return (day after tomorrow) to tell me everything in detail. She may have told you about some ghastly Kennedy Foundation symposium that I am supposed to take part in in Washington. That's this week-end and I'm going to try to weasel out of it so that we can stay up here on the island instead and she can tell me all about your adventures together. The idea of engaging in a symposium with a bunch of biologists on the subject of birth defects, and then being loaded on a bus to go to a black-tie dinner at the Shrivers, depresses me so much that it makes my back teeth ache. I'm going to try and worm out of it somehow.

I've got almost 50 pages done on the play—that's about half—and the progress I've made makes me feel very happy. Incidentally, this is more about hospital life than about the military, but in any case I have found that I have always written best when thinking about places and events that caused me misery.

I really miss you but, as you say, it won't be too long before we'll be together again and chew over our various experiences. Do take care of yourself. DRIVE CAREFULLY (slowly mainly), and keep reading. And WRITE me from time to time. I love you very much.

XXXXX

Papa

* Pascal Franchot Tone was one of the founders and presidents (1973–79) of Franklin College.

To Susanna Styron

November 10, 1971 Roxbury, CT

Dear Sue:

I'm writing this while you are undoubtedly in the depths of some Turkish opium den, and hope the mails are fast enough so that this will reach you in Lugano around the time of your arrival. We received your itinerary of the trip throughout Greece and Turkey and it sounds fabulous. Also received was your postcard from Greece with your description of your ouzo-drinking bout below decks with the crew. You sure do get around for a gal of sixteen.

Your ma and I went to a preview of Neil Simon's new play,* directed of course by M. Nichols, and then (this was last night) went out with Mike for dinner—a fine time, really, but as usual I am getting more and more fed up with Fun City and can't wait to get back here in the country. The play was funny enough, but instantly forgettable—not at all like the drama of your paw's, which is nearing completion; that is, I'm about halfway through the second of two acts. It's both very sad and very funny, this play I'm writing, and the best news I can send you so far is that Bob Brustein—of or than whom there is no finer judge in the world—listened to me read the first act not long ago, and absolutely adored it, instantly offered to stage it at Yale, where no doubt it will be put on late this spring. Naturally, to get Bob's kind of professional reaction and to find it so wholeheartedly positive and favorable is an enormous boost to my morale and I am proceeding in high spirits.

Little wildly interesting news otherwise, except to say that we all miss you very, very much and can't wait to see you. As for the African trip of mine—as you know it was postponed, not cancelled; Myles Turner still earnestly wants to make the safari, and it now looks as if we will probably go around the 20th of January. That means that I'll be able to drop in on you in Lugano either after the trip or before, probably the latter. I am very much looking forward to seeing your groovy school and meeting your pals and associates. Among other things, this is the longest stretch of time in

* Neil Simon (b. 1927), American playwright. *The Prisoner of Second Avenue* ran on Broadway from November 1971 until September 1973. It was later made into a film starring Jack Lemmon and Anne Bancroft.

about 20 years that I have not been to Europe and I am getting a real pang of longing for the old country. Your brothers and sisters are all fine and they send you their fondest love. The Montessori teachers wrote a note home saying that Al was going through, or had started just today, a phase which Maria Montessori had called "immersion in reading." Indeed, the teacher said that Al had gotten so infatuated with the printed page that she had really embarked upon a veritable "reading drunk," which is O.K. with me. I don't know what she's been reading—probably not Tolstoy—but I'd rather her turn into an alcoholic on print than to ruin her little eyes squinting at the boob tube. Sundance and Juniper are well and happy and send their love too.

Much love,
Daddy

To Robert Penn Warren

November 22, 1971 Roxbury, CT

Dear Red: Sorry not to have answered your rich and abundant letter sooner, but I have been spending a lot of my time this fall in the house on the Vineyard (toward the year's end, or after the end of summer, I find I get a good amount of writing done living up there for a few weeks as a bachelor) and somehow your letter got delayed in being forwarded. Anyway, I enjoyed the hell out of it, reading your account of life in that part of France and I'm delighted that things seems to be going so satisfactorily, if not downright buoyantly for la famille Warren. What a gas, as the kids would say, that you are living as nostalgically, within the shadow of Stendhal. I don't quite know what my own reaction would be to such proximity—probably it would at least have me off re-reading The Red and the Black and countless Beyle-can works I have too long neglected also.*

Which brings me to a much belated need to tell you how much I liked Meet Me in the Green Glen.† I had finished it—in a glow of excitement

* Marie-Henri Beyle (1783–1842), best known by his pen name Stendhal, was a French writer who helped develop realism in novels such as *The Red and the Black* (1830).

† Warren's novel *Meet Me in the Green Glen* (New York: Random House, 1971).

and just before I left the Vineyard a week or so ago, wanted to write you about it, didn't have your address (your misplaced letter not being in my hands), tried to call Albert, missed him, etc.—a whole comedy of communication-failure. Anyway, I want to say here and now how strong a work I think it is—the language as usual rich and flowing and superbly suited to the subject-matter, the characters (especially the amazing Cassie) brilliantly alive, and all welded together by the infallible Warren narrative drive. I envy the consistent energy of the book, there never seems to be the slightest let-down in the forward thrust of the story, and as always brooding over all, is that moral imagination which has made you the unique writer that you are. The trial—to cite just one fine sequence in the book—is one of the best episodes of its kind I've ever read. I could go on and on, and want to talk to you about it sometime soon, but hope it's O.K. if I leave you for the moment simply with the impression of how enormously impressed with the novel I am—if that means anything. Not only impressed, to repeat myself once more, but truly bouleversé which is what I think the French say when they mean even more than that.

My own work, speaking of work, has taken a rather bizarre turn. I am within a few pages of finishing, of all things, a full-length play, entitled IN THE CLAP SHACK, set in the venereal disease ward of a Naval Hospital during W.W. II. I've astonished myself by doing this thing but felt irresistibly compelled to do so and am rather tickled that Bob Brustein likes what I've done so far well enough to have offered to stage it at Yale this coming spring. This means of course that the novel I've been doing has been temporarily put aside but I expect to get back to it this winter. Playwriting I've found is a remarkable experience—tough in many ways, the need for discipline great but in certain aspects so free and easy that I wonder why I didn't take it up a long time ago.

Things are about the same, meaning getting worse, with people running amok on the streets, pollution, and Nixon. However, all the family here is fine and miss the Warrens—will especially miss your annual December shebang. Susanna has orbited out of sight, having already this fall been to Turkey and Greece but is now back in Lugano, where I feel she may be a little lonely in her bachelor girl's apartment after the first flush of freedom. I'm sure she'd be panting to see you if you get to that part of Swizzera and her address is Franklin College, Lugano.

Incidentally, I'll be proud to be in your anthology, and suggest you write my agent for the business side of the thing: Don Congdon, c/o Harold Matson Co., 22 East 40th St., N.Y. 10016.

Hope we can link up over there before long. Keep in touch and love to you all from all of us.

Bill

To Susanna Styron

December 2, 1971 Roxbury, CT

Dear Sue:

I've been a terrible correspondent these past few weeks but I have of course thought of you every day—sometimes 5 or 6 or even 7 times a day—and if there's any such thing as telepathy I think you would know about it and respond to my vibrations since when I think of you I really DO THINK. For one thing, your Ma and I were just a tiny bit made morose over the tone of one of your last letters—you seemed lonely in your single gal's apt. and I began to wonder if we had done the right thing in agreeing to let you live alone—and so I thought a lot about you then. But then Barbie, whom we saw over here one week-end, said she'd gotten a letter from you at about the same time, and you didn't sound lonely at all, and then your MA got that call from you over Thanksgiving in Baltimore, and she said you sounded very cheery, so my sadness about you was alleviated. One thing I don't want you to feel is real regret perhaps over having made the wrong decision about living by yourself. Having lived alone myself in Paris, I know what it is of an evening to look at the four walls, as they say. Yet on the other hand I'm very much aware of the fact that you do have a bunch of good friends and the opportunity to see them most any time you want to, so I'm sure that takes up a lot of the strain, and makes most of your solitariness a passing thing. But if it <u>does</u> get to be too much of an emotional hang-up, living like that, please don't hesitate to change your rooming arrangements, either now or next semester. There is no point in being even the slightest discontented when there's no need for it and you can get around it.

But the main thing is—and it is very hard to believe—you will be here very, very soon. I am stunned by the notion that once again the hideous season of Christmas is upon us, but knowing that you will be here warms the cockles of my old heart, and if for no other reason than to please my darling daughter I PROMISE that on Xmas day I will be nice, courteous, loving, trustworthy, jolly, outgoing, forbearing, sweet, tender, generous, affable, and a saint. I can't wait to see you, and my impatience is shared by at least 7 other members of this family, human and non-human, and countless other denizens of this county, commonwealth and nation. I will have my play done by then, God willing, and since anytime I finish a work I dwell in a kind of (perhaps misguided) ecstasy for several weeks you will find me in even more of a jolly Santa Claus mood than you ever thought possible.

I must say goodbye now because I've got to write a letter to a lady in Budapest who wrote a fine essay on my work. She also wrote me a letter and sounds very open-hearted and intelligent, so maybe you will want to meet her when you go to Hungary next semester. I won't say anything about you now—awaiting your approval—but she does sound like someone special and I'm sure she'd like to show you around when you go there.

Everybody sends love—Pete, Tom, Al, Mom and me, Marj, Gino, Juniper, Sundance, the two birds whatever their names are (God, are they noisy!), Tom's two chameleons, let's see also Nicky, the milkman, Tommy's Cleaners, Lloyd Green, New Milford Laundry, Vulcan Basement Waterproofing (I'm going to sue them), and I could go on and on, but am waiting for Xmas. . . .

10,000 Tons of love,
Daddy

To Susanna Styron

January, 1972* Goldsboro, NC

Dear Sue:

A sign on the front of the grandest hotel in this part of N.C. reads:

FINEST FOOD IN TOWN

BREAKFAST	60 c
LUNCH	1.00
DINNER	1.50 HP

And it was quite good too!

Love, Daddy

To Claire White

January 5, 1972 Roxbury, CT

Dear Claire: I don't mean to mix up metaphors, but thank you for sending me the pleasure of your box. Could this be symbolic? I've always wanted a box of yours and now I've got it, but never in my wildest dreams did I think it could be so crazy, so beautiful, or so Gothic! It drives me crazy. I've wondered what to do with it (knowing only that I want it constantly within my reach) and have decided to use it, on alternate weeks, as a receptacle (1) for small cigars and (2) for used razor blades. Several things about the box remain enigmas to me. The skull is great, but on the other panels I can't tell the difference between (a) a tit, (b) an ass and (c) a stomach with a navel. However, it all joins into one erotic frolic, and hope I shall have the pleasure of your intimate company soon again.

Much love,

Wm.

* Postcard from Downtowner Motor Inn, Goldsboro, North Carolina.

To Willie Morris

January 25, 1972 Roxbury, CT

Dear Willie:

Here is that piece of Red Warren's that you wanted, and I hope you can find what you need in it. Send it back at your leisure.*

Rose and I spent last Saturday night at Jason Epstein's in Sag Harbor and tried to raise you numerous times on Sunday by telephone but to no avail. I'm really sorry because we all wanted to see you and knock down a Bloody Mary or two. But let's get together soon.

Louis Rubin wrote to say that you had told the students that you couldn't come down to UNC in March. I'm not sure whether I want to go either, but I'll still consider going especially if you'll reconsider, with the view in both of our minds of putting on a Bill & Willie Show which seemed to be so successful at Duke last year. Let me know if you want to do it and I'll get to work and line up some good parties, sippin whiskey, handball games, poontang, etc.

My play IN THE CLAP SHACK is going to open the season at the Yale Drama School in the fall and I want you to be there for the first on-stage short-arm inspection in American theatrical history. How is your work coming? Let me hear everything.

Rose joins me in boundless affection
Bill
TRICIA LOVES COX†

* Unknown attachment.

† A sticker that Bill attached to the letter. He attached them to several envelopes around this time as well. The reference is to President Nixon's daughter Tricia, who had married Edward Cox on June 12, 1971.

To James and Gloria Jones

February 4, 1972 Roxbury, CT

Dear James + Moss:

Good news to hear that you are coming over here to this side of the pond later on in the month. We're really looking forward to seeing you so much—long time, no?— and want to throw a gala party for you all and Irwin + Co., filled with beautiful girls, fancy studs, and all your old good friends. Please let us know immediately when you'll be here, what your schedule is, etc., so that we can begin laying plans. I have no more money left, since I went crazy and bought a Jaguar XJ6 sedan that cost more than Nixon's limousine. However, my wife Rose has a few dollars left from Scott Tissue and so we'll make out all right for a party for you if we stick to beer, and no groovy broads or fancy studs of an order higher than Lila Kelly (remember?) or Ed Trzcinski. I think maybe, come to think of it, we can hire the back end of Clarke's for about $50. So please communicate right away about arrival time, where you're staying, how long, etc., so we can do the thing up brown.

Rose sends love to you all and joins me in saying that we are dearly looking forward to seeing your radiant, fat, grinning, abstemious, mothergrabbing faces again.

Love,

Bill

To Susanna Styron

February 7, 1972* Roxbury, CT

Dear Sue: It was wonderful getting your wonderful letter and hearing about all the fine times you are having in Rome. I am really <u>blue</u> with envy—that is 10 times more envious than being green—at the thought of you immersed in the glories and beauties and sheer pleasures of that most favorite city of mine.

* On one of the Nat Turner "Power of Self Determination" cards, Styron wrote above the image on the front, "He looks a little like Harry Belafonte, I think."

Everyone is tickled to death about your getting into Yale. You may be interested to know that your favorite person—John Schereschewsky—is exuberant over your admission and is claiming for himself almost all the credit for having made you so wise and bright. But everyone is overjoyed at the idea of your being a Yalie and I know you're going to have a marvelous time there.

If you see Jack, tell him that—alas—the African Trip is off. Myles Turner had to postpone the hike until even later in the spring, which made it impossible for me since I have a speaking engagement then. So it's really too bad in a way but I'm still entertaining hopes for someday . . . Someday . . . Meanwhile, I'm doing healthy hiking in the Roxbury hills.

Guess What!! The Mustang is no more, since in an excess of reckless affluence I traded it in on the most beautiful Jaguar you've ever seen. Actually it's such a great car I plan to live in it. The enclosed piece of the brochure should give you an idea what it's like and I hope it'll also help entice you back here so you can drive it. It is truly elegant without being pretentious and I've just gotten over my guilt about buying it. Terry of course is ecstatic. Actually I paid for it with my money from Paul Newman. The movie incidentally is being filmed next fall in New York and it looks as if John Huston will direct it.

The enclosed check is to be considered a little birthday present. Do take care of yourself and drive carefully when you drive—save yourself for the Jag. Prague sounds wonderful and I know you're going to really flower and flourish in Rome after gray Lugano. We all miss you so much and send you our dearest love.

Daddy

To Philip Roth

February 25, 1972 Roxbury, CT

Dear Philip:

What has happened about your super country Joint? Let me know. We need some friendly neighbors. That is a great house.

I too have been brooding about mortality and have been filled with Kierkegaardian despair believe me.

In the midst of this Angst, I found the solution. I bought a $9,000 XJ6 Jaguar, and feel much better.

Stay in touch,
W.S.

To Susanna Styron

March 28, 1972* Roxbury, CT

Dear Sue:

I am writing this thinking that you will be back from Russia in a week or so and when you read this you have had many—I hope—marvelous experiences. Also, doubtless, a lot of disheartening ones, but that is the trouble with travel in general and also partly—as you have discovered—with Russia. I'll be fascinated to learn what you felt about that incredible place, so please let me know at the earliest opportunity. I wrote Elana and Ray from Paris right after I saw you in Rome and can only hope that in the midst of the confusion you made some connection.

I had a lovely time in Paris with Jim and Gloria after I saw you, or left you, in Rome. Nothing madly exciting, but just a nice placid routine with of course more than one happy encounter à table at places like the Brasserie Lipp and La Coupole. The Joneses are really dying to have you up there for a visit so please don't hesitate to call them if you want to spend a few days with them. I say this without prejudice or favor. They are enormously fond of you so you will not discommode them by a visit. They want you! As soon as I got back here from Paris I had to go down South for that wretched lecture tour in Va. and N.C. The U of Va was a drag—I felt like a pariah in that smug place, almost no one showed up for my talk!—but this was cancelled out by my turn-out at the U of N.C.—nearly a thousand students, all rapt and worshipping except for the usual phalanx of half a dozen or maybe a dozen black folk who did their usual childish gig of trying, unsuccessfully, to embarrass me by walking out.

* On "Mrs. William Styron, Roxbury" stationery, with *Mrs. William* crossed out and *Mr. Irving* written in by hand.

Anyway, I think I'm going to transfer my state allegiance from Va. to North Carolina. The kids in Chapel Hill are really amazingly on the ball.

Under separate cover I am sending you some (a pair) of arch supporters, your size, and I hope you receive them in good shape and don't thereafter let your feet go flat. Other news: Sundance had 11—count 'em—11—puppies and so the house here in Rox has turned into some ghastly veterinary asylum. But the "kids" are beautiful. Though blind.

Oh how all of us miss you—especially me. Do write soon. They tell me that at Yale all they are waiting for is the arrival of Swinging Sue Styron. My play is definitely going to be put on next fall and first readings begin in a week or so, supervised by Bob Brustein. Pray for me. Love to Jack and Corda and you.

XXXX DADDY

To *The Atlantic Monthly*

May, 1972* Roxbury, CT

It was fun to see Gore's reaction.

I was very much amused by Gerald Clarke's clever and witty portrait of my friend Gore Vidal.† It somewhat embarrasses me therefore to register a complaint about a statement, attributed to me, which caused Gore to react so unhappily. Mr. Clarke says that I once told him that there were "only five big writers in the country today"—a group that included Mailer, Capote and myself but not Gore Vidal. Would that I possessed either the conceit or the self-assurance to so breezily set up a Board of Directors for American letters, but alas, I'm a mass of insecurities, besides being firmly convinced that literature is neither a track race nor a gentleman's club. What I do recollect is that Mr. Clarke asked me to name some American writers whose work I admired. I named several, including Mailer and

* Reprinted as "Vidal Blue," *The Atlantic* 229 (May 1972).

† Gerald Clarke, "Petronius Americanus: The Ways of Gore Vidal," *The Atlantic* 229 (March 1972).

Capote. It would never in the world have occurred to me to mention Gore, although if I really had been playing the little game that Mr. Clarke claims that I was playing, and if I were allowed a second rank, Gore definitely would have been included somewhere between five and ten, which to my mind is not bad at all.

To Susanna Styron

May 15, 1972 Roxbury, CT

Beloved daughter O'Mine: I've been planning to write you every day for a week or ten days now but all sorts of odd things have interfered. A couple of days ago I had to go down to Yale to hear a reading of my play. It went off fine, I thought (and Bob Brustein and others thought likewise); it made everyone laugh a lot, which is an excellent sign. It's going to be put on down there sometime late next fall and a director named Ed Sherin has taken on the job of directing. Among other things he directed The Great White Hope on Broadway, which I liked very much, and I like him too so I think we'll get along very well. Another thing that's occupied me is an interview I was asked to do with Daniel Ellsberg about the Pentagon Papers.* A group in New York called the New Democratic Coalition is putting out a publication and it turns out that Ellsberg wanted me to be his interviewer. So I did, and found it a rather fascinating experience. Ellsberg is a real fanatic and that quality comes out in his every word. But he is also quite earnest, likable, open, and in many ways charming so I found the hours I spent with him quite enjoyable and rewarding. He thinks Nixon is practicing actual genocide in Vietnam—genocide which is quite on the scale of the Nazi orgy in Germany—and I must say that after the events of the past two or three weeks I am inclined to agree with him.

As for your existential "wrassling," I'm sure that I don't have to tell you that your pondering and wondering and troubling are only extensions of what people have been doing ever since they had the capability of thought, which is to say hundreds of thousands of years. Gods and the idea of a

* "Responsibility and the Exhilaration of Power," *Pointing to the Presidency,* a special publication of the New Democratic Coalition of New York (1972).

God were of course born out of just this troubled pondering, so it may or may not be a consolation to you that your intense wonder and turmoil about the meaning of the human condition is, in fact, a part of the human condition—or at least as it is experienced by sensitive and questing souls like yourself (no joke). It may just be that there is no reason or purpose to existence. Many great men—thinkers and artists—have thought this to be true, yet have not despaired over this assumption but have created great work through their very vision of mankind enduring triumphant over the sheer purposelessness of the universe, and in spite of the bleak and soulless aspect it so often presents. The whole concept of tragedy is of course embodied in this notion.

But I've often had the feeling that the existential dilemma is a very subjective matter, entirely depending upon the individual and the circumstances of his life, and that we "Western intellectuals" with our wrenched and tormented psyches have often imposed the need to find a purpose which may be in the end only an exercise in masochism. A fisherman in the Arabian Gulf finds purpose in life by fishing, a Wyoming sheepherder by tending his sheep and remaining close to Nature and that big sky. On a somewhat higher level intellectually, a person like James Joyce, a profoundly pessimistic man at bottom, could find reason and purpose through these moments termed "epiphanies"—instances of intense revelation (through love, or a glimpse of transcendental beauty in the natural world) which gave such a sense of joy and self-realization that they justified and, in effect, ratified the existence of him who experienced them. In other words, the existential anguish becomes undone; through moments of aesthetic and spiritual fulfillment we find the very reason for existence. The creative act in art often approaches this, but it can work on humbler levels as well. If you'll pardon my pointing to my own work, I think I tried to render this quality of revelation—"epiphany" in a part of Nat Turner. I'm thinking of the passage beginning on p. 119 of the Random House edition (you may want to re-read it) where Nat as a little boy is waiting on the table during a spring evening and experiences the combined ecstasy of (a) being alive and healthy in the springtime, (b) being appreciated as a human being, and (c) being given some marvelous unspoken promise about the future. For him at this moment all these things were enough. Existence and its joys justify everything and remain sufficient.

All the foregoing is of course ridiculously crude, off-hand and sketchy.

What you have brought up has been the subject of the life-work of dozens of bearded old professors from Uppsala to Yale. But they are at least honest observations and they may give you a few hints about what your old dad has thought from time to time.

I certainly miss you very much and for that selfish reason am happy as I can be that you are going to Yale, despite your rather gloomy observations about the place. At this point I really wouldn't have too many dread qualms about Yale. You are certainly the most beautiful, and vigorously independent person I know and I fully respect your desire to keep that independence intact but I honestly think you exaggerate your fears of a threat to your continued operation as a free spirit. In any case, try not to fret over it.

Also, do drive that lovely new car of yours carefully, especially this summer when the Latin people get their customary madness on the highway. I'll talk over Andy's scholarship problems with your Ma. As for the typewriter, I'd be glad to send you the money for it. How much?

Best love from
Daddy

To Frederick Exley

June 8, 1972 Vineyard Haven, MA

Dear Frederick:

The state of Iowa is filled with rich farmers who make pots of money selling hogs in places like Dubuque and Sioux City which we poor suckers in turn remunerate by buying bacon at $1.19 a pound. These rich farm bastards in turn support fat institutions of learning like the University of Iowa, which should be able to pay a decent fee for writers to come and titillate the same farmers' daughters with their (Thomas Wolfe's phrase) creamy thighs. I will agree to come to your class for expense money but only against my better judgment. I am not a particularly venal person but I feel that we writers deserve honest pay for honest work (and that includes appearing at classes) as much as do doctors or lawyers and certainly more than politicians. Actually with me the amount of the money involved is really immaterial (my father-in-law was a clever scoundrel who in 1934 bought 9,000 shares of IBM at $8.00 a share and left them to my wife), it is—to be trite—the principle of the thing. In other words, I'd feel more comfortable about it if John Leggett could squeeze one of those hog's tits and get me, say, as little as $250, but in any case I will come out there for expenses if those cheap bastards can't cough up anything. Let me know when this deal takes place.

Young kid I knew well—only 20 years old, an aspiring writer—died very tragically and unexpectedly last September. He was a passionate admirer of your work, wanted to meet you, etc. I'll tell you more about him when I see you. He came from a rich family and this spring they started a literary festival in his memory at Taft School, where he graduated from. Arthur Miller, Jerzy Kosinski and I kicked off the first event.* Maybe you would consent to go there next spring. Anyway, we'll talk about that too.

Faithfully

B.S.

To Mike Mewshaw

September 27, 1972 Vineyard Haven, MA

Dear Mike:

I enjoyed Walking Slow very, very much.† It is a great leap from Man in Motion—which as you know I also liked—and that is saying something. Your sense of narrative flow is impeccable and also I think you've substantially deepened your feeling for character—specifically, Carter is a much more mature, sympathetic and believable figure than the hero of Man in Motion. Also I'm delighted with your deft ability in handling subsidiary characters—Eddie Brown and [Unknown] are both raucously alive. In short, I think Walking Slow is a real achievement and I hope you're proud of it—you should be. What really sustains the book, I think, is a continuous and unobtrusive yet most effective strain of comic insight which somehow nicely ventilates the pervading seriousness of the book yet never

* Jerzy Kosinski (1933–91), a novelist best known for his novels *The Painted Bird* (1965), *Being There* (1971), and *Steps* (1969), which won the National Book Award.

† Michael Mewshaw's second novel, *Walking Slow* (New York: Random House, 1972).

calls attention to itself. This sense of humor is one of your solidest gifts. Hang on to it, for it's invaluable.

I hope you're enjoying Spain. I've never spent much time there but my daughter Susanna—age 17—just returned from a long summer all over the country, where she became great pals with Luis Miguel Dominguín.* Although she assures me the attachment was innocent, there were some very funny photographs in certain Spanish magazines, the captions of which identified her as the bullfighter's inamorata, his first American love since Ava Gardner. It made me feel a little odd and not so young, especially since Dominguín is exactly my age.

When you get to be a well-known writer—which you are on your way to becoming—you must avoid at all costs any interviews, especially with little epicene pricks from Esquire such as the one you mentioned in your letter. There is nothing much to be said about that disaster except that from the very outset of the interview he felt himself clearly so superior and was so patronizing (I remember him once alluding to the fact that "the best of your work" was behind me) that I could hardly have expected it to be any better. But I let it be a lesson: avoid all interviews! . . .

Best to you both and keep in touch.

Bill

To Frederick Exley

September 29, 1972 Vineyard Haven, MA

Dear Fred:

I'm in receipt of your various interesting and informative communications and just wanted to say that I am looking forward to my sojourn to Iowa City very much. I am as yet uncertain about the exact date but I as-

* Born Luis Miguel González Lucas, Dominguín (1926–96) was a famous bullfighter who took the name of his father, bullfighting legend Domingo Dominguín. Luis Dominguín counted Pablo Picasso among his friends, and had affairs with actress Ava Gardner and model China Machado, among others. In 1954, he married actress Lucia Bosé, and had a son, Miguel Bosé, a Grammy-winning singer. In 1959, the rivalry between Dominguín and his brother-in-law, Antonio Ordóñez, was chronicled by Ernest Hemingway in *The Dangerous Summer*.

sume that the idea of sometime during the first week in November still stands. I enjoyed your graphic description of the festivities chez Bourjaily and appreciate your warning about eschewing their hospitality since I was planning vigorously to eschew it anyway. Thank God for old Iowa House, where I hope you will make me a solid reservation. A trip to Chicago also sounds like a good deal of fun and I'll leave in your hands whatever plans might be made in the carnal or "fun" sense. From your description of the city in your fictional memoir you seem to know your way around, and perhaps you will introduce me here and there as Dr. Penis, pronounced whichever way you chose.

I just got back from New Orleans where I delivered a kind of talk at a cornpone affair called the Deep South Writers Conference, but mainly occupied my time in eating those fantastic Gulf oysters and in other animal pursuits. I am now closing up my house here on the Vineyard and am heading soon for Roxbury, Connecticut, which is the address you can reach me at. My play—In the Clap Shack—opens in December at the Yale Repertory Theatre and I've got to get down near New Haven in order to deal with casting and other preliminaries. There are already ominous rumblings about the play, largely due to its subject matter—syphilis and gonorrhea—and I'm steeling myself for the inevitable attack, a mean little book of essays entitled "William Styron's In the Clap Shack, 10 White Urologists Respond."

Let me know of any further developments on the Iowa City scene. My telephone number in Connecticut, incidentally, is (203) 354-5939. Stay in touch.

All best,
Bill S.

To Bob Brustein

October 18, 1972 Roxbury, CT

Dearly Belovedfolk:

It was great to receive your letter and to know that things over there must be so much more pleasant in the long run than over here, where people are still knifing each other at random, "cutting up" (their wives and boyfriends), and in general making a terrible mess of the contemporary scene. The Yale Daily News has just announced on its front page a mad rapist at loose on the campus and I would fear for Susanna's "security," except for the fact that she is really by now such a femme moyenne sensuelle.* It turns out that she turned her last few weeks in Spain into an extraordinary caper with Luis Miguel Dominguín and she brought back a sheaf of clippings from the Madrid equivalent of Paris-Match, showing her in photographs running away from photographers à la Brigitte Bardot and then later being trapped by reporters into such admissions as: " 'I will go anywhere on earth that Luis Miguel goes,' said the lovely 17-year-old North American student of French and Spanish literature." She pretends to indignation at such journalistic mendacity but of course loves every bit of it and carries the clippings around with her everywhere. Her roommate at Silliman is Bobby Shriver.†

Speaking of Shriver, we gave a big bash up here for Connecticut fat cats for fund-raising, got Sarge to come, and raised $10,000 in a night, which seemed to me prodigious but was rather disappointing to the state political pros. Cleve and Francine Gray and Freddie and Florence March were among our co-hosts, and they told me to be sure to send their love to you.‡ Although probably a lost cause, the McG. Campaign is looking considerably more sprightly now than it did in the recent past. The revelations about the Republican party's criminal dealing are really extraordinary and if truly brought out into the open could turn things around. But this is a wild hope.

Everybody—including us, of course—enormously admired your piece on the London scene in last Sunday's Times.§ It was so preposterously intelligent and articulate in the midst of that sheet (or shit) which usually is such a collection of tired inanities and press-agent pufferies. And I'm de-

* A riff on "un homme moyen sensuel"—a man of average tastes and sensibilities.

† Robert Sargent "Bobby" Shriver III (b. 1954) is the current mayor of Santa Monica, California.

‡ Cleve Gray (1918–2004), American abstract expressionist painter. He was married to the author Francine du Plessix and lived in Warren, Connecticut. Actress Florence Eldridge was married to actor Fredric March; they owned a home in New Milford, Connecticut. The property was later sold to Lillian Hellman as well as Henry Kissinger.

§ Brustein wrote a regular column from London, beginning with his piece "London vs. New York: A Tale of Two Cities," *The New York Times,* October 15, 1972.

lighted to see that you are going to do it on a regular basis. Also David Pearce (God bless him, in spite of all) has sent us some Xerox copies of your pieces in The Observer, to which he subscribes. They're terribly good and make me believe that I could fall in love with the theatre if I lived in England, even in a non-Elizabethan time. You de bes' critic, yassuh!

Arthur Miller's play opened in Boston and though as you know I am very friendly with Arthur maybe it is my budding rivalry as a fellow playwright which makes me interested in the early response.* Danny Bell (we are both on the board of the American Scholar) told me in New York the other night that it may be the worst play he has ever seen. Which would have saddened me several years ago, but now (as a playwright) gives me a small, secret yuk-yuk. Though I hope it's not all that bad.

I've not gotten down to N.H. yet to see the Molière and the Ribman but hope to do so in the next week or so. As a matter of fact, of course, it will be essential. Rose didn't see the Molière but loved A Break in the Skin. I've talked to Alvin several times.† He seems most happy about the way things are going this season and we are getting together within the next few days, to talk about preliminary matters, and I hope I can see both the Molière and the Ribman in his company. I heard a stunning recording of There's a Star-Spangled Banner Waving Somewhere on the radio, so mawkish that it almost made me come and I learned where to send away for a copy, which should be arriving in a few days, and I want to supply it to Phylis so he can use the song as a curtain-raiser. I'll consult you further later in regard to your thoughtful advice about a British production. Right now all I want is for the Yale caper to go off well.

You've probably heard that Bill Preston and Elsie are Splitsville. It saddens the hell out of me but I can understand why all Nonie (bless her, she's in good shape) can do is laugh and laugh.

Diabolique was wonderfully sweet during the September days.‡ We went to Naushon several times and again to Lambert's Cove a couple of evenings. I've mastered the radio, incidentally, and have discovered that you can call anywhere on earth through the New Bedford marine opera-

* Arthur Miller, *The Creation of the World and Other Business* (1972).

† Alvin Epstein, associate director of the Yale Repertory Theatre under Brustein, directed Styron's play.

‡ The *Diabolique* was a boat jointly owned by Styron and Brustein.

tor, so we actually rang up Roxbury, Conn., while anchored in Tarpaulin Cove. It beautifully weathered a near-hurricane around Labor Day, and Tom Hale has now pulled it up for the winter. I'll be sending you our bill sometime, but there's no hurry.

We miss you enormously, your cats and chicks, and will be looking forward to your December arrival with celebration. Kisses, love, stay in touch.

Bill

To Bob Brustein

October 30, 1972 Roxbury, CT

Dear Bob:

The enclosed truly gruesome account from the Gazette* is not intended to depress you (as much as it did me) but to impress upon you (as it did me) the incredible value of a ship-to-shore radio-telephone such as we have on Diabolique. The poor wretch in the Gazette story should not, of course, have abandoned the boat because it remained afloat and had he stayed aboard probably the worst consequence would have been an extremely uncomfortable night for all concerned. But had he had a radio like the one we had installed (that kind of boat of his must have cost several thousand more than ours and therefore he should have been able to invest in one) he could have had all sorts of assistance on the spot within minutes. In any case, it's the saddest story about the sea that I've heard of in a long time. Can you imagine what memories this guy has to live with for the rest of his life?

I'm enclosing the accumulated boat bills, some of which date back well into the summer. I've deducted from the grand total items which had to do with my personal use of the boat after you left, such as gas and certain things that had to be attended to when the boat filled with water during a wild storm on Labor Day. These total $45.33. If you'll check on all this

* October 1972 issue of *The Vineyard Gazette* (Vineyard Haven, Massachusetts).

and approve it and send me a check for $541.65 I'll pay off the robbers. God Knows it seems to be a rich man's sport but, as John Hersey said to me, if you try to balance out the cost against the relatively few man-hours of pleasure you'll go bonkers—J.P. Morgan's dictum about yachts applying as well to our little beauty as to Onassis's or Sam Spiegel's. The greatest single item, you'll notice, is the invaluable radio which I had mistakenly thought we'd already paid for. After Mr. Jaeger's ordeal, I think you'll agree that it is well worth the cost. And, exorbitant as Tom Hale's outfit is, they do take care and pride in their work. During that bad storm they were right on top of that boat, cosseting it and pumping it and soothing and nursing it. Also, please fill out the enclosed contract (all it needs is your signature) and send it back to the shipyard as soon as convenient.

We've enormously enjoyed hearing from you and savoring vicariously the good London life. As you might know, I've had a moderately virulent case of Anglophobia for many years (your ancestors did not fight the motherfuckers as mine did, you immigrant), but you make things sound so pleasant and exhilarating that you could almost entice me into a few weeks in London Towne. Rose was going to come over with Ann Mudge to see the opening of Jay Allen's musical about Victoria, but at the last minute Mudge got cold feet so Rose also decided not to go. Me, I've been working but have been interrupted by a couple of trips to talking engagements I foolishly agreed to—one in New Orleans at L.S.U. which was redeemed by the truly excellent provender that is offered in restaurants all over the city (if the Vineyard had just one of the hundreds of oyster bars that are all over New Orleans it would make living there perfect)—and the other this week at Iowa City, whither I was lured by the crazy Fred Exley (did you read A Fan's Notes? A curiously brilliant and hilarious book with a lot of torment underneath), who got the University to pay me a lot of money and held out the ultimate enticement, or corruption: after the Iowa stint, a big bash in Chicago at a super suite in the Playboy Towers (Exley is making devious use of Hugh Hefner) with all sorts of rabbits named Flopsy, Mopsy, and Michele.

Alvin Epstein was up here not too long ago to talk about the play. It was fairly rewarding; he wanted me to make some minor dialogue changes, which seemed reasonable enough, so I did. I haven't been in touch since but I hear they are auditioning for—among others—Magruder; and one of Susanna's friends, who apparently—at age 17 or 18—was one of the few good things in the film version of A Separate Peace, is trying out for the role . . . I shall be closer to matters at Yale after I return from Ioway and the bunnies.

Miller's play as you doubtless know is apparently in even worse shape than when I last wrote you about it. Zoe Caldwell is now in the starring role, after two previous defections, and the same thing goes for the leading man. If anything remotely like this happens to Clap Shack I may be reached c/o General Delivery, Lima, Peru.

We miss you both enormously and send great love and can't wait for your appearance (you've got to come up here) but will mourn Norma's absence.

Much love from us,
Bill

To Willie Morris

November 7, 1972 Roxbury, CT

Dear Brother Willie

I sent a letter on this stationery* to Gene Genovese, telling him that I thought that Nat Turner looked a little like the younger Dick Nixon. Gene wrote back to say that he really looked like Booker T. Washington. I just got back from reading and talking at the U. of Iowa, returning by way of Chicago where I was a free-loading guest at the Playboy Towers and where everything you can imagine goes on. Or carries on. Happy to have your letter awaiting me, especially since I have tried many many times to call you in the past few months but finally gave up, finding you about as obtainable as Adolf Eichmann must have been when he was hiding out in Argentina. It was great to hear about your book and its down-home heroine and I do hope you'll let me take a look at it when a manuscript or galleys become available. I sure was sorry to hear about Ichabod Crane,

* Again, the Nat Turner stationery.

though, and I know how sad it must have made you feel, having lost Tugwell and Beauregard in the same way myself. We gave them a Jewish burial, though, on account of my wife Rose.

Try to get over here sometime very soon. My daddy (just turned 85) sent me a fantastic Wayco (Wayne County) ham from Goldsboro, N.C., and we'll fry it up and have it with grits, red-eye gravy, and Jack Daniels. Also, I'll have a ticket to Clap Shack for you if you come over—that's December 15 . . .

Bill

To Bob Brustein

November 15, 1972 Roxbury, CT

Dear Bob: Received your lively letter which was much appreciated, also the boat check which is sent on to the M.V. Shipyard. We've all enormously enjoyed your accounts of London goings-on. They gain special luster when juxtaposed against your dispatches in the Sunday Times: that last one—comparing the privacy of England with our state of affairs here—was truly excellent. We look forward to those pieces with great anticipation.

Alvin led the first reading of The Clap Shack a couple of days ago and I think it went off terribly well, given the fact that it was held on the third floor of The Blossom Shop right up from David Dean Smith and all the traffic hubbub from below made it a little difficult to concentrate. Jeremy Geidt—as you may know—is Dr. Glanz and I think he'll be fine for the role, despite the British accent. He seems also to relish the part and likes the play a lot. I think we came up with a rather remarkable "find" in the lad playing Magruder. His name is Miles Chapin (son of Schuyler Chapin, the new head of the Met. Opera), is 18 years old with some past acting experience, is the very soul of wistfulness and innocence, rather plump with his hair parted in the middle and wears granny glasses. His reading was quite good (though as Alvin points out, he will need considerable work) and has mastered a nice, authentic-sounding mid-South accent. I was frankly very pleased with the boy and think that he will be a hit once he gets fitted into the role. Paul Schierhorn is playing Budwinkle and is doing a fine job—at least the reading was fine . . . Lineweaver is being done by Nick Horman who is good but for my money doesn't play (or didn't read) the part nearly as flamboyantly or as "campy" as it should be. Alvin assures me, though, that Horman is a good actor who—once he gets into the role—will be able to turn on all the necessary fruity mannerisms, so that reassures me. Joe Grifani, naturally, is fine as Stancik, as is Michael Gross as Dadaris. The only part missing at the moment is Schwartz, which Joe read but, being a wop, was really unsuited for. Alvin is now engaged in a search for the Jew-boy. All in all I was very pleased and excited by the potential that was shown at the reading and am looking forward to your appearance at the last rehearsals because I know you will want to add a few of your very special licks to the production.

Strange to admit, I am getting a little of those pre-production jitters. I thought that I would be able to go through all this with more sang-froid than I might fail to display, let us say, upon the publication of a novel, but am just as nervous about this baby as I am about a book. People with names like to go along with your impression that the play might be a little too American for a British audience. Arthur Miller is going to see it this coming Wednesday with Francine and Chris Gray, and I'm interested in knowing his reaction.

But enough about the play. Suffice it to say that I'm considerably more [unknown] than I was when I wrote you the early news. Random House will have its version soon—complete with photographs—and I'll send you the first copy.

I'm delighted that you enjoyed Africa, despite the customary annoyances. I had the feeling that it would turn you on as it did me. It's astounding how Africa imprints itself on the memory in a way that no other place seems capable of doing.

Your Sunday Times articles continue to be greatly enjoyed. Our Man in London does an exceedingly good job. I was especially taken by the piece on Arden. What a wild tale, and you told it exquisitely.

Meanwhile, I keep working away in this amazingly mild and temperate winter, as much as I can eschewing the streets of New York, which more and more are beginning to resemble some hideous habitat of hyenas in the Ngonogoro Crater.

We miss you all and are looking forward to your early arrival on the Vineyard and picnics on Naushon, and other island delights. Al says she now wants to give Danny an all-over body massage while he reads to her from Playboy, which has become her favorite quality lit.

Love to all,
Willie

To Frederick Exley

November 30, 1972 Roxbury, CT

Dear Fred:

I received my fancy shirts in good shape, for which many thanks, also for the "Iowan" dispatches and your various communications. I thought Sharla did a very nice job indeed—despite the "homespun philosopher" tag, which vaguely makes me feel like James Whitcomb Riley—and I will write her a thank-you.*

I've had time to reflect on our Iowa and Chicago escapade and feel it was an enormous success—especially the tab we laid onto Hugh Hefner. But those Playboy guys were genuinely nice and, God knows, generous and hospitable. I hope you had a good time again in Chicago on Thanksgiving. Terry Southern once told me about how, during the filming of Dr. Strangelove, Slim Pickens (the cracker Texas pilot who had really never left Texas or California before) arrived via BOAC in London where he was met by a Rolls-Royce full of J. Arthur Rank, button-down, very Oxford proper types. After being seated in the Silver Cloud, one of the flunkies, in a very proper British voice asked what Mr. Pickens would like to look forward to in London in terms of creature comforts. His reply: "Gennamun, all a man needs when he goes anywhere is three square meals a day, lots of tight pussy, and a warm place to shit." Thereby cementing Anglo-American ties.

That thing about Linda and her poem and her hang-up is truly baf-

* James Whitcomb Riley (1849–1916) was an American writer and poet best known for creating "Little Orphan Annie" and the "Raggedy Man."

fling, though. However, it doesn't seem to me too surprising. Remind me, when next I see you, to tell you some wise thoughts I have on the matter, gleaned from experience.

It doesn't look as if we'll be able to touch base on Christmas or thereabouts because of geography problems. However, do keep in close touch. My wife Rose tells me to remind you (she's a great fan, pardon the expression, of yours) that you must come here and be a guest and we'll throw you a party that will curl your toes. Also the Taft School nearby definitely wants you in the spring to be on the memorial program I told you about.

Kiss all the groupies for me.

Your pal in Jesus,
Bill

Styron's play, In the Clap Shack, *premiered on December 15, 1972, at the Yale Repertory Theatre.*

To Bob Brustein

January 2, 1973 Roxbury, CT

Dear Bob:

I trust you are back safe and sound from your African adventures. Let me know how it all went, as I am eager to learn whether your experience was as fine as mine when we went to Kenya and Tanzania with H.R.H. Khan several years ago. It was totally unforgettable and I hope you had the same kind of time.

Opening night for the "Shack" was a laff riot. Unbelievably hideous weather—mercifully no snow—and the curtain was 20 minutes late due to the fact that the busload of theatregoers I had invited up from New York got stranded somewhere on Bruckner Boulevard for a long time. Mercifully, they had plenty of booze and arrived only five minutes after the delayed curtain. Being classically nervous, I saw little of the show, skulking in the lobby or spending most of the time at the Ol Heidelberg downing doubles to soothe my psyche. But I was told on good authority that it was a fine performance and that the audience loved it. The party at your place was a huge success. The caterers turned out a smashing supper and everybody (over 100 head) got drunk and it cost a fortune but what the hell. The busload of drunks got back to N.Y. at 3:30 AM during which trip my friend Bobby White tried to attack six of the lady guests, and I was told that Joe Fox indecently exposed himself.

I expect you've seen the clinker of a review by Clive Barnes.* I suppose I should be grateful to him for "admiring" me as a writer, but I found it pretty ghastly that the review was so totally negative. As I think you are aware, I had no ambition to write King Lear but I do think the play has some virtues, including a fairly original theme, some sharply drawn characters and a lot of moments of both pathos and comedy. The laughter I heard that night—and it was considerable—certainly didn't come from a machine. Then what possesses a reviewer like Barnes that he offers not a solitary word of approbation, that he saw no value whatever in the work? . . . Rose and Susanna have been in Guatemala looking at the Mayan ruins and the other kids have been skiing. Meanwhile, Alexandra made the trip by plane alone from New York to Baltimore.

How is Norma? Hope all goes well with her physically-wise. Give her a hug and a kiss, and also tell Danny that Al is crocheting a jock strap for him to wear this summer on the fantail of the Diabolique. Incidentally, I'm enclosing two bills, one for storage and one for the installation of the hawse pipe, which is a dandy invention and will allow us to swing the anchor directly overside from the foredeck and to stow it permanently there. You can send me your check for ½ at your leisure.

Everyone sends love and we are panting to know about Africa.

Send us the gnus.

Jambo,

Pill

* Clive Barnes, "Playwriting Debut for Styron," *The New York Times* (December 17, 1972). Barnes wrote that "the subject matter makes [*In the Clap Shack*] sound more original than it in fact is . . . the play is rather conventional." After critiquing nearly every aspect of the play, Barnes wrote that "Mr. Styron exaggerates everything."

Styron abandoned work on The Way of the Warrior *and began a manuscript entitled* Sophie's Choice: A Memory.

To Bob Brustein

January 22, 1973 Roxbury, CT

Dear Bob, Happy to receive both of your communications. Your long letter cheered me up a great deal after the early and creepy reception from the distinguished members of the press. Jesus, what ignorant pricks! But things have improved immeasurably since then and I feel much better about the play on my own! For one thing, it actually got a couple of swell reviews—a rave in the Hartford Courant and a boff-o (or is it sock-o?) in, of all places, Variety. Then (from what I hear, since I haven't been back since opening night) the performances have been knocking the audiences in the aisles. Our friend Phil Roth went a week or so ago with Howard and Alvin and all said that the effect was really tremendous. As you know, Philip is rather hard to please and he was wild about it, saying among other things that Schwartz was the best "stage Jew" he'd ever seen, but liking the whole thing enormously. And I know Philip well enough to feel that if he hadn't liked it, his reticence would be vast. Howard and Alvin are both hugely delighted by the way things are going, so fuck Barnes and all the rest.

Also thanks for your letter from Boyd. I spoke to Howard about it and he said he would send him a copy of the finished version of the script immediately. It could be great fun to see it done in London. . . . I haven't seen hide nor hair of Phillip, whom I thought I was going to put together a tape for the sordid part of the production. I've also sent an order off through the mail for "There's A Star-Spangled Bannner," as sung by the original troubadour, Elton Britt, but haven't received it, mail order places being notoriously slow. If you or Norma are in touch with P., please tell him to contact me as soon as possible because I would love to get that part of the production grooved in, so to speak.

We saw the Miller play in a preview last night and it was, alas, all the frightful things that have been bruited about. There's some really clever stage business here and there but that's about all—mostly it's a long Jewish joke about God. Jews as playwrights shouldn't joke about the Creation. It all ends up sounding like cheap lower East Side vaudeville, and I'm afraid that's about the level of Arthur's play. Mainly, though, it just doesn't hold together, doesn't have any vision; also it's badly marred by the Augustinian assumption that sex really is the evil behind human misery. This aspect is also done joking but it doesn't work since it was never a good message and especially hard to take in the 1970s.

Love and miss you all and are looking forward to your arrival in Dec, but tell Norma that our heart breaks at the thought that she can't be here. Also Al is bereft at the thought of being deprived of those throbbing embraces of Danny's, those wild nights of lust, that thrusting tool.

Oh well, there is always next summer and the decks of the Diabolique.

À bientôt,

Bill

To Philip Roth

January 29, 1973 Roxbury, CT

Dear Philip:

I have not "committed the cruelty" of reading either Podhoretz or Howe more than once but I do have some lingering impressions.* As one who is no stranger to such all-out attacks, I think I can both analyze and judge the nature of this kind of knee-in-the-groin criticism with, possibly, a little bit more astute familiarity than some writers.

. . . The first was from Stanley Kauffmann, who blasted Nat in the Hudson Review. It was not really a rancorous piece like Howe's but it was nearly as negative, saying that as literature the book was kaput, valueless. Shortly after this Kauffmann wrote a revealing review of another novel in the Atlantic. I can't at the moment recall what novel he was reviewing but it was someone you and I would consider a respectable writer and was receiving much acclaim in the press. Kauffmann put the book down from the first word, saying that it fell into a category of novels like Ship of Fools,

* Norman Podhoretz and Irving Howe, "Philip Roth Reconsidered," *Commentary* (December 1972).

In Cold Blood (though not strictly a novel), and Nat Turner—"big" books by decent writers which nonetheless had gained fame and favor not through any intrinsic worth but because their reception had been "rigged" by publishers and the media. I remember that as I read this review I suddenly became aware of the reason for Kauffmann's hostility in the long Hudson Review piece. It was really because Nat Turner had been such a smashing success, not only in literary but commercial terms. I had noticed this tendency in Kauffmann in his New Republic film reviews, to blast what I thought were pretty good movies (Tom Jones was one) when they were both popular and critical successes, and he was using the same old bludgeon on me. For the truth of the matter is that to say as he did that the success of Nat Turner was "rigged" is tantamount to saying that the favorable criticism it had received—from people like Philip Rahv and Alfred Kazin and Vann Woodward among others—was duplicitous and hypocritical, by men who were lying through their teeth. And then when it became clear to me how large a component in Kauffmann's critical lexicon was the idea of "success," I began to realize the motivation for his negative appraisal of my work. It is of course too glib and easy to accuse all critics of being afflicted with the vice of envy—but I'm positive given the evidence, that this was Kauffmann's trouble. My "success."

When criticism gives the impression of an inability to find virtually any value in work which many others (including those of high distinction) have regarded highly, you may be certain that the critic is deviously motivated. I know that there are all sorts of rebuttals to that proposition—the emperor's clothes syndrome, for one—and of course there is the famous example of Dwight Macdonald's demolition job on By Love Possessed.* But everyone with any real literary sensibility (including me) knew that Cozzen's book was bloated, badly written and incredibly overrated, and we were tickled to death by Macdonald's attack. The point I'm trying to make is that, despite the inevitable shift in values over a long period of time, there is generally speaking, a sound instinct abroad in both the critical and public mind as to what constitutes a major writer or a major work. The consensus is usually pretty accurate, too—the consensus among those who count, that is. In the late thirties and early forties, when Clifton

* Dwight Macdonald, "By Cozzens Possessed—A Review of Reviews," *Commentary* (March 1958).

Fadiman was raking Faulkner over the coals in the New Yorker, I (who had just started to read books like The Sound and The Fury) knew in my 15-year-old head that Fadiman was a misguided imbecile.*

I will come to Norman and Irving (don't they run a delicatessen somewhere?) in a moment, after a last reference to the kind of criticism I'm talking about. The other major (non-black) attack on Nat Turner came from Richard Gilman in The New Republic. This long piece, like Howe's, was aggressively rancorous, and it called Nat mediocre if not worthless. Much of Gilman's motivation had to do with the poisonous thesis (that he was then dishing out) that whites could not understand or evaluate black life and letters, and the essay revealed to me also (rather startlingly, I must say) that Gilman could barely write grammatical English. But mainly Gilman, like Howe, undercut the thrust of his argument by his refusal to acknowledge any value in my work at all . . . But in his insistent and nattering negativism he resembled Howe, and therefore—after the initial smart had worn off (one has to admit it that it does hurt)—I realized how easily he could be dismissed. For no one can legitimately take unto himself the authority to deem as worthless work in which too many other people of taste and intelligence have discovered great value.

Which brings me to Norman. His attack on you is, quite simply, weird. What is "the New Class" anyway? Nowhere does he successfully or convincingly define it, this New Class. Whatever it is, you are its spokesman and he is greatly and clearly disturbed by your "success." Of all people, Norman being troubled by success!! Of course, his concern with your success is somewhat different from the success-obsession of Kauffmann, who, I hate to say (because I used to know and rather like him), is a failed "creative" person for whom I honestly believe success in others acts like poison. Norman's pain over your success derives, as far as I can tell, from ideological considerations, and they are pretty simple-minded. Simple-minded and, I might add, very close to Philistine. His statement that the purpose of your work has been largely to offer documentary evidence "for the complacent thesis that the country is inhabited exclusively by vulgarians, materialists, boobs and boors" reminds me of those scandalously reactionary pieces that used to appear in Time or Life back in the forties and

* Clifton Fadiman, "Faulkner, Extra-Special, Double-Distilled," *The New Yorker* (October 31, 1936); "Mississippi Frankenstein," *The New Yorker* (January 21, 1939).

fifties, putting down honest writers and praising Herman Wouk. Given Norman's political and social reorientation I am not really surprised at this line, but I am amazed at how little subtlety he demonstrates. He sounds like Spiro Agnew. And indeed I think that's the crux of the matter, and it's such a tired situation that it borders on the absurd: an honest writer who has not shrunk from viewing life and society head-on once again being taken over the hurdles by someone who himself has abandoned literary standards even as he embraces Neanderthal social values and politics.

Despite the disclaimer to the contrary, Podhoretz really resents your treatment of the Jews and I would say that this resentment is at the heart of both his and Howe's assaults on your work. Had you not written Letting Go and When She Was Good it would have been difficult for both of them, but it immeasurably helps their strategy (part of which, or I should say a major part of which is to damn you for bearing false witness against Jewish life) to be able to say in effect, "Look, we are not after Roth for his nasty portrayal of Jews, because see how ugly he paints WASP life too." At least that's my reading of the matter. Howe's mind is vastly more penetrating and complex than Podhoretz's and of course he possesses, basically, a finer literary sensibility. But I can't get over the feeling that the rather well-hidden but overriding animus in Howe's piece has to do with your treatment of Jews. I don't mean to say that Howe is so unsophisticated as to think that Jewish life, any more than that of any other minority, should be exempted from the writer's right to portray it with as much severity as is compatible with his vision of the truth. I do think, however (and I've seen it in the pages of Dissent) that Howe is, quite unbeknownst to himself, possessed of an old-fashioned Jewish defensiveness which caused your work (despite his early praise of it) to stick in his craw as painfully as it did in the throats of those rabbis. Literarily speaking, the intensity of his attack on you rarely makes much sense and he often seems to lapse into arcane double-talk when he runs out of logic in trying to make a point. His entire attack on Portnoy, for instance, is to me nearly incomprehensible since it fails to acknowledge the fact that whatever its defects the book works; the animating spirit behind the novel is of such vigor as to make it quite academic whether the book is a group of skits, or has imperfect "development," or whatever. This is why earlier on, rather self-indulgently, I made the comparison with the Gilman treatment of Nat. The point is that, whatever its flaws, Nat Turner worked in a very special way for people, and it totally begs the question whether, as Gilman insisted, I had found the "wrong voice" for Nat, just as it begs the question that Howe is offended that Portnoy "never shuts up." For most people the book worked beautifully—whatever the mystery behind it—and throughout his piece Howe gives himself away by protesting too much. Also I think his taste has become degraded. I thought Last Exit to Brooklyn, with which he compares you unfavorably, was one of the most shrill, turgidly overwritten books I'd ever read.

At any rate, at too great length, these are my reflections, for what they're worth. In regard to Howe's piece, and on the purely mundane level, it is still curious to me that I've not heard a single person—in the great literary jungle we all sometimes venture into—mention a word about it, nor indeed about Commentary, where, if memory serves me right, that Macdonald attack on Cozzens was published. And I recall with what noisy glee that piece was received everywhere! I would only suggest that the crashing silence surrounding Howe's "reconsideration" of you means that, if many people read it at all, which I doubt, the unfair and hectoring tone which Howe adopted so bored people—as it did me—or turned them off, that they simply lost interest.

Well, you're forty now and old enough to know you've just got to take such shit. Wait till you're forty-seven* (I can barely write it), boy, then you'll know what the wintry touch of mortality really feels like. However, we can get our walking sticks out when you come back in the spring and hobble through the Connecticut woods, in the late summer of life for you, I in the early autumn.

Yours in the slime we sometimes find
ourselves up to our asses in—Bill

* Styron consciously struck out "seven."

To Mia Farrow

February 7, 1973 Roxbury, CT

Dear Mia: I received your nice cards warning me about calls from your agent, but Mr. McIlwane (is that the way you spell it?) was most pleasant on the telephone, and I now have recently had the opportunity of getting together with David Brown, who also has struck me as a capital fellow, really. Seems that he and Mr. Zanuck have a movie company or something and they would very much love to do a movie with you starring and me writing the script. The idea sounds good to me.

But before I met Mr. Brown (David, that is) I came up with another notion. I know that when you and I talked last you spoke of your disaffection with some of the kooky roles you had played in the fairly recent past, and I could understand your feeling. However, I also wondered if this weren't the perfect moment to cast you in Lie Down in Darkness, of course as Peyton, who was a little kooky, but, more importantly, tragic and potentially a splendid role for an actress of your caliber. Over the years LDID has been optioned more times than I can count, and there have been many treatments and several scripts, but for various reasons (usually cowardice and inertia on the part of the producers) nothing ever panned out.

In 1962, John Frankenheimer took an option on the book, and lined up Natalie Wood to play Peyton and Hank Fonda to play the father. A friend of mine, Richard Yates (author of a fine first novel, Revolutionary Road), wrote the screenplay.* Then something happened; the story goes that Natalie's agent persuaded her that the role of Peyton would destroy her virginal, all-American image, and when Natalie backed out so did Fonda and eventually Frankenheimer. All that was left was Yates's script—a good one, I think.

I recited the foregoing history to David, and it interested him enormously. He has of course asked to see the script, and I am in the process of getting it into his hands. I have not re-read the script in the intervening ten years, but I do remember it being strong and faithful to the book, and

* Richard Yates, *William Styron's Lie Down in Darkness: A Screenplay* (Ploughshares Books, 1985).

especially sensitive to the nuances of Peyton's rather complex character. I spoke to Yates over the phone (he now teaches in the Midwest) and he still expresses his faith in the script, with the reservation that it was, after all, written ten years ago and would doubtless need some revision, if only to take advantage of the more liberated situation movies find themselves in in A.D. 1973. I would doubtless collaborate in whatever rewriting and revisions are necessary.

At any rate this is a tentative feeler, pardon the expression, to ask you if this interests you and maybe excites you as much as it does me and, apparently, David Brown. I have a feeling that Dick Zanuck will be taken by the idea too. You are one of the very few actresses who has the range and subtlety to grasp a sad and complicated girl like Peyton Loftis, and I believe the time is ripe for the film . . .*

To Bob Brustein

April 23, 1973 Roxbury, CT

Dear Bob:

Enjoyed your last letter and, needless to say, your visit to New Haven—all too brief as it was. Now the play is, as they say, history but I hope it won't be embalmed in history, since I'm looking forward to a few more productions here and there from time to time. The Random House edition, incidentally, will be appearing imminently, complete with photographs, and I'll airmail you a copy as soon as I get one.

Good to hear about your Vineyard arrival although you seem to be having such a fine time that only a pleasant retreat like our island could ease the re-entry shock into the Citadel of Democracy. A weird atmosphere prevails here now—a kind of obverse side of the radical violence

* Styron had long hoped that a film of *Lie Down in Darkness* would be made. He had written his agent Elizabeth McKee on December 14, 1956, hoping that Eva Marie Saint would sign on for the role. Neither that film version nor this one ever made it into production. Styron's daughter Susanna is currently working on a new film based on Yates's script.

scene, with apathy on the campuses, political and otherwise, nostalgia for the 50's, etc. Indeed, I think in certain respects the 70's might resemble the Eisenhower years.

My novel about the Marine freak hero is coming along well, though at a time when Poirier proclaims Mailer the equal of Hemingway and Fitzgerald and potentially as great as Faulkner I feel very weak and humble as a writer.* I'm possibly taking a week off early in June to tour Holland with Rose and Bobby and Claire White (she's Dutch-born). Plans are skimpy so far, and iffy, but iffy I do come I might stop by in London for a fort with you chaps. I'll let you know well in advance.

You should enjoy writing your Times pieces since they are very elegant jobs indeed. We all enjoyed the piece on English actors enormously. Right on. I've done a long piece for The Book Review on Malcolm Cowley's farewell look at the Lost Generation, and have been told it will be on page 1. I'll send it to you in May, if you don't get it anyway.

A stupid boat bill is enclosed, but necessary, I think, in order to preserve the metal on the darling Diabolique. Just send a check at your leisure, anticipating, however, at the painful moment of check writing some lovely hours to come at Tashmoo, etc. Love to all from all of us.

—Bill

To Philip Roth

May 23, 1973 Roxbury, CT

Dear Philip:

It is testimony to your enormous gifts as a writer that—despite the fact that I am doubtless the only American male with two balls who has a real congenital aversion to baseball and who has avoided books on the subject like the plague—I read The Great American Novel (on a trip to Virginia) with the greatest delight and hilarity. It's a wonderfully funny and good book, be proud of it and, again, fuck the reviews.

At any other time I would be glad to nominate Reynolds but I'm al-

* Richard Poirier, often called Mailer's most astute critic, had just published *Norman Mailer* (New York: Viking, 1972).

ready nominating or seconding Peter Matthiessen and I really don't like to get in the habit of over-exposure. One begins to look a little like Glenway Wescott or Leon Edel. But there should be no trouble in finding someone. What a "club" that is, that outfit.*

Someone sent me Kazin's new book. Although less nasty, he treats me a little like Howe treated you—the work of a lifetime dismissed in 200 words. You come off a lot better. As for Mailer, get this: "We are at his mercy."!! Fuck them all.

Watergate saves us all. Remember when Mencken was asked why, if he hated the U.S. so, didn't he leave, he replied: "Where else can you get a 3-ring circus for the price of a morning newspaper?" To which now add the tube. See ya soon,

Bill

P.S.: TGAN is just fine. FUNNY! A lovely book.

Random House published In the Clap Shack *on June 15, 1973.*

To Susanna Styron

July 16, 1973 Vineyard Haven, MA

Dearest Sue:

I received your wonderful letter and read it and am writing this while awaiting one of our typical summer Vineyard invasions. Naturally it's another Kennedy invasion. Teddy called me up several weeks ago, saying that he and two other senators who are members of the Senate Interior Committee (Bible of Nevada, and Johnston of Louisiana) would be having a public hearing on the Islands Trust Bill on the Vineyard today, and would I mind "hosting" a clambake. So your Ma and I are hosting a clambake on our beach for about 75 people, most of them supporters of the bill.

* The American Academy of Arts and Letters.

Typical Styron deal. How I get into things like this I'll never know. Next summer I'm spending in Lacoste. Anyway the weather is really heavenly, which is one nice thing, after yesterday which saw a miniature tornado and over an inch of rain.

As usual, I came up here with the idea in mind that perhaps for once I would be free of the social nightmare. What should happen, however, a few days after we arrive is that Sinatra calls and says he's coming up on a boat. The boat was fairly modest by Sinatra standards—100 feet but the de luxe equipment was the same—color television, seven crew members and Frank's new valet, a grinning black man who comes a-running at the shouted command, "Abraham!" We did have a nice time, however, for a few days, moseying over to Nantucket, spending the night in one of the posh staterooms, and watching John Mitchell squirm on the color TV. To my great surprise, Frank is violently anti-Nixon, maybe because he wants Agnew to be president. Incidentally, he sent you his love and invited you and the family to Palm Springs for Thanksgiving.

He told a funny joke. A very portly Jewish fellow is running for the train, when he stops to weigh himself on one of those scales that also tell you your fortune. The card read: "You still weigh 260 pounds. You're still Jewish. And you missed your train."

I was a little sorry to hear that you're not exactly ecstatic about your present abode. I gather the chaps and girls aren't exactly topflight, as they say at posh clubs, but I also sensed that things aren't entirely gloomy and that basically you are having a pretty good time of it. Naturally, all the gang here misses you terribly and if you want to come back earlier you will be greeted with open arms, but I think maybe you will decide to hang in there for the full stretch.

When you do come, you will find everyone in great shape—if all goes as well as they are going now. I am writing well—which is to say I eke out my painful 600 words a day—and your Ma is in fine spirits and batting the old tennis ball at furious speed. Tom is a big tennis hound too and plays a lot with Fain Hackney, who barely beats him.* Polly and all of us were greatly relieved that her heart was not involved in her condition, which seems to have improved a bit. Poor sweetheart, she can't do any

* Fain Hackney (b. 1960) is the only son of Lucy and Sheldon Hackney, the Styrons' close friends and neighbors.

great exercising still but she does get around quite actively with her friend Dinah and all the other friends who flock to the house, and drives to the beach and to parties up-island. All in all, I'd say she's enormously better in all respects than what I gather was a bad spell in Spain. Alexandra is head of something she calls the "Max Smart Park Avenue Detective Agency" and Natalia d'Almeida* (I forgot to tell you the d'Almeidas are here) and Elizabeth Hackney† and her co-investigators. Yesterday she was busily taking notes and investigating the brutal rape and murder of Lady Godiva at the West Tisbury fair. She discovered that the perpetrator was Si Bunting,‡ who has been visiting for a few days. Alexandra immediately had him electrocuted, without benefit of trial.

By the time you get back they will, I think, have closed in on Nixon, and if he is not impeached he will certainly have his powers—which were tending in a very malevolent direction—seriously impaired, perhaps allowing Congress to exercise some of its powers which have been fumbling and subordinate for too long under Tricky Dick.

Anyway, be good and tranquille until you arrive. The Diabolique will be ready to take you on many picnics—especially to Lake Tashmoo which will soon have to be called Lake China, but that is a sad story, too long to go into here.

Much love from all of us, but especially from your

dear old dad

Xxx

P.S. I paid your phone bill. Also I'm enclosing proof of your Vineyard riches. Buy me a beer in Oak Bluffs.

* The daughter of the Styrons' close friends George and Ann d'Almeida.

† The Hackneys' youngest daughter.

‡ Josiah Bunting III (b. 1939) is the author of several books of fiction and nonfiction. He was the headmaster of the Lawrenceville School and the president of Hampden-Sydney College.

To Charles H. Sullivan*

May 15, 1974 Roxbury, CT

Dear Charlie:

I have often thought over the years since Quantico that you may have been the single most important factor in my having ever gotten a commission. You were clearly Number One from the very beginning and I through the accident of alphabet was always in close proximity to you. As a result I'm almost certain that I squeaked through PCS largely because I was hanging onto your coattails, or dungaree tails. Oh, I suppose if I had been a <u>complete</u> foul-up I would never have made it, but I'm certain that the fact that we were mates helped a great deal.

At any rate, I was happy to hear from you again after all these years. I was also most appreciative of your reaction to my work, and I thank you for troubling yourself to express your feelings. Your observations about blacks in the service are most perceptive and telling, and if the plantation analogy you make is depressing it is obviously true. Inside the service and out, the same thing applies—stagnation.

I was never really cut out for military life, but once a marine always a marine, as you doubtless know. The Corps still holds for me a strange fascination; it is a very special place, and although I'm glad I chose another career I am not being at all fatuous when I say that I am a better man for having served in the Marines. It was plain from those Quantico days that you would make a great success at it, and how glad I am that you found a good life there.

May your life in retirement (my God, military people retire young!) be just as good. I hope to have another book out soon, and will appreciate your reaction, pro <u>or</u> con. Meanwhile, once more thanks for the words after all this time.

Sincerely,
Bill Styron

* Charles H. Sullivan was a friend of Styron's from the Marine Corps. Sullivan was a career officer who had served in Guadalcanal before being sent to officer training at Princeton.

To Louis D. Rubin, Jr.

July 8, 1974 Vineyard Haven, MA

Dear Louis:

I should stop giving interviews.* The one you saw was not a terribly good one, mainly because I was in France suffering from a surfeit of exhaustion, wine and oysters, and I said some rather unconsidered things which you rightly caught me up on. However, I have since then been in receipt of the MS of the interview that Ben Forkner sent me and have submitted it to some pretty drastic editing. I sent it back to Ben and I do hope that I will also be able to see a final draft. Please tell him this if you see him, since I do not know if I really edited it harshly enough. Oddly enough, though, although I would rephrase it more gracefully, I find the part that you quoted me in your letter the <u>least</u> offensive of the things I said.† I mean the stuff about Nat being "ignorant of his own pride" etc. Because I actually think that the <u>real</u> Nat, the Nat I was referring to, <u>was</u> ignorant of his own undertaking, the enormity of what he was doing and so forth. I really do. I think that there is a great deal of a posteriori evidence (and there are several historians who have commented on this) that Nat may not have been dumb, in your words, but that he was very definitely a psychopath, dangerously over the edge, who hadn't the faintest notion of the way to foment a workable revolt. In other words, I'm saying that in actual fact my book <u>did</u> give him the complexities and nuances of character and intelligence which the historical Nat lacked. I'm afraid I'll have to stand by that, but you may be absolutely correct in saying that the flaw in the interview lies in the <u>way</u> I said all this. I thought that I had cut out what might be the most offensive parts, but if you will re-read what I have sent to Ben and tell me specifically how I can further improve it, I would appreciate it.

Alas, upon reading the interview I found most of that part that you felt to be "fascinating" etc. to be unacceptable, and have deleted most of it.

* Ben Forkner and Gilbert Schricke, "An Interview with William Styron," was conducted in France in April 1974 and published in *The Southern Review* (Autumn 1974); reprinted in West, ed., *Conversations with William Styron*.

† Styron wrote Rubin a postcard on July 29 indicating that "I toned down at least some of the 'race' references that you felt were rather out of order."

My reason is very very simple (and again due to my weak state in France): NO writer should reveal such a detailed outline of a work-in-progress, it's absolutely asinine, and therefore although I've retained a good hint of the plot and theme I've cut out all those details which at this stage of the game is to cut my own throat.

But thanks for the good interest and suggestions and I'll try to improve the abortion even further.

Yrs,

Bill

To Susanna Styron

July 19, 1974 Vineyard Haven, MA

Dear Sue:

We thoroughly enjoyed your long letter about your life as a pedagogue in Spain. Although much of it sounds like a drag, a lot of it indicates that you are also somehow managing to enjoy yourself. I would figure that life in Spain can't be all bad.

Polly showed up a couple of days ago all wreathed in smiles, feeling very good, and ready for the Vineyard whirl. The horse from Amenia is being brought up tomorrow, and I think your sister is looking forward to being an equestrienne again—though why I don't know, since I find those dumb beasts insufferably boring. Otherwise la famille is doing its usual Vineyard bit. I like it up here of course, but I am beginning to think that maybe these island summers constitute something in the nature of a rut. I am contemplating perhaps a single summer away from here—Malaga maybe—in order to break the too monotonous sameness of the routine. The post office, picking up the Times at Leslie's, putting up with Lillian—it gets to be a bit much, or a bit much of the same. One little diversion is nice: Tommy and I have become mad "Jarts" aficionados—you know, that game which is half darts, half horseshoe pitching. I generally beat old Tom, but he is still nutty about poker and usually skins his Hackney and Dahl pals, which makes up for his defeats at my hands in Jarts.

Your Mama told me about your letter in which you were brooding over taking off a year at Yale and concentrating on the film. I think we should wait until you get back here next month before any final decision is made. I am not precisely dead set against your plan—as a matter of fact I think it has some points—but I do think we should talk it over carefully. Apropos of which, I wanted to mention Armand Deutsch, a gentleman with whom we had lunch yesterday.* Mr. Deutsch, who is called Ardie, is the man who plucked you out of the water some years ago when you almost committed suicide by swimming out to Sinatra's yacht. He remembered the incident well. At any rate, he is very rich, a cousin of Phil Stern's, and lives in Beverly Hills where he is partly associated with the film business. He is a partner in fact of David Wolper, the documentary film maker who was briefly connected with Nat Turner, and he told me that if you are really serious and decided to spend next year making films he thought there would be no trouble getting you the kind of job you might want with Wolper. I said to him that I'd pass this along to you for what it's worth. At any rate, let us keep this in mind and go over all the pros and cons when you get here in August.

We all miss you and are anxiously awaiting your return to this little bower of Eden. Next week-end Willie Morris is throwing a Dixieland party down in East Hampton, and your Mom and I are going—staying with the Stantons—after which Jim and Gloria will come up here to stay for a week or 10 days. Maybe you'll get here in time to see them. I know to you it is like coals to Newcastle, but I have made a fantastic gazpacho and want you to try it out.

Be good and pray for your famille from time to time. Miss you very much.

Much much love,

Papa

* Armand S. Deutsch, the eldest grandson of Julius Rosenwald, was the intended victim of the kidnappers and murderers Nathan Leopold and Richard Loeb. A close friend of Frank Sinatra, "Ardie" was also in the inner circle of Ronald and Nancy Reagan. As Todd Purdum wrote in his *New York Times* obituary on August 18, 2005, "He shared a box at Dodger Stadium with Jack Benny and then with Walter Matthau, traveled the world with the publisher Bennett Cerf, lunched regularly with the director Billy Wilder and had dinner every Christmas for years in the Beverly Hills home of James Stewart." Deutsch also wrote a memoir, *Me and Bogie: And Other Friends and Acquaintances from a Life in Hollywood and Beyond* (New York: Putnam, 1991).

To Frederick Exley

Spring, 1975 Patmos, Greece

Dear Fred: I'm staying here on this island where St. John the Divine wrote the Book of Revelation. It makes it real weird for a lapsed Episcopalian. The Aegean here must be as beautiful as Hawaii. My host is Sadri Khan (son of the Aga) and we live rather well indeed. I've been able to get some work done, and hope to be back in the U.S. and on Martha's Vineyard around the end of June. Hope you can pay Rose and me a visit this summer.

Your pal,

Bill

To Carlos Fuentes

January 4, 1976* Hotel Meridien, Martinique

Dear Carlos:

I am writing you from French soil in the hope that this portends that I may soon come to "the mainland" and pay you a visit.

We missed you on the Vineyard at Thanksgiving but drank several toasts in memory of your and Sylvia's visit last year.

Together with two others, Rose and I (plus son Tom and Alexandra) chartered an 80-foot sailboat and sailed down here from Antigua—a week's trip, with stops at Guadeloupe and the incredibly primitive island of Dominica.

The French accomplished their de luxe style much better on the mainland than in their far-flung outposts. This hotel is straight out of "The Clockwork Orange," a super-Hilton all tricked out in plastic with hordes of package-tour trippers from Paris + Lyons (plus a large sprinkling of Italians), wretched service and (most profoundly ironic) abominable food. However, I did manage to climb to the peak of that splendid volcano, Mt.

* The Styrons were on vacation with the Brusteins.

Pelée, at risk of near-total exhaustion but with an exhilarating thrill of triumph somewhat like that of Hillary and Maurice Herzog.

Belated thanks for the photographs you sent some time ago. Rose was especially appreciative since they were very flattering. I don't know when there will be a Styron visit to Paris—we feel a little déracinée since the Joneses moved away from the Île St. Louis—but do not be surprised if you receive a visitation within the next few months. I am eagerly anticipating not only seeing you both again but a delectable taste of those tamales Suzette.

Rose joins in fond regards to tout Fuentes.

Abrazos,

Bill

To Burke and Evangeline Davis*

April 9, 1976 Roxbury, CT

Dear Folks:

That was a very lovely time you showed us, as they say in the vernacular, and me and my wife Rose are still glowing with the warm aftermath. Many, many thanks for your combined generosity.

Primary things first. Somewhere near Emporia, Va., we stopped at a Stuckey's to let the girls pee, and I bought for $1.45 a bag of shucked pecans, idea in mind to fulfill the eggplant recipe. To make a long story short: it was <u>everything</u> you said it was. Up here in Roxbury last night we tried it out and it was a <u>triumph</u>. It is so good that it will have to go into the standard repertory.

We received the books (incidentally, Burke, all the way down Rt. 301 Rose read your Jefferson book to the kids and now I know more about T.J. and Virginia than I ever did; however, three miles beyond Skippers, Va., I

* Burke Davis (1913–2006), noted Southern writer of biographies and historical novels, best known for his nonfiction works on the Civil War. Like Styron he had strong ties to both North Carolina and Virginia; from 1940 to 1980 he was married to Evangeline McLennan Davis.

didn't feel that ozone fix you said I would passing the N.C. line, smelled more like hydrocarbons & tobacco); they arrived the day we got back and we are most grateful.* I have the Va. Quarterly Review here in my studio with young Burke's story and will write him my reaction as soon as I read it in the next day or two.

My falling-down ankle, the result of those pre-revolutionary streets, is perfectly well now, after a brief swelling that night in Goldsboro. I just walked seven miles today to prove my resilience.

My dear old daddy is, at 86, pretty spaced out. After being in his great years a Jacksonian Democrat, he is now in his ancient age reverting to old ancestral fears, and thinks the niggers are going to do him in. Says one of them, named William, whom he hired to clip the hedge, has stolen the clippers and has sold them—a godawful thing he broods about 24 hours a day. Wants to kill the black sonofabitch. He used to be very gentle, an egalitarian.

Please come to see us on the Vineyard this summer. Any day, any time. My wife Rose will write you. Much thanks again for everything and fond best,

Bill

To Robie Macauley

August 9, 1976 Vineyard Haven, MA

Dear Robie:

I want to thank and congratulate you on the neat and, indeed, eloquent way in which your reply dealt with Ms. Ozick and her hysteria.† She is clearly a True Believer and the only way in which she can be handled is

* Burke Davis, *Getting to Know Thomas Jefferson's Virginia* (New York: Coward, McCann & Geoghegan, 1971).

† Cynthia Ozick, "A Liberal's Auschwitz," took issue with Styron's argument that the tragedy of the Holocaust was "ecumenical" and "anti-life" rather than Jewish. See William Styron, "Auschwitz's Message," *The New York Times* (June 25, 1974). Robie Macauley defended Styron in *The New York Times Book Review,* August 8, 1976. Ozick admonished Styron for making Sophie Zawistowska Polish Catholic rather than Jewish, and renewed her critiques of *Sophie's Choice* as recently as a 2005 speech at Harvard.

through words like yours: cool, temperate and wise. I'm glad you underlined the fact that nowhere did I minimize the terrible suffering of the Jews. But you did me a favor and you also did a favor to people in general by pointing out that where totalitarianism is concerned everyone suffers ultimately and that it is not only shallow and naive but extremely dangerous to think otherwise.

Sincerely
Bill Styron

To Susanna Styron

October 17, 1976 Roxbury, CT

P.S. I forged your signature on the automobile deed and Mrs. Vanderhoop is sending me the check next week, which I will deposit in your acc't in Dry Dock.

Dear Susanna:

I love your letter from Heathrow, especially its safe and satirical remarks upon the Briddish—how completely I agree! Do send me more letters—with comments, please, upon the Spanish and the French, both of which I like more than the beastly Briddish with their mediocrity.

I am enclosing your Mass. ballot, in case you want to exercise your sacred and divine right to vote. I do think it might be a good idea even if it is a lot of trouble. Your trouble would involve, I think, having to go to the American Consulate in Madrid and having it witnessed by an official there. But hurry! Nov. 2 approacheth.

This afternoon Polly left all agog to fly to Nice, thence to Italy. She was so excited I thought she'd pop out of her skin. We had a fine time while she was here—fixing oysters and crabmeat. She has become so adult—it's hard to believe, and she and her adored and adoring Charlie make a fine pair.

Your grandfather is now ensconced happily at River Glen in Southbury, about 10 minutes drive from here. I chartered a Piper Aztec from the Vineyard and Willie Morris and I flew down to N.C. to pick him up last Tuesday. He is pretty alert for his 87 years, cheerful, only now and then vague or confused, and asks often for his beloved granddaughter Susanna whom he misses. Drop him a postcard now and then: c/o River Glen, Southbury, CT, 06488.

The N.Y. Times Magazine wants to devote a whole Sunday issue (or nearly whole) to an article I intend to write on capital punishment.* As you know, the reactionary U.S. Supreme Court restored the death penalty and plans are afoot to execute large numbers of people, starting with three states: Texas, Georgia and Florida. I intend to go to one of these states (probably Florida) and do a long and detailed study of one of the condemned. In Florida there is a white boy exactly Tommy's age awaiting the electric chair for murdering a little girl of 12. Chances are I'll hone in on this case. It of course means an interruption of "Sophie" but my feelings are so strong about the awfulness of the death penalty that I think the time worth it—especially when it'll be read everywhere (including Spain) and just may have some effect in altering people's consciousness about the matter.

Out walking with Sundance and Aquinnah yesterday I happily lit up a post-lunch cigar which Aquinnah immediately snatched from my hand and chewed in half. In my rage I threw my walking stick at the little beast but the stick missed and broke in splinters on the asphalt. I could tell that Aquinnah was just laughing. Life in Roxbury goes on just as it always has.

Much love,

Daddy

To Susanna Styron

November 16, 1976 Roxbury, CT

P.S. Mrs. Vanderhoop sent me her check for BMW, so all is O.K. in that department, thanks to various forgeries.

Dear Susanna:

Looks like the South is going to rise again. Thanks to your absentee vote in Mass and Polly's absentee vote in Roxbury our peanut-picker won

* Styron never wrote the article.

and everyone is quite happy hereabouts.* What Jimmy is really up to, however, remains to be seen. Your mother and I spent the election evening (I am reporting this as counterpoint to your description of election night in Paris, which I loved) at Michael and Alice Arlen's on Firth Avenue. We drove in my swank new Benz and all sorts of old friends were arrayed around the five TV sets—Bruce Jay Friedman and Jackie Kennedy (you might mention this to Albina), Norman Mailer (we're back on speaking terms), and a lot of other folks I can't recall at the moment. It was an exhilarating thing to see Carter win, but there is a curious lull at the moment, as if people really can't figure out what this odd farmer is going to do about China, the Russians, the Economy, etc.

I loved your letter from the beautiful city and indeed I was wrenchingly nostalgic by the notion that my little girl was writing me from the place where 25 years ago (God!) I had such a good-bad time. I say that because basically I loved it but I did have some weary and lonely hours. I'm so glad that you've found friends to enjoy. I did too but it took me a long time and I pined away at the Hotel Liberia (rue de la Grande Chaumière, right around the corner from the Dôme in Montparnasse) and some nights I got so homesick I thought my heart would bust in twain. I think that is why out of sheer necessity I was able to write The Long March in a burst of 5 or 6 weeks at that dinky little hotel—loneliness is sometimes fruitful, though not often. I know what you mean about "things going to happen to you," that feeling of anticipation. Paris helps create that feeling on its own. What a gorgeous city. I also felt that there was "something big" and that I was going to find it. So I'm sure, you will. It's a great time of life and I think that your passion for the movies will pay off. I'm not knocking on my own chosen profession—I still think that "the novel" when it is working on eight cylinders is a majestic form of expression—but I do think that films are marvelously exciting at their best and it must be tremendously exhilarating for you to be involved in movies, knowing that eventually you will do something that fulfills your "vision." I'm babbling . . . I'm so happy for you to be having the time of your life in that wonderful metropolis. Even if you are a bit queer about food and only eat Granola and other unspeakables.

* The election of James Earl Carter, Jr., as President of the United States.

Sophie is coming along well though as usual slowly and painfully. Along with its blessings, the wretched and insufferable part about "the Novel" is this dimension of Time—the sheer months and years it takes to get the thing finished. But I'm moving along with some sense of progress. I read some of it out loud to Bob Loomis and Hilary last week-end and I think they liked it a lot. It is so terribly weird to dare do what I am doing. I'm the only American writer (that is, writer as a member of my identifiable literary generation) who has faced the Holocaust head-on, the Concentration Camps, and I have made the amazing decision to embody the victim as a non-Jew. Certainly the hell I went through about Nat Turner will be a serene summer outing to what I will get for Sophie, or because of it. But I can't go back. I'm committed like a bird in flight or a Boeing 747 in take-off and can't go back! I have such an intense love-hate relationship with this work. Sometimes I can't bear facing the pages, other times I feel it will be as good as anything written by anyone in this or any other decade.

Following are some random jottings and thoughts and reminiscences about happenings here since last I saw you.

Last week-end a fine masterpiece of a party here chez Styron for Francine Gray and her book (which has gotten excellent reviews generally and is doing very well).* Big sit-down bash for 30 people. Among those present: Millers, Sadri and Katy, Matthiessen and Maria (lovely gal), Warrens (looking fine), Millers, Tom Guinzburg (with pretty gal who is a Lie Down in Darkness adorer, always makes me feel good), Allens, Ed Doctorow (a truly superb gent). Smashing event. Marqués de Cáceres Rioja wine went over big, also my Va. ham. I gave a beautiful toast to Francine and her book. Several of us stayed up until 4:30 AM. Woke next day to find to my horror that in my generosity I had given away to the male guests all of the Havana cigars in my humidor.

I'm taking Tommy down to see Duke soon. He's such a bright boy with such poor grades (like his father). I hope he likes Duke, the best school now in the South (he'll never make Yale or Harvard).

He got kicked in the foot by a horse, X-ray revealed only a bad bruise.

* Francine du Plessix Gray, *Lovers and Tyrants* (New York: Simon and Schuster, 1976).

God, how I hate horses! I also hate that devilish Aquinnah, who can be charming but who chews everything in sight, worse than that goat Feather.

Sorry to hear that you want to do a film on a drop-out prostitute. Couldn't you make a movie about a nice American boy who voted for Gerry Ford and wants to open a new Big Mac place somewhere near Danbury?

Grandpop is flourishing at River Glen (he loved your letter but can't write back and told me to send love to you) and eats like a horse. Imagine, 87! It really turns out the poor sad Eunice in her dementia was starving him with Pepsi-Cola. Right out of Faulkner. But now he's doing wonderfully, we pick him up and bring him here almost every day. Daphne is adorable to him and today, mirabile dictu! he and Terry ate chitlins together.

It is hideously cold, the coldest autumn all over the U.S. in 15 years. But barta to the weather, we'll survive. I still take my walks.

In the Clap Shack, my sole foray in drama, is going to be produced in—of all places—Barcelona! Can you imagine! Do you think we should all go to opening night, armed with ampoules of penicillin?

Looking forward enormously to the Xmas expedition. Right now it appears that we will show up in Paris on Dec. 17th thence to Klosters, although I'll be damned if I will be caught on skis. What a blessing to spend a Yuletide, without ulcers, in a foreign ambience. All I want you to do when I arrive in Paris is to take me to the nearest outlet for Belon #00 oysters. I'll buy all that any of us can eat.

Must shut up now. Please tell Albina that I got her nice note a week or so ago and would have replied but lacked her address (she didn't write it down). I send my fond regards chez Casati and am looking forward to a happy get together in December.

Polly sends adorable heartwarming letters from Italy. Can't wait to see her as well as you, my beloved Numero Uno fille.

Much much love,

Daddy

To Willie Morris

May 3, 1977 Roxbury, CT

Dear Willie:

Jim and Gloria told Rose and me the other night about your mother, and I wanted to say (for both of us) how sorry I am. It is, I know, a terrible wrench to suffer and I am thinking of you—all the more, I'm afraid, because my own poor old daddy seems to be failing badly, losing practically all of his memory, and all I can do is help him go to the toilet to do the peepee and stand there cursing God as he dribbles. Who thought up this idea of the end of life anyway? My daddy never fails to remember Willie Morris though, which is something.

I'll be seeing you at the Matthiessen-Guinzburg-Styron 50th party soon (I'm 66 but it doesn't matter).

Thinking of you,
Bill

To Herbert Mitgang*

June 17, 1977 Roxbury, CT

Dear Mr. Mitgang:

I am sure that you were never at a party with James Jones or myself, and I am also willing to believe that you don't have a shovel. I'm sorry that you didn't see that these references were metaphorical.

Contrary to the reaction you received about your obituary report, most of the readers I canvassed did not really think your piece was either fair or

* James Jones died on May 9, 1977, and Mitgang penned the *New York Times* obituary on May 10. He had written an indignant note to Styron on June 14, 1977, in reaction to Styron's piece in *New York* magazine: "A Friend's Farewell to James Jones," *New York* (June 6, 1977). This piece was collected in the first edition of *This Quiet Dust* but was replaced by a different piece on Jones for the second and later editions. "Apparently, you did not like my obituary report on Jones," Mitgang wrote. "Most readers thought it fair and respectful." He questioned Styron's ability to recognize the "difference between a news report and a eulogy," finishing by admonishing Styron that "I don't have a shovel." Mitgang to Styron, June 14, 1977.

respectful. This had less to do with the so-called facts, which in general you set down with accuracy, but with a certain tone and lack of balance which invaded the piece and left most of the people I know who read it with a bad taste in the mouth. Just one example would suffice; it has to do with Jones's life-style which you so gratuitously emphasized throughout at the expense of his work. I am speaking of the brief passage where you deal with Hemingway and Jones.* There because of your emphasis and tone the reader is left with the distinct impression that it was pure and idealistic for Hemingway to abstain from writing movie scripts and somehow rather venal for Jones to do so (although of course many fine writers including Faulkner and Fitzgerald pursued this way of making money). There are many other places in which this kind of animus, whether unconscious or not, comes leaking out, and despite your disclaimer to the contrary many readers noticed it.

Certainly no one expected any writer for the Times to compose a eulogy, nor do I think that the piece was really composed in a spirit of ill-will. Maybe you just had a bad day. But my own feeling, reflected in a consensus of practically everyone I have talked to, is that you did Jones a disservice.

W.S.

* Mitgang's obituary included Jones's quote about Hemingway: "One has to be an egomaniac to be a writer, but you've got to hide it. . . . Hemingway was more concerned with being an international celebrity than in writing great books. He worked harder on his image than on his integrity. He was a swashbuckler who didn't swash his buckle or buckle his swash." Seemingly reacting to this critique of Hemingway, Mitgang wrote: "Unlike Hemingway, however, Mr. Jones continued to be criticized as a writer, regardless of his themes. Unlike Hemingway, he did not avoid writing for films and turning out books clearly designed for the commercial market. And, unlike Hemingway, he had gone to Paris, not in his youth, but in his flourishing mature years." Mitgang, "James Jones, Novelist, 66, Dies; Best Known for 'Here to Eternity,'" *The New York Times* (May 10, 1977).

To Elizabeth Hardwick

September 30, 1977 Roxbury, CT

Dear Lizzie:

I was unable to get to the memorial for Cal at the American Palace Theatre—I heard it was fine—but I did come to Boston for that ceremony.* I was quite awed by it even though I think that Cal would understand why for me—a Virginia boy brought up "low church"—all that incense smelled of popery. But it was, as they said, majestic.

I can't tell you, though, how I will cherish that trip we made to Russia together. Cal's face in repose at that table was so moving as the Fiedenenkos and Cousinses yammered away. And that walk through Red Square at night and the lousy salami sandwiches, and Cal's sweet, sardonic resignation. Just to have been with him in a place like that during his last month or so—and with you—is something I will always treasure. I wish I had had the chance to tell him that after that drunken party at Vog's dacha in Penedelkino, Yevtushenko and I got a couple of bottles of champagne and went out in the moonlight and sat until dawn at Pasternak's grave. I think Cal would have relished that, but the next morning I was so hungover that I barely made it on the Aeroflot Flying Fortress to London.

Oh well, Lizzie, what can you say? A wonderful man. Wonderful memories. I hope to see you before long.

Much love,
Bill

To Stuart Wright†

September 30, 1977 Roxbury, CT

Dear Col. Wright:

Thanks for your letter with its agreeable surprises. I am sending the copy of <u>In the Clap Shack</u> back to you, signed, by separate mail. I appreci-

* Lowell had died on September 12, 1977.

† Stuart Wright (b. 1948), bibliographer and private-press publisher in Winston-Salem, North Carolina. His imprint, Palaemon Press, issued several limited editions by Styron. Styron gave Wright his only set of galleys for *Sophie's Choice*.

ate the handsome photos, also the clipping from Bell Wiley's book.* It is most illuminating, especially since it is true that the general impression one gets of that war is of life without erotic joys. Wiley sets the record straight.

As for publishing something of mine, I am taking the liberty of sending your letter on to a professor at Virginia Tech who knows all my work and who has done a bibliography of my so-called "oeuvre."† He is very bright and engaging and may have some good ideas for you. I imagine you will be hearing from him soon. I hope something develops.

Thanks again.

With kindest regards,
Wm Styron
Maj-Gen CSA

To Stuart Wright

October 12, 1977 Roxbury, CT

Dear Col. Wright:

I hope that by now you've been in touch (or he with you) with Jim West at Va. Tech. It seems that he knows of a thing (unpublished) which I had forgotten—a spoken tribute, rather brief in length, to Robert Penn Warren which I gave several winters ago in New York City.‡ I think it might be just right for your series. The MS is with my papers at Duke, and Jim will ferret it out if you decide that you want it.

* Bell Irvin Wiley (1906–80), Civil War historian who studied under Ulrich B. Phillips at Yale and later worked at the University of Mississippi, Louisiana State University, and Emory University.

† James L. W. West III, *William Styron: A Descriptive Bibliography* (Boston: G. K. Hall, 1977).

‡ Styron delivered the tribute to Warren at the Lotos Club in New York City, April 10, 1975, and it was published as *Admiral Robert Penn Warren and the Snows of Winter* (Winston-Salem, N.C.: Palaemon Press, 1978). The first edition was signed only by Styron; a second edition in 1981 was signed by both Styron and Warren. This piece was eventually collected in *This Quiet Dust.*

Appreciate the Forsyth Co. book.* I used to know a lot of Winston-Salem boys when I was at Davidson, but I've lost touch with them. I also spent a very frustrated night at the Zinzendorf Hotel. I'd come up to visit a W-S. girl who, in the fashion of the time, rejected me, and I had to pass the night at the hotel listening through those thin walls to the most impassioned erotic activity one can imagine. That is my forlorn memory of Winston-Salem.

I will be here Xmas and will look forward to your generous gift.

Best regards,

Wm Styron C.S.A.

To Stuart Wright

November 12, 1977 Roxbury, CT

Dear Col:

I think perhaps the piece should be called "Admiral Robert Penn Warren and the Snows of Winter"—("a tribute by William Styron"—if you so wish). I don't think there is any further permission needed from Duke. I already signed a release sent to me by Jim West. I think there should be a note to the effect that it was a speech given by me at the Lotos Club, N.Y.C. (4/10/75) and there should be somewhere a copyright © by William Styron, with the year.

Herewith also a snapshot. It was taken at Luxor, Egypt, in March 1967 (by my wife Rose). There is no other photo I can lay my hands on but I think it's right nice anyway. The personae (l. to r.) are Red Warren, behind him (partly hidden) his wife Eleanor Clark, his daughter Rosanna, his son Gabriel (foreground), my daughter Susanna, me, my daughter Polly.

I hope all this is satisfactory. I am eagerly looking forward to the final product. Incidentally, I'm sure I can get Red to co-autograph the pam-

* Wright was a coauthor of *Forsyth: The History of a County on the March* (Chapel Hill: University of North Carolina Press, 1976).

phlet with me if you would like it—certainly any number up to 250 or so. Let me know.

Yours in the rebel cause.
W.S.
Gen. C.S.A., etc.

P.S. The piece is hardly literature, I see upon re-reading, but certainly nice enough as a speech before some assembled drunks.

William Clark Styron, Sr., died in Southbury, Connecticut, on August 10, 1978.

To Willie Morris

August 11, 1978 Roxbury, CT

Dear Willie:

I thought you would want to know that my dear old father died Thursday night, in peace and no pain. In a little over a month he would have been 89, so with three good wives and rich life behind him there is sadness but no grief. He was really fond of you and I think he remembered that plane ride from N.C. with as much wonderment as you and I did.

See you soon,
Bill

To Danny Robb*

September 21, 1978 Roxbury, CT

Dear Danny:

I had a great teacher at Duke University, who sent me on my way as a writer. Go to a good school and have the luck to find a teacher who cares: that is my advice.

Sincerely

William Styron

P.S. Also, it doesn't hurt to do an enormous amount of <u>reading</u>.

To Roxbury Zoning Board

September 23, 1978 Roxbury, CT

Gentlemen:

I would like to build a wall in front of my property on Rucum Road in Roxbury.† The wall would extend the full length of my property, approximately 300 feet, and would be a maximum eight feet in height. The bottom four feet or thereabouts would be of stone, which in turn would be surmounted by approximately four feet of wooden palings. It would be attractively built. The reason for this wall is to effectively shut out the noise and sight of traffic from my house and studio, both of which are built very close to the road. During most of my residence in Roxbury for the past twenty-four years Rucum Road has been a quiet and peaceful street. In the last two or three years, however, the road has become one of the busiest in town, largely due to the establishment of the housing development at the top of Rucum Hill.

I am a writer who works at home and whose livelihood depends literally on reasonable peace and quiet. The new influx of traffic with its nearly

* Danny Robb, a fifteen-year-old boy, had written to Styron asking how he got started in his career.

† The town said the proposed eight-foot wall was too high. The Styrons built a four-foot wall and planted many fir trees.

endless stream of cars, trucks and construction equipment causes at times distraction and noise which I find nearly intolerable. A wall with its necessary height of eight feet would, I am almost certain, provide an effective barrier against this intrusion and allow my family and me the quiet and privacy we need. The proposed wall would satisfy all reasonable aesthetic requirement and would prove to be no traffic hazard whatever. I respectfully request that the Zoning Board accede to this proposition.

Very truly yours,
William Styron

To Peter Matthiessen

December 24, 1978 Roxbury, CT

Dear Peter: I'm sorry not to have been able to get together with you last week (or week before) but have been in a kind of delirium finishing Sophie which has removed all of me except my tonsils—and even they are going. Am off to Venezuela until Jan. 15 and trust we will all get together soon after that. I'm finishing Snow Leopard and it is plainly a masterpiece.* After my recuperation a few drinks will be in order. Keep in mind the idle delights of Salt Cay.

Love to Maria, Porter†

* Peter Matthiessen's 1978 nonfiction account of his two-month journey to Crystal Mountain in the Himalayas.

† "Porter" was Matthiessen's nickname for Styron, given during chess matches in Ravello in the early 1950s and used for his entire life.

To Bertha Krantz*

January 4, 1979† Spice Island Inn, Grenada

Dear Bert:

Hope this gets to you in time for the printer. Otherwise I'll fix it in galleys.

Last line of book should now read (p. 889):

"This was not judgment day—only morning. Morning: excellent and fair."‡

Off to the Orinoco tomorrow.§ See you mid-month or thereabouts.

Fond regards,
Bill S.

To Susanna Styron

March 21, 1979 Roxbury, CT

Dear #1 Susanna:

I so much enjoyed getting your letter about Sophie. I had hoped that you would like it—you were a sort of "pilot" for the book—and the fact that it got to you, as they say, means a whole lot to me. As you must know by now I am a slow creator but I put an enormous amount of thought and energy into the work. Taking so long in a sense increases the risk—suppose it's a Bomb after all those years? suicide time!—and although I hate to admit it I am rather anxious to know whether the book works on all the various levels I've sought. Your reaction (and there are not as yet many people who have read it) makes me think that I might have succeeded in the way I wanted to, and your words made me happy. One of the many things I cherish in you, my #1 daughter, is your common-sense sensibility—this is really a higher form of critical acumen than most professional critics

* Bertha Krantz was the chief copy editor of Random House; she edited all of Styron's books.

† Styron forwarded this note to Bob Loomis in April of 1998.

‡ The last line of *Sophie's Choice*.

§ The Orinoco River in Venezuela.

possess—and when you tell me that the book affected you in the way it did, I know that you are being honest with me as well as being a first-rate critic (what Va. Woolf cherished as "the common reader"), and that pleases me immensely. I'm even glad that you had to look up a few words in the dictionary—shows I'm still keeping you on your toes.

I had an interesting thing happen the other night in regard to the book—or I should say two interesting things. This was when your mother and I were down at the Warrens in Fairfield, right after coming back from Salt Cay (about which more in a minute). There was an English editor there named Tom Rosenthal, who had very much wanted Sophie for his own firm, Secker and Warburg, and with whom I had been in correspondence. By this time he knew he could not have the book, having been out-bid by Cape, but was very good-natured about the loss. Of course he had read the galleys and the fact that, after having lost in the bidding, he could still rave to Red Warren about the book seemed to me to endorse the worth of the book more than anything. What he told Red in my presence was simply this (a) it was one of the finest novels he had ever read and (b) it was far and away the best work yet written about the Holocaust, better than any Jew (and he himself was Jewish) had remotely approached. This of course made me feel very good, even though he added as an aside that certain Jews in the U.S. were likely to hate the book. Which brings me to this—

Later, a foolish ass of a Yale professor of English named Harold Bloom (whom I later gave a vigorous tongue-lashing to, though for other reasons) told me that the head of the American Jewish Committee, an immensely powerful organization which practically controls Israel among other things, had told him that the word was out that Sophie was violently anti-Semitic and would be "dealt with" accordingly.

So as you see, it looks as if the next few months are going to be very lively. Can it really be that the furor over Nat Turner is going to be duplicated? Stand by for further communiqués.

You missed an extraordinary extravaganza at Salt Cay. The high point was the week spent by your beloved friend Willie Morris in company with the "3 Widows," Gloria Jones, Muriel Murphy and Lady Hardwicke. Willie outdid himself in professional Southern sentiment, reading from old Civil War chronicles and letting the tears drain happily down his jowls while twilight fell over the sea and the Daiquiris flowed down his throat like molasses. Willie is a character, drunk or sober, and I'm sure that the piece he is going to do on me and Sophie in the Book-of-the-Month Club News will be a small masterpiece.* In every respect Salt Cay remains Paradise, and I hope it is not sold in the near future, so that you can avail yourself next year once again of its incredible charms. The only time it even got slightly draggy was when, toward the end, it got commandeered by an overwhelming preponderance of your people (including your three siblings) and we began to get eaten out of house and home, right down to the last bouillon cubes.

I am reminded now by myself to thank you for the various H'wood publications you have sent, including the H'wood Reporter with its fanciful remarks by Swifty Lazar.† Such nonsense he speaks! Incidentally, I have heeded your admonitions about Swifty and given him wide berth in regard to "deals." My agent Don Congdon has refused to have anything to do with the transaction which Swifty was trying to promote when I was out there. You may remember that Swifty had said that if Don allowed them to have a one-shot chance at selling Sophie he would get a million dollars and give Don the commission. Don's explanation to me as to why he turned the idea down was sublimely simple: Don is almost certain that he himself can get more than a million. So much for Swifty's dreams!

I loved your descriptions of Jimmy Baldwin and the fag Jesuit. Jim, of course, I've always been enormously fond of; it does my heart good to know that he still feels the same way after all these years. Do you realize that there was a year—it must have been around 1963 or 1964—when Jimmy must have been among the 5 or 6 most famous people in the world? More famous than Sinatra. Or Henry Kissinger. Or Shirley Temple. He had to wear white-face for disguise.

I'll probably be coming out to see you in a month or so. I hope you'll tell me more about your reaction to Sophie. Meanwhile, chin up in that

* Willie Morris, "William Styron," *Book-of-the-Month Club News* (Midsummer 1979).

† Irving Paul "Swifty" Lazar (1907–93) was a talent agent who was given his nickname by his client Humphrey Bogart. Lazar represented many prominent actors and authors, including Lauren Bacall, Ernest Hemingway, Larry McMurtry, and many others.

"revolting" place, as you called it. You can only go on to better things. I love you beaucoup much.

Your devoted,
Daddy

To Willie Morris

April 2, 1979 Roxbury, CT

Dear Willie:

I was deeply touched by your letter and so grateful to you for expressing yourself about Sophie in the honest and eloquent way you did. I value your judgment over and above anyone I know, and your expression of confidence truly filled me with joy. As I recollect, you were dead right about Nat Turner, and I have the feeling that your predictions about Sophie will turn out to be accurate, too. Also, I know that your B.O.M. piece will be splendid. After finishing a long work like Sophie I guess it was inevitable that I have been feeling a kind of post-parturition gloom. Bless you for turning that feeling around and helping give me the inner comfort I've needed. Finally, I'm tickled half to death that you perceived the book's intrinsic Southernness. We mustn't ever let that go.

Ever in fondest gratitude
Bill

To Philip Roth

April 3, 1979 Roxbury, CT

Dear Mr. Rothstein: Count your blessings. At least I placed your opus before that of Mr. Wouk, who is much older than you (and much more Jewish). Consider this: I could have linked When She Was Good with Irving Wallace. So you come off pretty clean. Also my new work contains the famous Jewish country club joke which you once related, although naturally I don't attribute this to you. This is something you may also wish to take up with your attorneys. Hope to see you in late May although I may be in Albion before then and will ring you. For the first time in my life, like the Arabs, I've made the limeys pay a bundle.

—B.

To Willie Morris

May 30, 1979 Roxbury, CT

Dear Willie: A small printing outfit out in California does beautiful limited editions of short works by writers—usually 500 copies.* I've given them permission to print SHADRACH, and I wanted you to know that the edition will bear the dedication "To Willie Morris" which in three words is a way of expressing my friendship for you. It will be published in mid-summer and you will, of course, get several of the first copies.

As ever,

Bill

Sophie's Choice *was published by Random House on June 11, 1979.*

To Charles H. Sullivan

July 5, 1979 Vineyard Haven, MA

Dear Charlie:

Hope you've gotten through Sophie's Choice by now. It's doing extremely well, better than I anticipated + very near the top of all best seller lists and generally fine reviews, also sold to the movies (Alan Pakula, who

* The story was published in an edition of three hundred copies. William Styron, *Shadrach* (Los Angeles: Sylvester and Orphanos, 1979). The story also appeared as "Shadrach," *Esquire Fortnightly,* November 21, 1978, and was collected in *A Tidewater Morning.*

did "All the President's Men") for a nice bundle.* So I'm beginning to believe the 5 years' sweat were worth it.

On your way to New Hampshire why don't you stop off here at my summer place on Martha's Vineyard? It would be great seeing you again and I have an ulterior motive: I am returning to a novel about the Marine Corps I temporarily set aside to write Sophie and would be happy to pick your brains about the Corps if you would permit it. Anyway, hope all goes well with you.

Sincerely

Bill S.

To Prince Sadruddin Aga Khan

July 5, 1979 Vineyard Haven, MA

Dear Sadri:

As I opened your letter from the appropriately named M./Y. EROS I thought to myself that those sweaty afternoons with Shorty (inspiring me as she did to the subsequent love scenes with Leslie Lapidus) surely paid off. Grateful as I was to you for the Patmian adventure, I was just as grateful for your letter and for the knowledge that you liked and appreciated the book and its contents. I was also of course very touched that Katy cared for the book as she did. You two are among the tiny handful (friendship aside) of the readers I cherish.

From remote Patmos you were doubtless unable to get much of an idea of Sophie's progress (it was only published a couple of weeks ago) but I am pleased to say that it is doing exceedingly well, surpassing at least my own expectations. The book jumped from nowhere to 2 on the N.Y. Times best-seller list, where it remains this week, and I only have to dislodge a moronic thriller by someone named Ludlum to reign supreme (at least for a while). In the meantime the novel is 1 on the local scene in Boston, N.Y., and Washington. The paperback sale, to Bantam (owned jointly by a

* The film of *Sophie's Choice,* directed by Alan J. Pakula, opened on December 8, 1982. The film was nominated for five Academy Awards, and Meryl Streep won Best Actress for her performance as Sophie.

Kraut publishing firm and Fiat, so much for our WWII enemies), was for $1,575,000—not quite a record for fiction, but close to it. So I think all this indicates that one can still make a success with quality as well as trash. The reviews have been in general extremely good—the only notable dissents coming from The N.Y. Review of Books, where the book was raped by a totally obscure academic from Queens College, and, predictably, from The New Yorker with a contemptible little kiss-off which told much more about The New Yorker than it did about Sophie.* I am enclosing some material for your inspection. The editorial from The Washington Star, incidentally, was read aloud to me over the phone by Teddy Kennedy, who called me up in great excitement at 10 P.M. to say that he had never seen a novel given such attention in a national newspaper.

Your sympathetic letter meant a great deal to me. No matter what the reception a book gets (that is, in the media) the important reaction is from a friend whom one truly trusts and I could easily tell the intensity and the perception you gave to the book. One of the big surprises (you alluded to this matter) is that I have received no noticeable backlash at all from the Jews. As a matter of fact, you could have knocked me over with a broomstraw when I opened (with some trepidation) an envelope from Commentary and discovered therein no snide warning of coming controversy but a warm letter from Norman Podhoretz—who certainly must be the archbishop of the Jewish right wing—telling me that the book was "marvelous" and wishing me every success. So I am delighted to report that everything so far has come up smelling, as they say, like roses. (No word from the Poles as yet, I think some problems there eventually.)

I hope that I'll be able to come to see you in Geneva toward the end of August or a bit later in September. I've been invited to go to Yalta by the Soviet Writers Union—an invitation I may or may not accept. In any event, I want to come to Europe on general principles (nostalgia); also Sophie is being published in England in September and I've tentatively agreed to be there. However, I'll keep you posted. Maybe you'll save a room for me—I think Rose might link up with me later in September. We

* Robert Towers found "it difficult to regard *Sophie's Choice* as even a noble failure" in "Stingo's Story," *The New York Review of Books,* July 19, 1979. The *New Yorker* review of June 18, 1979, called the book "an elaborate showcase of every variety of racial prejudice and guilt" and "loaded with overwrought sentences."

miss you both very much and are panting with envy over your return to Patmos, especially aboard that lewd vessel, the Eros.

Much love to you both from us folks here,

Bill

To Ben Crovets*

September 1, 1979 Vineyard Haven, MA

Dear Mr. Crovets:

That was an amazing letter you wrote me about Sophie. It is a small world indeed. The reason I'm certain that "your" Sophie and "mine" must be the same girl is that I did know her in 1949 (not 1947, as I wrote in the book) and also she did live, as I did, in a rooming house on Caton Avenue—something I did not mention by name in the book.† Those two facts clinch her identity. The story about the boyfriend was spooky indeed. I met a boyfriend, who seemed harmless enough, and if it's the same boyfriend you mentioned I must have sensed something violent in him. But practically all of my book is invented, so to speak; I never really got to know Sophie very well and in fact I left the Caton Avenue house after only a few weeks' residence, and never came back.

I do thank you for writing me such an interesting letter. Should you dredge up any other memories of Sophie, or have any idea as to what might have eventually happened to her, I'd be fascinated to hear from you. Meanwhile, my best thanks for what you wrote me.

Sincerely

William Styron

* Ben Crovets, a Wantagh, New York, resident who wrote to Styron suggesting that he had known the original Sophie in Brooklyn in 1949.

† Jim West offers a detailed account of the various women whom Styron put together to create Sophie. She was chiefly a combination of the physical attributes of an actual Polish Catholic Sophie whom Styron knew in Brooklyn in 1949 and the personality of a woman named Wanda Malinowska whom Styron dated in 1949. See West, *William Styron: A Life*.

To George Target*

October 16, 1979 Roxbury, CT

Dear Mr. Target:

Thanks very much for your long, rich, vivid and appreciative letter. It is good indeed to get such a reaction—especially from England where I'm afraid my literary fortunes have never fared too well. I'm rather tickled that you were driven back to The Joys of Yiddish, since that is the book I used to forge most of my Yiddish in the first place. Also I was flattered that you should link me with John Fowles—a most impressive writer. Thanks again for your message. It helps to know that one is making contact with a truly receptive reader.

Best wishes,

Wm Styron

To Charles Sullivan

October 22, 1979† Roxbury, CT

Dear Charlie:

I received your letter (also the earlier one) in addition to the extremely useful material on the Marines in Nicaragua. This, together with other bits and pieces I'm beginning to accumulate (plus Burke Davis' book on Puller), should really begin to build up an invaluable reservoir of information.‡ I happen to know Burke Davis (he lives in my old neck of the woods in Virginia, and we have the same editor at Random House) and I don't

* George Target (1924–2005), British novelist and World War II veteran who spoke out vigorously against the failings of organized religion. He had sent Styron a lengthy fan letter praising *Sophie's Choice* and comparing Styron to Thomas Wolfe and John Fowles.

† Enclosed with this letter were inscribed copies of Styron's books. In *Lie Down in Darkness,* Styron wrote: "To Charlie, the man who dragged me kicking and screaming through Officer Candidate School and made me the Marine I still am. Affectionate regards, Bill Vineyard Haven, Mass August 1979." In *Sophie's Choice,* Styron wrote: "To Charlie, Warmest best wishes from his old classmate. Semper Fidelis Bill—Martha's Vineyard 1979."

‡ Burke Davis, *Marine! The Life of Chesty Puller* (Boston: Little, Brown, 1962).

quite understand how or why I've not read his Puller book—but it is a lack soon to be rectified. I really appreciate your great help in all this, as I am straining at the bit, so to speak, to get back to work. Yes, you're absolutely right, The Way of the Warrior is a free translation of the word Bushido and—as you will eventually see, I hope—there is a very definite irony having to do with the Marine officer class—you mentioned this in an uncannily accurate way. I do thank you for the various information you've supplied, and I hope I can call on you from time to time for further wisdom.

It was just great seeing you and Dorothy—however briefly—last summer and we'll certainly have to get together again. At the end of November—the 30th, to be exact—I am giving a talk and receiving an honorary degree at Fla. State University in Tallahassee. I'd like to think that I might get further south to St. Pete along about that time, if you're free for a day or so. I'll keep you informed.

Sophie has dropped a rung or two on the best seller list but it's still doing beautifully according to Random House—into its sixth printing and 225,000 copies in print. So I'm feeling no pain about my most recent baby.

Anyway, stay in touch and I trust everything goes happily with you and Dorothy.

All best—Bill

Sophie's Choice *won the inaugural American Book Award for Fiction.*

To Philip G. Prassas*

January 2, 1980† Roxbury, CT

Dear Mr. Prassas:

I noticed you sent a copy of your Harper's letter to Aldridge. I'd be absolutely delighted if somehow you would see fit to sending a Xerox copy of this letter of mine to Aldridge, too, without comment.

Best wishes,

—W.S.

Dear Mr. Prassas

I am very appreciative of your recent letter with its lively defense of me against John W. Aldridge. While I am quite honestly touched and grateful that you should rise to such a defense, I hope you won't be offended when I say that I think you are taking Aldridge far too seriously. In the same mail as your letter I received a letter from a woman, a professor of English at a large Eastern university, who has also written many reviews in intellectual journals. Her name would be familiar to you; I am not acquainted with her personally. She wrote: "Your book is assuredly the most powerful American novel I have read in years and years. The only novel of Faulkner's that affected me as much is Absalom, Absalom. Next to Sophie's Choice, Mailer, and recent Bellow and Malamud pale, and Cheever and Updike seem very minor figures. I will teach this novel every year (as soon as it comes out in paperback), for it is a masterful achievement of the first rank."

I did not quote all this at such length in order to aggrandize myself, or out of insecurity. I have received since publication of Sophie literally hundreds of letters, in the same vein, from intelligent readers of roughly the same high literary standard of this woman. Aside from this, Sophie has received, generally speaking, the most favorable reviews (from critics I respect) of any of my novels. It has received (like all ambitious works) a

* Prassas wrote a letter to Lewis Lapham, editor of *Harper's,* after John W. Aldridge's "Styron's Heavy Freight" appeared. Prassas included his letter to Lapham and Aldridge's review in a letter to Styron on December 20, 1979, labeling Aldridge's piece "a smug hatchet job," which, like the *Turner* critiques of the late 1960s, "don't even qualify as literary criticism."

† This letter consists of the short note and the long letter.

certain amount of harsh criticism—but even most of this harsh criticism has been embedded in reviews which tend to regard the book as a good book with certain serious flaws. I take such reviews with good grace, since almost none of these reviewers approached the book with Aldridge's built-in hatred and animosity; he is quite unique among his colleagues in regarding Sophie as a failure with no redeeming features. His crocodile tears shed for my hoped-for but unrealized success are laughable in their transparent dishonesty. He has been praying for my "failure" for years, and it must drive him half-wild to realize that he has been overwhelmingly outvoted.

But most of this is really beside the point, which is why I suggested that you are taking Aldridge much too seriously. The point itself is that Aldridge's own credentials are by now seriously questionable and shaky. Writers have the right to scrutinize critics for their intrinsic quality, just as critics do writers, and by now Aldridge's deficiencies as a literary arbiter are pathetically obvious. I hesitate to employ such an old cliché, but one really is tempted to ask: John W. Who? In even rather subtly savvy literary circles his name arouses no interest, rings no bell of recognition. It may be known that he is a sycophant of Norman Mailer, but that is about all. Well into his 50s he has not the shred of the reputation of his truly distinguished critical contemporaries: George Steiner, Hugh Kenner, Irving Howe—men who, unlike Aldridge, have illustrated the necessity of critics engaging our attention through a rich command of linguistics, history, philosophy, religion, sociology and other intellectual disciplines. There is no cerebral resonance in Aldridge, which is why he seems so provincial, so empty, so pompous, and why in the end he doesn't matter.

But I do most heartily thank you again for your concern. Strangely enough, the once-great Harper's has become the weird bellwether of philistinism (not, as its editor would like to think, the vanguard of intellectual inquiry), and Aldridge fits that philistinism like hand in glove. We need people like you to keep an eye on these dispiriting frauds, masquerading as the elite. For your thoughtfulness and effort, I am grateful.

Sincerely,

William Styron

To Lillian Hellman

April 2, 1980 Roxbury, CT

Dear Lillian,

I returned from a week-long trip to Mississippi to find your letter. I am hastening to answer it, because I am afraid that the young Chink lady reporter with her single quote from me—"It's unfortunate all around"—left you, and the general Times reader, with a sense of ambiguity which I certainly didn't intend.*

Least of all did I intend my words in any way—in the slightest way—to be construed as an endorsement of Miss McCarthy's sentiments. Surely you must know that. I found what she said about you to be as vicious, mendacious and appallingly tasteless as did most of the other people I've talked to about the matter. Certainly I have very little regard for Ms. M., personally or otherwise, in any case. I've only met her once or twice and was rather put off by her archness and smugness in each case. After Nat Turner appeared she made some very ugly remarks about my work which were quoted extensively in an Italian newspaper. So aside from being no fan of the lady, I was utterly repelled by the statement she made about you in public.

But, this said, I think it is "unfortunate" (and this is as strong a word as I would care to use) that you decided to sue this woman, as bitchy and outrageous as the statement was. The key complaint you have against me is embedded in your sentence: "I really don't feel the anger I might have once felt about your lack of defense of me." But the fact of the matter is this: you don't need any defense. Let me tell you this: you are a fine and enduring writer whose work in several forms has touched millions of people, and whose life has stirred countless people, too. By contrast, La

* Styron is referring to his comment quoted in Michiko Kakutani, "Hellman-McCarthy Libel Suit Stirs Old Antagonisms," *The New York Times* (March 19, 1980): "'It's unfortunate all around,' was all William Styron had to say." The lawsuit stemmed from Mary McCarthy's comments on *The Dick Cavett Show* in January 1979. In the appearance, McCarthy said that Hellman was "overrated and dishonest" and that "every word she writes is a lie, including 'and' and 'the.'" Hellman filed a defamation suit against McCarthy, Cavett, and the Educational Broadcasting Corporation (which aired Cavett's show). Although sparked by McCarthy's television remarks, Kakutani's article delineates the feud's roots in "hostile traditions within the intellectual Left."

McCarthy is a literary careerist whose best creative work is distinctly second-rate or less, and whose critic work—always marred by cleverness, vindictiveness and an amazing amount of sheer bad writing—has already begun to look shopworn and dated. Against such an adversary you need no defense at all, save one: silence.

This is all that I believe to be unfortunate about your part in the matter: that you rose to her bait and allowed yourself to be encouraged to enter into a probably long and costly lawsuit (with a questionable resolution) rather than to shrug it off and refuse to get down to Miss M's level. What she said about you was loathsome and, of course, in itself a lie but so outlandishly hyperbolic as to be absurd. Had she said—just for example—that you were a card carrying Party member until the year 1960 (or that you were a lesbian, or that you had committed a fraud) you would probably have a sound case. But the very grossness of her statement—I was about to say, a kind of sublime silliness—paradoxically protects McCarthy, since it is so ludicrous that it plainly defies belief. The few people I know who saw the show all felt that the statement, and the patently vicious way she uttered it, reflected far more tellingly upon McCarthy than upon you. That is why I think the lawsuit is "unfortunate." It has nothing to do with my undying regard and affection for you.

I am glad that you took up my defense in the face of an attack from some other writer, whomever he may be, and I appreciate it, but I fail to see what it has to do with the matter at hand. It is only what I would expect from a good friend, but in friendship there should be no quid pro quos.

If I had bothered to answer the attacks on me (remember Nat Turner, when I was, in print and in public called a "Fascist," "morally senile," "degenerate," etc?) I would by now be prematurely withered and spent. The trouble with you, I fear, is that you cannot accept the fact that you are really a wonderfully powerful and enduring writer. When, a number of years ago, Elizabeth Hardwick attacked you in a disgustingly gratuitous and mean-spirited way, many people, including myself, were appalled.* But I was profoundly disturbed at the extent of your disappointment in me—or resentment, or whatever—when I refused to join those who

* Styron refers to Elizabeth Hardwick, "The Little Foxes Revived," *The New York Review of Books* (December 21, 1967).

sprang to your defense in print. It was, God knows, no lack of loyalty that prompted my refusal but only an abiding feeling, then as now, that such insults, no matter how insufferable, are best endured in silence, and that we somehow begin to weaken our hard-bought integrity by lowering ourselves to battle with those who are demonstrably vicious or second-rate.

Naturally, I don't except you to agree with any or all of the above, but I do expect you to believe in my fondest love for you which, despite falterings and differences, has never failed.

Bill

To Donald Harington

April 2, 1980 Roxbury, CT

Dear Don,

It was good indeed to hear from you again. Also very interesting to hear that you're in Pittsburgh. Pittsburgh was the first "big" city that I ever saw, at about ten or so, when I would come up to Fayette Co., Pa., to see my Yankee (mother's) relatives. I thought it was unbelievable to be able to eat lunch in a department store (Joseph Horne's), and the Liberty Tube was the first tunnel I ever traveled through. Also, I saw my very first stiff when a rakish older lad (about 15) took me to the Allegheny County morgue. Finally, my mother was a graduate of the University of Pittsburgh—must have been in its very early days, before the grandiose Cathedral of Learning. You're in good hands.

Now as to Mailer—I'm holding you to your word not to be libelous—it is a dull story. We had been for several years, back in the Fifties, what I thought were known as good pals. He lived not far from here, in an old farmhouse in Bridgewater, and he and his wife Adele and Rose and I saw a good deal of each other. I thought our relationship was going along swimmingly. I admired Mailer and his work, and I knew that he liked me and admired my own writing. Then one day, out of the blue (I can remember the date perfectly, March 13, 1958, because it was the day my daughter Polly was born), I got a perfectly shocking letter from Norman. He accused me point-blank of having made "atrocious remarks" about Adele, and in so doing betraying forever our friendship. He also said that if he heard any more about my slanderous ways he would beat the shit out of me. I thought at the time that there was no foundation in his accusation, and was horrible hurt; I really suffered. In all honesty now, come to think of it, I really may have said some remarks about Adele. She was very aggressive. . . . I probably remarked on this to some tattletale, who promptly got back to Norman. Hence his rage. But in the end (after the initial shock) I didn't care. A true friend would not have written such a vicious letter, would have wanted to talk it out instead. So I finally said, Fuck it, and that was the end of our relationship. I've never really regretted it.

I hope the preceding can be of some use to you, though you must vow to be discreet and, as you say, forbearing, forgiving, etc.

I am in a terrible funk, having contracted an almost terminal bronchitis while sleeping for two nights in the Bilbo Suite (named after the late senator and demagogue) in the Governor's Mansion in Jackson, Mississippi. Anyway my near terminal bronchitis is the result of having commenced smoking innocently at the age of 14 (all this data confirmed by the new Smoking Report of Surgeon General of the U.S.). I'm shooting to make 60, which is due to come along in a shockingly short time (I'm one year younger than Jimmy Carter who, according to The Washington Post, is spending his evenings reading Sophie's Choice)—but if these fucking attacks continue to lay me under like they are now doing, I'll be sleeping in HIS Bosom any time now.

I relished your reminiscence about John Irving. I'm sending you a copy of Sophie, autographed, by return mail. Stay in touch and Believe in Him.

Bill

Styron delivered the commencement address at Duke University in May 1980.

To James L. W. West III

August 18, 1980 Vineyard Haven, MA

Dear Jim:

You're absolutely right about Daddy Grace, except that the interesting thing is that there were two prophets, and both were the inspiration for Daddy Faith.* The other Newport News impresario was the Elder Solomon Lightfoot Michaux and he had a rival temple in the Negro section of N.N. (generally known as Jefferson Avenue).† I never could get them straight except that they had a large influence in the town in those days—among the Negroes, that is. The city in the Thirties was close to 50% and Niggertown was sheer hell, with more knifings, cuttings and murders per capita than any city in the U.S. outside of (for some unknown reason) Chattanooga, Tenn. The district where most of the mayhem went on, incidentally, was called Blood Fields (not Bloody). Dr. Joseph Buxton, the surgeon who delivered me (and the father of my father's second wife) had to go in there every Saturday night and sew up the victims. I saw the mass baptisms of both Daddy Grace and the Elder Michaux many times. They were held in the shallow water near the Little Boat Harbor, where the ferry to Norfolk docked (supplanted in the Fifties by a tunnel). Thousands of Negroes showed up from all over Va. & N.C. Tidewaters and I remember the Fox Movietone newsreel people also covered it. Quite a sight, all those black people (mostly women) in their white turbans and robes, hollering Hallelujah.

It would make a nice article and I hope you proceed with it. All goes well here, more or less, given our mortal condition on earth. Stay loose.

Yours,
B.S.

* A key character in Styron's *Lie Down in Darkness.*

† Solomon Lightfoot "Elder" Michaux (1885–1968) was a radio evangelist, entrepreneur, and founder of the Church of God Movement. Charles Manuel "Sweet Daddy" Grace (1881–1960) was the founder and first bishop of the predominantly African American United House of Prayer for All People.

To Philip Roth

October 5, 1980* Roxbury, CT

Dear Philip: This is our next president feeding America.† The Deeter attack on fags was fascinating and horrible. She may be our next Secretary of H.E.W., so watch your step. I've got to go to Dartmouth to be idiot-in-residence for the early part of this week but will get in touch for dinner soon.

—B.S.

To Willie Morris‡

April 30, 1981 Roxbury, CT

Dear John: I doubt very much that I'll be able to forge anything so elaborate as a complete inaugural address, but it may be that I can find the time for a few eloquent lines. If I can, I'll do it, for it is plain that we cannot allow the mean opposition to even contemplate taking over a city which is a nice place to live largely because of your leadership. I find Fourex natural membranes, however, less abrasive than Trojans, and I hope I can expect a gross of such in recompense.§

Yrs ever,

Bill S.

* Postcard of Ronald Reagan bottle-feeding a chimpanzee.

† Reagan was the subject of other notes between Styron and Roth. In an undated postcard from 1985 or 1986, Styron wrote that he was "saving a lovely true Reagan story until I see you next—soon, I hope."

‡ The letter was addressed to John O. Leslie and was a response to another of Morris's prank letters. Leslie was the mayor of Oxford, Mississippi, and a friend of both Morris and Styron. Morris wrote Styron on April 27, 1981, on Leslie's stationery asking him to replace Morris as Leslie's speechwriter.

§ This payment in prophylactics was in reference to Leslie's/Morris's offer to have "anything in my drugstore" in payment.

To Willie Morris

May 28, 1981 Roxbury, CT

Dear Willie:

Your Mississippi piece is absolutely splendid—so tellingly right and beautiful.* I'm proud of you for having written it for so many reasons. Not the least of these is the fact that once and for all it makes manifest the tremendous humanity of the state (and therefore, by indirection, the South in general), and wipes out forever any claim on the part of the North to moral superiority. But I also just loved the writing—the richness and the passion. It is a beautiful piece and will be read, I believe, for a long long time to come. (Life did a great job, too, in the presentation.)

The new president of France, Mitterrand, offered me and Arthur Miller round trip transportation by Concorde if we would come to his inaugural.† So we went, paraded down the Champs-Élysées, went to the Arc de Triomphe, had a drunken 2-hour lunch at the palace, got drunk, got laid, and now I'm back. Such adventures do not come without their price, though. Since I've returned I've been suffering from (at the outset, at least) the worst attack of gastritis I've ever had (horrible nausea for 48 hours which made me contemplate suicide), followed by bronchitis which is still pestering me dreadfully. Can the clap be far behind? All this to help usher in the first left-wing administration in a quarter of a century.

IT IS TIME TO SETTLE DOWN AND STOP THIS TRAVELING ABOUT.

Willie, thanks for Miss. piece again, and give my love to Dean and Larry. And do stay in touch, as usual.

Always,

Bill

P.S. The check for my Ole Miss show arrived in good shape.

* Willie Morris, "Coming on Back," *Life* (May 1981), reprinted in *Shifting Interludes: Selected Essays* (Oxford: University Press of Mississippi, 2002).

† Styron wrote about the event in "A Leader Who Prefers Writers to Politicians," *The Boston Globe* (July 26, 1981), collected in *Havanas in Camelot* as "Les Amis du Président."

To Ian Hamilton*

July 1, 1981 Vineyard Haven, MA

Dear Mr. Hamilton:

I saw Cal Lowell off and on during the years after I first met him—in Paris with Lizzie in the early 1950s—until the year of his death. I admired him enormously, always had great affection for him, and always wished I knew him better and saw more of him. He was enough my senior for me to be able to regard his response to my own work as big-brotherly, in the benign sense of the phrase, and I cherished the fact that he once told me that my The Long March was one of the finest short novels he had ever read. He could be painfully frank, though, telling me once that my novel Set This House on Fire had some very good things in it but was quite a bit too long (which it probably is).

One night back in the early 1960s—it was just before one of the episodes which led to his being put away in an institution—I recall listening to him rave in the most ferocious way about Stalin. I always believed Stalin was a monster myself and had no illusions, but Cal's rage was obsessive and monumental; he said that by comparison Hitler was a saint, that no one in the history of the human race had committed such evil. I thought Cal was going to have apoplexy. I mention this only because his fury, in retrospect, seemed to be connected with the fact that only days later he was institutionalized. It was one of those strange, unsettling evenings that sticks in the mind.

I rather regret that my best and most sustained recollection of Cal is connected with a trip that he and Lizzie and I, together with several other American writers, took to the Soviet Union during the late spring of the year of his death (1977). The regret has to do with the fact that it was the last I ever saw of him. The writers' conference we attended in Moscow was the joint effort of the Soviet Writers Union and an American outfit called the Charles E. Kettering Foundation, dedicated to furthering Soviet-American relations. Cal (and I think Lizzie) seemed as skeptical as I about the potential fruitfulness of the trip but it could be regarded as a nice all-expenses-paid-for junket to a new and fascinating country, so we set off in

* Author of *Robert Lowell: A Biography* (New York: Vintage, 1983).

fairly good spirits. Before we got to Moscow I enjoyed seeing two examples of Cal's disregard for convention—a nonconformity which I had seen him display before and which I really admired. Cal chain-smoked (I have little doubt that this contributed to his failing health) and on the Boeing 747 we were seated in the non-smoking section, although the smoking area had been requested. Cal smoked anyway, much to the annoyance and finally the fury of a non-smoker whose protests to the stewardesses were of no avail. Cal referred to this man contemptuously as an "environmentalist," and kept smoking the entire way to Frankfurt, despite all efforts on the part of the staff to make him stop. I was rather tickled by his obstinacy; after all, it was Pan American which had made the mistake in seating, and he was standing by his rights.

Our group leader was a rather fussy bureaucrat from the Kettering Foundation who annoyed us all, but especially Cal, by his worry that the members of the group might exceed expense account limits in certain situations. We stopped over briefly in Frankfurt where we were housed at the very swank Frankfurterhof Hotel. There we were cautioned by the gentleman in question that, because of the expensiveness of the place, we should display caution and discretion in ordering, especially meals. This was offensive—after all we were grownups, even dignitaries of sorts, the Kettering Foundation was well-heeled—and no one was more insulted by the edict than Cal. To my great delight, Cal led a revolt in the restaurant and in clear sight of the man in charge ordered four of the most sumptuous and expensive bottles of white German wine that any of us had tasted. It was a clear victory of individual choice over bureaucracy.

But I began to detect a tired and melancholy strain in Cal. Before lunch in the bar of the hotel the next day we had Bloody Marys and I remember Cal speaking of Boris Pasternak, whose work he admired passionately; he said that he wanted to visit his grave, and spoke of death. "We all have one foot in the grave," I distinctly remember him saying, though of course having no inkling then of what this might foreshadow.

I have always felt myself a little less sensitive than perhaps normal to the purely physical moods of others, but in Moscow even I could tell that Cal seemed extremely tired. Even so, he could be very funny as he so often was in that low-keyed but abrasive way. We were lodged in a hotel called the Sovietskaya, a one-time palace of the Czarist days now reserved for V.I.P. visitors. It is a high-ceilinged, dark, gloomy place which, despite its history, has no charm whatever. When we entered the place one of our colleagues, a droll Russian-born scholar of Soviet literature named Vera Dunham, gestured despairingly and said: "This is the Russians' Waldorf-Astoria." To which I recall Cal replying: "My God, what is their Hilton like?"

Cal seemed to need a lot of sleep. Once in this dismal hotel when he and Lizzie and I were waiting, seemingly interminably, for food we had ordered at one of the "buffet" counters on an upper floor, Cal got restless and excused himself and disappeared. He was gone and for a long time, until Lizzie got a little nervous and I went up to his room to see what he might be doing. Opening the door, I found him on the bed, stripped to his underwear and sound asleep. It was as if he had become so exhausted that he had had to plunge into sleep without a word to anyone.

I'll never forget how touched I was at the boring writers' session when I would glance over and let my eyes rest on the brooding, sorrowing Beethovenesque head. I don't know why that head and face so often touched me so through sheer presence—so much suffering contained there, I suppose. Hence the wicked and caustic wit which was so delicious (and sometimes cruel)—a way to turn one's self away from suffering.

I don't know whether Cal got to visit Pasternak's grave or not—Lizzie would remember, I'd imagine. Certainly not on the night before we all left Moscow—I to go back to New York, Cal and Lizzie, I believe, to Leningrad. We spent a fine drunken evening at Vosnesensky's dacha Peredelkino—an event notable among other things for the presence of Yevtushenko, who was making friends again with Andrei after a long estrangement.* Perhaps because of Cal's fatigue he and Lizzie went home early. Yevtushenko and I went to Pasternak's grave and sat until dawn talking and drinking Bulgarian champagne. Yevtushenko toasted Cal as "your greatest poet."

Sincerely
William Styron

* Andrei Andreyevich Voznesensky (1933–2010), Russian poet and writer whom Lowell called "one of the greatest living poets in any language."

To Willie Morris

August 16, 1981 Vineyard Haven, MA

Dear Willie: Your observations on John Gardner, received today, were right on target.* Why the fuck couldn't he have said all that originally, the fink?

Gloria was up here for a few days and we had a great time. She told me of the Doubleday contract and that's great news for you.

I thought the enclosed from The Village Voice might interest you. Apparently the asshole Lewis Lapham has just resigned from Harper's—that once-great magazine, thanks to you, which he has helped to kill.† The sadness is unbearable.

See you soon.
Stingo

To Duke University‡

August, 1981 Roxbury, CT

I think that it is necessary only to ask yourselves whether Harvard or Yale would consent to having a Nixon library associated with their names in order to realize why Duke must not permit the proposed library and archives. Duke has become a truly great university. To establish any connection, no matter how informal or tenuous, with the works of a man who brought such disgrace to his high office would be a smear on the image of the institution we all cherish and respect. There would seem to be no reason, other than that of misplaced vanity, for Duke to wish to be the location for these archives, which are doubtless of historical importance but

* Styron refers to Gardner's freshly written headnote to his critical review of *Sophie's Choice,* which was reprinted in Arthur D. Casciato and James L. W. West III, eds., *Critical Essays on William Styron* (Boston: G. K. Hall, 1982). Gardner qualified much of his original criticism of the novel in this headnote.

† Styron wrote later in August to Morris, "Incidentally, it turns out that Lewis Lapham was not just 'resigned,' as reported, but fired, which is all the more justice."

‡ Styron wrote this when Duke was considering whether to allow its most famous graduate, President Richard Nixon, to house his presidential library at the university.

which could find suitable lodging elsewhere. In the 1950s my great teacher and mentor, William Blackburn, helped lead the successful fight to prevent Nixon from receiving an honorary degree from Duke. It must be remembered that this was even before Nixon became involved in the criminal activities of Watergate. It is with Professor Blackburn's memory in mind, but also the self-esteem which I'm sure I share with thousands of loyal Duke alumni, that I vigorously protest this threat to our university's fine reputation.

To Willie Morris

January 12, 1982 Roxbury, CT

Dear Willie:

I'm just back from Venezuela and the Brazilian jungles to face this incredible arctic weather. I was in an Indian village 300 miles up the Orinoco River and ran into "Knuckles" Kazin—he's become a Baptist missionary.*

Seriously, Kazin has moved to Roxbury, and I'm mortified that I might have to have social intercourse.

Thought you'd like to see the enclosed—especially the part on RPW.

I learned just yesterday that Sophie was voted by the Paris book critics circle, or whatever, as the best novel published in France in 1980. There is some justice.

How goes the novel and your other work? Am looking forward.

Ever,

Bill

* Alfred Kazin.

To Amelie Burgunder*

May 15, 1982 Roxbury, CT

Dear Amelie,

I wish I could be encouraging about the special screening of Sophie, but I really have discovered that I have very little muscle where this movie is concerned. I was not really made to feel very welcome on the set (though I did go very briefly about three times) and so I don't really feel I have much influence. I had rather hoped to have a screening benefit for my old prep school, Christchurch, but have been reluctant to approach Pakula or anyone about this. I don't really mean to imply that Pakula, or anyone, has been unfriendly. Pakula has in fact been most solicitous about my reactions to the script, and I think (unlike some directors) he would be horrified if I were to express a negative reaction to his "translation." But, as I say, I just don't feel that I have any real influence on such matters as screenings. Pakula and the company are now in Yugoslavia doing the European part of the film, and will be there through the first week in June. I will try to bring up your screening when next I see him—but, if past experience means anything that may not be for a very long time. I wish I could be more positive but, as you can gather, I'm somewhat in the same boat.

Love, Bill

To C. Vann Woodward

June 18, 1982 Vineyard Haven, MA

Dear Vann:

We are still so sad over Glenn, and I wanted you to know that you are in our thoughts constantly.†

I hear the good news that you'd probably be coming up to visit the Hackneys before long. I hope you will prolong your stay to visit the Styrons too.

* Amelie Burgunder was married to Rose's brother Bernei.

† Woodward's wife, Glenn Boyd McLeod, who had passed away.

Willie Morris called to say that he will be giving a big speech on Nov. 3 at the Peabody Hotel in Memphis on the state of the South (Faulkner gave the speech 25 years ago). I said that if you'd go I'd fly down with you. He'll be writing you. It might be fun. Anyway, we're looking forward to seeing you soon.

As ever,
Bill

To Edward Bunker*

July 10, 1982 Vineyard Haven, MA

Dear Eddie:

Thanks for sending me these two truly excellent pieces. They are frightening and written with beautiful intensity—also they told me a lot about things I didn't know. I wonder if the racial horror is any better now, ten years later.

It was great seeing you up here on the island. Try to come back sometime—our welcome mat is always out for both of you. But in any case I hope we can get together in the Apple after the summer's end.

Thanks again for letting me see these fine articles.

Yours,
Bill

* Bunker (1933–2005) was an ex-convict who taught himself to write in prison and went on to a successful career as a writer, actor, and screenwriter. As his widow, Jennifer, wrote, "There was no greater friend to Eddie than Bill. He was generous beyond measure to his friends and to other writers. He once called me with a question when he was filling out an application for a Guggenheim Fellowship for Eddie. He was in a deep depression but somehow managed to complete the application because he knew how much Eddie needed it."

To Susanna Styron

July 11, 1982 Vineyard Haven, MA

Dear daughter Sue:

We were delighted to get your letter and to hear all the good news about your work, bella Roma, etc. There had been an item in The N.Y. Times about the incredible heat in Italy, so I imagine that you had to suffer through that, as you said. June weather here was about the worst in memory—damp, cold and gloomy—so you didn't miss anything. But July in general has been quite wonderful—blue and hot but not too hot—and it's like the Vineyard summers of yore. We really miss you. It is not the old island without your smiling (sometime) face. For some reason the social life this summer is more pleasant (perhaps just a little less boring) than usual. Same old faces—Buchwalds, Wallaces, Phillipses, etc.—but everybody's in a fairly good mood, given the deplorable state of the world, and so the evening parties are reasonably nice. Miss Hellman, I fear, is utterly insane and loathsome to everyone, but is mercifully immobilized by her cigarette, her blindness, feebleness and venom and so can really bite no one seriously. I take Aquinnah faithfully for 4½ mile hikes each morning and am feeling fit as a fiddle. Tom and Al are here most of the time so we have a lot of laughs. My gorgeous new car works like a charm (a birthday present to me from your mother, which I paid for), and the writing goes well, too—I'm back on the Marine Corps novel. Alan Pakula called for a long time a week or so ago, said the film was in great shape, said I had to come down and see the rough cuts, or whatever, but I suspect that these are more of his empty promises. I have not seen a single frame of that movie and am beginning to very much doubt that I'll see any of it before it's finished. I gather that all writers of novels are treated this way by filmmakers.

I envy you being in beautiful Italy. Hope I can come over to see you before too long. Give hugs and kisses to the Zajacs and have a splendid plate of fettuccine with gorgeous wine and think of your devoted

Dad XXX

who sends great love

To Ben Crovets

July 26, 1982 Vineyard Haven, MA

Dear Mr. Crovets:

Still no word from our Sophie, so I suspect she either went a long way off (back to Europe?) or met some unkinder fate. I never learned her last name, either. Perhaps the movie, when it appears in December, will cause her to surface, but I doubt it. Meanwhile, if you ever hear anything, let me know.

Sincerely

Wm Styron

To Susanna Styron

July 31, 1982 Vineyard Haven, MA

P.S. I was worried about paying my bills the other day when I went to the P.O. and out dropped a check for $91,000—all French royalties. Vive la you know qui.

Dear darling #1 daughter,

It was lovely talking to you on the telephone the other day, and also getting your various communications. I'm so glad everything is going so well; you really seem contented and that makes me happy. I'm so glad you were not on the road that Aug. 1 week-end especially after hearing about those 44 French kids being slaughtered on the highway. Bad as things are in the dear old U.S., it seems (knock on wood) that our highways are a bit safer than in Europe. So drive carefully!

You asked about politics. Politics stink worse than ever, with Reagan at the helm—an accredited moron in charge of the greatest country on earth. You asked about George Shultz.* Bill and Wendy Luers† apparently

* George Pratt Shultz (b. 1920), American economist and statesman; Secretary of the Treasury (1972–74) and Secretary of State (1982–89).

† William Henry Luers (b. 1929), diplomat and former U.S. Ambassador to Venezuela and Czechoslovakia. He served as president of the Metropolitan Museum of Art in New York for thirteen years. Bill and his wife, Wendy, became very close friends of the Styrons.

know him well (they aren't here quite yet, but I'm going to quiz them on the guy) and I've been told that they think highly of him—of his personal character and his motives. But it's hard to say, really, since I think that Shultz is just as manipulable an item in the hands of the Calif. Power brokers as Reagan himself is. I think the whole country is being run by the military-industrial leaders (a few of them, immensely powerful) who would love to see such horrors as the war in Lebanon escalate into a larger conflict. Bush's brother is out of the race in Conn., as you no doubt know, which means a truly tough fight for Toby against Weicker. I'm beginning frankly to believe that, with the hysteric mood of the country being what it is, Toby may be the underdog in the battle. And this in spite of the fact that people are beginning to see Republican Reaganomics as the sham it is.

Carlos and Sylvia* are here and we're having a lovely time. Carlos may be the only truly intelligent man I know. He and I are going to be telephoning García Márquez (in Mexico City) soon about the ABC interviews with Castro I told you about. Also Carlos and I are cooking up a trip to Nicaragua in December, with García Márquez as a fellow traveler—no pun intended. It would greatly help my Marine Corps novel (the one I interrupted to do Sophie) if I could get at least a brief feel for Nicaragua, where so many Marine horrors took place during the 1920s. Meanwhile, I've started fooling around with a reminiscent sad-funny chronicle of my 1946 summer trip to Trieste aboard a cattle boat from Newport News. Tomorrow Sylvia's putting me on Mexican TV with a crew from Boston coming down. The social whirl whirls pleasantly and we see a lot of Buchwalds, Phillipses, Marquand, Jules, even Lillian—with whom your mother just today, took a horrific nude swim in L's Jacuzzi, ugh. Tom is off to Texas. I'm off to W. Chop with Aquinnah to mail this to you with much much love. I'll send more soon.

Love you,
Daddy

* Carlos Fuentes and his wife, Sylvia.

To Susanna Styron

August 18, 1982 Vineyard Haven, MA

Dear #1 Daughter:

I am sitting out at the end of the dock in beautiful sunlight writing this in a chair. If the handwriting is a little goofy looking it's because of the unaccustomed position. Aquinnah is next to me, looking very self-satisfied (she's so spoiled) and has her eyes trained on the lawn, ready to howl at any intruder, canine or human. Thus, the lazy pace of these summer days. Carlos and Sophia Fuentes have left, with plans afoot for Carlos and me to go to Nicaragua this winter. I would probably try to make the trip coincide with a trip to see Castro, after Carlos and I huddle with García Márquez in Mexico City. All this, I might add, I would like to think might come after a trip to Italy to see #1 daughter. I miss you so much, as does all of the fam., and I am plotting a way to get to Rome before too long. I love your various communications. Your description of a week-end in the country with the Russians was wonderful.

Eddie Bunker and his girl Jennifer were here and that was fine. Eddie got on especially well with Gene Genovese, also visiting—the chemistry between the San Quentin alumnus and the ex-Brooklyn slum kid was just right. Other social events have included a mammoth party your mother gave for Bill and Wendy Luers (guests included Buchwalds, Kay Graham, and Carl Bernstein and his current companion Margaret Jay, wife of the ex–British ambassador), and last night a horrible party at the Edgartown Yacht Club that Walter Cronkite gave for his 90-year old mother. It was supposed to be a traditional dance for the old lady, but about a week or so before she had been knocked down on the beach by a gigantic poodle, breaking her leg, so she showed up in a wheelchair. The Buchwalds and Styrons were the youngest guests by about 20 years, the others being drunken old retired admirals and other of the Edgartown Yacht Club ilk.

The enclosed article does not quite do justice to my Mayhew Seminar appearance. The reporter describes the audience as being "perplexed," but I think my approach went over the head not of the audience but the reporter himself who is about 18, very solemn and wanted, I think, a pompous lecture on Art and Life and Other Important Topics. Also, if I was "uncomfortable" at the lectern it was because the temperature was about 98°.

I'm finishing the galleys of my book of essays, This Quiet Dust, and Random House has done a most fine printing job. The book is much longer than I thought it would be—you'll get one of the first copies. Also, the book of Mitterrand's writings, to which I wrote the introduction, has received to my surprise a great deal of attention, and that's nice.

Your brother Tom has broken silence in Texas to say that he's having a fine and busy time. Polly has taken over the Roxbury house, which pleases us and Al—well, Al is the No. 1 swinger of the H.T.R. and the island in general, as you can imagine.

More guests tonight—Francine and Cleve Gray, my friend Marie-Eugénie de Pourtales from Paris. Will the madness never end?

I'll write more soon. Meanwhile, much love from Aquinnah and me, on the dock.

Daddy

To Susanna Styron

September 3, 1982 Vineyard Haven, MA

Dear #1 Daughter:

The summer is almost over and the thundering hordes have departed the premises (I hope) for good. In sheer numbers the visitors this season have been all but unmanageable. I must confess, however, that the summer has been in general quite enjoyable, even your mother's obsessive tennis being tolerable. Carl Bernstein and his current girlfriend Margaret Jay, just left and I must say that it was entertaining having them around. Tomorrow (day before Labor Day) your mother and I are departing upon one of the most decadent adventures I've ever had. This is to charter a plane and go down to East Hampton, where Craig Claiborne has invited 75–100 people to one of the great feasts of the century—25 chefs (literally) from the best restaurants in New York (French, Italian, Chinese) turning out presumably great food for the visitors. I would not under any circumstances have undertaken the ludicrous enterprise had it not been for Gloria Jones (with whom we'll be staying) who said she would break my arm if I didn't come. I will have more to report on this orgy at a future date.

Your mother will be going with Al to Roxbury soon but I will stay up here for a few more weeks (during the season of merciful quietude) to get some work done. The galleys of This Quiet Dust, my book of essays, have arrived and look quite handsome. I'll make sure you get a copy. We've loved your letters; your story about Mario and his faith in the Styron name and puissance was much appreciated. My only momentary discontent comes from the fact that my sidekick and faithful companion Aquinnah suffered some sort of relapse due to heartworm treatment; while she is in no great danger she will have to remain quiet for a long time, and this means that I won't have her palship on my essential daily walks. Oh well.

I'm still brooding over a trip to Rome. You might be surprised some day before long. Tom seems to be very happy down in Texas and Polly is a constant resident in Roxbury. So things are well. Al—the No. 1 girl of the Island—asks me to send lots of love. Which I do, along with lots of my own.

Love you molto,
Daddy

This Quiet Dust and Other Writings *was published by Random House on November 30, 1982. The film of* Sophie's Choice *premiered in December.*

To Willie Morris

December 28, 1982 Roxbury, CT

Dear Willie:

Thanks for the nice review from Memphis. So far as I know, it is the only good review my modest book of essays received. An English professor from someplace like Rutgers (naturally) lambasted me in The N.Y. Times Book Review and the others followed suit.* It was really perplexing, since This Quiet Dust really didn't set itself up as a showy or ambitious work

* Thomas Edwards, professor at Rutgers and editor of the literary quarterly *Raritan,* wrote "Rhetoric Doing the Work of Thought," *The New York Times Book Review* (November 21, 1982).

but simply a collection of casual pieces which might be savored for the relatively simple essays they were. I guess I've got to simply resign myself to the fact that critics will seize almost any opportunity to show off their malice; in any case, I realize that English professors hate the guts of writers in general. But thanks for the Memphis piece.

The good news is that the movie of Sophie is doing incredible business in the eight major cities where it's showing. It's really quite a fine movie—not the same as the book, of course—but a splendid adaptation in which Meryl Streep (who's going to win an Oscar) does an absolutely fantastic job. I hope you see it before long. We had a great world premiere in N.Y., benefit for Amnesty International (sold out), and I went down for the gala Southern premiere in Richmond, also a benefit for Christchurch School and a great success. The Governor read out a citation and the day was called Wm. Styron Day and I felt I'd come a long way from being a little nose-picker down in the Tidewater.

Speaking of governors, Wm. Winter* got a fine laudatory article in the Times in regard to his educational program. The South is rising again!

When you coming up to Yankee land? It's been too long. Stay in touch and best to all my Oxford buddies.

Yrs ever Stingo

To Mary Buxton†

February 16, 1983 Roxbury, CT

Dear Mary: Your letter was written with great good spirit and warmth and I hope I can reply in kind, at least in part.

* William Forrest Winter (b. 1923) served as the fifty-eighth governor of Mississippi from 1980 to 1984 as a Democrat.

† Mary Wakefield Buxton was related by marriage to Elizabeth Buxton, Styron's first stepmother. Buxton wrote a piece, "Journeys," for *The Southside Sentinel* (serving Virginia south of the Rappahannock River), which celebrated Elizabeth. "One of the crosses Aunt Elizabeth had to bear in life was being the stepmother of William Styron . . . [she] dedicated a portion of her time to keeping young Bill in line and he later sought his revenge by writing *Lie Down in Darkness* in which Aunt Elizabeth was portrayed as one of the most dreadful women ever depicted in American literature. I thought he exagger-

Let me begin, though, with a true reminiscence. When I was 22, the age of the narrator in Sophie's Choice, and living in New York, I came down with a truly wretched case of hepatitis. In those days, right after World War II, it was a very serious and unfamiliar disease, and I'm sure I came as close to dying as I ever have. While recuperating, I received a letter from Elizabeth. The gist of her letter was this: while she was happy that I had recovered, she hoped from her heart that I realized that I had brought the illness on myself, that by the loose and debauched life I had been living—drinking, irregular habits, etc.—I had no one to blame but myself for my close call with oblivion. I was still very weak when I read her words, barely able to get out of bed, and they made—to say the least—a bleak impression on my spirit. In short, I can say—some 35 years later—that it was one of the most hateful and poisonous letters a boy of 22 ever received from a vindictive stepmother, and it made me feel like hell. Therefore, I really can't accept your gentle suggestion that Elizabeth was representative of stepmothers in general, who are traditionally despised by their 13-year-old children. I was no longer 13, like Luke vis-à-vis Virginia, or your sister's stepson. I was, rather, a young adult in full command of my sensibilities, and I still hate Elizabeth for that loathsome, disgusting letter with its terrible freight of puritanical malice. The only reason—as always—that I didn't write back and tell her to go fuck herself was because of my father, and my desire not to make that good man unhappy. How he lived with her for so long in apparent bliss is a cosmic mystery.

Of course I "forgave" her—whatever that means. Until she died, she and my father visited our family and we had some fine times together. I think she had sincere affection for all my children. There were moments when in a sort of pitying way I had warm feelings for her. But she was a grim woman and I'm sure that had my father married her, say, five years earlier, when I was just a child, I would have been destroyed. I'm amazed to this day that I allowed myself to have anything to do with her. I rather regret that in the TV documentary you saw there was more time spent on her than should have been—a disproportionate bulge which I thought was a flaw in the film. And I'm very sorry indeed that Buck was hurt. But I would be insincere now if I didn't register my true feelings.

---

ated." More recently, Mary published a similar account as "The 'Evil' Step-Muse," *Virginia Living* 5, no. 3 (April 5, 2007).

You're partially right, certainly, about my father's true nature in matters of race. The book version of the old man was considerably idealized and you are correct in saying that he kept most of the prejudices of his post-bellum Southern generation. But there had been many moments in the past when I had glimpsed in him the sight of a genuine liberal struggling to escape from the flesh of a reactionary (he did in all actuality, as I said in the book, resign as president of the Va. chapter of the Sons of the Revolution when that group endorsed Senator Joe McCarthy) and so I think my portrait wasn't too far off.

I'm glad all is going well with you and Chip. I think of the Tidewater often though it's been many years now since I've visited the Peninsula. Your letter was, at heart, filled with good will and an undercurrent of happiness, and I hope that state is always yours.

Faithfully and with love always
Bill

P.S. Rose sends her fondest.

To Willie Morris

May 8, 1983* Cannes, France

Dear Willie: The Cannes Film Festival would be poontang heaven for a young stud but since I am President of the Jury I have to act real moral and drink mineral water. I'm having a good time but 22 movies in 10 days is a bit much even for a film buff like me. I'll be back around the last of May and hope we can have a good ole boy reunion.

Stingo

* Postcard, "La Piscine de l'Hôtel Majestic et les jardins du Casino."

To Willie Morris

July 6, 1983 Vineyard Haven, MA

Dear Willie:

I'm so glad you felt the same way I did about the Hamptons. That damn place has always filled me with anxiety but the week-end in question I thought really exemplified the place at its worst. Needless to say I adore Gloria, as you do, but Matthews and I both agreed passionately that it is a terrible mistake to invite such a mob for any kind of festivity. There was absolutely no communication with anyone, so that you end up more in a state of constant irritation and even hostility than in the conviviality that such an event is supposed to produce. Except for seeing you, and one or two other people I care for, the whole week-end was for me a terrible and depressing washout, and I made a solemn vow never to go back to that area unless I can be assured that the social life will be under control. You're absolutely right: the people there do move in packs, and it is very close to disgusting. I've always cherished my few friends there, but at the same time I've always detested the place for its umbilical cord relationship to the worst aspects of N.Y. City: chic food shops and dreadful cocktail parties and shrinks and gynecologists driving BMWs and, mainly, seeing the same damn people over and over and over again. Believe me, and I mean it: Martha's Vineyard has its drawbacks but it is a slander to say that in any way it resembles the Hamptons. I can live my own life here, and work, and I know it would be impossible to do that there. I think the greatest indictment came from Peter and Maria Matthiessen, who told me that they've gotten so fed up with this madhouse aspect of the place that they've seriously considered moving away.

Anyway, it was great to see you and I'm very much looking forward to that book of yours. Will you get me an early version to read? Tell Matee Daniels that all the intellectual Jews up here are rooting for him to win; they know he will push their cause down there and it will mean a lot more copies of highbrow quarterlies being sold in the great state of Mississippi. Vann Woodward is coming up for a visit in a week or two. We'll hoist a glass in memory of all the good old times.

Yrs in Jesus
& Jerry Falwell,
As ever,
Bill

To Carlos Fuentes

July 17, 1983 Vineyard Haven, MA

Dear Carlos: I'm sorry you couldn't have made it up here for a brief vacance. The weather has been splendid and I miss our Immanuel Kantian promenades.

Your Harvard speech was absolutely excellent and I've heard very fine reverberations.* I'm sure its effects will be strong and persuasive—despite the official resistance—and you certainly had an enormously influential podium. It was a triumph of reasoned exhortation.

Keep me posted on developments in regard to the Canadian powwow. I think it could be very fruitful indeed.

Abrazos Stay in touch
Bill

To Edward Bunker

November 28, 1983 Roxbury, CT

Dear Édouard Bon Coeur:

I have tried to contact you many times recently by telephone but got either no answer or a mysterious busy signal. The latter baffled me, and I wondered why there should be a busy signal when otherwise no answer. This conjured up visions of someone lurking around, not answering the phone but making calls, etc. However, it seems plain that you have not been home for some time and I hope this reaches you.

For one thing I wanted to let you know how certain efforts I have made to procure you some loot have been making out. By the time I was able, at the beginning of the fall, to make inquiries about funds and fellowships at the American Academy of Arts and Letters, to which I belong, it turned out that all of the candidates and applications had been processed for this year—the deadline was early last summer. So while this put you out for

* Fuentes was Harvard's commencement speaker in 1983 and aroused controversy because of his outspoken criticism of American foreign policy and President Ronald Reagan.

the current year, you are still eminently qualified for the next go-round in the coming year. I should point out that these fellowships are not terribly munificent—I mean, you can't live off them—but they amount usually to several thousand bucks nonetheless, and are pretty good in terms of recognition. So please keep this in mind for 1984, as I'd be glad to push the matter and I think you'd have an excellent chance to get a fellowship. Many writers who are not nearly as classy as you have gotten these grants.

This idea may simply appall you, and if it does read no further—but did you ever consider teaching? I don't have to tell you how many good writers have taken this route, and should it not make you unhappy to think about it I believe I might be able to pull some kind of influence in this direction. If you are interested that is another thing you can let me know about, and I shall make the appropriate moves.

You may not believe it, but I am far, far into a new novel which pleases me enormously. My liver has acted up to the extent that I barely drink anything anymore—so it is just me and Aquinnah, taking our walks in the woods together. I hope we can get together before too long, perhaps in the holiday season, but at the moment, I am totally mystified as to your whereabouts. As I say, I hope this reaches you in good shape, and that you are likewise in good shape. Why don't you give me a call if the carrier pigeon delivers this to you safely.

Yours,
Bill

To Frederick Exley

December 24, 1983 Roxbury, CT

Dear Fred: If you don't get a Guggenheim, it will be through no fault of mine.* I laid it on so thick (saying such things as: In 25 years of making recommendations there is no candidate so highly regarded in my eyes, etc.) that they will either buy it or reject it out of hand as preposterous, perhaps even indecent. I am used to such humiliations as the Signed First

* Exley received a Guggenheim Fellowship for 1984.

Edition Society. The other day I got a fan letter saying, in all seriousness, that my work combined the best of James Joyce and James Michener.

Merry Xmas,
Bill

To Charles Sullivan

February 1, 1984 Roxbury, CT

Dear Charlie:

Many thanks for the splendid cigars, which were here waiting for me after a trip to Mexico. I'm about ready to head south again, since despite the fact that moments of New England winters are exhilarating, enough is really enough and some of these days around 10° with the wind blowing are really monstrous. Who knows, I may end up on your doorstep. Anyway, the cigars are excellent. They are proof of something I've long maintained (in spite of wisdom to the contrary): that the best Tampa cigars are really of very highly maintained excellence, close enough to Havanas to make a more than passable substitute (Imagine, it's been 20 years since the Cuban Embargo!). Anyway, I am grateful to you for the thoughtfulness.

My Marine Corps novel is coming along well, and sometime before long I'd like to talk to you about it seriously and at length, and maybe solicit your advice and observations.

As you will recollect very well, WWII ended before a lot of us got to the Pacific, thus shattering dreams and creating ambiguities. My own dream was shattered because a large part of me wanted to fight the Japs and prove my courage and all that sort of thing. After all, this is what the USMC had been training me to do for a long time, and I felt quite let down when in August 1945 we all heard the news at Quantico. On the other hand, another part of me was quite relieved that Hiroshima prevented me from having my ass shot off. I would be dishonest if I didn't say that. At any rate I ended the war with profoundly mixed feelings, and a large part of this new novel is concerned with these complicated attitudes toward courage, idealism, patriotism and, most importantly, The Bomb.

The story is told as if I (called Stingo—remember him?—who is the first person narrator) had been perhaps nine months or a year older, and then—instead of having his career terminate at Quantico—had been of the right age to be involved in the fighting as a platoon leader on Okinawa. Due to a freak accident, which is no fault of his own, he escapes combat, which causes him enormous and real frustration, since he not only honestly wants to prove himself in action but also feels that he has let his platoon down badly because of his absence. Shortly after this—recovered from the accident—he rejoins his unit on Okinawa, finding that most of his platoon has been shot up in one of the final battles, and the island is now secured. Thus he has truly escaped hearing a shot fired in anger. During the mopping-up operations, however, which are virtually danger-free for our hero, a fellow officer is horribly and mortally hurt in a booby trap and dies in the narrator's arms. Back on Saipan (this incidentally is based on theoretical action with the 2d Division, which as you may remember was involved in the later stages of the campaign—8th Marines), Stingo's previous macho courage does a flipflop and he finds himself no longer this gutsy young officer but utterly terrified. Though he has not experienced battle, he has seen its horrible effects and thus he loses his bravery. His terror, of course, is compounded by the fact that he knows he will be participating in the invasion of Japan (Operation Coronet, November on Kyushu) and that his chances are slim indeed for survival. The previous study in machismo turns into a study of fear. However, when the bomb drops on Hiroshima he is saved. It would be easy to say that his joy knows no bounds—he feels joy but it is hardly boundless, being shadowed by too many other factors: Hiroshima itself and his own continuing agonized conscience.

This is a crude description. However, this is the first novel I've heard of which deals with that very important dilemma—the conscience of those, like myself, whose lives were directly saved by The Bomb.

In these post-war years I've had a very easy solution to those situations when—at a party, say—someone inveighs against our national morality and the "crime" of Hiroshima. I simply walk out of the room. My life was saved by the bomb, and this novel is an attempt at an explanation of that uncomplicated fact and its consequences; therefore, it is about individual survival vs. mass death, and a lot of other thorny issues.

I've gone on at such length—I hope not too boringly—because I thought you might be interested in how the Marine Corps still haunts the imagination of someone like myself who—though I did not make it my career—was powerfully influenced by its effect on me many years ago.

I'd be interested in your response to this story. Naturally, since it is a novel, I'm going to feel free to depart from pure fact from time to time and go off on flights of fancy. I'd also like to think I might call on you from time to time, not just for technical advice, perhaps, but to get your feelings about the larger picture. I think this will be a very good novel if I can get it put together.

Many thanks again for the glorious cigars. Stay in touch.

Faithfully yrs as ever
Bill S.

P.S. I hope you're in good shape after the operation. In case you're interested—my father had a near lethal heart problem when he was about our age, recovered, never had another ill or tremor, and I buried him happy as a clam two months short of his 90th birthday.

To Willie Morris

March 3, 1984 Roxbury, CT

Dear Willie:

Thanks so much for the photo and text about my narrow escape on the road in Magee, Miss. I have a drinking problem, as you know, and I would not like the world to know it but a little too much wet goods which I took on up Hwy. 49 an hour or two earlier was the cause of the near-catastrophe. Also, fortunately for the reputation of both me and her, the 19 year old darling of impact was performing upon me an illegal act known in Italian as F_LL_T_O and ran off into a hayfield unscathed and unreported by the press.

Anyway I'm O.K. now. This has been a miserable cold winter and I'm yearning for sunshine. I often think of my old pal in Oxford. Tell the Mayor I got the Avenue magazine he sent. I thought it was quite a fine piece on you, Willie, unlike so many journalistic portraits which betray all sorts of hidden hostilities and jealousies.

The problem with being a writer of some note is that one can fuck off forever and never get a word written, I'm not exaggerating when I say that this spring—if I had responded to all the invitations—I could have been a merry-go-round that would have taken me to eight separate countries on three continents. As it is, I do have plans to go to Japan in May (paid for with lots of Yen by Japanese Broadcasting) because my new novel is about fighting the Japanese; and that same month I am also going to East Germany and Czechoslovakia. Fortunately, I will have enough of the book done by then to make me feel somewhat freer to relax.

Sophie has sold nearly 200,000 copies in hardback in France, hence I'm a national hero there, hence I've even been read by François Mitterrand (who told me "j'aime la pauvre Sophie") hence Rose and I are going to a state dinner at the White House when he comes here in three weeks. Do you think I've sold my soul, when it takes all I can to avoid vomiting when President Goo-Goo (as John Marquand calls him) appears on the TV screen.

Willie, stay in touch. I miss you a lot and I'll be looking forward to an early reunion. Your old friend,

Bill

Tell Dean how wonderful I thought her kids were (also her).

To Edward Bunker

April 1, 1984 Roxbury, CT

Dear Eddie:

Once again, it has not been for lack of trying that I haven't gotten in touch with you. I guess I'm the helpless product of the telephone age, and when I call a dozen times and get no answer I figure you're incommunicado. I should know better, and place more reliance on the written word.

Anyway, I did want to say that I deeply lament the loss of your friend. My heart ached when you wrote me the news (a time I tried to call you) and I know how it hurt you, because I know how it would hurt me (and will someday); who was it said that a dog "is a tragedy waiting to happen"? The buggers—they get under your skin in a certain way. They aren't our species, but somehow the love we feel for them is a confirmation of our link with Nature. We certainly feel the loss of a good dog more keenly than the loss of a mediocre human being—which again has to do with our mysterious connection with the natural order. I grieve with you and join in an affectionate goodbye to old Dusty.

I'm delighted that your work is pounding away so well and look forward to reading the fruits. I think that it is wise of you to want to get this one off your back first. There is absolutely nothing wrong with wanting to make some good bucks to clear the way for the other work—I can name you at least ten fine writers who have done this, not starting with, but including, Faulkner.

Christ, writing is a horrible row to hoe. I'm coming along—well, I think—but each line is so tough, and the completion seems such a distant and impossible thing, that I can understand Conrad saying that there was hardly a day that he approached his writing desk without wanting to burst into tears. I'll get it done somehow, but I feel such envy for those guys who can just pour it out like some bodily fluid—semen, I guess, or shit, depending on how honest or good they are.

Let's get together in the month of April—sometime and someplace without fail. We have things to talk over and it would be great to see you again after so long.

Regards as always,
Bill

P.S. I'll tell you about my evening at the White House with Mitterrand as dinner partner.

To Mattie Russell

May 24, 1984* Roxbury, CT

Dear Mattie: I am sending these letters to you as a curiosity—a rather sad one. The correspondent is a young man named Jerry Marcus of Queens, N.Y. I'm not exaggerating when I say that I've received hundreds of these letters, written to me over the past 6 or 7 years. I never read them because they are incredibly long-winded and the handwriting is terrible. I never answer but the letters have been coming almost every week—as if I were a confessor to whom he was spilling his entire life. I send these to you merely as an example of what writers are sometimes exposed to. Sorry not to have seen you at grad. Best, B.S.

To Robert Loomis

February 22, 1985 Roxbury, CT

Dear Bob:

I just wanted to set down a few random reflections on the manuscript which you may want to tuck away for future reference. By the time the book is done I may have altered my feelings some, but I rather doubt it.

I'm afraid I feel very much as you expressed yourself as feeling on the phone. Just as you said something to the effect that this was the first time you felt you had to express a major criticism (naturally, I am not quoting you accurately)—this time in regard to the first part of the book—so I feel just as strongly, also for the first time, that your editorial sensibility has allowed you to miss the essential solidity and thrust and importance of that part of the work. I have discarded a great deal of earlier material, and struggled very hard to find this book's architectural integrity; it is essential to that integrity that the central part of the work be framed by these two longish journal sections.

So far as I could tell you missed seeing the basic rightness of this first

* On the back of the postcard is a note from Marcus: "Bill, What I have dreaded has happened. . . . I met Gabina the Russian lesbian Jewish émigré while shopping with my wife . . ." etc.

section. I actually did not intend it to have the same kind of swift "authority" of the rest of the book. It is admittedly slow, deliberative, contemplative, introspective; it is the diary of a young man close to a nervous breakdown because of fear. If it does not engage the reader in a quickly unfolding tale I could not care less; however, I do believe that within its tension—the night problem, the swim, the forced march, the scene with the shrink, etc. I regret that you didn't seem to recognize the great deal of careful writing that made this a cohesive whole. On reflection, I have not been able to agree at all with your feeling that Stingo reacts in an unconvincing way to the Captain. Also, contrary to your view, I feel that the foreshadowing is done the way it should be done, dropping the right hints concerning the future.

This is not to say that I think the section is by any means perfect. You were correct, I think, in feeling that the music store scene with Mozart strikes a jarring note after the Beethoven in the swimming scene. I've felt that that episode was extraneous and distracting anyway (as is the little paragraph about reading Proust) and these will be cut out.

Recently I read the long title piece of Ed Doctorow's LIVES OF THE POETS, as I imagine you have.* I admired it enormously—a static, reflective, almost monotonously self-absorbed work that has great power. His work and mine couldn't be more different, but in certain ways I've strived in this section for a similar effect of irony, humor and desperation. I think I have achieved it and I'm just sorry that you apparently have not been able to perceive what I think I have successfully achieved. Of course, I could be wrong—everyone is deluded from time to time—but it is absolutely essential; it will stand just as it is, and while as always I am sure you are such a good editor—it will remain in this form as the beginning of the book. (As I think I told you, similar journal entries—though not as lengthy—will end the book, after the Bomb has fallen and the marines, as they actually did, go to Nagasaki.)

After all this is said, I am glad that you liked the way the central narrative moved. It is coming along smoothly and I think I'll have a finished MS sooner than you might think.

* E. L. Doctorow, *Lives of the Poets: Six Stories and a Novella* (New York: Random House, 1984).

I wouldn't have written at such length if I still didn't think you were the best editor in the business. I suppose the making of books wouldn't be nearly so interesting if there weren't occasionally obdurately held points of view like mine, but I did want to get it down for the record, in addition to expressing my continued admiration and respect.

In Duke's name
Bill

PS How is Mrs. Yorke?

To Louis D. Rubin, Jr.

June 18, 1985 Vineyard Haven, MA

Dear Louis:

I had meant to write you long before this about Teacher—a fine idea, I think—but suddenly realized with dismay (and a sense of apology) that I had let a long time pass.* Forgive me the lapse, but I think the real reason I didn't respond was my inability to come up with a suitable subject, hard as I might try. The sad fact is that I can't remember any teachers who commanded my respect or devotion in the years before college and William Blackburn. The Commonwealth of Virginia, you may recollect—and I am fond of pointing out—ranked 48th in education during the years of my upbringing, also during the ascendancy of Harry Byrd who put what little money the state had into a highway system to get tourists safely to Jamestown and Williamsburg.

Most of my teachers (mainly female, of course) were therefore of limited quality—many of them simply ignoramuses. There was a Miss Thorpe who taught Music Appreciation and mangled the names of all the great composers (Dworack, Saint-Sayens, Hayden), a Miss Pitts who was a decent sort and tried to teach me Latin in a totally incomprehensible Tidewater accent, an ogrish male math teacher in his 50s named "Coach"

* Louis Rubin, ed., *An Apple for My Teacher* (Chapel Hill, N.C.: Algonquin Books, 1987), collects a dozen writers' essays on influential teachers.

Kriegler whose interests were obviously in football; and, most memorably, the eponymously named Miss Ball, a real looker who I'm still convinced, in full view of the class, aroused herself (I'm sure unconsciously, after all this was the 1930s) by pressing her groin against the corner of her desk. All of my teachers seemed to be characters out of Kings Row, with the mentality of Ronald Reagan.*

I'm sorry to send you this depressing report—so belatedly—but that is the real and honest reason I don't think myself qualified for your excellent venture. I wish you good luck on it, though, and would love to read the final essays.

Hope all goes well with you.

All best,

Bill

P.S. In case you're interested, there will be a 12,000 word excerpt from my new book in the August issue of Esquire.†

To Philip Caputo‡

October 6, 1985 Roxbury, CT

Dear Phil:

I've read your piece and this is just a brief note to tell you that I think it is just fine—poised, sensitive, intelligent, with a nice undertone that I can only describe as abrasively witty. Very nice indeed. I take no exception to anything and feel you were (despite worries) quite discreet. Naturally,

* *Kings Row* is a 1942 film starring Ronald Reagan, based on Henry Ballamann's controversial 1940 novel about the duality of small-town life. By "mentality," Styron may be referring to a scene in the film in which Reagan's character, after having his legs amputated by a sadistic surgeon, asks, "Where's the rest of me?"

† "Love Day," an excerpt from *The Way of the Warrior,* was later included in *A Tidewater Morning* (1993).

‡ Philip Caputo (b. 1941) is an American author and journalist. Winner of a Pulitzer Prize in 1973, Caputo is best known for his Vietnam memoir *A Rumor of War,* which Styron reviewed: "A Farewell to Arms," *The New York Review of Books* (June 23, 1977). Styron praised the book, calling it a "remarkable personal account of the war in Vietnam." This review was also collected in *This Quiet Dust.*

I've lost your phone number, or left it on the Vineyard, so do call me when you get a chance and let me express my feelings more directly and in detail.

All best,

Bill

Roxbury: 203-354-5939

Styron admitted himself to Yale–New Haven Hospital for suicidal depression on December 14, 1985.

To Peter Matthiessen

December 16, 1985 Roxbury, CT

Dear Peter:

I've gone through a rough time.* I hope you'll remember me with love and tenderness. I wish I'd taken your way to peace and goodness. Please remember me with a little of that zen goodness, too. I've always loved you and Maria.

Love

Porter

* Rose recalls that Bill began "going down the tubes" over Thanksgiving 1985 on Martha's Vineyard—the last Thanksgiving the family would celebrate there for nearly a decade. The week following Thanksgiving, Bill gave a speech in Virginia and it was a disaster. Soon after, Bill and Rose went to a literary fund-raiser at the circus. Norman Mailer was dressed as a strongman, Erica Jong was dressed as a fairy, and Bill, not in costume, was "a portrait of horror." The next day, Rose checked him into Yale–New Haven Hospital.

To Mia Farrow

February 21, 1986 Roxbury, CT

Dear Mia:

I've been out on the street for a while and am feeling very good once more. I will miss your cheery voice on the telephone, which was one of the few tolerable features of my detention. Except for the superb hospital cuisine (crabmeat au gratin, broiled snapper en papillote) it is one feature I will miss very much. You were a dear to think of me. My head and soul have been put back into working order—perhaps better than before, for whatever that's worth—and I divide my time between work and the new indoor-outdoor jacuzzi, very Finnish in this brisk weather. Come over sometime and try it out. You were wonderful in Hannah, which is the first movie I saw after I was sprung. I hope I see you before too long, not just the great sound of your voice wishing me well.

Love

Bill

To Philip Caputo

April 5, 1986 Roxbury, CT

Dear Phil:

I tried to call you recently but discovered that the number you gave me in your letter had been "changed to an unpublished number." I appreciate very much your letter of March 10, its encouragement and good will and faith. I went through an extremely grim period between early December and early February but I'm happy to say that I've pulled out of it nicely and am in the process of finishing the job of putting myself back together. Depression is a horrible and mysterious malady; the only good thing to be said about my form of the illness is that such depressions almost always resolve themselves for the better, even after forcing one to the very edge of the abyss.

I'm sorry about the fate—at least up until now—of your truly excellent article. There is a great deal of truth to the fact that I've abandoned the book I told you about; however, it's really not so much abandonment as extreme alteration. It's much too complicated to go into here but the gist of what I want to say is that I've completely reconstructed the novel—to a degree that would make what I told you quite erroneous—although I fully intend to retain the section that was in Esquire. Naturally I'd like to see the article published—in Esquire or elsewhere—and naturally, too, it would require a certain amount of rewriting in view of my change of plans for the book. But in case you still want to do the piece, and I gather you do, I'd be glad to talk to you about the changes that would be necessary to make. Maybe you'd want to discuss this by phone, if so, please call me here in Roxbury, where I'll be until early June.

Let me say again how grateful I am to you for your letter. Corny as it may appear, it seems that only a marine can be truly aware of another marine's suffering; you gave me a nice jolt of good cheer. Thanks from the depths, I'm pleased and proud of your friendship. Do write or call.

Yours ever

Bill S.

To Donald Harington

April 13, 1986 Morne Trulah, St. Lucia

Dear Don: I am writing this from the isle of St. Lucia, a beautiful, rather less well-known speck, 40 miles long, about halfway down the Antillean chain, just south of Martinique. I've been to these islands many times but this is my first visit to St. Lucia, and the weather is perfect this time of the year. I'm leaving in a few days so I'll probably mail this from New York.

Part of my visit has been recuperation. Your letter (along with your address) passed away from me last summer, disappearing as my life almost did, and that is why I never answered your kind words about the piece in Esquire.* I didn't quite realize it at the time but I was being swallowed up in a fearsome mental illness known as depression—"the black dog," as Churchill called the relatively mild version that seized him from time to time. Mine progressed very slowly albeit inexorably through summer and

* "Love Day," *Esquire* (August 1985).

fall until in mid-December I was hospitalized at Yale–New Haven with about as serious a form of the malady as it's possible to get. I was there for nearly seven weeks.

I'm happy to report that I'm close to fully recovered. Depression in fortunate cases (the majority, really) seems to be self-limiting and runs its course until the victim comes out the other end of his nightmare more or less intact. In the meantime, however, it's Auschwitz time in the heart of the soul—a form of madness I wouldn't wish upon a literary critic. They give you drugs and a rather innocuous and simple-minded type of psychotherapy, but the real curative is rest and time. Depression—aside from crushing any joy whatever—destroys the health by destroying sleep, appetite, libido and all the other things that make life worth living. It's a long way back but (and I hope it doesn't sound trite) one is somehow made stronger by the crucible of the experience. I've begun writing again during the past four weeks (depression also wrecks the intellect, for a long time I was incapable of reading a daily newspaper) and feel very close to normal. Hallelujah, I say every morning now, because for many mornings last winter, I didn't think I'd last the day.

I would be very pleased indeed to read your lost cities of Arkansas book and also let you know my reaction.* Do send a copy of the galleys to Roxbury, where I'll be in a few days. It sounds like just the kind of book I'd love to sink my teeth into, and you'll certainly get my response which I'm virtually certain will be positive knowing your feeling about Arkansas and the depth of your empathy.

If I'm lucky and can husband my new-found strength, I'll finish that Marine Corps book within a couple of years and ask you for <u>your</u> blessings on it, along with that of Jesus.

Yours,

Bill

* Donald Harington, *Let Us Build Us a City: Eleven Lost Towns* (San Diego: Harcourt Brace, 1986).

To Philip Caputo

July 4, 1986 Vineyard Haven, MA

Dear Phil:

Life down there with all that fishing seems so idyllic that I've got half a mind to chuck this Vineyard scene and come to Key West. But I do imagine that the heat is a little intimidating at the moment, so if I do take you up on your suggestion and come, I'll doubtless do it in the fall. Anyway, it was good to hear from you. The Statue of Liberty event which I've been following on TV seems such a gross piece of commercialism that it makes one lose the vestiges of one's patriotism. A wonderful Alabama lady,[*] age 84, who lives up here in the summer quite rightly and indignantly asked why the TV coverage of the Liberty show couldn't have been government sponsored, with no beer commercials. The gov't, she also said rightly, should have paid for the restoration of the statue instead of having Lee Iacocca hustle the project. It would have cost the taxpayers ¼ the cost of a ballistic missile.

All my depression has disappeared, even the vagrant shadows that were hanging around when I saw you, and I'm well into a revised version of the book along the lines I spoke to you about. I feel good about the new version, and work is slow as usual, but fairly steady.

I'm pleased that you and Esquire are pleased about the article.[†] I've reread the Xerox of the piece which you sent me and I'm sure your revisions will fit in well. In the draft that I've read I only have two or three small items that I'm concerned about and which, as a favor, I wish you'd eliminate in the final version. I think when I was getting deep into my illness I may have mentioned them to you but much of that time is fuzzy to me so at risk of repetition I'll mention them again. On p. 26 there is my criticism of William Gass which I wish you'd get rid of.[‡] I do feel that way but I honestly don't think there's any need to alienate a fellow writer in print. Also, I wish you'd tone down my observations about academics. "Creeps"

* Virginia Foster Durr (1903–99) was a civil rights activist and the mother of close Styron friend and Vineyard neighbor Lucy Hackney.

† Philip Caputo, "Styron's Choices," *Esquire* (December 1986).

‡ William H. Gass (b. 1924), American novelist, essayist, and philosopher. His novel *The Tunnel* won the National Book Award in 1995.

they are—many of them—but that's too strong a word for me to want to be quoted as calling them. Finally, in the last few paragraphs I'm not too happy about that very ambiguous reference to "skullduggery." I don't want to suggest that either of us censor what I might have told you in a perhaps indiscreet moment but I'm not happy with the way that remark stands at the moment.

How goes your work at the moment? Well, I hope. In the next life I'm going to have a Pontiac dealership instead of writing novels. I've been reading a lot more recently about the Vietnam war. Bill Broyles' book on his return to Vietnam (Brothers in Arms) is quite remarkable, I think, as a retrospective document by a combat veteran.* Have you read it? Also, I just finished another good but depressing (pardon the word) chronicle about Vietnam vets, Payback by Joe Klein. I imagine you've read it; as a matter of fact, Klein uses a quote from A Rumor of War as an epigraph to one of the book's sections. I'm trying to get a line on some work dealing with the most badly wounded survivors of the war. Do you know of any such book? There's an enormous amount already written on the psychological damage (I've just read Wounds of War by a psychiatrist, Herbert Hendin) but if you could suggest anything in particular about physical casualties, I'd like to know.† I suspect you can understand my reason for wanting this kind of information, since as I told you a horrible wounded Marine figures centrally in the version—the new version—of my book.

In case you ever want to chat about anything my number up here is 617-693-2535. I intend to be here at least until mid-September and probably past that.

Keep pulling in those big fish and stay in touch.

All best

Bill

* Bill Broyles, *Brothers in Arms: A Journey from War to Peace* (New York: Alfred A. Knopf, 1986).

† Herbert Hendin and Ann Pollinger Hass, *Wounds of War: The Psychological Aftermath of Combat in Vietnam* (New York: Basic Books, 1984).

To Peter Matthiessen

October 18, 1986 Roxbury, CT

Dear Peter,

I had never noticed, until I saw the extraordinary jug handles in the David Levine cartoon in NYRB, what gigantic ears you have but this does not lessen my belated appreciation of Men's Lives. I was too fogged up to read it when the galleys arrived last winter, and too dilatory this summer, but I read it recently and think it's just splendid. Some of the best stuff I've ever read on men of the sea, laboring men, and I'm sure it'll become both a classic and a monument to the folk you've so eloquently written about. A truly fine book.

I also thought the Indian presentation the other night at PEN was an eye-opener and very successful in its general appeal and informativeness. How did the deposition go?

Let me know if I can help (though I don't know how) and keep in touch.

Ever,

Porter

To Willie Morris

May 15, 1987 Roxbury, CT

Dear Willie:

I'm enclosing a couple of articles from The N.Y. Times for your perusal. One of them, as you can tell, is by yours truly—it came out last Sunday.* The other, by Tom Wicker, is about a Mississippi native and is self-explanatory. Joe Ingle, who is the minister who runs the Southern Coalition in Nashville (and whom I visited on my way down to Oxford) asked me to bring the plight of Johnson to your attention in the hope that you might be able to pull a string or two to help save this poor fellow. It really does appear that this is a case of another truly innocent victim. I wonder

* William Styron, "Death Row," *The New York Times* (May 10, 1987).

if that friend of yours in the legislature, about to become the next Speaker, might pull enough weight to at least get the governor to delay the execution so that a full examination of Johnson's case might be made. It seems to me that it would be horrible if in this instance an innocent man should be gassed at Parchman.

Speaking of Parchman, I wanted to chime in and endorse the feelings in your recent letter that that trip we took (and indeed the whole visit to Miss.) was one of the most memorable events in recent years. Tom had the time of his life. He is of course one of your greatest fans among a legion of fans, and keeps talking about the trip as one of the greatest experiences he's ever had . . . Furthermore, I was absolutely bewitched by your adorable Jane Rule. That picnic she threw in the Charleston cemetery, at the foot of the grave of Mr. James Crow, was one of the paramount picnics in a lifetime of grand picnics; please tell her for me how much I admired that wonderful provender, as well as admiring her, for herself, boundlessly.

I'm greatly looking forward to <u>Taps</u>. I don't really know what to say about the Korean War, except perhaps that it remains one of the most completely forgotten military conflicts in Western history. It would be a terrible thing to die in any way but most wars leave at least a mark on history. Korea left no mark. To have died in that war would have been to perish in total oblivion. I suppose there was some merit in America helping save the South Koreans from the Kommunist Menace—but <u>why always Americans</u>, thousands of us?

I've distributed the Elvis T-shirts from Graceland to various girls. They were more effective than caviar or Rolex watches.

Stay in touch and thanks again for a glorious visit.

Your ole buddy,
Stingo

P.S. I greatly appreciated the note from Gov. Winter—an admirable man whose fame still spreads far and wide in Yankeeland.

To Charles Sullivan

August 1, 1987 Vineyard Haven, MA

Dear Charlie:

I've been intending to write you—about, among other things, getting you to look out for the August Esquire—but realized I'd left your address in Roxbury. I would have telephoned you but figured (obviously incorrectly) that you had already fled the St. Pete heat. Anyway, I'm glad you got the Esquire with my reasonably healthy-looking mug on the cover.* It was a pretty good issue to appear in, since I gather this one has received quite a bit of attention and has sold out in many places.

I really haven't abandoned the USMC novel, in fact I've returned to a re-working of it along the line you and I have discussed (Saipan, the zealot officer bearing down on a suspected "radical" enlisted man, etc.) so it may be that what I've got now is two novels going simultaneously (like Balzac and Tolstoy, not bad people to emulate). At any rate, the long piece you read in Esquire is something that can stand alone as a "novella" or short novel whether or not I decide to extend it into something longer, which I'll probably do.

The weather up here has been marvelous, despite trouble with the crops; the driest June & July since 1946. Lots of people in and out, as usual, lots of socializing but reasonably good fun.

The president of France has just awarded me the Legion of Honor. There'll be a ceremony in N.Y. or Washington in the fall. That little red ribbon may be the only thing I'd rather wear than the Congressional Medal.

I imagine we'll be here through most of September. I hope you all can drop by for a visit on your way to N.H., or while there. Stay in touch.

Your Well and Reasoned Friend
Bill

* Styron appeared on the August 1987 cover of *Esquire* with John Updike; the issue contains Styron's novella *A Tidewater Morning*.

To Willie Morris

October 15, 1987 Roxbury, CT

Dear Willie,

I thought your piece on Faulkner's Mississippi was just great.* You captured so much both of the beloved state and the man himself. I am eagerly looking forward to the Geographic with the pictures—I know it will be sumptuous.

Also, please tell Richard Ford how grateful I am for the book of stories.† I'd read several already in Esquire but both reacquaintance with the old and work I'd never read made for wonderful reading. Thank you for the present. I hope we can all get together someday before long.

Because of the long journey I'm not going to press you to come to my Legion of Honor ceremony but it would be splendid if you could make it. Afterwards I've hired a Frog restaurant in N.Y. where we will be having catfish coquilles, chitlins Lyonnaisse, grits Bercy and Brunswick County (Va) Scuppernong 1972.

À bientôt I hope
Stingo

To Gavin Cologne-Brookes‡

October 20, 1987 Roxbury, CT

Dear Mr. Cologne-Brookes,

I would welcome the opportunity of meeting you and talking to you when you come here next spring and I hope we could have a fruitful and enjoyable get-together. At the moment I know only that I must be in California on March 29 through April 1st or 2nd but outside of that I expect to

* Willie Morris, "Faulkner's Mississippi," *National Geographic* 175 (March 1989).

† Richard Ford (b. 1944) is a Pulitzer Prize–winning writer. Styron refers to Ford's 1987 short-story collection, *Rock Springs* (New York: Atlantic Monthly Press, 1987).

‡ Author of *The Novels of William Styron: From Harmony to History* (Baton Rouge: Louisiana State University Press, 1995) and *Rereading William Styron* (Baton Rouge: Louisiana State University Press, 2013).

be here in the early spring and would welcome you. I don't know precisely what I can contribute to your thesis but I could try to do my best.

You must feel very odd, "the only Briton" writing about my work. I don't feel quite like Edmund Wilson, who called your countrymen "the despicable English" and really had quite a vitriolic animus about Britain, but it is true that I've felt no warmth about England over the years and plainly the feeling is mutual. Nothing at all personal, as we say, nor do I mean to be condescending when I say that not some, but many, of my good friends are English. But it is remarkable how some countries will take certain writers to their hearts and virtually ignore others. The best example, in my own case, can be seen in a list of books that was sent to me some time ago—a list I imagine you've heard about: the 20 "best novels" by living Americans, drawn up by some British book association or other. It contained novels by every single U.S. writer I consider my peer (Roth, Updike, Bellow, Mailer, etc. etc.) and quite a few novels by writers I would completely disdain—but not one of my works was on the list. Strangely, when I beheld this list I was not in the slightest bit surprised. Totally aside from the absurdity of such lists (noblest dogs, best soaps, worst diseases) I had, through long experience with the British reaction to my work, always expected to be ignored and this list was a simple validation.

But I would certainly be happy to have you have a drink or two with me (I've gone off the hard stuff but still go for a bit of beer or wine) and also break bread and take walks in the woods with me and my dog Tashmoo—although the glory of spring comes late to the Connecticut countryside. So plan to come ahead, keeping in mind the problem of the dates I mentioned. I'll also be happy to receive the preliminary writing you've done and give you my commentary for what it's worth—I'm a very poor judge of the contents of my own box or bottle. But I'll be honest, at least, and carefully try to assess your argument.

Sincerely,

William Styron

P.S. Jim West wrote very warmly and admiringly about you.

To Louis D. Rubin, Jr.

November 16, 1987 Roxbury, CT

Dear Louis,

I'd be pleased and honored to be a founding member of the Fellowship of Southern Writers and I thank you for inviting me.* I had a few qualms at first, since I have a sneaking suspicion (perhaps unfounded in truth) that such of your editorial and critical founders as Messrs. Sullivan and Simpson† have a rather tepid view of my work, and I thought that I might not feel terribly comfortable being associated with them (or vice versa). But since you say "all of us" want me in the group I take this as an assurance and will put my qualms at rest. The group sounds as if it might have fruitful activities in the future and that would be fine with me. You are certainly correct in your assumption that I would not like to get connected with some self-conscious new Agrarian movement, a kind of Southern Mafia whose aims would certainly not be in accord with what I would feel to be a strong and meaningful literature. But you make it clear that the fellowship has more intelligent goals, so count me in. As for suggestions regarding membership, there instantly come to my mind Reynolds Price and Willie Morris but I'm sure you all have considered these worthy gents already.‡

I have followed the progress of Algonquin Books with great pleasure, and have seen the name crop up in all sorts of nice places. You are to be congratulated for bringing such inventiveness and vitality to this good venture. I've read more than a few of your productions, and had a special response to Hopkins' <u>One Bugle No Drums</u> because of my brief but intense connection with the Korean War.§ It was an exceptionally fine memoir. All of your books, incidentally, are beautifully turned out.

* The Fellowship of Southern Writers was founded in 1987 by a group of authors to encourage the literature of the South. Charter members included Styron, Rubin, Robert Penn Warren, C. Vann Woodward, Cleanth Brooks, Shelby Foote, and several others.

† Southern literary critics Walter Sullivan (1924–2006) and Lewis P. Simpson (1916–2005).

‡ Morris was never elected to the fellowship.

§ William B. Hopkins, *One Bugle No Drums: The Marines at Chosin Reservoir* (Chapel Hill, N.C.: Algonquin Books, 1986).

The enclosed clippings explain themselves. I thought you might like to see them. There is one (probably intentional) inaccuracy in the article from Mississippi, viz., Henry Kissinger was definitely not present.*

Faithfully,

Bill S.

To Willie Morris

November 24, 1987 Roxbury, CT

Dear Willie,

Following is the passage I believe you wanted from my speech about Jim:

"I never knew an artist whose style was so inimitably and faithfully a reflection of himself. Let me give you an example which is surely going to disturb the liberals who hear these words. You were not a bigot, but take the word 'nigger,' which I often heard you use in conversation with a certain casual and disarming precision that was almost breathtaking. You were the only man I ever knew upon whose lips that word had no connotation of ugliness or animosity but instead was uttered with a kind of large, innocent, open sense of fraternity, and I often wondered at this, at how it would be, until I realized that in that word, or at least in the way you spoke it, there were profound echoes of your great predecessors Sherwood Anderson and Dreiser and, above all, Mark Twain—whose peculiarly border sensitivity, part Southern, part Midwestern, but achingly American, you inherited in full measure."†

I hope this will be of help. I can get you the whole speech if you need it but this is, I believe, the pertinent passage.

Willie, your visitation was wonderful and Mayor Leslie's speech was superb. Everyone felt that your presentation was the highlight of the eve-

* In an article in *The Oxford Eagle* (November 12, 1987), Morris playfully slipped Kissinger's name into a list of notables present at the dinner where Styron was awarded the Legion of Honor.

† Unknown speech about James Dickey (1923–97), the poet and novelist best known for *Deliverance* (1970).

ning and I am so grateful to you for turning up in Sodom and making the event a splendid one. Several people have requested copies of the "letter" and I have had quite a few Xeroxes from that issue of the Oxford newspaper. I am enjoying wearing my pretty little rosette in my lapel, just as Pop Bill enjoyed his. It really is, somehow, the supreme honor. I saw Norman Mailer at a party and he asked me if I thought it would help me get laid in Paris. I told him that you couldn't get laid in Paris if you were an American until they named an avenue after you. He was plainly just jealous.

I'm sending this off to you rapidly, as per your instructions. Hang loose and give my best to all.

Ever,

Stingo

To Louis D. Rubin, Jr.

November 25, 1987 Roxbury, CT

Dear Louis,

I very much appreciate the Woodson book.* It is beautiful and much of his work does, of course, bring back the atmosphere of the Virginia where I grew up.

I hope I didn't sound too querulous about the critics who are on board. You're absolutely right about a general lack of unanimity in any group regarding a person's work, and that's the way it should be, really. I guess I just can't shake my prickly feeling about most critics, especially professional Southern ones and their often insistent chauvinism. But I'm happy to be in the group.

I neglected to tell you, incidentally, how much I approved of your own critical demolition of Stephen Oates' bio. of Faulkner.† My reasons are threefold. First and most importantly, the book is the mawkish and appalling disgrace you said it was. Secondly, Oates wrote a biography of Nat

* William L. Tazewell, *Down to the Sea with Jack Woodson: The Artistry of a Distinguished American Illustrator* (Chapel Hill, N.C.: Algonquin Books, 1987).

† Stephen B. Oates, *William Faulkner: The Man and the Artist, a Biography* (New York: Harper and Row, 1987).

Turner after my book appeared; all well and good except that Oates has taken every opportunity he can to denounce me (usually in interviews) and in fact took a nasty swipe at me in the introduction to his own book.* Thirdly, he is a plagiarist. On the last page of his Faulkner book, he quoted a whole passage of my description of Faulkner's funeral without attribution (he left out direct quotes for most of the passage)—something I was going to call to the attention of his publisher but somehow forgot. Thanks for doing such a well-deserved chop-up of this pious fraud.†

Yrs,

Bill

To Prince Sadruddin Aga Khan

December 12, 1987 Roxbury, CT

Dear Sadri & Katy,

Like the bad penny, Kosinski always turns up—as you can see, at the moment of my divine apotheosis. I really thought that Kosinski should have gotten the Légion d'Honneur, not I—maybe he will, maybe I'll use my influence with Mitterrand to get him one, and at least a "Chevalier" for Kiki.

Anyway, the enclosed clippings will describe the goings-on last November when I finally entered heaven.

I hope to be able to come and pay you dear people a visit before too long. Rose and I both miss you very much.

The Right Wing is in panicky despair over the Summit and its aftermath. No Evil Empire to hate! I was invited to the Soviet Embassy to meet Gorbachev and sat listening to him at a table where my companions were—get this—Joyce Carol Oates, Norman Mailer, Billy Graham, Paul

* Stephen B. Oates, *Fires of Jubilee: Nat Turner's Fierce Rebellion* (New York: Harper and Row, 1975).

† In November 1991, Oates and Styron exchanged letters about the alleged plagiarism. Oates was faulted by the American Historical Association for "misuse" (a category of misconduct that the association's professional division created for Oates's work) rather than plagiarism. The debate over his alleged offenses was still raging a decade after the initial accusations.

Newman and Henry Kissinger. Could you conceive of an odder group of table-fellows?

Stay in touch.

Much love,
Bill

To Lewis Steel*

December 31, 1987 Roxbury, CT

Dear Lew, I appreciate your kind comments about Sophie's Choice. You know, in the end (if we are honest with ourselves) we writers write at least in part to create some ultimate effect upon a reader—especially readers whose minds and sensibilities we respect—and so it is enormously gratifying to receive a response like yours. It makes so much of the sweat and effort worthwhile. I'll never forget our courtroom days—it's a vivid part of my memory—and it was good hearing from you and to feel that same valuable continuity remains unbroken.

Faithfully, Bill S.

P.S. Did you know that Ida Schenkman, that bailbondswoman, tried to cheat me out of $10,000? After three years I got it back.

* Steel was the attorney who represented Tony Maynard, on whose behalf Styron testified in 1974. Maynard's manslaughter conviction was thrown out, but he had spent seven years in prison and was wounded during the Attica rebellion. Steel wrote in 2008, "After the trial we developed a friendship which unfortunately floundered on the shoals of Nat Turner."

To Willie Morris

January 6, 1988 Roxbury, CT

Dear Willie, It looks as if Uncle Shelby has joined forces with Mike Thelwell and Herbert Aptheker.* The enclosed is from a review from the exceedingly dull George Garrett about an exceedingly dull 20-pound historical novel by someone named Thomas Flanagan. It's bad enough that the darkies jumped me but a white Mississippi boy? I thought he knew better.

It was great hearing your Yuletide voice. I've heard fine things about your book and am eager to get a look.

I'm off to Nicaragua with Carlos Fuentes. If I don't come back, remember that I loved America and the ideals for which she stands, also the United States Marine Corps, Duke University, and my dog Tashmoo, more than I could even express.

Your friend,
Stingo

To Philip Roth

March 4, 1988 Roxbury, CT

Dear Philip: You have your dwarf, I have Jerry Marcus. His weekly letter is enclosed.

He has been writing me a letter like this, at least once a week, for nearly 10 years. I almost never read them and always throw them away, because they are such a mess. I am his intellectual garbage pail. He writes me about anything that comes to his mind, books, movies, random thoughts, anything. He is an orthodox Jew, and teacher (substitute high school) in

* George Garrett, "Young Fenians in Love and History," *The New York Times* (January 3, 1988), was a review of Thomas Flanagan's 824-page *The Tenants of Time* (New York: Dutton, 1988). In the review, Garrett cited Shelby Foote's "displeasure with Mr. Styron's liberties with and distortions of the character and story of Nat Turner—'If I write a story about a very tough little western badman, that is very different from pretending to write a story that I made up out of my head and call him Billy the Kid. I have no right to do that to Billy. No one has.'"

Long Island City. He is about 45, I think, and has terrible sex problems with his wife whom he hates. He is quite intelligent, really, but insane. He holds the N.Y. City Arm Wrestling championship. He has sent me his picture. He has the physique of a horse. I can't get him off my back. He calls me on the phone a lot but I almost never let myself talk to him. He calls me Bill.

I didn't read this (letter, ha!) very carefully—I never do—but somewhere I notice he mentions you. He always talks a lot about writers, mainly Jewish writers.

I wish he would write you instead of me.

I'll trade him for your dwarf.

Here is a joke: What's 6 miles long, green and has an asshole every 3 feet?

Ans: The St. Patrick's Day Parade.

See you on the 11th.

—BS.

To Carlos Fuentes

April 24, 1988 Roxbury, CT

Love and congratulations on your great honor.* Sorry unable to be with you. Will see you soon in New York to celebrate.

Bill and Rose

William Styron was awarded the MacDowell Medal for outstanding contribution to the arts in the summer of 1988.

* Fuentes was awarded Spain's $87,000 Cervantes Prize, often considered the top honor for Spanish-language writing.

To Philip Caputo

August 7, 1988 Vineyard Haven, MA

Dear Phil:

John Hersey told me that he thought that if I write you at your old Key West address it would be forwarded to you—I hope this reaches you. Several things have impelled me to write you after such a long silence on my part. I tried to get in touch with you by phone a number of times a long while ago but misplaced your number and couldn't find it since you were unlisted. Then one thing or another kept stalling my writing you. I'm a very poor correspondent. Anyway, talking with John was a pleasure, since we spoke about you, and I also had a call not too long ago from Margot Kidder*—a knockout lady, incidentally—who said she had seen you in Key West. Furthermore, Rose belatedly passed on an announcement of your wedding—for which warm congratulations—and to this must be added the coup de grâce: I gather you are going to be living in Connecticut. At least, that was the word I got from John. If this is true I hope it means that we will be neighbors. At any rate, I'm delighted by your new domestic condition and hope that it is true that you are becoming a Connecticut Yankee, then we can hoist a glass or two. I use the word glass advisedly since ever since my mental meltdown, which you wrote about, I have limited my drinking to 2 or three glasses of wine in the evening, never more, and have not had a drop of the hard stuff since at least the time since I last saw you. Amazing—I never thought there would be a day when I didn't have my ritual jolts of Cutty Sark at eventide, but there it is and I don't miss the jolts at all.

I also wanted to tell you, with vast belatedness, that I read Indian Country with great excitement and admiration. It really contains some of the very best and most penetrating writing, in my opinion, and I hope that if we have some sort of reunion in Connecticut I'll be able to elaborate at greater length on your achievement.

My own writing has been somewhat spasmodic but I'm proceeding apace, trying to finish a piece based on a trip Carlos Fuentes and I took to Nicaragua, and also I'm midway in a grand exposé of what it's like to suf-

* Kidder (b. 1948) is an actress best known for playing the role of Lois Lane opposite Christopher Reeve in four Superman movies.

fer from melancholia. The fiction is churning slowly and may turn out to be something I'm proud of if I can get it set solidly on the rails of my imagination—or what's left of it in this demented era.

I hope you receive this and also receive renewed expressions of my highest esteem, as the French say when signing off.

Yours,

Bill S.

To Stuart Wright

October 6, 1988* Roxbury, CT

Dear Stuart,

Although I can't prove it, I have good reason to suspect that you stole the diary which you recently returned to me at my request. When Jim West visited you, you told him that I had either given you the diary or had sold it to you—you couldn't remember which. Your obscurity in this matter taxes my credulity, and my belief is further stretched by the bill of sale you enclosed from the House of Books. I find it virtually impossible that this particular rare book dealer, which I recall having had a high reputation, would have come into possession of anything so intimate as a boyhood diary, written by a well-known contemporary author, without having notified the author and authenticated the item, and I received no such notification.

But although I think you stole the diary let us for a moment, purely for the sake of discussion, assume that you had gotten hold of it from the House of Books or—since the bill of sale does not assign the diary directly to you—from someone else who did. To me it is appalling that you would have visited me so many times without ever once mentioning that you had this book in your possession. A person with your expertise in manuscripts and rare books would surely have known that a boyhood diary is something that does not normally appear on the market and that

* Styron sent Louis Rubin a copy of this letter with a cover note reading: "Dear Louis, You may want to circulate this letter to certain concerned parties. —Bill." Styron also provided the letter to Jim West and others.

its very presence there makes it suspect. You must have known that I would have been curious as to its whereabouts. Therefore even in the unlikely event that you had obtained the book by honest means, your failure to mention it to me—or, more honorably to restore it to me—is indefensible and a despicable breach of trust.

You spoke rather patronizingly, when you returned the diary, of my having been a good and generous friend to you, as if by returning it you were doing me a favor. I can only say that my sentiments could not be less reciprocal and that I regret ever having let you into my house.

William Styron

To Willie Morris

November 16, 1988 Roxbury, CT

Dear Willie,

Dean and Larry sent me the news clips about the premiere of Good Old Boy, and I must say I was delighted and envious.* I want you to know that the event has inspired me to try to teach my new little black lab, Dinah, to drive. There are quite a few dogs in the neighborhood that drive but they are used to automatic. Dinah is going to be the first dog in Litchfield County, Conn., to drive stick shift. Anyway, I wish I'd been there and I hope I get a cassette.

Your buddy,
Stingo

* Morris's *Good Old Boy* was made into a TV movie titled *The River Pirates*, which premiered in 1988.

To Phillip Horne*

December 6, 1988 Roxbury, CT

Dear Mr. Horne,

I was very pleased and also quite touched to receive your long and generous letter concerning my work and my father—they are both, as you point out so correctly, intertwined. I was also happy to receive the pictorial history of N.C. State. All of the book was engrossing but naturally I was especially captured by the parts having to do with the period circa 1910 when my father was there. They filled me with a curious nostalgia—if you can feel nostalgia for something or some time that you yourself did not personally experience. But, then, I am often prompted to live imaginatively in my father's past rather than my own. I was moved by your perceptions regarding my relationship with him; it was very complex and, indeed as you say, devoted though not without its prickly aspects—that would be quite natural, also, I'm sure. But in general I was quite bowled over and greatly impressed by your reflections on paternal relationships, N.C. State past and present, the Va.-N.C. border country, Nat Turner, your reading of my work and all sorts of other lively topics. It did me a great deal of good to read your letter. I was in rather sour spirits on the day it came, and the honesty and feeling of your words did a great deal to buoy me up.

I'm quite fascinated by your idea of somehow memorializing my father at State. Naturally I have no objections at all, but the idea of your melting some of those hard corporate hearts at Tenneco fills me with both awe and trepidation. But if you think you can pull it off you certainly have both my approval and blessing. I looked at the face of my father in that yearbook page which you so kindly sent me and thought how tickled he would really be—deep down, in spite of his natural inclination toward self-effacement—and so I wish you well. It is with some astonishment that I record here the fact that next October 1st will be his 100th anniversary.

Certainly I'd be happy to talk over anything further that you have in mind (including having you show up here with ham in hand, or arms) and I'd be very well disposed to a meeting. Probably the best time for me (and

* Director of Gift Planning (1987–93) at North Carolina State University, where a memorial fund in Styron's father's name was established in 1989. Horne suggested to Styron that he collect and publish in book form the three stories in *A Tidewater Morning.*

I imagine for you) would be after the Holiday horrors are over and (for me) sometime after January 10th when I'm planning to return from a short trip to the Caribbean. Why don't you mark a tentative time to call me here—(203) 354-5939—though of course I'd welcome a call or letter, really, at any time. Meanwhile, please believe me when I say that your letter meant a great deal to me, and I'm grateful for it.

Sincerely

William Styron

To Willie Morris

February 9, 1989 Roxbury, CT

Dear Willie,

All the folks around here—family and friends—did indeed adore "Good Ole Boy." It is utterly charming and you should be proud that the folks in Tinsel Town did such a loving and warm job of transferring your words to the screen. Thanks for sending it. I am off to California for a short while to see Susanna and am taking the cassette you so kindly sent to show to her stepson Tavish, age 10.

My black lab pup Dinah leaps and bounds in the air like a god-dam gazelle. I wish you could see her, I believe she may be as unique as that grotesque tree-clenching bulldog from South Carolina. I don't know whether I sent you the enclosed flyer from last summer—The MacDowell Medal has been given to such figures as Robert Frost, Edmund Wilson, Miss Hellman, Mailer and Updike. Norman M., who was on the jury, confided to me recently that I nosed out Saul Bellow for the honor, which made me believe that us Southern Presbyterians are coming back into our own.

Rose joins in love.

Stingo

To Willie Morris

July 1, 1989* Vineyard Haven, MA

Dear Willie, I saw on page 3 of The Southern Register something I consider to be the final apotheosis: pictures of you, me and "Knuckles" Kazin all in an intimate lunch. I've re-read your Geographic piece on Faulkner's Mississippi with great appreciation and this reminds me that I'll be seeing you in August.† Don't know exactly when I'll arrive but I do hope to spend an extra day or two—probably before the 3d. My friend François ("Frank") Mitterrand has invited me to "be at his side" in Paris on Bastille Day, July 14, so I'm goin' and will bring you back some hog-jowl pâté.

See you soon. Your buddy,

Stingo.

To James West

October 21, 1989 Roxbury, CT

Dear Jim,

The main reason it's taken me quite some time to write you is that for a week recently I was legally blind. Not to sound melodramatic, really, but the cataract in my left eye (the worst one) got rapidly more opaque and I was seeing things as a blur. To complicate matters, the drops I was taking to dilate my pupils, and which greatly helped my vision, were prohibited for several weeks before the operation last Wednesday, and so for many days I was groping my way around, able to see large objects and able to perambulate, but pretty much of a washout when it came to either reading or writing. The operation, however, was a complete and rather astounding success. There is a world-class eye clinic in, of all places, Waterbury, Conn., about 10 miles from here, and I had it done there. I'd been told how remarkable the procedure was, and how dramatically successful it was supposed to be—but I had to have it to truly believe it. It was a pain-

* Postcard of Edward Degas' *A Cotton Office in New Orleans* (1873).

† Willie Morris, "Faulkner's Mississippi," *National Geographic*, vol. 175 (March 1989).

less operation which took less than 20 minutes, after which I wore a patch over the eye overnight and came back to the clinic the next day for the "unveiling." Since that moment I've been able to see like a healthy ten-year-old. I have a brand new permanent lens made of plastic that allows me to see objects as I haven't seen them in the several years since the cataract began to act up. Colors are especially amazing—particularly reds and browns, and I've been able to perceive this autumn foliage with breathtaking freshness. I really feel as if I've been reborn. I may do the other eye in a few months—it may be that this new eye will compensate adequately enough, at least for a while, so that I can delay the other operation. At any rate, I feel greatly unburdened and sing hallelujahs for the science of ophthalmology.

Before the operation my sight was so bad that it actually prevented my reading a speech in Richmond whither I'd gone to address a huge flock of Va. English teachers at the Hotel Jefferson. Even though I'd had the speech (the essay I wrote on my grandmother) blown up to Cyclopean size I was unable to see it well enough to read, so I spoke impromptu and answered questions, which seems to satisfy them well enough. Not long before that I was in Norfolk at Old Dominion University, where there was a huge crowd, assembled largely I suspect because I was the prodigal hometown boy returned to his native hearth. I'm enclosing an interview I did before the gathering, which you may find interesting. There is a reference to depression toward the end, which reminded me to tell you that the Vanity Fair article has been postponed until December, ostensibly because at the magazine they are so enthusiastic about the piece that they want to make it a special feature.* Christmastime is a notorious season for melancholia so, who knows, it may deter a few people from slitting their throats as they contemplate more useless garbage in their Yule stockings.

I'm delighted to hear of your pleasant new ménage in Belgium. It sounds as if you have a wonderful setup and I have a feeling that you're going to enjoy yourself (along with the family) immensely. I envy you all that Belgian cuisine.

The jamboree in Raleigh for my father's 100th was a tremendous suc-

* William Styron, "Darkness Visible," *Vanity Fair* (December 1989). This 15,000-word piece was expanded into book form in 1990.

cess. The whole family (including husbands) was there for a splendid Sunday barbeque which was delectable despite the weekend's continuous rain. Phillip Horne, the entrepreneur behind the show, outdid himself by prevailing on Bob Loomis (who was present) to get Random House to produce a lovely little 8-minute film about my father and Newport News and me and my career, so called. They got Tom Wicker* to come down to N.N. and narrate the film from the Hilton Village piece. It was a truly lovely little presentation and they showed it as a prelude to my speech before a 900-member audience; it quite bowled me over, and my daddy would have been beside himself with the praise they bestowed upon him. I wish you'd been able to be there.

I'll write further soon; meanwhile enjoy beautiful Belgium.

As ever,

B.S.

To Jack Zajac

November 2, 1989 Roxbury, CT

Dear Jack,

It was lovely of you and Corda to come to my public exhibition—such a bore it must have been—but it was wonderful going to Santa Cruz and having that good dinner with all the friends. Also, grim as it was, the trip through the Mall was memorable, and I'm grateful as usual for your hospitality. I got to New York right on schedule, much of the trip made endurable by reading these Smithsonians. I was especially taken by the article on George Rhoads (Oct. 1988) and his remarkable Rube Goldberg machines. I've known George ever since our Bohemian days in New York in the late 40s. He lived in total squalor (as did I) and, being poverty-stricken, we often dined off of government surplus canned fish. He took the photograph of me that adorned the first edition of Lie Down in Darkness. For years he painted rather murky paintings and it's lovely to see that he's come into his own.

* Thomas Grey Wicker (1926–2011) was a journalist and columnist for *The New York Times*.

Thanks again to you guys for everything. Rose was fascinated by Corda's info on yeast and will be in touch.

Ever thine,
Bill

To Bob Brustein

December 3, 1989 Roxbury, CT

Dear Bobby, I greatly appreciated what you said on the phone about my Vanity Fair essay. I hope you know that you are the Ideal Critic (in the best sense) and that I value your opinion more than almost anyone I know (or don't know), and so when you express such a reaction I feel tremendously fulfilled. So as always I'm very grateful to you. And I'm looking forward to seeing you bientôt.

Ever, Bill S.

To Robert Bruccoli

December 9, 1989 Roxbury, CT

Dear Mr. Bruccoli,

Thank you for sending me the reader's report on Lie Down in Darkness, with its many apprehensions concerning the book's steamy passages. Actually, the book was pretty heavily censored by the publishers and an account of this appears, I am told, in the 1980 volume of Studies in Bibliography in an article by Arthur D. Casciato.* Thanks again for sending me the item.

Sincerely William Styron

* Arthur D. Casciato, "His Editor's Hand: Hiram Haydn's Changes in Styron's *Lie Down in Darkness*," *Studies in Bibliography* 33 (1980).

To Charles Sullivan

December 23, 1989 Roxbury, CT

Dear Charlie,

I want to thank you and Dorothy for the magnificent box of citrus fruit. It will be greatly relished and, I'm sure, quickly devoured by the mob of family and friends who are gathering here this Xmas weekend.

Your call was also greatly appreciated and it reminded me that I'd been out of touch for quite some time. In the past year I've had physical problems which have set me back a little, fortunately not too far back. Last winter I began to notice that my right arm had lost strength and was malfunctioning. When shaving or combing my hair I found I couldn't properly rotate my wrist, and at certain angles I dropped things like coffeepots. I went up to Mass. General Hospital and checked in with a neurologist, who after various tests decided I had a nerve compression in the fifth vertebra of my neck, and this was preventing my biceps from working properly; in fact, the right bicep had atrophied 40%. I was able to trace this back to an injury I'd received at Camp Lejeune in 1951: during a stream crossing exercise I'd been forced up against a wire cable and my neck had caught the blow, sending a kind of shock down my arm. Neck and arm were quite painful for a few days, but I was young, of course, and eventually everything healed and so forgot about it. Anyway, the docs said an operation was necessary to prevent total atrophy of that arm muscle. So I had the operation and lo and behold the surgeon discovered a broken ligament from that 1951 stream crossing incident, a ligament which had calcified and caused the entire problem.

The operation was a total success and now the arm is 85% functioning, which satisfies me for all intents and purposes, especially since the prediction is that recovery after another six months or so will be virtually total. But I'm still amazed that the USMC accident should rise up and strike me 37 years later.

In October I also had a brand new lens implanted in my left eye. The cataracts I'd been born with, and which caused me problems at Parris Island & Quantico in 1945 (I managed to get a waiver) finally became quite opaque this past year, especially the one in the left eye, which got so "thick" that I was legally blind. Then came this amazing operation (in

Waterbury, nearby) which was totally painless, took less than 20 minutes (I'd dread a dentist visit more), and left me with 20/20 vision without glasses, looking at the world and its bright colors with such freshness that I felt—and still feel—like Adam in the garden of Eden. So we can bemoan much of our modern technology but, my God, when technology works such miracles one can't help but feel full of praise.

So, one step back, two steps forward. That seems to be the way of the body as one gets older, or am I being too generous and optimistic? I'm glad your ticker is mending well.

I'm glad I talked to you about the censorship of letters in the Pacific during WWII. I finally have made a breakthrough, I think, in my USMC fiction, a short novel involving the narrator (a Stingo prototype), and Ollie North–type zealot of a company commander who is determined to prevent an enlisted man sending love letters to his sweetheart because the letters are explicitly erotic. But that's only the main theme, or the dominant theme—the other theme, as is usual in much of my work, is the misuse of power.

I might be consulting you by phone again in the near future if you don't mind. I'm off to St. Barts with the family—a wonderful French island with grand food and grander beaches. Hope to be in touch before long. Fond regards to Dorothy.

Semper fi,
Bill

Isn't what's happening in E. Europe astounding?*

* Styron refers to the revolutions of 1989 and the fall of communism, events that began in Poland and quickly spread to Hungary, East Germany, Bulgaria, Czechoslovakia, and Romania.

To Gavin Cologne-Brookes

February 15, 1990 Roxbury, CT

Dear Gavin,

Herewith the Vanity Fair essay for your perusal. As I think I told you the piece caused a tremendous commotion here and as a result I'm turning it into a small book for Random House, enlarging and elaborating here and there. The piece has already been contracted for by journals in France, Italy, Germany and Spain. Typically, no one in England seems to have wanted to publish it, though probably Cape will do it as a book since Random House is doing it.

I appreciate your comments about the movie of Sophie. My reactions have been quite similar to yours. I think on a certain level the film works pretty well—in a linear sense, capturing the essence of Sophie's story vis-à-vis her past and revelations about Auschwitz. But I deeply regret other parts. The sadomasochistic relationship which I established between Sophie and Nathan was softened to the point of absence. The double suicide at the end was totally unprepared for, not a hint of Nathan's obsession which led up to that event. Also, one of the reasons that Peter MacNichol's reading of "Ample Make This Bed" is so bad—aside from the horrible obviousness, which you pointed out—is MacNichol himself, entirely too callow for the role, especially with that glutinous accent from God knows where in Dixie, certainly not Tidewater Virginia. The moment I cringed most severely was when he was about to fuck, or something, Meryl Streep and exposed those pathetic little skinny legs of his. What a hoot.

I can only give you a provisional answer to your query about using my cottage to work in for a month or so in the spring. Certainly the invitation I gave you still holds, but there are one or two things it depends upon. Rose and I have a friend who has been renting the place for quite a few summers, and he probably will want it again; however, it may be that he won't be able to come until mid-June or July, in which case you would be welcome to have it. I usually go up to Martha's Vineyard on June first, so there may be an overlap if you come in mid-May but that would be O.K. so far as I'm concerned. Let me say that while I can't give you any definite word at the moment, the prospects would seem good, so what I'd like to do is wait a few weeks before giving you a definite promise. I hope this won't strain your schedule. I know that you would want a firm idea fairly soon so I'll do my best to let you know before too long. I'm delighted your novel is progressing to your satisfaction, and I'd like to be able to give you shelter for a while.* Stay in touch.

Faithfully,
Bill S.

To Willie Morris

July 28, 1990 Vineyard Haven, MA

Dear Willie,

I'm enormously pleased, of course, that you are going to tie the nuptial knot. I'd heard rumors of this event as a possibility but your confirmation delighted me. I'm eager to meet JoAnne† since, among other things, you have impeccable taste in girls/women/females/dogs and I know she fills the bill in every respect.

I've had trouble prying myself off this island and so it looks as though a late July visit to the Magnolia State will be at the very least delayed until a later date. The reason for all this is largely my upcoming book Darkness Visible, which is an expanded version of the essay I wrote on depression in Vanity Fair. The book, even before publication, seems to be attracting a lot of attention and as a result I've had to do a lot of annoying but (to Random House, at least) necessary publicity. I'm here right now doing a segment for Diane Sawyer for a forthcoming "Prime Time" ABC program, and the same network is doing an hour-long documentary on depression (Aug. 29) in which I'm featured somewhat against my will—inadvertently, really—I've found myself in the process of becoming a lead-

* In a letter from April 14, 1990, Styron added that "our residences will overlap for a couple of weeks but that's perfectly all right with me since I trust that we will be independent of each other as much as either of us would wish. Jimmy Baldwin, for instance, had the same arrangement over a much longer period of time and there was no sweat. I trust you will have some sort of vehicle because this place as you know is a long way from nowhere."

† JoAnne Prichard Morris was Willie Morris's second wife. She was the executive editor at the University Press of Mississippi from 1982 to 1997 and is currently an editor at the *Jackson Free Press.*

ing guru on melancholia, and God Knows where it will end. The book is officially slated to be published Sept. 27th but copies are due any day now and I'll make sure you get a mint example, signed by your old pal and fellow sufferer. They are making a first edition of 75,000 copies, which is a lot, but Jason Epstein told me that he thought it would sell forever. Everybody seems to be a victim of the malady these days, and my message is fairly simple: tough it out, brothers and sisters, for one day you will get well.

But I've got to get back to the novel since I'm very uncomfortable in the guru role except in the short term.

Your beautiful piece in Esquire on Celia reaffirmed my belief in the beauty and constancy of English prose when written by a loving and gifted hand such as yours.* I heard nothing but awed praise for your essay from every quarter.

Stay in touch and let's lay plans for an early get-together. Dinah and Tashmoo send their love to you, as does my other girl Rose.

Your steadfast pal,
Stingo

To Mike Mewshaw

October 21, 1990 Roxbury, CT

Dear Mike,

I greatly appreciate your letter about Darkness Visible—totally aside from the pleasure in hearing from you again. It must be a kind of reverse culture-shock to come back to God's Country (!) after so long a stay in the real Arcadia. For me the USA loses quality incrementally from day to day—it's in virtual decay on all levels, morally, spiritually and physically, best typified by a drive out of New York City (as I do with some frequency) where the potholed roadways and shocking slums juxtaposed against the skyscrapers make it all appear like a rich Bangladesh on the verge of collapse. I've got half a mind to pull my roots and live in France,

* William Morris, "The Blood Blister," *Esquire* (October 2, 1990).

where I've been often recently (thereby defying the foreboding I expressed in my little book) and where life still seems sweet instead of fear-ridden and mainly hideous.

I'm rather astonished at the way Darkness Visible has caught on. There are 140,000 copies in print at the moment, according to Random House, with no end in sight. Curious to think that a slender little volume about lunacy may provide a meal ticket for my superannuated years.

I'll be fascinated to see Year of the Gun.* John Frankenheimer can be an inspired director. He once had an option on Lie Down in Darkness; nothing came of it, though through no particular deficiency of his. My view on the movies is: take the loot and run with it, and I assume that happily you've been bestowed with loot. Run with it.

Good to hear of your residence in Ch'ville. I hope this means that our paths will cross more often now. Remember me to Slim please, and keep a stiff upper lip in these weird times.

Yours,
Bill

To Thomas Guinzburg

February 1, 1991† Roxbury, CT

Dear Tom,

Since the time when we agreed to become judges for the Turner Tomorrow Award, Carlos Fuentes, Peter Matthiessen and I have begun to have severe doubts concerning the worth of the enterprise and we want to take this occasion to set down our objections. Plainly the award was conceived in the spirit of idealism and with the best of intentions. But it now appears that what we had assumed might be a contest that would produce works of literary merit has really become a scramble by writers of questionable talent to cash in on a basically flawed concept.

* The film Frankenheimer made of Mewshaw's novel.

† This letter also appears in the Matthiessen Papers with a handwritten yellow Post-it note stamped with Styron's address in Roxbury: "Pete man, Here is the letter with your good points incorporated. See you soon Porter."

None of us questions the fact that, in gifted hands, a fine futuristic novel could be written about survival and prosperity on the planet and even that positive solutions to world problems might be credibly created by a novelist of genuine vision. But as the contest seems to be shaping up, it is highly doubtful that such a work will be produced or indeed that we would be presented with any book that could come close to meeting the literary standards that the three of us would feel obliged to impose.

Reports in the press, which we have no reason to doubt—especially since you have publicly verified some of these reports—have indicated that the bulk of the contributions are frivolous and certainly opportunistic. In any case, to produce a novel within the space of a year—on demand, so to speak—would seem an activity in which literary principles are almost bound to be compromised. We would not wish to give an award to any work which is so likely to be meretricious.

In short, none of us believes that the Turner Tomorrow Award will elicit entries of sufficient merit to warrant our giving a prize. We are therefore stating this view explicitly so that before the time of judging comes you and others connected with the award will be forewarned about our almost totally negative frame of mind We will quite understand if, because of our position, you will wish to substitute other judges in our place, and that might be the best solution. Copies of this letter are going to Nadine Gordimer and Wallace Stegner, and in the interest of fairness we hope you will make available copies to the other judges, to whom we have no access, so that they also may have an opportunity to agree or disagree with our position.*

Sincerely,

Bill

* Styron explains the Turner award fiasco in "We Weren't in It for the Money," *The Washington Post* (July 16, 1991). This was Styron's answer to Jonathan Yardley's attack on the judges in *The Washington Post.*

To Louis D. Rubin, Jr.

March 24, 1991 Roxbury, CT

Dear Louis,

Many thanks for the data on the Styron relatives on the Outer Banks. It turns out that there are more Styrons around than I had ever imagined. I was at an airline counter in San Diego not too long ago, trying to work out some sort of travel deal, when the agent pressed a button on his computer and found a William C. Styron of such-and-such an address in Raleigh, N.C. Precisely my name—obviously some unknown cousin. I will definitely subscribe to The Mailboat.*

I thought you'd like to see the enclosed from the San Francisco Examiner, especially since you are alluded to as the benign cupid who put together the Styron-Burgunder connection. I'll always be in your debt.

You did a great job with Algonquin and should be proud and rest contentedly on your well-deserved laurels.†

I'm sorry I can't make Chattanooga but will look forward to other sessions with the good ole boys.‡ Hope you all have fun.

Yrs,

Bill

To Philip Roth

January 3, 1992 Roxbury, CT

Dear Philip:

For my sins, I'm off to India, where I fully expect to get stuck (sucked?) by a Sikh; however, even if I don't get back I wanted to say I'm sorry your book, etc., prevented our getting together to talk about Operation Shy-

* The Styron name is fairly common in eastern North Carolina, particularly in Carteret County and along the Outer Banks. *The Mailboat,* edited by Karen Willis Amspacher on Harkers Island, was a periodical devoted to coastal North Carolina history and folklore.

† Rubin had just retired from Algonquin Books, turning over control of the company to his son Robert and cofounder Shannon Ravenel.

‡ The Fellowship of Southern Writers met biennially in Chattanooga, Tennessee.

lock. It's a splendid book as you must know, energetic and challenging, perhaps your best yet and you should be relaxed and proud. I really would like to talk to you in detail—there's so much richness in the book to deal with. I'll be back on the 18th of Jan.—thank God only two weeks eating curry and ghee (and a fly or two) so I'll contact you and we'll talk. Rose is staying until the first week in February.

I mentioned you at some length in The Nation (your Halcion siege) and I hope they sent you a copy, as I requested.* You also might want to look at my reflections on WWII in the current Newsweek.†

Have a happy New Year. You eminently deserve it.

In Jesus' name
—B

To Arthur Schlesinger, Jr.

March 1, 1992 Roxbury, CT

Dear Arthur:

This month the University of Georgia Press is publishing a book called The Return of Nat Turner by a white historian named Albert Stone.‡ I've not read it but from responsible sources I've heard that it's basically an attack on my book—a novel that I'd thought after 25 years (this year is its silver anniversary) had enough integrity and had grown venerable enough to be free of such molestations. I gather that once again the attacker, like the blacks in 1968, seems unable to comprehend the prerogatives of the historical novelist and is attempting to lambaste me on the narrowest of historiographical principles.

Needless to say I'm sick of this kind of vulgar ignorance, which could be dismissed as the work of a yahoo were it not for the mischief it might

* Roth fictionalized his own encounter with Halcion in his novel *Operation Shylock* (New York: Simon & Schuster, 1993).

† William Styron, "Prozac Days, Halcion Nights," *The Nation* (January 4/11, 1993), and William Styron, "The Enduring Metaphors of Auschwitz and Hiroshima," *Newsweek* (January 11, 1993).

‡ Albert E. Stone, *The Return of Nat Turner: History, Literature, and Cultural Politics in Sixties America* (Athens: University of Georgia Press, 1992).

cause in these wretched times of political correctness. Aside from being aware that you might simply be interested in this phenomenon per se, I was wondering if you might know someone in the historical field, sympathetic to ole Nat, who might want to head this guy off at the pass and deal with him in a review somewhere.* Any suggestions you might have, at this moment of my renewed martyrdom, will be greatly appreciated.

Love to Alexandra

As ever

Bill

To Carlos Fuentes

June 28, 1992 Vineyard Haven, MA

Dear Carlos,

I've been engrossed in reading The Buried Mirror and wanted to tell you what a splendid work I think it is.† It has told me so much and brought together so many historical strands that I'm fairly astonished at how you've managed to do it—creating this intricate tapestry with such consummate skill. I might add that your gifts as a novelist are eminently on display, for

* Schlesinger replied that he didn't "blame" Styron "for a certain irritation" over the Stone book. "It seems really idiotic—or malicious—to stir up twenty-five years later a controversy that was both mischievous and meaningless at the time." "I have mentioned the Stone book to a number of historians," Schlesinger went on, "none of them has ever heard of Stone. The feeling is that the book will probably be stillborn and that attacks will only [give] it undeserved publicity. . . . This, I think, is Vann Woodward's feeling, for example. Probably stoic indifference is the best policy. This too will pass—and ole Nat will remain." Schlesinger then commented on his participation in a conference in Seville for the Columbus quincentennial. "Poor Chris—another casualty of political correctness. If he had known all the things he would be held accountable for five hundred years after, I doubt that he would have bothered to discover America." Styron wrote Schlesinger on July 1, 1992: "Dear Arthur, Thanks for sending me the TLS review of the book on Nat Turner. On balance, not too bad, though I think Norman (as well as I) would be amazed by: 'Mailer-ish on the belief that exposition is the great clue to character.' That's a brand new wrinkle in Nat Turner criticism." See Michael O'Brien, "Elegy for Virginia," *The Times Literary Supplement* (June 5, 1992).

† Carlos Fuentes, *The Buried Mirror: Reflections on Spain and the New World* (Boston: Houghton Mifflin, 1992).

the book has tremendous narrative drive and has held me spellbound for the past few days.

I wish I could feel as sanguine and enthusiastic about this country of mine. The Supreme Court decision on kidnapping (especially Mexicans) is one of the most astoundingly arrogant judicial edicts ever to be handed down by any tribunal anywhere. It makes me want to hang my head in shame for our vaunted democratic process. I honestly do think that the U.S.A. is sliding down the tubes and there seems to be nothing in the future (certainly no presidential candidate) to arrest the process.

I have however been able to arrest the prostate process about which I was so distressed when we talked on the phone a week or so ago. I was so badly blocked that I'd almost resigned myself to the terrible Roto-rooter operation but since then I've been saved by a little pill called Hytrin. This is a medication known as a "smooth muscle relaxant" which works subtly on the bladder outlet to permit freer urine flow. I've been on Hytrin for some time now and most of my mealtime anguish (getting up several times to deal with blockage and a weak dribble) has been alleviated. If you haven't already been put onto this pill, I urge you to do everything you can to try it. No side effects that I can detect, and my urologist (who's head of the department at Harvard Medical School) says he feels that it's only a matter of time when this pill (which has been approved by the F.D.A. to lower high blood pressure but not for prostrate trouble) will be the panacea for all but the most intractable problems.* (The F.D.A., he says, is typically dragging its heels for complicated and nasty reasons I won't go into, though it has to do with money.) Anyway, do get your doc to put you on this pill if you still need treatment (the generic name is Terazosin).**

Young Carlos came by here some time ago in his beautiful Pussymobile, and spent the night and then disappeared in quest of, I'm sure, those treasures the Pussymobile is made for. It was lovely as usual to see him.

Will be awaiting your arrival in September. Meanwhile, love to Sylvia and stay in touch.

Abrazos,

Bill

* See William Styron, "Too Late for Conversion or Prayer," first published (in English) in *Havanas in Camelot*.

** A sign of superannuation and the mortician's knock—old guys talking about their prostates!

To Willie Morris

June 13, 1993 Vineyard Haven, MA

Dear Willie,

I don't think my conversation on the phone with you the other day could possibly convey the extent of my enthusiasm for New York Days.* It's simply a wonderful book, rich in anecdote, history, language and feeling. I think that when the final accounting is made, the book will rank not only as one of the finest renditions of the 1960s but, quite simply, as one of the great memoirs of the century. It is an overwhelmingly splendid achievement that has left me gasping for superlatives. It's so damned readable—I couldn't set it aside for a minute—and I reveled in your continuously captivating prose. I hope you're very proud of what you've done. I'll be at the party in New York; I wouldn't miss it, and would travel from Tibet to be there.

As ever,

Stingo

P.S. The MS is now in the hands of my summer neighbor, pushing 90, Virginia Foster Durr, who loves the book.

* Morris's 1993 memoir about his days as the editor of *Harper's*.

To Gavin Cologne-Brookes

May 3, 1994* Roxbury, CT

Dear Gavin,

Since we were last in touch I've had a few physical problems which, fortunately, I've managed to beat pretty well. In this era of high-tech medicine one manages to dance and skip one's way along life's perilous path just a few steps ahead of the undertaker. As a matter of fact, my problem was never life-threatening but not a barrel of laughs, either. Last summer and fall I began to notice that my right shoulder and arm were not functioning too well. So I went up to Boston to MGH (Massachusetts General Hospital, also known as Man's Greatest Hospital) for tests and they discovered a great deal of arthritic buildup which was causing nerve compression in the neck vertebra and consequent loss of muscle strength. So early in December I had a 5-hour operation. For a week afterward I was in real pain but that went away and the good news, finally, is that the operation seemed to halt the deterioration and I'm improving. I'm quite relativistic about this whole matter; although I'll probably never again have full strength I'm not really dysfunctional, not in a wheelchair, have fine appetite, can still get it up, etc. So what the hell, existence could be a lot worse.

Your mention of Death of a Salesman prompts me to reflect on the fact that just last night in New York, I saw Arthur's new play Broken Glass.† As usual, it got savaged by the critics here but will probably be a big hit in London. Arthur is quite amusing about all this. I think he no longer expects the U.S. critics to give him so much as the time of day but of course he feels that so long as the Brits love him in the passionate way they do, he's home free. It's good to be loved somewhere.

A Tidewater Morning came out here last fall and did quite well for a slim book of stories but set no record on the best-seller lists—something I hadn't expected anyway. The reviews were in general quite good and the

* Styron attached a clipping from *Random House Magazine* with a photo of President and Mrs. Clinton presenting him the National Medal of Arts. Styron circled and identified "movie director Billy Wilder" looking on.

† Arthur Miller's *Broken Glass* ran at Manhattan's Booth Theatre from April 24 to June 26, 1994.

book has been contracted for in all European countries except Germany, for some odd reason, where I really could care less about publication. Jim West remarked that the one review from England he saw—from, I think, the Sunday Times—may have been the single nastiest review he's ever read about any of my work, including the Nat Turner garbage. Basically, though, reviews don't seem to touch me in the way they used to; good, bad, or indifferently stupid, they just roll off my thickened hide. One piece of recent news is the fact that this year Random House will be bringing out Nat Turner in their beautiful new resurrected Modern Library. It's a superb edition of selected books, all "classics," and I'm happy to be a member of the club.

I'm also pleased to hear about your book, both mine and yours. The U.S. odyssey sounds like it could be enormously entertaining. As for the one on yrs. truly, I hope the tone is properly obsequious and you will treat me with the fawning deference I deserve. Incidentally, are you dealing with Darkness Visible? It's astounding, the ripples that little book continues to create. Enclosed is a recent spin-off. I'll be here in Rox. until June 1, then the Vineyard. Let me hear from you sometime.

As ever,

Bill

P.S. How is your offspring faring? Robust, I hope.

To Edward Bunker

August 18, 1994 Vineyard Haven, MA

Dear Eddie,

I called you the other day to tell you that (among other things) I looked at Reservoir Dogs and I thank you for digging it up for me.* The summer has been so filled with weird social events that I wasn't able to get to it until now, but I do appreciate you sending it. I agree with you that it isn't terribly good but it has some remarkable stuff in it and represents, I guess,

* Bunker appeared in Quentin Tarantino's 1992 film in the role of Mr. Blue.

a mode of filmmaking in which violence is pretty much taken to the limit. Rose got up and left at the point where the cop was about to be burned up and didn't come back even when I told her he was saved. I found the whole thing pretty gut-turning, too, but it was worth seeing and I thought you turned in a delightfully Bunkeresque (whatever that means) performance.

It looks as if the Clintons are on their way, which will make the social whirl even more horrendous. Fuentes and Gabriel García Márquez are going to be here and a dinner is planned wherein, I suspect, García Márquez will be pushing Clinton for making peace with Castro. At least, that seems to be the idea at the moment. I look forward to the Clintons' arrival with mixed fascination and dread. But I will probably take Hillary for a walk on the beach again—she is a good ole woman, as they say down South, and deserves compassion for having taken so much ill-deserved abuse.

The enclosed Modern Library edition of Nat Turner proves that I'm some sort of classic. I think it's a beautiful edition. I can't remember whether you may have read the introduction or not. Anyway, stay in touch.

Ever,

Bill

To George D'Almeida*

November 2, 1994 Roxbury, CT

Dear George,

I am deep into your beautiful epic verse and enjoying it immensely. I have to take it in slow draughts—it is so rich—but the total effect is so far greatly moving, like certain music. It will sustain me through this chill November, and I thank you.

Many years ago—27, to be exact—I remember sitting in my Vineyard living room, with you present while I went over the jacket copy (finding

* D'Almeida, a painter and poet, was a friend from Rome in 1959. George's mother married Paul Warburg, who owned a large estate on Martha's Vineyard, so they became friends on the Vineyard as well.

mistakes) of Nat Turner. After all of the misery it went through, Nat is now reincarnated in The Modern Library, which I reckon establishes it as at least a minor classic (in the catalog it roosts between Laurence Sterne and Thoreau) and at any rate makes me feel that the book—if I may use the unpolitically correct allusion—has triumphed over darkness.

That was a lovely time seeing you guys on the Island—much better, I might add, than when the Clintons arrived, which had its nice moments but was also noisy and chaotic.

Love to all & stay in touch.

Bill

P.S. I hope you read the new introduction.

To Willie Morris

November 29, 1994 Roxbury, CT

To: Willie
From: Stingo

Willie, you are about to enter into an amazing new phase in your life, take it from me, who has been in that phase longer than I would like to admit. It has been told that the distinguished Supreme Court justice Felix Frankfurter, then in his late sixties, sent a telegram to a colleague on his sixtieth birthday which read: "Welcome to the great decade!"

Willie, Felix Frankfurter was off his rocker. Let me tell you, the sixties really suck. Your wiring and your plumbing begin to go haywire, things start to crack and leak—the name of the game is dysfunction. You will find that this is the decade of eroding religious faith, and you will lose the radiant belief that so sustained you as a Baptist from Yazoo City. No man, you will discover, can continue to profess devotion to a Deity who thought up anything so ludicrous as the prostate gland.

But there are wondrous compensations. You will discover that, with the waning of the old ardor, you will be overtaken by an even more intense love of dogs and children. You will continue to appreciate the joys of gastronomy, though there are only limited ways to give flavor to soft food. You will learn the pleasures of slow motion, like the three or four minutes to get out of the front seat of a car. And Willie, when you sense a deliriously lovely young girl eyeing you on the sidewalk, and you think of the old days when they used to fawn over you and ask you up for coffee, and then she asks you if she can help you across the street—then you know that age itself is a glorious compensation, and that respect is a more beautiful attribute than anything so tawdry as lust.

But mainly, Willie, as you enter Felix Frankfurter's grisly decade, take comfort from the supreme knowledge that you have the abiding love of your friends, not only here in Connecticut, where Rose and I and Dinah and Tashmoo are thinking of you, but throughout the world—literary and otherwise—where your name is honored as an imperishably lovely writer and one of the indisputable life-enhancers of our time. HAPPY BIRTHDAY!

To Peter Matthiessen

February 7, 1995 Roxbury, CT

Dear Peter,

You were incredibly brilliant the other night, what with your orotund and enormously effective declamation of my rich beautiful prose, not to speak of your oleaginous and, I might add, entirely justified praise of my work—I just wanted to say how grateful I am for laying it on with the moving thickness I deserve.

Also I'm greatly pleased that Mr. Watson proceeds at such a happy pace—keep me informed of progress.

And let us reunite in some fine sociable way very soon.

As ever,

Porter

To Peter Matthiessen

March 17, 1995 Roxbury, CT

Dear Peter,

I know there are no words to help assuage the bottomless pain that you and Luke and family are feeling, but I did want to say that I've been thinking of you constantly.* There's very little I can do, I know, but you helped me through my darkest times, and if there's any way I can help you at this moment I am here.

We send love to all of you
Porter

To Robert L. Byrd†

April 10, 1995 Roxbury, CT

Dear Bob,

I thought that the enclosed book should be put among my papers, since it is an important work relevant to The Confessions of Nat Turner.‡ The attached letter from Magda Moyano will partially explain it.§

Until she sent me this thesis on John Hartwell Cocke, I had reached an impasse in the writing of Nat Turner. After I read the work, the outline of the rest of the book became clear: I would use John Hartwell Cocke as a model for Nat's master, Samuel Turner, and also use Bremo Plantation as a prototype for the kind of environment Nat would be reared in. The book proceeded well and smoothly after I made that decision, but it really

* Matthiessen's grandson was killed by a hit-and-run driver.

† Then director of the Special Collections Library at Duke University.

‡ Boyd Boyner, "General Hartwell Cocke of Bremo," Ph.D. dissertation, University of Virginia.

§ Styron met Magda Moyano, a young translator, on a trip to Mexico for the Inter-American Foundation in 1963. Although her father was Argentinian, Moyano's mother was from Fulvana County, Virginia. Moyano was a descendant of John Hartwell Cocke, master of Bremo Plantation in Virginia. It was Moyano who led Styron to Boyner's study of this progressive slave owner.

did require the serendipitous acquisition of this work by Coyner to make the breakthrough.

I thought it would be a good addition to my collection.

Best regards,
W.S.

To Philip Nobile*

April 10, 1995† Roxbury, CT

Dear Mr. Nobile:

Your lengthy letter deserves a lengthy reply.

I think I have tried to face up to the sins of our culture, to use Garry Wills's term, as well as any American writer.

But there are so many pious and hypocritical points of view suggested in your letter—from those of the Pope and the Church to that of the ignorant and misinformed Eisenhower to that of the admirable Garry Wills—that I find it hard to adequately express my contempt for the idea of apologizing to Japan, much less explaining the many reasons why such an apology would be outrageous—the most important being that the lives of thousands of potential invading troops on the mainland of Japan (myself included) were almost certainly saved by the dropping of the atomic bomb.

Despite the Emperor's sanctimonious "deep sadness," the Japanese have never officially apologized for their appalling atrocities against civilians in Asia and against Allied prisoners of war, scores of thousands of whom died in conditions approaching those of the Nazi concentration camps, and whose ordeal has recently been definitively chronicled in Prisoners of the Japanese by Gavan Daws.‡ By contrast, the Germans have admirably confronted their Nazi past, and Americans have dealt soul-searchingly not

* Nobile authored *Judgment at the Smithsonian: The Bombing of Hiroshima and Nagasaki* (New York: Marlowe and Co., 1995).

† This letter was written in response to Nobile's letter to Styron on April 7, 1995, requesting Styron's opinion of the United States' apologizing to Japan on the fiftieth anniversary of the atomic bomb.

‡ Gavan Daws, *Prisoners of the Japanese: POWs of World War II in the Pacific* (New York: William Morrow, 1994).

only with slavery and our sins against Native Americans but also with our criminal war in Vietnam, culminating at this very moment with the remarkable confessions of Robert McNamara.

The Japanese have steadfastly refused, as a nation, to accept guilt for their recent history (this has been scathingly documented by Ian Buruma in The New York Review of Books), but until they do, our future, and theirs, will be in danger.* I am convinced from the evidence that the Japanese were not ready to surrender, and that, tragic as it was, the dropping of the atomic bomb was a historical necessity. But even if this were not so, there would be a need for Japan to accept blame for its atrocious past (of which Pearl Harbor was only a small component), and that they have not done so remains a moral outrage and an offense to humanity.

Sincerely,
William Styron

To Editor, ***The New York Times***

April 23, 1995† Roxbury, CT

To The Editor:

In "Mr. McNamara's War" (editorial, April 12) you savagely attack Robert S. McNamara's acknowledgment of error in Vietnam as "prime-time apology and stale tears," declaring that he "must not escape the lasting moral condemnation of his countrymen."

No mea culpa deserves such contempt. It is true that his comes late—very late—but it should be saluted, not scorned. This country can never be truly reunited until the Vietnam wound is closed. Mr. McNamara, by his admission, has taken a long step toward the healing. What he needs now is company. The presidents of those years are dead, but most of the other warlords are still among us. Let's hear from them.

You state: "Fifty-eight thousand Americans got to come home in body

* Styron is referring to Buruma's many articles in *The New York Review of Books* in the early 1990s, among them "The Devils of Hiroshima" (October 25, 1990) and "Ghosts of Pearl Harbor" (December 19, 1991).

† The writer William Manchester also signed this letter.

bags. Mr. McNamara, while tormented by his role in the war, got a sinecure at the World Bank and summers at the Vineyard."

These are the facts. Robert S. McNamara became Secretary of Defense on Jan. 21, 1961, and resigned on Nov. 29, 1967. On Jan. 19, 1968—nearly two months later—the United States high command reported the total number of Americans killed in Vietnam as 16,459.

Our bloodiest years in Vietnam lay ahead. By the end of 1969 there would be 39,893 dead. Your final figure is correct: 58,135. But that was more than six years after Mr. McNamara left the Pentagon. So if it was Mr. McNamara's war, was it not also Mr. Rusk's? Mr. Bundy's? Mr. Clifford's? Mr. Rostow's? Mr. Laird's? And—last, but certainly not least—Mr. Kissinger's?

As writers we have always taken a solemn view of our responsibilities as Americans. Fifty years ago we served in the United States Marine Corps. We vigorously denounced the war in Vietnam—though never the brave men who fought there—and we openly, often bitterly, disagreed with all who were prosecuting it, including Mr. McNamara.

We welcome his acknowledgment that the United States was wrong then, believing that America can never be damaged by an act of contrition, and we invite all those who stood with him to join him now on his knees.

William Styron
William Manchester

To Philip Roth

June 21, 1995 Vineyard Haven, MA

Dear Philip,

I'll certainly refrain from any contact with the press in regard to your book, as per your request. After reading the New Yorker excerpt, which was splendid, I'm looking forward to the whole thing—I've got the bound galleys here and I'm sure the rest of the text will live up to the terrific New Yorker sample.*

* Philip Roth, "The Ultimatum," *The New Yorker* (June 26, 1995).

I appreciate your birthday note. Oh God, it's hard, hard—I mean, it's not really hard, or as hard as it used to be, and that's the trouble although to be quite honest I'm rather pleasantly surprised that I'm not yet ready to be fitted for an implant. Maybe just some kind of brace.

Stay in touch.

Your buddy,
Bill

P.S. While cooking fried chicken the other night Daphne mused wistfully about you. I think she wants some dick, like the old days.

P.P.S. You might want to look for a long memoir of mine in The New Yorker sometime before long. It's a non-fiction version of the ordeal I memorialized in that play "In the Clap Shack."*

To Peter and Maria Matthiessen

July 7, 1995 Roxbury, CT

Dear Peter and Maria,

Thanks from my heart's bottom for the splendid pen recorder which Al delivered to me safely. Now on my walks with my beloved poochies I'll be able to record some of the aphorisms for which I'm famous ("Cogito, ergo sum"; "virtue is its own reward"; "a foolish consistency is the hobgoblin of little minds," etc.), and have them at hand hot for the typewriter and posterity.† It is my finest birthday present—even surpassing an inscribed copy of Newt Gingrich's 1945 (which he was honest enough to call a "potboiler)."

Love and stay in touch
Porter

* William Styron, "A Case of the Great Pox," *The New Yorker* (September 18, 1995), collected in *Havanas in Camelot.*

† Styron mentions Descartes' "I think, therefore I am," Cicero's "Virtue is its own reward," and Ralph Waldo Emerson's "A foolish consistency is the hobgoblin of little minds."

To C. Vann Woodward

January 1, 1996 Roxbury, CT

Dear Vann,

Charles Joyner asked me to be present at Coastal Carolina Univ. later this month to be on stage with you for a conversation about Southern matters.* I told him that I'd be glad to do it if I can work out the right dates. Since I've got to give a talk in Orlando, Fla., on January 24th, the best date for me would be Jan 25th-26th. Would this be convenient for you? Please let me know.

In that fine essay of Joyner's on Nat Turner, which you gave me, he made the point that David Walker's famous Appeal expressed rage and hatred at black people not because they were black but because slavery had so profoundly degraded them. This love-hatred motif was something I tried to express in Nat Turner but apparently our Nobel laureate, Ms. Morrison, has not been able to perceive that. Enclosed is some more of Ms. Morrison's wisdom.

Happy New Year,
Bill

To Mia Farrow

January 16, 1996 Roxbury, CT

Dear Mia, When you get this I will be, God willing, asprawl on the sands of Anguilla (thinking of you in a snowdrift. Ho! Ho! Ho!).

I'm enclosing Toni Morrison's statement about my Nat Turner, along with a page from a very long essay on my book that will soon be published by Charles Joyner, a distinguished historian of slavery.† You will see that

* Charles Joyner is Burroughs Distinguished Professor of Southern History and Culture at Coastal Carolina University and author of several books on American slavery.

† Charles Joyner, "Styron's Choice: A Meditation on History, Literature, and Moral Imperatives," in Christopher Morris and Susan A. Eacker, *Southern Writers and Their Worlds* (College Station: Texas A&M University Press, 1996). See Toni Morrison, "The Art of Fiction No. 134," *The Paris Review* (Fall 1993). Morrison responded to questions about Styron's novel: "Well, here we have a very self-conscious character who says things

he quotes Eugene Genovese about the matter that Toni Morrison chokes on. I think it explains the whole thing very well.

I'll be back in 10 days or so and will call you for another walk, dinner, whatever. Stay warm.

Love,

Bill

To Mike Hill*

August 6, 1996 Vineyard Haven, MA

Dear Mr. Hill,

I'd be glad to participate in your film on Apollo 8, which sounds exciting indeed, and I thank you for the invitation.

The essay in question was the introduction to a book of photographs taken by various astronauts on several flights.† This book was published at least 10 years ago by, I believe, the firm of Clarkson N. Potter and was edited by my friend Carol Southern, who now has her own imprint under her name at Random House. Oddly enough, I've forgotten the name of the book (the copy I have is in my house in Connecticut) and I'd also

---

like, I looked at my black hand. Or, I woke up and I felt black. It is very much on Bill Styron's mind. He feels charged in Nat Turner's skin . . . in this place that feels exotic to him. So it reads exotically to us, that's all. . . . He has a right to write about whatever he wants. To suggest otherwise is outrageous. What they should have criticized, and some of them did, was Styron's suggestion that Nat Turner hated black people. In the book Turner expresses his revulsion over and over again . . . he's so distant from blacks, so superior. So the fundamental question is why would anybody follow him? What kind of leader is this who has a fundamentally racist contempt that seems unreal to any black person reading it? Any white leader would have some interest and identification with the people he was asking to die. That was what these critics meant when they said Nat Turner speaks like a white man. That racial distance is strong and clear in that book."

* Mike Hill, filmmaker who made an audio recording of Styron in the fall of 1996 for a documentary about Apollo 8, the first space mission to circle the moon in December 1968. Hill served as a consultant on the PBS documentary *Race to the Moon* (2005).

† In his foreword to Ron Schick and Julia Van Haaften, *The View from Space: American Astronaut Photography 1962–1972* (New York: Clarkson N. Potter, 1988), Styron recalls the hush that fell over a small group of friends watching the televised Apollo 8 mission during a party. He later identified the host as Leonard Bernstein.

forgotten that the essay had been reprinted in Final Frontier. If you have a copy of the full essay, that's fine. I mention the publishing history of the piece only to point out that the original could be found in that book and, I'm sure, located by contacting Carol Southern at Random House.

In any case, as I say, I'd be quite willing to read the essay for you. I'll have considerable free time here on the Vineyard this summer, and will probably be back in Connecticut by mid-September and will have time there, too. What I guess I'm saying is that I'm flexible and can, within reason, tailor my time to suit your schedule. I think the best thing might be for you to telephone me here on the Vineyard so that we can set up a time.

As you can tell, I was incredibly moved by that mission and so I'm very happy to be able to help you out.

Sincerely,
William Styron

To Gavin Cologne-Brookes

August 29, 1997 Vineyard Haven, MA

Dear Gavin,

I'm sorry to have been out of touch for so long but your kind letter gave me an opportunity to re-establish lines of communication. I hate to say it, but I've gotten so accustomed to telephones and faxes that letters are becoming a bit strange to me; I gather that's a fairly common symptom nowadays.

I'm glad your domestic life is thriving and that fatherhood is such a happy estate for you; it is something very special, and without it I would have felt quite foreshortened spiritually (despite the frequent hecticness). Also I'm pleased to hear about your various writing projects. I enjoyed reading that introduction to Writing and America, with its attention to Nat Turner. President Clinton has been vacationing on this island and I've seen quite a bit of him; in fact we had him to dinner. At one point, when Nat came up in conversation, he blurted "Surely I come quickly . . ." and you could have knocked me over with a broomstraw, hearing that line from the last part of the book. He then went on to tell me how he'd read

Nat in 1969 and how it had been a "transformative" work for him; needless to say, I was tickled to get all this from the Prez or POTUS ("Pres. of the United States") as he is designated by the Secret Service.

I thought you might be interested in the enclosed journal, published by the National Endowment for the Humanities. Jim West's biography is going to be published in the late winter of the coming year and I think it's quite a good job. Needless to say, I have mixed feelings about being focused upon in such a way. I think it best that writers' biographies appear not while they're alive but gone to the great writers' colony in the sky. I really dread all the attention the book is going to get, with all the attending bullshit. ("Mr. Styron has always been a somewhat problematical figure in modern American letters," etc.)

Best news at the moment is that my daughter Susanna has just finished directing (and written the script for) a movie based on my story "Shadrach," starring Harvey Keitel and Andie MacDowell. It was filmed down in North Carolina, where I saw some of the production. I think it may turn out to be a terrific film.

Best of luck to you on your writing. What pain it is! But also what joy eventually, when it turns out well. I'm sure you'll prevail.

All best to you & your fine family,

Bill

To Philip Roth

November 16, 1997 Roxbury, CT

Dear Philip,

After I called you, several weeks ago (getting no answer) I learned from our pal Dick Widmark that you had gone back to N.Y.C., "to be among my people."* I do hope you are feeling more congenially situated in your own ethnic group than in this washed-out enclave of Wasp yokels. All October I was on the talk trail—Arkansas (will you believe it? Arkadelphia, home of Jim McDougal & Whitewater), Tennessee, Cincinnati and

* Richard Widmark (1915–2008), actor and neighbor of Styron's in Roxbury, Connecticut.

Boston, plus Richmond—making enough to pay for the new kitchen here in Roxbury. Big bucks.

I had wanted to mention the loathsome du Plessix. Although she always irritated me I never quite shared your rage—that is, until I read an odious piece she wrote for The New Yorker following the demise of Diana.* You doubtless saw it: how she, du Plessix, having always eschewed the cult of celebrity to the point of taking People magazine to the garbage "with ice tongs," found herself "bawling" over the loss of one who was a paradigm of all suffering women who had been repeatedly betrayed by cads, etc. etc. Even for du Plessix it was sickening, and when I read it I finally understood your, shall we say, animus and I realized that the woman is utterly lacking in both taste and shame.

I hope we can discuss this and more savory matters in the near future and trust you'll contact this web site when and if you return to the Hills. Stay in touch.

Bill

P.S. I've misplaced your N.Y. address and am sending this to Cornwall Bridge for forwarding.

To Gavin Cologne-Brookes

[Unknown], 1997 Roxbury, CT

Darkness Visible is in its 19th paperback (Vintage) printing.

I get "you-saved-my-life" letters like this almost every day.†

This letter was handed to me by a very young woman at a party at a writers' conference in Idaho, ironically at the house where Ernest Hemingway shot himself.

* Francine du Plessix Gray, "Department of Second Thoughts," *The New Yorker* (September 15, 1997).

† The letter thanks Styron for the "book that was every bit as responsible for saving my life as the surgeon and internist who put my body back together after my suicide attempt."

To Robert and Claire White

January 9, 1998 Roxbury, CT

Dear Bobby & Claire,

I've been reading Stanford White's letters with a lot of pleasure.* He was a wonderfully gifted writer and probably would have made a fine writer if he hadn't turned to other fields. Architecture was much better appreciated than writing in those years so he plainly made the right choice.

I thought you'd like to have this calendar.† I am the pin-up boy for May, as you will see, even though Claire and I are June children.

Have a Happy New Year.

Willum

To Philip Roth

March, 1998 Roxbury, CT

Philip: My father always said: Beware of Jews with crystals.‡

BS

* Claire Nicholas White, *Stanford White: Letters to His Family* (New York: Rizzoli, 1997).

† Styron refers to a 1998 calendar entitled "A Literary Companion," issued by the Library of Congress. The writers whose pictures appear therein include Poe, Eliot, Rebecca West, Pasternak, Capote, Hughes, and Gertrude Stein.

‡ Uri Geller had sent Bill a crystal after the two met at a birthday party, and Styron forwarded Geller's note to Roth.

To Edgar L. Nettles*

May 24, 1998 Roxbury, CT

Dear Mr. Nettles,

I'm most appreciative for your generous letter with its many touchstones of memory for me. I remember "Miss Cosby" so well from sixth grade and hope you will give her my very best wishes after so many, many years. You might tell her that not too long ago, after I gave a talk at a college in Florida, I was approached by a lady who had been a colleague of hers at the Hilton School. This was Virginia Saunders, who I believe had taught me in third grade. So it has been rather wonderful to have contact with these most influential people in my past.

Your memories of my father also touched me, and I thank you for sharing them. He was indeed an extraordinary man and one to whom I also owed a great deal. He supported me wholeheartedly in my struggles to become a writer, and I was tickled by your description of his presentation of "Nat Turner" to the barber. A moment like that was my spiritual payback for his faith in me.

Please also tell "Miss Cosby" that like her, I have a vivid memory of being Marley's Ghost in "A Christmas Carol." I remember wearing white grease paint and my appearance (I guess I must have been about 12) scared the daylights out of the little 6-year-old tykes in the front row of the auditorium.

Hilton Village, with its river and pier and sycamores, was a paradise for a kid. Thanks once again for helping me to summon up memories, and for your thoughtfulness in writing me.

Sincerely,
William Styron

* Edgar L. Nettles was a coworker of Bill, Sr., at the Newport News shipyard. His wife, Frances C. Cosby, was Styron's sixth-grade teacher. Reading "A Tidewater Morning" prompted Nettles to write Styron.

To Amelie and Bernei Burgunder

July 13, 1999* Vineyard Haven, MA

Dear A&B: I appreciate greatly your gift of that perfectly beautiful linen shirt. Cotton I've got, wool I've got, but linen is a swank new addition to my summer wardrobe—here on the Vineyard which, according to New York magazine (which is my authority on all things) is a "center of high fashion." Love, Bill

To James L. W. West III

August 10, 1999 Vineyard Haven, MA

Jim:

This is the eulogy I gave for Willie at the Methodist church in Yazoo City last Thursday.† It was even hotter than at Faulkner's funeral in 1962, if that's possible. Willie would have been amused that for the mourners the heat was a near-death experience.

B.S.

* This postcard is from the "Writers and Their Familiars" series (photographs by Jill Krementz). The photograph is of Styron walking with his dog Aquinnah in Roxbury. As the caption reads: "William Styron with Aquinnah, Roxbury, Conn., April 29, 1979. William Styron (b. 1925) has written some of the most important novels of our time, including *Lie Down in Darkness* (1951), *The Confessions of Nat Turner* (1967), and *Sophie's Choice* (1979)." Aquinnah, a golden retriever, "had attributes that were nearly human, but she also possessed all-too-human failings," Styron recalls. "For instance, when I taught her how to drive, she insisted on staying on the left-hand side of the road. So that ended her driving career, which made it all the better for our wonderful daily walks together." The co-editor of this volume, R. Blakeslee Gilpin, sold Styron the stamp for this postcard and canceled it at the West Chop, Massachusetts, post office.

† This note accompanied the manuscript of Styron's eulogy for Willie Morris, which was published in *The Oxford American*, September/October 1999, and in a book of tributes called *Remembering Willie* (Jackson: University Press of Mississippi, 2000).

To Bob Brustein

February 11, 2000 Roxbury, CT

Dear Bob,

You must be insane. By now you should know that the only people who are given the Nobel Prize are large American Negro mammies and 87-year-old Salvadoran poets. But I must say it was terribly sweet of you to think of me in that way and to shoot off that letter to the weird trolls in Stockholm who handle such matters.

In an indirect way your endorsement (in the profoundly unlikely event of my copping the prize) would very likely hasten the demise of America's most famous playwright. For according to our friend Philip Roth, it is only the prospect of the Nobel Prize that keeps Arthur Miller alive October to October. Were the garland to descend on me, in this or any other year, my Roxbury neighbor—according to Philip—would not last another month.

You'd have more than some of your snotty reviews to answer for.

But I am grateful to you for the loving thought and send my love in return.

Ever,

Bill S.

In the spring of 2000, Styron's depression returned, much more seriously than ever before. He ended up having shock treatments against his will and was contemplating suicide.

To Edward Bunker

June 14, 2000 Roxbury, CT

Dear Eddie,

That was a half insane idea of mine and of course one that would put you in jeopardy.* Forgive me for the loony thought and I hope you still consider me

Your devoted Brother
Bill

P.S. Do call me, though, I'm suffering.

To James L. W. West III

June 15, 2000 Roxbury, CT

Jim, Read this <u>after</u> reading MS.†

Dear Jim,

The depression makes it hard for me to write but I did want to tell you of the plans I had for ending the novel.

The book is <u>not</u> unequivocally pro-Bomb. It ends with a confrontation between Paul and the Reverend and Isabel, in which Paul maintains that Truman could have been held culpable if the Japanese were on the verge of surrender. But since there is no evidence of this, Truman was perfectly justified in his decision. The novel ends on a note of reconciliation, with Paul asserting to his stepmother and the minister: <u>Let History be the judge</u>.

B.S.

* Styron had asked Bunker to procure a suicide cocktail for him and Bunker urged him to take a few days to think it over.

† The unfinished manuscript of Styron's *The Way of the Warrior*.

To Edward Bunker

June 16, 2000 Roxbury, CT

Dear Eddie,

I've gone quite daft with my depression—can hardly write a letter—but as a follow-up to my postcard/letter which you may or may not have received by now, I want to ask your forgiveness for suggesting to you that you partake in any such harebrained scheme.* I value your friendship more than almost anything and now hope that you will pardon me for putting your own well-being in jeopardy.

If you don't answer I'll certainly understand but hope you will call me sometime.

Ever,

Bill

To Edmond Miller

January 30, 2001 Roxbury, CT

Dear Ed,

I must say it was brave and generous of you to travel all the way to Richmond and back to Wilmington in a major blizzard, all to participate in a black tie event, much of which must have been pretty boring.† The governor of Virginia, incidentally—he of the Lay Down in Darkness line—was at my table, and allowed as how I was among the first to know in advance that he was to be chosen as Chairman of the Republican National Committee, I really felt I'd hit the Big Time.

* Bunker replied, "I have to tell you that you're one of the best friends I've had in my entire life. You've done so many favors for me that I can't begin to count them. There is nothing [in] the world that I would not do for you."

† "An Evening with William Styron" was held in the grand lobby of the Library of Virginia on December 2, 2000, when Styron was quite frail from the depression, which, he explained, had "mutated into a physical decline." This celebration featured tributes by Meryl Streep, Kevin Kline, Jim West, Peter Matthiessen, Mike Wallace, and Bruce Hornsby.

I do appreciate your concern for my health. I was still a little wobbly that evening, having been not long out of the hospital. But now after two more months I think I can safely say that I'm nearly 100% restored, and have gained back enough weight to be, at 170 pounds, just where I should have been for many years. It is a vile and detestable illness whose only saving grace is, as I've noted in print, that it is conquerable. I really feel fine.

Aside from the egregious Gov. Gilmore I thought the evening wasn't really too bad after all. I heard that most importantly the event raised a lot of money for the Library of Virginia. But beyond this it seemed to me the evening expressed some faith in literature, in the written word, and no one will quarrel with that.

Thanks for your various kind remarks, which bring cheer to my heart. Stay well. Spring is right around the corner.

Best, as ever,
Bill S.

To Brooke Allen

April 29, 2001 Roxbury, CT

Dear Brooke, One of Cynthia Ozick's chief failings is simple pretentiousness and I think you did a fine job of exposing her on this ground.* Thanks for sending me your review. I suppose I'm more irritated by her attacks on me than I should be.† If there were any validity in her accusations about "Sophie's Choice"—that it "corrupts" history by (among other absurd claims) trying to supplant the Jewish Anne Frank with the Polish Catholic Sophie—I'm sure the book would long ago have been exposed as a fraud or worse. But Ozick stands alone in her mewling complaint, refusing to

* Brooke Allen reviewed Ozick's *Fame and Folly* for *The New York Times Book Review* on June 9, 1996.

† Ozick's essay "A Liberal's Auschwitz," in her collection *The Pushcart Prize,* took writers like Styron to task for not emphasizing the Holocaust's "specifically Jewish martyrdom." Robie Macauley's review of that essay in the June 27, 1976, *New York Times* prompted Ozick to clarify her position and Macauley to defend Styron in the August 8, 1976, Letters to the Editor.

permit any historical suffering that is not Jewish. Anyway, you've pointed out expertly those many places in which the empress is starkly unclothed. Thanks for the good work!

Love, Bill

To Jeffrey Gibbs*

October 10, 2001 Roxbury, CT

Dear Mr. Gibbs,

I'm most grateful to you for your generous letter about Sophie's Choice. It heartens me to get a letter like yours since I get discouraged from time to time about the future and value of fiction and about the hard job of writing; words like yours are like a good dose of adrenaline and allow me to take hope. Certain details you mention are especially pleasing to me—the pull and allure of great music, for instance. Without music I would have been unable to write a single serious line and I'm delighted that I may have helped cause your own renewed involvement with Bach and Beethoven.

There is a continuity in literature. How gratifying it is to me to think that my work may have inspired you in some way to create your own. It's important—essential I should say—that books, which are lifelines to the future, continue to be written and read. I hope you'll persist in your own quest to explore, as you put it, the darkest side of humanity and that you will find the right way of expressing what you have to say. I'm touched to think that my work may have helped in that valuable process.

Sincerely

William Styron

* Jeffrey Gibbs (b. 1971), Florida-born poet and writer who read *Sophie's Choice* as an undergraduate in 1992 and credits the book with changing his life.

To Gavin Cologne-Brookes

February 11, 2002 Roxbury, CT

Dear Gavin,

We have indeed been out of touch too long—my fault—but I'm delighted to learn that you're going to be in New York in March, and I'm sure we'll be able to get together for a reunion. We could certainly at least have lunch or dinner and I'd like to think you may have time enough to come up here to Conn. for a visit of whatever length.

At the time I received your earlier letter (Jan. 2001) I was recovering from a horrible recurrence of my chronic illness, the black dog, which sent me to the hospital, actually two hospitals, from June of 2000 until the following November. It was a sudden major depression (induced, I'm certain, paradoxically, by the malefic effect of an anti-depressant) which metamorphosed from a mental disorder to a generalized physical breakdown that nearly killed me. I lost over 40 pounds, developed pneumonia, had an eating disorder that caused me to be fed through an abdominal tube, and was bedridden for months. I'll fill you in on the gorier details when I see you. Fascinating to say, however, I've made an almost complete recovery, gaining back just the right amount of poundage to put me at the optimum weight I should have had for years. But it was an incredible ordeal which, having taken me to the very brink, makes me now feel like a lucky Lazarus. I've resumed my usual schedule and that includes writing, giving talks, and making flights to such far-off destinations as the Caribbean and California. I've given readings this past year at Howard, Yale and Princeton.

You wrote me about your memoir about traveling around the U.S. in a bus, something you also talked to me about sometime ago. I wonder if it's in such shape that you'd like me to read it. Now that I'm in good physical condition I'd very much like to take a look at it so if you'll bring it along on your N.Y. visit it would give me great pleasure to give it a reading.

It's not quite true that (at least in my case) a prophet is not without honor in his own country. The enclosed photos were taken at an upscale housing project in progress in my hometown of Newport News.* The de-

* Styron attached a photo of himself in the gazebo in Styron Square and another photo of him and Jim West in front of the sign for the city of Newport News.

veloper has named the community Port Warwick—after, of course, the town in Lie Down in Darkness and Styron Square is the project's focus with other thoroughfares named Loftis Avenue and Nat Turner Boulevard. In addition, I was asked to give names to the dozen or so streets, avenues and squares and so we have (all named after U.S. literary figures) such squares as Emily Dickinson and William Faulkner, streets named after Eugene O'Neill and James Baldwin, along with Herman Melville and Walt Whitman Boulevards. I'm sure it's unique in America and very exciting to think of the genuine nod made to culture instead of the banal Woodbine Street and Mayflower Avenues.

I'm certainly looking forward to seeing you in March, Gavin, so do stay in touch about such matters as where you will be and how we can contact each other. It will be great to see you again.

My best to you and your growing family.

As ever,

Bill

To Readers*

Roxbury, CT

I hope that readers of Darkness Visible—past, present and future—will not be discouraged by the manner of my dying. The battle I waged against this vile disease in 1985 was a successful one that brought me 15 years of contented life, but the illness finally won the war.

Everyone must keep up the struggle, for it is always likely that you will win the battle and nearly a certainty you will win the war.

To all of you, sufferers and non-sufferers alike, I send my abiding love.

William Styron

To be made public at my death and published in all subsequent editions of Darkness Visible.

* Styron sent this note to his biographer and friend Jim West with a note dated June 5, 2000: "Jim: I'm having a very bad time. I hope to make it through but in case I do something to myself I trust you will make the enclosed letter public and also bring it to the attention of Random House. As ever, Bill."

ACKNOWLEDGMENTS

FIRST, I WOULD LIKE to make special acknowledgment of Edmond Miller. When Ed learned that I was casting a net far and wide to retrieve my husband's existing correspondence (Bill, in my memory, never kept copies), he generously pointed me to certain letters in Duke University's Rubenstein Library and suggested plumbing other writers' archives at Yale, Princeton, the University of Texas, the University of Mississippi, the University of North Carolina, and the Morgan Library. I am most grateful to him.

James L. W. West III, Bill's biographer, was an invaluable resource and frequent adviser who was in close contact with Bill and me for decades. The book Jim put together of Bill's early correspondence with "Pop" inspired me to write an introductory essay on their unique father-son relationship and then to pursue this volume.

It is especially fitting that Bob Loomis ushered this project from a computer file into print. Beyond being Bill's classmate at Duke and his incredible editor for almost fifty years, Bob was ever ready to encourage us. He approached Bill's private correspondence as he did Bill's fiction, with great sensitivity and steadfast principle. Ben Steinberg has been a splendid ally at Random House, where we also profited from the sharp touch of copy editors.

I am indebted, too, to Robert Byrd, head of the Special Collections Library at Duke University, and to his responsive staff, especially Will Hansen, who found and sent me documents I needed when I could not return to Durham myself. I am also indebted to Richard Workman and Katherine Kelly, who were at the Ransom Center in Austin, Texas, when I visited; to the patient personnel who guided me through Harvard's Houghton Library and its Law School Library, as well as those at the Library of Congress; to James Baldwin's sister Gloria Smart; and to our dear neighbor and pal Mia Farrow, who lifted my spirits by presenting me instantly with Bill's original handwritten letters to her. There are many others whose friendship I so value: they sustained me through the search.

Finally, Blake and I agree that this collection would never have seen the light of day without the endless hard work and imaginative contributions of Christina Christensen. She has our deep appreciation.

Rose Styron
April 2012

I feel fortunate to give credit to the many institutions that generously supported this work over the years. The John Hope Franklin Fellowship program at Duke University, the Gilder Lehrman Center at Yale University, and the Center for the Study of the American South at the University of North Carolina at Chapel Hill all provided crucial assistance for my work in Bill's papers. Above all, this volume would likely have taken another decade if it had not been for the unstinting support and flexibility of the United States Studies Centre at the University of Sydney: in particular, I am grateful to Margaret Levi, Rebecca Sheehan, Sean Gallagher, Andres Vigano, Geoffrey Garrett, Brendon O'Connor, and Craig Purcell. A special related thank-you to Shane White for all of his support and interest in this and other projects. I am also grateful to my colleagues at the University of South Carolina, where this project finally made it into print.

My advisers and mentors have provided encouragement and enthusiasm throughout this process. I owe particular debts of gratitude to Joe Flora, Harry Watson, Tim Marr, Glenda Gilmore, Anne Fadiman, and Bertram Wyatt-Brown. John Stauffer has selflessly given me inspiration, support, and counsel; I cannot wait to share this work with him. Last but by no means least is David Blight, who, aside from being my model of scholarship and teaching, is the best cornerman any young academic pugilist could hope for. David has gone out of his way to help me stretch beyond staid disciplinary boundaries and always proves a wise and loyal friend.

Simply put, this collection would not have been possible without James L. W. West III. In addition to donating a wide assortment of Xeroxed letters, Jim patiently read galleys of the manuscript and generously shared his unparalleled expertise. Rose and I are very grateful for his countless contributions.

I must thank Rose for the opportunity to edit this collection. I had become consumed with all things Styron after my first month in Bill's papers at Duke and I leapt at her invitation. Rose is an astounding person, all the more so for being able to remember a dinner party in Rome in 1952 or the identity of a nickname in a letter five decades old. It has been a privilege to edit these letters with her.

My deepest thanks are to my wife, Abbey, who not only put up with the endless transcriptions and piles of Xeroxes on the kitchen table, couch, and floor, but also endured the 100,000-plus miles of travel the collection entailed. While sharing my enthusiasm, offering a critical ear, and listening to lots of talk about William Styron in 1948, 1968, and beyond, she also gave birth to our son, Bear. I would be lost without Abbey's loving support. Someday I hope she or Bear will crack this book open to see the fruits of those many late nights and early mornings.

R. Blakeslee Gilpin
April 2012

FIRST AMERICAN EDITIONS OF WILLIAM STYRON'S BOOKS

Lie Down in Darkness. Indianapolis: Bobbs-Merrill, 1951.

The Long March. New York: Random House, 1956.

Set This House on Fire. New York: Random House, 1960.

The Confessions of Nat Turner. New York: Random House, 1967.

In the Clap Shack. New York: Random House, 1973.

Sophie's Choice. New York: Random House, 1979.

This Quiet Dust and Other Writings. New York: Random House, 1982. Expanded edition, New York: Vintage, 1993.

Darkness Visible: A Memoir of Madness. New York: Random House, 1990.

A Tidewater Morning: Three Tales from Youth. New York: Random House, 1993.

Inheritance of Night: Early Drafts of Lie Down in Darkness. Preface by William Styron. Ed. James L. W. West III. Durham and London: Duke University Press, 1993.

Havanas in Camelot: Personal Essays. New York: Random House, 2008.

The Suicide Run: Fives Tales of the Marine Corps. New York: Random House, 2009.

INDEX

Page numbers in **boldface** refer to recipients of letters.

ABOUT THE EDITORS

Rose Styron is a poet, journalist, translator, and human rights activist. She has published three books of poetry: *Thieves' Afternoon, From Summer to Summer,* and *By Vineyard Light.* At the forefront of the field of international human rights since she joined the board of Amnesty International USA in 1970, she has chaired PEN's Freedom to Write Committee and the Robert F. Kennedy Human Rights Award. Currently, for the Academy of American Poets, she co-chairs, with Meryl Streep, Poetry and the Creative Mind.

R. Blakeslee Gilpin is the author of *John Brown Still Lives! America's Long Reckoning with Violence, Equality, and Change,* winner of the C. Vann Woodward Prize for the best dissertation in Southern history. His writing has appeared in *The Boston Globe, The American Scholar,* and *The New York Times.* An assistant professor at the University of South Carolina, Gilpin specializes in the history, literature, and culture of the American South. He is currently at work on a new biography of William Styron.

ABOUT THE TYPE

This book was set in Garamond, a typeface originally designed by the Parisian typecutter Claude Garamond (1480–1561). This version of Garamond was modeled on a 1592 specimen sheet from the Egenolff-Berner foundry, which was produced from types assumed to have been brought to Frankfurt by the punch cutter Jacques Sabon.

Claude Garamond's distinguished romans and italics first appear in *Opera Ciceronis* in 1543–44. The Garamond types are clear, open, and elegant.